"This student-friendly book is an ideal accompaniment for an undergraduate class. Kubicek's accessible style, engaging questions, and comprehensive knowledge makes *European Politics* simply the best textbook I have found for instructing a class in the politics of Europe."

—Richard Arnold, Muskingum University, USA

"An innovative, analytical approach to European politics. Kubicek tackles the major institutional and policy questions in Europe, providing a strongly comparative approach to domestic institutions, integration, and post-Cold War and post-communist politics. Indispensable for any course on the topic."

—Patrick H. O'Neil, University of Puget Sound, USA

"With Europe as a continent at a crossroad, Paul Kubicek takes a broader view of European politics. This is an excellent contribution both to scholarly and non-academic debates bringing an up-to-date perspective on the current affairs of Europe. Kubicek's writing style makes content accessible and his insights provide a sharp angle to Europe's most pressing contemporary issues."

—Theofanis Exadaktylos, University of Surrey, UK

"Kubicek provides a rich and insightful account of politics in Europe, which makes this book stand out among other volumes on the same topic. He identifies common threads among the politics in different European political systems, while also highlighting the distinctive features of each national system and of the European Union. Kubicek does so by transcending, but not ignoring, the usual divide between Western and Eastern Europe and between national and supranational politics."

—Kostas Kourtikakis, University of Illinois at Urbana-Champaign, USA

European Politics

European Politics surveys the history, institutions, and issues that are essential for understanding contemporary European politics. Exploring a central question—"what is Europe?"—this text's thematic approach helps students compare politics in individual countries and see the political big picture in the region. *European Politics* examines not only countries already in the European Union but also those eligible to join to give students the most comprehensive picture of Europe's evolution in a globalized world.

Key changes for the new edition:

- Fully revised and updated to include coverage of recent elections, public opinion data and key topics such as refugees, Russia and Ukraine, Syria, more on the economic crisis, and Brexit;
- Expanded and revised opening chapter explaining Europeanization, multi-level governance, and the fissures in Europe;
- Greater and updated coverage of theory, multi-culturalism, and the EU.

This timely, in-depth text will be essential reading for anyone interested in European politics.

Paul Kubicek is Professor of Political Science at Oakland University, USA.

European Politics

Second Edition

Paul Kubicek

LONDON AND NEW YORK

Second Edition published 2017
by Routledge
2 Park Square, Milton Park, Abingdon, Oxon OX14 4RN

and by Routledge
711 Third Avenue, New York, NY 10017

Routledge is an imprint of the Taylor & Francis Group, an informa business

First Edition published by Pearson Education, Inc. 2012; Routledge 2016

British Library Cataloguing in Publication Data
A catalogue record for this book is available from the British Library

Library of Congress Cataloging in Publication Data
Names: Kubicek, Paul, author.
Title: European politics / Paul Kubicek.
Description: Second edition. | Milton Park, Abingdon, Oxon ;
New York, NY : Routledge, 2017. |
Includes bibliographical references and index.
Identifiers: LCCN 2016046311| ISBN 9781138671591 (hardback) |
ISBN 9781138671607 (pbk.) | ISBN 9781315616919 (ebook)
Subjects: LCSH: Europe—Politics and government.
Classification: LCC JN5 .K83 2017 | DDC 320.94—dc23
LC record available at https://lccn.loc.gov/2016046311

ISBN: 978-1-138-67159-1 (hbk)
ISBN: 978-1-138-67160-7 (pbk)
ISBN: 978-1-315-61691-9 (ebk)

Typeset in Sabon
by Florence Production Ltd, Stoodleigh, Devon

Contents

List of illustrations

Figures

Tables

Preface

I finished writing and editing this edition of *European Politics* in late 2016. Amid all the dramatic events in 2016, including the refugee crisis and war in Syria, Brexit, and the US presidential election, the twenty-fifth anniversary of the collapse of the Soviet Union and the final dénouement of Cold War received relatively little attention. I myself recall a class I took at that time, during which our professor, who had distinguished herself both in academia and in government service, was bewildered by the unexpected collapse of communism and disintegration of the Soviet Union. She observed that the world that she knew, a world predicated on divisions between East and West, had ended and that we, members of a new generation, might be better placed to look upon the emerging European and world order with a fresh set of eyes. In the initial post-Cold War years, there was a palatable sense of Western triumphalism and optimism, including discussions of the "end of history" as liberal democracy was seen to be ascendant, without a viable ideological challenger. While there were some immediate post-communist crises—the wars in the former Yugoslavia were the bloodiest in Europe since World War II—one could point to positive signs, including the growth of democratic institutions in most of post-communist Europe and more push for European integration, spearheaded by the European Union (EU).

The first edition of this textbook, written nearly a decade ago, was an attempt to look at a unifying Europe with a "fresh set of eyes." Drafted after the introduction of the euro and the expansion of the EU in 2004 and 2007, it exuded, in many ways, a sense of optimism or at least one of possibility for a more united, democratic Europe. However, even then there were signs of possible trouble, including concerns about terrorism and immigration. By the time the book was published, Europe was in a full-blown economic crisis, with some pondering the viability of the euro, the EU, and the social-democratic model in many European countries.

The second edition of this text focuses more on these developments, as well as the refugee crisis in 2015–2016 that had reverberations both at the EU level and within individual states. Momentum for a more unified Europe has clearly been lost. Indeed, with the Brexit vote in June 2016, the pendulum appears to be swinging the other way. This is not to say that the EU is doomed or that wholesale political changes within European states are likely. What is apparent, however, is that there is much political uncertainty across Europe, as new actors have emerged to challenge the idea of a single Europe, both in terms of its institutions as well as its fundamental values. While the book still takes a broad comparative approach and focus on common trends across the continent, the question about the future of Europe is far more open-ended than before. While one could argue that some events give cause for worry, one consolation, I hope, is that students will find the study of contemporary Europe interesting and engaging and will learn to appreciate competing perspectives both on where Europe has been and where it might be headed.

Numerous acknowledgements are in order. When I began my academic career, I did not consider myself a "Europeanist." "*East* Europeanist," perhaps, but not one with continent-wide expertise. To the extent that I am a bona-fide "Europeanist" today, I became so only with time and often through teaching. Thus, thanks must first go to my former students (in Turkey, Ukraine, Slovenia, and in the US), as this book is in part an outgrowth of how I learned to teach various classes on European and EU politics, often incorporating insights and feedback from students. Among my academic colleagues, numerous individuals stimulated my interest in European political issues and provided me with opportunities or inspiration to pursue research in the field. I would like to make special mention of Ilter Turan, Zvi Gitelman, Ronald Suny, Kevin Deegan-Krause, Amie Kreppel, Rudi Rizman, John McCormick, and Frank Schimmelfennig. Much thanks must be given to the numerous reviewers who provided feedback and suggestions on how to improve upon the first edition. I have tried to incorporate them into this volume, which no doubt resulted in many improvements. I thank Andrew Taylor and Sophie Iddamalgoda at Taylor and Francis for supporting this second edition and assisting in numerous large and small ways to produce a more engaging text.

Lastly, thanks to Alyce, Jonah, and Asher. They have been both companions on adventures throughout Europe as well as a constant source of support, for which I am most thankful.

Map of Europe

The fall of the Berlin Wall: A transformative moment of Europe

Chapter 1

Introduction: What is Europe?

In my view, the best place to begin an examination of European politics is with an anecdote from a trip to Berlin, a city that has been the locale of world-altering events throughout the past century and is once again the capital of Germany. I am standing in the center of the city, just outside the Brandenburg Gate. Although it has long been a symbol of the city, Brandenburg Gate is perhaps best known for the events that occurred there in November 1989. The Berlin Wall, the icon of the Cold War and a divided Europe, stretched in front of its western façade. In that month, the Berlin Wall fell, and Berliners from both the western and eastern halves of the city scaled the wall to celebrate the end of communism. The scene of jubilant crowds celebrating on top of a structure that was associated with violence and repression was one of the defining images of the end of the Cold War and of the twentieth century.

A tourist approaches me, asking, "Where is the Wall?" Ironically, he is from the divided island of Cyprus, which until recently also had a wall through the middle of its capital city. I tell him that it has been removed from here and one has to look elsewhere in the city to see areas where it still stands. He walks away disappointed, and I reflect on the fact that indeed, if one did not know the history, one could easily walk around and through the Brandenburg Gate and never know what had transpired here. Perhaps this is a good thing, a reflection that the Cold War division of Europe and of Germany is a thing of the past.

Yet, history is clearly present, if one wants to look. Just north of the Brandenburg Gate is the refurbished Reichstag, the German parliament building, which the Nazis purposefully set on fire in 1933 to justify repression of their opponents. South of the gate is Hitler's bunker, where, presumably, he committed suicide in the waning days of World War II. Adjacent is a memorial to victims of the Holocaust, a square city block of giant coffin-like boxes laid out in rows. There are not many old buildings of the type one would find in central Paris, Prague, or Porto, a reminder that Berlin was subjected to massive bombing by the Allies in World War II. Just east of the gate is the hulking Soviet (now Russian) embassy, a vivid reminder of the Cold War. A couple of blocks further one sees concrete barriers reminiscent of the Wall, but these now surround the US Embassy, structures that are now *de rigueur* in the post-9/11 world.

Perhaps such physical reminders of Berlin's past are beside the point. Since the fall of the Wall, Berlin has turned into a giant construction site, and the symbol of today's Berlin is arguably a new, if garish to some, commercial complex on Potsdamer Platz. Asking young Berliners to reflect upon their past may elicit the response *Wir sind jetzt alle Deutsche* ("We are now all Germans") or, even, *Wir sind jetzt alle Europäer* ("We are now all Europeans"). They did not experience the Cold War and the division of their city.

Look closer, however, at two older ladies chatting amicably on the park bench. Despite sharing a common language, they grew up in two different countries (West and East Germany) with diametrically opposed political systems. The aged pensioner walking with a cane is a veteran of Hitler's army, although, becoming a citizen of West Berlin after the war, he says he completely embraces democratic values and his wartime allegiance to the Third Reich is no longer relevant.[1] The businessman rushing to a meeting—could he have been, as hundreds of thousands of East Germans were, employed by the *Stasi*, the communist secret police? Further along you see a group of dark-haired young men speaking a language that is clearly not German. Perhaps they are some of the millions of people of Turkish heritage now living in Germany, or maybe they were part of the wave of Syrian refugees that streamed into Germany in 2015.

Establishing the main theme

European Union (EU) collection of twenty-eight countries (as of 2016) that aims for economic, political, and social integration in Europe. The EU possesses its own political structure and assumes an important role in formulating public policies.

The breaching of the Berlin Wall, the end of communism, and the subsequent expansion of the **European Union** (EU) in the 2000s to post-communist states can be seen as evidence of a "new" Europe, one that is breaking down barriers and unifying countries and peoples. This perspective, reflected in many parts of this text, scraps the older notion of dividing Europe into various parts (e.g., "Eastern" or "Southern" Europe) and emphasizes both the common features of European political systems and societies today and the drive, at the transnational level, to unify the continent in political and economic terms. Institutionally, this push is spearheaded by and manifested in the EU, but it also has social and cultural dimensions, ranging from mass tourism to the ubiquitous Irish pubs, Spanish tapas bars, Italian pizzerias, and French bistros throughout Europe to the multi-national composition of European football (*soccer*, in American parlance) clubs and the wildly popular Eurovision pop music contest to formation of a common "European" identity. Looking at various aspects of European unity in the mid-2000s, perhaps, in retrospect, the pinnacle of Euro-optimism, some spoke of Europe as the new "superpower."[2]

This is not to say, however, that a single, united Europe is, in fact, the current reality, as one can point to a number of divisive issues and problems, such as heated debates over immigration and multi-culturalism, desires to uphold one's own national power and identity, and concerns about the downside of globalization and economic integration and how best to promote economic growth. Indeed, if the first edition of this text, written mostly prior to the European debt crisis that emerged at the end of the 2000s, took a more optimistic tone, one will find in this second edition—written mostly in 2016—more skepticism about prospects for a united Europe, reflected in divergent responses and heated debates over economic crisis of the late 2000s (which extended into the mid-2010s in several states) and the refugee crisis of 2015–2016, which led some countries to close their borders and argue for re-considering basic tenets of European integration. Some observers suggested that due to these problems the EU had reached a "breaking point" or that it was "on the verge of collapse."[3] This was, notably, *before* the 2016 vote for "Brexit"—British withdrawal from the EU—which led to even more economic and political uncertainty, both in Great Britain and across Europe, as some feared (or welcomed) the prospect of a weakened or dismantled EU.

This book explores the notion of "one Europe," both how it can help describe, analyze, and explain contemporary European politics as well as its limitations that have become more apparent in the 2010s. Of course, a complete understanding of the drive for European unity would weave together various cultural, economic, historical, and sociological threads into a complex fabric. This book gives attention to each, but, as a text for a course in European politics, it focuses on political institutions, political culture, and various domestic and international political challenges facing European states and citizens today.

Europeanization a process emphasizing how national-level political processes and practices have become more similar over time and informed by transnational European-level concerns and institutions.

One key concept that stretches across these issues and will appear, at least implicitly, in each chapter, is **Europeanization,** an often contested notion that highlights how changes in national-level political systems can be attributed to the developments of European integration.[4] Europeanization is, however, a multi-dimensional process that can be understood in a variety of ways. A top-down, diffusion-oriented conceptualization focuses mostly on the EU, emphasizing how formal and informal rules, procedures, styles, "ways of doing things," and beliefs and norms develop in the EU policy process and are then incorporated into domestic political systems.[5] An example of this type of Europeanization is the adoption of a common currency, the euro, which was the outgrowth of closer economic integration among states and takes away powers traditionally exercised at the state level. Europeanization, however, can also be conceived in a bottom-up fashion, examining in particular how the rise of a pan-European identity among citizens contributes to common practices and the empowerment of continent-wide political institutions. It can also be viewed as a process—driven by factors such as common economic and social challenges as well as transnational communication—that leads to political convergence across Europe, as ideologies and parties align similarly in different national contexts and electorates respond to the same stimuli.[6] However one defines Europeanization—this volume will look at all of these possible elements—it clearly is a process that transcends the borders of individual states, blurring traditional, state-level concerns of comparative politics with those of international relations. Looking beyond Europe itself, one should also note that the quest to transform Europe—historically a region of intense conflict and bitter national rivalries—into a more coherent, stable, and peaceful entity is one of the great issues in international politics and, potentially, represents a model for other regions.

Yet, recognizing the EU's motto, "Unity in Diversity," it is also worth remembering the different historical experiences of European peoples and the peculiarities of their domestic political institutions and socio-economic systems. The EU, while important, has not made the nation-state obsolete. Despite Europeanization in a number of fields (e.g., media markets, environmental policy, interest groups, political culture), "one Europe" in its fullest manifestation is a highly contested notion that has not been realized and is far from an inevitability or given for the future. Despite the pledge in the 1957 Treaty of Rome to create an "ever closer union of peoples," many reject a united Europe as a normative goal. Schisms—both between countries and within them—are real, and often Europe does not speak with a single authoritative voice or act like a superpower. For example, despite vowing "never again" in the wake of the Holocaust and asserting that managing the disintegration of Yugoslavia would be the "hour of Europe,"[7] European countries sat largely idly by while genocide occurred in the Balkans in the 1990s. In 2015, German Chancellor Angela Merkel asserted that sheltering refugees was a reflection of European values, but it was clear from the responses of countries such as Poland, Slovakia, Denmark, Great Britain, and Hungary that leaders in those states held different values or priorities.

Indeed, to preview an overarching theme of this volume, one that I believe gives one purchase on understanding much of what is transpiring in Europe today, one can point to tensions between the logic of Europeanization and the pull of domestic politics. By "logic of Europeanization," I embrace a functional perspective (developed more in Chapter 3) that argues that for practical reasons, numerous international issues require cooperation and integration. One could argue that it "makes sense," in aggregate economic terms, for the small and medium-size countries in Europe to work together, eliminate trade and investment barriers, allow labor to move freely, and develop a common currency to cement a common market. It "makes sense" for issues such as environmental protection to have a pan-European dimension, and, in terms of foreign policy, a united Europe is a far more capable global player than one that is divided and working at cross-purposes. This perspective was adopted by the founders of today's EU, and has long been embraced by political leadership on the continent. Indeed, up through the 2000s, the idea of a single Europe was attractive to many, as post-communist states made numerous reforms to qualify for membership in a club which they believed yielded significant benefits.

However, one can push the "logic" of functionalism only so far. One can debate, for example, how far economic integration "logically" should go, with many (some using the advantage of hindsight) arguing that the adoption of the euro may have been a step too far, given the problems that emerged within a decade of its creation. More significantly, perhaps, political considerations may trump the "logic" or "objective good" of a more united Europe. Trade and immigration may, as most economists would argue, make the whole better off, but both can create losers as well. Some companies are unable to compete, and some individuals lose jobs. Integration means surrendering national sovereignty, which many may value as they continue to have a closer political and emotional connection to their national states. States may thus be weaker—or, at least, many citizens may believe their states to be weaker—inside the EU, in which they may have to go along with the decisions of more powerful states or, perhaps even worse, of faceless "Eurocrats" in Brussels. Many in Europe also believe the EU and Europeanization have long been driven by the preferences of economic or technocratic elites, who have lost touch with the "common" people. In the 2010s, these perspectives, captured by growing **Euroskepticism** throughout the continent, gained more political traction. Indeed, fears of immigration, perceived loss of national power, and backlash against political elites were all factors that drove the "Brexit" vote, a vote that proponents claimed allowed Britons to "take their country back" and is the clearest indication yet that Europeanization is not an inevitable or irreversible process. To put it somewhat differently, it now seems clear—to answer a riddle posed about European

Euroskepticism doubt or fear of the prospect of greater European unity and a stronger role for the EU.

Greece bailout: Members of left wing parties shout slogans behind a burning European Union flag during an anti-EU protest in the northern Greek port city of Thessaloniki, Sunday, June 28, 2015

© Giannis Papanikos AP/PA Images

integration—that integration is not like a bicycle that you have to keep pedaling and from which one cannot get off.

Furthermore, even under the rosiest scenario of those embracing the notion of "one Europe," it is clear that Europe will not politically unify to have a single government. Instead, scholars try to capture the current reality by referring to **multi-level governance**, meaning that political power is territorially dispersed (and often contested) among European-level decision-makers in the EU, national-level political leaders and institutions, and, in many countries, sub-national or regional actors. The idea of multi-level governance does not wholly contradict the idea of "one Europe." Rather, multi-level governance recognizes that European-level institutions and rules are *one* of the defining characteristics—but not the *only* characteristic—of political life in Europe today. In this way, use of multi-level governance requires one to take approaches that bridge the disciplinary divide between comparative and international politics, as "states no longer serve as the exclusive nexus between domestic politics and international relations."[8]

multi-level governance
idea that political power in Europe is territorially dispersed among European-level decision-makers in the EU, national-level political leaders and institutions, and, in many countries, sub-national or regional actors.

This book embraces the idea of multi-level governance, which reflects both how the EU and Europeanization have advanced but also that individual states (and in some cases, regions within states) remain important actors. While not a text on the EU, it recognizes that the EU plays a key role in European politics. The rise of multi-level governance, epitomized by the expanding reach of the EU, can thus be seen as a "watershed in European political development."[9] Earlier, traditional approaches to European politics that are rooted exclusively in domestic political institutions or that tack on brief consideration of the EU as a sort of after-thought thus do not capture the broader reality of Europe today. At the same time, however, national governments (and, as clearly evidenced in the case of "Brexit," voters) still matter. Study of European politics should, as suggested above, weave together comparative and international politics in a way that the study of Middle East or Latin American politics (where the Arab League and Organization of American States, respectively, are relatively weak actors) would not. This might make a more complex presentation, but such is political life in contemporary Europe.

Defining Europe

Before proceeding further, one should address a central definitional question: What is Europe? While the question appears simple enough, it can elicit a number of different answers.

Geography

At a most basic level, one could define Europe as a continent defined by geography. However, the borders of Europe, unlike those of Africa or South America, are not clearly delineated. Excluding islands, one can say that Europe stretches from Scandinavia in the north to the Mediterranean Sea in the south and from Portugal and Spain in the west to . . . well, therein lies the problem. Indeed, by focusing on its eastern border—wherever that may be—one might argue that Europe is less a continent and more a peninsula (or series of peninsulas) of Asia (thus, some refer to "Eurasia"). Students in elementary school often learn that Europe stretches eastwards to the Ural Mountains, thereby encompassing part of Russia. Many would dispute Russia's European credentials, but by this definition several other post-Soviet states, including Armenia, Azerbaijan, and Georgia, would be European by virtue of lying west of the Urals. By similar logic, Iraq and Syria could even be considered part of Europe. Perhaps one could follow another long-standing tradition[10] and argue that the border between Europe and the Middle East (usually defined as part of Asia) is the Bosphorus Strait, which bisects sprawling Istanbul, the largest city in Turkey and at one time, when it was known as Constantinople, the capital of the Byzantine (Greek) Empire. Yet, Turkey has been declared eligible to join the EU, which, in crucial ways, trumps mere geography in defining Europe. Of course, many oppose Turkish membership in the EU, and, if Turkey is allowed to join, the boundaries of Europe might stretch further: On what grounds could Georgia and Armenia then be excluded? For that matter, what of Israel, which, even though it has been deemed ineligible to join the EU, participates in the European basketball and football championships and the Eurovision music competition? Suffice it to say that consensus on Europe's geographical borders remains elusive.

Europe as an idea

Perhaps, one might say, Europe today is best conceived as an idea, or even as a political or social *project*. Put in the jargon of social science, Europe is a construction,

Cold War
ideological conflict from the end of World War II to the late 1980s–early 1990s between the US and its allies and the Soviet Union and its allies. As a consequence of the Cold War, most of Europe was divided into two ideological-military blocs.

not a geographical entity but a product of human agency.[11] Notably, during the **Cold War**, "Europe" as a united political or social unit did not exist. Instead, Europe had to be modified by adjectives. Western Europe not only had clear geographic borders but was also defined by its democratic political systems and opposition to Soviet-inspired communism.[12] Most classes and textbooks on "European politics" were—and in many cases, still are—overwhelmingly devoted to this part of Europe. Eastern Europe, in contrast, was defined by its communist political and economic systems and in opposition, in its ideological orientation at any rate, to the "decadent," "imperialist," capitalist West. Since the end of the Cold War, the division of the continent into two opposing ideological camps is over, although the old West/East division still has some meaning while some now speak of an emerging North/South division on the continent.[13] Such observations, however, do not undermine the claim that today's Europe is more unified than at any previous time in modern history. Still, however, one could ask, what lies behind this "Europe"?

Note that citizens of most nation-states would not normally ask this question of their own countries. Most Americans, Britons, Poles, Germans, Italians, Spaniards, and so on, beset as they might be with internal divisions in their own countries (think "red states" versus "blue states" in the US, English versus Scots, or northern versus southern Italians), could nonetheless agree on a set of values or traditions—regardless of how vague or banal—that help define their national identity. Countries usually have a history with a set of narratives or myths on which they can draw. Europe, with a history of conflict and populated by diverse peoples living in dozens of national states, has no such luxury. There is no "founding father" of Europe that resonates like George Washington does for Americans, a singular event like the French Revolution, or a unifying cultural figure like Shakespeare for the English or Cervantes for the Spanish. How then can one define Europe? Or, to put it differently, what is Europe for?

Europe as an economic community

Helene Sjursen, a Norwegian political scientist, suggested that there are three possible answers to this question.[14] First, one could view Europe—best epitomized by the early history of the EU—as a "problem-solving entity," based on economic citizenship, functionalism, and material economic interests. Arguably, this was the main basis for European legitimacy in the formative years of the EU. However, as we'll see in Chapter 3, in the 1990s the EU and concomitant processes of Europeanization began to move beyond mere economic concerns, and in discussions of EU expansion to former communist countries, an economic definition or conception of Europe was far less pronounced and compelling, giving way to moral, cultural, and political claims.[15] In other words, as "Europe" has grown in recent years and new issues and challenges have emerged, its definition and mission have changed.

Europe as a cultural community

An alternative conception of Europe, according to Sjursen, would be a value-based community, based upon social and cultural citizenship and drawing a firm line between Europe and other states and actors. From this perspective, Europe would be an entity that seeks to revitalize traditions and memories of distinctly "European" values, to forge a "we-feeling" as a basis for integration. Ironically, Mikhail Gorbachev, the last leader of the Soviet Union (1985–1991), advanced this type of argument, maintaining, "Europe from the Atlantic to the Urals [a phrase used by French President Charles de Gaulle in the 1960s] is a cultural-historical entity united by the common heritage of the Renaissance and the Enlightenment."[16] What precisely that "we-feeling" is would be a subject of dispute and may crucially depend upon what Europe is trying to define itself against. Former West German Chancellor Helmut Schmidt wrote an interesting essay entitled "Who Doesn't Belong in Europe," where he argued that for cultural reasons Russia, Ukraine, Belarus, and (Muslim-majority) Turkey lie outside.[17] Since Turkey has applied to join the EU, it is the Turkish case that has elicited the most debate on the questions of "what" or "where" is Europe. According to Pat Cox, former President of the European Parliament, "This [Turkish membership in the EU] is the most difficult question of all. . . . It's about how we define Europe."[18] On this issue, religion—if not pious belief then at least a Christian heritage—is often used, especially by those who oppose Turkish membership, as a marker for what defines "Europe," but, of course, Christianity is far from unique to Europe[19] and, as noted in Chapter 9 of this volume, secularism is increasingly embraced as a "European value," as many Europeans have turned away from religious belief and practices. Alternatively, some Europeans,

A man waves a French flag on top of a destroyed tank belonging to forces loyal to Libyan leader Muamar Qaddafi in Ajdabiyah, March 27, 2011

In focus

European political values

Individual countries, one might say, rest upon core political values. These values are usually promulgated in their constitutions. "Europe," of course, is not a single country, and it lacks a common constitution. If, therefore, one is to conceive of "Europe" as an already existing or at least a potential political community, on what values does it rest? What documents would express these values?

To the extent that the EU is the most powerful expression of European unity, one should expect that if "Europe" rests on political values, they could be found in EU documents. Indeed, this is the case. As we'll see in Chapter 3, the EU is built on a foundation of various treaties that date to the 1950s. Each of these treaties—while focusing on construction of institutions or development of policies in particular issue areas—includes statements of political vision and values. Specific rhetoric and the overall emphasis of these statements have changed over time. For example, the 1957 Treaty of Rome, which sets the goal of "an ever closer union" of peoples in its first preambulatory clause, does not mention the terms "democracy" or "human rights" in its entire preamble, emphasizing instead elimination of trade barriers, balanced trade, and coordination of commercial policy. In contrast, the 1992 Maastricht Treaty confirms Europeans' "attachment to the principles of liberty, democracy and respect for human rights and fundamental freedoms and of the rule of law" in its third preambulatory clause, subjugating economic issues to later in the document. The ill-fated Constitutional Treaty of 2004 stated in its first preambulatory clause that it draws inspiration from "the cultural, religious and humanist inheritance of Europe, from which have developed the universal values of the inviolable and inalienable rights of the human person, freedom, democracy, equality and the rule of law," and goes on to mention the goal of "peace, justice and solidarity throughout the world" (second clause) Europeans' "common destiny" (third clause) and the continent as a "special area of human hope" (fourth clause). This document, ambitious as it was, was not approved, but the 2009 Lisbon Treaty, its replacement-of-sorts, puts democracy and freedom front and center, including—at the risk of sounding a bit repetitive—both the clauses from the Maastricht Treaty on the attachment to democracy and human rights and the first clause from the Constitutional Treaty linking such values to historical and cultural inheritances.

While one can debate both how effectively these documents and the EU as a whole work in practice—issues we'll return to several times in the text—as well as their eloquence or coherence compared to national constitutions, the overall message is clear—the EU, whose goal is to eliminate divisions in Europe, is built on political values. Given the EU's importance in the construction of "Europe," it makes it easier to view the latter as more than mere geography or an economic arrangement to bolster trade and more as a political community.

Critical thinking questions

1. Do you think common values such as commitment to democracy and human rights are enough to form a cohesive political community among countries with different histories and political experiences?

2. The US started as thirteen separate states but over time evolved into a more cohesive political community. What factors facilitated this? Do you think conditions to form such a community in contemporary Europe are as propitious as those in early US history?

as we will note below, define "European values" in a way that distinguishes them from those of the US. Some of these values would be, in addition to secularism, a commitment to social solidarity, a welfare state, supranational governance through the EU, and multi-lateral international institutions. Of course, not all Europeans would want to draw such a sharp distinction with the US, and some would even suggest that Europe needs to embrace many aspects of the American system.

Europe as a political community

Finally, one can imagine Europe in more inclusive terms, defined not culturally but as, in Sjursen's words, a "rights-based post-national union" based upon political citizenship and appeals to universal standards and rights. In this vein, political legitimacy within states and within the EU would rest upon political support and legally entrenched fundamental rights and fealty to democratic procedures. In contrast to a cultural model, this rests upon universal values. This sentiment was captured in the 1990s with the assertion that the repressiveness and violence associated with the rule of Slobodan Miloševic in Serbia somehow was not befitting of a "European" country and made Serbia a justifiable target of European political and economic sanctions. As noted in the **In focus** boxed feature, expression of a more political idea of Europe has been included in various EU documents. From examination of these materials, one definitely gets a sense that Europe stands for something universal, and although, naturally enough, Europe would have to have some geographic parameters (e.g., Mexico or Canada are not part of Europe), all humanity could, vicariously at least, embrace Europe's vision and values. Such a conception would obviously benefit states like Turkey who seek to join Europe (here defining the parameters of Europe as the EU) but arguably do not meet cultural criteria. Turkish Prime Minister (now President) Recep Tayyip Erdoğan made this argument in 2004 to press the Turkish case, noting that "the EU is neither a union of coal and steel, nor of geography, nor only of economies. It is a community of political values."[20]

Why it matters

One might suggest that such debates over the definition of Europe seem too abstract or are mere rhetoric. However, they do matter for several reasons. First, as noted in Chapter 11, many European states, thanks to immigration, are already culturally diverse, and the need for immigrants will grow in coming years, so narrower definitions of the EU as a cultural-based entity will poorly serve a dynamic, multi-cultural Europe. Second, as noted, they have great relevance when considering both possible EU expansion to Turkey, Bosnia (another predominantly Muslim state), and beyond, as well as Europe's relations with neighboring states that clearly do not meet minimal geographic definitions to qualify as "European." In particular, a rights-based, universalist conception of Europe could be used to advance replication of the "European model" far beyond the boundaries of Europe whereas adherents of a culturally defined Europe would argue that Europe could not export its values or institutions. Finally, and perhaps most importantly, a rights-based identity would best serve those interested both in "deepening" European integration (e.g., such as adopting a single constitution for the EU or re-structuring of EU institutions to better involve European publics), as it expressly views Europe in political terms. If Europe is primarily about economics or culture/values (the latter narrowly defined), then the rationales for both deepening and widening the EU to other states may be essentially over and the "European project" largely complete with Europe's "*re-unification*" in 2004 and 2007, when most of the post-communist states of Eastern Europe joined the EU. If, however, there is to be a broader, more ambitious European *political* project, then the EU could advance a more political or rights-based identity for itself. As Thierry de Montbrial of the French Institute of International Relations argued, the core concepts of the EU are democracy, rule of law, human rights, secularism, market economy, security, and solidarity. "What we want to achieve in Europe," he claims, "is a new kind of political unit, whose identity is based on these concepts."[21]

A provisional definition

For now, we'll let these debates lie, although they will be taken up throughout this text. Clearly, it is hard to reach a clear verdict on what Europe is or what it seeks to become. At present, the safest route is to note that the substantive meaning of Europe is subject to much debate and is still evolving. Europe and European are, in short, constructed and contested terms. However, this caveat of sorts does not solve the present problem of how to delineate the subject of study for this volume. For a solution, I defer to the EU, which declares that only "European" states are eligible for membership. Obviously, therefore, all twenty-eight members of the EU are European, as are candidate countries, including Turkey and several states in the Western Balkans (e.g., Albania, Serbia, Montenegro). Countries that have been invited to join the EU but have chosen to stay out—Norway, Switzerland, and Iceland[22]—are also, by this standard, European, and will be periodically mentioned in this text. However, most of the post-Soviet states, including Ukraine, Belarus, Armenia, Georgia, and, most significantly, Russia, while having close relationships with the EU and, in some cases, an Association Agreement, have not been explicitly recognized as potential members of the EU. Therefore, by the paradigm I adopt, they will not be covered as European countries in this text, although the EU's relations with these states will be discussed in the final chapter.

Why study Europe?

In the not-so-distant past, few would have asked the above question. However, at the dawn of the twenty-first century, some might argue that Europe is outmoded or passé and that other regions of the world deserve more of our attention. Some speculate that this century will be the Chinese century, and there is little question that China—and that other Asian giant, India—are rising powers in the global economy. Former US President Barack Obama declared that the US needs to make a "pivot to Asia" in its foreign policy, implicitly de-prioritizing Europe. In addition, after 9/11, the 2003 invasion of Iraq, and, in the 2010s, the rise of the Islamic State

(ISIS) in parts of Iraq and Syria, the Middle East has been an important area of focus, especially for the United States.

Europe is a world power

Europe, however, is no peripheral player in either the world economy or in the global battle against terrorism. True, the individual countries within Europe are at best medium-sized states. The days of a world dominated by European "Great Powers" such as Great Britain, France, and Spain are long gone. However, when Europe is regarded as a collective entity, which reflects in part the accomplishments of the EU, a different picture emerges. The EU has created a single economic market among its members. Comprising, as of 2016, twenty-eight countries and over 500 million people,[23] the total EU economy is the largest in the world (23.75 percent of the global total), as seen in Figure 1.1. The United States (22.34 percent) comes in a close second, followed by China (13.28 percent). Moreover, even though China and India are important and growing countries, their impact on the world economy is primarily a function of their sheer size (1.3 billion and 1.1 billion people, respectively), not *per capita* income of each individual citizen, which remain below average for the world as a whole. When one looks at this variable, as seen in Figure 1.2, one clearly sees that leading European countries, as well as the EU as a whole, rank among the wealthiest and most highly developed areas in the world, a point confirmed by other data such as educational achievement and public health.[24] Europe is also the dominant actor in terms of international trade—in 2014 the EU had over $8 trillion in exports compared to $2.3 trillion for both the US and China—and Germany's trade surplus ($260.5 billion in 2014) is eclipsed only by China's ($383 billion).[25]

globalization
multi-faceted process that refers to the diminishing importance of national borders and increasing ties that connect countries and peoples of the world. Some welcome and champion it; others believe globalization is an economic or cultural threat.

While **globalization** and "Americanization" are at times almost used interchangeably—with McDonalds becoming the literal (and often despised) symbol of globalization[26]—one should recall that there are a number of important European firms in the world economy that compete and often out-compete their American or Japanese rivals—Nokia, Siemens, Bosch, BMW, Daimler-Benz, Ericsson, Cadbury-Schweppes, Airbus, British Airways, Vivendi, DHL, Pearson, Fiat, Royal Dutch Shell, Vodafone, Carrefour, Nestle, Renault, British Petroleum, Novartis, Unilever, and British-American Tobacco, just to name a few. One hundred forty-two European companies were in the 2015 Global Fortune 500, whereas only 128 were American. Many recognizable "American" brands—including Budweiser, which in the summer of 2016 re-named itself "America"—are now part of European companies.[27] Defining globalization differently—by tourism, Internet traffic, or investment flows—Europe similarly comes out on top.

However, as Table 1.1 reveals, Europe is not a fully fledged superpower, at least when one looks at military aspects of power. No EU member ranks in the top fifteen in terms of number of people in the military,[28] although collectively EU countries do have a sizeable number of men and women in their militaries. Many, however, are in the reserves, and EU countries as a whole spend much less than the US on the military. They cannot come close to the Americans (or Russians, for that matter) in terms of projecting military power or employing the most technologically advanced weapons. The main nuclear powers remain the US and Russia. As for the

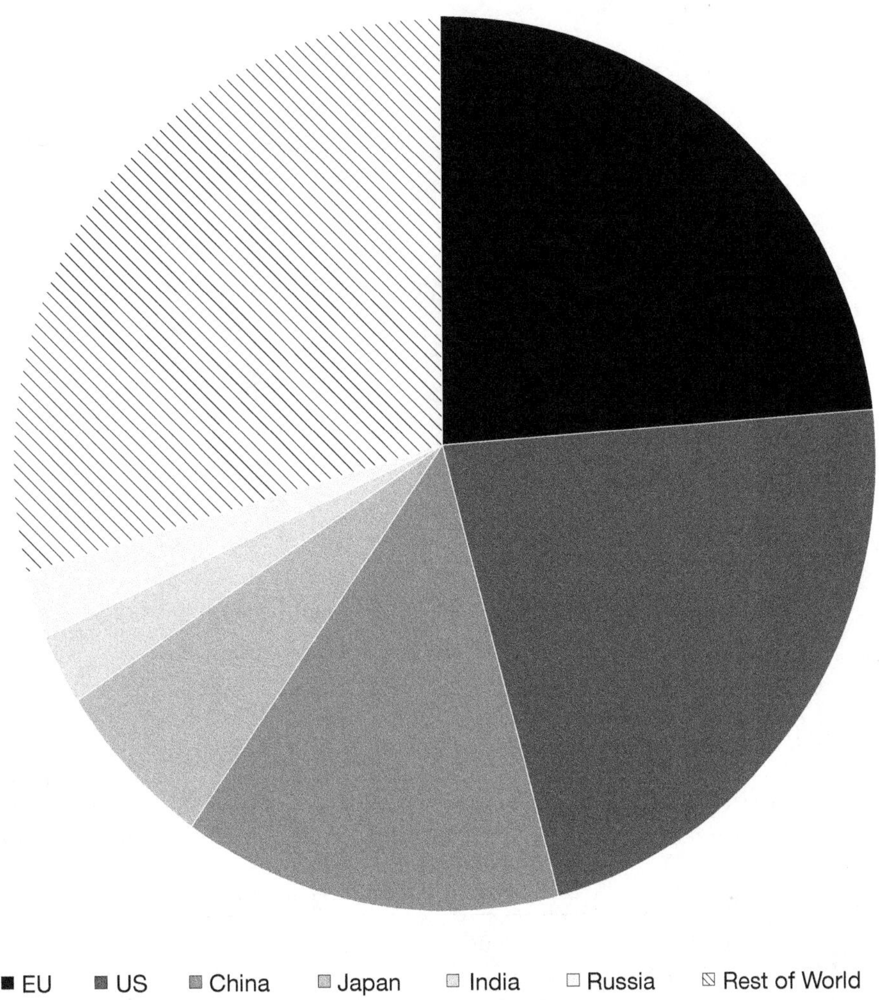

FIGURE 1.1 Distribution of 2014 world gross domestic product (GDP), by country/region

World Bank Data from 2014, available at www.worldbank.org

soft power
use of non-coercive and non-military instruments of power, such as diplomacy, economic assistance, and power of example, to exert influence in world affairs.

EU itself, as opposed to the individual militaries of European countries, it possesses only a 60,000 person rapid-reaction force. An all-out military conflict between America and Europe—a fear that I have, to my amazement, heard occasionally from my own students—seems both far-fetched and, should it come, likely to be very one-sided. Moreover, one could argue that even if Europe has the capability to act militarily, it often has little will to do so alone (e.g., the war in Iraq in 2003, intervention in Syria's civil war) and even in cases to stop genocide, as in Bosnia and Rwanda in the 1990s or Darfur in the 2000s, Europe refused to take the military initiative.

This is not to say Europe is not a powerful force in international affairs. Instead, it relies far more on "**soft power**" (e.g., economic assistance and trade policy,

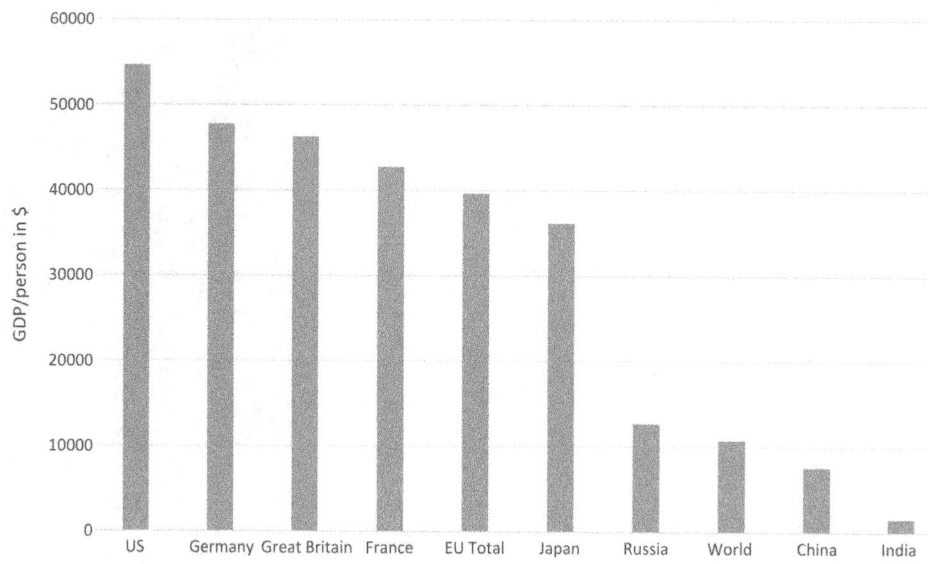

FIGURE 1.2 GDP per person (in $) in selected countries/regions

World Bank Data from 2014, available at www.worldbank.org

TABLE 1.1 Military capabilities of various global powers

Country or region	*Total armed forces, 2014*	*Military spending in 2014 $ billion*	*Military spending % GDP 2014*	*Deployed nuclear warheads*	*Aircraft carriers*	*Attack aircraft*
EU	2,149,000	205	1.4	450	8	1671
Germany	178,600	34.7	1.2	0	0	169
Great Britain	154,700	60.0	2.0	150	1	168
France	312,350	47.0	2.2	300	4	284
US	1,381,500	610	3.5	4760	19	2785
Russia	1,287,000	84.6	4.6	4380	1	1438
China	2,993,000	200.9	1.9	260	1	1385
Japan	259,800	45.9	1.0	0	3	287
India	2,749,700	50.9	2.5	90–110	2	809

Source: Stockholm Institute Peace Research Institute (SIPRI) Yearbook, 2015, available at www.sipriyearbook.org, World Bank (www.worldbank.org), and www.globalfirepower.com, and http://ec.europa.eu/eurostat/statistics-explained/index.php/Government_expenditure_on_defence, accessed June 26, 2016.

hard power
use of the military and other coercive measures such as economic sanctions to exert influence in world affairs.

diplomacy, multi-lateral institutions, moral authority, culture) than on "**hard power**," exemplified by military might. As defined by Joseph Nye, "soft power" suggests that "a country may obtain the outcomes it wants in world politics because other countries want to follow it, admiring its values, emulating its example, aspiring to its level of prosperity and openness."[29] To the extent that Europe can market itself as a democratic zone of peace, be more generous in foreign assistance than the US, engage in more public diplomacy, and is less intent than America upon using military muscle to force states to comply with its preferences, it is, at least according to Europhiles, becoming more and more influential around the world. Some maintain that Europe is a "transformative power," having great economic and political influence across one hundred countries in the "Eurosphere," a collection of states in Europe, Africa, and the Middle East that are connected together by sizable economic, and, in many cases, historical and cultural ties.[30] Across a wide range of issues—corporate mergers, genetically modified food, data privacy, the environment, airplane engine emissions, human rights—Europeans set the standard, forcing others to abide by European law and norms (or regulations). One writer claims that "Europe's weapon is the law," meaning that the EU's regulations and use of conditionality for aid and trade are producing an invisible but unstoppable "Europeanization" of laws and economic practices throughout this "Eurosphere."[31]

As for being eclipsed by the struggle against terrorism, one should note that in the 2000s European troops were on the front lines with Americans in both Afghanistan and (more controversially and less universally) Iraq. Moreover, Europeans have been the victim of numerous terrorist acts—discussed more in Chapter 12—and homegrown, Islamic terrorist cells are a grave worry. In this respect, Europe is thus a major theater in the "war on terror," and some, even prior to the rise of ISIS, speculated that extremist groups that could emerge in democratic European states actually present a larger threat than groups based in the Middle East or South Asia.[32]

Europe as a source of political ideas and institutions

Enlightenment
intellectual movement that began in the seventeenth century in Western Europe and emphasized human reason, material progress, and individual rights

liberalism
ideology that emphasizes the rights of the individual and limited government; a basic idea behind modern democracy and capitalism.

There has always been a powerful philosophical and historical argument for the study of Europe. Europe was the birthplace of democracy—both in its ancient Greek variants and in more "modern" forms that arose in Great Britain centuries before the creation of the US. Europe was also home to the **Enlightenment**, an intellectual movement that began in the seventeenth century that sought, in broadest terms, the political and intellectual liberation of humanity by emphasizing the power of human reason (over that of religious dogma), material progress, and enlightened individual self-interest. The Enlightenment spawned a search for new ideas in the sciences, arts, and social life. The most fundamental ideas on which contemporary democracies are based—limited government, separation of powers, rule of law, religious tolerance, capitalist economic systems, civil rights—found earliest expression during the Enlightenment among various European thinkers. The bases of **liberalism**, the ideology that animates most contemporary democracies,[33] were articulated by the English writers such as John Locke (1632–1704), John Stuart Mill (1806–1873), and the Scottish economist Adam Smith (1723–1790), whose *Wealth of Nations* (1776) is considered the classic exposition of capitalist thought. The French Revolution of 1789, with its slogan of *liberté, egalité, fraternité*, was an inspiration to millions around the globe and is often argued to be the one of the foundations for the still-potent ideology of nationalism.[34] The study of European politics is thus, in part, how the rise of democratic ideas gave rise to democratic institutions and how those institutions have adapted to new challenges over time.

It is also worth mentioning that the two greatest ideological challengers to liberal democracy—**fascism** and **communism**—arose in Europe. Fascism is most associated with Hitler's Third Reich in Germany (1933–1945), but it was first put into practice by Benito Mussolini in Italy (1922–1943). It rejected the very premises of individual rights, preferring instead to invest authority in an all-powerful, militaristic state. Fascism was defeated in World War II by an alliance of democratic and communist states (an alliance that is at times forgotten), and the post-war period through the late 1980s was defined by the Cold War, a struggle between democratic capitalist states and their erstwhile communist allies, led by the Soviet Union. Communists rejected capitalism as inherently unjust, preferring state ownership and planning of the economy to secure economic equality. Communism's moral and utopian impulse, however, could not be realized, because in practice communism produced an all-powerful, repressive state that denied basic democratic rights to citizens. In literal and figurative terms, Europe was the front line in the Cold War, which divided the continent into two antagonistic halves. Communism ended in Eastern Europe in 1989–1991, and since then major steps have been taken to foster democracy in Eastern Europe and integrate the entire continent.

fascism
ideology associated with Hitler and Mussolini that glorifies the state and rejects ideas of democracy and individual rights.

communism
ideology associated with the Soviet Union that aspires to create utopia but in practice led to state domination over economic and political life.

Europe as case study for political science

It is also worthwhile to study Europe as part of broader study of comparative politics and international relations. While every region or country of the world offers something to these sub-fields of political science, Europe represents a great laboratory to illustrate political concepts and test numerous theories of the discipline. As noted, Europe is central in any study of democratic practices. On this score, one could also add that there is a diversity of democratic institutional arrangements in Europe (e.g., in electoral systems, in types of political executives), making it a useful region to study for any student of comparative politics. The movement to democracy in the 1990s in post-communist Europe also figures prominently in the so-called "transitions literature" that examines recent waves of global democratization. Their experience may offer lessons to would-be democratizing states elsewhere. While on-balance capitalist, the different mix of free market and statist economic orientations among European states offers a great opportunity to compare varieties of capitalism. Because Europeans enjoy free and open political systems that are based upon popular participation, one can see how political culture matters in shaping political institutions and outcomes. Thanks to the success of the EU, Europe is the primary focus for theories of regional integration. On the other hand, ethnic conflict, most recently in the former Yugoslavia, reveals the continued power of nationalism in a supposedly "post-national" continent. Numerous issues connected to globalization—immigration and adjustments to a more multi-cultural political environment, structural economic reform to enhance competitiveness, and the search for solutions to transnational problems (e.g., climate change, organized crime)—also figure prominently in Europe. Where possible, this book tries to connect our discussion of Europe to larger debates and theories in political science.

A European model?

Lastly, and certainly most controversially, one could suggest that Europe not only presents an empirical field for the study of politics but also a normative (values-based) one. In other words, Europe represents a model of how political, economic, and social life *should* be organized. We have already mentioned how some writers regard contemporary Europe as a new superpower. This normative line of argument, however, goes even further and suggests that Europe is not only powerful but also a type of moral exemplar, worthy of study *and* emulation. Jeremy Rifkin, for example, develops this argument by referring to the "European dream" that, in his view, is more compelling than the better-known "American dream" as a source of inspiration both for Europeans and for a wider global audience.[35] Paradoxically, he argues that Europe today is abandoning the emphasis on individualism and material progress spawned by the Enlightenment and is instead focusing on sustainable development, community, and quality of life issues.

European social model
the highly developed welfare state found in many European countries that is funded by high taxes and provides numerous economic and social benefits to citizens.

Much of his argument rests on claims about what might be called the **European social model**, which emphasizes the role of the state in providing social welfare for its citizens. For example, most European states have nationalized and universal health care,[36] free or very low-cost universities, paid maternity benefits,[37] and generous unemployment and child support provisions. Europeans also work far less each year than Americans or Japanese do,[38] and they are allowed to retire earlier. Whereas some might contend this is just a reflection of laziness, the fact is that in the 2000s workers in several European states were more productive than their American peers. True, taxes are higher in Europe than in the US and there are signs that this system is in need of a major overhaul in several countries. Whether the European social model can survive in today's globalized world is an important subject we will consider in Chapter 10.

Some in Europe would go even further, however, and posit that various aspects of the European social model *define* Europe today. More often than not, this point is framed not only in terms of institutions but as part of modern-day European culture, a feature that distinguishes Europe from the United States. For example, Jürgen Habermas, a well-known German philosopher, argues that European identity is built upon a separation of religion from politics, a belief in the power of the state to correct the failures of the market, a party system that explicitly confronts the negative results of capitalist modernization, an ethos of solidarity, a moral sensibility (part of which, according to him, has resulted in a continent-wide ban on the death penalty), and deference to supranational and international authority.[39] Habermas and those that adhere to this view would argue that on these fronts not only is Europe different from America—a country that many Europeans associate with intense religiosity, unbridled patriotism, widespread violence, and an obsession for individual wealth—but also better.

One should note that not all would agree with Habermas or have taken kindly to the idea that movement toward a more unified Europe, perhaps a political union, is one that is supportive of or congruent with democracy. Today, Euroskeptics abound in Europe. After "Brexit," this is most clear in Great Britain,[40] but political figures from nationalist parties are lobbying for "Franxit" for France or "Nexit" for the Netherlands, both countries that in 2005 rejected a Constitutional Treaty for the EU that was designed to strengthen EU institutions. On the other side of the Atlantic, the idea of a European superpower has rung some alarm bells. One British journalist, appealing to an American audience, wrote in 2003 that "it is not too late for the United States to help stop the European superstate from becoming a reality."[41] Robert Kagan, a prominent American neo-conservative writer, acknowledges the numerous differences between Europe and America, maintaining, "Americans are from Mars and Europeans are from Venus," which, in his view, compliments Americans as stronger and "real men."[42] Charles Kupchan, a liberal American scholar, goes even further, suggesting that the coming "clash of civilizations" will not be the West versus Islam or China but, instead, could be Europe versus the US.[43]

Fears of open, hostile conflict between Europe and the US can be easily exaggerated. Madeline Albright, the former US secretary of state, offered an addendum to Kagan's points, noting that Mars and Venus—as Roman gods—got along well and even produced children together, including Harmonia, the Goddess of Concord.[44] Despite real differences on a number of important issues during the presidency of George W. Bush—Iraq, climate change, the US prison camp at Guantanamo Bay, Cuba—Europeans and Americans share a number of basic values, including a commitment to democracy and human rights. Bush's successor, Barack Obama, was quite popular in Europe, although many in Europe were extremely alarmed by the prospect of a President Trump. As noted above, Europe offers no military threat to the US. Focus on differences overlooks the numerous projects—democracy promotion, anti-poverty and anti-AIDS programs, nuclear non-proliferation, international peacekeeping operations—in which Americans and Europeans have worked together.

Moreover, one would be unwise to dismiss the broader European project. After World War II, who would have imagined that France and Great Britain would be allies of Germany within less than a generation? In the 1980s, who could have imagined that the Berlin Wall would fall, prompting dramatic yet peaceful changes that would allow previously Western European institutions such as the EU and NATO (North Atlantic Treaty Organization) to expand eastward? In the 1990s, many—including Henry Kissinger, the worldly and eminent former US secretary of state—expressed doubts that the euro would ever exist, and yet, in 2002, euros replaced the national currencies of twelve countries, and more countries later joined the eurozone. This is not to say that we will see, in Winston Churchill's words in 1946, a "United States of Europe" in our lifetimes. That would clearly be pushing things too far. Nor is this to say that all is well in Europe. Playing on another comment of Churchill's about democracy, one British historian suggested—before the Brexit vote—that "the Europe we have today is the worst possible Europe, apart from all the other Europes that have been tried from time to time."[45] To Euroskeptics inside and outside of Europe, one might therefore ask if their vision of Europe would be as prosperous and peaceful as one in which Europe became even more integrated.

One Europe, or many?

Much of this chapter has discussed the idea that European states and societies are moving closer together and that there is utility in looking at commonalities across individual countries. Each chapter includes an **Is Europe one?** section that illustrates the extent of European unity on a particular issue. However, the question is not purely rhetorical. Please be mindful of the question mark. In other words, while the idea of a single Europe helps set up a narrative for the text, it is not a pre-judgment on either the empirical reality or on what Europe should become. The "logic" of integration may not always fold, and it has often been challenged on various grounds. One therefore can and often should look critically at the very idea of "one Europe." Europe is, after all, made up of more than thirty countries, each with its own history, system of government, cultural and sub-cultural traditions, and, in most cases, language.

True, historians might discuss Christianity as a common cultural tradition in Europe or feudalism as a common feature of the region's socio-economic development, but one can argue whether either retains relevance today. Christianity has been torn by schisms, some of which led to violence (e.g., the Thirty Years' War in Europe, 1618–1648), and, debates over Turkey's place in Europe notwithstanding, it is less and less salient as a political or cultural force in most of Europe today. Feudalism has long been eclipsed by industrial development, either in its capitalist or communist forms, and it makes little sense to invoke this as a unifying force in Europe today. As opposed to unity, in modern times Europe has known far more conflict, prompting Jean Monnet, often thought of as the father of European integration, to remark that "Europe has never existed; one has genuinely to create Europe."[46] Perhaps the greatest common denominator in Europe today—at least politically speaking—is the universal establishment of democracy[47] (a factor that by the 2010s serves to leave Russia out of discussions of "Europe"), but, as we shall see, European democratic institutions differ from country to country, and many are of recent origin.

Thus, in contrast to the discourse on European unity, one can also speak of numerous divisions that are a source of conflict or at least potential conflict among European countries. Obviously there have been numerous wars among European states. A partial listing of major conflicts since the seventeenth century would include the Thirty Years' War; the Ottoman conquests in the Balkans and subsequent siege of Vienna (1683); the Seven Years' War (1756–1763), fought globally between France and Britain; the Napoleonic Wars (1803–1815); the Crimean War (1853–1856); the Prussian-Austrian War (1866); the Franco-Prussian War (1870–1871); the First and Second Balkan Wars (1912–1913); World War I (1914–1918); the Polish-Soviet War (1919–1921); World War II (1939–1945); the Cold War (1940s–1991); and the wars after the breakup of Yugoslavia (1991–1999). A student of modern European history could thus argue, with only slight exaggeration, that for more than 300 years major European states were either at war, preparing for war, or recovering from war. Today, war among the larger European states seems impossible, even inconceivable—France, for example, is not preparing for war with Great Britain or Germany.[48] To the extent that there is conflict or security concerns in today's Europe—this is the focus on Chapter 12—it is mostly on its eastern edges (e.g., Turkey, Russia and Ukraine) or generated by non-state actors, in particular, terrorists. In historical perspective, then, the geopolitical situation in today's peaceful Europe is the exception, albeit one for which we can be grateful. While some Europeans would like to say that this past is behind them, or, perhaps, that historic conflicts are now manifested in jokes about one's erstwhile enemies or played out on the football pitch, occasionally one does see vestiges of Europe's past wars rear their head. For example, when Germans began to talk seriously of reunification in early 1990, many French, Polish, and British figures were apprehensive, remembering what a previously strong and united Germany had done a half century earlier.[49]

Moreover, even though a major war between large European states seems inconceivable, there are still divisions and important differences among countries in Europe. In most general terms, one can point to four distinct peoples, cultures, or linguistic groups in Europe: a Germanic one (e.g., German, Swedish, Dutch) in the north, Slavic (e.g., Polish, Bulgarian, Slovak) in the east, Latin (e.g., Italian, French, Portuguese) in the south, and Celtic (e.g., Irish, Scottish, Breton) on the western fringe. Stereotypes regarding each abound (e.g., the hardworking and stoic German, the amorous and passionate Italian, the fatalistic Pole), and, perhaps, these do capture some real differences. There are also a variety of religious traditions: Catholic, Protestant, and Orthodox Christians (and numerous variants with respect to the latter two categories), Jews, and, increasingly, Muslims. This has been both a source of past conflict and, particularly with the arrival of non-Christian immigrants, current debates and tensions. Ideological divides may seem less salient today than during the Cold War, but one can still speak of how vestiges of communist rule account for sociological, cultural, and economic differences between West European and former communist states, and many countries, particularly those like Portugal, Spain and Greece, hard-hit by the economic crisis of the 2000s, have acute political divisions along the traditional left-right political spectrum. The fact that the very definition of Europe is contested has led to some conflict, as some countries, such as Ukraine and Turkey, have been excluded from the most grandiose incarnation of Europe—the EU—on the grounds that they do not, as yet, fully embrace "European" standards or principles.

Even within the EU—with members committed to common values—there are regular battles over the budget and the distribution of power between larger and smaller countries and between richer and poorer ones, the latter of which became particularly salient during the economic crisis of the late 2000s. On various foreign policy matters, there are splits between those states that harbor more goodwill towards America or see their interests align with those of the US (e.g., Great Britain, Poland) and those that, for historical, ideological, or purely pragmatic reasons, are more apt to oppose some of Washington's initiatives (e.g., France, Greece). These have been most salient with respect to intervention in the Middle East, an issue briefly highlighted in this chapter's **Is Europe one?** feature. In economic orientation, one can identify differences between states that have a more free market approach (e.g., Great Britain, Ireland, Finland, the Netherlands) and those that have more of a socialist tradition with a large state sector and state regulation over the economy (e.g., France, Sweden, Italy, Slovenia). Even though most European states do have well-developed social welfare programs, there are variations across countries and regions. Among the citizens of Europe, one can also point to differences in political culture defined by national lines, economic conditions, or historical experiences, a topic we shall explore in more detail in Chapter 9. One can argue whether all of these types of differences are more salient than the common features across European countries today, but the simple point is that one cannot and should not uncritically treat Europe as an undifferentiated whole.

Is Europe one?

European involvement in Iraq and Libya

Although Europeans and Americans both espouse freedom and democracy, and most European countries are in NATO with the US, Europeans and Americans have not always seen eye to eye on foreign policy matters. In recent years, this has been clearest in the Middle East, particularly with respect to the US-led invasion of Iraq in 2003. However, in this case, as well as the NATO intervention in Libya in 2011 to support an uprising against the dictatorial government of Muamar Qaddafi, one also saw clear divisions within Europe.

While the war in Iraq was unpopular among European publics—there were massive demonstrations against it in many European capitals—many countries did send troops to Iraq. These included Great Britain, Italy, Spain, the Netherlands, Denmark, Portugal, Norway, Poland, Romania, the Czech Republic, Slovakia, Latvia, Estonia, Bulgaria, Albania, Hungary, and Bosnia. Of the twenty-seven members (or, in 2003, soon-to-be members) in the EU, more than half (fifteen) sent troops—hardly evidence that Europe refused to support the US. True, only a few countries deployed a large number of troops: The British sent 46,000 men and women; Italian forces peaked at 3,200; Poland's at 2,500; Spain and the Netherlands sent roughly 1,300 troops each. In contrast, Estonia sent only forty (about a tenth of the *per capita* US commitment of troops) and Slovakia and Lithuania just over a hundred each.[50] Still, the willingness of many post-communist states to support the US was notable, with then-US Secretary of Defense Donald Rumsfeld remarking on the "new Europe," as opposed to France and Germany, traditionally viewed as the leaders of the EU, which refused to send any troops at all.

By the summer of 2009 all non-US forces were withdrawn from Iraq, a reflection of the rising costs (and ambiguity in the mission) of occupation and rising anti-war sentiment. Still, the fact that many governments sided with the US was testimony to the strength of the Atlantic alliance. On the other hand, the fact that Europe was so divided, with two of the largest EU members opposing the war while many "old" (e.g., Britain, Italy, and the Netherlands) or soon to-be or "new" EU members (e.g., Poland and Slovakia) sent troops, provided further evidence that the quest to forge a united Europe, at least on some important foreign policy matters, remained a chimera.

In 2011, in the wake of the "Arab Spring" uprisings, the Western alliance faced a new crisis. While authoritarian regimes were relatively peacefully removed in Tunisia and Egypt, an armed uprising in Libya was engaged with government forces, and the country was sliding into civil war. The US, along with several of European states, called for action, and, unlike in Iraq, secured a UN mandate for intervention.[51] Furthermore, in this case, there was clearly more of an urgent humanitarian dimension—Libyan government forces were poised to attack Benghazi, the center of the rebellion, and there was little doubt there would be massive bloodshed—and the security concern, namely a massive wave of refugees, was also less hypothetical than Saddam Hussein's alleged reservoir of weapons of mass destruction (which were never found). However, the war in Iraq had not gone well, and many, particularly in the US, were loath to send in troops to occupy another Arab country. In this case, the US chose, in a phrase that President Obama later had to try to live down, to "lead from behind," as the British, French, and Canadians took the lead in launching air strikes. However, the US did employ cruise missiles in support of this mission, as well as providing ammunition to the British and French, who ran out of materiel. As in the case with Iraq, other European countries offered modest amounts of support—mainly in enforcing a naval blockade. Participants in this mission included Italy, Spain, Belgium, Norway, and Denmark, but only two post-communist states (Bulgaria and Romania). As with Iraq, Germany elected not to intervene, demonstrating again that Europe could not act as one in a key foreign policy decision. Ultimately, Western intervention helped remove Qaddafi from power, but, as with Iraq, it failed to prevent the country from sliding into civil war and becoming a terrorist haven.[52] This has made Western leaders even more reticent to intervene in the region, even as, in the case of Syria, the humanitarian and security costs have been immense.

Critical thinking questions

1. What factors do you think best account for why some European countries supported intervention in Iraq and Libya and others did not?
2. Why do you think Americans tend to be more supportive of overseas military campaigns—Iraq is but one example—whereas Europeans frequently are not?

social cleavages
lines of division within a given society, produced by socio-demographic factors such as class, region, ethnicity, and age.

Equally significantly, one must recognize that there are important divisions or **social cleavages** within countries. In other words, just as it would be mistaken to focus exclusively on the commonalities of Czechs and Germans as Europeans, one should also recognize that there are notable differences among people within the Czech Republic or Germany. Many of these cleavages are well known to social scientists: class, gender, occupation, urban/rural divides, age, region (e.g., West versus East Germany), and ethnicity (e.g., ethnic Czech versus a Czech citizen of Roma [Gypsy] heritage). Sometimes, these differences have manifested themselves in open, armed conflict or terrorism, as has been the case in Northern Ireland (Catholics vs. Protestants), Bosnia (Serbs/Croats/Muslim Bosniaks), and Turkey (Turks vs. Kurds). As we'll note in Chapter 7, some cleavages, particularly ethnic and linguistic ones, have fueled separatism in countries such as Spain and Belgium. Most of the time, however, while these cleavages do not garner dramatic headlines, they are the stuff of politics, contributing to the formation of competing political parties, social movements, and interest organizations.[53] These issues are taken up in more detail in Chapters 8 and 9.

This text takes up many of the themes suggested in this opening chapter. In contrast to many treatments of today's Europe that are rooted exclusively in comparative politics at the state level, this book devotes more attention to the EU, processes of Europeanization, and the workings of multi-level governance. The next two chapters provide brief historical background. One focuses on domestic political developments, particularly the continent-wide emergence of democratic, capitalist systems, while another traces the development of the EU, the main institutional form for a "one Europe." The next set of chapters (Chapters 4 through 9) focuses on political institutions and political culture. It begins, however, with consideration of the institutions and policies of the EU, recognizing that the EU is central to much of European politics today and that processes of Europeanization emanating from the EU have a great impact on domestic political institutions. Coverage of domestic political institutions (e.g., parliaments, executives, courts, parties) follows, and these chapters largely eschew country-by-country analysis, looking instead at patterns across the continent and comparing and contrasting various features. Within these chapters we shall also consider how Europeanization affects state-level institutions and decision-making. Finally, the last three chapters take up a variety of contemporary issues that have relevance across a wide number of countries, looking for factors that are helping to pull European states closer together and those that create problems of governance at both the national and international levels.

The fall of the Berlin Wall, as noted at the outset of the chapter, was a key event in opening up possibilities for a freer, more united Europe. Germany and Europe as a whole have changed dramatically in the past twenty-five years. Over this period, Europeans have had other events to celebrate, but, for those pushing for an institutionally more capable EU or a more dynamic, competitive economic environment on the continent, much work remains to be done. Many now suggest Europeanization may have gone too far, and that states need to assert themselves against a too-powerful EU. The expectation is that after reading this book you will gain insights into these contemporary issues, as well as the history, political institutions, and complex political, economic, and social forces that define European politics today.

Application questions

1. What characteristics do you associate with the term "Europe"? What makes Europe distinctive from, say, the US, Australia, or Canada?
2. In recent years, how has Europe tried to use its "soft power"? Under what conditions is reliance on "soft power" more likely to succeed?
3. Do you see Europe as a successful actor on the world stage? If so, how? Where? If not, what prevents Europe from being a "superpower"?
4. Do you believe, like Habermas, that Europe offers an attractive model? What might be problems with the European social model?
5. Do you agree there is a "logic" of Europeanization? How far do you believe Europeanization can go? Do you believe Euroskepticism is a more potent political force?

Key terms

Cold War	7
communism	16
Enlightenment	15
European social model	17
European Union (EU)	2
Europeanization	3
Euroskepticism	4

Additional reading

Calleo, David. 2003. *Rethinking Europe's Future*. Princeton: Princeton University Press.
Utilizing perspectives from history, economics, politics, and philosophy, this book traces the development of Europe's political economy. It also raises important questions about whether and how Europe can build on its past achievements and overcome contemporary challenges. Although intended for a scholarly audience more so than other books mentioned here, it would be very useful to students taking classes on modern Europe.

Delanty, Gerard. 1995. *Inventing Europe: Idea, Identity, Reality*. New York: St. Martin's Press.
An oft-cited source that takes up, from a historical and constructivist position, the question, "What is Europe?". Delanty's core argument is that the definition of Europe has changed over time, and that it is a reflection of particular economic, social, international, and ideological contexts.

Hooghe, Liesbet, and Marks, Gary. 2001. *Multi-Level Governance and European Integration*. Lanham MD: Rowman and Littlefield.
Important source on how the growing power of the EU and delegation of authority to sub-national (regional) governments is eroding the power of the nation-state. This presents a more nuanced picture of governance in Europe, particularly how the different levels (pan-European, state, sub-state) interact with each other.

Reid, T.R. 2004. *The United States of Europe: The New Superpower and the End of American Supremacy*. New York: Penguin.
This book, written by a journalist who was stationed in Europe, compares the US and Europe on a number of fronts and argues that Europe is eclipsing the US in several key respects, including economic performance and international influence.

Rifkin, Jeremy. 2004. *The European Dream: How Europe's Vision of the Future Is Quietly Eclipsing the American Dream*. New York: Penguin.
Perhaps one of the strongest "pro-Europe" manifestos, this book examines the development of a particular European "model" and why this is more compelling, both within Europe and as a global model, than the American "dream."

Notes

1 Lest one think this is completely hypothetical, in 2006 Günter Grass, Germany's most famous post-World War II author, admitted that he had served in the German army in the later stages of the war. This revelation puts a shadow on Grass's moral authority within Germany and as a world literary figure. Pope Benedict XVI was also compelled to join Hitler Youth during World War II.

2 T.R. Reid, The United States of Europe: The New Superpower and the End of American Supremacy (New York: Penguin, 2004).
3 For a solid review of challenges facing the EU, see Jim Yardley, "The Breaking Point," *New York Times Magazine*, December 20, 2015, p. 38–57, and George Soros and Gregor Peter Schmitz, "The EU Is on the Verge of Collapse—An Interview," *New York Review of Books*, February 11, 2016.
4 For detailed discussion of Europeanization in a variety of fields, see Paolo Graziano and Maarten P. Vink, eds. *Europeanization: New Research Agendas* (New York: Palgrave, 2007).
5 For more on this concept, see Maria Green Cowles, James Caporaso, and Thomas Risse, eds. *Transforming Europe: Europeanization and Domestic Change* (Ithaca NY: Cornell University Press, 2001), and Kevin Featherstone and Claudio Radaelli, eds. *The Politics of Europeanization* (Oxford: Oxford University Press, 2003).
6 Daniele Caramani, The Europeanization of Politics: The Formation of a European Electorate and Party System in Historical Perspective (Cambridge: Cambridge University Press, 2015).
7 This was the phrase of Jacques Poos, the Foreign Minister of Luxembourg, rebuffing possible American intervention in the early stages of the conflict. Quoted in Noel Malcolm, "The Case Against Europe," *Foreign Affairs* 74:2, March/April 1995, p. 68.
8 Gary Marks, Liesbet Hooghe, and Kermit Blank, "European Integration from the 1980s: State-Centric vs. Multi-Level Governance," *Journal of Common Market Studies* 34:3, September 1996, p. 372. See also Hooghe and Marks, *Multi-Level Governance and European Integration* (Lanham MD: Rowman and Littlefield, 2001).
9 Hooghe and Marks, *Multi-Level Governance*, p. xi.
10 Pocock argues that the first delineation of Europe was made by ancient peoples who plied the waters of the Bosphorus. They developed myths and folk-tales that in effect gave the name "Europa" to the lands to the West, and "Asia" to the lands to the East. From J.G.A. Pocock, "Some Europes and Their History," in Anthony Pagden, ed. *The Idea of Europe* (Washington: Woodrow Wilson Center Press, 2002), p. 56.
11 See Gerard Delanty, *Inventing Europe: Idea, Identity, Reality* (New York: St. Martin's Press, 1995), and Pagden, *The Idea of Europe*.
12 Some states, such as Switzerland and Austria, were officially neutral in the Cold War, but their political systems would qualify them as Western European. Arguably, it was Turkey's alignment with the West in the Cold War—Turkey joined NATO in 1952—that helped it gain recognition in 1963 as geographically eligible to join the fledgling European Economic Community.
13 Charlemagne, "The Myth of the Periphery," *The Economist*, March 27, 2010.
14 Helene Sjursen, "Introduction—Enlargement in Perspective," in Sjursen, ed. *Enlargement in Perspective* (Oslo: ARENA, 2005), p. 8. See also Sjursen, "Why expand? The Question of Legitimacy and Justification in the EU's Enlargement Policy," *Journal of Common Market Studies* 40:3, 2002, p. 491–513.
15 Jose I. Torreblanca, The Reuniting of Europe: Promises, Negotiations and Compromises (Aldershot: Ashgate, 2001).
16 Mikhail Gorbachev, *Perestroika: New Thinking for Our Country and the World* (New York: Harper and Row, 1987), p. 190. The irony, of course, is that many Europeans saw the Soviet Union separate from Europe and Gorbachev himself, although a reformer, was leader of an undemocratic state.
17 Helmut Schmidt, "Wer nicht zu Europa gehört," *Die Zeit*, October 11, 2000.
18 "Turkey's EU Bid: Resistance is on the Rise," *Business Week*, February 9, 2004.
19 Indeed, in its heritage, like Judaism and Islam, it is an "Asian" religion. Jesus (and Moses and Abraham) was not a European.
20 *New York Times*, October 3, 2004, p. 13.
21 Thierry de Montbrial, "Debating the borders of Europe," *International Herald Tribune*, May 21, 2004.
22 In 2009, after a severe economic crisis, the parliament of Iceland approved a measure to make an application to join the EU. It is highly uncertain whether Icelandic voters, however, will eventually approve EU membership.

23 As of this writing, the timing of "Brexit" is uncertain. In any event, the larger point—that "Europe" broadly defined has a larger economy than the US—still holds.
24 The European Union has achieved near universal (99+ percent) literacy, as compared with 95 percent in China and 69 percent in India (World Bank data, from 2010/2011). As for health, average life expectancy in the EU is 81, compared to 76 in China and 68 in India (World Bank data, 2014).
25 All data from the World Bank, www.worldbank.org.
26 As an example, even *The Economist* employs a Big Mac index to gauge prices and purchasing power across countries.
27 Other brands include Texaco, Amoco, Snapple, A&W Root Beer, Dr. Pepper, Random House, Dunkin Donuts, Holiday Inn, Dial soap, Bazooka bubble gum, Baskin-Robbins, and even Ben and Jerry's, now owned by Unilever, a Dutch company. See Jeremy Rifkin, *The European Dream: How Europe's Vision of the Future is Quietly Eclipsing the American Dream* (New York: Penguin, 2004).
28 Italy, with 320,000 active duty personnel as of 2015, ranks eigteenth, after countries such as Columbia, Vietnam, South Korea, and Egypt. Turkey (fourteenth largest at 410,500 people) has the largest force in Europe, excluding Russia. See www.globalfirepower.com/active-military-manpower.asp, accessed June 26, 2016.
29 Joseph S. Nye, *The Paradox of American Power* (Oxford: Oxford University Press, 2002), p. 8.
30 Mark Leonard, *Why Europe Will Run the 21st Century* (London: Fourth Estate, 2005).
31 Leonard, *Why Europe*, p. 35.
32 Zachary Shore, *Breeding Bin Ladens: America, Islam, and the Future of Europe* (Baltimore: Johns Hopkins University Press, 2006).
33 I use liberalism here in its classic and European sense, meaning a belief in limited government, individual rights and choice, and tolerance toward differing views. In this view, liberalism is associated with democratic governments and free-market economies and virtually all Americans, whether they recognize it or not, are liberals. I recognize that Americans often define the term liberal differently, denoting a political position left of center that often endorses a more interventionist role of the state in the economy. However, any reader of the conservative British publication *The Economist* will immediately notice how it generally praises "liberal" policies and programs.
34 Classic works on nationalism that identify it as a modern phenomenon arising at the time of the French Revolution include Ernest Gellner, *Nations and Nationalism* (Ithaca: Cornell University Press, 1983) and Eric Hobsbawm, *Nations and Nationalism Since 1780* (Cambridge: Cambridge University Press, 1992).
35 Rifkin, The European Dream.
36 Whereas some would contend that the quality of health care in the US is superior, the fact is that the US spends more on health as a percentage of its national wealth (about 15 percent, twice as much as Sweden or France) and has a lower life expectancy than most Western European countries.
37 Whereas in the US new parents gained the right in the 1990s to take twelve weeks of unpaid leave, Swedish mothers get up to sixty-four weeks off at two-thirds pay.
38 Reid claims that in 2003 Americans worked on average 1,976 hours, 400 more than German or French workers and 200 more than British workers. See Reid, *The United States of Europe*, p. 155.
39 Timothy G. Ash, Free World: Why the Crisis of the West Reveals an Opportunity for Our Time (New York: Penguin, 2005), p. 47–48.
40 Anyone wanting to familiarize herself with the British Euroskeptic position need only pick up a copy of a British tabloid newspaper such as *The Sun* or *The Daily Telegraph*. A more erudite Euroskeptic account can be found in Malcolm, "The Case Against Europe," and in Christopher Booker and Richard North, *The Great Deception: Can the European Union Survive?*, 2nd edition (London: Continuum, 2005).
41 Gerard Baker, "Against United Europe," *Weekly Standard*, September 22, 2003.
42 Robert Kagan, *Of Paradise and Power: America and Europe in the New World Order* (New York: Alfred Knopf, 2003), p. 3. This reference draws from the 1992 book *Men Are from Mars, Women Are from Venus* by John Gray.

43 Charles Kupchan, *The End of the American Era* (New York: Vintage, 2003).
44 Taken from remarks made at the William Davidson Institute at the University of Michigan, March 24, 2004.
45 Timothy Garton Ash, quoted in Roger Cohen, "Britain's Leap in the Dark," *The New York Times*, June 25, 2016.
46 Quoted in Rifkin, *The European Dream*, p. 200.
47 This is not to say that democracy is not threatened in parts of Europe, including, in the 2010s, in Hungary, Poland, and Turkey. These cases are discussed more in later chapters of this volume.
48 There are, of course, security issues in the Balkans and growing worries in some quarters of a resurgent Russia, but conflict between major powers in Europe—as opposed to local, secessionist conflicts such as Kosovo, Abkhazia, or Chechnya—is not a major worry.
49 Margaret Thatcher wrote that she had conversations with French President Francois Mitterand (1981–1995) about how to "check the German juggernaut." Quoted in Tony Judt, *Postwar: A History of Europe Since 1945* (New York: Penguin, 2005), p. 639.
50 Data come from Christopher Blanchard and Catherine Dale, *Iraq: Foreign Contributions to Stabilization and Reconstruction* (Washington: Congressional Research Service, 2007), available at http://fpc.state.gov/documents/organization/99533.pdf.
51 UN Resolution 1973 had a limited mandate, to protect civilians and enforce a no-fly zone. Critics of the intervention, notably Russia, claimed the US and its allies overstepped their authority in attacking Libyan government targets.
52 Alan Kuperman, "Obama's Libya Debacle," *Foreign Affairs* 94:2, March/April 2015, p. 66–77.
53 The classic work on social cleavages in advanced industrial states in Seymour M. Lipset and Stein Rokkan, *Party Systems and Voter Alignments: Cross-National Perspectives* (New York: Free Press, 1967).

Srebrenica 1995: Fifty years after World War II, another genocide in Europe

Chapter 2

Political and economic development in Western and Eastern Europe

On July 11, 2015, local, regional, and international dignitaries, including former US President Bill Clinton, gathered in Srebrenica Bosnia, where, twenty years previously, the worst massacre in Europe since World War II occurred. In July 1995, over 8,000 Bosnian Muslim men and boys were killed by Bosnian Serb forces after United Nations (UN) peacekeeping forces ignominiously withdrew under pressure from the Serbs. This tragedy was later labeled an "act of genocide" by a UN war crimes tribunal and the International Court of Justice. Clinton and others duly paid homage to the victims, pledging "never again" would the world turn its back on such crimes against humanity. Among the speakers was Serbian Prime Minister Aleksandar Vučic, who planned to offer words of conciliation. In the 1990s, however, Vučic was a leader of the Serbian Radical Party, and he was a staunch supporter of the Bosnian Serbs and their military commanders, several of whom were subsequently put on trial for war crimes. As he prepared to speak, protesters in the crowd unfurled a banner reading "For one Serb, we will kill 100 Muslims," a statement Vučic himself made in the week after the Srebrenica massacre. Rocks and bottles were thrown in his direction, and he was hastily evacuated from the scene.[1]

This event illustrates a number of important points. First, history casts a shadow over the present, as wounds created in the past do not always easily heal. This is true not only with relatively recent episodes (such as the war in Bosnia) that are in the living memory of most Europeans, but also for more distant events such as the Holocaust, World War II, nationalist uprisings in the nineteenth century, and centuries-old battles against Turks and Arabs. Not only do past events often color contemporary political debates, but broad historical patterns help account for political and economic development and shape today's culture and values. Secondly, history is contested. Whereas Srebrenica is viewed by Bosnian Muslims as their Auschwitz, many Serbs believe that claims of genocide are a lie and are evidence of Serbia's mistreatment by the international community. Other questions for historical debate include responsibility for past conflicts, the case for separatism (e.g., Scotland, Catalonia), the relative merits of different development strategies, one's place (or not) in the current EU, and, more broadly, national (as well as European) identity. On a related note, one should keep in mind that history can also be abused and that historical analogies only stretch so far. Memories of the war in Bosnia are used by some to stereotype ethnic groups. Angry Greeks, upset at EU-imposed austerity measures, compare German Chancellor Angela Merkel to Hitler. Memories of Ottoman invasions of Europe are invoked in contemporary debates over Muslim immigrants. Lastly, whereas one can understand history as an unchangeable given, it can also be viewed as something to be overcome. Certainly, those who wish for peace and reconciliation in Bosnia adopt this perspective, and the entirety of the EU project could be interpreted as a means to overcome nationalism and put many historical ghosts to rest while embracing values such as democracy, rule of law, and respect for human rights, features that themselves evolved over time and today increasingly define what it is to be European. Whether or not this has been successful is one of the major themes of this book.

This chapter serves as a historical overview of Europe, recognizing that in order to understand many of the contemporary political issues and debates in Europe and to discuss where Europe might be heading, it is imperative to have some idea of where Europe has been and how, through various means, certain "European" ideas and practices developed and took root. It will focus on broad trends that helped shape the present, in particular the development of states, democratic institutions, and economic systems. It is intended to be more a cursory treatment than a comprehensive history.

It is difficult, notwithstanding the discussion of "One Europe" in the previous chapter, to isolate a single European history. Historically speaking, Europe was divided, often profoundly so. Rather than focus on discrete national histories, this chapter will focus on general patterns of development in Western and Eastern Europe.

Western European development

Countries in Western and Eastern Europe developed differently in several key respects, and one could argue that the Western European experience largely defines in substantive terms what Europe "means" today. Thus when Eastern Europeans stated in the 1990s that they wanted to rejoin Europe, they were asserting that they wanted to enjoy what *Western* Europe already had, as democratic, capitalist systems had become the norm for the continent. Understanding how Western European states evolved is thus a logical first step in understanding contemporary discussions of "Europe."

The emergence of nation-states

A fundamental institution in the study of political science is the **state**, a political association that exercises authority over a territory and its inhabitants. In English, state and country are often used interchangeably, although one can distinguish the two by noting that it is the state, as an organization, that rules over a given country/territory. Although other political associations (e.g., tribes, empires) have existed throughout human history, modern, centralized states first arose in Western Europe. Whereas there were more than 1,000 different European mini-kingdoms or principalities in the fourteenth century, by the end of the nineteenth century, one could speak of a dozen major states in Western Europe.

state

a political association that exercises authority over a territory and its inhabitants.

State formation

How did states form? Although some might want to harbor more romantic notions, examination of European history reveals that today's European states are, in essence, winners in a brutal survival-of-the-fittest conflict among competing political entities. In simple terms, today's states with their territorial boundaries are largely the result of military conflict. In Charles Tilly's well-known formulation, "War made the state and the state made war."[2] In the case of Great Britain, for example, most date the emergence of the current English state to 1066, when William the Conqueror (from Normandy, part of today's France) invaded and won the English crown. In France, early French rulers in the Middle Ages subdued provincial rulers in regions such as Brittany and Burgundy. Switzerland, one of Europe's oldest states, traces its foundation to 1291 with the creation of a confederacy among three Swiss cantons (regions) that fought against foreign rule. In Scandinavia, Denmark, due to military prowess and dynastic unions, gained dominance by the time of the Kalmar Union in 1397, but Swedish revolts in the 1500s led to the creation of a separate Swedish kingdom, which eventually extended its dominion to Norway (independent only since 1905) and Finland (independent since 1917). Spain was united in 1492, when the last Moors (Muslims) were driven out of southern Spain, but the Spanish government, even with its vast wealth thanks to its colonies in the New World, exercised weak authority over its many disparate regions.

Other states in Europe are more recent creations. The Netherlands, which was part of the Spanish Kingdom, gained independence in 1648 after an eighty-year struggle. In 1830, French-speaking socialists and Dutch-speaking Catholics successfully rebelled the rule of a Protestant Dutch king, thereby creating Belgium, which was ruled by a German king. Italy and Germany were the last two major Western European states to form. Both had well-established cultures and economically vibrant regions but lacked political unity. Italy, divided into a host of regions and city-states (e.g., Naples, Florence, Venice, Rome), was unified only in 1861 thanks to the combined military efforts of the rulers of the region of Piedmont and the revolutionary Giuseppe Garibaldi. In the early 1800s there was an effort to unite the numerous German principalities, but a single Germany did not come into being until 1871, when various German regions were brought together thanks to the military victories of Prussia (one such German region, centered in Berlin) over Denmark, Austria-Hungary, and France. Austria, where German is also the primary language, became a separate state only in 1918, after the dismemberment of the multi-ethnic Austro-Hungarian Empire.

Intense military competition on continental Western Europe prompted the formation of more centralized governments. State power in turn led to technological, administrative, and economic growth.[3] Early European states, of course, did not perform all the functions of states today, most notably provision of social welfare and universal education. However, their primary activities—taxation and military recruitment—put resources into their hands so that they could consolidate their power in Europe and, eventually, globally, as they established colonies in the Western Hemisphere, Asia, and Africa.

The doctrine of sovereignty

sovereignty
the exclusive right of a ruler or state to exercise political authority over a territory and people; in various ways, this doctrine is being challenged by today's EU.

Two features distinguish modern European states from their predecessors: the doctrines of **sovereignty** and nationalism. Sovereignty refers to the exclusive right of a ruler to exercise political authority over a territory and people. It suggests that the ruler is supreme, that is, not needing to share power with any other social or political entity, such as a religious establishment or regional authority. Put forward initially as a legal doctrine by Jean Bodin (1530–1596), sovereignty suggested that the ruler (a king) was not subject to any human law, answering only to God or natural law. As it evolved, sovereignty included the principle of non-interference in the affairs of other states. States were therefore sovereign, able to do whatever they wanted over the territory they ruled. As ideas of democracy expanded, the notion of popular sovereignty developed, meaning that it was the people or nation that was sovereign, not an individual monarch. To the extent that supranational organizations such as the EU and global economic forces are undermining the "power of the people," many worry about both how state sovereignty and democracy will fare as European states draw closer together.

nationalism
belief that primary source of an individual's identity belongs with a broader collective, the nation; often used to argue for the independence and power of the nation.

Nationalism: Fostering a sense of identity

Establishing sovereign control over a territory was but a part of state formation in Western Europe. States also had to rule over a population. In order to facilitate political control, rulers needed to employ more than repression and coercion. States needed to gain legitimacy, a sense among the people that state authorities have a right to rule over them. Previously, rulers had attempted to legitimize their rule and claim sovereignty through use of religion, claiming a divine right to rule. As the power of the religious establishment, however, came under assault and, in some cases, monarchies were overthrown or were forced to make compromises with groups in society, notions of "divine right" became untenable. Instead, leaders attempted to foster a sense of loyalty, an affective link between the state and the people under its control. In most European countries, this was accomplished by the development of **nationalism**.

nation
a group of people united by various traits (e.g., language, culture, history) that often aspire for a state of their own.

Nationalism has many possible definitions.[4] For our purposes, we can define it as a belief that locates the source of individual identity within a broader collective, the **nation**, which is also the central object for loyalty. The nation can also be defined in various ways. Some endow it with more objective, observable traits (e.g., a common language, religion, history) that unify its various members and give a nation political and social coherence. Others would emphasize that nations are constructed, built upon myths or imaginations of the past or of a common destiny. For nationalists, the boundaries of the state (an organization) should correspond with those of the nation (a people). Nationalism, in other words, posits that nations should have their own states, and state power is legitimate to the extent that it fulfills the need for the nation to rule itself. However, the push for a more united Europe in many respects seeks to transcend nationalism and create a pan-European identity. Suffice it to say, at least for now, that this project is controversial among those still beholden to more conventional ideas of nationalism.

Not all nationalisms, however, are the same. Obviously, the particulars of French nationalism, Danish nationalism, Italian nationalism, etc., will differ. Broadly speaking, however, one can point to two different types of nationalism:

civic nationalism
a more inclusive idea that defines the nation on the basis of common citizenship and/or acquired characteristics such as acceptance of certain political values; examples include Great Britain, France, and the US.

ethnic nationalism
a more exclusive form of identity that stresses features such as heredity and religion that are allegedly intrinsic to the people; a historical example is German nationalism.

civic nationalism and **ethnic nationalism**. Civic nationalism defines the nation on the basis of common citizenship and/or acquired characteristics such as acceptance of certain political values. It tends to be more inclusive. Many Western European states have a predominantly civic view of the nation. Whereas citizenship might be defined by birth, one can also "become" British or French, for example, by moving to the country, accepting its basic political values, and becoming a naturalized citizen. To the extent that civic nationalism emphasizes membership in a political community, it is rather similar to patriotism, love of one's country. Ethnic nationalism, on the other hand, stresses features such as heredity and religion that are allegedly intrinsic to the people. It tends to be reactive and less inclusive, positing clearer divisions between "us" and "them," the latter of which cannot truly become part of "us." Although more common in Eastern Europe, it does have one Western European variant worth mentioning: Germany. Because Germany existed as a cultural entity long before it was politically unified, it could not have a nationalism based upon a common citizenship. Its earliest nationalists tended to be intellectuals who emphasized the cultural uniqueness, if not superiority, of the German people. According to Wilhelm von Humboldt (1767–1835), a relative liberal and the founder of the University of Berlin,

> There is perhaps no country that deserves to be free and independent as Germany, because none is so disposed to devote its freedom so single-mindedly to the welfare of all. The German genius is among all nations the one which is least destructive, which always nourishes itself, and when freedom is secured Germany will certainly attain an outstanding place in every form of culture and thought.[5]

Understanding the roots of German nationalism, which even in the nineteenth century was directed against the British, French, and Jews, goes a long way toward explaining some of the darker moments in twentieth-century Europe.

One might also note that many states had trouble establishing any form of state-centered nationalism. This was especially true in multi-ethnic states such as Belgium (split between Dutch speakers and French speakers) and Spain (with sizeable non-Spanish peoples such as Basques, Catalans, and Galicians).

Nationalization of politics

Nationalism was put forward as an objective and ideology by political elites and intellectuals. Its goal was to create a more coherent, homogeneous nation-state, one in which the political boundaries of the state would correspond with the cultural boundaries of the nation. This was not an easy task, often because even though nationalism was advanced in the name of the people, the people themselves had little feeling of nationalism. In the words of Massimo D'Azeglio, a leading figure in the drive to unite Italy in the 1860s, "Now that we have made Italy, we have to make Italians."

The nationalization of politics was thus an important theme in many states, lasting at least into the early part of the twentieth century.[6] More parochial, sectarian, peripheral, or local identities had to give way to a national identity. In nationalization's initial stages, center-periphery cleavages predominated, with state elites interested in consolidating their authority by forging a coherent national whole. Particulars varied from state to state: In Germany, the main battles were in overcoming longstanding local identities; in the Netherlands, the division was between Catholics and Protestants; in Scandinavia, the urban/rural divide was important.

Over the course of the nineteenth and twentieth centuries, nationalism's hold grew stronger throughout Europe. Much of this was the result of the expansion of state power, meaning that the state made nations.[7] Common curricula in public education helped spread the national idea and standardize language. Media such as radio and newspapers also played a role, as people began to connect, however vicariously, with other citizens in the state. Economic growth contributed to the growth of more cosmopolitan cities, where people from different parts of the country interacted with each other. The growth of transportation networks led to the development of national economies. Over time, the development of capitalism contributed to the growth of class antagonisms, meaning that left-right political cleavages between workers and owners increasingly defined political life, as territorial or ethno-linguistic divisions receded in importance. Diversity gave way to standardization. Whereas in the 1700s multiple languages were spoken in France and Germany was a collection of small princely kingdoms, by the early twentieth century, one could speak without hesitation of a French or German nation that was both culturally and politically unified.

Origins of democracy

Europe is not only the birthplace of the modern state. Europeans were also the first to develop democratic forms of government. Indeed, one of the main themes of European history has been the expansion of democracy, both in terms of its spread to more states and in terms of creating a more inclusive citizenry with political rights. Today, **democracy**, defined in simplest terms as a system of government based upon free and fair elections with universal suffrage and respect for civil and political rights, is fundamental to the political idea of Europe.

democracy
a system of government based upon free and fair elections with universal suffrage and respect for civil and political rights.

The genesis of democracy in Great Britain

Several European countries claim a long democratic history. Iceland maintains that its parliament, the *Althing*, which dates to 930, is the world's oldest legislature. Other Scandinavians such as the Danes and Swedes point to their experience with their own *tings* (assemblies) among various tribes in the Middle Ages as precursors to their own democracies. The Swiss date their democracy back to the initial formation of a Swiss Confederacy in 1291.

Most accounts, however, focus on Great Britain as the birthplace of modern democracy. Britons refer to their parliament, which dates from 1265, as the "mother of all parliaments." The origins of British democracy are usually traced to 1215 with the signing of the Magna Carta, an agreement between the king and feudal barons that protected the latter from abuses by the former. This was an important milestone towards constitutional liberalism, meaning that the power of the state was limited by law. However, the Magna Carta, by itself, did not envision democracy in the sense that the people would henceforth enjoy the rights to elect their leaders. On the contrary, the unelected monarch was still sovereign, and the earliest English parliaments were also unelected bodies of wealthy, landowning nobility. In the 1600s, the power of the monarch was more directly and seriously challenged, thanks in part to the growth of an urban merchant class that wanted political power to go along with its wealth.[8] The English Civil War of the 1640s, which had both political and religious dimensions, led to the overthrow and eventual beheading of King Charles I. In 1688, the (Protestant) monarchy was restored, but the king was allowed to assume the throne provided he recognized the supremacy of parliament, thereby limiting the power of the Crown still further and making Britain the first constitutional monarchy. This event, together with passage in 1689 of a Bill of Rights, was an important milestone toward the development of British democracy, although, because voting rights were severely limited, it is problematic to refer to Great Britain in the 1700s or 1800s as democratic in the contemporary sense. Political and civil rights were only gradually extended to most Britons in the late nineteenth and early twentieth centuries.

Enlightenment and the democratic idea

Whereas the first stirrings of limited government and constitutionalism in Europe date to the Middle Ages, democracy remained both spatially and substantively limited. Most states were monarchies, and most residents could not participate in politics. Democracy came about later, and often only gradually. While democratic development can be understood as a consequence of economic growth and modernization, its philosophical roots lie in the intellectual revolution of the Enlightenment.[9]

The core idea of democracy, of course, dates back to ancient Greece. The term "democracy" derives from the Greek language and means "the people (*demos*) rule." However, ancient Greeks did not have any well-developed notion of individual rights or political equality, both of which underpin modern democratic states. These principles arose during the Enlightenment in the seventeenth and eighteenth centuries. As noted in Chapter 1, the Enlightenment and its ideals distinguish Europe from other regions of the world. Enlightenment thinkers elaborated ideas of natural freedom. Many believed that government should be limited and based upon a **social contract** between the rulers and the ruled, with the rulers enjoying the right to rule only as long as they protected individuals' political and civil rights. They also argued for the liberation of people from both state and religious authority. Denis Diderot, the editor of the famous *Encyclopedia* (1751–1765), the gospel of sorts for the Enlightenment, stated that salvation would arrive "when the last King was strangled with the entrails of the last priest."[10] The Enlightenment provided inspiration for the French Revolution in 1789, which overthrew one of Europe's strongest monarchies and had ripple effects across the continent, as more and more people were drawn to its slogan of "*liberté, egalité, fraternité*" (liberty, equality, solidarity) and its proclamation of universal manhood suffrage.

social contract
idea from various thinkers of the Enlightenment that government rests on a contract, with rulers having the right to rule only as long as they protect peoples' political and civil rights.

Democracy expands

The idea of giving the people a say in their government was put into practice in several European states in the nineteenth century. True, definitions of "the people" were usually limited to the upper classes, but one should recognize that even a narrow application of popular sovereignty constituted a major break with the past, when kings were subject to no law and people were subjects of the crown rather than citizens. Voting in competitive elections, the *sine qua non* of democracy, became widespread, and most states featured some sort of parliamentary institution that was supposed to reflect the popular will. Again, this should not be equated with modern democratic practice. Only a minority of the people could vote. Civil and human rights were not universally respected. However, political power was gradually transferred from monarchs and put in the hands of assemblies that made some sort of claim to represent "the people." The dates in which parliamentary representation and universal manhood suffrage were established are presented in Table 2.1.

A few comments are in order. First, the path to democracy varied from state to state. Whereas in some states, such as Great Britain, Sweden, and Denmark, democracy evolved in a relatively peaceful fashion, in some countries, such as France, Italy, and Spain, it was the product of wars and domestic upheavals. As Charles Tilly notes, there is no singular path to democracy.[11] Secondly, the degree of democracy—as measured by parliamentary supremacy—varied throughout Europe. Whereas in Great Britain and in the Netherlands elected parliaments and prime ministers became the main political players, in Germany executive authority in the figure of the Chancellor (Prime Minister) was accountable to the Kaiser (Emperor), not the parliament. In Belgium, King Leopold II (1865–1909) wielded wide powers, and he was able to use his position to establish a brutally repressive and murderous regime in the Congo in Africa. This was not, to be sure, the only European colonial possession. Great Britain, Spain, Portugal, the Netherlands, and Germany established control over most of Africa and large parts of Asia, and subject peoples in these regions did not enjoy the fruits of democracy. Indeed, John Stuart Mill (1806–1873), mentioned in the previous chapter as a champion of liberalism, defended British colonialism as a largely benign and progressive development, as self-rules and democracy were inappropriate for (in his terms) "backward" or "uncivilized" peoples.[12] In the twentieth century, these subject peoples would demand their rights, pointing to the contradiction between European embrace of ostensibly "universal" rights and colonial subjugation. Lastly, not all early European "democracies" functioned very well. Italy's was (and still is) marked by corruption, and ostensibly democratic governments in Spain and Portugal were wracked by instability throughout the 1800s and in practice functioned more like oligarchies that concentrated power into the hands of very few individuals.

TABLE 2.1 Development of parliamentary representation and voting in Western Europe

Country	*1810*	*1820*	*1830*	*1840*	*1850*	*1860*	*1870*	*1880*	*1890*	*1900*	*1910*
Norway	A									B	
Great Britain			A								B
Switzerland				AB							
Belgium			A						B		
Netherlands				A							B
Italy						A					B
Denmark				A							B
Spain						AB					
France							AB				
Germany							AB				
Sweden						A					B
Finland										AB	
Portugal											AB

A: Start of continuous parliamentary representation; B: First universal manhood suffrage
Source: Adapted from Tilly, *Contention and Democracy in Europe 1650–2000* (2004), p. 214

Expansion of suffrage

The final stage in the growth of European democracy was the expansion of the vote to groups that were previously disenfranchised. Whereas by the mid-1800s men—usually only men of property—enjoyed the vote in most European states, no state was democratic in the twenty-first century sense of that term. For example, in the 1830s less than 5 percent of the population enjoyed the right to vote in Switzerland, the Netherlands, and Great Britain. At this time, urban industrial workers and ordinary peasants and farmers, not to mention all women, were often deemed unfit to participate in politics by their social "betters." In the middle and late 1800s these disenfranchised groups pressed for voting rights in several European countries. It was largely due to pressures "from below," particularly from the working class, not the goodwill of elites or a culture of equality, that more people were given basic democratic political rights.[13]

The first restrictions to go were those that discriminated by economic standing or literacy. As seen in Table 2.1, from the mid-1800s to the early 1900s, property restrictions and literacy tests were lowered and eventually removed, leading to universal male suffrage. Age restrictions were also gradually lowered, so that by the end of World War II, 18 became the usual age for voting eligibility in Europe. The last disenfranchised group to win the vote was women. Women had lobbied aggressively for the right to vote, especially in Great Britain and the Netherlands, but they were unable to achieve success until after World War I. As seen in Table 2.2, Scandinavian states tended to be the first to expand suffrage to women. Italy, Belgium, and Greece granted women equal voting rights only in the aftermath of World War II, and in Switzerland, it was not until 1971 that Swiss men, in a referendum, agreed to give the vote to their wives, mothers, and daughters.

The table shows the year that women gained equal voting rights with men. In some cases, women were allowed to vote in local elections or subject to different age qualifications prior to gaining full equality with men.

TABLE 2.2 Granting of female suffrage in Western Europe

Country	*Year*
Finland	1906
Norway	1913
Denmark	1915
Iceland	1915
Austria	1918
Germany	1918
Netherlands	1919
Sweden	1921
Ireland	1922
Great Britain	1928
France	1944
Italy	1946
Belgium	1948
Greece	1955
Switzerland	1971

Economic development

The Industrial Revolution and early capitalism

Western Europe's ascendance to world economic dominance, which it would maintain until the end of World War II, can be dated to the Industrial Revolution of the 1700s. True, there were important antecedents to Europe's economic takeoff: the discovery of the "New World," which supplied markets, raw materials, and precious metals; profits from the slave trade, which was intimately tied to agricultural production in colonies in the Americas; technological change; and urbanization.

As with constitutional government, Britain was a leader, developing a textile industry in the early 1700s.[14] Development of the steam engine led to breakthroughs in both transportation and early industrial production. Mechanized power contributed to the growth of factories, which were both economically more efficient and fostered more urbanization. By the early 1800s France, the Netherlands, Belgium, and several German states, particularly Prussia, also became industrial powers. By the end of the 1800s, factory towns popped up across the continent.

Without a doubt, the industrial revolution led to great economic progress, at least measured in terms of gross output and the development of new products. While the specifics of each economic system varied from state to state, early industrialization was based on **capitalism**, which rested on private ownership, competition among economic producers, and minimal state intervention in the economy. The father of capitalist thought, the Scottish Enlightenment thinker Adam Smith, wrote in *Wealth of Nations* in 1776 that the pursuit of individual self-interest would lead to an improvement in general welfare.

capitalism the economic system that rests on private ownership, competition among economic producers, and minimal state intervention in the economy; developed in much of Western Europe in the 1700s and 1800s.

Despite the enormous technological progress and immense social change wrought by capitalism, many critics emerged to advocate a different path. Industrialization, while producing immense profits for the owners of capital, also created a working class that worked long days in dangerous conditions and lived in squalor. Child labor was commonplace; the drive for profits kept wages low. Righting the perceived wrongs of capitalism thus became a major political struggle. The best known critic of capitalism was the German political economist Karl Marx (1818–1883), who argued that capitalism dehumanized workers and needed to be thrown off by a workers' revolution, which would lead to the development of communism, a classless society in which there was no private property and all people were equal. Marx's ideas would be the inspiration for revolutionary activity throughout Europe—most notably in 1848 and 1870—and, after his death, a version of his vision was put into place in the Soviet Union.

The rise of national economies

Capitalism, at least envisioned by its early advocates, rested upon the actions of individuals. Later industrializers tended to rely more upon state planning or financing for economic development. This was best exemplified in Germany, where Friedrich List (1789–1846), pressed for the economic unification of German states and urged protectionist measures (e.g., imposition of tariffs) to shield German industry from competition from Great Britain and other more developed states.[15]

Although List did not live to see it, the unified German state would grow rapidly thanks to economic nationalism and state encouragement of construction of modern industries, particularly iron, steel, and chemicals. By the early twentieth century, the state was taking the lead in the economic life of many European states. Nationalism, however, was tempered by growing cross-national economic ties. Ultimately, however, national competition—in economics, armaments, and imperial expansion—spilled over in military conflict.

Turmoil in Europe, 1914–1945

While European history is marked by a variety of political, economic, and technological accomplishments, Europe had a nightmarish first half of the twentieth century. Wars, genocide, and repressive governments caused some 60 million deaths.[16] Economic depression led many to doubt the virtues of capitalism and democracy. Although advocates of a united Europe might emphasize, as did the draft Constitutional Treaty of the EU in 2005, that Europe is a region of "special area of human hope," one should be mindful of the darker side of Europe's past.

This turmoil affected both Western and Eastern Europe. Indeed, both World Wars started in Eastern Europe, and the majority of the military casualties, civilian deaths, and victims of the Holocaust were from Eastern Europe. Politically, however, some of the most important developments in this period occurred in Western Europe. In particular, after World War I (1914–1918), weak democratic governments in Italy and Germany fell to mass movements espousing a militant form of nationalism and a cult of a powerful leader. This was fascism, which explicitly rejected the norms of liberal democracy by emphasizing the rights and powers of the state over the individual and rejecting ideas of equality and tolerance. The first Fascist leader to come to power was Benito Mussolini (1883–1945) in Italy, who organized his "blackshirts" in a struggle against communists and socialists and, promising to restore order, assumed power after unleashing his supporters in a march on Rome that forced the government to resign. Within a few years, Mussolini stripped the Italian parliament of powers, banned opposition parties, and put the press under government control.

Far more dangerous was Adolf Hitler (1889–1945), who modeled Mussolini's tactics while adding elements of Social Darwinism, eugenics, and anti-Semitism (which was far from unique to Germany) in an effort to cultivate his German "master race" and a new *Reich* that would last a thousand years. After 1930, when the Great Depression hit Germany, sparking hyperinflation, massive unemployment, labor unrest, and the possibility of a communist seizure of power, Hitler emerged as a popular figure. His Nazi Party gained 18 percent of the vote in 1930 parliamentary elections and 37 percent in 1932. Conservatives, thinking they could control Hitler, supported his appointment to Chancellor (Prime Minister) in 1933. Afterwards, however, he passed laws banning other political parties and trade unions, passed a series of anti-Jewish laws, and, as *Der Führer* (The Leader), he demanded the unquestioned obedience of the German people. He began to rearm Germany in an effort to secure more *Lebensraum* (living space) for Germany.

Germany's invasion of Poland in September 1939 marked the beginning of World War II, which engulfed most of the continent. It was during the war that Hitler committed his greatest crime, the Holocaust, as millions of European Jews (as well as Roma [Gypsies], Soviet prisoners of war, ordinary Poles, homosexuals, Jehovah's Witnesses, and socialists and communists) were sent to labor and death camps. It is worth mentioning as well that others—in France, the Netherlands, Poland, Austria, and elsewhere—collaborated with Hitler, although thousands of people also tried to save Jews from the gas chambers.

The invasion of the Soviet Union, as well as the declaration of war against the United States in December 1941 after Pearl Harbor, proved to be Hitler's greatest mistakes. Eventually, the alliance of the Soviet Union, Great Britain, and the US pushed the armies of Germany and Italy back. Hitler committed suicide as the Soviet army advanced on Berlin. His thousand-year *Reich* lasted just over twelve years, but was responsible for the deaths of millions, including the genocide against 6 million European Jews.

Post-war development

The end of World War II opened an important new chapter in European history. Whereas the Cold War division between Western and Eastern Europe dominated international politics, within Western Europe democratic governments took hold. Capitalism was tempered with the emergence of a welfare state and, in order to prevent future conflicts, states began the process of economic and political integration.

Cold War divisions

After World War II, the two superpowers—the US and the Soviet Union—divided Europe into spheres of influence. In Western Europe, the US, with economic assistance delivered under the **Marshall Plan**, helped rebuild countries devastated by war and fostered democratic, capitalist systems. In Eastern Europe, behind what Winston Churchill called the "Iron Curtain," the Soviets imposed communism. The two former allies viewed each other with suspicion and formed rival military blocs. Germany, occupied by both the Soviets and the Western powers (the US, Great Britain, and France) was divided into two states. West Germany, as we shall see in the **In focus** section, became both a political and economic success story. East Germany, on the other hand, became a repressive police state under communist authority. The competition of the Cold War—which occasionally turned "hot" in places such as Korea and Vietnam—lasted for more than forty years, ending with the collapse of communist regimes in Eastern Europe in 1989 and the reunification of Germany in 1990. But, as noted in the **Is Europe one?** section with respect to today's Germany, vestiges of Cold War divisions remain.

Marshall Plan
US economic assistance program directed to Western Europe after World War II; often credited with the post-war economic recovery in Western Europe and helped cement ties between the US and European governments.

(Re)Democratization

Consolidating democracy became a major political project in post-war Western Europe. Indeed, the existence of democracy would become, in many respects, *the* distinguishing feature of the region and an indicator of its successful political development.

For democratic states that prevailed in the war (Great Britain) or that were neutral and escaped conflict (Ireland, Switzerland, and Sweden), democratization was not a pressing issue. Similarly, many previously democratic states that were occupied by the Germans (e.g., the Netherlands, Norway, Finland, Belgium, Denmark) were able to reestablish themselves with relative ease, often with their pre-war political leaders returning from exile and resuming leadership. In many of these countries, a high degree of consensus on basic policies (e.g., the welfare state) and the general moderate orientation of the parties on the left and the right facilitated coalition governments and, for the most part, post-war political stability.

Some countries had more difficulties in establishing democratic governments. In Italy, fascism had been defeated, but the nineteenth-century constitution, which established Italy as a constitutional monarchy, was no longer tenable because the monarchy had been discredited by its association with Mussolini. A popular referendum turned Italy into a republic in 1946. In 1948 Italy adopted a new constitution that guaranteed individual rights, and in elections that year the Christian Democrats, benefiting from covert US support, defeated their communist rivals. The Christian Democrats would dominate Italian politics for the next four decades, but Italian governments were troubled by problems of corruption and were typically fragile coalitions that had an average lifespan of one year.

One would have thought the West German case would be difficult as well. Germany's attempt to install democracy after World War I failed. Overcoming the legacy of Hitler—recalling that millions of Germans voted for him and presumably supported him during the war—obviously presented many problems. The Western allies helped oversee a process of de-Nazification, but clearly not every Nazi Party member could be punished for political affiliation. The allies also helped draft a new constitution that included federalism, judicial review, and a higher electoral threshold for parties to enter parliament, thus creating a more coherent party system. As in Italy, the Christian Democrats, led by Konrad Adenauer, dominated political life, but there was no specter of a communist takeover. Emphasizing moral renewal—a welcome message for many—and the need for Germans to both confront their past and move forward with a new stronger, democracy, Adenauer ruled Germany until 1963. Thanks to the government's ability to provide stability, the German "economic miracle," discussed more in the **In focus** section, European economic integration, and a great deal of consensus within German society on basic priorities, democracy succeeded.

Ironically, France, with a longer democratic tradition and nominally on the winning side in World War II, was more problematic. France was split between groups on the political right and left. More nationalist and conservative forces allied with Charles de Gaulle, leader of the anti-Nazi French Resistance. He was opposed by those on the political left, particularly the communists, who also had contributed heavily to the Resistance. All the main actors wanted a new constitution, but they could not agree on particulars. De Gaulle opposed the 1946 Constitution, which established the principle of parliamentary supremacy, but, as proportional representation voting led to growth of many parties, it was hard to form stable coalition governments. The final straw was a colonial crisis in French-ruled Algeria. With French paramilitary forces in Algeria threatening to invade France itself, the

In focus

The post-war miracle in West Germany versus relative decline in Great Britain

Great Britain was on the winning side in World War II. Germany lost and was divided into two. These facts are well known. As seen in Figure 2.1, at the end of the war *per capita* income in Britain was more than 50 percent higher than that in West Germany. However, by 1958 the total West German economy was larger than that of Great Britain, and by 1973 its *per capita* income eclipsed that in Britain. In the wake of the German "economic miracle," Britain, with one of the lowest economic growth rates in Europe in the 1960s and 1970s, looked like the new "sick man of Europe." Britons began to wonder who really won the war. How does one explain the different experiences of these two states?[17]

Note first their similarities. In both states, state spending represented a sizeable part of the economy. For example, between 1950 and 1973 government spending rose from 30.4 percent to 42 percent of GDP in West Germany and from 34.2 percent to 41.5 percent in Great Britain.[18] Many of these funds went to social welfare programs—health care, pensions, education, and housing. Moreover, in both countries the state pursued interventionist policies to help equalize incomes and regulate private enterprise. Tax rates, reaching more than 80 percent, were high. In the immediate post-war years, both states had rapid recoveries. Within a decade, however, the two countries were on separate paths.

The roots of Germany's "economic miracle," ironically, go back to the 1930s, when the Nazis invested heavily in communications, chemicals and metallurgy, and vehicle manufacture. Much of its economic infrastructure, including many of its manufacturers and banks, survived the war. The destruction that did occur allowed the Germans to build from scratch, constructing new, more efficient factories. Britain, which had less damage, had an older industrial core. Relative to Germany, it was declining *before* World War II, and after 1945 Britain continued its pre-war policies of under-investment, limited research and development, and low-risk, low-reward business strategies. It also emerged from war heavily in debt, had higher defense expenditures, and, through the 1960s, supported several colonies in the developing world. The famed British economic John Maynard Keynes observed during the war itself:

> If by some sad geographical slip the American Air Force (it is now too late to hope for much from the enemy) were to destroy every factory on the North East coast and in Lancashire (at an hour when the Directors were sitting there and no one else) we should have nothing to fear. How else are we to regain the exuberant inexperience which is necessary, it seems, for success, I cannot surmise.[19]

Similar arguments can be made with respect to labor relations.[20] The British trade unions, which survived the war, were strong players in the economy, eventually becoming a burden on the economy as their resistance to change and insistence upon full employment at any price hampered economic growth. In the 1970s, when the government advanced tepid reform plans, the unions wielded the strike weapon and created multiple political crises. In contrast, the West German trade unions, while strong in membership, were essentially new creations, lacking the institutional ability to flex their muscles independently in the post-war period. Instead, the key aspect to Germany's social market economy was cooperation among the state, employers, and workers, with workers agreeing to be less militant and to hold down wages (thereby freeing up funds for investment) in return for steady employment. The fact that West Germany was also willing to import cheaper labor—from southern Italy, Turkey, and Yugoslavia—also helped keep German companies more competitive.

Government policies also differed. The Germans, as had been the case in the late 1800s, developed close and productive ties between private business and the state, which helped guarantee favorable loans for businesses and supplied much of the capital for investment and research. The high value of the Deutschmark meant that imported raw materials were relatively cheap. Even though German exports were costly, they quickly developed a reputation for quality that allowed them to compete extremely well in global markets. In contrast, British companies did not enjoy positive state patronage in terms of access to needed capital. Instead, political pressures often forced them to build plants and distribution centers in uneconomic parts of the country in order to appease local politicians and unions. Whereas state ownership of business was far more prevalent in Britain than in Germany, the British economy remained far less planned than elsewhere in Europe. This was not necessarily a good thing, as the economy lacked any sort of strategic ambition. For example, while German car companies—Volkswagen, BMW, and Mercedes—became world champions thanks in part to pragmatic state policy, the British car companies, which had been dominant in Europe in the early 1950s, collapsed, with the remains of the last independent British car maker, British Leyland, purchased by . . . BMW.

Why this discussion of "ancient history"? First, the German success (in addition to that in France, Italy, Scandinavia, and elsewhere) points to the fact that "big government" can work. Indeed, the recovery in post-war Europe was attributable in large part to an activist state. Secondly, this history helps explain the condition of both Britain and Germany today. Ironically, however, today their roles are somewhat reversed. As we'll see in Chapter 10, Britain's decline fueled the rise of Margaret Thatcher, whose tenure in office (1979–1990) witnessed the unraveling of Britain's collectivist consensus and the introduction of a more free-market approach. Because of Germany's success, there was no such reform impulse. By the 1990s, chronic double-digit unemployment and sluggish growth had made Germany's "economic miracle" seem, indeed, like ancient history. It was difficult for German leaders to push through reforms, thanks in part to the power of German unions and their unwillingness to abandon a system that has served their interests for so long. However, in the 2000s Germany clearly became Europe's economic and political leader, leading some to wonder if Germany had become, perhaps, too powerful.

Critical thinking questions

1. What lessons (if any) does the West German "economic miracle" have for contemporary Europe and beyond?
2. What lessons (if any) does the successful consolidation of democracy in West Germany have for efforts to construct democracy in other parts of the world, e.g., the Middle East?

government turned to de Gaulle, the only man deemed to have the credibility with the military to end the crisis. He agreed to serve, but only if France adopted a new constitution with a stronger presidency, which he saw as his rightful position. Thus, in 1958, the French Fifth Republic, with its semi-presidentialism system (a strong president but also a prime minister) was born.

A few West European countries had a more arduous path to democracy. Spain had suffered under the military dictatorship of Francisco Franco since 1939, when his forces, with the help of Nazi Germany and fascist Italy, prevailed in a brutal civil war. It was only after Franco's death in 1975 that Spain was able to democratize. Portugal, the poorest country in Western Europe, similarly suffered under the dictatorship of Antonio Salazar (1932–1970). Like Spain, Portugal democratized in the 1970s. In Greece, elections had been held in 1946, even as the country was embroiled in civil war, but sharp political divisions (between left and right, monarchists and republicans) made governance difficult, contributing to a military coup in 1967. Civilian, democratic rule was reestablished in 1974. Thanks in part to the assistance of the European Community (forerunner of the EU), all three states became stable democracies in the 1980s.

Reconstruction and the rise of the welfare state

After World War II, economic reconstruction was a top priority, necessary for the survival of democratic governments. Rebuilding would not be easy. The devastation from the war was enormous, and there was a political imperative to get economic life back to normal as quickly as possible.

The economic recovery in Western Europe was predicated upon several policies. First, because of the lack of private resources, the state took the lead in investment, planning, and often exercising ownership over industries. Reliance on the state as the engine for growth was driven both by necessity and a widespread feeling that *laissez-faire*, free-market capitalism, had to be managed and/or constrained in order to avoid the economic dislocations that preceded World War II. In the words of the famous Austrian economist Joseph Schumpeter, "The all but general opinion seems to be that capitalist methods will be unequal to the task of reconstruction."[21] Second, the US provided $13 billion in economic assistance—over $100 billion in today's dollars—to Europe to assist in rebuilding through the Marshall Plan. Third, by the 1950s several European states began to push for freer trade and economic integration. These early efforts—which were the first steps toward creation of the EU—are covered more in the next chapter.

There was, it should be noted, no single economic model, although in all states, state spending—for both investments and for social welfare—rose far above pre-war levels, and millions of workers moved off the farms and into manufacturing and service jobs in the cities. France went furthest with state planning, which included nationalization of industries, an interventionist industrial policy, state promotion of exports, and economic programs that set national goals and techniques of production.[22] In Italy, pre-existing ties between the state and businesses were revitalized, with the state providing credits to priority sectors and (less productively) favored clients. In Britain, state takeover of many economic enterprises (e.g., transport, utilities, mining) was at the heart of the program of the Labour Party,

TABLE 2.3 Economic growth in post-war Western Europe

Country	Average annual growth rates				
	1950–1958	*1958–1966*	*1966–1973*	*1973–1980*	*1980–1990*
Austria	6.1	4.4	4.9	2.5	2.1
Belgium	2.4	4.3	4.8	2.3	1.6
Denmark	2.3	4.9	3.2	1.0	1.7
Finland	4.0	5.0	5.1	2.2	2.9
France	4.2	5.3	4.9	2.2	2.1
West Germany	8.7	5.3	3.9	1.8	2.0
Great Britain	1.8	3.1	2.9	0.9	2.4
Greece	6.7	6.9	7.7	3.0	1.4
Ireland	0.8	3.3	5.0	4.3	3.4
Italy	6.1	5.7	4.6	3.1	2.0
Netherlands	3.8	4.8	4.9	2.1	1.9
Spain	5.4	7.3	7.1	3.3	3.0
Sweden	2.7	4.3	3.3	1.5	1.8
Switzerland	3.8	5.0	3.8	0.3	1.8

Source: Data are Total GDP converted at Purchasing Power Parity (PPP). Taken from Groningen Growth and Development Centre at www.ggdc.net, accessed on June 10, 2007

which defeated Churchill's Conservatives in elections in 1945. In West Germany, there was little state ownership and explicit planning, but the state did play a role as mediator between workers and employers to ensure economic stability. As noted in the **In focus** section, the result was an economic "miracle."

European economies began to rebound quickly.[23] Growth rates in the 1950s and 1960s—the so-called post-war "Golden Age"—exceeded those in the US. Data are presented in Table 2.3 and in Figure 2.1. As one can see, growth rates remained impressive in most states into the 1960s, producing, as seen in Figure 2.1, a steep increase in *per capita* GDP (gross domestic product) by 1973. Moreover, even with various economic crises and the decline in average growth in the 1970s and 1980s, West Europeans in 1990 were still markedly richer on a *per capita* basis than in 1973. The best performers were West Germany, as well as poorer states such as Greece and Spain, which started from a lower base. Economic growth, in addition to providing a better quality of life for citizens—flush toilets, refrigerators, color television, automobiles, and washing machines were the norm for a growing middle class—also contributed to the preservation of democratic systems of government.

welfare state
a feature of Western Europe after World War II that featured government provisions for free health care and education, state-provided pensions, unemployment insurance, subsidized housing, and other goods; paid for by higher taxes, but often supported by parties both on the right and left.

Finally, one should mention one other component of the socio-economic system that developed in post-war Western Europe: an extensive **welfare state**. The recognition in the post-war years that the state would have to take a leading role to ensure public health and provide support to the infirm, aged, and orphaned spurred the creation of new government programs, such as Britain's National Health Service, established in 1948. The state thus played a role in the economy not only to facilitate growth but also, in the words of John Maynard Keynes, to satisfy the "craving for social and personal security."[24] As the historian Tony Judt observed, many believed the state could foster "social cohesion, moral sustenance and cultural vitality.[25]

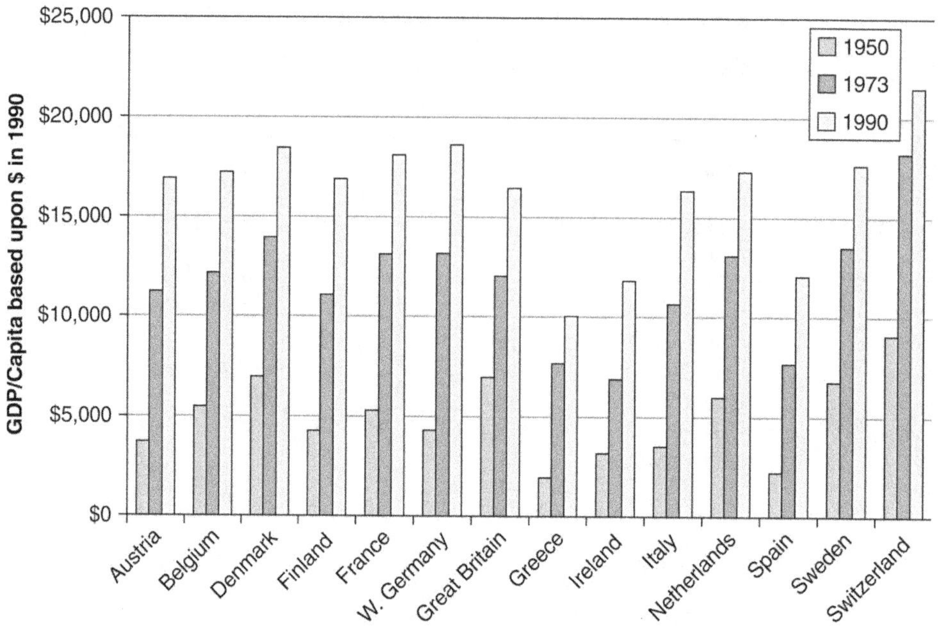

FIGURE 2.1 GDP/Capita in post-war Western Europe

Data are GDP/Capita based upon 1990 dollars at Purchasing Power Parity. Taken from Groningen Growth and Development Centre at www.ggdc.net, accessed on June 10, 2007

The welfare state encompassed many policies, including free health care and education, subsidized housing, state-provided pensions, generous vacation allowances, unemployment insurance, and daycare and maternity leave. These were, to be sure, expensive, and state spending rose in each successive decade from the 1950s to the 1990s, reaching by the late 1980s more than 50 percent of the total GDP in Sweden, the Netherlands, France, and Italy. In order to pay for these programs, marginal tax rates were set high (often over 80 percent), which meant that many elements of the welfare state helped redistribute income from the rich to the middle class and poor. As a result, inequality declined in Western Europe.

The welfare state had an ideological edge, with growing parties on the left typically advocating more extensive social welfare programs. However, even Winston Churchill, hardly a socialist, conceded that "there is no firmer investment for any community than putting milk into babies."[26] In Britain, a so-called collectivist consensus between Labour and the Conservatives oversaw construction of a generous welfare state throughout the 1950s and 1960s. Speaking of the British case, one writer noted that

> British capitalism has been compelled, by the sheer pressure of the British people, acting through our effective democratic institutions, to do what we used to say it would never, by definition, do; it has been forced to devote its productive resources to raising the standard of life of the population as a whole.[27]

In West Germany, the social-market economy, which saw a pronounced redistributive role for the state, was developed under center-right Christian Democratic governments. France's statist economic system was furthered by de Gaulle, ostensibly a right-wing political figure. Parties on the right in Austria, Belgium, the Netherlands, Norway, Italy, and elsewhere championed welfare policies. Bargaining among the government, business associations, and trade unions often provided the underpinning for state policy. Few parties advocated *laissez-faire* capitalism.

What were the consequences of this system? As noted in Table 2.3, Western Europe saw high levels of economic growth, especially before 1973. While it may be hard to argue that the welfare state was the primary cause of economic growth, one could point to rising education levels and better public health as factors that contributed to growing labor productivity. Although Britain, as noted in the **In focus** section, began to fall into relative stagnation, numerous studies confirmed through the 1970s a positive link between the expansion of the state sector and economic growth.[28] Redistributive policies also cut poverty rates, which were (and remain) far lower in most parts of Western Europe than in the US. Sweden and Finland, which had two of the most developed welfare states—ruling Social Democratic parties tolerated private ownership but taxed high-earners very heavily—became two of the wealthiest countries in the world, a remarkable achievement for countries that as recently as the 1930s were undeveloped by Western European standards.[29] Aside from the bottom line, Europeans would point to quality of life issues (e.g., leisure time, cleaner and well-planned cities, social cohesion) to argue for the superiority of the European social model.

In many respects, then, post-war Western Europe was a success story. Most countries in the region had stable democratic governments and were generating respectable figures in terms of economic growth. By the 1970s, however, in several countries growth began to decline. While this did not threaten democracy, it did lead some to call for overhauling aspects of the socio-economic model and the welfare state. These challenges—which continue through today—are reserved for later discussion in Chapter 10.

Eastern European development

The political history of Eastern Europe, as we shall see, differs in many ways from that of Western Europe. Whereas Western Europe has built upon centuries of political and economic development, particularly the emergence of democracy and capitalism, Eastern Europe, in many ways, has in recent years tried to overcome its more troubled past in order to establish institutions and policies similar to those in Western Europe.

Eastern Europe as a land of empires

Whereas, similar to Western Europe, several independent kingdoms appeared in Eastern Europe in the medieval period, in the more modern period, as seen in Figure 2.2, much of the region was encompassed by larger empires, political structures that grouped together a variety of nations or peoples in which one nation or group tended to have political dominance. These were empires of the Germans (Prussians), Russians, Turks (Ottomans), and Austria-Hungary (Habsburgs). These empires controlled much of the region until the end of World War I.

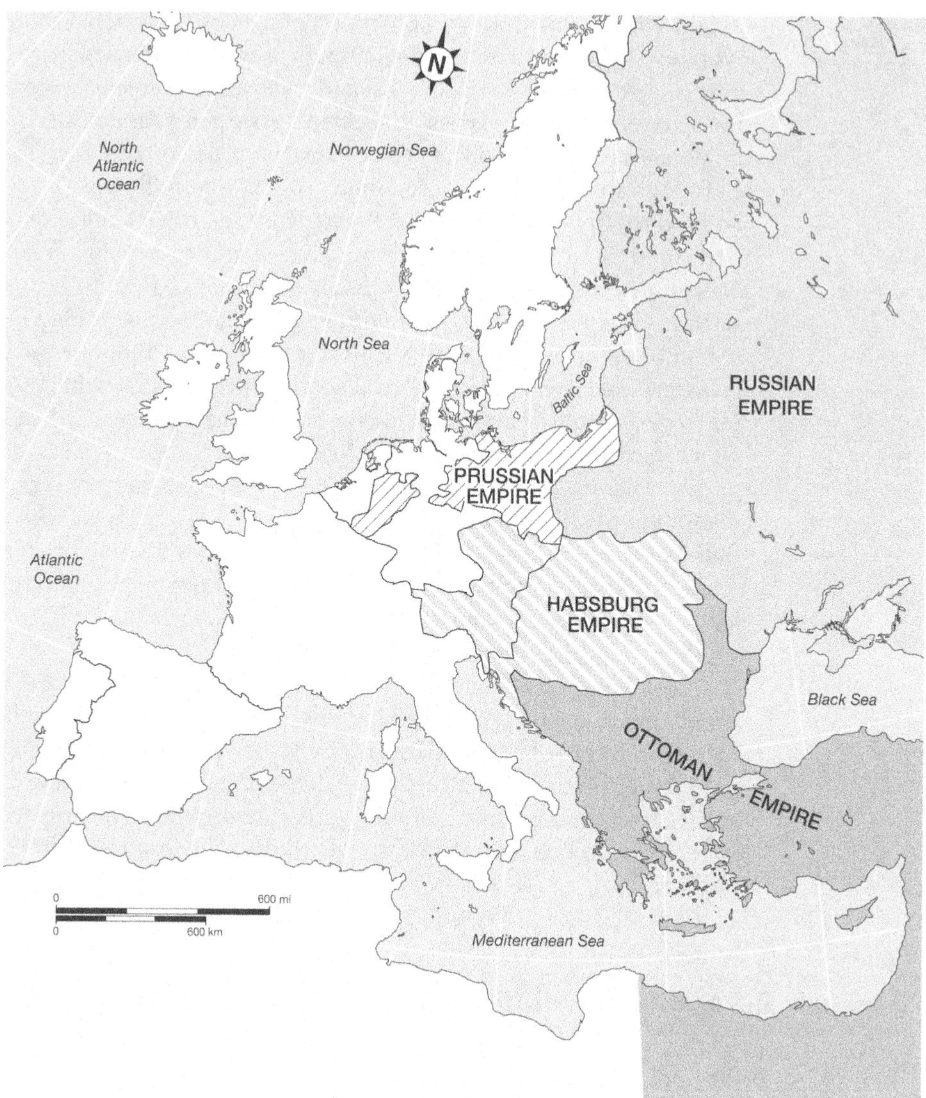

FIGURE 2.2 Eastern Europe in 1825

Being part of an empire meant several things. Obviously, East European peoples were not sovereign. They did not rule themselves. They had no state of their own. Civil and political rights were limited. Eastern Europe thus did not experience the political liberalization and gradual democratization that marked much of Western Europe. Economic development was also far less dynamic than in Western Europe. Most of the people in the region were poor peasants. Illiteracy rates in some areas exceeded 90 percent. In the words of one scholar, East European peoples became "hewers of wood and drawers of water for alien masters."[30] True, some empires, in terms of political repression and economic opportunity, were better (e.g., the Habsburgs) than others (e.g., the Ottomans or the Russians), but the key point is that the peoples of the region lacked political independence.

Imperial legacies arguably matter today. In a simple sense, it mattered who ruled over you. It is no accident, many would contend, that the most advanced, democratic states in the region today—such as the Czech Republic, Slovenia, and Hungary—are former Habsburg lands that were economically more advanced over a century ago, whereas those that experienced longer Ottoman rule and/or Russian influence, such as Bulgaria, Romania, and Albania, are both poorer economically and have had more difficulties consolidating effective democratic governments. In Poland, there were vast differences among the Habsburg, Russian, and German ruled areas, with the German regions far more urbanized and industrialized, especially compared with the eastern regions controlled by Russia.[31] Poles will sometimes even note that even today one can still discern differences in their own political culture among a "Germanic" west and Baltic coast, a "Russified" east, and the former Habsburg lands of Galicia in the south.

The end of empires, political independence, and the failures of democracy

The political environment in Eastern Europe changed dramatically after World War I, which marked the defeat and collapse of all four empires. With the end of imperial rule, new countries (e.g., Czechoslovakia) were formed, and others (e.g., Poland) reappeared on the map. The watchwords in redesigning post-World War I Europe, borrowing from US President Woodrow Wilson's Fourteen Points, were democracy and self-determination. Democratic systems of government were established with the help of the victorious Allies. Significantly, however, not every group of people was given its own state: Czechs and Slovaks shared Czechoslovakia; Slovenes, Croats, Serbs, Macedonians, and other peoples became citizens of the Kingdom of Serbs, Croats, and Slovenes (later renamed Yugoslavia, meaning "land of the Southern Slavs"). Many states also had large numbers of ethnic minorities, including Jews, who had no state of their own.

The hopes that some had for the region were, for the most part, not realized. Democracy did not take root, save in Czechoslovakia. In general, democratic governments lacked stability and a strong sense of legitimacy from the populace. They could not solve challenging socio-economic issues. More controversially, one might suggest that the peoples of the region—poorly educated, with little tradition of self-rule or tolerance and often holding grievances against ethnic minorities or other states—did not possess a democratic political culture. Democratic governments fell to military coups in several states, including Poland, Bulgaria, and Lithuania. In Yugoslavia, tensions among Serbs, Croats, and other nationalities—dramatically leading to the assassination of Croatian leaders on the floor of the national parliament—led the king to disband the Yugoslav parliament and establish a royal dictatorship in 1929. The king of Romania declared himself dictator in 1938. In several states, pro-fascist movements, taking inspiration from Italy and Germany, challenged democracy and whipped up animosity toward Jews and other minorities. Only in Czechoslovakia, blessed by higher levels of economic development and led by Westernized intellectuals Tomas Masaryk and Eduard Benes, did democracy survive, even though within the country Slovaks complained of discrimination and arrogance from the more numerous and better-off Czechs.

World War II and the communist takeover

On top of the domestic challenges, there were also international tensions in the region. The peace treaties of World War I did not create homogeneous nation-states, meaning that political borders did not correspond with ethnic or cultural borders. The desire to redraw the borders thus became great rallying cries in "revisionist" states such as Hungary and Bulgaria, not to mention Germany, where grievances against the Treaty of Versailles contributed to the rise of Hitler.

World War II started in Eastern Europe. In 1938, Germany occupied part of Czechoslovakia, eventually taking over much of the country by early 1939. That fall, Germany and the Soviet Union attacked and dismembered Poland, which led Britain and France to declare war on Germany. In 1941, Germany attacked the Soviet Union, and much of the fighting in World War II occurred along the Eastern Front. Germany found some allies (e.g., Hungary and Bulgaria) in the region. Most of the Holocaust's infamous death camps—such as Auschwitz, Treblinka, Belzec, and Majdanek—were in Poland. Of the 6 million Jews killed in the Holocaust, half were Polish citizens. Most of the others also came from Eastern Europe.[32] The memory of the Holocaust is an important—and at times highly charged—issue in the region, and only after the fall of communism have some states looked closely at what happened and the role of their own citizens in this genocide. During World War II, Yugoslavia was also engulfed in a three-way civil war among Nazi-backed Croats, Serbs, and communist fighters.

The war was far more devastating in Eastern Europe than in Western Europe. Poland lost 6 million people, a fifth of its population; more than 1 million perished in Yugoslavia; Romania lost half a million soldiers and civilians combined; the Soviet Union lost up to 20 million people to fighting, disease, and death camps. Economic losses were also staggering.[33]

While there was some homegrown resistance against the Germans, most of Eastern Europe was "liberated" by the Soviet Union. Despite promises made by the Soviets in the Yalta Agreement of February 1945 to hold "free and unfettered elections," they did not allow democracy to take root in the countries and regions they occupied.[34] Non-communist politicians were harassed, often driven from the country. Secret police forces were established to root out "unreliable elements." Communist parties "won" rigged elections. The communist economic system was established. By the end of the 1940s, Germany was divided into two countries, mirroring the political division of Europe between a democratic, capitalist West and a communist East.

Communism in Eastern Europe 1945–1989

Communism lasted in Eastern Europe for more than forty years. Most of the region adopted the Soviet model of communism and remained allied with the Soviet Union. The major exceptions to this pattern were in Yugoslavia and Albania, where local communist leaders—Jozef Tito and Enver Hoxha—prevailed in their wartime conflicts and imposed their own versions of communism in their countries. Some East Europeans may have supported communism because of its promises of a better life and social equality—appealing given the region's recent past history—but the imposition of communism owed more to Soviet force than popular demand. Vladimir Tismaneanu reflected that:

> The new structures erected on the ruins of those smashed and increasingly atomized societies had to be carbon copies of the Soviet ones: rubber-stamp parliaments, communist control over all spheres of life, establishment of concentration camps for the extermination of politically unreliable elements, and the institution of a command economy, where private property was virtually eliminated and replaced by state ownership of all resources.[35]

Those who dissented risked loss of a job, imprisonment, even death.

Communism transformed Eastern Europe. The economic priority was industrialization, which meant that new factories and cities were constructed. Literacy became near universal as these states experienced socio-economic modernization. Living standards for many went up, as there was substantial economic growth in the 1950s and 1960s.[36]

This is not to say that communism was a paradise. It was not. Political freedoms were virtually non-existent. Farmers were pushed off their land into collective farms. Living conditions for many workers were squalid. Consumer goods were in short supply, and people had to wait years to obtain an apartment, car, or goods such as a washing machine. Despite promises to overtake the Western model, communism never did. East European economies never acquired a reputation for making quality products (as did West Germany, for example), were cut off from most of the world, and were not driven by consumer demand. For a relatively advanced economy like that of Czechoslovakia, the results were particularly dire. Whereas in 1938 Czechoslovakia's standard of living was comparable to that of Belgium and higher than in Austria or Italy, by 1960 Czechoslovakia had not only fallen behind all of these states but was poorer than it had been in 1938.[37]

When given a chance, there were efforts to reform and/or escape from communism. These occurred in Hungary in 1956, Czechoslovakia in 1968, and Poland in 1980–1981. The first two reform efforts were crushed by Soviet invasion. The last, given inspiration by the Catholic Church and Pope John Paul II, formerly a bishop in Poland, and spearheaded by the independent trade union Solidarity, ended with a declaration of martial law by the Polish government. Many tried to leave communist Eastern Europe; more than a hundred were killed trying to get over, around or under the Berlin Wall, which was built in 1961. There were some brave individuals, labeled dissidents, who lived under communism and campaigned for human rights and freedoms. However, many of these people were jailed and seemed, at the time, to be politically marginalized.

The end of communism

Despite a veneer of stability, Eastern European regimes were never fully secure. They failed to win widespread legitimacy. Economic problems made it clear that the regimes would never deliver on promises of a material paradise. Although most citizens did not face daily violence or coercion, most knew that they were not free and, thanks to the efforts of institutions such as American-supported Radio Free Europe, they knew that life in the West was better. Lastly, many citizens resented the presence of Soviet troops in their countries. It was not until 1989, however, that they were able to throw off the yoke of communism.

Why did communism collapse in 1989? Note the two parts of this question. The first part—communism's collapse—could be answered by invoking several of the factors mentioned above (e.g., low legitimacy, economic problems, repression). By focusing on these factors, one might conclude that the collapse of communism was simply inevitable. In retrospect, this might be true, yet few saw it coming, and it is important to remember that these factors had existed for years and communism survived.

By 1989, however, several factors converged that made the overthrow of communism possible. First, economic problems were becoming more acute, whether measured by overall growth rates or shortages of products. Average citizens and elites increasingly lost faith in the system. Corruption was increasingly a problem as well. However, this discontent had no sizeable outlet until the Soviet leader, Mikhail Gorbachev, began to encourage political and economic reform, both within the Soviet Union and in Eastern Europe. Gorbachev encouraged greater freedom of expression and economic experimentation, and, crucially, he did not send Soviet troops into the region to suppress reform efforts.

civil society
networks and associations of citizens that are independent of the state, argued by some to be instrumental in the collapse of communism and development of democracy in Eastern Europe.

Gorbachev's reforms helped activate **civil society** within Eastern Europe.[38] By civil society, one refers to networks and associations of citizens that are independent of the state. Organizations in civil society campaigned for greater freedom and respect for human rights. Civil society did not seek to battle with authorities with violence. Rather, the point was to confront the regimes with moral claims and to develop an "alternative society" composed of those who rejected the official ideology and create new forms of media, culture, and informal educational institutions. Many were led by dissidents. Obvious examples would be the Solidarity, "flying universities" (*ad hoc* lectures on political topics in private homes) and the Catholic Church in Poland, the Charter 77 citizens' initiative in Czechoslovakia, and human rights and environmental groups that emerged in the late 1980s in Hungary.

The collapse of communist governments throughout the region occurred very quickly, within a matter of months in the second half of 1989. Poland was, in many respects, the leader, thanks to its well-formed civil society centered on Solidarity. With the economy in deep crisis, the government reached out to Solidarity and the Catholic Church in negotiations in February 1989. Lech Walesa, the leader of Solidarity who had been placed under house arrest earlier in the decade, said he would be willing to talk to the devil himself if it would save Poland. These negotiations led to elections in June of that year, in which the communists were decisively defeated. By September 1989, Poland had a new, non-communist government led by Solidarity. In Hungary, talks between the government and opposition led to various reforms (including the opening of the border with Austria) and an agreement to hold new elections. In East Germany, protesters from religious, human rights, and environmental organizations, openly supporting Gorbachev when he visited East Berlin, put more and more pressure on the government. On November 9, 1989, a government spokesman—mistakenly it turned out—announced that citizens now had the freedom to travel and leave the country. That night, East Germans began to pour over and through the Berlin Wall, as East German border

Solidarity demonstration in Poland, 1988

Is Europe one?

Bridging the gap between East and West Germany

The reunification of Germany in 1990 can be considered a microcosm for the idea of a single Europe. Borders were torn down as people, separated by political arrangements made after World War II, agreed to live in a common state. A Solidarity Pact pledged financial support from the West to the East. Democracy and capitalism spread eastward. The adjectives "West" and "East," it was assumed, would soon become a thing of the past.

Over two decades later, the euphoria of reunification is long faded. Whereas the stark divide of the Cold War era is no more, some Germans refer to a continued "wall of the mind" between the *Ossis* (those in East Germany) and the *Wessis* (those in West Germany). One German politician suggested that "We might be the first country which has, by unifying, created two peoples."[39]

Each side has a host of complaints to make about the other. From 1990 to 2010, West Germany gave nearly $2 trillion (about $30,000 for every West German) to the East to assist in the construction of new housing and infrastructure, social welfare, and environmental cleanup. No one expected the costs to be this high. Not only did West Germans see a tax increase, but the entire economy experienced a deep crisis in the 1990s because of the financial costs of reunification. Many areas of the former East Germany now have newer and better roads, rail terminals, hospitals, and airports than in the West. To the extent that economic performance of much of the former East Germany still lags behind West Germany, many West Germans wonder where their money has gone. The answer, according to many, is for generous social welfare programs for the "lazy," "unskilled," and—most gallingly—"ungrateful" *Ossis*. Shockingly, in 2004 a poll found that 24 percent of *Wessis* believe it would be better if the Berlin Wall was still up.[40]

Despite the money spent in the East, many *Ossis* feel shortchanged. The installation of capitalism in the former East Germany meant that many of the East German companies went bankrupt. The unemployment rate in the former East Germany hovers above 15 percent, twice that in West Germany. GDP *per capita* is approximately 70 percent the West German average.[41] Many *Wessis* came to East and bought cheap property, and they are resented for their wealth and perceived arrogance. An idea (later scrapped) by one West German entrepreneur to build a theme park outside of Berlin that would "recreate" the East German experience—grey buildings, police watchtowers, bad food and service, tin-can East German cars, crumbling infrastructure, arbitrary "arrests" of patrons—was not well received by those who had actually lived under such conditions. Many East Germans report that they feel like second-class citizens and report feelings of *Ostalgie*, nostalgia for aspects of East Germany. True, one of their own—Angela Merkel—became chancellor in 2005, but Merkel's support for cutting subsidies for the East has not won her much support in her home region.

Public opinion polls reveal the gap that still exists between West and East. For example, the European Social Survey in 2014 found that those living in the former East Germany are significantly less likely to trust the government and political parties, are less satisfied with their lives and the state of German democracy, and less inclined to believe that the political system allows people to have a say in government. They are also more in favor of government efforts to reduce income inequality and more likely to believe that immigration makes Germany worse off.[42]

What are the political effects? The former East German communists, renamed first the Party of Democratic Socialism and now the *Linke* (Left) Party, regularly receive over 20 percent of the vote in the former East Germany, and, although some consider it a pariah party, they are part of the ruling coalition in two regional governments in the East. Some East Germans are also turning to the far right. In the 1990s, "skinhead" attacks on ethnic Turks and other minorities were a major cause for concern, and the 2000s and 2010s far-right parties—which are inevitably compared to the Nazis—won seats in local and regional elections in parts of eastern Germany. The anti-immigrant group Pegida (Patriotic Europeans Against the Islamization of the Occident) has been particularly active in eastern Germany. With *Wessis* now arguing they need to pull back their support for the East—government subsidies to eastern Germany still account for tens of billions a year, although the Solidarity Pact formally ends in 2019—it is clear that regional divisions within Germany remain a festering problem.

The fate of Germany may be cautionary. One could fairly ask, if Germany is still not truly "reunited" twenty years after the fall of the Berlin Wall, how long will it be before one can speak of an undivided or single Europe?

Critical thinking questions

1. Who would you expect to be most nostalgic about the old East Germany? Why would they feel that way?
2. Should West Germans continue to transfer money to the East to make economic conditions in Germany more equal?

guards were confused about their orders and did not stop them. Within a year East Germany would cease to exist as a separate state. In Czechoslovakia, protests and strikes in late November 1989 led to the "Velvet Revolution"[43] and the installation of Václav Havel, a playwright and leading dissident who had been dismissed two months earlier as "morally insignificant" by the government, as president.[44] In Bulgaria, the government also agreed to new elections. Only in Romania, which suffered under perhaps the most brutal and megalomaniac dictator in the region, Nicolae Ceausescu, was there violence as government troops clashed with protesters in December 1989, and, after his fall from power and flight from the capital, Ceausescu and his wife were executed after a brief trial.

The post-communist transformation

The collapse of communism in Eastern Europe in 1989 was a cause for massive celebration. With the end of Soviet domination and authoritarian rule, many hoped that the division of Europe would end and that East Europeans would quickly be able to overcome the communist past and enjoy democracy, peace, and prosperity. However, elation gave way to a hangover as people began to realize that the road ahead would not be easy. In some places, as noted in the **Is Europe one?** section on reunified Germany, there is even a nostalgia for the past as citizens of former communist countries have had trouble adjusting to a democratic, free-market system.

A prevailing issue in Eastern Europe since 1989 has been the transition from communist rule toward a more democratic polity and more market-based economic system. The challenges to this dual transition—creating democracy *and* a market—seemed formidable. There was no tried-and-true formula that states could adopt, and no guarantee of success. As the decade unfolded, it became clear that states would pursue a different mix of policies and that there were reform leaders (e.g., Hungary, Estonia, Czech Republic, Slovenia), reform laggards (e.g., Romania, Slovakia), and states or regions engulfed by widespread violence (e.g., Croatia, Bosnia, Kosovo). By 2000, most states could claim success, meaning that democratic systems worked relatively well and that their economies had mostly recovered from an arduous reform period. By 2007, ten post-communist states had joined the EU, and several more were clamoring for closer ties and eventual membership.

Establishing democracy

Whether the states of Eastern Europe could establish stable, democratic governments in the wake of communism's collapse was a major question in the region for much of the 1990s. Whereas there was widespread support for creation of democratic governments, there were concerns that the transition to democracy would not be easy. Few of the states had prior success with democracy. Economic dislocations in movement to capitalism would be severe. The specter of nationalism could reemerge and thwart political liberalization. The international environment was uncertain. Ralf Dahrendorf suggested that the most challenging part of the transition would be the "hour of the citizen,"[45] which would take more time to develop than new political and economic institutions. Some alarmists feared that over a generation of communist rule had created a "Leninist" political culture among both elites and masses that did not possess the levels of public trust and tolerance and willingness to compromise necessary for democratic politics.[46] President Havel, speaking to fellow Czechoslovaks in 1990, lamented that "the worst enemy" of reform was "our own bad qualities—indifference to public affairs, conceit, ambition, selfishness, the pursuit of personal advancement and rivalry."[47]

Ultimately, most states succeeded in building democratic systems. Elections were held, and many parties ran, offering voters a genuine choice. Most parties ran on platforms to preserve civil and political freedoms, and many explicitly looked to Western Europe as a positive example. In several states, such as Poland, Estonia, Czechoslovakia, and Hungary, voters immediately embraced anti-communist parties rooted in the dissident movement. These states became leaders in the reform process. New constitutions were adopted or previous ones were amended to guarantee democratic freedoms. A lively, if at times low-quality, media developed. Public opinion surveys found publics in most states thought having democracy was good, and support for non-democratic alternatives—military rule, a dictatorship, a return to communism—was low throughout most of East-Central Europe, especially among Slovenes, Czechs, and Hungarians.[48] Post-communist publics were not always enamored with their governments, but rather than turn to non-democratic actors, they voted out incumbents when given a chance. This was the pattern in a number of states, including Poland, Hungary, Lithuania, and Bulgaria.

Western assistance to post-communist Europe was also substantial. From 1989 to 1995, Western countries pledged $86 billion to assist post-communist Europe, and the largest donor was the European Union.[49] Both NATO and EU expansion was undertaken with the idea of supporting and encouraging democratization. Non-governmental actors in Western Europe (e.g., universities, businesses, women's groups, human rights groups) also invested and partnered with actors in Eastern Europe to encourage political, economic, and broader social change.

This is not to say there were no problems along the way. Establishing an independent and capable judiciary was one of the top challenges, as well as developing a civil society supportive of democratic institutions. Nationalist politicians in a number of countries, taking advantage of economic uncertainty and making various historical claims, tried to stoke conflict by making claims against minorities and/or other states.[50] With the exception of the former Yugoslavia, however, this did not lead to widespread violence or derail the democratization project. Czechoslovakia did split up, peacefully, into two countries (the Czech Republic and Slovakia) in 1993, and some states, such as Romania and Slovakia, led by former communist parties or by leaders who presided over corrupt, nationalistic governments, remained "reluctant democratizers" throughout much of the 1990s. In many of these states, the EU and other international organizations played a positive role, offering material incentives for reforms, monitoring the environment (in particular with regard to media and minority rights), and strengthening the hand of minorities and opposition parties against political incumbents that were ambivalent or hostile to reforms.[51] Table 2.4 reports "freedom scores" for several states in the region in the 1990s, reflecting the different pace of reform. These data, compiled by Freedom House, judge states based upon political

TABLE 2.4 Freedom House scores for selected post-communist states

Country	*1989*		*1991*		*1993*		*1995*		*1999*		*2012*	
	PR	*CL*	*PR*	*CL*	*PR*	*CL*	*PR*	*CL*	*PR*	*CL*	*PR*	*CL*
Poland	4	3	2	2	2	2	1	2	1	2	1	1
Hungary	4	3	2	2	1	2	1	2	1	2	1	2
Czechoslovakia/ Czech Republic	6	6	2	2	1	2	1	2	1	2	1	1
Slovakia	n/a	n/a	n/a	n/a	3	4	2	3	1	2	1	1
Bulgaria	7	7	2	3	2	2	2	2	2	3	2	2
Romania	7	7	5	5	4	4	4	3	2	2	2	2
Yugoslavia/Serbia	5	4	6	5	6	6	6	6	5	5	2	2
Croatia	n/a	n/a	3	4	4	4	4	4	4	4	1	2
Albania	7	7	4	4	2	4	3	4	4	5	3	3
Estonia	n/a	n/a	2	3	3	2	2	2	1	2	1	1
Latvia	n/a	n/a	2	3	3	3	2	2	1	2	1	1
Russia/Soviet Union	6	5	4	4	3	4	3	4	4	5	6	5

Source: Freedom House, at www.freedomhouse.org, or see Freedom House's annual publication, *Nations in Transit*

rights (PR) and civic liberties (CL) on a scale from one to seven, with one being the most free. These data allow us to classify states as leaders or laggards, although one can see that over time, thanks in large part to international encouragement as well as an improving economic environment, some of the laggards have managed to catch up to the "leaders."

One is tempted to suggest, in fact, that by the 2000s political life in most of East Central Europe had become "normal." True, there were some interesting developments:[52] the election of twin brothers as President and Prime Minister of Poland in 2005; the inability of Czech parties to form a government for half a year after 2006 elections; and the return of Bulgarian Tsar (King) Simeon II, who served as Prime Minister from 2001 to 2005 and became the first monarch in history to ever be elected head of government in democratic elections. However, in most countries, the main political patterns are similar to what you would find in Western Europe: a social democratic left that was progressively becoming further and further removed from the communist past, a conservative right that was either tied to the Church or a free-market ideology, a liberal—in the European sense—center, and a few extremists haunting the political margins and winning the votes of the disaffected. But the big debates and questions—Will post-communist states become democratic? Can economic and political reform be done simultaneously? Will they make enough progress to join the EU?—seem to have been largely settled, although, as we'll explore in subsequent chapters, there have been some disturbing developments in the 2010s, in particular in Hungary and Poland, that might make one question how secure democracy is in this region.

Establishing capitalism

In addition to creating democratic political systems, post-communist leaders in Eastern Europe also faced the task of creating a new economic system, one that would not be state-directed but instead rely upon free markets, entrepreneurship, and private property. There was no blueprint for dismantling the communist economic system, and, more so than on the issue of democratization, the pace and scope of economic reform generated great controversy.[53]

The reason for this is that economic reform would be painful. Guarantees created by the old system (e.g., state-determined prices, subsidies for enterprises) would be taken away. Freeing prices would mean inflation. Taking away state subsidies and direction would create chaos and possibly bankrupt many enterprises. Some of the communist welfare state would also be dismantled. Many individuals would be, in the short term at least, "losers" during the transition. Living standards would decline, and many individuals would feel far less economically secure in the free-market system.

shock therapy name for economic reform programs in post-communist Europe that emphasized a rapid move from communism to capitalism.

The precise mix of reforms varied from country to country. Poland, eager to shed its communist past, launched "**shock therapy**" economic reforms designed to make a rapid break with the past. The political rationale for shock therapy was that publics might become frustrated with economic reforms and vote to undo reforms. This generated the belief among many reformers that political reality meant that they only had a limited amount of time to reform. Better then, in this view, to do as much as possible as quickly as possible.

Other states, such as Hungary, Slovenia, and Romania, undertook more gradual reforms. Advocates of gradualism sought to minimize the pain of reforms. Moving too fast, they thought, would be too costly. Moreover, by moving slower, one could wait until one set of reforms was consolidated and then move on to another reform, creating less chaos. Whereas they recognized the risks of lengthening the reform period, their position was that the fragile democracies in the region could not survive the "shock" of shock therapy.

In all cases, however, economic reform entailed taking the state out of the economy and allowing the market to function. This meant freeing prices, allowing private business and ownership of land, fostering competition, encouraging foreign investment, ending state planning and letting individual producers make economic decisions, and, most controversially of all, privatizing enterprises owned by the state by either selling them at auction, distributing shares of companies to their workers and managers, or giving all citizens vouchers with which they could buy shares of companies on newly formed stock markets.

privatization process by which state-owned enterprises in Eastern Europe were sold or otherwise transferred to private individuals; it was often controversial, as it produced inequality and was subject to corruption.

Each type of **privatization** had its pluses and minuses (e.g., vouchers were more "democratic" but, unlike auctions, did not raise money for the state), and this issue was one of the most controversial of all, as individuals and groups made various political, economic, and even moral claims to obtain economically valuable assets. There was no single model of privatization. The Czechs were famous for their vouchers, which seemed like an effective strategy until revelations of corruption were brought to light in 1997. The Poles, given the heritage of Solidarity, preferred management-employee buyouts, which was a very protracted process and ultimately left many Polish workers unhappy. The Hungarians sold off their enterprises—often to foreigners—which allowed them to generate more revenue but left many wondering who in the end benefited from the process. Ultimately, by whatever strategy and whether it was done quickly or slowly, most of the state's assets were privatized. Throughout the region, however, ordinary workers expressed frustration with the outcome, and few felt that privatization had delivered on its promises.[54]

What were the results? Certainly, as seen in Table 2.5, there was pain: inflation, unemployment, economic decline. The retreat of the state and the nebulous legal environment meant corruption flourished. Inequality increased. Some—younger, better-skilled workers—fared well, and many of these individuals found jobs in the newly expanding service economy or with international companies. Others, especially older workers in blue-collar jobs, fared far less well, as their factories shut down and they lacked skills to find work in the new economy. "Losers" protested against government policy, which, in the cases of Romania in 1991, Poland in 1993, and Bulgaria in 1997, helped bring about the collapse of governments.

As seen in Table 2.5, there is evidence to suggest that the "shock therapy" approach in those states that reformed more rapidly, such as Poland and the Czech Republic, was a superior strategy, as these states saw growth by the mid-1990s. Anders Aslund, who advised several governments in the region, argues that the record conclusively shows that those who were slower to adopt reforms or moved more gradually (e.g., Romania, Bulgaria, and, further east, Ukraine and Russia) did worse.[55] The World Bank, assessing the experience in the region, argues that focusing solely on the speed or sequence of reforms ignores other factors (e.g., initial starting points, country-specific variables) that also matter. The general picture is that a

TABLE 2.5 Results of economic reforms in post-communist Europe

Country	*Avg. annual inflation, 1990–1996, %*	*Avg. unemploy-ment, 1990–1996, %*	*First year of economic growth*	*Real GDP 2000 (1990 = 100)*	*Private sector share of GDP, 1999*	*Foreign investment, 1991–1998, $ per capita*	*GDP/Capita, 2014, $*
Poland	116.3	13.2	1992	144	65	386	14,343
Czech Republic	30.9	2.9	1994	99	80	995	19,530
Hungary	25.7	9.9	1994	109	80	1,666	14,028
Romania	121.4	8.1	1993	82	60	215	9,997
Bulgaria	115.5	11.5	1994	81	60	n/a	7,851
Estonia	47.4*	4.1*	1995	85	75	1,279	20,161
Lithuania	136.5*	5.4*	1994	67	65	n/a	16,507
Slovenia	64.0	12.5	1993	120	55	n/a	23,999

Source: World Bank, *Transition: The First Ten Years* (Washington: The World Bank, 2002), and online data from www.worldbank.org, United Nations Conference on Trade and Development (UNCTAD), online at www.unctad.org, Austrian National Bank (Osterreichische Nationalbank), *Focus on Transition* 1, 1997, available at www.oenb.at

*Data available only from 1993–1996.

commitment to reforms was key and that reforms needed to build momentum to begin to produce positive results. Vacillating between one course and another or adopting only partial reforms (as occurred early on in Romania and Bulgaria or later in Russia) was not the recipe for success.[56]

Regardless, as the case with democratization, the laggards did, on many indicators, catch up. By the late-1990s, most states could claim the "worst" was over. Return to the communist past was politically and practically impossible. Shops in cities such as Prague, Budapest, and Riga were full of all sorts of goods, including luxury products. New factories were being built. Slovakia, for example, on a *per capita* basis had by 2010 the most autoworkers in the world. Although in terms of *per capita* income post-communist Europe still lags behind Western Europe, growth rates in the mid-2000s approaching 10 percent a year in countries such as Slovakia, Estonia, and Latvia would make the average German or Italian quite jealous. Some, as noted in Chapter 10, even suggested that Eastern Europe, economically speaking, had important lessons to offer for Western Europe.

This is not to say all is fine. As seen in Table 2.5, whereas such countries such as Slovenia have living standards that approach those in Western Europe, other states, including Romania and Bulgaria, remain relatively poor. In 2014, both Albania and Bosnia had GDP *per capita* under $5,000. Unemployment is still a major problem, ranging in 2014 from about 6 percent in more successful states such as the Czech Republic to over 11 percent in Bulgaria to 28 percent in both Bosnia and Macedonia.[57] The gap between the capital cities and the countryside is very pronounced in most states, with thousands migrating to the cities in search of work, even at low wages. The economic crisis of 2007 to 2010 also hit the region hard, a topic covered more in-depth in Chapter 10, and economic difficulties were cited in 2015 as one reason these states could not take in more refugees, an issue discussed in Chapter 11.

The tragedy of Yugoslavia

While nobody would claim the post-communist transition was easy in East Central Europe, the worst-case scenarios were largely averted. The great exception, of course, was the former Yugoslavia, whose constituent parts and peoples became embroiled in several wars, resulting in over 200,000 deaths, some 2 million refugees, and, on a continent where most thought such things could never happen again, genocide.

Explaining the breakup of Yugoslavia

In retrospect, such a development does not seem entirely surprising. As seen in Table 2.6, Yugoslavia was an amalgam of seven main different national groups representing three religions who, prior to 1919, had never before lived in a single country. Levels of economic development varied widely—with Slovenia and Croatia far more advanced than Kosovo or Macedonia. Most republics had sizeable numbers of ethnic minorities (e.g., Serbs in Croatia, Albanians in Serbia and in Macedonia). To top it all off, many of the groups had histories of conflict with others, and some in each national group felt that the idea of a "South Slav" union denied their own nationality its right to self-determination. Jozef Tito, the communist leader, managed to keep a lid on potential conflicts, but after his death in 1980, economic decline and nationalist politicians—chief among them the Serb leader Slobodan Miloševic—began to pull Yugoslavia apart. Warren Zimmerman, the last American ambassador to Yugoslavia, argues that:

> The breakup of Yugoslavia is a classic example of nationalism from the top down—a manipulated nationalism in a region where peace has historically prevailed more than war and in which a quarter of the population were in

TABLE 2.6 Ethnic composition of Yugoslavia

Ethnic group	*Main religious affiliation*	*Population*	*% of national total*	*% of total in Bosnia**
Serbs	Orthodox	8,140,000	36.3	37
Croats	Catholic	4,428,000	19.8	20
Muslims**	Islam	2,000,000	8.9	40
Slovenes	Catholic	1,754,000	7.8	n/a
Albanians	Islam	1,730,000	7.7	n/a
Macedonians	Orthodox	1,340,000	6.0	n/a
"Yugoslavs"	Mixed	1,219,000	5.4	n/a
Montenegrins	Orthodox	579,000	2.6	n/a
Hungarians	Catholic	427,000	1.9	n/a

*Full name is Bosnia and Herzegovina
**This category refers to ethnic Slavs who speak Serbo-Croatian, not Albanians, Turks, or Roma.

Source: 1981 Census Data (last full census in Yugoslavia, presented in Denitch, *Ethnic Nationalism: The Tragic Death of Yugoslavia* (Minneapolis: University of Minnesota Press, 1996), pp. 29, 234

> [ethnically] mixed marriages. The manipulators condoned and even provoked ethnic violence in order to engender animosities that could then be magnified by the press, leading to further violence.[58]

The end of Yugoslavia

After Tito's death, rumblings of discontent and manifestations of nationalism emerged in Yugoslavia. The first activity was in Kosovo, a region within Serbia that is considered the birthplace of the Serbian people but by the 1980s had a population that was 90 percent ethnically Albanian. As Albanians began to mobilize to assert their rights, Serbs responded with their own claims, including a memorandum in 1986 published by the Serbian Academy of Sciences that referred to a "genocide" occurring against Serbs in Kosovo. Miloševic seized upon this idea, and employed authoritarian methods to strip Kosovo of its autonomy. Other national groups became nervous about Miloševic and the possibility that he would try to create a "Greater Serbia."[59] When Yugoslavia held regional elections in 1990—a result in part of the wave of reform that occurred elsewhere in the region in 1989—nationalist politicians fared well. Both fearing Serb nationalism and tired of subsidizing poorer regions of the country, many Slovenes and Croats clamored for independence. Efforts to save federal Yugoslavia—both internally and internationally—failed. US Secretary of State James Baker famously declared that "we have no dog in this fight."[60] The final straws were the declarations of independence in June 1991 by the Slovenian and Croatian legislatures, moves that were widely supported within both republics—with the obvious exception of the ethnic Serb communities in Croatia.

War and "ethnic cleansing"

The breakup of Yugoslavia led to violence. Slovenia, where there were few ethnic Serbs, fought a brief ten-day war and secured its independence. In Croatia, where there were areas with Serb majorities, local Serbs declared themselves separate from Croatia and were supported by the Serb-dominated Yugoslav National Army. Serbs seized control of large areas of Croatia and shelled cities such as Dubrovnik, Vukovar, and the Croatian capital, Zagreb. In early 1992 UN peacekeepers were sent to enforce a ceasefire.

The worst fighting, however, occurred in Bosnia-Herzegovina (hereafter Bosnia), which was the most heterogeneous of all the regions of Yugoslavia and had territory claimed by both Serbs and Croats. The main division among the three groups in Bosnia (Bosnian Muslims [or Bosniaks], Serbs, and Croats) was religion, but it is perhaps worth mentioning that the Muslims in Bosnia had to rank as among the most secular of all Muslims in the world. In January 1992, Serbs in Bosnia proclaimed their own Republic of the Serb People. On March 24, 1992, Miloševic and the Croatian leader Franjo Tudjman, ostensibly enemies, met and agreed to divide up Bosnia.[61]

Although one could foresee that Bosnia would be engulfed by fighting, international peacekeepers did not arrive, making the claim in 1991 by Jacques Poos, Luxembourg's Foreign Minister, that Yugoslavia would be "Europe's hour," utterly fatuous.[62] As had occurred in Croatia, local Serb forces mobilized and drove non-Serbs—mainly Muslims—from their homes in what would be euphemistically called "**ethnic cleansing.**" Ethnic Croats did the same, and by the end of 1992 Muslims controlled only a small percentage of Bosnia's territory. Efforts to negotiate a peace agreement led nowhere, and the bleeding wound of Bosnia—a six-hour drive from Vienna or Venice—created a moral crisis for Western governments. In the summer of 1992, images of Muslims in Serb "concentration camps" were transmitted on television, invoking memories of Auschwitz and prompting many to label the violence a genocide and call for international intervention. Sarajevo, the multi-ethnic Bosnian capital, was put under siege and its residents targeted by snipers.[63] As noted at the outset of this chapter, the worst single massacre during the war occurred in Srebrenica, where 8,000 unarmed Bosnian men and boys were killed by ethnic Serb forces. This event so shocked the world that at last NATO was compelled to do something.

ethnic cleansing
euphemism used to refer to ethnic-based violence which occurred in the former Yugoslavia, including the massacre of civilians in Srebrenica in 1995.

The conflict in Bosnia came to an end after NATO began bombing Serb positions. In November 1995, US President Bill Clinton managed to get Miloševic, Tudjman, and Bosnian President Alija Izetbegovic to come to Dayton, Ohio to negotiate and finally sign a peace agreement. The Dayton Accord put a NATO-led force of over 40,000 international peacekeepers into Bosnia and Croatia, and agreed to create a single Bosnian state with two "entities"—a Muslim-Croat Federation and the *Republika Srpska* (Serb Republic). It also required all governments to cooperate in the hunt for war criminals and to allow refugees to return to their homes, and it set up a means for international financial assistance for rebuilding in both Croatia and Bosnia. Progress on a number of fronts was slow. It was only in 2011 that Ratko Mladic, the Bosnian Serb commander at Srebrenica, was captured in Serbia and extradited to The Hague to stand trial before the International Criminal Tribunal for the former Yugoslavia.

The fighting in Kosovo

The next major conflict was in Kosovo, where the process of Yugoslavia's breakup started in the 1980s. Interestingly, while fighting raged in Bosnia, Kosovo was tranquil, in large part because the leader of the Kosovar Albanians, Ibrahim Rugova, an admirer of Mahatma Gandhi, believed that Albanians should follow for both moral and practical reasons a strategy of non-violent resistance against the more powerful Serbs. Rugova was pointedly *not* invited to Dayton, however, leading many Kosovar Albanians to question his approach. By 1997, insurgents in the Kosovo Liberation Army (KLA), supported by some of their co-ethnics in Albania proper, emerged to attack Serbs in Kosovo. In reprisal, Serbs began to attack Kosovar civilians.

In March 1999, NATO began a bombing campaign against Serb positions both in Kosovo and in Serbia itself. This action lacked authorization from the United Nations and aroused great international controversy. Tens of thousands of refugees fled to Macedonia and Albania, and a large-scale humanitarian crisis loomed. After six weeks of bombing, which inflicted heavy damage in Serbia and produced at minimum hundreds (Serbs claimed several thousand) of civilian casualties, Miloševic agreed to pull out of Kosovo, which became a UN protectorate and was occupied by 50,000 peacekeepers. Since the conflict, international administrators have overseen reconstruction efforts, helped conduct elections, and prevented conflict, although Serbs—perhaps 5 percent of the population—claim that they have been the targets of violence from Albanians.

Endgame: Miloševic's defeat

The final denouement of the conflict, however, occurred in Serbia itself. Opposition to Miloševic had been growing throughout the 1990s, not only because he championed an aggressive foreign policy but also because the conflict and international sanctions were devastating to the economy. Corruption thrived, whereas the average Serbs were hit hard by an unemployment rate of over 50 percent and inflation that topped 5,000,000,000,000,000 percent (that is *not* a typo) between October 1993 and January 1995.[64] In October 2000, many believed that opposition leader Vojislav Kostunica defeated Miloševic in Serbian presidential elections, prompting widespread protests when it was clear the government falsified voting returns. Facing massive civil unrest, Miloševic resigned, and in March 2001, after an armed stand-off, he was arrested by Serbian police on a corruption charge and subsequently turned over to international authorities to stand trial for war crimes. His trial began in 2002, but he died in his prison cell in March 2006, before the court could render a verdict.

Within Serbia in the 2000s, there has been intermittent progress toward a more liberal democracy, even as Montenegro, the one Yugoslav republic that remained united with Serbia, declared independence in 2006, and Kosovo declared independence in 2008, although the latter has yet to gain sufficient international recognition to occupy a seat at the UN. Taking action to purge the military and government of those who were parties to war crimes and allowed corruption to flourish has been a major challenge for post-Miloševic Serbian governments. A pro-Western prime minister was assassinated in March 2003 by a rogue policeman with ties to nationalist groups, and nationalist parties continue to do well at the polls. Serbia did issue, in 2010, an official apology for the massacre at Srebrenica, although it stopped short of using the word genocide, and numerous alleged war criminals have been apprehended and put on trial. In March 2016 Radovan Karadžic, the political leader of the Bosnian Serbs during the war in Bosnia, was found guilty of genocide for his role in the Srebrenica massacre by the UN tribunal in the Hague and sentenced to 40 years in prison. While many would call this justice, it will not heal all the wounds caused by the fighting in Bosnia, whose memories, as noted at the opening of this chapter, remain a source of tension in the region.

Application questions

1. Why did Western Europe, as opposed to another region of the world, rise to global pre-eminence? Does this early history make Europe unique and therefore make it less likely that ideas such as democracy and limited government, which developed in Western Europe, can take root elsewhere?
2. Most people, regardless of where they live, would claim that they are patriotic or nationalistic. Many would argue that these are positive traits. How can one explain why some countries have more positive manifestations of nationalism and others—particularly in Eastern Europe—have tended to have more negative ones? Do you think globalization and economic integration will allow Europe or other parts of the world to "overcome" nationalism?
3. Given widespread belief today in the superiority of free and open markets, what relevance does the post-war success of statist welfare policies in Western Europe have today?
4. How specifically might the legacy of past empires matter for countries in Eastern Europe today? Are there still important political, social, or cultural differences that make this region somehow less "European"? Given the different historical experiences of peoples of Europe, what is your understanding of the term "European"?
5. Why do you think the international community did not act preemptively to prevent conflict in Bosnia? What do the atrocities there show about the idea of "Europe"?

Key terms

Additional reading

Davies, Norman. 1998. *Europe: A History*. New York: HarperCollins.
An account of Europe from its prehistory to modern times, with most of the focus on the twentieth century. Extremely lengthy (more than 1,000 pages long), but a very handy reference work.

Judt, Tony. 2005. *Postwar: A History of Europe Since 1945*. New York: Penguin.
An encyclopedic account of developments in both Western and Eastern Europe since World War II. Judt's work covers both major political and economic developments as well as social history and popular culture. Judt is particularly useful on the issue of the development of the welfare state.

Mason, David S. 2005. *Revolutionary Europe 1789–1989: Liberty, Equality, Solidarity*. Lanham MD: Rowman and Littlefield.
Examines intellectual and ideological trends in Europe since the French Revolution, including nationalism, fascism, communism, and liberalism.

Schopflin. George. 1993. *Politics in Eastern Europe*. Oxford: Blackwell.
A relatively short treatment of the region, focusing on developments since 1945 as well as the revolutions of 1989.

Tilly, Charles. 2004. *Contention and Democracy in Europe, 1650–2000*. Cambridge: Cambridge University Press.
A major scholarly work that examines how states and democratic governance arose in Europe. One of its major themes is that social conflict, including outbreaks of internal and inter-state violence, has been an important force for political development in Europe.

Notes

1 "Surfaced tensions," *The Economist*, July 11, 2015.
2 Charles Tilly, "Reflections on the History of European State-Making," in Charles Tilly, ed. *The Formation of National States in Western Europe* (Princeton: Princeton University Press, 1975), p. 42.
3 See Paul Kennedy, *The Rise and Fall of the Great Powers* (New York: Random House, 1987), and Charles Tilly, *Contention and Democracy in Europe, 1650–2000* (Cambridge: Cambridge University Press, 2004).
4 For an excellent collection of works on nationalism, see Anthony Smith and John Hutchinson, eds. *Nationalism* (Oxford: Oxford University Press, 1995).
5 Quoted in Liah Greenfeld, *Nationalism: Five Roads to Modernity* (Cambridge: Harvard University Press, 1992), p. 276.
6 Daniele Caramani, The Nationalization of Politics: The Formation of National Electorates and Party Systems (Cambridge: Cambridge University Press, 2004).
7 Ernest Gellner, *Nations and Nationalism* (Ithaca: Cornell University Press, 1983), and Benedict Anderson, *Imagined Communities: Reflections on the Origin and Spread of Nationalism* (London: Verso, 1991).
8 The classic source is Barrington Moore, *Social Origins of Dictatorship and Democracy* (Boston: Beacon Press, 1966).
9 For general works on this topic, see Roy Porter, *The Enlightenment* (New York: Palgrave, 2001), and Dorinda Outram, ed. *The Enlightenment* (Cambridge: Cambridge University Press, 1995).
10 David Mason, *Revolutionary Europe 1789–1989: Liberty, Equality, Solidarity* (Lanham MD: Rowman and Littlefield, 2005), p. 21.

11 Tilly, *Contention and Democracy in Europe*, p. 34–41. His analogy is that democracy is like a lake, which can form in a limited number of contrasting ways. It is not, in his view, like an oil field (unique to very special conditions) or a garden (which can be cultivated by anyone with the proper skill).
12 John S. Mill, Considerations on Representative Government (1861), Chapter IV.
13 Dietrich Rueschmeyer, Evelyne Huber Stephens, and John Stephens, *Capitalist Development and Democracy* (Cambridge: Polity Press, 1992), and Tilly, *Contention and Democracy in Europe*.
14 For more on the British case, see Robert Allen, *The British Industrial Revolution in Global Perspective* (Cambridge: Cambridge University Press, 2009).
15 Roman Szporluk, *Communism and Nationalism: Karl Marx versus Friedrich List* (Oxford: Oxford University Press, 1991).
16 Mark Mazower, The Dark Continent: Europe's Twentieth Century (London: Penguin, 1998).
17 This account draws heavily from Tony Judt, *Postwar: A History of Europe Since 1945* (New York: Penguin, 2005), p. 354 -359.
18 Judt, *Postwar*, p. 360.
19 Judt, *Postwar*, p. 358.
20 Mancur Olson, *The Rise and Decline of Nations* (New Haven: Yale University Press, 1982).
21 Judt, *Postwar*, p. 63.
22 Peter Hall, *Governing the Economy: The Politics of State Intervention in Britain and France* (Cambridge: Polity Press, 1986), Chapter 6.
23 Barry Eichengreen, ed. *Europe's Postwar Recovery* (Cambridge: Cambridge University Press, 2003).
24 Quoted in Judt, *Postwar*, p. 73.
25 Judt, *Postwar*, p. 361.
26 Quoted in Judt, *Postwar*, p. 538.
27 Alan Warde, *Consensus and Beyond* (Manchester: Manchester University Press, 1982), p. 26.
28 See Hall, *Governing the Economy*, p. 29–30.
29 Judt, *Postwar*, p. 364–367.
30 Robin Okey, *The Demise of Communist East Europe: 1989 in Context* (Oxford: Oxford University Press, 2005), p. 4.
31 David Turnock, *The Economy of East Central Europe 1815–1989* (London: Routledge, 2006), p. 76, 88.
32 Interestingly, even though Bulgaria was allied with Germany, it did not surrender its Jews to Hitler and the SS. One wonders how the fate of Jews would have been different if other states did not cave in to Hitler's demands to turn over their Jews for annihilation.
33 Tony Judt, *Postwar*, p. 18–19. For comparison, Poland lost 20 percent of its pre-war population; Germany lost only one-fifteenth and France one in seventy-seven.
34 When Roosevelt told Stalin he wanted the Polish election to be pure like Caesar's wife, Stalin responded, "They said that about her but in fact she had her sins." Charles Bohlen, *Witness to History*, quoted in Gale Stokes, ed. *From Stalinism to Pluralism: A Documentary History of Eastern Europe Since 1945*, 2nd edition (Oxford: Oxford University Press, 1996), p. 23.
35 Vladimir Tismaneanu, *Reinventing Politics: Eastern Europe from Stalin to Havel* (New York: Free Press, 1992), p. 24.
36 See data in J.F. Brown, *Eastern Europe and Communist Rule* (Durham: Duke University Press, 1988), p. 504–505.
37 Judt, *Postwar*, p. 171–172.
38 Excellent treatment of civil society in the region can be found in Tismaneanu, *Reinventing Politics*, Chapters 4 to 6.
39 Wolfgang Nowak, a former minister in the government of Saxony (region in formerly East Germany) in "Getting back together is so hard," *The Economist*, September 18, 2004, p. 58.

40 "Getting back together is so hard."
41 See reports in *Deutsche Welle*, "German unification—Subsidizing the East," October 2, 2012, and "Eastern Germany is Western Germany's Trillion Euro Bet," September 24, 2010.
42 On-line data analysis from the 2014 European Social Survey, available at http://nesstar.ess.nsd.uib.no/webview/.
43 The exact derivation of the term is disputed. Many allege that it arose because the important meetings of the Czechoslovak opposition occurred in the Magic Lantern Theater in Prague, which has velvet curtains and carpeting. Others contend that the name simply implies softness and non-violence. Indeed, in Slovak the event is simply known as the "Gentle Revolution."
44 Quoted in Stokes, *From Stalinism to Pluralism*, p. 154.
45 Ralf Dahrendorf, *Reflections on the Revolution in Europe* (London: Verso, 1990).
46 Vladimir Tismaneanu, *Fantasies of Salvation: Democracy, Nationalism, and Myth in Post-Communist Europe* (Princeton: Princeton University Press, 1998), and Ken Jowitt, *New World Disorder: The Leninist Extinction* (Berkeley: University of California Press, 1992).
47 Valcav Havel, "New Year's Day, 1990," in Stokes, *From Stalinism to Pluralism*, p. 252.
48 According to the 1999 World Values Survey, over 70 percent of those in Hungary, Poland, Romania, Estonia, and Slovenia thought having democracy was a good thing. Serbia and Croatia ranked as primary exceptions, and further to the east in Russia and Ukraine non-democratic attitudes were more prevalent. Online analysis from www.worldvaluessurvey.org. For more on public opinion in the region, see Richard Rose, *Understanding Post-Communist Transformation: A Bottom Up Approach* (London: Routledge, 2009).
49 Okey, The Demise of Communist East Europe, p. 181.
50 For example, in Romania, the government courted the support of openly anti-Semitic, anti-Hungarian, and anti-Roma forces, some of which openly expressed admiration for both communist dictator Nicolae Ceaucescu and the World War II fascist leader Ion Antonescu. In Hungary, Ivan Csurka, vice-chair of the Hungarian Democratic Forum, wrote in 1992 about the need for Hungarians—implicitly referring to Hungarian minorities in Slovakia and Romania—to create their own "*Lebensraum*," a term most famously associated with the Nazis.
51 Paul Kubicek, ed. *The European Union and Democratization* (London: Routledge, 2003), and Milada Vachudova, *Europe Undivided: Democracy, Leverage, and European Integration* (Oxford: Oxford University Press, 2005).
52 Many of these fears stem from the rise of "populism," an admitted nebulous term, in the region. See collections of articles devoted to this topic in *Journal of Democracy* 18:4, October 2007, and *Problems of Post-Communism* 55:3, May/June 2008.
53 Excellent sources on the economic reforms in the region are The World Bank, *World Development Report 1996: From Plan to Market* (Oxford: Oxford University Press, 1996); Anders Aslund, *Building Capitalism: The Transformation of the Former Soviet Bloc* (Cambridge: Cambridge University Press, 2002); and The World Bank, *Transition: The First Ten Years* (Washington: World Bank, 2002).
54 Paul Kubicek, *Organized Labor in Postcommunist States* (Pittsburgh: University of Pittsburgh Press, 2004).
55 Anders Aslund, "The Advantages of Radical Reform," *Journal of Democracy* 12:4, October 2001, p. 42–48.
56 World Bank, *Transition*, p. 16.
57 Data from the World Bank, online at www.worldbank.org.
58 Warren Zimmerman, "Origins of a Catastrophe," *Foreign Affairs* 74:2, March/April 1995, p. 12. See also Bogdan Denitch, *Ethnic Nationalism: The Tragic Death of Yugoslavia* (Minneapolis: University of Minnesota Press, 1996).
59 Good books on Kosovo are Julie Mertus, *Kosovo: How Myths and Truths Started a War* (Berkeley: University of California Press, 1999), and Tim Judah, *Kosovo: War and Revenge* (New Haven: Yale University Press, 2002).

60 Quoted in Richard Holbrooke, *To End a War* (New York: Random House, 1998), p. 27.
61 Misha Glenny, *The Balkans: Nationalism, War, and the Great Powers* (New York: Penguin, 2001), p. 633.
62 Quoted in Noel Malcolm, "The Case Against Europe," *Foreign Affairs* 74:2, March/April 1995, p. 68.
63 For accounts, see Zlata Filipovic, *Zlata's Diary: A Child's Life in Sarajevo* (New York: Penguin, 1995), and Tom Gjelten, *Sarajevo Daily: A City and Its Newspaper Under Siege* (New York: Harper, 1997).
64 James Lyon, "Yugoslavia's Hyperinflation, 1993–1994: A Social History," *East European Politics and Societies* 10:2, Spring 1996, p. 293–327.

EU President Herman Van Rompuy of Belgium and European Commission President Jose Manuel Barroso of Portugal accept the Nobel Peace Prize award on behalf of the European Union in Oslo

Chapter 3

The development of the European Union

In October 2012, the Norwegian Nobel Committee awarded the Nobel Peace Prize to the European Union (EU). In its press release, the committee noted that the EU and its forebears had "for over six decades contributed to the advancement of peace and reconciliation, democracy, and human rights in Europe . . . [and] helped transform most of Europe from a continent of war to a continent of peace." Prior to bestowing the award at the formal ceremony in Oslo, the chairman of the committee lauded the EU's many accomplishments, praising in particular its expansion to post-communist Europe, noting that this action "may have amounted to the greatest act of solidarity ever on the European continent."[1] Such language echoed the language of the 1957 Treaty of Rome—one of the seminal documents in the history of European integration—which called for "an ever closer union among the peoples of Europe."

This award, one could argue, was well-deserved. The EU has helped make war among previously hostile European countries "unthinkable," the aspiration laid down in the 1950 Schuman Declaration, which laid the steps for a more united Europe. At the same time, however, as the chairman of the Nobel Committee noted, the EU is not perfect; he noted many of its controversies and shortcomings, including the failure to prevent the tragedy of Srebrenica, mentioned in the previous chapter. Others would be more critical. Indeed, at the same time that the EU received its award in Norway—ironically a country that is clearly eligible to join it but has declined to do so—Euroskepticism, if not Eurohostility, was on the rise in many parts of Europe. Greeks were protesting EU-imposed austerity measures, and debt problems in countries such as Spain, Portugal, and Italy made many fear for the future of the euro, the common currency used in most EU members. Nationalist, anti-immigrant parties, which are harshly critical both of the powers of the EU and the open borders it has promoted, were on the rise in many countries. By 2016, amid both continued economic difficulties and an influx of refugees and migrants (both of which will be discussed in subsequent chapters), anti-EU voices grew louder, including in Poland and Hungary, two countries that a decade before had enthusiastically joined the EU. In 2016 Britons voted, 52 percent to 48 percent, in favor of "Brexit"—leaving the EU—a development that stands in stark contrast to the Nobel Committee's praise of the EU in 2012 and made some fear for the EU's very survival. One observer suggested that the "idealism" of the "noble enterprise" of the EU had vanished; rather than fording the stream of numerous challenges confronting it, "it is sinking in the mud."[2] These issues are examined in more detail in subsequent chapters.

This chapter generally has a more sanguine tone. As suggested in the opening chapter, the idea of a single Europe may be best embodied in the EU, an organization that includes, as of 2016, twenty-eight European countries—with further expansion possible—committed to the goals of economic, political, and social integration of the continent. Created after World War II with a limited mandate and perhaps idealistic aspirations (and having different names over time), the EU has grown in scope, becoming an important political and economic actor and advancing processes of Europeanization. Discussion of every major political issue in contemporary Europe has some dimension that includes the EU, which makes it difficult to examine European politics by exclusively focusing on institutions or issues within individual states.

Despite its significance, the EU is not always well understood or appreciated—indeed, many Europeans revile it. Former US Secretary of State Madeline Albright said that one must be "a genius or French" to decipher its workings,[3] and even the French no doubt have some problems comprehending its Byzantine-like bureaucracy and myriad of rules and regulations. Entire courses could easily be taught just on the EU or on some of its policies. Our task, in a text that aims to present a broad survey of European politics, is far more modest. It eschews examination of arcane details or the minutiae of the EU. However, as noted, a fundamental grasp of the EU—its rationale and historical development, its institutions, its policies in key areas—is essential to understand contemporary European politics. This text therefore devotes two chapters to the EU, and places them before consideration of domestic-level institutions and actors. This chapter focuses more on the historical development of the EU through the 2000s, providing a building block for the subsequent chapter that examines its institutional structure and several of its core policies.

What is the European Union?

Before jumping into the origins of today's EU, a good starting point might be to define what the EU is and how it differs both from national states and from other international organizations. Although the EU has its own flag, anthem (Beethoven's "Ode to Joy"), holiday ("Europe Day" on May 9), motto ("Unity in Diversity"),[4] laws, regulations, and governing structures, the EU is not a single state, as is France or Germany. It is an organization made up of national states. As of 2016, it has twenty-eight members (Great Britain, as of this writing, is still in the EU) and twenty-four official languages.[5] While these states are said to have "pooled" their authority or sovereignty together in the EU, they remain free to leave it at any time. The EU exists, in a basic sense, only because its members allow it to function. In a strict sense it thus has, unlike states that establish their own control and sovereignty over a territory, no life of its own. Viewed in this light, the EU is not that much different from other international organizations, and its actions can be understood as policies that conform to the interests of its member states. Such a perspective is known as **inter-governmentalism,** which stresses the powers of the member states within the EU.

inter-governmentalism view of European integration that argues that the guiding force behind integration is the interest and power of individual nation-states.

Yet, one can clearly see that the EU is not just another international organization. Not only does it cover a wide number of issues (e.g., trade, social policy, environment, security), but it also offers to those who reside within its borders rights as citizens, all of whom carry an EU passport. It taxes its member-states to give it financial means. It has its own military force and issues its own currency, both competencies that traditionally have been the sole prerogative of nation-states. Most importantly, it possesses legal power above that of member-states. In other words, on a host of issues enumerated in EU treaties and legislation, it has authority, and its decisions, enforced by its own institutions, trump those of national governments. This is very different than, for example, the United Nations (UN). The UN Security Council can make a decision and require members to accede to UN demands, but enforcement is sporadic at best, and five major states (the US, Russia, China, Great Britain, and France) have a veto on the UN Security Council, so the UN cannot compel them to do anything. In contrast, on most issues in the EU, no state has a veto, there is a court to arbitrate disputes and enforce decisions, and states are required to adopt EU laws and directives into their national law. The UN has no such equivalent. This aspect of the EU—the power that it has above that of its member-states—is referred to as **supranationalism,** and the goal of those who want to see a stronger EU is to strengthen its supranational elements.

supra-nationalism
view of European integration that emphasizes the powers the EU has gained over nation-states so that it can compel them to act in certain ways.

There is, of course, a tension between inter-governmentalism, which emphasizes the interests, rights, and powers of states, and supranationalism, which essentially wants to take power away from states and invest the EU with greater authority. This tension has played itself out historically, with the two perspectives ascendant at different times, and in the institutional make-up of the EU, which includes elements of both. Over time, the EU has become increasingly supranational, although it is still far from the point where one could talk about the irrelevance of nation-states in Europe. The EU does matter as an independent institution—it now has *de facto* a life of its own—but individual countries in Europe continue to matter as well. At present, one might best think of the EU as something in between a federal government—such as the US, Australia, or Canada—and an international organization, with its final stage of development still unknown.

integration
sustained and institutionalized interaction among states and social actors that fosters a harmonization of policies; usually rests upon creation of an international organization such as the EU.

What is the EU designed to do? The key term here is **integration**. Integration is not merely cooperation, which occurs all the time in the international arena. Integration suggests something wider than an agreement on a limited set of issues (e.g., arms control, trade). Rather, it refers to a process of sustained and institutionalized interaction among states and social actors that fosters a harmonization of policies. Integration requires institutional arrangements, and it implies as well that states pool their powers or sovereignty together in such a way to create a larger whole (the EU) out of the sum of its parts (member-states). One can imagine different levels of integration, such as moving from a free-trade zone to a common market to economic and monetary union. In less than fifty years, the EU has traversed this territory. One can also discuss different types of integration, such as economic, political, and social. Although there are a number of organizations in the world that may aspire to foster some level of integration (e.g., Arab League, Organization of American States), few have made much progress or have real powers. There are various regional trading blocs, such as the North American Free Trade Agreement (NAFTA), but none come close to the EU in the level of economic and political integration. Ultimately, the EU serves to create a common set of policies throughout Europe and promote, as noted above, an "ever closer union" among its peoples.

Rationale for European integration

Why would one want to pursue European integration? Realist theory in the field of international relations—which stresses the desire for states to maintain sovereignty—has some difficulties explaining it,[6] and, in broad historical perspective, European integration sounds like an idealistic, fanciful, perhaps impossible notion. Europe, after all, had been the scene of two horrific wars in the first half of the twentieth century, not to mention previous centuries of strife and warfare.

Political goals

Yet, it was precisely those wars and the desire for peace that inspired post-war European leaders to search for new, pan-European solutions to Europe's problems. When Robert Schuman, the post-World War II French foreign minister considered one of the founding fathers of today's EU, first proposed a limited plan of economic integration—the aforementioned Schuman Declaration—his stated goal was make future wars "not merely unthinkable but materially impossible."[7] The core idea was that by fostering economic **interdependence**—that is, strong ties among states so that they rely upon each other for their individual well-being—the need and incentive to go to war would be removed. If by destroying your enemy you also destroy the basis for your own livelihood, war becomes less desirable. As integration and interdependence take root, one could also argue that such sustained cooperation would weaken feelings of nationalism, which were viewed by many as the cause of World War II. The goal, which was truly ambitious and in some ways revolutionary, was to create a peaceful continent. Regardless of what one may think of the EU—and it has plenty of critics—there is little doubt that it has succeeded in attaining this overarching goal. This was the primary rationale for its selection as the 2012 Nobel Peace Prize winner. War today among Great Britain, France, Spain, and Germany—previously bitter rivals—is inconceivable.

inter-dependence the idea that connections (e.g., political, economic, social) between countries make them dependent on each other; often attributed to globalization; many argue this has decreased the likelihood of war.

Economic goals

Above and beyond creating a more peaceful Europe, proponents of integration would point to concrete economic benefits. Andrew Moravcsik argues that integration has been driven largely by the economic interests of states and social actors, not pure idealism.[8] The economic arguments in favor of integration are several. Free trade, which was the primary point of emphasis in the first decades of the European project, would allow states to specialize in areas where they had comparative advantage, and all states would benefit through the trade of more efficiently produced goods. Indeed, one could argue that much of the post-World War II recovery in Europe was trade-driven, and exports in all EU countries increased after economic integration began. By building a common market, the middle- and small-sized European states could also take advantage of economies of scale and pool resources and thus better compete economically with larger states like the US and Japan. Moreover, certain aspects of integration (e.g., the Common

Agricultural Policy or CAP) were deemed essential to states to develop and support sectors of their national economies. For poorer member-states, EU development, cohesion, and regional funds have been important sources of revenue in national budgets.

Other objectives

euro
common currency used by most members of the EU; came into being in the late 1990s.

With most aspects of the common market achieved by 1992 and the monetary union launched with the common currency or **euro** (€), European integration is no longer just about economics. It has, as argued below, "spilled over" in a host of other concerns. Many transnational issues (e.g., pollution, crime, immigration, security) require international cooperation, and the EU has taken on responsibilities in these fields. European integration also allows Europe to pursue collective goals in foreign affairs, ranging from fostering democracy in neighboring states to deploying peacekeepers to troubled regions. Within Europe, as the EU has deepened its authority into new fields (e.g., social policy, education, good governance practices), some believe the EU can socially integrate Europe and help laggards in some fields meet higher standards. Some even see a united Europe as a means to balance US power or to present an alternative vision to American-style capitalism and its values.[9] In short, as idealistic as the EU may seem, one can fashion a realist-style argument that EU integration should be pursued so that European states can be more powerful than they would be on their own.

Arguments against the European Union

Of course, European integration has numerous critics. "Euroskepticism" takes on a variety of forms, ranging from "soft" variants that object to specific policies or question the wisdom of integration in certain areas to "hard" Euroskepticism that advocates withdrawal from the EU (as seen in the 2016 "Brexit" vote) and/or a dismantling of the EU itself. Euroskepticism attracts adherents across the political spectrum.[10] Some ground their objections to the EU on pragmatic or non-ideological grounds: The EU demands that its members democratize and ensure rule of law, but it itself lacks openness, transparency, and a real connection to people; it has a costly and inefficient bureaucracy that unnecessarily imposes another layer of governance in Europe; and it has complicated decision-making procedures. Other objections to the EU are more ideological. For those on the nationalist right, often concerned with national power and/or free markets, the EU's supranationalism has eroded national sovereignty, imposes thousands of unnecessary regulations on businesses, and, through fostering open borders, has facilitated excessive immigration and undermined states' security. Most nationalist-oriented European political parties, including the National Front in France, the Swedish Democrats, the Danish Peoples' Party, and Jobbik in Hungary, are strongly anti-EU. For some on the left, the EU is alleged to harbor a "neo-liberal" agenda that restricts states' ability to fund social welfare programs and, in some cases in the 2010s, has imposed austerity on its members. Far-left parties that have campaigned against the EU and/or fundamental EU policies include Syriza in Greece and the Left Bloc and Community

Party in Portugal—in both states these parties entered into government in 2015—as well as *Die Linke* (The Left) in Germany. As noted in the introduction to this chapter, Euroskepticism appears to be on the rise in many quarters in the 2010s, evidenced by the success of anti-EU parties, the outcome of the "Brexit" referendum, as well as public opinion surveys that find low levels of trust in the EU in many countries.[11] Developments such as these have led some to question the long-term future of the EU,[12] and we will examine them throughout this volume.

Origins of the European community

The original idea for a united, democratic Europe goes back several centuries. Some contend that the Holy Roman Emperor Charlemagne (800–814) should be seen as the *Pater Europae* (Father of Europe), as he was the first to unite Western Europe after the fall of the Roman Empire and was the forebear to subsequent German and French monarchies.[13] Charlemagne, of course, was an emperor, not a modern-day democrat. Once nation-states had formed, the connection between European integration and democracy was most clearly advanced by the German philosopher Immanuel Kant (1724–1804), who argued in *Perpetual Peace* (1795) for a confederation of European democratic states that would help secure peaceful international relations. Nineteenth-century communist leaders envisioned working-class revolutions that would do away with national states. After World War I, the idea of pan-European integration took on new life, with the French foreign minister Aristide Briand proposing a European Confederation of States and various British intellectuals supporting a European socialist confederation. World War II obviously obliterated any plans for European unity, but during the war anti-Fascist groups kept the dream of a united Europe alive.

Post-war roots

The devastation of World War II convinced many that new political arrangements would have to take hold in Europe. Every country in Western Europe had some sort of federalist movement, and those favoring a united Europe found a prominent spokesman in British wartime leader Winston Churchill. In a famous speech delivered in Zurich in September 1946, he called on Europeans to replace "rivers of blood" with "a kind of United States of Europe" that would give people a "sense of enlarged patriotism and common citizenship."[14] This goal received the backing of the US, which was worried about the spread of Soviet influence and wanted West Germany reintegrated into Europe. Specifically, the US encouraged those states receiving Marshall Plan money to work together and embrace free trade, and various international bodies were put together to help with distribution of aid and reconstruction.

Immediately after the war, there were numerous efforts to promote European integration. In 1948, various governmental and non-governmental organizations sponsored a Congress of Europe, which attracted over 1,200 political figures to discuss European unity. The Congress produced a number of recommendations, including a call for "economic and political union" as an "urgent duty." In 1949, the inter-governmental Council of Europe was created, which was essentially a consultative body, although it did create in 1950 a European Court of Human Rights, which has frequently been used by individuals to defend their rights against abusive governments. In 1952, a treaty was signed for a European Defence Community (EDC), which envisioned a pan-European security organization. It failed to take root, however, because the French National Assembly refused to ratify it, citing concerns about West German remilitarization and encroachments on French sovereignty.

European Coal and Steel Community (ECSC)
a precursor to today's EU; formed in 1951 among six countries, it was a supranational organization that integrated coal and steel production and distribution.

Despite problems with more grandiose schemes for European unity, there was one success. In 1950, Jean Monnet and Robert Schuman, both French officials, proposed a "High Authority" to integrate and oversee the development of French and German coal and steel industries, two key sectors for the military and for general economic development. Konrad Adenauer, chancellor of West Germany, accepted what became known as the Schuman Plan, which had been developed secretly and without British input. France and West Germany invited others to participate in this scheme. The result was the **European Coal and Steel Community (ECSC)**, formed in 1951 and the precursor to today's EU.

Treaty of Rome
signed in 1957, this expanded early integration efforts with the goal of a common market and an "ever closer union" of European countries.

The ECSC was limited. It covered only two industries and had only six members —France, West Germany, Italy, Belgium, the Netherlands, and Luxembourg. Great Britain was invited to join, but, preferring to emphasize its relations with its colonies and with a history of wanting to remain apart from political ventures on the continent, it stayed out. Scandinavian countries also refused to join, and no offer was made to Spain or Portugal, which had non-democratic governments at the time. Monnet, who assumed the leadership of the organization, wanted it to be a purely supranational and centralized organization with a High Authority (later called the Commission), assembly, and court, but, because states were unwilling to cede total authority to this new entity, an inter-governmental Council of Ministers was added as well. All of these institutions are found in today's EU and are examined in detail in the subsequent chapter.

The formation of the European Economic Community

European Economic Community (EEC)
another earlier version of the EU, created in 1957, which was charged with lowering trade barriers and creating a common market for goods, labor, and capital.

The ECSC's economic impact was limited, but its importance was in providing a "psychological space for Europe to move forward" and serving as a "political vehicle" to overcome French-German hostility and put European integration in motion.[15] Paul Henri-Spaak, the Belgian foreign minister, took the lead in organizing a conference in Messina, Italy in 1955 to consider further integration. The result was the **Treaty of Rome,** signed in March 1957, which created the Euratom (which sought cooperation in the field of nuclear power) and the **European Economic Community (EEC)**.[16]

The EEC joined together the members of the ECSC in a far more ambitious project. Its stated goal was creation of an "ever closer union" of European peoples that would be realized in the first instance with a common market, in which goods, labor, services, and capital could move without hindrance across national borders. This was a momentous break with the past, which had been dominated by economic nationalism.

TABLE 3.1 The evolution of the European Union

1950	Schuman Plan for Franco-German integration
1951	Treaty of Paris forms the six-member ECSC
1957	Treaty of Rome establishes EEC
1966	Luxembourg Compromise allows national vetoes
1967	EEC, ECSC, and Euratom form European Community (EC)
1973	Great Britain, Denmark, and Ireland join EC
1979	First direct elections for European Parliament
1981	Greece joins EC
1986	Spain and Portugal join EC
1986	Single European Act (SEA)
1992	Common Market created
1993	Maastricht Treaty approved by all members; EU formally created
1995	Austria, Finland, Sweden join EU
2002	Euro introduced in twelve countries
2003	Nice Treaty enters into force; EU Convention publishes draft Constitutional Treaty
2004	Cyprus, Czech Republic, Estonia, Hungary, Latvia, Lithuania, Malta, Poland, Slovakia, and Slovenia join EU
2005	EU Constitutional Treaty rejected in France and the Netherlands
2007	Bulgaria and Romania join EU
2009	Lisbon Treaty ratified by all member states
2010	Creation of the European Financial Stability Facility, a response to the debt crisis in several states that use the euro
2013	Croatia joins the EU
2016	British voters endorse "Brexit," which will lead to Britain's negotiated withdrawal from the EU

Reaching this goal would not be easy, and several stages were envisioned. First, states would have to lower trade barriers, eventually removing all barriers to trade in goods. The six countries would also form a customs union, meaning they would have a common trade policy vis-à-vis the rest of the world. Certain policies, such as a competition policy, freeing of internal markets, tax harmonization, coordination of state planning, and mutual recognition of product standards, would have to be in place to help ensure a level playing field among the actors. To protect agriculture, a major concern of the French, the EEC agreed to create the CAP, which would ensure a higher price for agricultural products. The emphasis was overwhelmingly on economic goals. The Treaty of Rome functioned largely as an "economic constitution," not one with explicit political elements.[17] However, the implications of the Treaty were clearly political. In the words of Spaak, "Those who drew up the Rome Treaty . . . did not think of it as essentially economic; they thought of it as a stage on the road to political union."[18]

functionalism
idea that integration would move slowly, step-by-step, based upon pragmatic, functional goals, not idealistic schemes.

The functional approach

Why did economics predominate the early years of European integration? What theories can one employ to explain this process? Most discussions of European integration invoke the idea of **functionalism**, meaning that successful European integration would have to rest on functional, tangible goals and programs and not overarching idealistic schemes. Schuman was clear about this, acknowledging that "Europe will not be made all at once, or according to a single, general plan. It will be built through concrete achievements, which first create a *de facto* solidarity."[19] Economic issues were judged to be more amenable to integration because states could find common ground, and they did not touch upon items like foreign policy or cultural issues, seen to be the sole prerogative of states. In particular, one could argue that issues of "low politics," typically outside of view or concern of the wider public—the technical elements of economic integration—would be less subject to nationalistic pressure compared to issues of "high politics" that are more in the spotlight. In the words of one historian, the initial steps of integration were a deliberate "de-dramatisation of European politics."[20] The ambitious goal of continental peace was not to be achieved through a grandiose project, but through incremental steps, starting with economic cooperation and negotiation, in which one could make concrete, tangible achievements. This notion is supported by the failure of the more ambitious and supranational EDC. Rather than creating a supranational security arrangement among Europeans, the American-led NATO alliance became the key structure for West European security.

Proponents of integration, however, did not intend to stop just with economic integration. From the beginning there was a political impulse, one designed to foster deeper political integration as well. The idea, known as **neo-functionalism,** was that economic integration would incrementally "spill over" into other issues.[21] Neo-functionalists took economic interdependence as a given, and its proponents argued that government officials and interest organizations in individual states would realize it was in their interest to develop larger markets and coordinate policies through supranational mechanisms. However, as integration proceeded in one sector, it would, by necessity, expand into others, as more policies would have to be pursued at levels of governance above the individual state. This logic of "spillover" would produce more and more integration, encompassing political as well as economic realms. Monnet put the matter best:

neo-functionalism
idea that economic integration would build momentum and gradually "spill over" into political and other realms.

> Once nation-states and their leaders find themselves bound by rules, infringement of which will destroy common policies that are to their own advantage, these institutional bonds will serve not only to inhibit the occurrence of conflict, but also to mediate it if it does occur. Little by little this method of conducting policy in common will spread to all sectors of interstate relations until the members of the Community no longer deal with each other on a bilateral basis. At this point they will have become a federation just as the provinces of France were assembled in a national state at a moment favorable to a change in this status.[22]

federalists
those who sought to expand the powers and supranational orientation of institutions of European integration.

Monnet's adherents—known as **federalists**—sought to expand the power of the institutions of the EEC and give them a more supranational orientation.

This (neo-)functionalist perspective long dominated discussions of the European integration, but it has been challenged by differing perspectives. Andrew Moravcsik grounds his explanation of EU development on inter-governmentalism, stressing how integration serves the interests of both state and non-state actors. However, the overlying notion is that these actors retain some autonomy, that they are not subject to a deterministic logic that makes progressive, linear integration virtually inevitable.

While Moravcsik would acknowledge that technocratic actors within the EU and in individual states may be drawn to supranational approaches, this is not necessarily the policy preference of all actors, some of whom wish to preserve prerogatives of national power. Moravcsik and other inter-governmentalists would note that the history of European integration is one of ups and downs, as state leaders have often been decisive in braking or speeding up the process. The institutional arrangements of the EU are also, in his view, the result of bargaining among various actors with various amounts of power.[23] This theoretical debate between neo-functionalists and inter-governmentalists remains relevant today, as the former would emphasize how the benefits of integration logically lead to supranational outcomes, while the latter would argue that these outcomes are shaped—and can be unmade, most clearly evidenced in the "Brexit vote"—by actors, including voters, who may take more into account than an economic cost-benefit analysis. Indeed, as noted in the opening chapter, it is this tension—the "logic" of integration vs. the political reality that may limit how far integration or "one Europe" can go—that constitutes one of the main themes of this volume, one that is developed in several of the subsequent chapters.

Obstacles to integration

After the signing of the Treaty of Rome, the federalists had trouble realizing even their more limited vision of a common market. Part of the problem was technocratic, meaning the sheer task of coordinating a myriad of economic policies was difficult. Politics, however, also entered into the picture, as states wanted to ensure that they were being treated fairly by the EEC and, more broadly, that the EEC served their interests. In this respect, "spillover" was not an automatic or necessarily smooth process, and, over time, as European integration took up more political questions—tax policy, immigration, security, a common currency—"bureaucratic tinkering" outside the eyes of the state authorities (or the wider public) was no longer sufficient.[24] In this respect, Moravcsik's inter-governmental analysis is persuasive in pointing out how *states* held up or forwarded the progress of European integration, which did not automatically or magically occur.

The power of states—and their leaders—to slow down the process of integration was manifested most clearly during the rule of French President Charles de Gaulle (1958–1969). De Gaulle was in favor of European integration, as a means to contain Germany and counter American power, but only insofar as it served French interests. In particular, de Gaulle favored the CAP as a means for other European states to support French agriculture.[25] He twice vetoed a British bid to join the EEC, arguing it would disrupt the cohesion of the existing organization and lead to unwanted US influence. He also favored an inter-governmental approach—a "Europe of nation-states"—and vehemently objected to supranational proposals, including efforts by EEC to acquire its own revenue and reduce national veto powers. In 1965, France boycotted the work of the EEC, paralyzing the organization. The result was the "Luxembourg Compromise" of 1966, which noted that the EEC would work for unanimity if "very important interests" were at stake, *de facto* preserving states' vetoes on matters they chose to view as "very important." De Gaulle, however, was not the only problem. By the 1970s, as many European economies began to slow and the world economy experienced oil and currency shocks, states looked to national, not European solutions. Integration stalled, and many began to speak of "Eurosclerosis."

Early accomplishments

This is not to suggest that the Treaty of Rome was a failure. There were some notable accomplishments. In 1967, the ECSC, the EEC, and Euratom merged, forming the European Community (EC). By 1968, tariffs on industrial products were eliminated, and the EC formed a customs union for purposes of international trade. Intra-European trade increased dramatically. In 1970, the EC acquired its own independent source of revenue, secured from a portion of tariffs levied on non-EC goods and a portion of a value-added tax (a type of sales tax) employed by member states. In 1974, the EC established a Regional Development Fund, which was used to promote economic development in less well-off areas (e.g., southern Italy and Ireland, later Spain, Greece, and Portugal). In 1979, voters directly elected the European Parliament for the first time. In the 1970s the EC also took early steps toward monetary union by creating the European Exchange Rate Mechanism (later called the European Monetary System) to lower inflation and end dramatic currency fluctuations, both of which had become problems. Most significantly, perhaps, the EC expanded to more countries. First, after its two rebuffs by de Gaulle, Great Britain was admitted in 1973, taking the plunge on a larger, more supranational organization after spearheading the creation of the inter-governmental European Free Trade Association (EFTA) with Scandinavian states. Ireland and Denmark joined with Britain, and the British and the Danes became prominent voices for more inter-governmentalism within the EC. Greece, Spain, and Portugal joined in the 1980s, once they had thrown off the shackles of authoritarian rule.

The road to Maastricht and formation of the European Union

The first few decades of European integration included some notable accomplishments, namely that states that have once been bitter rivals decided to pool their sovereignty and cooperate on a host of issues. This very fact should not be underestimated. Progress on several key issues, however, did remain modest. The goal of a common market was not achieved. Inter-governmentalism remained the norm. Other issue areas, such as foreign policy and the environment, received only modest levels of attention at a pan-European level. For many, "Eurosclerosis" seemed to better describe the status of the EC than the vision of an "ever closer union" articulated in the Treaty of Rome.

By the end of the 1990s, however, the European integration project had new momentum. The Maastricht Treaty, signed in 1991, formally transformed the EC into the EU, which also assumed powers over a host of issues. The end of the Cold

War opened up possibilities for further expansion and the unification of the continent. Many countries gave up their currency and adopted the euro. In the first decade of the new century, the vision of Monnet, Schuman, and other early advocates of European integration, which had looked utopian only a few decades before, looked closer and closer to being realized.

More impetus for integration

European integration gained renewed vigor in the late 1980s, thanks to the efforts of an unlikely duo: British Prime Minister Margaret Thatcher (1979–1990), who was suspicious of the EC as a socialist project, and the Frenchman Jacques Delors, a federalist and supranationalist *par excellence* who served as the head of the European Commission from 1985 to 1995.

Thatcher viewed the EC as ideologically suspect and hopelessly inefficient, and she launched many attacks on the EC, extracting concessions in 1984 on budgetary issues because of British "over-payments" to the EC budget. However, she did support open markets and competition. To the extent that the proposed and delayed common market would advance free markets on a European level, she was in favor of fulfilling the terms of the Treaty of Rome. The EU Commission under Jacques Delors agreed, stating that "Europe stands at the crossroads. We either go ahead—with resolution and determination—or we drop back into mediocrity."[26] The result was the **Single European Act (SEA)**, adopted in 1986. It contained a strict timetable to remove all trade barriers (e.g., non-tariff trade barriers, differential tax rates, lack of standard regulations) and create a common market by 1992. The common market would ensure not only free movement of goods, but also of capital (money for investment) and of people. Customs regulations essentially ended, and individuals living within the EC were free to reside, work, or study in any EC country.[27] With the adoption of the Schengen Agreement in 1985 and its gradual expansion, border checks across much of Europe also became a thing of the past.

Single European Act (SEA)
adopted in 1986, it put forth a timetable to remove all barriers to trade and create a common market by 1992 and expanded the powers of the European Community to new areas, such as the environment.

The SEA contained other measures—expanding the role of the EC to areas such as the environment and research and development, augmenting the powers of the European Parliament, and, perhaps most significantly, limiting use of national vetoes by introducing qualified majority voting—that were not to Thatcher's liking, but she agreed to it for the sake of forging a freer and common market. The SEA also mentioned the goal of monetary union, to which Thatcher vehemently objected, but she believed that it would never happen.[28] As noted below, it did, thanks in no small part to the efforts of Jacques Delors, who made creation of a single currency a top priority.

As if that were not enough, international events, namely the collapse of communism, opened up more opportunities for the EC. Delors, emphasizing his role as a policy entrepreneur, suggested that Europe also move closer to political union, which would necessitate an expansion of EC power in a variety of fields. In 1990, Delors, backed by France and Germany, announced an Inter-Governmental Conference (IGC) on European Political Union, which had a broad mandate to suggest internal reforms and expansion of EC powers.

The Maastricht Treaty

Maastricht Treaty
signed in 1991, it formally created the EU and expanded the scope of European integration, including creation of the euro and a Common Foreign and Security Policy.

The result was the Treaty on the European Union or, as it as better known, the **Maastricht Treaty,** so named because a draft version of it was approved in 1991 in Maastricht, a city in the Netherlands. This document ranks as important as the Treaty of Rome in the annals of European integration, perhaps even "one of the most important developments in world politics in the latter half of the twentieth century."[29] It made many changes. First, it formally created the European Union, a three-pillared organization that includes the old EC (the economic pillar), a pillar for a new Common Foreign and Security Policy (the so-called second pillar), and a third pillar on Justice and Home Affairs, which covers issues such as immigration and criminal activity. Each pillar was designed to have its own rules, with the latter two more inter-governmental in design.[30] Second, the treaty spelled out a timetable for monetary union and criteria under which states could join it. The Maastricht Treaty thus led to the birth of the euro. Third, the treaty established EU citizenship, which took on a physical manifestation with the distribution of EU passports.[31] Fourth, it made several institutional reforms: It strengthened the powers of the European Parliament; it gave the European Council an explicit agenda-setting role; it expanded the use of qualified majority-voting in the Council of the European Union; and it established a Committee of the Regions. All of these institutions are discussed in the next chapter. Lastly, within the EC pillar, the EU, as a neo-functionalist might have expected, expanded into new domains: education, culture, public health, infrastructure, labor market policy, and consumer protection.

The Maastricht Treaty was not popular in all quarters of Europe, and even as it was drawn up one could see that it was the result of various compromises: Spain, Portugal, and Greece, among the poorer members, demanded more financial assistance; France was adamant that monetary union have a set schedule; Germany insisted on strict criteria to join a single currency; Britain rejected any reference to a "federal union," thus leaving the Maastricht Treaty to assert that it was "a new stage in the process of creating an ever closer union among the people of Europe." Still, this was not enough to satisfy all critics. Thatcher, no longer Prime Minister but Baroness Thatcher of Kesteven in the British House of Lords, railed against it, but the British House of Commons, after much debate, ratified it. The Danes, Euroskeptics like the British, rejected it, with just over 50 percent voting no in a referendum in March 1992. Six months later, only 51 percent of French voters, long thought to be Europhiles, voted in favor. On a second attempt, after Denmark secured opt-outs on the common currency and defense, Danes approved it. In 1993, Germany, where the public remained unsold on the euro, became the last to ratify the treaty, where it had been challenged in court by Germany's *Land* governments.

Post-Maastricht developments

From the mid-1990s through the 2000s, the pace of European integration quickened. Not content to establish simply a common market in which goods, capital, labor, and services could move freely, advocates of a more united Europe pushed forward

In focus

The adoption of the Lisbon Treaty

In 2005, French and Dutch voters rejected the EU's Constitutional Treaty, a document that was three years in the making and designed to replace all existing EU treaties with a single document. The word "constitution" indicated that this was a far more explicitly political document than previous treaties, one that some feared would create a European superstate and spell the end of each country's sovereignty. Its rejection was therefore hailed in many quarters. *The Economist*, a British newsweekly that was never particularly keen on the Treaty, claimed that the "dream of deeper political integration and, in the 1957 Treaty of Rome's famous phrase, 'ever closer union', is over."[32] However, European leaders did not abandon the notion that major reforms of the EU were needed. Eighteen of the twenty-seven EU members had ratified the Constitutional Treaty, and many wanted to salvage something, although they were more reluctant to employ the term "constitution."

In December 2007, the leaders of the EU met in Portugal and signed a new treaty, known as the Lisbon Treaty. Unlike the Constitutional Treaty, the Lisbon Treaty would not replace earlier EU treaties with a single document; rather, it would amend existing EU treaties. According to José Sócrates, the Portuguese Prime Minister, the Lisbon Treaty "is not a treaty for the past. This is a treaty that will make Europe more modern, more efficient, and more democratic."[33] Similarly, according to a statement on the EU's website, the Lisbon Treaty will "provide the EU with modern institutions and optimized working methods to tackle both efficiently and effectively today's challenges in today's world."[34]

The Lisbon Treaty is not markedly different from the Constitutional Treaty. Angela Merkel, Germany's Chancellor, acknowledged that "the substance of the Constitution is preserved. That is a fact."[35] It changes voting procedures within EU institutions (discussed more in the next chapter) and increases the powers of the European Parliament. It includes a provision for a Citizens' Initiative in order to connect the EU to the population. Perhaps its most visible change is the creation of the post of President of the European Council, a *de facto* President of Europe, who would be selected by the heads of European governments. Some of the differences with the Constitutional Treaty are of a more symbolic nature: There is no reference to the term "constitution"; it makes no mention of EU symbols such as the anthem and flag; the Charter of Fundamental Rights is referenced but not formally included; opt-outs (Great Britain and Ireland for Justice and Home Affairs, Poland and Great Britain for the Charter of Fundamental Rights) are recognized; and the EU will not have a "Foreign Minister" but instead a "High Representative in Foreign Affairs and Security Policy," although this individual will have the same role envisioned in the Constitutional Treaty. A few changes are more substantive. National parliaments will have a greater role in EU decision-making, including a mechanism whereby they can challenge the legitimacy of EU proposals. While the old pillar structure of the Maastricht Treaty is formally abolished, there is explicit recognition that the Common Foreign and Security Policy will remain subject to its own rules, including unanimous decision-making.[36]

Overall, though, the most important difference was that the Lisbon Treaty, as noted, amended, but did not wholly replace, existing treaties. Thanks to that provision, its drafters hoped that member states would not feel an obligation to submit its ratification to popular referendums, which doomed the Constitutional Treaty. José Manuel Barroso, President of European Commission, noted that referendums were "more complicated" and "less predictable" and asked (rhetorically?), "If a referendum had to be held on the creation of the European Community, or the introduction of the euro, do you think these would have passed?"[37] Valéry d'Estaing, the former French President who was responsible for drafting the Constitutional Treaty, confessed that the Lisbon Treaty differed little from the earlier document but that "subtle changes" were adopted to "head off any threat of referenda by avoiding any form of constitutional vocabulary." He also noted that the earlier proposals were "hidden or disguised in some way," hardly reassuring given that greater transparency was supposed to be one of the aims of the reforms.[38] The Belgian foreign minister acknowledged that "The aim of the Constitutional Treaty was to be more readable; the aim of this [Lisbon] treaty is to be unreadable. . . . The Constitution aimed to be clear, whereas this treaty had to be unclear. It is a success."[39] Needless to say, such statements cannot be found on the EU's website that purports to explain and answer questions about the Lisbon Treaty.

Initially, the Lisbon Treaty seemed destined to suffer the fate of the Constitutional Treaty. Although most states—including France and the Netherlands—ratified it by overwhelming majority vote in parliament,[40] in Ireland a popular referendum is required to ratify new EU treaties. In June 2008, as they had done seven years before with the Nice Treaty, Irish voters voted "No" (53.4 percent against), despite the fact that all three major parties in Ireland lobbied for it and Ireland had been historically a major beneficiary of EU largesse. Various reasons were put forward for its rejection, including Irish fears of loss of sovereignty, military neutrality, and EU tax harmonization policies. Others noted that at 500 pages, the Lisbon Treaty was simply too long, a collection of "unintelligible drivel" put forward by the "dictatorship" of Brussels that, in the words of Ireland's representative on the European Commission, "no sane or sensible person" would read in full. Research conducted by the Irish government indeed found ignorance among both "yes" and "no" voters, but this may simply reflect that voters do not want to understand the "fiendish complexity of the EU."[41]

The Irish vote made it impossible for the Lisbon Treaty to go into force in early 2009 (as was planned) and threw the EU into a new crisis. Luxembourg's Jean-Claude Juncker stated, "This vote doesn't resolve any of the European problems, it almost makes every European problem bigger. It was a bad choice for Europe. There is no Plan B."[42] Although a few leaders, such as Václav Klaus, the Euroskeptic president of the Czech Republic, declared the treaty dead, other states went ahead with the ratification process. By May 2009, all EU members, save Ireland, had approved it through parliamentary ratification.[43]

Could Ireland, comprising approximately one percent of the EU population, stand alone? Although some suggested that the Irish could perhaps try to argue that voter approval was in fact not necessary, it was politically impossible to simply have a revote in parliament after the measure had been submitted to and rejected by voters. Demanding a revote (which had also been done after the Irish rejected the Nice Treaty in 2001) risked the perception of "bullying" the Irish prime minister and, as *The Economist* colorfully put it, could amount to "leaving whisky and a loaded revolver in the study and expecting him to do the decent thing for Europe."[44] To placate the Irish, other European states agreed to some modifications in the Treaty (e.g., removing a provision that meant some EU countries would not have an EU commissioner), and a new referendum was scheduled. This time, the Irish government took great pains to educate voters and stressed that the Lisbon Treaty would not end Irish neutrality, legalize abortion, or mean Irishmen would be drafted into a European army, all fears that were expressed during the first referendum. Feeling pressure from other countries as well as humbled by an acute economic crisis, in October 2009 the Irish gave their blessing to the Lisbon Treaty, with

67.1 percent voting in favor. The following month, the Czech Republic's Klaus reluctantly gave the treaty his blessing, meaning it had been ratified by all member states. Herman Van Rompuy, former prime minister of Belgium, and Catherine Ashton, the EU Trade Commissioner from Britain, became the first President and "High Representative" under the Lisbon Treaty.

Some hailed passage of the Lisbon Treaty as a great victory, and it has a real impact on the machinery of the EU. However, the saga of the Lisbon Treaty is in many ways cautionary. Like the Constitutional Treaty, it fell victim (at least at first) to voters less than enamored with the idea of giving more power to Brussels. Moreover, given the fact that Ireland was the only state where it was put before voters in a referendum, it makes it difficult to argue that the adoption of the Lisbon Treaty is a means, among other things, to remedy the EU's perceived "democratic deficit." Skepticism and, in some cases, fear of the EU is widespread. In order to move forward—whether it be with institutional reforms ("deepening") or further expansion ("widening"), the EU will need public support. How to win over increasingly Euroskeptical voters is something that proponents of EU reforms must figure out.

Critical thinking questions

1. How significant are the changes made by the Lisbon Treaty?
2. How do the debates about the Lisbon Treaty illustrate the tension between supranationalism and inter-governmentalism?

new projects: the euro, which replaced the currencies of twelve countries in 2002; institutional reforms designed to make the EU stronger, more efficient, and more accountable to European citizens; expansion of the EU to more countries, so that by 2004 it contained more than twice (twenty-five to twelve) the number of members it had in 1992; and, last but certainly not least, new treaties designed to consolidate all previous treaties, build a stronger connection between EU institutions and citizens, and, perhaps, provide a basis for still further integration.

Because EU institutions are covered more fully in the next chapter, discussions of institutional reforms, including the EU's alleged "democratic deficit," are largely covered there, although the **In focus** section of this chapter reviews debates over the **Lisbon Treaty**, the most important post-Maastricht treaty adopted by the EU. Among the many important new EU policies and initiatives in the 2000s, we shall focus here on the two with the greatest importance: the adoption of the euro and expansion of the EU in the 2000s.

Lisbon Treaty
a reform treaty that, among other things, changes the voting rules within the EU and creates a *de facto* EU "president" and "foreign minister"; came into force in 2009.

The euro

According to Robert Mundell, an American Nobel Prize-winning economist, "The introduction of the euro is one of those epochal events that can only be understood in the context of long periods of history."[45] The history of the euro dates to the 1970s, when volatility in exchange rates threatened the European trading system, prompting the creation of mechanisms to tie the value of European currencies together. By the late 1980s, full monetary union—which had been discussed in the early 1970s but left undone—appeared to many, including EU Commission President Delors, a logical extension of the common market. In 1988, Delors chaired a committee to examine the question of monetary union, which a year later proposed a three-stage process to bring it to fruition. Still, the idea was highly controversial. Thatcher said that "it confirmed our worst fears" and was full of "Delorism socialism,"[46] and the Germans were loathe to part with their beloved *Deutschemark*. However, once provisions were put in place to create an independent central bank and enforce strict criteria to join the currency—together with French support for German reunification in 1990—the Germans, perhaps reluctantly, acceded. Monetary union could be hailed as "victory" of sorts for neo-functionalists, as it could be viewed as a logical outgrowth, a "spillover" of a common market, but was also, particularly for Delors and French President Francois Mitterand, a consciously political project, an affirmation of the unity of Europe.

Rationale for a single currency

Advocates of the euro, which in 1995 became the somewhat uninspiring name for the single currency, pointed to several advantages of having a single currency.[47] Most obviously, it would make travel and business easier. Tourists would no longer have to exchange money (and pay sizeable commission fees) when traveling among European countries, and businesses would no longer have to keep multiple accounts in different currencies and exchange money as a consequence of intra-European trade and investment. Put another way, having to exchange money at the border or convert prices from one currency to another cut against the grain of a single, common market. Imagine the US—a common economic market of fifty states—with fifty different currencies! The EU estimated that elimination of currency exchange expenses alone would save some $10 billion annually.[48] In addition, businesses would no longer be subject to exchange rate risk. Businesses prefer predictability to volatility. A single currency was thus seen as a boon to business, encouraging more trade and investment across borders and, consequently, generating jobs.

There were also less obvious economic advantages to the euro. A common currency, it was argued, would allow Europeans to compare prices easier and find better bargains. Additionally, many alleged that making the necessary reforms to join the euro—discussed more below—would especially benefit countries such as Italy and Greece that had chronic inflation and high budget deficits. The euro would thus inject a measure of fiscal responsibility into states where it had been, to say the least, rare. The euro was designed as well as an expression of European power, to give medium-sized European economies a means to compete globally with the almighty American dollar, which was the world's preferred reserve currency and standard unit of exchange for international transactions. Lastly, it was advocated as an important symbolic reflection of European integration and even European identity. As the French economist Jacques Rueff wrote in the 1950s, "Europe shall be made through the currency, or it shall not be made."[49] As national governments were allowed to put their own design on one side of the euro coins (the bills are standardized), one could argue that as a Dutch woman reaches into her pocket and pulls out coins graced by the images of an Irish harp, the Slovenian poet France

Prešeren, and Vienna's Belvedere Palace, she *feels* more European. In the words of Wim Duisenberg, the first head of the European Central Bank, "The euro is much more than just a currency. It is a symbol of European integration in every sense of the word."[50]

Meeting the requirements

One could not, however, simply sign up for the euro. A multi-national conversion of numerous currencies involving millions of people and literally trillions of euros was historically unprecedented. It could not happen overnight. Nor, for that matter, would it succeed if just anyone could join. Each aspirant to join the eurozone had to demonstrate that it was economically solvent and thus would not bring down the value of the euro or generate monetary instability. In this respect, joining the euro was like a marriage. Love may be most important, but it might still be worth looking at your prospective partner's financial situation before making a commitment, because upon the exchange of vows his debt becomes your debt. For countries that prided themselves upon fiscal responsibility—chiefly the Germans—this meant that chronic debtors and spendthrifts such as the Italians had to get their fiscal house in order.

convergence criteria
rules on inflation, interest rates, and debt that countries had to meet in order to join the euro.

Stability and Growth Pact
agreement among countries using the euro that is aimed to keep the euro stable; its primary provisions concern budget deficits, which must remain under 3 percent of GDP.

The Maastricht Treaty laid out **convergence criteria** countries had to meet to join the euro. These were low inflation, low interest rates, exchange rate stability, a budget deficit of less than 3 percent of gross domestic product (GDP), and a total debt ratio of 60 percent to the country's total GDP. These last two criteria proved to be the hardest for several states to meet. The Italians, Greeks, French, and Spanish had to cut government spending and even privatize companies to raise revenue and cut their debt. By 1997—the year before exchange rates were to be permanently fixed—eleven states met the criteria, although the EU showed remarkable flexibility in claiming that states such as Belgium (122 percent debt/GDP ratio) and Italy (121 percent debt/GDP ratio) made enough progress to be included.[51] Greece, which had not met the criteria in 1997, was allowed into the eurozone in 2001, although many speculated at the time (with good cause, as it turned out, an issue that we'll explore in Chapter 10) that Greek claims of meeting the criteria were at best dubious. In an effort to prevent future problems, prospective euro members agreed in 1997 to a **Stability and Growth Pact**, whose key provision is that states using the euro pledge to keep their annual budget deficits under 3 percent of GDP. To employ the marriage analogy again, this "vow" meant that the new spouse could not, after being wed, run up a big credit card debt.

Arguments against the euro

Not all Europeans were enamored with the euro. Arguments against its introduction fell into three broad categories.

First, there was the nationalistic argument. The euro would be managed by the European Central Bank (ECB, formally created in 1998), with oversight from various EU bodies. By "pooling" their sovereignty together in the euro, states surrendered the ability to conduct their own monetary policy—meaning setting exchange rates, interest rates, and the money supply. All of these can be employed by states to spur or slow down economic growth. Many feared giving control to the ECB, thinking that their own national level central banks should remain in charge of monetary policy. On a less technical but nonetheless important level, people tend to like "their" money. It is a reflection of their history, part of their identity. Replacing colorful bills with images of national heroes for the bland euro was, for many, not a good trade. Largely because of economic nationalism, as well as confidence that their economy would out-perform the eurozone, the British opted to retain their pounds and pence.

Those on the political left were nervous about the euro because of the above-mentioned constraints put on euro members via the Stability and Growth Pact. By limiting the ability of states to run budget deficits, some leftists—especially in Sweden and Denmark with their sizeable welfare states—feared that the ECB would order Stockholm or Copenhagen to cut generous health care, pension, and education benefits in order to meet euro criteria. Both the Danes (in 2000) and the Swedes (in 2003) in referenda rejected participation in the euro. Notably, these were the only two instances when Europeans were able to vote directly on joining the euro.

Finally, economists made technical arguments against the euro. Chief among them was the notion that the eurozone was not an "optimum currency area." What does this mean? In brief, the eurozone has a functional lack of labor mobility, does not have much wage flexibility, and does not have a strong central government able to dispense funds to areas affected by adverse local economic conditions or "asymmetric shocks." For example, if Spain were to experience economic problems due to a country-specific problem (e.g., natural disaster, a downturn in the business cycle, a bust in the local real estate market [which did occur in 2008–2009]), one could not expect Spaniards to move *en masse* to another country with better prospects or the European Union to be able to devote enough resources to pull Spain out of the crisis. Moreover, the Stability and Growth Pact—if strictly enforced—would limit the ability of Spain itself to do much about the problem. Although this type of argument seems arcane and hypothetical, it manifested itself in 2010, when Greece, Portugal, Spain, and Ireland, because of severe debt crises made worse by the global economic downturn, required a bailout from their European partners. This made some doubt the very viability of the euro as well as the European project as a whole.[52] This important development is taken up more fully in Chapter 10.

These arguments, however, did not prevail prior to the adoption of the euro. The economic and *political* rationale in favor of the euro proved too strong to overcome in twelve of the EU states. Unlike in the 1970s, in the 1990s European leaders fulfilled their pledge to create a monetary union.

The launch of the euro

The euro was officially launched as a medium of exchange on January 1, 1999, after exchange rates among all of the participating euro countries were permanently fixed in December 1998. Combining the values of, at that time, all eleven currencies, the euro was born with a value of $1.168. At this stage, the euro was only a virtual currency; one could keep a bank account or credit card in euros and even purchase euros electronically, but there were no euro coins or bills. Many stores, however, priced products both in euros and in local currency so that people would get used to "thinking" in euros.

The physical currency was introduced in January 2002. In the years before its appearance, there was extensive debate on what or who should appear on euro notes (generic representations of "European architecture" prevailed over depictions of actual [meaning "national"] people or places); whether the money should include Greek lettering spelling out "euro" (it does); and whether the Italians could form a plural for euros (*euri*) more in line with Italian (they could not). Despite fears of confusion and money shortages, the transition was incredibly smooth—ATMs dispensed euros, clerks were able to calculate prices and make change, and banks had enough money on hand. After a two-month transition period in which both older currencies and the euro qualified as legal tender, venerable currencies such as the French franc and Greek drachma had value only for collectors of obsolete money.

The effects and future of the euro

Like it or not, the euro is a reality. One can, however, ask a number of questions: How has the euro fared? Can its adoption be judged a success? What is its future?

In strictly economic terms, the euro has had a rather bumpy ride. Initially, it did fall in value—reaching a nadir of $0.83 in October 2000, losing nearly a third of its value after less than two years of existence. However, as seen in Figure 3.1, it bounced back, reaching a high of $1.60 in April 2008, although it later fell, due in part to the world economic crisis and fears debt defaults in countries such as Greece or Spain would have ramifications throughout the eurozone as well as the relatively poor performance of several European economies. By 2016, the global rise of the dollar across all currencies led the euro to ten-year lows against the dollar, a development no doubt welcomed by American tourists but also by European exporters, who are better able to sell their products to American consumers.

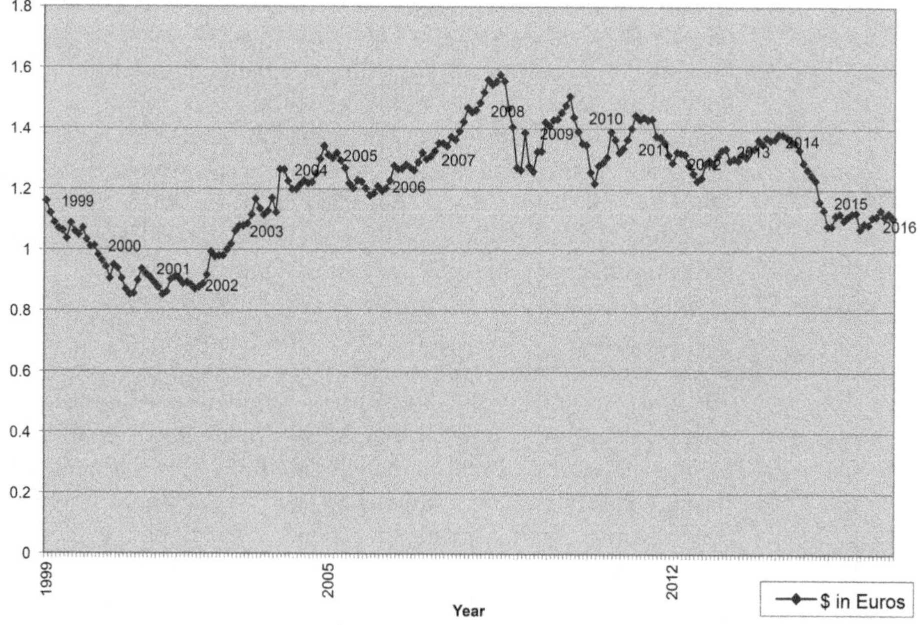

FIGURE 3.1 Dollar/euro exchange rate, 1999–2016

www.x-rates.com

Whether the euro has delivered on all of its promises is a subject of debate. Cross-border trade and investment have increased. The overall inflation in the eurozone has been low—about 2 percent a year.[53] However, France, Italy, and Germany—the largest euro economies—continued to have sluggish growth and high unemployment. Overall, growth in the eurozone from 2002 to 2006 averaged less than 1.4 percent, compared to 2.3 percent in Great Britain and 2.5 percent in Sweden,[54] suggesting there was not an immediate positive "euro effect" on growth, and in 2008 most European economies went into recession. Whether or not economic problems in Europe in the late 2000s and early 2010s were the "fault" of the euro can be debated—all three of the biggest euro economies have chronic problems that predate the euro, and it was problems in the US that triggered the global economic crisis in 2008—but many remain unsold on the promise that the euro will bring jobs and growth. Generating growth, managing debt, and holding together countries with competing economic priorities have been significant challenges in the 2010s, a topic explored in Chapter 10.

Since its introduction, however, the eurozone has expanded, albeit slowly. Micro-states such as Andorra, Monaco, and San Marino were *de facto* forced to adopt the euro after the currencies they had previously used (e.g., Spanish pesetas, French francs, and Italian lira) disappeared. On January 1, 2007, Slovenia, which joined the EU in 2004, became the first post-communist country to adopt the euro. Cyprus and Malta joined the eurozone a year later, followed by Slovakia in 2009, Estonia in 2011, Latvia in 2014, and Lithuania in 2015. Thus nineteen of the twenty-eight states in the EU now use the euro. Montenegro and Kosovo, which declared independence from Serbia in the 2000s, also use the euro as their currency, even though they do not belong to the EU. More EU members are expected to join the euro. Indeed, prior to joining, all new EU members in Eastern Europe pledged to join the eurozone. However, in the wake of the eurozone debt crisis in the late 2000s–early 2010s, enthusiasm for joining the euro in countries such as Poland and Hungary has declined.

Many of the largest debates over the euro within the eurozone concern the terms of the Stability and Growth Pact. Many states, particularly France and Italy, have complained that the 3 percent cap on budget deficits is too constraining. As early as 2001, the European Commission issued a warning to Portugal for its high budget deficit, threatening the imposition of fines. In 2004, chronic poor economic performance pushed Greece, Italy, France, and, ironically, Germany above the limit. The European Commission sought a reprimand and possible fines, but the Council of the European Union, where member states vote, refused to act. Ultimately, the EU agreed to loosen the Stability and Growth Pact, allowing states to exceed the 3 percent limit for a host of reasons, including public investments, pension reforms, and "any other functions, which, in the opinion of the Member State concerned, are relevant." In wake of the global financial crisis from 2008 to 2010, many states that use the euro began to run budget deficits well in excess of the 3 percent cap. The overall budget deficit in the eurozone rose to 5.3 percent of GDP in 2009, with Greece's the highest at well over 10 percent, leading some to wonder if the Stability and Growth Pact is truly dead and what would be the future stability of the euro.[55] These issues will be taken up in more detail in Chapter 10.

Expansion—Where is the border of Europe?

As noted in the previous chapter, one of the slogans of the 1989 revolutions in Central and Eastern Europe was "Return to Europe," and many post-communist political figures soon began clamoring for membership. Finding the case for expansion hard to resist (if still controversial in some circles), the EU-15 (the member states after the trouble-free accession of Sweden, Austria, and Finland in 1995) agreed to take in the newly democratic, albeit poorer, countries to the east. Making preparations for them to join the EU was a major preoccupation in the 1990s on both sides of the continent. By 2007, as seen in Figure 3.2, the EU expanded to include twelve new members.

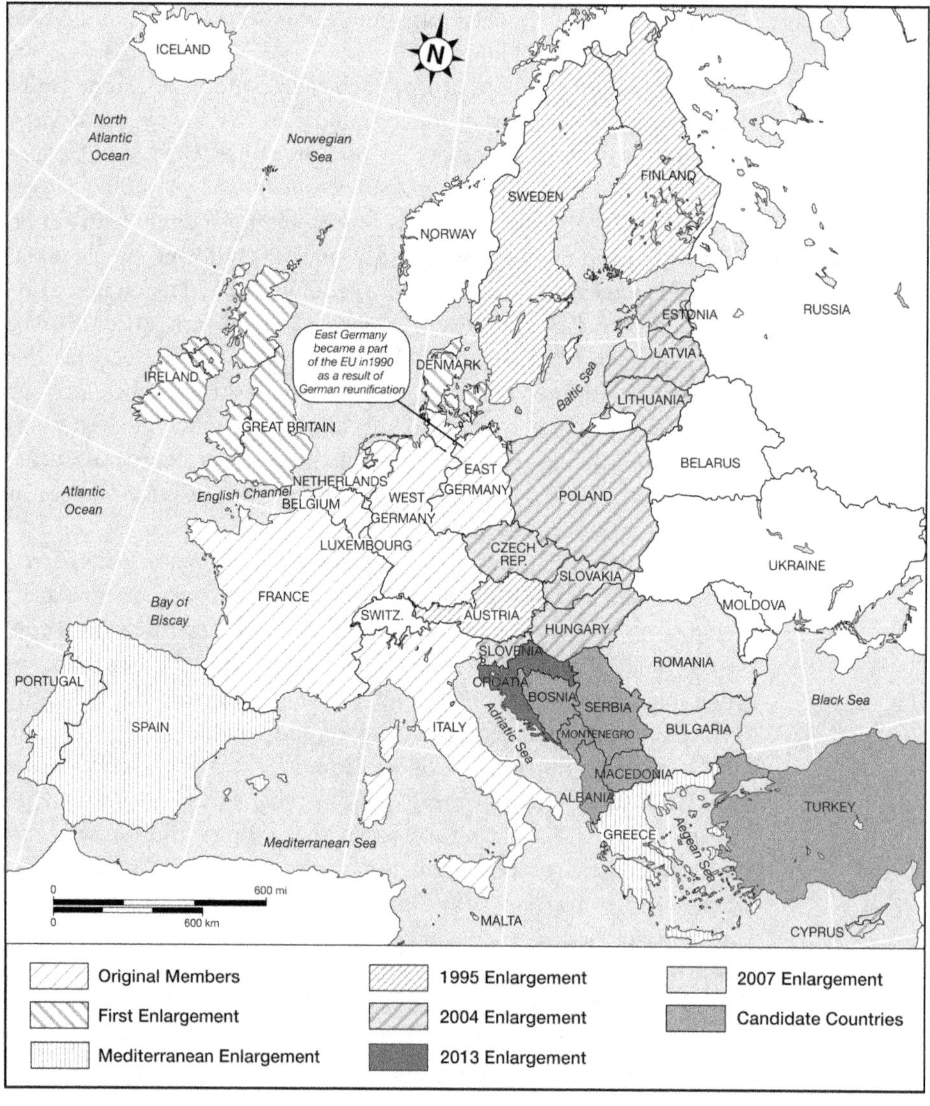

FIGURE 3.2 The expansion of the EU over time

Motivations for expansion

Why Eastern Europeans sought membership in the EU is easy to understand. The EU could be a major source of aid, it would help secure international peace and democracy, its influence would be helpful on more technocratic and legal matters of the post-communist transition, and, perhaps above all else, membership would be a potent symbol that these states were indeed European—for all that implied—and that they had "made it." In simple terms, the EU was a club of successful, secure, democratic, wealthy states. Who would not want to belong to such an organization?

The motivations of the EU are perhaps more difficult to decipher. After all, if you are in "the club," why would you want—to put the matter crassly—the "riff-raff" to join? Indeed, as noted below, there were potent arguments against expansion. Nonetheless, the EU decided, after some hesitation, that post-communist countries could join the organization. Why?

One might cite an economic rationale: the need to find new markets and trade partners. While at first this seems a compelling argument, the EU could have achieved this goal via free-trade agreements or by using various incentives (e.g., aid, access to the EU market) to encourage post-communist states to liberalize their markets to accommodate EU trade and investment. The EU has a host of such arrangements with other countries (e.g., a Customs Union that went into effect with Turkey in 1996, an Association Agreement signed with Ukraine in 2014). These arrangements would be a far simpler and less expensive option for the EU: New members would not complicate EU decision-making and place demands on EU Structural, Regional, and Cohesion funds.

Perhaps the main goal was to spread democracy and peace to a region with a troublesome past—remember that both World Wars started in Eastern Europe, and the wars in the former Yugoslavia in the 1990s alarmed many in Europe. Certainly, this was a stated objective, and it explains in part why Germany (bordering post-communist Europe) was more enthusiastic about expansion than, for example, France. According to former German Chancellor Helmut Kohl, "the policy of European integration [including expansion] is in reality a question of war and peace in the twenty-first century."[56] However, by the time the EU actually expanded, all of the new member states were stable democracies, and, arguably, the EU could have employed other mechanisms besides expansion to encourage peace and security. Moreover, NATO expanded in 1999 to Poland, the Czech Republic, and Hungary, and to the other post-communist EU members in 2004. These moves were probably sufficient to provide security to those countries.

Several analysts have suggested that purely materialistic or practical concerns are not sufficient to explain the EU decision to expand.[57] Instead, moral claims played a large role. Central and Eastern European states were European. Article 237 of the Treaty of Rome states that any European state can join (a clause that was applied in 1963 to affirm that Turkey is eligible for membership). These states wanted to "Return to Europe." They had suffered under communist repression. They were now building democracies and market economies. They looked to Europe for inspiration. In terms of material costs and benefits, the case for expansion was arguably somewhat thin. In terms of morality—and to some extent guilt—there was little that the EU could do but agree to expand.

Copenhagen Criteria
agreed upon in 1993, these specify that a country wishing to join the EU must be democratic, have a predominantly free-market system, and adopt all pre-existing EU laws and directives into their national legislation.

acquis communautaire
the existing body of EU laws, regulations, directives, and policies, which must be adopted by aspiring member states; by 2010, it numbered some 90,000 pages.

The roadmap to expansion was first laid out with promulgation of the **Copenhagen Criteria** of 1993, which stated that those who wished to join must be stable democracies (with establishment of rule of law and protection for minorities), have a predominantly free-market economic system, and agree to incorporate all aspects of the (then) 90,000 odd pages of EU law, directives, and policies, often referred to as the ***acquis communautaire***, or simply the *acquis*, into their national legislation. In the meantime, the EU would provide aid to help with economic restructuring, democratic development, and technical assistance. In 1998 the EU finally agreed to open accession talks with (at that time) six aspiring members. As more states (e.g., Slovakia, Romania) met the basic political and economic requirements of Copenhagen, the EU opened talks with them as well. By the end of the 1990s, a "big bang" expansion to a dozen states—including the small island nations of Malta and Cyprus—seemed imminent. Still, the process took some time and often was highly technical. As seen in Table 3.2, the EU and aspiring members had to conclude negotiations on thirty-five chapters of the *acquis*. For each, the EU had to be satisfied that the new member's laws were in accordance with EU policies and practices. This table also gives one a good idea of the reach of the EU in various policy realms.

The costs of expansion

This is not to say that all were pleased with the EU's plans or that the EU could easily absorb all the prospective members. The post-communist expansion would be far more difficult than the addition of Austria, Finland, and Sweden in 1995. This time, the EU was looking to add many more states and more than 100 million people. In terms of languages, cultures, and historical experience, the EU would become much more diverse. The sheer size of the new EU would complicate EU decision-making. Because each prospective new member (Poland and, to some degree, Romania excepted) was relatively small, there was no overcoming the fact that their accession would tilt the balance of power in the EU toward smaller states and away from the traditional powers of France, Germany, and Great Britain.

Most significantly, however, was the fact that post-communist states, unlike the entrants in 1995, were far poorer than the EU average, as seen in Table 3.3. Put in aggregate terms, what this meant was that the planned EU expansion to ten post-communist states—forgetting for a moment about tiny Malta and Cyprus—would increase the EU population by 28 percent, but its economic output by only about 5 percent. They would, without question, require massive amounts of EU assistance—tens of billions of euros—to meet EU standards in a number of areas (e.g., environmental protection, social policy). They would henceforth qualify for the bulk of EU Regional Funds, much to the consternation of Greece, Portugal, Spain, and Italy, which had previously been the primary beneficiaries of EU largesse. Thus, prior to their admission, there was a reworking of the EU budget to help wean older members off the EU dole gradually. Many of these states are very agricultural, with rates of agricultural employment—particularly in Romania (44 percent), Bulgaria (26 percent), and Poland (25 percent)—well above the EU average of

TABLE 3.2 Chapters of the *acquis communautaire* (EU law and policies)

Chapter 1: Free movement of goods
Chapter 2: Freedom of movement for workers
Chapter 3: Right of establishment and freedom to provide services
Chapter 4: Free movement of capital
Chapter 5: Public procurement
Chapter 6: Company law
Chapter 7: Intellectual property law
Chapter 8: Competition policy
Chapter 9: Financial services
Chapter 10: Information society and media
Chapter 11: Agriculture and rural development
Chapter 12: Food safety, veterinary, and phytosanitary policy
Chapter 13: Fisheries
Chapter 14: Transport policy
Chapter 15: Energy
Chapter 16: Taxation
Chapter 17: Economic and monetary policy
Chapter 18: Statistics
Chapter 19: Social policy and employment
Chapter 20: Enterprise and industrial policy
Chapter 21: Trans-European networks
Chapter 22: Regional policy and coordination of structural instruments
Chapter 23: Judiciary and fundamental rights
Chapter 24: Justice, freedom, and security
Chapter 25: Science and research
Chapter 26: Education and culture
Chapter 27: Environment
Chapter 28: Consumer and health protection
Chapter 29: Customs union
Chapter 30: External relations
Chapter 31: Foreign, security, and defense policy
Chapter 32: Financial control
Chapter 33: Financial and budgetary provisions
Chapter 34: Institutions
Chapter 35: Other issues

Note: Negotiations on all chapters must be successfully concluded prior to a state gaining admission to the EU.

about 5 percent.[58] Overall, the proposed expansions would double the number of farmers in the EU and put the CAP, already accused by its critics of eating up too much of the EU budget, under great strain. Lastly, the prospect of millions of relatively poor people having the right to move and work anywhere in Europe (this being one of the basic freedoms of the EU, freedom of labor) led to fears among many of the EU-15 states of a wave of economic migrants from the east. Germany and Austria, as “front-line states” were particularly worried. Imagine, many would tell me, if the United States opened its border to any Mexican who wanted a job!

TABLE 3.3 Economic comparisons: East vs. West

Country	*GDP/Capita*	*GDP Growth, 2005*
Slovenia	$17,700	3.7%
Czech Republic	$11,960	4.1%
Hungary	$11,210	4.0%
Estonia	$ 9,310	6.0%
Slovakia	$ 8,940	5.1%
Poland	$ 7,300	4.5%
Lithuania	$ 7,110	6.5%
Latvia	$ 5,800	5.5%
EU-15	$34,520	2.7%

Source: "Countries: The World in Figures," *The World in 2005*, The Economist Intelligence Unit

To limit some of these costs, the EU placed certain conditions on the applicants from Central and Eastern Europe. First, older EU members were given the right to restrict labor mobility from the new member states for up to seven years. Great Britain, Ireland, and Sweden chose to let their labor markets remain open to those who joined in 2004 (but not, interestingly, for Bulgaria and Romania, which joined later). As a consequence, hundreds of thousands of people from Central and Eastern Europe moved to these states—half of the 600,000 migrants to Great Britain from 2004 to 2006 were Poles.[59] While this phenomenon is changing the complexion of British, Irish, and (to a lesser extent) Swedish societies—which now have dozens of Polish groceries, bars, churches, and civic associations in addition to Polish waiters, hotel maids, and construction workers—their economies have continued to grow, and unemployment has not gone up. Secondly, CAP support to new states was phased in over a ten year period, giving the EU time to make more reforms to CAP. In addition, the EU-15 were allowed to put protectionist measures in place to guard against any risk of unsafe food from the east. Ironically, these actions—which people in applicant countries saw as discriminatory—were occurring at the same time that the EU-15 enjoyed, because of CAP subsidies, a trade surplus against the lower cost farmers in post-communist Europe.[60]

Fulfilling the criteria

As can be inferred from the above discussion, once the nitty-gritty of accession negotiations began, the luster of EU membership began to fade away. People in post-communist countries felt like they would be second-class citizens in the EU and that the EU was simply dictating terms to them. Some complained that adopting EU regulations (e.g., particularly in employment policy) would undermine their comparative advantage of lower labor costs on international markets and ultimately cost them jobs. Others began to talk of the EU as a new empire, which, like the Soviet Union, would cost states their sovereignty. By 2002, the percentage of respondents who thought EU membership would be a good thing fell to under

Supporters wave EU, Bulgarian, and Romanian flags during a welcoming ceremony for the two countries' entry into the EU, as of January 2007

© Thierry Charlier AP/PA Images

50 percent in Estonia (32 percent), Latvia (35 percent), Slovenia and the Czech Republic (43 percent), and Lithuania (45 percent).[61]

Despite some frustration on both sides, accession talks made progress. As discussed in the previous chapter, democracy became consolidated, even in laggards like Romania. As seen in Table 3.3, post-communist economies were growing faster than most within the EU, mitigating fears that these states would be hopeless economic burdens. As the technical chapters of the accession talks (e.g., industrial policy, competition policy, taxation) were gradually concluded, the question about expansion no longer was *if* or *who* but *when*. Ten countries—Estonia, Latvia, Lithuania, Poland, Czech Republic, Slovakia, Hungary, Slovenia, Malta, and Cyprus—were admitted on May 1, 2004. Bulgaria and Romania, which had more "catching up" to do, were let in on January 1, 2007.

In the 2004 expansion, the most problematic case turned out to be Cyprus. The island of Cyprus has been divided since 1974 between the internationally recognized Republic of Cyprus, sometimes known as "Greek" or "Southern" Cyprus, and the Turkish Republic of Northern Cyprus, created as a result of the 1974 invasion of Turkish armed forces and recognized by no state except Turkey. The EU and the United Nations (UN) hoped that the prospect of EU accession would further reunification talks, but a UN reunification plan, accepted by the Turkish side, was rejected in 2004 by voters in "Greek" Cyprus.[62] This outcome was seen as a defeat both to the EU and the UN, and now that they are ensconced in the EU, the Greek Cypriots are in an even stronger bargaining position vis-à-vis Turkish Cypriots in reunification talks.

The expansion to Romania and Bulgaria in 2007 proved difficult mainly because on certain key issues—particularly corruption and judicial reform—it was clear that

Is Europe one?

Comparing new and old members of the European Union

The expansion of the EU to primarily post-communist countries in 2004 and 2007 radically altered its composition. The newest members have very different histories and are much poorer than the EU-15. Their addition has forced changes in the EU budget and in the EU's institutional structure. Beyond these basic and obvious issues, however, how much has expansion changed the EU? Do the new member states have different policy preferences compared to older members? Does the widening of Europe somehow dilute the European project?

In certain respects there is little question that the countries of Central and Eastern Europe *are* different. For example, on foreign policy questions they generally tend to be much more Euro-Atlantic in orientation, meaning they value good relations with the US and often are not—much to the consternation of former French President Jacques Chirac, who suggested that they should know their place—willing to follow the French or German lead. This was clearest with respect to the US-led invasion of Iraq in 2003, which France and Germany opposed and most post-communist governments (if not their publics) supported, but it extends to other questions as well (e.g., planned placement of bases for a US missile-shield in Poland and the Czech Republic).[63] On economic policy, many post-communist states, particularly the Poles, Czechs, and Estonians, have, by many measures, more liberalized economies than states such as France and Italy and, like the British, are not amenable to efforts to construct a more "social Europe." Poland and the Baltic states are eager to expand the EU further to the east (e.g., to Ukraine), whereas France, Austria, and others complain of "expansion fatigue."

Moreover, the inclusion of post-communist countries has brought history back into the European Union.[64] Whereas Western Europeans, thanks to the EU, have overcome much of their tragic past and, for the most part, do not linger on the past (although the British arguably still get some pleasure out of aggravating the French), Eastern Europeans brought a fair amount of historical baggage into the EU. Examples include a difficult relationship with Russia, tensions among Slovakia, Hungary, and Romania on treatment of ethnic Hungarians, and disputes with Germany on the treatment of ethnic Germans after World War II. In 2015, when a wave of refugees, primarily from Syria, swept Europe, many Central and East European states, including Hungary, Slovakia, and Poland, were adamantly opposed to taking even a small number of refugees, citing not only the economic costs but also that they, in contrast to the French, Germans, or Swedes, lacked experience handling immigrants and developing a multi-cultural society. Looking ahead, the possible expansion of the EU to the western Balkans (e.g., Bosnia, Serbia) and Turkey (consider its troubled relationship with Greece and Cyprus) would add more historically based intra-EU tensions.

In terms of public opinion, one can point to some differences. However, for the most part they revealed that publics in new member states tended to be *more* enthusiastic about the European project. For example, Eurobarometer surveys from the fall of 2006[65] show that those in new member states (not counting Bulgaria and Romania, which joined in 2007) were more supportive of further enlargement (72 percent in favor in the new states, 41 percent in the EU-15), a common defense and foreign policy (84 percent to 73 percent) and a European Constitution (60 percent to 50 percent), exhibited more trust toward the European Commission (59 percent to 46 percent) and European Parliament (61 percent to 50 percent), and were more likely to have positive views of the EU (52 percent to 45 percent). Cynics might suggest that

they have not yet had time to become jaded about "Europe" and that they were not the ones who paid for the 2004 and 2007 expansions. Indeed, those in new member states, two years after joining, were considerably more likely (67 percent to 52 percent in older members) to claim that their country benefited from membership in the EU. Over time, Euroskepticism has emerged in a number of these countries. However, in a Eurobarometer survey from the fall of 2015, one still finds that those in post-communist states are more likely than those from the EU-15 to trust the EU (53 percent to 42 percent), to have a positive image of the EU (48 percent to 40 percent), and to believe that the EU is working for them (42 percent to 38 percent).[66]

Lastly, even though there are real differences across European countries on key issues (e.g., foreign policy, EU institutional reform, immigration, economic policies), the East-West divide is only one of the many cleavages in Europe, perhaps not even the most visible or important one, as a "North-South" divide between creditor and debtor states created tensions during the economic crisis of the early 2010s. Reassuringly, surveys reveal that publics on both sides of the continent rank the values of the EU similarly: human rights, democracy, peace, rule of law, and respect for other cultures. On this crucial measure, Europeans stand united.

Critical thinking questions

1. If you were a citizen in France or Germany, would you have favored EU expansion to post-communist states?
2. Has EU expansion strengthened or weakened the EU? Be able to employ specific evidence to support your case.

they did not meet EU standards. Nonetheless, in a move that honestly left some in Brussels scratching their heads, they were admitted anyway because little was thought to be gained by pushing back the accession date and dragging on negotiations indefinitely. In part recognizing what some would call a mistake, the EU, fearing that reforms would stop once they were admitted, has made aid to both conditional on continued progress.[67] In 2013, Croatia, which began accession talks in 2005, joined the EU, a development that was relatively uncontroversial, as Croatia was small, more prosperous than several states admitted in 2004 and 2007, and had made substantial democratic progress since the end of its conflict with Serbia in the 1990s.

There is little doubt that the EU's expansion to the east has created challenges for the union, as real differences exist between older and newer members of the EU, a point developed in this chapter's **Is Europe one?** section. Among other concerns, observers note that throughout post-communist Europe corruption remains a problem, one that is arguably worse now that "joining the European Union has produced temptingly large puddles of money to steal." One head of an anti-corruption agency laments, "Before accession, governments were under close scrutiny. Now the fight against corruption is not a priority."[68] Not only are chronic corruption issues eroding Eastern Europeans' confidence in political institutions, but they also temper EU enthusiasm for additional expansion.

Who's next?

The addition of Croatia in 2013 will likely not be the final expansion of the EU, although many in the EU have stated that they would like to take a break and concentrate on internal reforms and economic problems before absorbing still more members. Some might also add that given the above-mentioned concerns with the 2007 expansion, the EU is being extra careful in assessing states' readiness to join the EU. The EU began accession talks with Turkey in 2005, Macedonia in 2008, Montenegro in 2012, and Serbia in 2014. It also formally declared Albania a candidate country in 2014, and both Bosnia and Kosovo are interested in joining. Macedonia and Montenegro are quite small countries, and their candidacies are widely supported in Europe. Serbia, Albania, and Bosnia have more serious political problems and will likely prove more difficult, and Kosovo is not formally recognized as an independent country by all EU members. Turkey, however, is likely to be far more difficult for a number of reasons, not the least of which is that most Turks are Muslims. Some European governments, including those in France and Germany, as well as a large share of European public opinion, are against Turkish membership. This highly controversial issue is covered in more detail in Chapter 12. Beyond these states, one could also mention both Moldova and Ukraine, which as of 2014 have Association Agreements with the EU and are keen to join. However, the EU has yet to give them the green light by declaring them official candidate countries.

In the long term, one could imagine the EU expanding even further. After all, if one hails the EU as a great success story, why must it remain only European? Why could it not—indeed why *would* it not—want to extend the zone of peace and prosperity? Indeed, if Turkey is accepted, the boundaries of "Europe" could expand—to Georgia and Armenia (both Christian countries) on the eastern border of Turkey, perhaps to Lebanon, even to North Africa (Morocco's application in the 1980s was rejected on geographic grounds, but this could be revisited). *The Economist*, speculating on what the EU would look like on its hundredth anniversary in 2057, suggested that Israel and Palestine joined as its forty-ninth and fiftieth members (!) and that negotiations over Russian entry were in the works.[69]

Inconceivable? Imagine the highest hopes of Europe's architects in the 1950s compared to the reality today: a common market, single currency, twenty-eight members, and cooperation in numerous fields. Yes, there are serious problems, and, looking at the EU in the 2010s as opposed to 2000s, there is, it is true, less cause for optimism. Several crises—notably the refugee crisis—have led some to re-evaluate the role and powers of the EU. This topic will be more fully explored in Chapter 11. "Brexit" poses a different challenge and creates uncertainties both in Britain and in the EU as a whole. However, the EU has weathered crises before, and despite various controversies and setbacks, it does, as the Norwegian Nobel Committee noted, have much to celebrate over its sixty-plus years of existence.

Application questions

1. Give an example of how supranationalism can conflict with national sovereignty. Overall, what do states gain through the EU? Why do they need an organization like the EU to reap the benefits of closer integration?

2. Some envision the EU as a potential alternative to the traditional sovereign state. Would you agree? What does this mean, precisely? What might this say about not only the EU but also about politics in an era of globalization?
3. Given the history of Europe, few would have believed European integration could go as far as it has. How much further might it go? What might slow it down or stop it?
4. How does the EU fit into realist perspectives of international relations? Does its growth and success fundamentally disprove or undermine realism?
5. Some think the EU is like a bicycle, meaning you have to be pedaling and moving forward or you fall off. Others retort that you can stop and park a bicycle from time to time without getting off it. Which makes more sense? In other words, could Europe just "stop" and abandon grandiose reform projects?

Key terms

Additional reading

Europa (http://europa.eu)
Main portal to the EU's website. Excellent source of information and documents on the EU.

Gilbert, Mark. 2003. *Surpassing Realism: The Politics of European Integration since 1945.* Lanham MD: Rowman and Littlefield.
This book suggests how the emergence of the EU challenges the basic assumptions of realism, which has been the dominant theory in international politics. According to the author, other approaches may be more useful for understanding both the EU and global politics more generally.

Moravcsik, Andrew. 1998. *The Choice for Europe: Social Purpose and State Power from Messina to Maastricht*. Ithaca: Cornell University Press.
A classic source for European integration theory. Moravcsik is particularly interested in how realist perspectives about power can be used to explain the EU.

Nelsen, Brett, and Stubb, Alexander. 2003. *The European Union: Readings on the Theory and Practice of European Integration*, 3rd edition. London: Lynne Rienner.
This book contains historical documents related to European integration as well as reviews of the basic theories (e.g., functionalism, neo-functionalism) that have been invoked to explain the development of the EU.

Rosamond, Ben. 2000. *Theories of European Integration*. New York: Palgrave.
One of the shorter and more accessible texts that wades through what can be a very difficult topic to understand fully. This book lays out both the initial theories of integration and how they have been challenged and amended over time.

Notes

1 Text of the press release of October 12, 2012 and speech at the December 10, 2012 award ceremony can be found at www.nobelprize.org/nobel_prizes/peace/laureates/2012/press.html and www.nobelprize.org/nobel_prizes/peace/laureates/2012/presentation-speech.html.
2 Tim Parks, "Why the E.U. Had It Coming," *The New York Times*, July 10, 2016.
3 *The Economist*, October 21, 1999.
4 None of these, it might be worth adding, are mentioned in the body of the 2009 Lisbon Treaty, whereas they were formally enshrined as EU symbols in the ill-fated Constitutional Treaty, which was rejected by French and Dutch voters in 2005. Some thus might dispute calling them official EU symbols, but a statement of sixteen member states included in the final act of the Lisbon Treaty said that for them these will "continue as symbols to express the sense of community of the people in the European Union and their allegiance to it." They remain widely used within the EU.
5 The EU employs over 3,000 translators, and translation costs in 2006 were $1.3 billion. From *The New York Times*, December 6, 2006, p. A10.
6 Realists have tried to explain European integration by focusing on the calculation of costs and benefits to member states. However, one should also recognize that integration has been about values and a new way of viewing international relations. According to one observer—who gives some credence to realist interpretations—the states of the EU have "turned the theory and practice of nation-state behavior on its head." See Mark Gilbert, *Surpassing Realism: The Politics of European Integration Since 1945* (Lanham MD: Rowman and Littlefield, 2003), p. 10.
7 Quoted in John Pinder, *The Building of the European Union* (Oxford: Oxford University Press, 1998), p. 3.
8 Andrew Moravcsik, *The Choice for Europe: Social Purpose and State Power from Messina to Maastricht* (Ithaca: Cornell University Press, 1998).
9 T.R. Reid, *The United States of Europe: The New Superpower and the End of American Supremacy* (New York: Penguin, 2004), and Jeremy Rifkin, The European Dream: How Europe's Vision of the Future is Quietly Eclipsing the American Dream (New York: Penguin, 2004).
10 An excellent and multi-faceted critique of the European project is Noel Malcolm, "The Case Against Europe," *Foreign Affairs* 74, March/April 1995, p. 52–68.
11 For example, a fall 2013 Eurobarometer survey commissioned by the EU itself found that 26 percent of respondents across the EU thought things were going in the right direction in the EU, 31 percent have a positive image of the EU, and 31 percent tend to trust the EU, whereas 58 percent tend to distrust it. Highest levels of distrust

were in Greece (77 percent), Spain (71 percent), Portugal (68 percent), and Great Britain (67 percent). See http://ec.europa.eu/public_opinion/archives/eb/eb80/eb80_anx_en.pdf.

12 Jim Yardley, "The Breaking Point," *New York Times Magazine*, December 20, 2015, p. 38–56.

13 His remains are interred in a cathedral in Aachen, Germany, which each year bestows a Charlemagne Prize for the figure deemed to have done the most to promote European unity. Notably as well, *The Economist*'s European columnist goes by the pen-name "Charlemagne." See Charlemagne, "Long live the Karlings," *The Economist*, September 4, 2010, p. 56.

14 Randolph Churchill, ed. *The Sinews of Peace: Post-War Speeches by Winston S. Churchill* (London: Cassell, 1948), p. 198–202. Notably, however, he noted that Britain would not be the basis for such a scheme, which would have to rest upon France recovering "the moral leadership of Europe."

15 Tony Judt, *Postwar: A History of Europe Since 1945* (New York: Penguin, 2005), p. 158.

16 On the same day, a second Treaty of Rome created the European Atomic Energy Community (Euratom), which was structured like the ECSC.

17 James A. Caporaso, *The European Union: Dilemmas of Regional Integration.* (Boulder: Westview, 2000), p. 4.

18 Quoted in Derek Unwin, *The Community of Europe* (New York: Longman, 1991), p. 76.

19 Quoted in Uwe Kitzinger, *European Common Market and Community* (New York: Barnes and Noble, 1967), p. 37–39.

20 Luuk van Middlelaar, quoted in Ian Buruma, "In the Capital of Europe," *New York Review of Books* 53:6, April 7, 2016, p. 38.

21 The classic reference for neo-functionalism is Ernst Haas, *The Uniting of Europe: Political, Social, and Economic Forces 1950–1957* (Stanford: Stanford University Press, 1958). For a more recent treatment, see Wayne Sandholtz and Alec Stone Sweet, eds. *European Integration and Supranational Governance* (Oxford: Oxford University Press, 1998).

22 Quoted in Anonymous, "What Jean Monnet Wrought," *Foreign Affairs*, April 1977.

23 Moravcsik, *The Choice for Europe.*

24 Ian Buruma, "In the Capital of Europe," *New York Review of Books* 53:6, April 7, 2016, p. 38.

25 Moravcsik, *The Choice for Europe*, p. 181–196.

26 Commission of the European Communities, "Completing the Internal Market," *White Paper from the Commission to the European Council*, 1985, p. 55.

27 Sometimes one hears reference to the "four freedoms," which includes the free movement and exchange of services. This, however, has proven to be more problematic to implement.

28 Margaret Thatcher, *The Downing Street Years* (London: HarperCollins, 1993), p. 555.

29 Gilbert, *Surpassing Realism*, p. 220.

30 Foreign and Security Policy is typically formulated within the Council of the European Union by unanimous voting, with the Commission and European Parliament playing minor roles. Similarly, matters under the Justice and Home Affairs pillar are primarily the responsibility of the Council of the European Union. Proposals in the Constitutional Treaty, devised in 2003–2004, would have changed decision-making in both of these pillars, in particular by making Justice and Home Affairs subject to first pillar institutions. This document, however, was not ratified by all member states.

31 Passports are issued by national governments and include on their covers the name of both the individual country and the EU.

32 "The Europe That Died," *The Economist*, June 4, 2005.

33 Quoted in *The Irish Times*, May 12, 2008.

34 For more on what the Lisbon Treaty does, see information on the EU's website at http://europa.eu/Lisbon-treaty/index-en.htm.

35 Speech before European Parliament on June 27, 2007, quoted in *Brussels Journal*, December 11, 2007.
36 Sebastian Kurpas, "The Treaty of Lisbon: How Much of the Constitution Is Left?," Centre for European Union Policy Studies, December 2007.
37 Quoted in *The Irish Times*, February 8, 2007.
38 Quoted from *The Independent*, October 30, 2007, and *The Irish Times*, May 12, 2008.
39 *Brussels Journal*, December 11, 2007.
40 The Lisbon Treaty was actually approved unanimously by both houses of parliament in Italy!
41 *The Irish Times*, August 23, 2008, and Charlemagne, "Who cares about Europe?," *The Economist*, September 20, 2008.
42 Quoted on www.bloomberg.com, June 14, 2008.
43 The greatest challenges to Lisbon, besides Ireland, were in the German court system (over its effects on German federalism) and Czech President Vaclav Klaus, a strong Euro-skeptic who resisted granting his approval, thus delaying Czech ratification.
44 "Vote early, vote often," *The Economist*, July 26, 2008, and Charlemagne, "Bad times ahead," *The Economist*, October 18, 2008.
45 Quoted in Reid, *The United States of Europe*, p. 63.
46 Thatcher, *The Downing Street Years*, p. 708.
47 Good sources on the euro include Barry Eichengreen, *European Money Unification* (Cambridge: MIT Press, 1997), and Paul de Grauwe, *Economics of Monetary Union* (Oxford: Oxford University Press, 2000).
48 Reid, *The United States of Europe*, p. 67.
49 Quoted in "Holding Together: Special Report on the Euro Area," *The Economist*, June 13, 2009, p. 4.
50 Quoted in Reid, *The United States of Europe*, p. 66.
51 "Holding together," *The Economist*, June 13, 2009, has excellent background on the euro. See also Werner Atweiler, "The Euro: Europe's New Currency," at http://fx.sauder.ubc.ca/euro/euro.html, accessed April 11, 2010.
52 For a piece that discusses precisely this problem with respect to Spain, see Paul Krugman, "The Spanish Prisoner," *The New York Times*, November 28, 2010.
53 "Holding together," *The Economist*, June 13, 2009.
54 European Commission, *Economic Forecasts*, Autumn 2005.
55 "Holding Together," *The Economist*, June 13, 2009, p. 11. For an analysis of these issues prior to the financial meltdown, see William Buiter, "The 'Sense and Nonsense of Maastricht' Revisited: What Have We Learned About Stabilization in EMU," *Journal of Common Market Studies* 44:4, November 2006, p. 689–690.
56 Quoted in Steven Haseler, *Super-State: The New Europe and Its Challenge to America* (London: I.B. Tauris, 2004), p. 80.
57 See José I. Torreblanca, *The Reuniting of Europe: Promises, Negotiations, and Compromises* (Aldershot: Ashgate, 2001), and Helene Sjursen, ed. *Questioning EU Enlargement* (London: Routledge, 2006).
58 BBC News, "Brussels Plans Bulgaria-Romania Aid," February 9, 2004, online from http://news.bbc.co.uk.
59 "Romania and Bulgaria Join EU," *International Herald Tribune*, January 1, 2007.
60 Marian Tupy, "EU Enlargement: Costs, Benefits, and Strategies for Central and East European Countries," Cato Institute, *Policy Analysis* 489, September 18, 2003.
61 EU Candidate Eurobarometer Surveys, cited in Tupy, "EU Enlargement."
62 Elie Kedourie, "The Cyprus Problem and its Solution," *Middle Eastern Studies* 41:4, September 2005: 649–660, and *The Economist*, "A Greek Wrecker," April 17, 2004.
63 A good review of the foreign policy of new EU member states is Janusz Bugajski and Ilona Teleki, *Atlantic Bridges: America's New European Allies* (Lanham MD: Rowman and Littlefield, 2007).
64 Charlemagne, "The Burden of History," *The Economist*, May 19, 2007.
65 Eurobarometer 66, October–November 2006, available at http://ec.europa.eu/public_opinion/archives/eb/eb66/eb66_en.htm.

66 Based on national averages from Eurobarometer 83, Fall 2015, available at http://ec.europa.eu/public_opinion/archives/eb/eb83/eb83_anx_en.pdf.
67 "Romania and Bulgaria Join EU," 2007.
68 "Talking of Virtue, Counting the Spoons," *The Economist*, May 24, 2008.
69 "The European Union at 100: A Special Report on the European Union," *The Economist*, March 17, 2007.

Competing perspectives on Brexit in the British press

Chapter 4

Institutions and policies of the European Union

Whereas many have acknowledged Great Britain's often strained relationship with the EU,[1] few predicted the outcome of the June 23, 2016 referendum in which British voters were offered the option of "Brexit." The EU, after all, constitutes the world's largest market, London prospered as the EU's financial center (even as Britain remained outside the eurozone), and Britain's membership in the EU bolstered its global position. Prime Minister David Cameron, who had agreed in 2013 under pressure from Euroskeptic members of his own Conservative Party to hold this vote, had, in early 2016, used the prospect of Brexit to extract from Brussels numerous concessions, including restrictions on immigration and welfare payments to migrants, more powers for national parliaments, safeguards for the British financial sector, and a pledge that Britain would not be bound to any future political union.[2] He campaigned for "Remain." Some in this camp cast the vote in almost apocalyptic terms. *The Economist*, a conservative British newsweekly that is often critical of many EU policies, nonetheless came out in favor of continued EU membership, arguing that Brexit would entail grievous economic costs, "gouge a deep wound" in the heart of Europe, and "mark a defeat for the liberal order that has underpinned the West's prosperity."[3] Some also speculated that Brexit could unravel both the United Kingdom, as pro-EU Scots might opt for independence, and the EU itself, as opponents of the EU in other countries would be emboldened.

The "Leave" camp rooted its campaign in fears about EU overreach and the loss of British sovereignty and immigration, both from inside and outside the EU.[4] Many also viewed the EU—and globalization more generally—as something that benefitted elites but not ordinary people. Many Britons believed that cosmopolitan London had lost its "Britishness" or "Englishness." Images of the 2015 Syrian refugee crisis were also fresh in many people's minds. The pro-Brexit United Kingdom Independence Party's (UKIP) campaign included posters of dark-skinned refugees with the tagline "breaking point," and Boris Johnson, the former mayor of London and rival of Cameron's in the Conservative Party, compared the EU's designs on refugee policies with those of Hitler.[5]

The campaign was highly divisive, especially within the Conservative Party. A week prior to the vote, a pro-EU Labour member of parliament was murdered, with her killer shouting, "Keep Britain independent" as he attacked her. Campaigning for the referendum was duly suspended, but the last polls prior to the vote pointed to a narrow victory for "Remain."

This was not to be. "Leave" prevailed, 52 percent to 48 percent, with older, less educated, and more rural voters backing "Brexit," including large swathes of northern England that are typically strongholds for the pro-EU Labour Party. "Remain" was favored among young voters, those economically better off, and those in London (the leading magnet for immigrants), Northern Ireland, and, perhaps most significantly, Scotland. Whereas some celebrated the vote as a victory for democracy and the will of the people,[6] the fallout was immense. The British pound fell to a thirty-year low against the dollar, Cameron resigned as prime minister, Labour leader Jeremy Corbyn received a vote of no confidence from party members, and leaders of the Scottish National Party suggested Scots be given—as they had been in 2014—their own referendum for independence. Millions of Britons signed a petition asking for a re-vote. Adding to the confusion, many in the "Leave" camp conceded they had no plan of what to do next. Boris Johnson declared he would not serve as Cameron's replacement, and even Nigel Farage, the head of the UKIP, resigned his post. While Cameron said his government would not immediately invoke Article 50 of the Lisbon Treaty that would formally begin British withdrawal, European leaders indicated they wished the process, which could last two years, to begin as soon as possible. The Conservatives chose Theresa May to replace Cameron, and she announced that she would negotiate the best possible deal for Britain, although what that means and what she will actually be able to procure remains to be seen. Meanwhile, anti-EU figures in several countries, including France and the Netherlands, called for similar referendums. As of this writing, the final outcome of Brexit is unknown. Suffice to say this development stands in stark contrast to the 2012 celebration when the EU won the Nobel Peace Prize, and has prompted many supporters of the EU to re-consider what it is now capable of achieving.

This chapter continues our discussion of the EU, building upon the previous one that covered many of its important historical milestones through the 2000s. As noted in the opening chapter, the EU is the main institutional force behind Europeanization. Since the signing of the Maastricht Treaty in 1991, the EU has taken numerous initiatives both to "widen" (expand to more countries) and "deepen" (integrate in more policy areas). Today, Europeanization in a variety of fields—economics, the environment, justice, social policy, culture, even foreign policy—is often driven by the EU, whose rules, procedures, and norms are "incorporated in the logic of domestic (national and subnational) discourse, political structures and public choices."[7] Put differently, the locus of political decision-making in Europe has become, in many cases, the EU.

The political institutions of the EU—those bodies that make and enforce decisions—are therefore of foremost importance for a student of European politics. This is not to say that domestic political institutions—parliaments, prime ministers, and courts—do not matter. They do, but in many cases these institutions are either enacting EU policy or directives or are constrained from acting in a certain direction because of EU authority in that area. Moreover, as seen in the Brexit vote, different viewpoints on the EU constitute an important issue, one that can elicit passions on both sides. Scholars and observers of the EU debate how much weight one should put on the supranational and the intergovernmental aspects of the EU. The issue, in essence, boils down to where political power in Europe presently lies and which institutions matter the most.

This chapter focuses on EU institutions, leaving detailed examination of national level ones for subsequent ones. This is not meant as a statement that the EU matters more than national governments. Many treatments of European politics, especially those rooted more in comparative politics than in international relations, would reverse the order, including consideration of the EU only as in the last chapter or two. However, as mentioned earlier, the boundaries between comparative and international politics are blurred, not only within the discipline of political science but also in Europe itself. We cover the institutional "nuts and bolts" of the EU first to provide some continuity with the previous chapter, but also because the workings of the EU should not be considered a sort of afterthought. EU actions have continent-wide relevance. Thus, by necessity, discussion of the EU will appear in analysis of how domestic institutions operate in a Europe that is increasingly characterized by Europeanization and multi-level governance.

The EU has a complex governing structure. Like any government, one can point to legislative, executive, and judicial organs. These are identified in Figure 4.1. However, one must remember that the EU is not the government of individual states. Its structures blend together elements of inter-governmentalism, in which states are represented and their interests are given primary consideration, and supranationalism, which empowers EU structures and citizens directly, bypassing national governments. One issue to keep in mind is that while the supranational powers of the EU make it unique among international organizations and provide the basis for multi-level governance in Europe, intergovernmentalism remains a powerful force within the EU. Many of the most acrimonious debates within the EU revolve around the question of whether its supranational or intergovernmental elements should guide policy.

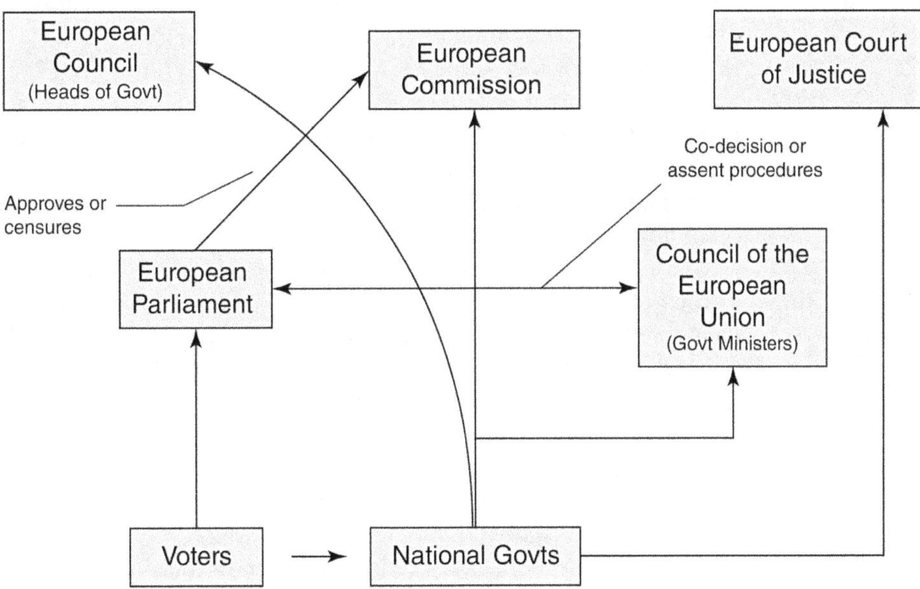

FIGURE 4.1 Institutions of the European Union

Institutions of the European Union

The European Commission

European Commission
executive body of the EU charged with drafting legislation and directives and overseeing implementation of EU policy.

Directorate Generals (DG)
departments within the European Commission akin to executive departments or ministries in a national government.

The **European Commission** is commonly viewed as the supranational executive body of the EU. It is responsible for overseeing the implementation of EU laws, policies, and directives. Furthermore, it is also responsible for developing the ordinary, day-to-day agenda of the EU and initiating legislation. It oversees the bureaucracy of some 25,000 "Eurocrats." It is housed in Berlaymont, a giant, austere building in what is known as the "European Quarter" in Brussels. The commission's work is divided up into thirty-three service institutions and departments called **Directorate Generals (DG)**, roughly similar to what might be a cabinet portfolio or division with a national-level executive branch. Each DG has its own staff and is overseen by an EU commissioner. Each country receives one commissioner, and some of the twenty-eight commissioners oversee more than one DG. The 2009 Lisbon Treaty, as originally formulated, envisioned reducing the number of commissioners to two-thirds the number of member states, but after the Irish voters initially rejected the treaty, this provision was dropped. States will continue to receive one commissioner each. Commissioners are nominated to their position by their national governments.

The European Parliament must approve the entire slate of the twenty-eight nominated commissioners; it cannot vote against an individual nominee. Commissioners serve five-year terms, and they take an oath upon assuming office, pledging to uphold the interests of the EU and be independent in carrying out their duties, thereby accept no national instructions on EU policy. In other words, the European Commissioner from Hungary, for example, is supposed to cease being "Hungarian" upon appointment to the Commission. He or she is supposed to think of the common good of the EU and all its members, not just Hungary. This makes the Commission, at least in theory, a supranational body. In practice, of course, it may be difficult for an individual to divorce herself from the interests of her country. Therefore commission seats are frequently divided up on the basis of the country's interests, although the most visible slots (e.g., foreign relations, industry, trade) are often given to larger countries.

The head of the European Commission, its president, is nominated by the Council of the EU. Presidents of the Commission, unlike the typical commissioner, usually have some political prominence: Jacques Delors (1985–1995) had served as French finance minister; Jacques Santer (1995–1999) had been prime minister of Luxembourg; Romano Prodi (1999–2004) was the former prime minister of Italy (a post to which he returned in 2006); José Manuel Barroso (2004–2014) was a former Portuguese prime minister; Jean-Claude Juncker (2014–present) also served as prime minister of Luxembourg. The president of the Commission, however, is only *primus inter pares* (first among equals). Notably, unlike a prime minister in a parliamentary system, he or she is not responsible for the selection of the other commissioners, as they are nominated by their own national governments. Seven commissioners also serve as vice presidents, including the High Representative for Foreign Affairs and Security Policy created by the Lisbon Treaty. The composition of the European Commission for the 2014–2019 term is presented in Table 4.1.

TABLE 4.1 Commissioners of the European Union, 2014–2019

Portfolio	*Commissioner*	*Country*
President	Jean-Claude Juncker	Luxenbourg
VP, High Representative for Foreign Affairs and Security	Federica Mogherini	Italy
VP, Budget and Human Resources	Kristalina Georgieva	Bulgaria
VP, Energy Union	Maroš Šefčovic	Slovakia
VP, Economic and Monetary Affairs	Valdis Dombrovkis	Latvia
VP, Digital Single Market	Andrus Ansip	Estonia
VP, Jobs, Growth, Investment, and Competitiveness	Jyrki Katainen	Finland
VP, Better Regulation, Inter-institutional Relations, Rule of Law, and Charter of Fundamental Rights	Frans Timmermans	Netherlands
Enterprise and Industry	Elżbieta Bienkowska	Poland
Transportation	Violeta Bulc	Slovenia
Trade	Cecilia Malmström	Sweden
Digital Economy and Society	Günther Oettinger	Germany
Enlargement and European Neighborhood Policy	Johannes Hahn	Austria
Agriculture and Rural Development	Phil Hogatn	Ireland
Financial Services and Capital Markets	Jonathan Hill	Great Britain
Competition	Margrethe Vestager	Denmark
Justice, Consumers, Gender Equality	Véra Jourová	Czech Republic
Climate Action and Energy	Miguel Arias Cañete	Spain
Taxation, Customs Union, Audit	Pierre Moscovici	France
Regional Policy	Corina Cretu	Romania
Health and Food Safety	Vytenis Andriukaitis	Lithuania
Research, Innovation, and Science	Carlos Moedas	Portugal
Education, Culture, Multi-lingualism and Youth	Tibor Navracsics	Hungary
International Cooperation and Development	Neven Mimica	Croatia
Migration, Home Affairs, and Citizenship	Dimitris Avramopoulos	Greece
Environment, Fisheries, and Maritime Affairs	Karmenu Vella	Malta
Humanitarian Aid and Crisis Response	Christos Stylianides	Cyprus
Employment, Social Affairs, and Labor Mobility	Marianne Thyssen	Belgium

The Commission is expected to work in close concert with other EU institutions and national governments. The various DGs have the political, legal, and technical expertise to largely run the day-to-day affairs of the EU. The Commission debates ideas for draft legislation, which often originate in the DGs. Decisions are usually made by consensus, although a majority vote within the Commission can be sufficient to pass proposals onwards to the European Parliament and Council of the EU, which must approve them in order for them to take effect. In this respect, one should emphasize that the Commission is not a legislative body, but it is intimately involved in the legislative process, as it drafts laws, regulations, and directives, issues opinions on proposed amendments, suggests amendments of its own, and, if necessary, can withdraw a proposal prior to a vote by the Council of the European Union or the European Parliament. The Commission also oversees the implementation of EU law, as the EU requires that member states transpose EU directives and policies into their own national legislation, an important mechanism in how Europeanization actually works. This gives the Commission a lot of power over national governments, as it sort of stands over the shoulder of national-level parliamentarians and bureaucrats to ensure that national laws are drawn up and enforced in accordance with the Commission's expectations. If states do not adopt or fail to implement EU laws and directives properly, the Commission then has the power to take offending states, institutions, or individuals to the European Court of Justice. In this respect, national governments surrender their sovereignty to the EU.

However, the Commission is not all-powerful. It must work within parameters defined by EU law and, above all else, is circumscribed by the more intergovernmental Council of the European Union (discussed below). However, the Commission has much *de facto* power to interpret matters as it sees fit, and its own interest is usually in expanding the competencies and supranational aspects of the EU.[8] For this reason, the Commission is a target for those opposed to deeper EU integration, and it is often accused for being too technocratic and opaque in its work. Notably, in the wake of corruption scandals in the 1990s, the power of the European Parliament to oversee the work of the Commission was expanded with visible effect.

The Council of the European Union

Council of the European Union inter-governmental body made up of national-level ministers that reviews and approves Commission proposals; also called the Council of Ministers.

Among all EU institutions, the **Council of the European Union** (formerly referred to as the Council of Ministers and not to be confused with the European Council, discussed later in the chapter) is arguably the most authoritative, as it is the body that is most empowered to decide what the EU should and should not do. Unlike the Commission, it is inter-governmental, and functions like a legislature insofar as it votes to approve the laws, regulations, and directives proposed by the Commission. However, the Council is not a single institution with a set membership, like a conventional state-level legislature. Rather, it is more like a collection of specialist subcommittees, whose composition changes depending upon the issue at hand. In other words, the Council of the EU is not a single council; it is a series of issue-specific councils, and it meets, in one of ten different forms,[9] about ninety times a year.

Each version or formation of the Council is made up of representatives from the governments of each member-state. The actual person occupying the seat, however, changes with the issue. For example, if the Council is discussing economic issues, then ministers of finance would typically represent their governments; if the issue is the environment, it would be environmental ministers; health ministers for health issues, and so on. There is no set term of office for those on the Council; individuals serve as long as they hold onto their national-level cabinet post. As governments change, however, the composition of the Council is altered. Formal meetings of the Council occur in the Justus Lipsius building in Brussels, and under the Lisbon Treaty its meetings must be open to the public when it votes on the Commission's proposals. Leadership of the Council rotates every six months according to a pre-determined order of countries. The selected country, not a particular individual, is then said to assume the presidency of the Council of the EU, which gives it greater visibility and ability to shape the EU's agenda. Some argue that a six-month rotating presidency is not particularly efficient. In practice, three successive Council presidencies, often referred to as a *troika*, cooperate to ensure some policy coordination.

The Council of the EU takes decisions on proposed legislation, which includes both directives that must be transposed into national law and regulations that are automatically binding on member states without any action by national parliaments. Its approval is required for anything to become EU law, although, as noted below, the European Parliament also has a voice in many areas of legislation. How the Council of the European Union makes decisions, though, is rather complicated and has been the subject of numerous disputes and changes. In the early period of European integration, decisions had to be unanimous. Unanimous voting on every proposal, however, could cripple the decision-making capacity of the EU, as even the smallest state de facto possesses a veto over policy. For this reason, the EU adopted a procedure of **qualified-majority voting (QMV)**. QMV prevents any one state from vetoing policy, but unlike simple majority voting (e.g., 50 percent plus one of the members would be needed to pass a proposal), QMV is designed to ensure that a larger majority of states favor an approved proposal. QMV was originally established with the Single European Act of 1986, but voting weights were altered by the Nice Treaty (which went into effect in 2003), and its scope expanded as a result of several EU treaties and agreements. It was again altered by the 2009 Lisbon Treaty, as explained below.

qualified-majority voting (QMV)
procedure used in the Council of the EU based upon weighted votes for each country; supermajority of votes required to pass legislation; phased out under Lisbon Treaty.

Under the QMV system as amended by the Nice Treaty, each country was assigned a number of votes, with larger countries receiving more votes. This was not strictly proportional. For example, Germany, with approximately 80 million people, received twenty-nine votes. However, Austria, with 8 million people (a tenth of Germany's population), received ten votes (over a third of Germany's allotment), and Malta, with less than half a million people (200 times less than Germany's population), received three votes, roughly a tenth of what Germany received. The rules for a proposal to pass were rather complex. First, the proposal must garner 255 of the 345 votes (73.9 percent), which is a sizeable "super-majority" of all votes. Secondly, under pure majoritarian logic, it must have the support of majority of the member states.[10] Finally, to prevent the smaller states from ganging up and imposing their will on the larger ones, the total votes in favor of a proposal must come from countries representing at least 62 percent of the EU's population. This final procedure helps ensure a degree of democracy: Those that represent a minority of the population cannot impose their will on the majority.[11] By comparison, note that in the US Senate a bill could pass with fifty-two votes from senators representing the smallest twenty-six states, whose population is less than 20 percent of the national total. In this respect, these procedures, although admittedly cumbersome, might look more "democratic" by ensuring that the requisite number of votes represents the majority of EU voters.

double majority
voting procedure for the Council of the European Union established by Lisbon Treaty; requires 55 percent of states representing 65 percent of population to pass proposals.

However, over time many began to view this system as unnecessarily complicated. The Lisbon Treaty changed the voting procedure from a QMV system using weighted votes to a **double majority** system. Under this system, a proposal is adopted if 55 percent of the states (sixteen of twenty-eight as of 2016) representing 65 percent of EU citizens approve it. An additional provision is that any blocking minority must compose at least four member states. Until March 2017, a member state could request that the Council use the old QMV system; after this date, double majority became the normal voting method. Thus, Malta and Germany now have equal votes out of the twenty-eight members for the first criterion in the double majority scheme, but Germany's size is represented more accurately in the second criterion. Whether this is "fairer" or not could be debated—the idea that proposals must pass with votes representing a super-majority of EU citizens holds under both schemes—but at minimum the double majority plan is far simpler than QMV.

Lastly, one should recognize that the Council of the European Union does not always use these voting procedures. True, there was a gradual expansion of QMV in earlier treaties, and one could argue that as the EU expanded to more states, use of QMV (or now, double majority) facilitates decision-making. Nonetheless, there are still some areas (taxes, culture, expansion, regional funds, foreign policy) that require unanimity. These issues are often considered more important or more sensitive to concerns about sovereignty, and thus by requiring unanimity, each state retains a veto over EU policy. In this way, the very voting system used by the Council of the EU combines—awkwardly, perhaps—inter-governmentalism with supranationalism, although, as with much in the EU, the push has been, over time, toward more supranationalism that would take away the power of any individual member state.

The European Parliament

European Parliament
the popularly elected legislature of the EU, which shares much decision-making power with the Council of the EU; only EU body elected by voters.

The **European Parliament** (EP) is the other legislative body within the EU and is the only EU institution directly elected by EU citizens. Because member-states are not directly represented in the EP, it functions more as a supranational institution than an inter-governmental one. It is housed both in the Espace Léopold (the largest building in Brussels's European Quarter) Brussels and in Strasbourg, France and (controversially) moves back and forth once a month at great expense.[12] It is elected every five years in European-wide elections by proportional representation. However, there is no single European party-list or pan-European party; national-level parties (e.g., the British Labour Party, the German Christian Democrats, Spanish Socialists) nominate their own candidates. Each member state receives a certain number of MEPs (Members of the European Parliament) based roughly on its population, although smaller states are disproportionately represented, as seen in Table 4.2. MEPs receive the same salary as members of their respective national parliaments, as well as a generous €262 per diem when they are in Brussels or Strasbourg. For the most part, MEPs are second-tier politicians, as those with more ability or possibilities would be more prone to serve in their national parliaments.

Once elected, members of the various national parties form blocs within the EP based upon party affinity. After the 2014 EP elections, eight blocs were formed, representing, in broad terms, the main party "families" in Europe. The largest were the European Peoples' Party (221 seats out of the 751 in the 2014 elections), composed of representatives of various conservative and Christian Democratic parties from the center-right, and the Progressive Alliance of Socialists and Democrats of European Socialists (191 seats), uniting Socialist and Social Democratic parties on the center-left.[13] Other blocs included the Greens, Liberals, and far-left parties. Interestingly, anti-EU parties such as the French National Front (FN), British Independence Party (UKIP), the True Finns, the Italian Lega Nord, and the Danish People's Party (DPP) won seats in the 2014 EP elections and formed two separate blocs, Europe of Freedom and Direct Democracy (forty-five seats) and Europe of Nations and Freedom (thirty-eight seats). Significantly, and worrisome

TABLE 4.2 Representation in the European Parliament

Country	*Population in millions*	*# of MEPs (2014)*	*MEP per million people*
Germany	80.8	96	1.19
France	65.9	74	1.13
Great Britain	64.4	73	1.13
Italy	60.8	73	1.20
Spain	46.5	54	1.16
Poland	38.0	51	1.34
Romania	19.9	32	1.61
Netherlands	16.8	26	1.55
Belgium	11.2	21	1.88
Greece	10.9	21	1.93
Czech Republic	10.5	21	2.00
Portugal	10.4	21	2.02
Hungary	9.9	21	2.12
Sweden	9.6	20	2.08
Austria	8.5	18	2.12
Bulgaria	7.2	17	2.36
Denmark	5.6	13	2.32
Slovakia	5.4	13	2.41
Finland	5.4	13	2.41
Ireland	4.6	11	2.39
Croatia	4.2	11	2.62
Lithuania	2.9	11	3.79
Slovenia	2.1	8	3.81
Latvia	2.0	8	4.00
Estonia	1.3	6	4.62
Cyprus	0.9	6	6.67
Luxembourg	0.5	6	12.0
Malta	0.4	6	15.0
Total	506.9	751	1.48

Source: 2014 population figures from Eurostat

to those favoring a stronger EU, in some cases (the FN, the UKIP, the DPP), anti-globalist, anti-EU parties won the most votes among all parties in a given country, a clear sign of rising Euroskepticism if not outright rejection of the EU.[14]

Within the EP, because no single grouping commands a majority among the numerous blocs, coalitions are necessary to pass proposals. Interestingly, studies have shown that MEPs do vote more along party/partisan lines than on national lines, showing perhaps that supranationalism has taken hold.[15] Like national legislatures, the workload of the EP is assigned to committees in policy-specific areas. EU Commissioners frequently appear before EP committees, and there is much cooperation between the specialized DGs and their EP counterparts. MEPs can speak in any of the twenty-four official languages, which can make its proceedings cumbersome.

The EP shares its legislative power with the Council of the EU. This is not, however, an equal partnership. In the early days of European integration, the EP was appointed and had purely advisory powers. Since 1979, however, when voters first elected it, the EP has steadily gained power vis-à-vis the Council. The SEA introduced a cooperation procedure, which gives the EP the right to review the Council of the EU's common position before a final decision is officially made. At this stage, the EP can reject or amend the Council's common position, and the Commission is also allowed to weigh in on the process. Ultimately, however, under cooperation procedures, Council had the final say, as it could override any action of the EP with a unanimous vote.

co-decision increasingly used mechanism in which EU actions and proposals must be approved both by the EP and the Council of the EU.

The cooperation procedure has largely been superseded by **co-decision,** created by the Maastricht Treaty and expanded in use by the 1997 Amsterdam Treaty and the 2009 Lisbon Treaty. The co-decision procedure is rather complicated, involving multiple readings of proposals in both the EP and the Council, but the gist of it is that for a proposal to pass it must be approved both by the Council (in this case, at present, by double majority) and by an absolute majority vote in the EP. If the two sides cannot reach agreement, a conciliation procedure is employed to hammer out differences. If there is no compromise, the act is not adopted. Thus, under co-decision, the EP has real legislative power, as its agreement is necessary for legislation to pass. There is also an assent procedure, usually used for the ratification of treaties and agreements, including expansion, that are negotiated by the EU. Under assent, the EP's approval is necessary, but it cannot offer amendments. In addition, the EP's approval is necessary for all non-compulsory items in the EU budget. Amie Kreppel argues that the EP is no longer a weak "multinational chamber of Babel" but instead a "transformative" legislature that plays a powerful role in EU decision-making.[16] Significantly, however, there are certain issues (e.g., foreign policy, some justice and home affairs issues) where the EP's powers remain purely consultative or advisory. Thus, while the EP is certainly more empowered than before, it is not yet co-equal to the Council.

The EP has also gained powers over the European Commission, although only the Commission has the formal right to actually propose legislation. In 1999, the EP forced Jacques Santer, then head of the European Commission, to form an investigatory body to examine charges of corruption within the Commission. The committee confirmed most of the allegations, and the EP was prepared to censure (in effect, dismiss) the European Commission. Before the EP could do so, Santer and the rest of the Commission resigned. In 2004, the EP forced two nominated Commissioners to withdraw from consideration. The principle of the EP as a check on the power of the Commission has thus been enshrined, and it now has the power to confirm the slate of nominated candidates to the Commission. In practice, this also means that the President of the Commission must be backed by the largest bloc in the EP, akin to a vote of confidence in a parliamentary system. Jean-Claude Juncker, a Christian Democrat, was nominated for the post of Commission President by the EPP in 2014.

As noted, the EP is the only body directly elected by voters, although elections to the EP have occurred only since 1979. The fact that the other EU bodies are not directly elected has led some to complain of a democratic deficit within the EU. Some even joke that measured against the EU's criteria for membership—a prospective member must be a democracy—the EU could not join itself! Despite such complaints, however, one cannot say that European voters have made the most of their opportunity to influence the EU, as turnout in EP elections is far lower than turnout in national elections. In 1979, for example, 63 percent of those eligible to vote turned out to vote for MEPs. In 2014, the figure was only 42.6 percent, the lowest turnout ever for EP elections, with exceptionally low turnout in some of the newer EU members such as the Czech Republic and Slovakia. Table 4.3 shows the turnout rates in select countries in the past five elections.

The European Court of Justice

European Court of Justice (ECJ) highest judicial institution in the EU, it upholds EU law and has the power to enforce decisions against member-states.

The **European Court of Justice** (ECJ) is the highest judicial organ in the EU and one that is clearly supranational in orientation. Housed in Luxembourg, the ECJ is composed of twenty-eight judges, one appointed by each of the member states for six-year terms by common concord among member states. The ECJ is empowered to hear cases that involve states, corporations, or individuals, and makes rulings on a range of issues, including provisions of the common market, rights of EU citizens, social policy, and interpretation of EU treaties. It issues preliminary opinions on matters sent to it by national courts. It can also sanction EU bodies as well as annul an action of the EU if such action violates EU treaties or fundamental rights of citizens; in this sense, it has the power of judicial review with respect to the EU's own institutions.

Since 1952, it has ruled on over 31,000 cases, including over 1,600 in 2015.[17] Decisions usually require only a majority of the judges, and many cases are heard before a panel of only three or five judges. There is also a subsidiary Court of First Instance to handle initial rulings on less complex cases. The role of the ECJ is crucial for the functioning of the EU. Without a body of law that is subject to definitive interpretation by an EU institution, the EU's decisions and policies would appear to be arbitrary and be subject to numerous disputes. If a state is found in violation of EU law, the ECJ has the power to issue fines. It did so most recently in 2012, when it fined Ireland over €3 million for failures to implement environmental rules.[18] While many ECJ decisions are rather technocratic or low-profile, occasionally

TABLE 4.3 Turnout in European Parliament elections, 1994–2014

Country	*1994*	*1999*	*2004*	*2009*	*2014*	*+/– 1994 (or 2004) –2014*
Great Britain	36.4	24.0	38.3	34.5	35.6	–0.8
Germany	60.0	45.2	43.0	43.3	48.1	–11.0
France	52.7	47.0	42.8	40.5	42.4	–10.3
Spain	59.1	64.4	45.1	46.0	43.8	–15.3
Italy	74.8	70.8	73.1	72.0	57.2	–17.6
Greece	71.2	70.2	63.4	52.6	60.0	–11.2
Netherlands	35.7	29.9	39.3	36.9	37.3	+1.6
Cyprus	n/a	n/a	71.2	58.9	44.0	–27.2
Czech Republic	n/a	n/a	28.3	28.2	18.2	–10.1
Poland	n/a	n/a	20.9	24.5	23.8	+2.9
Slovakia	n/a	n/a	17.0	19.6	13.1	–3.9
Total EU	56.8	49.4	45.7	43.2	42.6	–14.2

Source: Web pages of the European Parliament, www.europarl.europa.eu

it garners headlines, as in 2007, when it upheld a €497 million fine against Microsoft for abuse of its dominant position in the marketplace.

While the procedures of appointment are reminiscent of inter-governmentalism, judges on the ECJ, like European commissioners, are expected to abandon their national loyalties in order to interpret and apply EU law. Since the 1960s, the ECJ has become an important supranational institution. The primary elements of EU supranationalism—that EU provisions directly apply to individuals and that EU law supersedes national law—has been a guiding principle of the ECJ.[19] Writing in 1978 in *Simmenthal v. Commission*, the ECJ ruled that "every national court must . . . apply Community law in its entirety . . . and must accordingly set aside any provisions of national law which may conflict with it." Thus, the ECJ enjoys the power of judicial review at a supranational level and can void national laws if they are in conflict with EU law.

Overall, the ECJ has been an important player in propelling European integration forward. Its ruling in the *Cassis de Dijon* case of 1979—involving the importation into West Germany of a French liqueur—established the principle of mutual recognition of product standards, considered to be essential for the functioning of a common market. Analysts have suggested that the growing power and relevance of the ECJ shows functionalism in practice. In other words, the ECJ has helped expand EU powers by supporting the European Commission with expansive readings of EU treaties and by being sympathetic to interests and actors that have sought to acquire EU protections and privileges that are denied to them by member states.[20] The ECJ has thus been, to its critics, a site of "judicial activism," and worries about the powers of the un-elected ECJ and its bias toward promoting supranationalism led to special provisions being inserted into the Maastricht Treaty that would prohibit the ECJ from ruling in policy areas such as Justice and Home Affairs. National courts, especially in Germany, have also challenged the ECJ by asserting their rights to determine whether or not EU treaties accord with the national constitutions. Battles over the powers of the ECJ are a primary example of ongoing tensions between competing visions of the EU.

The European Council

European Council

EU body comprised of leaders of member states that sets broad goals for the EU; headed by president of the European Council.

The **European Council** (again, not to be confused with the Council of the EU) is where heads of government or state participate directly in the EU. It is therefore the quintessential inter-governmental body. It is a newer institution, created in 1974 as a forum for discussions among European leaders. It was formally incorporated into the EC in the 1986 SEA, and the Maastricht Treaty specifies that the European Council "shall provide the Union with the necessary impetus for development and shall define the general political guidelines thereof."

It meets at least twice a year and sets the general agenda for the EU as well as discussing the most important and controversial issues of the day. The more particular and technocratic, day-to-day issues concerning the EU are generally left to the expertise of the Commission. The European Council strives to reach decisions by consensus. Indeed, one of its main functions has been to smooth over major disagreements before divisive issues come to a vote before the Council of the European Union. Prior to adoption of the Lisbon Treaty, the presidency of the

European Council rotated every six months (in accordance with the previously mentioned presidency of the Council of the EU), and the incumbent's country was therefore said to have the presidency of the EU. This has now changed. Under the terms of the Lisbon Treaty, the European Council appoints an individual to serve as president of the European Council for a once-renewable two-and-a-half-year term. In 2014, Polish Prime Minister Donald Tusk succeeded Belgium's Herman van Rompuy in this position.

Since the 2000s, European Council meetings have become increasingly important to set goals and new initiatives for the EU, and some would argue that the energy for policy generation increasingly comes from the more high-profile European Council (whose meetings are well publicized and occasionally dramatic[21]) as opposed to the more technocratic European Commission. The creation of the post of president of the European Council was designed to elevate the importance of the European Council even further, although in the 2010s, particularly in response to the global economic crisis and the refugee crisis in Europe, it has become increasingly clear that it is Angela Merkel, Chancellor of Germany and therefore the leader of the EU's largest country, not the President of the European Council, who is the *de facto* "leader" of Europe.

Other bodies

The EU is far more than the institutions discussed above. It includes a host of more specialized agencies, think tanks, and service providers. Examples include the European Environmental Agency, the Office for Harmonization in the Internal Market, and the European Training Foundation. Agencies such as these are headquartered throughout Europe in an effort to spread out the EU bureaucracy, and most of these are unknown to European publics.

European Central Bank (ECB) ostensibly politically independent body of the EU responsible for management of the euro.

The most important specialized institution within the EU is the **European Central Bank (ECB)**, located in Frankfurt, Germany. This institution functions as the central bank for those states using the euro as their currency. Like the US Federal Reserve, it is politically independent, with a mandate to "maintain price stability" and "promote the smooth operation of payment systems," and it is expressly prohibited in Article 108 of the Maastricht Treaty from taking instructions from EU institutions or national governments. It was formally created in 1998, just before the euro was born, but evolved out of the European Monetary Institute, which was founded in 1994. The ECB's financial holdings are determined by subscriptions from member states, with largest economies (Germany, France, Great Britain, and Italy) making the largest contributions. The ECB is managed by a Governing Council and an Executive Board. As noted, the ECB is supposed to be entirely independent and professional in its operations. However, management of the euro, particularly its Stability and Growth Pact, which places a limit on states' budget deficits, has been a political issue, particularly in France and Italy. This will be discussed in more detail in Chapter 10.

Other bodies deserve brief mention. The Court of Auditors was established in 1977 to monitor the EU's financial affairs. It publishes an Annual Report, and, given widespread belief in the wastefulness and inefficiency of the EU, it has assumed a prominent role as a sort of watchdog. The European Economic and Social

Committee (EESC) was established by the Treaty of Rome and consists of 344 representatives of trade unions, employers, professional, and civic organizations appointed to four-year terms by national governments. The purpose of this body is to consult with other EU institutions and to provide a forum for "participative democracy" and "Europe with a human face."[22] The Committee of the Regions (COR), created by the Maastricht Treaty, consists of 344 representatives of regional and local governments, such as the *Länder* of Germany or the *voivodeships* (provinces) of Poland. It is purely a consultative body, providing a means for local officials to have their voice heard at the EU. It is also a nod to the principle of **subsidiarity**, explicitly mentioned in the Maastricht Treaty and meaning that decisions in the EU should be taken at the closest practical level of governance to the citizen. In other words, if it is strictly a local issue, it is not the business of the EU as a whole, and the COR provides a means for regions and municipalities not only to lobby the EU for particular items but also to tell it when not to rule in certain fields. Both the COR and the EESC are designed to put more democratic input into EU decision-making, although the fact that these two bodies have no binding authority is held up by some as proof of the overly technocratic, anti-democratic orientation of the EU.

subsidiarity

principle that decisions within the EU should be taken at the closest practical level to the citizen; often used to defend national or regional powers and argue against EU action in a given area.

How democratic is the European Union?

One of the longstanding criticisms of the EU is that it does not function democratically. In other words, it has a "**democratic deficit.**" As noted above, the only EU institution elected by voters is the EP, but even in this case, interest in EP elections is low, as evidenced by voter turnout. A common complaint—one voiced by the "Leave" side in the Brexit referendum—is that the EU is too distant and too complex for voters to understand, meaning that it does not "connect" with the citizens it purports to serve.

democratic deficit

idea that the EU suffers from a lack of democracy and connections to its citizens.

The democratic deficit of the EU actually has several dimensions.[23] First, the EU as a whole is rather isolated and not very well accountable to national parliaments, which are the primary bodies that represent voters. According to one set of observers, "governments can effectively ignore their parliaments when making decisions in Brussels."[24] Unfortunately, when up to 80 percent of the laws passed at the national level originate from the EU, one begins to wonder what purpose national parliaments even serve.[25] Second, as noted, the EP has historically been rather weak, not a co-equal legislature to the inter-governmental Council of the European Union, particularly with respect to the budget. It also lacks the ability to propose legislation (which is bestowed exclusively to the European Commission). Third, there are no real European-wide elections. EP elections are contested by national political parties, usually revolve around national-level political issues, and often draw people to the polls only so they can register a protest vote against their governments.[26] A prime example of this was in 2014, when the anti-EU UKIP and the French National Front placed first in EP elections; both votes were seen, in part, as a protest against the EU and the governing parties in Great Britain and France. Fourth, the EU, institutionally, cognitively, and psychologically, is too distant from voters, who often do not understand it or identify with it. A prime example of this occurred in 2009, when Herman van Rompuy, a former Belgian Prime Minister, was appointed to be the first to serve in the newly created position of President of the European Council. While this position was ostensibly designed to represent all EU citizens, a common response was "Herman van Who?", as most people had no idea who he was. As he was appointed and not elected, his democratic legitimacy was also subject to question.

Not all observers agree that there is a sizeable democratic deficit. Andrew Moravcsik, a well-regarded scholar who, as noted in the previous chapter, has a very inter-governmental perspective on how the EU works, notes that national governments, accountable to voters, still largely call the shots within the EU and that the EP has acquired substantial power over time. Moreover, the EU is quite transparent for a political institution (consider how easy it is to acquire all sorts of information from the EU's website, http://europa.eu/index_en.htm) and includes, as noted above, mechanisms for input from local and regional governments and civic organizations.[27] Others would argue that the EU should not be so concerned about democracy. Instead, it is and should remain a technocratic, regulatory state that, rather than doing what is popular, should focus on adopting policies to foster more effective and efficient international cooperation.[28]

Many discussions and actions in the 1990s and 2000s reflected concerns about the perceived democratic deficit. The Amsterdam Treaty established the procedure of co-decision that gave, in some areas, the EP equal powers with the Council of the European Union. It also made the European Commission accountable to the EP. However, it did not make the EP fully co-equal and did nothing to create a system of European-wide elections (e.g., popular election for the president of the Commission). There is no EU government for the EP (or voters) to hold accountable, and the EU still lacks a means for voters to choose between rival policy agendas among pan-European parties.[29] Yes, voters are linked to the EU through their national governments, but this tie to the EU seems tenuous to many in Europe. In 2009 and 2014, the EP made extraordinary efforts to increase voter turnout (e.g., media messages to encourage voting, use of Twitter and YouTube to communicate with younger voters). Voter turnout, however, continued to decline, demonstrating that the EP has yet to connect with its ostensible constituents.[30] Further ideas to strengthen the EU and its connections with citizens include more funding for the Euronews television station and creation of Europe-wide electoral districts to get away from the tendency that EP elections are, in effect, a collection of various national campaigns.

Interestingly, when voters are given a say, they frequently opt against decisions made at the EU level. Consider Denmark's initial rejection of the Maastricht Treaty as well as the Irish rejection of the Nice Treaty in 2001, the French and Dutch voters' "no" votes on the Constitutional Treaty in 2005, and the Irish rejection of the Lisbon Treaty in 2008, which was "undone" when they voted for it on a second attempt in 2009. As noted, in both 2009 and 2014 EP elections, anti-EU parties did well. The British referendum in 2016, discussed at the beginning of this chapter, is perhaps the most consequential of these anti-EU votes, constituting the first time that an entire country elected to leave the union.[31]

Public opinion surveys reveal problems of democratic legitimacy within the EU, although they are, overall, not as pronounced as portrayed by ardent Euroskeptics. Data from Eurobarometer surveys overseen by the European Commission are presented in Table 4.4. One finds that overall satisfaction with democracy in the EU is rather mixed, with figures lowest in 2015 in states such as Greece, Spain, and Italy that were most affected by the economic crisis and highest in newer member states in post-communist Europe. Compared to results from 2005, satisfaction with democracy in the EU did go down, but much of this was given by results from the countries with more severe economic problems. Interestingly, as also seen in Table 4.4, satisfaction with democracy in one's own country is also low in many countries, at times even lower than satisfaction with democracy in the EU. Different questions, however, reveal problems in terms of knowledge about the EU and about one's own empowerment or efficacy. For example, in 2015, across all twenty-eight member states, 42 percent of respondents stated that they did not understand how the EU worked, and the same figure believed that their voice counted in the EU, compared to 38 percent who believed that in 2005, and the 57 percent who believed in 2015 that their voice counted in their own country. Seventy-eight percent also believed the EU needed a "clearer message." And, while only 19 percent associated the EU with democracy, more people associated it with positive elements (49 percent for freedom to travel and work, 27 percent for peace, 26 percent for cultural diversity) than negative ones (23 percent for bureaucracy, 22 percent for waste of money, 11 percent for loss of cultural identity).[32]

What can be done about the democratic deficit or the perception of distance between the EU and its citizens? Some ideas, such as an elected president for Europe, might immediately come to mind, but, upon reflection, would be problematic (e.g., would this person really represent common EU or more narrow national or partisan interests; would he/she garner majority support)? Further empowering the EP could also be complicated, although the EP's powers have expanded over time while

TABLE 4.4 Satisfaction with democracy in the EU, 2005–2015

Country	*Satisfied with democracy in EU, 2015*	*Satisfaction +/- 2005–2015*	*Dissatisfied with democracy in EU, 2015*	*Dissatisfaction +/- 2005–2015*	*Satisfied with democracy in own country, 2015*	*Dissatisfied with democracy in own country, 2015*
Germany	48	+2	44	+1	71	28
France	42	0	43	+2	52	45
UK	40	−1	38	+3	63	33
Sweden	51	+8	41	−3	82	18
Netherlands	50	+9	44	−5	78	21
Greece	28	−21	66	+27	32	68
Spain	38	−22	48	+24	35	63
Italy	40	−11	48	+17	33	66
Poland	61	+9	22	0	55	39
Czech Rep	55	−3	34	−3	52	46
Hungary	52	−1	40	+10	38	61
Entire EU	46	−3	41	+6	52	45

Source: Eurobarometer 63 (2005) and 83 (2015), available at http://ec.europa.eu/public_opinion/archives/eb_arch_en.htm

participation levels in EP elections remains low. One could turn to elected national parliaments to counter the power of EU institutions, perhaps giving them some sort of "veto" over EU policy. This was part of the "deal" Prime Minister Cameron struck with the EU in 2016, but how realistic and effective this would be (or, conversely, whether it might stymie EU policy development and implementation) is unclear. Another institutional remedy for the EU's democratic deficit has been proposed by the French economist Thomas Piketty, who argues that too much of EU policy, particularly with respect to the euro, is guided by technocratic principles that are automatically imposed upon citizens. He supports creation of a separate "eurozone parliament" that would provide a more democratic means to govern the euro and manage issues such as bailouts and the debt crisis.[33] The practical effect of this proposal would empower France, Spain, and Italy while diluting Germany's voice in economic management, and it is highly debatable if Germany would agree to such a radical change. Most radically, one could suggest European-wide referenda to give publics a direct say over important EU questions, but it is doubtful that EU federalists (fearing popular rejection of integration) and member-states (fearing loss of control if voters, theirs or others, have more say) would brave this step.

Perhaps even more ambitiously, one could suggest that a change in the broader European political culture would boost the EU's democratic legitimacy. This position is most widely associated with the German political theorist Jürgen Habermas, who argues that the EU's fundamental problem is that it has built institutions through elite-designed "executive federalism" without building a "demos" (people who identify with it).[34] He thus argues for more efforts to link European publics together to build a community based on shared historical and cultural values that will in turn generate what he calls "constitutional patriotism." Empowering the EP, creating pan-European parties, and drafting a European constitution are all parts of this project, but it also includes a role for the intelligentsia and media that focus on continent-wide concerns and seek to transcend local allegiances and nationalism. He is, in a sense, echoing some of the more idealistic visions of European integration that emerged in the immediate aftermath of World War II but were abandoned for the more functionalist approach. Whether the political actors and the broader public in the EU is ready to take these steps is—to say the least—highly debatable. The question of construction of a common European identity will be taken up in more detail in Chapter 9.

What does the European Union do? Public policies of the EU

The EU plays an important role in many political, economic, and social issues in Europe and, over time, has acquired competencies in new areas. What it ultimately hopes to achieve or what it will ultimately become remains open questions, as explained in the **Is Europe one?** feature. Casting aside concerns about the future, however, today one might reasonably ask what current EU policies typically entail. The simplest answer is "a lot," although EU policy itself often tends to be extraordinarily technocratic and complex. As noted in Chapter 3, there are over

Is Europe one?

What is the final goal of the European Union?

Will Winston Churchill's stated aspiration in 1946 of a "United States of Europe" ever be realized? What will the EU become? Or, more precisely, what does it *intend* to become?

Natural as these questions are, they are very difficult to answer. Part of the reason is simply that they are speculative, and no one can know the future. However, a larger problem is that the final goal of the EU has never been spelled out. True, the Schuman Plan of 1950 envisioned itself as "the first concrete foundation for a European Federation," but, rhetoric of federalists such as Robert Schuman and Jean Monnet to the contrary, the subsequent treaty creating the European Coal and Steel Community only mentioned a "broader and deeper community among peoples." The Treaty of Rome and the Maastricht Treaty state an "ever closer union of peoples" as an objective, but such language purposefully avoids defining how "close" this union would ultimately be. The proposed Constitutional Treaty of the European Union, notably, was even vaguer, making reference to a "common destiny" or the goal of building a "common future." Nonetheless, it clearly was a step toward political union, and some compared its crafting to the constitutional convention in Philadelphia that ultimately formed the US.[36] However, its rejection in 2005 by French and Dutch voters left the whole idea of a European constitution up in the air.

Where, then, does Europe go? Neo-functionalist theories, of course, would argue that integration builds upon integration, and, one imagines, successive spillovers stop only once full political union has been achieved. Less charitably, one could invoke Robert Michels's "iron law of oligarchy" to argue that political institutions always seek to expand the scope of their influence, become more complex, and, for Michels, less democratic.[37] In other words, political actors and bureaucracies are never satisfied; they seek new missions for themselves, regardless of whether there is any objective need for them to do so. Euroskeptics would argue that the expansion of EU authority through the Single European Act, the Maastricht Treaty, and other more recent treaties exemplify this tendency, and that the creeping authority of the EU has gone beyond reason. After the adoption of the Nice Treaty, the decision to expand in 2004, and promulgation of a draft Constitutional Treaty, Europhiles appeared to be ascendant. The apparently unstoppable EU, however, ran into a more powerful force: its own citizens, as Dutch and French voters in 2005 and Irish voters in 2008 put a brake on treaties that would reform and presumably strengthen EU institutions.

By the 2010s, the EU was at a crossroads. While the Lisbon Treaty, after great controversy in several states—including Poland, Germany, the Czech Republic, Great Britain, and, obviously, Ireland—was finally ratified by all member states, it remains unclear what its impact will be. Despite fears by its critics, it does not create a European superstate. The EU remains a hybrid organization, containing elements of both inter-governmentalism and supranationalism. There has been a long debate over the wisdom of many EU policies, in particular, the CAP, as noted in the **In focus** feature, meaning that in some respects the EU could be scaled back and that neo-functionalism does not operate in a single, linear direction. Meanwhile, the numerous bailouts to solve the European debt crisis and the refugee crisis of 2015–2016 led some to believe that some of the accomplishments of the EU might be undone, in particular the euro and the Schengen Agreement that eliminated most borders within the EU. In this regard, the "Brexit" vote could be a harbinger, as parties hostile to the EU are gaining support in many EU states, including France, the Netherlands, Italy, Sweden, Denmark, Poland, Slovakia, Greece, and Hungary.

Risking a prognostication, it seems clear that there are political limits to European integration. Europeans are apprehensive about a host of issues—immigration, terrorism, threats from global economic forces, chronic unemployment. These issues are taken up in subsequent chapters. While some of these issues, in an objective sense, may lend themselves to more integration, there is little doubt that, in terms of the preferences of both many voters and political elites, there is more emphasis on national-level solutions and a disdain for the EU. Whereas the thirteen colonies could form the US, Europe, with its linguistic, economic, historical, and religious divisions, will not easily merge into a single state.

In this respect, it is easy to be skeptical of the future of the EU. Europe is not yet "one" and may never be. Nonetheless, there is little doubt that globalization is making the world a smaller place and compels international cooperation. One may look back at the 2010s as a period in which Europe took a breather, giving itself time to overcome its economic concerns and "enlargement fatigue." If the EU will not be a single state, it may be able to create a somewhat decentralized federation—modeled perhaps ironically on Switzerland, which has rejected EU membership, it would make decisions in a broad array of fields independently of member states. In the economic arena, one could say that Europe is already largely there. It could assume powers to cover all pan-European issues.

If this strikes you as too optimistic, imagine attending Churchill's speech in Zurich in 1946. Talk of a "United States of Europe" a year after World War II could easily have been dismissed as utopian. More than sixty years later, look how far Europe as come. In another sixty years, who knows what might be achieved?

Critical thinking questions

1. Looking ahead ten to twenty years, do you think European integration will deepen? In what ways?
2. In what policy area do you think EU integration has been least effective? Do you think the EU will abandon or retreat from efforts to pursue integration in this area?

100,000 pages of EU directives, regulations, and case law (referred to as the *acquis communautaire*), and one can easily get bogged down in the minutiae of EU activity. EU regulations extend into a wide variety of areas. Governments, of course, typically have a wide variety of detailed and sometimes arcane regulations, but critics of the EU suggest that in many areas the EU's rules are overly restrictive, unnecessary, or just plain ridiculous. For example, the EU has rules and regulations on the height of playground swings, the curvature of bananas, the trade of fresh and frozen bovine semen, and ratings of the quality of pig carcasses.[35] The discussion in this chapter is therefore not meant to be exhaustive. It focuses on several of the most contested and important EU policies.

The budget of the EU

A good place to start a discussion of EU policy is to look at its budget, which gives one some idea of its priorities and resources. As one can imagine, the budget is a source of contention, with some states, especially Great Britain, arguing that the EU spends too much money. Debates over the budget have become particularly pronounced in the 2010s, as austerity was being imposed in several member states while EU institutions requested more spending.[38]

Figure 4.2 presents a breakdown of the 2014–2020 EU budget, which reflects the fact that the EU operates on a seven-year budget cycle. Several items are worth noting. First, the overall budget of the EU, given its size and scope, is actually rather modest. The average budget over this cycle is €154.6 billion, a modest increase from the €130 billion spent in 2010.[39] While this sounds like a significant sum, it works out to about 2.5 percent of all public spending in the EU as a whole and only 1 percent of the national income of all EU members. This pales in comparison to the budgets of individual member-states, which often consume over 40 percent of the country's gross domestic product, and is far less than the nearly $3 trillion annual budget of the US. Second, one sees that a large portion of the EU funds are spent on economic development, and, in EU-speak, are put in categories with appealing names like "smart and inclusive growth," "sustainable growth," and "competitiveness."[40] Much of these funds are budgetary transfers through **structural funds** to less-developed countries in the EU as a means to create "cohesion," as well as some initiatives on competitiveness, infrastructure, research, and enterprise

structural funds
monies distributed within the EU from richer members to poorer member states to help the latter develop economically and meet EU standards.

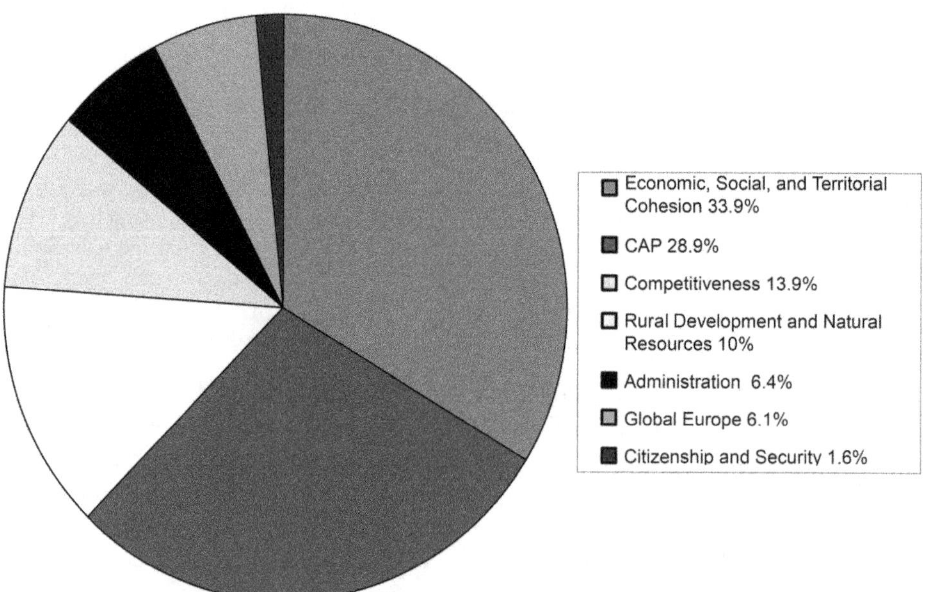

FIGURE 4.2 EU budget projections, 2014–2020

European Commission, *Multiannual financial framework 2014–2020 and EU budget 2014: the figures*, Brussels, 2014. Calculations include breakdown of larger categories reported by Commission

Common Agricultural Policy (CAP) controversial agricultural policy of the EU that helps ensure farmers' income, protects EU agriculture from foreign competition, and eats up a sizeable part of the EU budget.

development. Third, a sizeable portion of EU funds is still spent on the **Common Agricultural Policy (CAP)**, which is discussed in the **In focus** section. The figure for CAP in Figure 4.2 actually represents a sizeable decrease from earlier years, when it consumed 70 percent of the budget in the early 1980s and 45 percent in the 2006 budget. Despite sizeable EU aid efforts in neighboring countries such as Turkey and Ukraine, its foreign assistance/international affairs budget is relatively modest, as are its administrative costs.

Revenue for the EU comes from three main sources. In 2014, this included a portion from tariffs on goods entering EU countries (11.4 percent of the budget), part of the base of each state's value-added tax on consumers (12.3 percent), and,

TABLE 4.5 Contributors and beneficiaries of EU budget, 2014

Country	*Total national contribution, €, millions*	*Total EU expenditures in country, €, millions*	*Net contribution/ benefits per person, in €*	*GDP/Capita, EU 28 = 100*
Contributor				
Netherlands	6,391	2,014	261	131
Sweden	3,828	1,691	223	123
Germany	25,816	11,485	177	124
Austria	2,691	1,573	132	130
Finland	1,777	1,062	132	110
Denmark	2,213	1,512	125	125
France	19,574	13,479	92	107
Great Britain	11,342	6,985	68	109
Italy	14,368	10,695	60	96
Beneficiary				
Luxembourg*	232	1,714	2,964	266
Hungary	890	6,620	579	68
Lithuania	320	1,886	540	75
Greece	1,827	7,095	483	73
Malta	65	255	475	84
Latvia	244	1,062	409	64
Slovenia	327	1,143	389	83
Estonia	178	668	377	76
Poland	3,527	17,436	366	68
Portugal	1,637	4,943	308	78
Belgium*	3,660	7,044	302	119
Bulgaria	404	2,255	297	47
Czech Republic	1,309	4,377	292	85
Romania	1,353	5,944	231	55
Slovakia	625	1,669	193	77
Cyprus	143	273	144	62
Croatia	387	584	47	59
Spain	9,978	11,539	34	91
Ireland	1,425	1,563	30	134

Source: Interactive chart on EU Budget by the European Commission, available at http://ec.europa.eu/budget/figures/interactive/index_en.cfm, and population data and GNP (in purchasing power standards) from Eurostat. Data reflect all "rebates." *Expenditures include funds for hosting EU institutions; without these, Luxembourg and Belgium would be net contributors

In focus

The Common Agricultural Policy

The Common Agricultural Policy (CAP) is one of the largest and most controversial of all the EU's programs. Traditionally, it has consumed the vast share of the EU's budget, and debates over how to reform the CAP—or to scrap it altogether—figure prominently both within the EU and in international trade talks.

CAP's origins lie with the 1957 Treaty of Rome, which set the "common organization of agricultural markets" as a goal that would serve five objectives: increase productivity in agriculture, create a sufficient level of income for farmers, stabilize markets, guarantee a secure food supply, and deliver reasonable prices to consumers (Articles 39–40). Initial discussions on the CAP began in 1958, and most of its provisions were codified in the early 1960s. It replaced national agricultural support systems with a Europe-wide one, and established free trade in agriculture with common prices for products across Europe. CAP provided export subsidies to allow European farmers to be competitive with lower cost producers in international markets, and it set a target price for most agricultural goods (e.g., cereals, meat, dairy products), which guaranteed farmers a higher price for their products than what they would garner on a purely open, competitive market. In this way, CAP was a protectionist policy, insulating European farmers from world market forces and explicitly encouraging European consumers to buy European products. In its early years, the CAP's primary backer was France, which had a relatively large agricultural sector, envisioned agriculture as part of its national heritage, and viewed CAP as a trade-off for allowing the free trade of German industrial goods. For the French, the CAP was a means to make the rest of Europe pay for its agricultural subsidies. Put differently, Dutch and Belgian and German taxpayers were helping to ensure a good income for French farmers. However, to the extent that rural populations were a sizeable voting bloc—about 25 percent in many countries—CAP proved to be a political "winner" for many European leaders.[41]

It should be obvious that the objectives of CAP were contradictory. In particular, consumers were not served very well, because without the CAP they would enjoy lower prices for food, as cheaper imported products from, for example, the US or North Africa would be allowed into Europe. However, with CAP setting an artificially higher price for products, there was no cost advantage to potential imported products such as US wheat or Tunisian olive oil. Instead, Europeans consumed French wheat and Italian olive oil, and, predictably, farm lobbies emerged to lobby both national governments and Brussels for continued subsidies.

In certain respects, the CAP worked remarkably well. Because farmers were encouraged to produce and offered a high price for their goods, production soared, so that by the 1980s the EC had mountains of surplus butter, cheese, and meat that it could not consume or even unload. Large portions of each year's grain harvest were turned into fertilizer. However, thanks to export subsidies, European farmers could also sell their produce on world markets, even though producers elsewhere had lower costs because land and labor were more expensive in Europe.

While all looks great from the farmers' perspective, CAP has many critics. Historically, it consumed most of the EC's budget, and as fewer and fewer people worked the land—by the 2010s, even after the addition of post-communist countries, less than 5 percent of the EU's workforce was employed in agriculture—transferring a vast amount of money to a relatively small minority caused many to look twice at CAP. This was especially true in states that were less agricultural or had more efficient farms that did not need CAP support. Great Britain, particularly under Thatcher, became the primary critic of CAP, but others, including the Germans and the Dutch, began to ask why their taxpayers were supporting French, Italian, or Spanish agriculture. Moreover, consumers began to recognize that CAP was costly to them, as they would end up saving money if they could buy lower cost agricultural goods. In the 2000s, there were estimates that CAP cost the average consumer in Europe about €250 a year in terms of higher food costs and financial transfers to farmers and led to such absurdities that the EU ended up granting each cow a $913 subsidy![42] Lastly, data revealed that CAP overwhelmingly benefited large landowners who really did not need additional income. For example, in budget year 2003–2004, the queen of England received €360,000 from CAP. Data revealed that only 6 percent of the farms received 53 percent of the benefits, with 60 percent of the smallest farms getting only 10 percent of CAP funds.[43] Audits in 2009 found—in addition to Queen Elizabeth—German gummy bear manufacturers, Italian luxury cruise caterers, Prince Albert II of Monaco, and Spanish brandy distillers were recipients of CAP largesse.[44]

Reforming CAP is thus a major topic within the EU. The first serious efforts to reform CAP began in the 1980s, when the EC reduced price supports for many products and committed itself to budgetary discipline on the CAP. More concerted efforts to reform CAP occurred in the early 1990s under the leadership of Ray MacSherry, the Irish commissioner for agriculture. His reforms helped modify CAP so that it relied less and less upon price supports and instead gave a direct payment to farmers. Moreover, he proposed that CAP monies be better targeted to those farmers that really needed support, typically owners of smaller farms, not giant agri-businesses. The EC's trading partners also sought CAP reform, as they argued that export subsidies and tariffs prohibited free trade in agriculture and hurt poorer developing-world farmers who could not sell their products in the giant European market. Export subsidies were cut as part of international trade talks. Paradoxically, however, the new compensation packages for European farmers, which included direct payments and monies for taking land out of production (which helped eliminate the mountains of butter), actually added to the cost of CAP.[45]

New efforts to reform CAP were launched in the 1990s. One impetus was the outbreak of mad cow disease in Britain, which focused attention on food safety and environmental issues. These issues received additional attention thanks to the contamination of poultry products in Belgium in 1999 and in Germany in 2002 and the avian flu scare in 2005. Moreover, as the EU looked to expand to Eastern Europe—which is far more agricultural—it was clear that high levels of CAP spending were unsustainable. Germany, which in the past had deferred to the French on the CAP, also became more vociferous on the need for reform.[46] After often-acrimonious debate, proposals were put forward in the EU's Agenda 2000 reform program. They envisioned less money for price support and more utilization of direct payments to farmers. By 2003, CAP market support schemes, which had composed two-thirds of the CAP in 1990, were reduced to a fifth of CAP spending, and in the 2000s, under pressure from Great Britain and other countries that were opposed to CAP, price supports were cut in favor of funds for sustainable development, food safety programs, and efforts to promote alternatives to farming such as rural tourism.

CAP, however, remains under great pressure. Part of the problem was the 2004 expansion, which doubled the number of farmers in the EU. According to the Court of Auditors, in 2005 over 1,400,000 Polish farms applied for CAP support, more than France, Spain, and Italy (three of the largest CAP recipients) combined.[47] They were offered, at least initially, only partial CAP support. Polish farmers, for example, only received 25 percent of their CAP entitlement in 2004, 30 percent in 2005, and so on, until full CAP payments began in 2013. While many in Brussels (and no doubt Paris and Rome) may hope that many small-scale Polish farmers go bankrupt and find other employment, in 2013 Poland became the fourth largest recipient of CAP funds (after France, Italy, and Germany, and was very close to France in terms of CAP funds *per capita*), and post-communist countries (36 percent of the total EU rural population) overall received 23 percent of total CAP funds.[48] It is clear moving forward that the post-communist countries will put more pressure on CAP funding. For the 2014–2020 budget cycle, CAP is now subsumed under the heading "Sustainable Growth and Natural Resources," although, as seen in Figure 4.2, the traditional elements of CAP (labeled the European Agricultural Guarantee Fund by the EU) dwarf programs explicitly committed to rural development. Overall spending on traditional CAP, however, did decline from 36 percent of the EU budget in the 2007–2013 period, reflecting the impact of reforms adopted in 2013, that, *inter alia*, capped payments to larger farms, added targeted payments to younger farmers and those adhering to better environmental practices, simplified the payment scheme, and created measures for transparency on CAP disbursements, which it hopes will limit revelations that funds are going to "undeserving" recipients (e.g., European royalty).[49] CAP is also under pressure at the international level, as developing states complain that EU agricultural subsidies harm them by limiting their capacity to export their goods to the EU. The World Trade Organization (WTO) has won cases against the EU on the latter's sugar subsidies and on its banana import policies, but many of the EU's trade partners would like to see it further liberalize agricultural trade.

Critical thinking questions

1. Has CAP outlived its usefulness and original justification?
2. How might CAP conflict with other policies and goals of the EU and create tensions within the EU?

since 1988, assessments based upon the state's total gross domestic income (68.9 percent of the 2014 budget).[50] Note that most of the EU's budget is dependent upon funds transferred from member states[51] and thus is a source of tension between national governments and Brussels. Because of how funds are spent—overwhelmingly on structural funds and other assistance to less-developed areas and agriculture and rural development—some states are net contributors to the EU, whereas others, mainly poorer states, are net beneficiaries. Table 4.5 provides data from the 2014 budget. One sees that only nine states are net contributors, and three (Germany, the Netherlands, and Sweden) contribute at least twice as much as they receive from the EU. On the other hand, Poland, the sixth largest country in the EU, is the largest total recipient of EU funds. Most of the net recipients of EU funds are poorer than the EU average. Many are post-communist states or were hard hit by the economic crisis in the 2010s (e.g., Greece). As one could expect, there are disagreements between the better-off contributors and beneficiaries on the size and shape of the EU budget. This has been particularly true with respect to Great Britain, which has negotiated with Brussels the right to receive a "rebate" on its contribution, in part because it receives little funding from CAP. Nonetheless, the perception by many in Britain that the EU is just not worth it—Britain receives far less than it gives—animated the 2016 referendum on Britain's continued EU membership.

Policies of the common market

The most developed area of EU policy is in the vast number of laws and regulations necessary to establish and maintain a common market. This makes up the bulk of the pre-Lisbon Treaty "first" or "community" pillar of the EU, and important steps in the development of the common market were highlighted in the previous chapter. While one might think that creating a common market is easy—after all, one simply allows people, goods, services, and capital to move freely—it requires much policy harmonization in order for it to work effectively. In other words, it is not enough to remove a tariff and say that one can sell a French car in Germany. Among other items, one would want to ensure that the French car meets safety and emissions standards, that the French carmaker does not receive subsidies or other benefits that give it an unfair edge over its German competitors, and, perhaps, that French workers are free to form unions, receive a decent wage (or at least are not clearly exploited), and have good working conditions. In other words, there needs to be some assurance that trade is both free and *fair*.

Reducing barriers to trade

The policies of the common market thus reach into a number of areas. On the most basic level, physical barriers to trade and labor and capital flows have been removed: tariffs, quotas, customs offices, and border checks. One area of concern on this front is importation of products that are legal in one state into another where they are illegal. Such importation (e.g., marijuana legally purchased in the Netherlands) is prohibited, as states are empowered to enforce their own laws on banned or illegal goods.

In addition, the EU has moved to reduce fiscal barriers that can be barriers to trade and distort prices. An obvious example would be differential tax policies, which can make the same products more expensive in different states. The EU has thus made tax harmonization—particularly of the VAT, in effect the sales tax—a priority, setting a 15 percent minimum and working toward a single VAT across Europe. Excise taxes on alcohol and tobacco are also regulated under EU rules. And, of course, adoption of the euro makes it impossible for states to use exchange rates to gain trade advantages vis-à-vis others.

More difficult have been technical barriers to trade. These include items such as safety standards on products and even how products can be defined or labeled. As noted above, the *Cassis de Dijon* case of 1979 was crucial in setting the precedent of mutual recognition of standards, meaning that states must accept products that meet the minimum technical standards of the country of origin. Prior to this, there had been haggling over various points, including whether the cocoa content in British chocolate met the Belgian or Dutch standards to be called chocolate and whether or not Italian or French beer met the standards of German beer as defined by its famous 1516 purity law. In addition to mutual recognition, the EU has devised its own standards and regulations on a range of products, such as depth of automobile tire treads and allowable noise levels from lawnmower engines. EU regulations can be quite detailed and cumbersome. A proposal in 2006 required companies to register the use of 30,000 different chemicals, and the EU Commissioner for Enterprise and Industry estimates that the *annual cost* to European companies of complying with all EU regulations is €600 billion.[52]

Regulation

Many laws, however, do make life easier for businesses. As part of the single market, the EU passed directives to streamline and harmonize national legislation so that banks and insurance companies can set up businesses in other EU countries. Education operates under the principle of mutual recognition of diplomas and certification. The key notion in all areas of EU law is that of nondiscrimination, meaning that all EU products and all EU citizens must be treated equally without regard for national origin. Previous policies that favored one's own national companies (as was the norm in government procurement, for example) have been abolished. These measures can be controversial. For example, Austrian universities, less expensive than their German counterparts, have been, according to some, overrun with German students. However, under EU rules, Austria cannot favor its own citizens over foreigners.

The EU has set standards to maintain fair competition among European firms. Government support for particular enterprises is now regulated and cannot create unfair advantages for some firms over others. Of course, this is hard to enforce when many companies are owned wholly or in part by the state, but the idea is to create a more equal playing field and end the practice of state support for so-called "national champions." This has been felt most keenly in the airline industry, which used to be dominated by the flag carriers of various states (e.g., Air France, Iberia, Austrian Airlines), which could charge high prices because they had near monopolies on various routes. Air travel in Europe has been deregulated, and new, low-cost carriers (e.g., EasyJet, Ryan Air, Air Berlin, Wizz Air) are now offering services. The EU's competition policy has also prevented the merger of various companies, including in 2001 the proposed merger of the American companies General Electric and Honeywell, both of whom, because they do business in Europe, are subject to EU regulations. This decision provoked outrage across the political spectrum in the US, but, as Jack Welch, chairman of General Electric noted, one could not simply say "to hell with Europe." Instead, he maintained that "we have to do business with Europe, so we have no choice but to respect their law."[53] In 2004, the EU took on the juggernaut of Microsoft, eventually resulting in a judgment by the ECJ and a fine of €497 million for using its near-monopoly in operating systems to corner the market on operating software and work group servers. In addition to paying fines, Microsoft was forced to unbundle its Windows XP system from Media Player and to open up its operating system to goods provided by other companies.

Trade in services

Over a decade after the creation of a common market, free movement of services remained a problem. This emerged as a major area of focus for the EU in 2000s, particularly given the fact that services (e.g., financial, health care, education, retail) constituted 70 percent of overall EU GDP and employment. Even though labor, capital, and goods, with few exceptions, moved freely in the EU, and the EU affirmed the right of people to open businesses throughout the EU and receive services irrespective of the home country of the service provider, there were still various regulations and licensing barriers that prevented free trade in services. Part of the worry related to recognition of standards (e.g., could a Portuguese-licensed doctor practice in Germany?), and, after the 2004 expansion in particular, there were widespread fears that cheap service providers from post-communist countries would flood the more advanced countries. The "Polish plumber" was the archetypical figure, who, it was alleged, would, for example, move to France, charge less than French plumbers, and put French plumbers out of work. Campaigns for and against the "Polish plumber" raged inside the EU and among the mass public, with the Polish tourist board, as seen in the photograph below, even displaying a large billboard in Paris that featured a handsome Polish plumber inviting people for a visit. In 2006, the EU adopted a directive to liberalize trade in services, but service providers would have to meet the standards of the host country, not their country of origin, and some professions (e.g., health care, public transport, telecommunications, legal services) were exempted or subject to special measures. Provisions were also added to impose

Poland presents its new face to Europe

© JACQUES DEMARTHON/AFP/ Getty Images

restrictions for the sake of national security or the public interest. In 2013, the EU passed the European Retail Action Plan, devised to liberalize and enhance competitiveness in this sector. The EU's 2015 Single Market Strategy was also designed to generate freer trade in services, including improving recognition of professional qualifications, more protections for consumers (including in cases of e-commerce), and financing of start-ups and innovative service providers.[54]

Overall, while the EU claims to be a common market, it is clear that it is not yet a single economic space in the same way, for example, as the US. The most glaring omission, as noted in the previous chapter, is that it does not have a single currency for all its members—as of 2016, nineteen out of twenty-eight had adopted the euro. Furthermore, as suggested in the opening chapter—and elaborated in Chapter 11—the refugee crisis has prompted some countries to re-implement border controls, which could hamper trade as well as free movement of people. Even so, the EU has adopted literally thousands of regulations and directives to break down the myriad barriers to unfettered movement and competition among economic actors, and it is still moving, by and large, toward more economic integration. Although the idea of a single market is today almost taken for granted, it bears emphasis that its creation is arguably the greatest accomplishment of the EU.

Regional policy

As noted in the discussion on the EU budget, one of the major areas of EU spending is regional development within the EU. Although the Treaty of Rome established the European Social Fund (ESF), which has been and still is focused on stimulating employment, the first explicit effort to address regional disparities occurred in 1975 with the establishment of the European Regional Development Fund (ERDF). The main objective of the ERDF was to provide assistance for those regions of the EC that were less developed than the EC average. Initially, this meant that funds were transferred to places such as southern Italy, Scotland and Wales, Ireland, and rural regions of France. As the EC expanded, other regions—mainly in Greece, Portugal, and Spain—qualified for assistance. In the 1990s, a reunified Germany dipped into these funds to assist in the rebuilding of East Germany, and, after the 2004 and 2007 expansions of the EU, most of the ERDF monies are going to former communist countries. In addition, the Maastricht Treaty established a Cohesion Fund, which is devoted to providing assistance in the areas of transportation, competition, and the environment so that newer member states can meet EU standards. All three funds are components of the EU's structural funds, meaning that ESF spending is also directed toward less-developed funds and the goal of helping states meet EU criteria.

The vast majority of intra-EU assistance occurs through these funds. From 2000 to 2006, the EU disbursed €195 billion; from 2007 to 2013, the figure grew to €336 billion, the increase reflecting in part the addition of a large number of relatively poorer states; in 2014–2020, the figure is projected to be €352 billion, with nearly €200 billion coming from the ERDF, the largest single structural fund.[55] Whereas in 1975 regional policy consumed only 5 percent of the budget, its share has increased as the EU became more economically diverse. It grew to 15 percent by 1988, 36 percent by 2006, and has remained at roughly the same level since (37 percent in the 2014–2020 projected budget). Since 2006, the ERDF, the ESF, and the Cohesion Fund, although still technically separate, have been committed to three common objectives: convergence to EU standards by promoting sustainable development (Objective 1); regional competitiveness and employment (Objective 2); and cross-border cooperation (Objective 3). Over three-quarters of the funds are devoted to Objective 1, and include such fields as research and development, health, energy, transportation, and information technology. To qualify under ERDF, a region's income per person must be 75 percent or below the EU average; the threshold for the Cohesion Fund is 90 percent. It is important to note that the funds are devoted to regional, meaning primarily sub-national development. For example, regions in southern Italy or eastern Germany qualify for EU assistance even though Italy or Germany as a whole would not. For the 2014–2020 period, for example, Italy (€20 billion) and Spain (€19 billion) are slated to be the second and third largest recipients of ERDF funds, and even Germany will receive over €10 billion (Poland, with €40 billion, will receive the most).[56] Regions must apply for the funds, and the EU's COR helps oversee EU regional policy. These are not complete giveaways, as EU monies are expected to be matched by funding by national or regional governments.

As might be expected, the EU's structural funds are a subject of some controversy. Taxpayers in richer states do not relish the idea that their money is being taken from them and given to others. On the other hand, those who receive EU structural funds have fought hard to maintain their level of support. In this respect, the 2004 and 2007 expansions changed the calculus, meaning that some regions of Spain, Italy, Greece, and Portugal no longer qualify for ERDF monies. To remedy this, some money has been set aside so that these regions will be gradually weaned off the EU, and small amounts of money also remain available to sparsely populated regions of the EU (e.g., northern Finland and Sweden) and to the outermost regions, such as the Azores Islands of Portugal and French New Caledonia in the western Pacific.

Environmental policy

Environmental issues are now a top concern of the EU. Notably, the environment was not mentioned at all in the original Treaty of Rome. Initial discussion of environmental policy occurred only in the early 1970s. In 1981, the EU established a separate DG on environmental issues, and the SEA devoted considerable attention to environmental policy. Spurred in part by European publics that are very concerned about environmental issues, the EU has made environmental assessment an issue across a wide range of policy areas, including economics, transport, agriculture, and energy. The EU's commitment to environmental protection was reiterated in numerous documents in the 1990s, and in 1994 the European Environmental Agency (EEA) began operations. As amended by the 2003 Nice Treaty, the Treaty of the European Community now commits itself to preserving the quality of the environment and sustainable development (Article 2) and devotes Article 174 to environmental priorities.

In 2013, the EU adopted its Seventh Environment Action Programme, which governs EU policy until 2020. It states a number of priorities: climate change, biodiversity, human health, and sustainable development. It also emphasizes the need to better implement existing national-level and EU legislation, secure better information on humans' environmental impact, provide more investment for environmental issues, and, most significantly perhaps, "full integration of environmental requirements and considerations into other policies."[57] It also stipulates that the EU will also address international environmental and climate challenges. Within the EU, specific environmental competencies include policies regulating air quality, pesticides, waste management, "ecolabeling" for consumers, habitat preservation, emissions trading to reduce greenhouse gases, encouragement of organic farming, a ban on genetically modified organisms, and monitoring of compliance on environmental agreements and treaties. One clear accomplishment of EU environmental policy, which has often been driven by "greener" countries such as Denmark, Germany, Finland, and the Netherlands, has been to boost standards across Europe, and the EU has also taken a leading global role on environmental issues.

Despite EU interest on the environment, implementation has been a problem. EU directives are not always transposed into national legislation, and the EU has had to take member states to the ECJ to compel them to take action. Even on such a high-profile issue as greenhouse gas reductions as agreed to in the 1997 Kyoto Protocol, most EU states had great difficulty in meeting their commitments. The EU, however, did agree to the Kyoto Protocol's Doha Amendment in 2012, which imposes more binding reductions on its signatories. As before, the EU will monitor compliance among its members. Despite occasional protestations from some countries about the cost of environmental standards, this area is, overall, one in which EU policy engagement has widespread popular support. This is a reflection of a strong environmental conscience in most of Europe, an issue we'll explore further in Chapter 9.

Justice and Home Affairs
a growing area of EU competence, including border control, crime, terrorism, and provision of EU-wide rights to all citizens.

Justice and Home Affairs

One of the most rapidly evolving areas of EU policy is **Justice and Home Affairs,** which in the pre–Lisbon Treaty EU constituted a separate "pillar" of the union. This area covers a host of issues, most of which are managed by the DGs on Justice and Consumers and on Migration and Home Affairs. Issues under their purview include standard law-and-order concerns (e.g., immigration and border security, fight against organized crime, terrorism, human trafficking, drug policy, Internet crime), but also the defense of rights granted to all EU citizens. These include free movement across EU borders, the right to stand and vote in European and municipal elections,[58] rights of legal redress at the European level, and rights against discrimination. The EU has set up bodies to monitor and combat instances of racism, xenophobia, and anti-Semitism. The EU also tries to promote "active citizenship," which includes sponsorship of international youth programs, sister-city relationships, and EU-wide non-governmental organizations. Within the rubric of Justice and Home Affairs, there have been some notable accomplishments: the creation of Europol (European Police Office) in 1995; a European Arrest Warrant; the **Schengen Agreement** (originally signed in 1985 but incorporated into the EU in 1997) that eliminated border controls to facilitate the free movement of people,[59] and a Charter of Fundamental Rights adopted in 2000. The EU has repeatedly advanced a goal of a common visa and asylum policy and more coordination on

Schengen Agreement
signed in 1985, it eliminated internal border controls and guaranteed free movement of people among its signatory members. As of 2016, it includes twenty-six countries, including non-EU states such as Iceland, Switzerland, and Norway.

immigration. In 2014 it put forward an ambitious Justice Programme that awards grants for projects that help train personnel in matters of justice and law enforcement, make citizens aware of their rights and legal remedies, and promote cross-national cooperation on issues such as drug trafficking.[60]

Whereas cooperation on combating criminal activity has largely been forthcoming, some issues have been far less amenable to harmonization, as states have resisted a common, EU-wide standard. For example, despite repeated statements emphasizing the need for common guidelines in areas such as immigration and asylum, states have largely continued to maintain their own policies. While the EU has stated that it seeks more high-skilled immigrants, states continue to set their own immigration policies. This remains one of the most controversial issues of EU action. In 2015, amid the refugee crisis in Europe, the EU sought to impose a quota system for each country to take in a percentage of 120,000 refugees. This was highly controversial, especially in post-communist states, whose leaders claimed they lacked the funds and experience (if not the cultural sensitivity) to handle newcomers from the Middle East. Some suggested they would defy EU policy, which they portrayed as an imperialistic imposition on their state's sovereignty.[61] Great Britain, it is worth noting, is not a member of the Schengen zone, has opt-outs on EU migration and asylum policies, and refused to take part in this refugee-resettlement scheme, although it did make a separate commitment to take in some refugees. Nonetheless, many British voters blamed the EU for the wave of immigrants that entered Britain in the 2000s and 2010s, and immigration figured prominently as an issue in the Brexit referendum.

Dublin Convention

EU agreement, which came into force in 1997, which requires those seeking asylum to apply in the first EU country they enter. This was designed to coordinate EU asylum policy, but specific asylum policies still vary across member states.

As for asylum, various iterations of the **Dublin Convention**, which originally entered into force in 1997, have established rules that asylum seekers must apply for asylum in the first EU country they enter. This was designed to prevent "asylum shopping," in which refugees would try to get to countries such as Germany and Sweden with more liberal asylum policies. In theory, failure to abide by the Dublin Convention means that a refugee could be repatriated. However, this has been successfully challenged in court, and, amid the 2015 refugee crisis, countries such as Greece, Hungary, and Slovenia were so overwhelmed that they were unable to implement this agreement, meaning they either allowed refugees to pass through without processing them or turned them away. This crisis is explored more in Chapter 11. Furthermore, it is hard to imagine all EU countries adopting a common standard on citizenship and naturalization, let alone the EU creating a comprehensive bill of rights for all EU citizens that would supersede protections and responsibilities defined in national constitutions. In short, it is in this sphere, as well as in foreign policy, where inter-governmentalism remains strong and the integrationist impulse is far weaker.

As seen throughout this chapter, the EU aspires to do many things and has an ambitious agenda to become an even more powerful and effective actor. While many are skeptical about its future, it has already come further than many of its doubters could ever have imagined. The Lisbon Treaty and creation of a new President of the European Council hardly represent an endpoint of the EU's institutional development. It continues to entrench itself into the lives of Europeans and affects its member-states in profound ways. However, as seen in the 2016 British referendum, many Europeans are not convinced they or their country benefit from EU membership, and connecting the EU with its citizens/stakeholders remains a work in progress. We will explore, in later chapters, some of the profound challenges facing the EU in the 2010s. However, without wholly abandoning consideration of the EU—which impinges upon national-level politics in numerous forms—we now turn to fuller consideration of political institutions and practices within individual states.

Application questions

1. Why doesn't the EU adopt a purely parliamentary style of government, in which an elected parliament selects a prime minister and cabinet? Who would object to such an arrangement?
2. Do you agree that the EU has a "democratic deficit"? What could theoretically and/or realistically be done to make the EU more democratic?
3. From your understanding of EU institutions, can you give several examples of how the tensions between inter-governmentalism and supranationalism play out?
4. The EU spends a great deal of money redistributing wealth from richer countries to poorer ones. Whereas one might be able to understand how regional redistribution is plausible within a single country (e.g., think of transfers to eastern Germany, Scotland, or poorer parts of the US), how does such a scheme work in a multinational environment? Why would richer states agree to this?
5. After reading this chapter, are you more or less convinced about the need for European integration? Do you think the EU should go further in its stated goal of "an ever closer union of peoples"? At this point, what would tangible steps in that direction look like?

Key terms

Additional reading

Bomberg, Elizabeth, Peterson, John, and Stubb, Alexander, eds. 2012. *The European Union: How Does it Work?*, 3rd edition. Oxford: Oxford University Press.
Edited volume that focuses on the actors and policy-process of the EU. In addition to detailed information about specific EU institutions, includes chapters on democracy within the EU and how organized interests and lobbying impact EU policy.

Ginsberg, Roy. 2010. *Demystifying the European Union: The Enduring Logic of Regional Integration*, 2nd edition. Lanham MD: Rowman and Littlefield.
This book covers the historical development, institutions, and more contemporary policies of the EU. It is written with students in mind, meaning that most of its focus is more descriptive about the nuts and bolts of the EU, but it also includes some discussions about theories of EU integration and policy-making.

Hix, Simon. 2008. *What's Wrong with the European Union and How to Fix It.* Cambridge: Polity.
A provocative and lively text that does far more than simply describe how the EU works. Rather, it diagnoses problems both in the processes and outputs of policy-making in the EU, with particular attention to the question of garnering more public support and making EU institutions work more efficiently.

Journal of Common Market Studies, published by Wiley-Blackwell, website at www.blackwellpublishing.com/jcms.
Premier academic journal on the EU, with many articles on the functions and dynamics of EU institutions and on the evolution and effectiveness of EU policies. An excellent resource for research papers on the EU.

McNamara, Kathleen. 2015. *The Politics of Everyday Europe.* Oxford: Oxford University Press.
Theory-informed account of how the EU institutions and policies function and efforts the EU makes to gain popular support and legitimacy. Adopts a constructivist approach that assesses how ideas and concepts, such as the EU's cultural infrastructure, are developed. Recommended as an alternative to more standard nuts-and-bolts treatments of the EU.

Wallace, Helen, Pollack, Mark, and Young, Alasdair, eds. 2015. *Policy-Making in the European Union*, 7th edition. Oxford: Oxford University Press.
With contributions by leading scholars in the field, this book looks in detail at sectoral policies (e.g., agriculture, immigration) of the EU as well as theoretical perspectives on the EU's development. A very good reference for those looking for more detail about particular features of what the EU actually does.

Notes

1 For a book-length treatment, see Benjamin Grob-Fitzgibbon, *Continental Drift: Britain and Europe from the End of Empire to the Rise of Euroscepticism* (Cambridge: Cambridge University Press, 2016).
2 "Britain Receives Proposal for 'Better Deal' to Stay in the E.U.," *New York Times*, February 2, 2016. For more on Britain's relationship with the EU and the referendum, see Michael Emerson, ed. *Britain's Future in Europe: Reform, Renegotiation, Repatriation, or Secession* (Brussels: Centre for European Policy Studies, 2015), and Roger Liddle, *The Risk of Brexit: The Politics of a Referendum*, 2nd edition (London: Policy Network, 2016).
3 "Divided We Fall," *The Economist*, June 18, 2016.
4 "To These 'Brexit' Voters, English Identity Is Under Threat," *The New York Times*, June 17, 2016.

5 Roger Cohen, "For Jo Cox, Britain, Shun Hate," *The New York Times*, June 21, 2016.
6 See for example Charles Moore, "The European elite forgot that democracy is the one thing Britain holds most dear," *The Telegraph*, June 24, 2016, and Giles Fraser, "Brexit brought democracy back—now we need to start listening to each other," *The Guardian*, June 24, 2016.
7 Claudio Radaelli, "The Europeanization of Public Policy," in Kevin Featherstone and Claudio Radaelli, eds. *The Politics of Europeanization* (Oxford: Oxford University Press, 2003), p. 30.
8 Jonas Tallberg, "Delegation to Supranational Institutions: Why, How, and with What Consequences?," *West European Politics* 25, January 2002, p. 23–46.
9 The Council can meet in the following configurations, with a different mix of ministers for each: foreign affairs/defense; justice and home affairs; agriculture and fisheries; environment; economic affairs; transport and energy; education, youth, sports and culture; competitiveness; employment, social policy and health; and general affairs.
10 When acting on its own (e.g., not in response to a proposal from the Commission), a two-thirds majority is required.
11 This stipulation is almost always met by the weighted voting requirement, but it is possible that a proposal backed by all but three of the largest states would not meet this population criterion.
12 As a concession to the French, the EU agreed to hold the EP's plenary sessions once a month in Strasbourg. The "monthly move" of MEPs and staff to Strasbourg costs upwards of €200 million a year, and the EP itself has voted to hold sessions and regular committee work henceforth only in Brussels. However, the EP has no power to amend the agreement to hold sessions in Strasbourg. Thus, one can see how the EP is a weaker institution within the EU—it cannot even decide where it meets! See "A Parliament On the Move Grows Costly," *The New York Times*, June 29, 2011.
13 The most up-to-date information on the EP can be found at its website, www.europarl.europa.eu.
14 Data from the website of the European Parliament, cited above.
15 Amie Kreppel, *The European Parliament and the Supranational Party System* (Cambridge: Cambridge University Press, 2002).
16 Kreppel, The European Parliament, p. 1.
17 Basic facts and figures on the ECJ can be found at http://curia.europa.eu/jcms/jcms/P_80908/.
18 See RTE News, December 19, 2012, at www.rte.ie/news/2012/1219/359719-environment-court-fines/.
19 Key cases are those in 1963 that ruled that the Treaty of Rome placed constitutional obligations on members above that of their own laws and the *Costa v. ENEL* ruling (1964), which confirmed the primacy of EU law over national law.
20 Anne-Marie Burley and Walter Mattli, "Europe Before the Court: A Political Theory of Legal Integration," *International Organization* 47, Winter 1993, p. 41–76.
21 One example of this was in 2007, when, during discussion about re-weighting votes in the Council of the European Union, the Poles suggested they should have more votes because if it were not for Nazi Germany, there would be millions of more Poles. Suffice to say this did not sit well with the Germans.
22 More information on this institution is available at www.eesc.europa.eu.
23 Andres Follesdal and Simon Hix, "Why There Is a Democratic Deficit in the EU," *Journal of Common Market Studies* 44:3, September 2006, p. 533–562.
24 Ibid, p. 535.
25 *The Economist*, "Four Ds for Europe," March 17, 2007.
26 Mikko Mattila, "Why Bother? Determinants of Turnout in European Elections," *Electoral Studies* 22:3, 2003, p. 449–465. For the 2009 EP elections, see *The Economist*, June 13, 2009.
27 Andrew Moravcsik, "In Defense of the Democratic Deficit: Reassessing the Legitimacy of the European Union," *Journal of Common Market Studies* 40:4, 2002, p. 603–634.
28 Giandomenico Majone, *Regulating Europe* (London: Routledge, 1996).

29 Follesdal and Hix, "Why There Is a Democratic Deficit," and Charlemagne, "Not Normal," *The Economist*, January 20, 2007.
30 Charlemagne, "The Endless Election Round," *The Economist*, June 13, 2009.
31 In 1985, after a referendum, the Danish territory of Greenland negotiated its exit from the then-European Community. EU laws and directives do not apply in Greenland, which has substantial autonomy from Denmark.
32 These data come from Standard Eurobarometer 83 from the spring of 2015. Data tables can be found at http://ec.europa.eu/public_opinion/archives/eb/eb83/eb83_anx_en.pdf, accessed March 24, 2016.
33 Thomas Piketty, "A New Deal for Europe," *New York Review of Books*, February 25, 2016.
34 A good treatment in English of Habermas's fundamental ideas is his *The Crisis of the European Union: A Response* (London: Polity, 2012).
35 These examples were culled from a project in my class asking students to find the strangest EU regulation.
36 See *The Economist*, "The EU's Would-Be Founding Fathers," February 21, 2002, and Ben Crum, "Politics and Power in the European Convention," *Politics* 24, 2004, p. 1–11.
37 Robert Michels, Political Parties: A Sociological Study of the Oligarchical Tendencies of Modern Democracy (New York: Hearst's International Library, 1915).
38 Charlemagne, "Money Matters," *The Economist*, October 16, 2010, p. 66.
39 European Commission, Multiannual Financial Framework 2014–2020 and EU budget 2014: The Figures, Brussels, 2014.
40 In EU documents, "smart and inclusive growth" includes both monies for competitiveness and cohesion, as represented in Figure 4.2. Funds for CAP are under the heading "sustainable growth."
41 German farms, typically rather small and not particularly efficient, also benefited from CAP, and the German farm lobby, although not as well known as its French counterpart, nonetheless would help ensure German support for CAP for many years. See Tony Judt, *Postwar: A History of Europe Since 1945* (New York: Penguin, 2005), p. 306.
42 Jack Thurston, *How to Reform the Common Agricultural Policy* (London: Foreign Policy Centre, 2002), and Timothy Garton Ash, *Free World: America, Europe, and the Surprising Future of the West* (New York: Vintage, 2005), p. 155. More critiques of the CAP can be found in Noel Malcolm, "The Case Against Europe," *Foreign Affairs* 74:2, March–April 1995, p. 52–68, who calls it a "colossal waste of money."
43 Richard Baldwin, "Who Finances the Queen's CAP Payments," Paper from the Graduate Institute of International Studies, Geneva, December 2005.
44 "European Subsidies Stray from the Farm," *New York Times*, July 16, 2009, at www.nytimes.com/2009/07/17/business/global/17farms.html.
45 Desmond Dinan, *Ever Closer Union: An Introduction to European Integration*, 2nd edition (Boulder: Lynne Reiner, 1999), p. 344.
46 Christilla Roederer-Rynning, "Impregnable Citadel or Leaning Tower? Europe's Common Agricultural Policy at Forty," *SAIS Review* 23, Winter/Spring 2003, p. 133–151.
47 Court of Auditors, Audit of 2005 Budget, available through www.eca.europa.eu, accessed December 13, 2006.
48 See 2015 EU factsheet on agriculture in each member state, available at http://ec.europa.eu/agriculture/statistics/factsheets/pdf/eu_en.pdf.
49 For more on the post-2013 CAP reforms, see Johan Swinnen, ed. *The Political Economy of the 2014–2020 Common Agricultural Policy* (Brussels: Centre for European Policy Studies, 2015), as well as information from the European Commission at http://ec.europa.eu/agriculture/cap-post-2013/index_en.htm.
50 Data from interactive chart of the European Commission, available at http://ec.europa.eu/budget/figures/interactive/index_en.cfm.
51 The EU has few autonomous sources of funding, the largest of which is income taxes levied on EU employees, but these are a very small source of overall EU revenue.
52 "Regulatory Over-Reach?" *The Economist*, December 9, 2006, p. 70.

53 Quoted in T.R. Reid, *The United States of Europe: The New Superpower and the End of American Supremacy* (New York: Penguin, 2004), p. 105.
54 See press release on this proposal at http://europa.eu/rapid/press-release_IP-15-5909_en.htm.
55 Figures from the data portal at https://cohesiondata.ec.europa.eu/funds.
56 Figures from the data portal at https://cohesiondata.ec.europa.eu/funds.
57 See the EU's portal on this program at http://ec.europa.eu/environment/action-programme/.
58 Any EU citizen can run for the European Parliament or run in local elections, regardless of one's national citizenship.
59 Great Britain and Ireland did not sign on to the Schengen Treaty, and restrictions on free movement of peoples from the ten new members added to the EU in 2004 are in place until 2011. Norway and Iceland, not EU members, participate in this treaty.
60 More information on this program can be found at http://ec.europa.eu/justice/grants1/programmes-2014-2020/justice/index_en.htm.
61 "EU Governments Push Through Divisive Deal to Share 120,000 Refugees," *The Guardian*, September 22, 2015, at www.theguardian.com/world/2015/sep/22/eu-governments-divisive-quotas-deal-share-120000-refugees.

Austrian Chancellor SPOE, Werner Faymann resigns from office

© Ronald Zak AP/PA Images

Chapter 5

Parliaments and electoral systems

One does not usually think of Iceland and Austria as locales for political drama. Both are wealthy, stable, well-established democracies, better known for their natural beauty than contentious politics. Yet, in the spring of 2016, both captured headlines after unexpected developments. In Iceland, Prime Minister Sigmudur David Gunnlaugsson found himself mentioned in the leaked "Panama Papers" for setting up a shell company with his wife that created a possible conflict of interest. This, one might note, occurred in a country that was devastated by a financial crisis in 2008 created by reckless behavior of bankers and businesspeople, many of whom were sentenced to jail. Gunnlaugsson maintained he had done nothing illegal, and tried to maintain his office. Popular pressure on Gunnlaugsson mounted. His position, including within his Progressive Party, became untenable, and he resigned.[1] Parliament confirmed Sigurdur Ingi Johannsson, who had suggested there was nothing wrong with what Gunnlaugsson had done, as the new prime minister. This did not sit well with many in Iceland, and left-wing opposition parties pushed for a vote of no confidence in the new government. This failed, although in October 2016 Johannsson resigned after his party suffered a significant defeat in parliamentary elections, which saw the anti-establishment Pirate Party—yes, that's right—win third place by running on an anti-corruption platform.[2] No bloc of parties, however, won a majority in these elections, leading to more drama as various party leaders struggled to form a new government. Eventually, in January 2017, Bjarni Benediktsson of the center-right Independence Party became Prime Minister in a three-party coalition government, but he is also under a cloud for involvement with a shell company exposed in the "Panama Papers."

In Austria, Chancellor Werner Faymann of the Social-Democratic Party seemed secure as leader of a grand coalition government with the center-right Austrian People's Party. In April 2016, however, the Austrian political establishment was shaken by the results of the country's presidential elections, in which Norbert Hofer of the nationalist, anti-immigrant Freedom Party placed first in the initial round of voting and advanced to a run-off. While the Austrian presidency is primarily a symbolic office, the results were seen as a rebuke to the governing coalition and indicative of growing concerns in Austria about the influx of Syrian refugees and other migrants and the EU's open borders. In 2015, Faymann had embraced German Chancellor Angela Merkel's policy to welcome refugees, but switched his stance as public opinion and, in particular, his coalition partner grew increasingly concerned with the arrival of some 90,000 migrants and refugees into Austria. This about-face sparked a rebellion among many Social Democrats. Faymann was booed by party members in Vienna during a May Day event, typically a celebration for his left-wing party. Combined with the party's defeat in the presidential elections, Faymann was severely weakened, and he faced the prospect of losing a vote of no confidence in parliament or a move within the party to oust him as leader. Bowing to this reality, he resigned on May 8th.[3]

Two weeks later, Alexander Van der Bellen, a former Green Party leader who supports a border-free "United States of Europe," narrowly defeated Hofer in the run-off to become Austria's President. The drama was not over, however. The Freedom Party challenged the vote in court, alleging irregularities in ballot counting in several districts. In July, the Austrian Constitutional Court found enough problems with the election to annul it and order a re-vote in December, thereby giving a second chance to Hofer, who advocated for Austria to hold (as did Great Britain) a referendum on continued EU membership.[4] Ultimately, Van der Bellen prevailed with 53.8 percent of the vote, prompting one of his backers to half-jokingly declare, "Austria saves the world."[5] However, it is doubtful that the Freedom Party and like-minded nationalists and populists across the continent (and beyond) are a spent force.

The examples above are two of many (albeit among the more dramatic) in contemporary Europe that point to the importance and interplay of political institutions, which include the authoritative bodies that make decisions, the rules of the political game, and actors such as political parties that play a central political role. In both of these cases, there was a change in leadership and some instability and uncertainty, but, in the end, the institutions did their job. Political conflict was resolved peacefully through regularized, legally established procedures, and in both cases the political victors could claim they best represent the will of the people. While not all Icelanders or Austrians may have been pleased with the outcome, in neither case was democracy compromised.

The next several chapters of this book examine political institutions, the actors and structures that determine how political power is distributed and exercised. This is one of the core areas of political science. Aristotle, whom many consider the first political scientist, based his *Politics* on a comparative study of government in Greek city-states. He classified various types of government based upon who held power and in whose interest power was exercised. He identified monarchies, tyrannies, aristocracies, oligarchies, and democracies, We still classify governments based upon how political institutions are designed, often employing the same terms used by Aristotle.

In today's Europe, all countries have a democratic form of government. The modern form of democracy[6] is a system of government in which political leaders are chosen through free competitive elections and citizens have a variety of civil and political rights (e.g., freedom of speech, of assembly, to run for office) that allow them to gain information from different sources, express alternative viewpoints, and organize opposition to the government. Examples of democratic political institutions include elected parliaments and executives as well as courts and constitutions that help guarantee respect for political and civil rights and the rule of law.

These institutions, however, vary from state to state, both in their organizational design on paper and in their actual practice. Whereas all democracies in a most general sense give people the power to determine their government, various forms of political institutions help determine *how* people's preferences are represented and translated into policy. How these institutions are designed matters, and knowing how they function and interact among themselves, as illustrated in the examples above, is crucial to understanding how the political system in a given state operates. This chapter will introduce you to features of parliaments (often known better in American English as legislatures) in Europe, with subsequent chapters taking up executives, constitutions and legal systems, and political parties.

Functions of parliaments

National parliaments are the centerpieces of democratic governance in Europe, responsible for many important political tasks and often the only branch of government elected by voters. They are made up of individuals—often labeled members of parliament or simply MPs—who typically are given two general tasks that at times may contradict each other. On the one hand, MPs, as representatives of the people who voted them into office, are supposed to articulate and support the goals of their constituency, whether they be voters in a particular district or supporters of a certain political party. On the other hand, as public servants they are also charged with being responsible for the country as a whole. At times, it may be difficult to decide what should take priority—to defend the narrow interests of their constituency or to act in a manner that they think would be better for the country. This conundrum—who or what should elected representatives represent—has been an important concern in democratic theory.[7]

party discipline practice whereby elected officials and would-be candidates for office adhere to the party line, voting or endorsing programs backed by the party leadership.

In actual practice in most European democracies, MPs are expected to adhere to **party discipline**, meaning that they vote in accordance with the preferences of their party. This gives political parties a great deal of power, and it is easier and usually more accurate to think of the workings of parliament as more the interaction of a small number of political parties than as the activities of dozens or hundreds of individual MPs. Parliaments are organized around party blocs or factions. The leaders of the various party blocs structure the agenda and debates within parliament, in many cases micromanaging the details to include who should speak and for how long. This type of structure severely limits the powers and prerogatives of individual MPs. Relatively junior members of the party bloc that habitually break party discipline may risk losing the nomination of their party to run in future elections.

Parliaments are typically assigned a variety of tasks. Above all else, they are charged with making laws. Insofar as elected representatives of the people make laws, it is this lawmaking authority that, ultimately, makes European states democratic. Draft legislative proposals are debated in parliamentary sessions, and in several countries parliamentary committees play an important role in amending proposals before they are voted on by the whole parliament.

However, one should recognize that the lawmaking functions of most European parliaments are often rather *pro forma*. The reason for this is that most European states are parliamentary democracies, a feature we explore more in Chapter 6. For now, however, it is important to understand that, unlike in a presidential system (as in the United States), in most of Europe, parliament is responsible for choosing the executive authority (e.g., the prime minister and the cabinet), which is typically referred to as the government. The government draws up most legislative proposals and submits them to parliament for formal approval. Because of party discipline, MPs are expected to vote along party lines. Since, in most cases, the government

Is Europe one?

National parliaments and the European Union

In this chapter, we will largely isolate national-level European parliaments from issues surrounding Europeanization, assuming that parliaments' primary interplay is with voters who elect MPs and the government that presents proposals to parliament. We should realize, however, that one cannot easily isolate domestic politics from the European-level, as the EU has more and more influence over lawmaking in EU member states. Thus, in addition to debating and approving proposals drafted by governments, European parliaments are also expected to pass legislation required by the EU. What percentage of domestic-level legislation actually originates in Brussels—in the form of an EU regulation or a directive to transpose EU rules into national law—is difficult to say, as it depends how one counts individual legislative actions and varies considerably from country to country. For example, whereas critics of the EU in Britain claim that half or more of all laws in Britain originate with the EU, a study by the House of Commons put the figure at 9 percent.[8] Other counts of EU actions compared with adoption of national legislation in Ireland and Germany argue that, in these states, up to 80 percent of national-level legislation originates with the EU.[9]

Regardless of the precise figures, many see this as troubling. As noted in the previous chapters, some object to this on sovereignty or democratic grounds (e.g., national states and/or voters lose power), but several observers have suggested that the real "losers" in the process are national parliaments (NPs). Some argue that Europeanization means "deparliamentization," as real legislative authority is being taken away from NPs and given to the EU, where the European Commission typically drafts proposals that are then approved by the Council of Ministers and European Parliament. Much of the work of NPs in contemporary Europe is formally passing legislation to conform to decisions taken at the EU-level. One author concluded that because of the strong role of the EU, NPs "lack authoritative power over transnational policy-making."[10] True, national governments, via the European Council and the Council of the EU, are involved in EU policy-making, but those two forums include the executive branch (e.g., prime ministers and cabinet officials), not NPs. The net result is that NPs are no longer the locus of much decision-making. NPs are, at times, deprived of the right to deliberate over legislation and even represent voters. The lack of involvement of NPs in the EU is seen by some as another example of the "democratic deficit" of the EU.

NPs have attempted to remedy this situation. NPs have European affairs committees that attempt to influence or even control national decision-making within the EU. Some, such as those in Great Britain and Ireland, are advisory. In other cases, such as Germany, Austria, and Denmark, these committees have more power and can effectively order ministers to vote a certain way on EU proposals in the Council of the EU.[11] In this way, NPs can ensure that their preferences are represented in Brussels, although, because the EU employs double-majority voting for many of its actions, it is possible that a NP can express an opinion against a proposal but then be forced to adopt an EU directive into its national legislation. This can create a peculiar situation where parliamentarians would argue they do not want to adopt such a law but they "have" to do so. At this point, one could wonder if multi-level governance in Europe is stripping away too much power from nation-states and their elected representatives.

The EU itself recognizes that the lack of involvement of NPs in decision-making is a problem and has taken some steps to remedy the situation.[12] Since 1989, the EU has had a Conference of Community and European Affairs Committees of the Parliaments of the EU (COSAC, its French-language acronym), which meets twice yearly. This is a consultative body that provides a forum for communication and information, and it was formally recognized in a protocol to the 1997 Amsterdam Treaty.[13] According to that protocol, the COSAC can address to EU institutions any "contributions" that it deems necessary. The Amsterdam Treaty also stipulated that all European Commission consultative (e.g., research and background papers) documents be forwarded to national parliaments. Moreover, since 2006, as part of its "Citizens Agenda" to involve more actors in EU decision-making, the European Commission has agreed to provide copies of all proposals to NPs for feedback. There is also an Interparliamentary Forum between NPs and the European Parliament, as well as an electronic Interparliamentary Information Exchange, allowing MPs in any state to learn about the work of other NPs on EU issues.

In particular, NPs have been interested in enforcing the principle of subsidiarity, maintaining that certain decisions are best left to national-level, not EU-level, action. To this end, the Lisbon Treaty includes a Subsidiarity Control Mechanism, which employs a color-coded ("yellow cards" and "orange cards") scheme. If one-third of NPs agree that a proposal violates subsidiarity, this means it has a "yellow card" and the Commission is obligated to reconsider it. If a majority of NPs issue an objection, the proposal acquires an "orange card" and must then by submitted to the Council of the EU and the European Parliament. These powers, however, are purely advisory, as NPs cannot veto an EU proposal. As of 2015, in only two cases was the "yellow card" played (there were no "orange cards"). In one of these cases, the Commission withdrew its proposal; in the other, it went ahead with it, dismissing the objections by NPs on subsidiary grounds.[14] Suggestions for an even stronger role for NPs, for example, a second chamber of the European Parliament that would include MPs from NPs, have met stiff resistance from national governments.

While most observers do concede that deparliamentization, to a certain degree, is occurring and is a natural result of Europeanization, some scholars have tried to find a silver lining for NPs.[15] EU action in certain areas may create precedents for new policies, functioning as a "catalyst for parliamentary activity in those areas traditionally not subject to domestic legislation."[16] For example, prior to EU attention to gender equality or the environment, several states (especially in Southern Europe) had few laws on these issues. Because of EU involvement in these spheres, NPs understand that legislative action for these issues is desirable and necessary. NPs may then extend the principles of EU rules (e.g., pay equity in the workplace) to new national-level legislation (e.g., gender equity in paternal leave benefits). Moreover, EU involvement may facilitate policy transfer, as pan-European action on a particular issue may lead NPs to share data, learn about a particular field, and borrow "best practices" from others. The idea is that Europeanization will not only lead to legal uniformity across Europe but that the quality of legislation will actually improve across the continent.

Critical thinking questions

1. Do you view the existence of "European level" decision-making more as a necessity and logical outgrowth of common, transnational problems that require concerted action, or more as a deliberate usurpation of national power?
2. What actions or reforms might best balance the power of the EU and those of national-level parliaments?

commands the allegiance of the majority of the MPs, it is able to push through legislation because parliamentarians from the ruling party or parties are expected to support the government's initiatives. In many cases, parliaments also typically lack the staff or expertise to be able to take legislative initiative. MPs may draw up their own proposals—known as a "private bill" in the British system—but they stand little chance of passing unless they garner the support of the government. Thus, despite the fact that parliaments in Europe possess, on paper at any rate, supreme lawmaking authority, some argue that parliaments have become "reactive" or "rubberstamps," subservient to prime ministers and the cabinet.[17] We explore this more in the next chapter. In addition, others suggest that national-level parliaments have been significantly weakened by Europeanization, as more and more power is being transferred to the EU and that national parliaments increasingly do Brussels's bidding, not that of their own constituents. This contention is taken up in the **Is Europe one?** feature.

But, let us not push these positions too far. Most European governments—cabinet officials and prime ministers—answer to parliaments, and individual parliaments continue to matter. Just as parliaments vote in a government, they also possess, as noted at the outset of this chapter, the power to remove them with a **vote of no confidence**, meaning that a majority of MPs indicate that they will no longer support the government. Although rarely successful because it is seen as a drastic measure, this provides an important check on power, as parliaments can, if pushed, say no, and MPs can use the threat of a vote of no confidence to extract concessions from the prime minister and government. Sometimes when controversial measures attract public attention and dissent from within the ruling party's ranks (e.g., raising of university fees in Britain in the 2000s, proposals to change labor laws in France in the 2010s), the government will work with individual MPs for their support to ensure that the ruling bloc in parliament will not be subject to individual MP defections.

vote of no confidence
a parliamentary vote against the existing government that forces the government either to resign or call for new elections.

Parliaments also possess means to check or oversee governmental actions. These include "**question time**," in which government ministers are called before parliament to answer questions and are often subjected to close scrutiny, particularly from opposition parties. Parliaments also have committees (e.g., an environmental committee, an agricultural committee) charged with working with and, to some extent, keeping an eye on corresponding ministry of the government. These committees also serve as a place where interest associations or even individual citizens can present their case for reform in policy or against possible abuses of power by the government.

question time
practice in which government ministers are called before parliament to answer questions and are often subjected to close scrutiny, particularly from opposition parties.

While the general points made above apply across the continent, one should recognize that there are measurable differences in power among European parliaments. The Parliamentary Powers Index (PPI), developed by M. Steven Fish and Matthew Kroenig, measures the powers of legislatures on thirty-two dimensions, including the scope of the legislature's authority, its control over the executive branch, its administrative resources, and the power of courts to review legislation. Scores are from zero to one. In general, as one can see in Table 5.1, most European parliaments are relatively powerful—especially when compared to countries such as the US, Mexico, Brazil, Argentina, and Kenya that possess presidential systems—reflecting the fact that they are the primary decision-making bodies. There is, however, some variance in Europe, in particular in those countries with stronger presidents (e.g., including Cyprus, France, and Portugal, discussed in the next

TABLE 5.1 Parliamentary Powers Index (PPI) for select countries

Country	*PPI Score*
Germany	0.84
Italy	0.84
Czech Rep.	0.81
Great Britain	0.78
Poland	0.75
Hungary	0.75
Finland	0.72
Austria	0.72
Sweden	0.72
Romania	0.72
Portugal	0.63
France	0.56
Cyprus	0.41
US	0.63
Mexico	0.44
Brazil	0.56
Argentina	0.50
Kenya	0.31

Source: M. Steven Fish and Matthew Kroenig, *The Handbook of National Legislatures: A Global Survey* (Cambridge: Cambridge University Press, 2009). Data were gathered from 2002–2004, based upon a questionnaire administered to at least five country experts. The score is based upon parliamentary powers on thirty-two dimensions and can range from 0 to 1

chapter). True, this index measures formal powers—e.g., the British House of Commons is constitutionally supreme, free of any checks by courts or a written constitution, hence it scores relatively high—whereas actual practice may temper the powers of parliaments. However, when one takes into account that under parliamentary democracy parliaments possess ultimate power over the executive—a feature not found, for example, in the US, where there is more separation of power and presidents can enact measures by executive order—it remains true that European parliaments are powerful institutions.

That said, it bears mentioning that the process of producing legislation and the actual ability to exercise power differs from parliament to parliament. One obvious source of difference is whether a single party controls the majority of seats in the legislature or whether a coalition of parties must form in order to achieve a majority of votes necessary to pass legislation. The British parliament, for example, is typically dominated by two main parties, virtually assuring one party a majority in the parliament.[18] This is known as a **majoritarian system** of governance.[19] For a decade (1997–2007) Prime Minister Tony Blair of the Labour Party enjoyed large majorities in the House of Commons. Because of party discipline, members of the Labour Party typically backed the government on its legislative proposals; controversial issues such as the war in Iraq and education reforms were exceptions in which some Labour MPs voted against the government. As a result, Tony Blair managed to get most all of his legislation through the Parliament. In 2015, the Conservatives under David Cameron formed a government based on their control of 330 of the 650 parliamentary seats, a narrow (50.8 percent) majority, which meant that Prime

majoritarian system

political system that features two dominant parties, ensuring that one party has the majority of seats in parliament.

Minister Cameron had to ensure that there were virtually no defections from the Conservative MPs in any legislation his government advanced. In this way, one can argue that Cameron, who resigned in 2016 following the Brexit vote, possessed less power than Blair did, as the latter had more "wiggle room" to pursue his own initiatives and could risk a few of his party's MPs voting against a proposal.

Because of its majoritarian features, however, the British Parliament often *looks* relatively weak. Despite the at-times theatrical sessions of the House of Commons (particularly during question time), the outcome of parliamentary "debate" is rarely in doubt. The government takes care to line up the necessary majority, which may include in some cases concessions to individual MPs, thus making the passage of government proposals almost a foregone conclusion. However, even though the House of Commons might look like a rubberstamp, it bears emphasis that the prime minister possesses political authority only because he was selected by the parliamentary majority. That same majority could remove him at any time with a vote of no confidence, meaning that supreme or ultimate power continues to lay with the parliament.

coalition
an alliance of two or more parties in a parliament that together produces a majority that can pass legislation and elect a government.

consensus system
a political system in which governance depends upon coalitions among political parties because no one party has a majority.

The legislative process can be much more complex when a **coalition** is required to pass legislation. This means that two or more parties need to form an alliance in order to produce a parliamentary majority, which is often labeled a **consensus system** of governance because it rests on compromises between or among various political parties who are included in the legislative process. In this case, no single party can impose its will upon parliament. Under a consensus system, the members of the parliamentary coalition share both legislative and executive authority, with the latter submitting proposals to the ordinary parliamentarians for their approval. Examples of coalitional governments can be found in Germany. As seen in Figure 5.1, no German political party has secured a majority of seats in the past four elections to the *Bundestag* (lower house of parliament), although the Christian Democrats almost claimed a majority in 2013. As a consequence, parties have had to make coalitions in order to form a government. In 2002, the Social Democratic Party (SDP) and the Greens, both on the political left, formed a government. In 2005, the situation was more complex. With the parties on the center-right (the Free Democrats [FDP] and the Christian Democrats) and the parties on the center-left (the SDP and the Greens) pledging only to cooperate with each other and no party willing to make a deal with the far-left *Die Linke* (Left Party), there was no obvious coalition. After weeks of haggling, the SDP and the Christian Democrats agreed to forge a grand coalition of the two largest parties, making Angela Merkel of the Christian Democratic Union (CDU) Germany's first female chancellor. In 2009, when the SDP suffered a major setback at the polls and the FDP gained seats, Merkel refashioned the governing coalition, jettisoning the SDP in favor of the FDP, which, as free market champions, were ideologically closer to the Christian Democrats. In 2013, after the FDP failed to gain any seats, Merkel was compelled to seek a different coalition partner, and once again opted for a grand coalition with the SDP.

Because of the necessity to maintain a coalition in order to pass proposals through parliament, political life in countries with a consensus system is subject to more compromises than in Great Britain. Consider, for example, the period of the German "grand coalition" from 2005 to 2009, when Chancellor Merkel had to work with her center-left coalition partner (and erstwhile opponent), the SDP, to

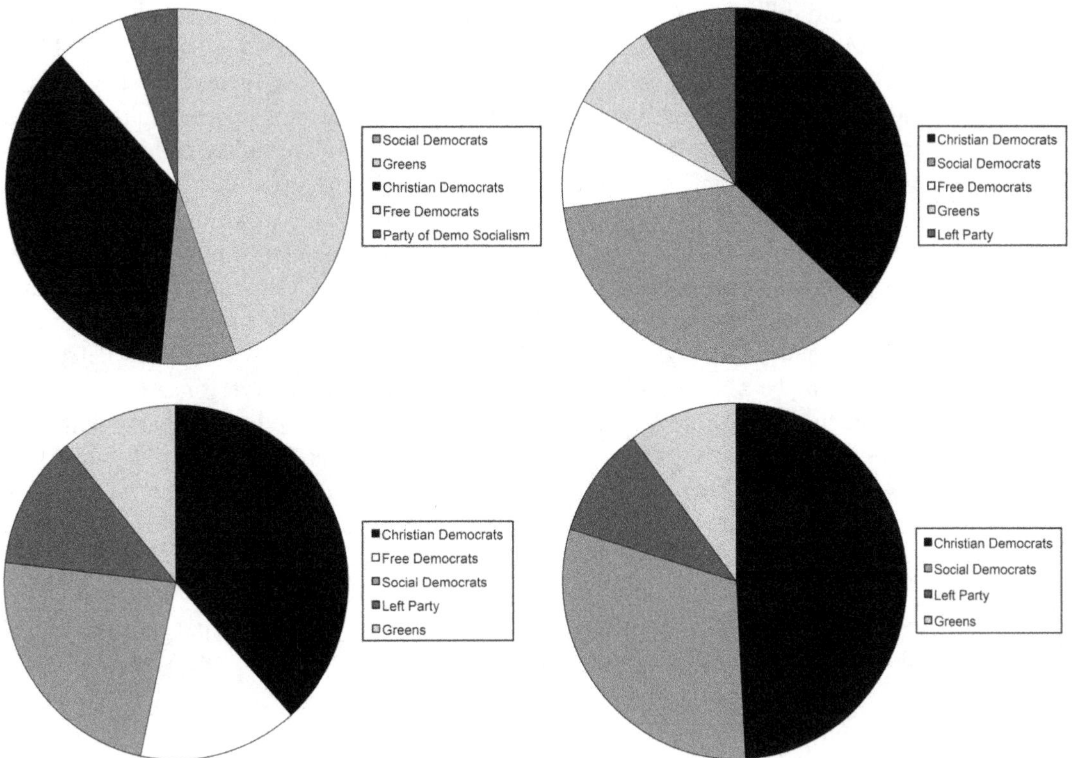

FIGURE 5.1 Seats in Bundestag after German elections, 2002–2013

Parties and Elections in Europe, available at www.parties-and-elections.eu/

pass legislation. Parliamentary committees in the German *Bundestag* also play a far more active role than in Britain, as the coalition partners and, at times, even the opposition parties have come together in committee to make amendments to the government's proposals. On the one hand, this makes the process of passing laws more cumbersome. Parties have to negotiate and make deals, and Merkel or any German chancellor will not get everything she might want. In some cases during the period of the CDP-SDP grand coalition, the two parties were unable to agree on substantive proposals in areas such as on taxes, health care, and labor market reform. Legislation deemed too controversial was watered down or put off for another day. Some decried this, even suggesting that Merkel was locked in a "cage" with the SDP,[20] and certainly this led to more uncertainty than in a pure majoritarian system, where the ruling party typically does not have to worry about securing passage of proposed legislation. However, one might retort that politics in Germany—and in other states such as the Netherlands, Sweden, and Finland that typically have parliamentary coalitions—will rest more on consensus than in cases where parties do not have to work with each other to get things done.

Coalitions are not always successful, however, and they can be difficult to form. For example, twenty-nine parties won seats to the Polish *Sejm* in 1991 elections, necessitating the formation of a six-party winning coalition. Needless to say, balancing the interests and positions of six different parties was difficult, although

Poland did manage to continue with its course of post-communist economic reforms for two years before the coalition collapsed and new elections had to be held. In 2006, the Czech Republic went without a government for several months because there was a 100-100 tie between the right and left parties in parliament, making it impossible to produce a coalition. In 2009, the Dutch government collapsed because one of the coalition partners withdrew. In 2010, the same occurred in Belgium, which, after new elections, went nearly a year (353 days) without a formal government because no coalition could be formed among the eleven political parties that won seats to the Belgian parliament. December 2015 elections in Spain did not produce a majority party or a workable coalition; a re-vote in June 2016 delivered similar results, although Mariano Rajoy of the conservative People's Party was expected to be able to cobble together a coalition with a very narrow majority. Also in June 2016, the Croatian government fell after the leading party withdrew support for a technocratic prime minister who had been installed in office only five months earlier. Dynamics such as these, which require either new elections or negotiations among parties to form a new government, obviously introduce more instability and unpredictability into a political system.

Whether or not a country requires coalitions is likely to be a function of how many political parties are present in parliament. The number of parties, as we shall see below, is in turn often determined by the country's electoral system.

One parliament or two?

unicameralism a system with only one parliamentary (legislative) body.

bicameralism a system with two parliamentary bodies.

Before examining that topic, however, it is worth noting one other obvious structural difference in European parliaments. Parliaments may be either **unicameral** (having only one "house" or legislative body) or **bicameral** (possessing two legislative bodies). Unicameralism is far simpler, as legislation must pass through only one body. Unicameralism tends to be associated with smaller countries and those without sizeable minority groups or regional divides. As seen in Table 5.2, most European states, particularly those with smaller populations, are unicameral. Bicameralism is by definition more complicated, as bills must pass through two legislative chambers, making the process of legislation more difficult, especially if different parties or coalitions control each legislative chamber. One could argue, however, that the presence of another legislative body serves as a check on abuse of power, or, as is the case in federal systems such as Germany and Austria, that a second chamber provides a means for regions or sub-national governments to be represented.

Bicameralism, however, does not work the same in all states. In Great Britain, the unelected House of Lords—whose members are appointed or inherit their positions—has very limited power, able to at most delay legislation. Similarly, in France the indirectly elected Senate, chosen by an electoral college of regional councils, is politically weaker than the National Assembly, which has the final say on all legislation. In Italy, in contrast, the Chamber of Deputies and Senate are coequal in legislative powers, with the Senate (uniquely among bicameral systems) even enjoying the right to remove the government with a vote of no confidence.

A referendum to alter the balance of power between the chambers by decreasing the power of the Senate failed in December 2016, leading to the resignation of Prime Minister Matteo Renzi, who had backed a number of institutional changes which he believed would help advance economic reform.[21]

Other cases, such as the Netherlands, Belgium, and Germany, fall somewhere in the middle, with the "upper house" of the legislature possessing some real power but subordinate to the "lower house," which, among other items, enjoys the right to name the prime minister (note how these labels can lead to confusion). The precise division of power between the two chambers is often complex. For example, in Germany, the "upper house" of the legislature, the *Bundesrat*, is where Germany's sixteen regions (*Länder*) are represented, with each *Land* sending members to the *Bundesrat* based upon its population. Legislation that is deemed to affect the *Länder* is put on a separate track, meaning that in these cases the *Bundesrat*'s power is equal to that of the *Bundestag*, the "lower house" of the German parliament. In other words, on these questions that are ruled to affect the *Länder* (e.g., transportation, health, education; most questions fall on this track), both chambers must give their approval. If different parties control the *Bundestag* and the *Bundesrat*—which has often been the case and occurred again in 2010—passing legislation can be very difficult. Even if the same party controls both chambers, it could be that the members of the *Bundesrat*—less accountable to the executive branch and perhaps more independently minded as they represent a distinct region—would complicate the passage of legislation. For this reason, bicameralism inherently puts the German chancellor in a weaker legislative position than the Norwegian, Bulgarian, or Swedish prime ministers, who work with unicameral legislatures. For matters that are deemed not to be of direct interest to the regions (e.g., foreign policy), the *Bundesrat* enjoys only a suspensive veto over policy, meaning that if it rejects a measure it can be overridden by the *Bundestag*, which has the final say.

One additional structural issue concerns the size of parliament. As one would expect, larger countries have larger parliaments, so that the ratio of voters to an MP is not unmanageably high. For example, the French National Assembly has 577 members, the German Bundestag has 598,[22] and the Italian Chamber of Deputies has 630. In contrast, the Estonian State Council has only 101 members, the Slovenian National Assembly has ninety, and the Icelandic *Althing* a mere sixty-three.

TABLE 5.2 Unicameralism and bicameralism in Europe

Unicameral States:	Albania, Bulgaria, Croatia, Cyprus, Denmark, Estonia, Finland, Greece, Hungary, Iceland, Latvia, Lithuania, Luxembourg, Macedonia, Malta, Montenegro, Norway, Portugal, Serbia, Slovakia, Sweden, Turkey.
Bicameral States:	Austria,* Belgium,* Bosnia and Herzegovina,* Czech Republic, France, Germany,* Great Britain, Italy, Ireland, Netherlands, Poland, Romania, Slovenia, Spain, Switzerland.*

*Federal State

Source: Author's compilation

How are parliaments elected?

electoral systems
rules and mechanisms that determine how candidates or parties win elections.

plurality systems
voting system in which voters vote for candidates and whichever candidate gets the most votes wins.

proportional representation
voting system in which voters typically vote parties and parliamentary seats are divided based on the proportion of votes each party receives.

Knowing that parliaments are elected bodies, one natural question would be, how are they elected? **Electoral systems**, meaning the rules and mechanisms that determine how candidates or parties win elections and thereby gain positions in government, vary from country to country. The nature of a country's electoral system can have a profound effect on its overall political structure, and the study of the design and consequences of electoral systems is a major topic in comparative politics.

One issue to consider is the term of office of parliamentarians. Put another way, the question is, how often are parliamentary elections? The short answers are that it varies and that it depends. It varies because the term of parliamentary office is different from country to country. In most European states it is four (as in Germany, Sweden, Spain, Romania, and Poland) or five (as in France, Great Britain, Italy, and Turkey) years. It depends, because most European parliaments do not have fixed terms of office, unlike, those, for example, of the US Congress. Elections can be called before the term actually ends, necessitated either by a vote of no confidence in the government or the prime minister choosing to dissolve parliament and have early elections. These are features of parliamentary systems of government, which are common in Europe and explored more in the next chapter.

Under what rules are elections held? Whereas all European countries are democracies, meaning that elections are free and fair and voters have a meaningful choice among parties and/or candidates, they do not all have the same type of electoral system. Here we will discuss mechanisms for parliamentary elections, leaving consideration of presidential elections—important in countries such as France, Poland, and Romania—to the subsequent chapter. In general terms, legislatures can be elected through one of two methods: **plurality systems** (sometimes called, erroneously, majoritarian systems) and **proportional representation.** Both are,

TABLE 5.3 Plurality and proportional representation systems compared

Plurality	*Proportional representation*
Country divided up into districts.	Country may (e.g., Spain) or may not (e.g., Netherlands) be divided up into districts.
One person represents each district.	Districts have multiple members.
Parties nominate a single candidate to run in a district.	Parties present voters a list of several candidates.
Voters vote for a candidate.	In closed list systems, voters vote for a party; in open list, STV, or mixed systems, they can vote for a candidate.
Candidate with most votes—plurality—wins; "winner take all."	Seats divided up based upon proportion of votes received; more than one "winner."
Used in Great Britain and variation used in France.	Used elsewhere, in various forms.

in the broadest sense, democratic, because they offer voters a choice of candidates or parties. Their fundamental logic, however, is very different. Each system has its own advocates who argue for its superiority over the other one. The most essential features and differences between these systems are displayed in Table 5.3.

Plurality voting systems

single-member district plurality system (SMDP) used in Great Britain, a plurality system in which the country is divided into districts and voters choose one representative per district; winner-take-all system.

run-off election a second-round election in which candidates that receive a certain number of votes in the first round are allowed to run; used in France.

two-ballot plurality system used in France, it requires a run-off election under plurality rules if no candidate in a given district receives a majority of the vote in the first round of voting.

Only two European countries—Great Britain and France—use plurality voting, although, thanks to British influence, it is used elsewhere, such as the US, Canada, India, and Australia. The British system is often upheld as the "purest" type of plurality voting. It is called a **single-member district plurality system (SMDP)**, sometimes referred to as first-past-the-post. The basics are relatively simple. The country is divided up into electoral districts (650 at present in Great Britain), ideally with each roughly the same in terms of population.[23] Candidates, usually nominated by a party, run for office hoping to represent a particular district. Voters in that district vote for one candidate. The candidate with the most votes in a given district—in other words, the one with a plurality (not necessarily a majority of 50 percent plus one)—wins. There is only one winner in each district, making it a winner-take-all system, as the winner wins the seat and the other candidates get nothing.

In these respects, elections in Britain look very similar to US congressional elections. It is important to emphasize, however, a core difference. Because the British have a parliamentary form of governance, the vote for a particular candidate is both a vote for an individual and a vote designed to tip the balance of power in parliament in favor of a particular party so that it may select the prime minister and cabinet. In the US, legislative and presidential elections are separate, so the choice of one's representative in Congress has no bearing on who is elected president.

The French electoral system works a little differently. Again, the country is divided into districts (577), and voters vote for a candidate. However, in order to win the election in the first round a candidate must get a majority of the vote. If there are several candidates and no one wins a majority, all the candidates that poll over 12.5 percent of the vote are entitled to enter a **run-off election,** held a few weeks later. The candidate who gains the plurality of the vote—not necessarily the majority—in the second round wins the seat, making this method of voting a **two-ballot plurality system.**

This system is more complex than the British one, and it functions in a manner that is not obvious at first glance. Consider hypothetical cases for two districts, as displayed in Table 5.4. In each case, several candidates have the right to advance to the second round of voting. The question is who wins in the second round. In District 1, three candidates—the Communist, the Socialist, and one from the center-right Republicans—advance, whereas one from the Greens does not. If voting in Round 2 repeated the results of Round 1, the Republicans would win (even assuming the left-leaning Greens vote for the left-leaning Socialists in Round 2). If all the non-Republican parties combine their votes, however, this coalition will defeat the Republicans. Thus, parties have incentive to make a deal, with one throwing support tothe other—presumably the Socialists would support a Communist candidate in another district—and, in this case, the Socialists take the seat, even though the Republican candidate won the most votes in Round 1. District 2 is more complex. Here four candidates advance, and if one followed the same logic as in District 1, the parties on the Left—the Socialists and Communists—would get 45 percent of the vote in the second round, enough for this alliance to win over an easily predictable alliance of the Republicans and the Democratic Movement (MD), both center-right parties. The wild card here is the nationalist, xenophobic National Front (FN), viewed as a pariah by other political parties, which officially have refused to cooperate with it on the national level. The question, though, is whether the Republicans will make an appeal to try to court FN voters (e.g., by proposing crackdowns on immigration or cuts in public assistance to minority groups) and/or even try to persuade the FN candidate to drop out of the race and throw his support to the Republicans. If the FN keeps its candidate in the race and FN voters vote for him, the Left wins. If the center-right alliance makes some sort of deal with the devil of the FN, it wins. Thus, even though the FN is a relatively small party—and it does have much capacity to win seats on its own under plurality rules—it still can play an important role in French elections.

Proportional representation

party list
rank-order list of a party's candidates for office; used in a proportional representation system to determine which individuals will end up serving in parliament.

Proportional representation (PR) in various forms is far more common in Europe. The purest form of proportional representation is found in the Netherlands. There are no separate electoral districts. Instead, the entire country is treated as a single district with 150 members, the number of seats in the *Tweede Kamer* (one of the chambers of the Dutch parliament). Parties compose a **party list** of individual candidates, ranking them in order. A full party list would contain 150 names, one for each possible seat. Voters then make their choice. Most countries with PR employ a closed-list system—meaning voters make a selection only among the competing parties. This occurs, for example, in Turkey, Portugal, and Spain. In other countries such as Sweden, the Czech Republic, Estonia, and the Netherlands, there is an open-list system, meaning voters have the option to show preference for a particular

TABLE 5.4 Illustration of French two-ballot plurality system

Candidate/Party		*% vote Round 1*	*% vote Round 2*
District 1			
Michel Rivard	Communist	20%	
Maria Vert	Greens	5%	
Caroline Bodin	Socialist	33%	58%
Laurent Monet	Republicans	42%	42%
District 2			
Sophia Blanc	Communist	13%	
Maurice Zidane	Socialist	32%	45%
Amie Govier	Republicans	35%	42% without FN, 55% with FN
Jonah Cohen	MD	7%	
Jacques Charlot	FN	13%	13%? or does it vote for the Republicans?

candidate, not merely a party, by ticking off that person's name on the ballot. In practice, however, few voters exercise this choice, opting instead to vote only for a party, as they would in a closed-list system.[24] In both systems, seats are then doled out in proportion to the percentage of votes the party receives. If, for example, the Dutch Labour Party gets 20 percent of the vote, it would win approximately thirty seats, 20 percent of the total of 150 seats. In this case, the candidates ranked one to thirty on the Labour Party's list would gain seats. The unlucky soul at number thirty-one would not. Obviously, those at the top of the list have the best chance of winning seats, and are chosen by the party for their ability, experience, and loyalty. Party-list voting—particularly a closed-list system where voters have no say over candidates—thus discourages maverick or upstart candidacies.

Other countries have variants of this basic PR system. Most commonly, the country is broken up into multi-member districts (as in Sweden [29], Poland [41], Spain [52], Turkey [79], Slovenia [9], and even tiny Malta [13], among others). Each district has a certain number of parliamentary seats, which can vary, as more populous districts usually receive more seats. Parties present a list in each district—which can vary from district to district to include more local candidates or be exactly the same across all districts—and seats are then determined based upon the proportion of vote received in each multi-member district. This allows for some geographic representation—although a voter still cannot identify his/her individual representative, as under plurality voting where each representative is connected to a unique district—and gives smaller, regional parties a chance a greater chance to win seats. In addition, some countries, such as Sweden, Denmark, and Austria, reserve a proportion (roughly 12 percent in the Swedish case) of seats that are held-back as a "top-off" to ensure that the final distribution of seats mirrors the national vote as closely as possible. In Greece and Italy, a proportion of seats is held back and given to the highest vote-getter, a practice that helps generate a parliamentary majority but skews the results in a disproportionate manner. So, for example, in the 2013 Italian elections, the center-left Italy Common Good coalition barely outpolled the center-right coalition (29.5 to 29.2 percent), but because of rules that award extra seats to the winner, the center-left has 54 percent of the seats in the Chamber of Deputies.

electoral threshold the minimum percentage of votes necessary to win seats in a proportional representation system; varies from country to country.

Significantly, electoral systems also vary in terms of the minimal **electoral threshold** of votes needed to gain seats in parliament. The Netherlands has the lowest, with a party needing only 0.67 percent of the vote to win a seat in parliament. Turkey has the highest, at 10 percent, which could produce a highly skewed electoral result if too many small parties fail to meet the threshold. Some countries (e.g., Spain) have a district-level, as opposed to national-level, threshold, which allows regional parties to gain representation. Most countries have a threshold somewhere in the middle, at 3 to 5 percent, which eliminates the smallest parties from gaining seats. Table 5.5 shows the electoral results for recent elections in the Netherlands, Turkey,[25] and Slovakia, the last of which has a 5 percent electoral threshold. Clearly, the electoral threshold has an impact on both the number of parties that gain entry into parliament and on the overall proportionality of the system.[26] In particular, one sees that the higher the threshold, the larger number of "wasted votes," votes cast for a party that, because it fails to meet the threshold, does not win any seats in parliament. Voters for these parties are therefore not represented in parliament.

Some countries go further with their adaptations. Germany and Hungary (and Italy from 1993–2001) have a mixed system, in which some seats are determined by plurality voting and some are determined by PR, but the overall logic of the system is such that the total number of seats are distributed proportionately. In Germany, this is known as **personalized proportional representation.** German voters get to vote twice. On one side of the ballot, as seen in the picture below, they vote for a candidate that represents a single-member electoral district, similar to how Britons vote. Half of the *Bundestag* is elected this way. On the other side of the ballot, voters choose a party, with each *Land* serving as a multi-member district for purposes of proportional representation. The percentage of votes a party receives on the second side of the ballot determines its total number of seats per *Land*, meaning the overall logic of the system tends to be in accordance with PR. For example, let's say that Christian Democrats wins 40 percent of the votes in a *Land* with forty seats. This means—keeping the math simple—it would be entitled to sixteen seats (40 x .4) from that *Land*. If it won ten seats from district-level (plurality) voting, it would receive the remaining six from its *Land* party list. If the party won fourteen seats outright in district-level voting, it would then get the remaining two from the party list. If it won all twenty seats at stake on the district side of the ballot in this *Land* (remember, half of the seats are determined by the candidate voting) outright, it would be able to claim all twenty. The result is an "overhang" of four seats, as from a purely PR standpoint it is entitled to only 16. The extra "overhang" is then simply added to the total in the *Bundestag*. In each of the recent German elections there have been several "overhang" seats, meaning that the actual number of seats occupied by MPs in the *Bundestag* is higher than the set figure of 598. After 2013 elections, for example, it was 631, and is likely to be different after future elections as the precise number of "overhang" seats changes. Lest one get bogged down in minutiae, the key point is that the overall outcome of the German system in terms of the number of seats awarded to parties looks as if it was PR. District voting, in addition to providing geographic representation, only helps determine the actual individuals who will serve in the legislature.

personalized proportional representation used in Germany, whereby half the seats are determined by votes for a candidate in a district and half the seats are determined by nation-wide proportional representation; voters therefore vote twice in each election, once for a candidate, once for a party.

There is a still more complex system, which is used in Malta and in Ireland: the **single transferable vote (STV).** Under this system, for example, Ireland is broken up into forty-two districts, and voters rank-order candidates, meaning they assign one as their first choice, one as a second choice, and so on. The votes are tallied for each candidate. If a candidate receives a certain minimum number of first-place votes (e.g., 25 percent + 1 in a four-candidate race, 20 percent + 1 in a five-candidate race), she is elected. Her "extra votes"—those she did not need to be elected—are then weighted and given to the candidates ranked second on the ballot. For example, suppose a candidate only needs 1,000 votes to be elected, but she received 1,200 votes. The second choice on those 1,200 ballots would be weighted (in this case, by a ratio of 200/1000, or .2) and distributed among the candidates. Once another candidate meets the threshold, his second-place (or, possibly, third-place) votes are also duly assigned to other candidates until all the seats in the district are filled. If no candidate wins a seat after the first count (before second choices are distributed), the candidate with the lowest number of votes is eliminated and his/her votes are transferred to other candidates in accordance with the preferences marked on the ballot. Without question, this system is quite complex.[27]

single transferable vote (STV) used in Ireland and Malta, a complex form of PR in which voters rank-order candidates, winning candidates must win a certain threshold of votes, and votes for losing candidates may be transferred to others.

TABLE 5.5 Effect of electoral thresholds on representation

Country/Party	*% votes, nationally*	*% seats in parliament*
Netherlands, 2012		
People's Party for Freedom and Democracy	26.5	27.3
Labour Party	24.7	25.3
Party for Freedom	10.1	10.0
Socialist Party	9.6	10.0
Christian Democratic Appeal	8.5	8.7
Democrats 66	8.0	8.0
Christian Union	3.1	3.3
Green Left	2.3	2.7
Reformed Political Party	2.1	2.0
50+	1.9	1.3
Party for the Animals	1.9	1.3
Slovakia, 2016		
Smer ("Direction")	28.3	32.7
Freedom and Solidarity	12.1	14.0
Ordinary People	11.0	12.7
Slovak National Party	8.6	10.0
People's Party	8.0	9.3
We Are Family	6.6	7.3
Bridge	6.5	7.3
Network	5.6	6.7
Christian Democratic Movement	4.9	0
Turkey, 2011		
Justice and Development Party	46.7	61.8
Republican Peoples' Party	20.9	20.3
Nationalist Movement Party	14.3	12.9
Democratic Party	5.4	0
Youth Party	3.0	0
"Wasted Votes"		
Netherlands	1.3	
Slovakia	13.3	
Turkey	18.1	

Source: Electoral outcomes as reported on Parties and Elections in Europe, www.parties-and-elections.eu/

alternative vote
a type of SMDP in which voters rank-order candidates, and second- and third-choices from voters of losing candidates are considered until one candidate gets a majority of votes; used in Australia but rejected by voters in Great Britain.

There are, one might also note, forms of preference voting that are compatible with plurality, single-member district voting as well. One idea is the **alternative vote** system in which voters in a district would rank order candidates. The winner would need a majority—not a plurality of votes. If no one received a majority, the lowest ranking candidate would be eliminated and the second-choice votes of those that voted for her would then be added to the totals of the other candidates. Such elimination of candidates and additional tallying of votes would continue until one candidate reached a majority. This system has been used in Australia, and in 2011 voters in Great Britain were given the choice in a referendum to adopt it. This proposal was backed by smaller parties, such as the Liberal Democrats, who argued that it would allow people to cast their "true" choice without fear of their vote being entirely

In focus

The relative merits of plurality systems vs. proportional representation

Earlier in this chapter we discussed the mechanics of different electoral systems and made only a brief reference to some of their consequences. The importance of electoral systems, as well as the relative merit of one type of system over another, are contested topics both in academic circles and in many European countries (e.g., Great Britain, Italy, Turkey) that have considered or have actually changed their electoral system in recent years.

Those favoring plurality systems make several points.[28] First, many would echo the claims of Duverger and note that plurality systems tend to produce two-party (or, more accurately, perhaps, predominantly two-party) systems, as seen in Great Britain, France (multi-party but a system with historically strong left and right blocs based on party alliances), and, beyond Europe, in Canada, Australia, and the US. Two-party systems ensure that one party will be able to form a majority, obviating any need to form a potentially messy and unstable coalition government. In addition to being cumbersome to manage, coalitions are also problematic from the standpoint of democratic theory. They are often created through a process of bargaining or "horse-trading" among political elites, behind the scenes and beyond the power of voters. In addition, coalition government may give undue influence to small parties (e.g., historically the case with the Free Democrats in Germany), who become the "kingmakers," creating or destroying government by throwing their support to one party or another. Coalitions can therefore be held captive by the interests of a small group, complicating the efforts of the government to adopt policies that may have wide support among the population.

A two-party system also makes parties compete for the "median voter," the hypothetical voter occupying the middle of the political spectrum. In other words, plurality systems encourage moderate, large, catch-all parties. In contrast, under proportional representation, more extremist parties can gain seats and, as seen with the case of the *Die Linke* (former Communist) Party in Germany in 2005, complicate the formation of a government. In France, in contrast, the two-ballot plurality system has prevented the extreme right FN from winning a large number of seats. Moreover, historically speaking, some would argue that the PR system in Weimar Germany (1919–1933) facilitated the rise of extremist politics, epitomized by the emergence of the National Socialist (Nazi) Party.

In addition, plurality systems ensure geographical representation (although PR systems can make some accommodation for this), making individual members of parliament more clearly accountable to a particular constituency. Moreover, by getting to vote for a candidate—not merely a party as with a closed list PR system—voters can weigh the particular merits of individuals (e.g., ethics, experience) and not just the party's ideology.

Advocates of PR point to several flaws with plurality systems. Under plurality systems, election results tend to be skewed, meaning the number of seats a party wins does not match the number of votes it receives. For example, in British elections in 2001 and 2005, the Labour Party won a clear majority (63 percent in 2001, 55 percent in 2005) of seats in the House of Commons, allowing Tony Blair to remain prime minister. In each case, however, the Labour Party received a minority (41 percent in 2001, 35 percent in 2005) of votes. In 2015, David Cameron became Prime Minister, when the Conservatives gained a narrow majority (50.8 percent) in parliament even though they won only 36.9 percent of the vote. On the other side, the third-place Liberal Democratic Party received 22 percent of all votes in 2005 but only 9.6 percent of the seats. A similar outcome (23 percent of the vote, 8.8 percent of the seats) befell the Liberal Democrats in 2010, and in 2015, while their vote declined to 7.9 percent, they were virtually eliminated from parliament, garnering only eight of 650 seats (1.2 percent).

The reason for this skewed outcome lies in the presence of smaller "third parties" and the winner-take-all nature of SMDP. In short, it does not matter how much an individual candidate wins by, as long as she receives more votes than other candidates. Smaller parties which do well to gain a sizeable fraction (10 to 20 percent) of the overall vote will likely place first in relatively first districts, the requirement to win the seat for that district. Adding up votes and seats across districts, the percentage of vote they receive overall will not correspond to the percentage of seats—this has been the consistent outcome for Britain's Liberal Democrats. In France, which uses a different version of plurality voting, there are also skewed results. For example, in 2012 the various left-wing parties in France received just under 40 percent of the vote in the first round of voting for the National Assembly, but, after both rounds of voting, received 57 percent of the seats. Thus, even though the majority of French voters did not, when given initial choice, vote for the left, it was able to secure a parliamentary majority.

Compare this outcome to those in Table 5.5. There is much more proportionality between votes received and seats won. The greatest proportionality is in the Netherlands, where the threshold of entering parliament is under 1 percent of the vote, meaning that even the smallest parties can win seats and few votes are "wasted" on parties that win no seats. The proportionality has often been far less in the Turkish case, in large part because of the 10 percent threshold requirement. In most PR systems, though, there is a closer correspondence between votes and seats. In the 2013 German elections, for example (see Figure 5.1), the Christian Democrats were the leading vote getters, receiving 41.5 percent of the vote. In the British case, such a result would almost assuredly produce a majority in parliament. In the German case, however, the Christian Democrats won only 49.2 percent of the seats, a far more proportional result and one that ultimately necessitated a coalition government.

For defenders of PR, this is an issue of fairness. How "fair" is it, they would assert, that a majority of voters in Britain vote against the Conservatives in 2015, but the Conservatives win a majority of seats? From their perspective, the results of elections under PR more closely resemble the actual preferences of the voters. Advocates of PR would thus claim it is more "representative," and that, unlike plurality systems, every vote counts.[29] Under a plurality system, many votes are "wasted," making no difference whatsoever to the final outcome. Moreover, because voters in two-party plurality systems have fewer meaningful choices,[30] it is alleged they are unable to vote their true convictions, settling instead for the lesser of two evils. PR, then, in short, is more representative, offers more choices, and, it is also argued, results in higher voter turnout.

What of the argument against coalitions and in favor of more moderate, two-party systems? True, sometimes coalitions are difficult to manage, but they require a more consensual form of politics, ensuring that the policies that are adopted have broad political support. Moreover, the expectation that parties will have to form coalitions with each other may lead to less adversarial politics. As for governability, the political scientist Arend Lijphart maintains that PR systems perform better in terms of economic performance and in minority and female representation. Additionally, although cabinets under PR may be less durable, the changes from government to government are less radical than under plurality systems, when one party tends to wholly displace the other.[31] As for small parties having too much power, one could say the same about factions or unelected interest groups in two-party systems. Geographic representation may sound nice in principle, but we know that parties can gerrymander districts, drawing lines in such a way that they can ensure their candidates will be elected by friendly electorates. Although this is often considered a problem in the US, there are plenty of "rotten boroughs" in Great Britain that are so overwhelmingly oriented to one party that elections are essentially meaningless.

Many of these points solicit rebuttals. Why should parliament reflect all the divisions in society? Might it be better to force the disparate elements of a country to transcend their differences and join larger, more moderate catch-all parties instead of offering separate parties for, example, Catalans or Northern Italians or women or communists or racists? True, PR may work well for prosperous Sweden or Finland, but Lijphart does not discuss Weimar Germany (1919–1933) or the failed French Fourth Republic (1946–1958), which had a PR system and high levels of political polarization and instability. As for turnout, any number of factors can account for that aside from type of electoral system (meaning correlation does not mean causation), and gerrymandering can be thwarted if the drawing of districts is left to more neutral parties (e.g., courts or non-partisan commissions).

How might one resolve these points? Obviously, one can compare cases and look and see which system is "better" on the basis of certain criteria. Another means may be to look and see who is clamoring for change, thereby revealing dissatisfaction with one system over another. France, for example, controversially switched to PR in 1986—albeit for only one election once the governing party calculated they would actually do better under the previous system, with which French voters were more accustomed. In Great Britain, the Liberal Democratic Party—not surprisingly—has made electoral reform its top issue, and in the late 1990s the Labour Party appointed a commission to make suggestions. After the Liberal Democrats formed a coalition with the Conservatives in 2010, they were able to put the idea of moving to an alternative vote system—already used to elect the mayor of London—to voters in 2011. As noted in the text, this failed, but whether it was because Britons truly like the SMDP system or because they found alternative vote too confusing is difficult to say.

However, proving perhaps that the grass is always greener on the other side, the Italians in 1993 switched from a pure PR system to a mixed system that was primarily (75 percent) based upon district voting. This was done with the goal to eliminate smaller parties and introduce some rare stability into Italian politics. Alas, neither happened, and as regional parties such as the *Lega Nord* benefited from district voting, Italian politics became arguably even more polarized. In 2006, Italy returned to a pure PR system, resulting in a nine-party coalition government. One might suggest that the problem in Italy is less PR or plurality than, simply, Italy itself.

Interestingly, most of the new democracies in Europe have adopted a PR system or, as in the case of Hungary, a mixed system. One could muster this as evidence that institutional designers in these countries concluded that PR is better or more democratic, but as increasingly authoritarian Russia abandoned a mixed system in favor of pure PR in 2005, one might make the simple observation that choice of electoral system is not the decisive factor in judging the quality of democracy. Both systems can work, and both offer a version of democracy. Echoing Ken Gladdish, one might simply argue that the advantages of one system over the other hinges upon the particular circumstances (e.g., cleavage structures, economic stability) in a given country.[32]

Critical thinking questions

1. Can you say that one type of electoral system (plurality or proportional representation) is more "democratic" than the other?
2. What are advantages to voting for a candidate instead of a party? What might be some disadvantages?

"wasted." Others found the scheme quite difficult to understand, even though, its supporters argued, the Irish successfully employed the more complex STV system, even before use of computers and electronic voting! However, this referendum failed, meaning that Great Britain still uses the first-past-the post method of voting.

Consequences of electoral systems

Does any of this matter, or is it only of academic interest? Many would argue that the choice of electoral system has great consequences. Each system has pluses and minuses and its own defenders, and further discussion on these particulars is provided in the **In focus** section. For now, however, one should understand and appreciate arguably the greatest consequence of an electoral system: its effect on the number of parties in a political system. In a famous pronouncement called **Duverger's Law**, French political scientist Maurice Duverger suggested that SMDP systems like the British tend to produce a two-party system, that PR tends to produce a multi-party system, and that France's two-ballot plurality system favors a multi-party system with two dominant blocs of parties.[33] One could add as well, which was seen above, that the lower electoral threshold in a PR system also tends to produce more parties.

Duverger's Law
idea that the type of electoral system will help determine the number of political parties.

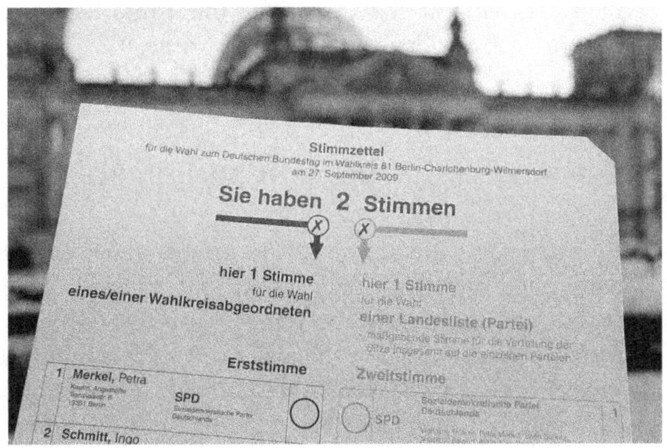

A German election ballot: Voters select both a candidate and a party

© MICHAEL GOTTSCHALK/AFP/Getty Images

One can easily see how some aspects of Duverger's Law might work. For example, in the Netherlands, even if a party wins only 2 percent of the vote, it still wins seats, and can use these seats as a basis to champion certain positions, win further support, and perhaps even serve in a coalition government. In short, under PR smaller parties survive and get some representation. They "matter" more, and individuals will vote for them feeling that a vote for them counts and is not "wasted," as arguably happens when people vote for "third parties" in SMDP systems like Great Britain (and the US). Indeed, the US represents perhaps the best-known example of Duverger's Law working in a SMDP system, as polls show that Americans would like to have more electoral choices but most realize that voting for a party besides the Democrats or Republicans is likely to be a "wasted" vote. Hence, two parties dominate.

The logic underpinning Duverger's Law may be sound, but does the evidence always support it? Malta has the purest two-party system in Europe—and uses PR-STV. Since Greece and Spain democratized in the 1970s, both countries, despite using PR, also had, more or less, a two-party system, although by the 2010s both countries had a more fractionalized, pluralistic political landscape. In contrast, whereas Great Britain has traditionally had a two-party system, the Liberal-Democrats have established a solid niche, winning parliamentary representation for more than twenty years and even winning over 20 percent of the vote in 2005 and 2010 elections. True, they won less than 10 percent of the seats—which raises a different issue of how SMDP tends to skew outcomes (see the **In focus** section)—but they have survived, even forcing creation of a coalition government in 2010, as their presence in a closely divided parliament prevented a single party from enjoying a majority. The Scottish National Party is also a major force in Britain as a "third party," but it does well because of concentrated regional support, allowing it to win many districts. Britain thus no longer has a pure two-party system. Critics have suggested that Duverger got cause and effect backwards, and that the true story is not that PR produces many parties but that a highly fractured polity, with multiple lines of division or cleavage (e.g., religion, class, ethnicity, region, nationalism) led political elites to choose a PR system that would facilitate power-sharing.[34] Indeed, when Italy adopted a more plurality-based system in 1993 (which it later abandoned), it did not appreciably reduce the number of parties. Still, rather than use the term "law," perhaps one could refer to this as a tendency, one that is supported by evidence outside of Europe.[35]

How representative are European parliaments?

In addition to knowing about electoral systems and their consequences on party systems, one might also wonder what sort of people are elected to parliament. This gets to the important question of representativeness: Do representatives reflect—literally—their constituents and/or the make-up of the country? This question can be answered in several ways by looking at the composition of European parliaments. For example, one might wonder about the representation of women, who are typically—because women live longer than men—the majority in most countries. Data on this topic are presented in Figure 5.2. As one can see, in the past two decades the relative percentage of women in European parliaments has grown, although they still remain a decided minority in most countries. Women are best represented in Scandinavian countries, Germany, the Netherlands, and Spain, where in 2016 over a third of all MPs in all of these countries were female.[36] Some countries, such as France, have tried to redress gender inequality through quota laws, requiring political parties to nominate a certain percentage of women for office. In Great Britain, the Labour Party since the 1990s has made an explicit effort to nominate more women for office, albeit for "safe" seats. The results of both efforts, as seen in Figure 5.2, are fairly sizeable in terms of progress over time. In general, studies have found that systems that use proportional representation are likely to have more female representation, whereas countries that do not, such as France, Great Britain, and the US (19.5 percent in 2016) rank among the lowest in the developed world. In Europe, the lowest percentage of female parliamentarians is found in post-communist Europe and in Turkey.

In other ways, one also finds that MPs do not accurately mirror the country in which they serve. For example, while "European" minority groups—for example, Scots in Great Britain, Catalans in Spain, Hungarians in Romania—are usually represented roughly proportionally to their numbers, other minorities (e.g., Turks in Germany, North Africans in France, Africans and South Asians in Great Britain) fare less well. For example, despite the fact perhaps as many as 5 percent of all people in France are Muslims, only one Muslim was elected in 2007 from mainland France to serve in the National Assembly. In 2012, eight foreign-born French citizens were elected, which can be seen as progress, but given that 10 percent of French are foreign-born, it is clear that the National Assembly does not reflect the ethnic

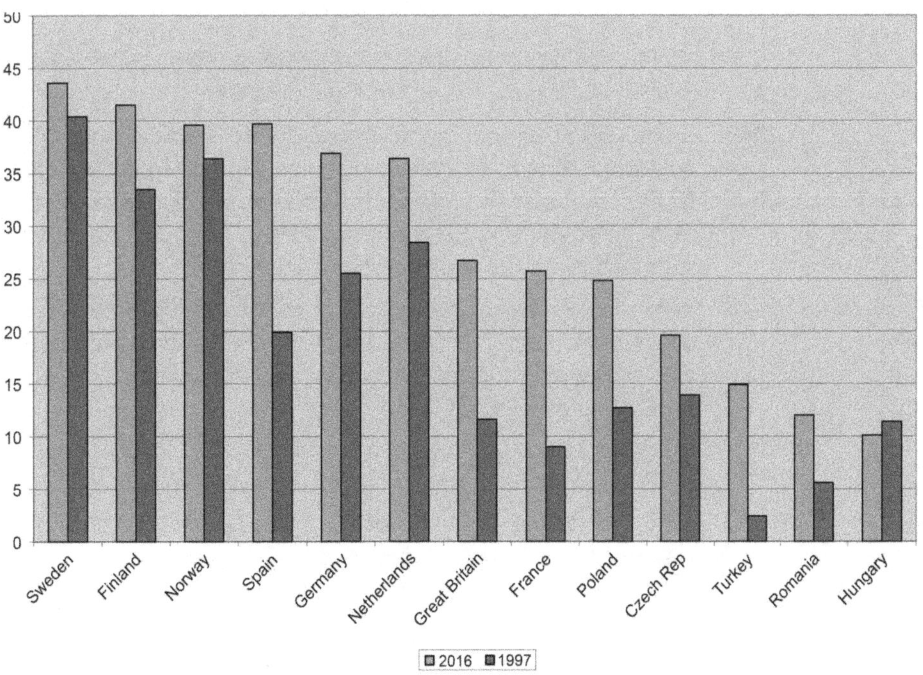

FIGURE 5.2 Percentages of female parliamentarians by country

Inter-Parliamentary Union, at www.ipu.org/wmn-e/classif.htm, accessed May 17, 2016. Data are as of April 1, 2016. Data are for both houses of parliament if the country has a bicameral system

diversity of the country. Turks and other immigrants in Germany have fared almost as poorly, although in 2008 the Green Party elected a German of Turkish heritage as one of its co-leaders. In terms of social class, most parliamentarians, as one would expect, are well-educated professionals. Lawyers, business people, and academics are typically over-represented compared to blue-collar workers, housewives, and (perhaps most obviously) the unemployed, although parties on the political left, particularly those with strong ties to trade unions, have made efforts to recruit candidates from the working class. Some countries (e.g., Romania, Serbia, Turkey), one might add, buck this pattern and have a reputation of electing a large number of "thugs" to parliament. Fistfights among legislators, for example, are sadly not uncommon events in Turkey.

Most parliaments, of course, do not witness such drama, and the more mundane, day-to-day operations of European parliaments rarely grab headlines. However, they are essential players in European democracies, representing voters, passing legislation, and, in parliamentary systems, selecting the prime minister. Maintaining the support and confidence of parliament, as illustrated in examples from Iceland and Austria, is essential for any government. We'll examine in the next chapter the different institutional arrangements for executive authority and how presidents and prime ministers interact with and, in some cases, usurp the powers of parliaments.

Application questions

1. Would you favor changing the electoral system in your country? What electoral system do you believe would function best?
2. Some believe a proportional representation electoral system can be bad because it allows "extreme" parties to gain seats in parliament. One could counter that it is important that all voices in the country, even "extreme" ones, be represented. Looking at cases in Europe or thinking of your own country, do you see this as a problem with proportional representation?
3. Why do you think women are better represented in the parliaments of Scandinavian countries than in Great Britain, France, or post-communist states? Should parties adopt "affirmative action" style policies or quotas to ensure better female representation?
4. What is meant by the idea of a "wasted vote"? How does this occur under SMDP and PR? What, if anything, can be done to eliminate this problem?
5. Why would a country have a bicameral legislature? Are there advantages/disadvantages to bicameralism?

Key terms

Additional reading

Doring, Herbert, ed. 1995. *Parliaments and Majority Rule in Western Europe*. New York: St. Martin's.

A comparative treatment of how Western European parliaments function. Unlike most works, it is organized around topical themes (e.g., relations between ministers and MPs, use of question time) than a country-by-country description.

Gallagher, Michael, and Mitchell, Paul, eds. 2006. *The Politics of Electoral Systems*. Oxford: Oxford University Press.

A survey of the design and effects of electoral systems in twenty-two countries (twelve in Europe), as well as general information on how different types of systems function.

Lijphart, Arend. 1999. *Patterns of Democracy: Government Forms and Performance in Thirty-Six Countries*. New Haven: Yale University Press.

This is a classic source that contrasts majoritarian and consociational forms of democracy. Many of the theories about why political institutions matter and how they might be better designed come from Lijphart's work.

Norris, Pippa. 2004. *Electoral Engineering: Voting Rules and Political Behavior*. Cambridge: Cambridge University Press.

This book looks at the interplay between electoral systems and political behavior, especially voting. In particular, it looks at how the choice between plurality and proportional representation systems affect the behavior of parties and voters.

O'Brennan, John, and Raunio, Tapio, eds. 2007. *National Parliaments within the Enlarged European Union*. London: Routledge.

Provides both an overview of interactions between the EU and national parliaments as well as several case studies on how individual parliaments, including those in new EU member states, work with the EU.

Notes

1 "Iceland PM Steps Aside After Protests Over Panama Papers Revelations," *The Guardian*, April 5, 2016.
2 "Iceland's Premier Resigns as Vote Strengthens Pirate Party," *The New York Times*, October 31, 2016.
3 "Austrian Chancellor Resigns Abruptly Amid Surge in Right-Wing Sentiment," *The New York Times*, May 9, 2016.
4 "Austrian Court Orders Another Presidential Vote," *The New York Times*, July 2, 2016.
5 "Austria Rejects Far Right in Test of Trump's Effect," *The New York Times*, December 5, 2016.
6 In Aristotle's time, Greek city-states practiced direct democracy, where citizens themselves made or approved many of the laws. Assemblies were chosen by lot, not competitive election. Today, because populations are larger, representative democracy—in which voters select people to represent them—is the norm, although, in some cases (e.g., use of referenda in countries such as Switzerland), one finds use of direct democracy in Europe.
7 A classic source on this question is Edmund Burke, "Speech to the Electors of Bristol" (1774), available in E.J. Payne, ed. *Select Works of Edmund Burke* (Indianapolis: Liberty Fund, 1990).
8 Briefing paper by Vaughne Miller, "EU Legislation," at www.parliament.uk/commons/lib/research/notes/snia-02888.pdf, accessed April 26, 2010.
9 For a calculation on Ireland, see http://eulaws. freetzi.com. For a report on Germany co-authored by Roman Herzog, the former German president, see "EU Threatening Parliamentary Democracy, Says Ex-German President," *EU Observer*, January 15, 2007, available at https://euobserver.com/institutional/23250. Both accessed May 26, 2016.
10 Vivian Schmidt, "European 'Federalism' and Its Encroachment on National Institutions," *Publius* 29:1, 1999, p. 25. See also John O'Brennan and Tapio Raunio, eds. *National Parliaments Within the Enlarged European Union* (London: Routledge, 2007).
11 Tapio Raunio and Simon Hix, "Backbenchers Learn to Fight Back: European Integration and Parliamentary Government," *West European Politics* 23:4, 2000, p. 142–168.
12 Summary of actions on this issue can be found in "National Parliaments and the EU," Euractiv.com, August 1, 2008, at www.euractiv.com/en/euelections/national-parliaments-eu/article-174732, accessed December 4, 2009.
13 The website for COSAC is www.cosac.eu/en/.
14 Report from http://ec.europa.eu/dgs/secretariat_general/relations/relations_other/npo/subsidiarity_en.htm#procedure.
15 See Sonia Mazery, "The European Union and Women's Rights: From the Europeanization of National Agendas to the Nationalization of a European Agenda," *Journal of European Public Policy* 5:1, 1999, p. 131–152, and Francesco Duina and Michael Oliver, "National Parliaments in the European Union: Are There Any Benefits to Integration?" *European Law Journal* 11:2, March 2005, p. 173–195.
16 Duina and Oliver, "National Parliaments," p. 176.
17 Michael Mezey, *Comparative Legislatures* (Durham NC: Duke University Press, 1979), p. 36.
18 Great Britain does possess other parties, and in 2010 the Liberal Democrats garnered enough seats to compel creation of a coalition government. This, however, was an exceptional development, and in 2015 Britain returned to single-party government.
19 This terminology comes from Arend Lijphart, *Democracies: Patterns of Majoritarian and Consensus Government in Twenty-One Countries* (New Haven, CT: Yale University Press, 1984).
20 "Set Angela Free," *The Economist*, September 19, 2009.
21 "Italian Voters Have Rejected Mateo Renzi's Constitutional Reforms," *The Economist*, December 5, 2016.
22 Or, more accurately, at least 598, as peculiarities of the German election law allow for additional members of parliament to be elected and seated in the *Bundestag*.

23 In practice, this is rarely achieved. For example, in Great Britain most districts include about 70,000 voters, but figures range from over 100,000 on the Isle of Wight to several districts with under 50,000 in Wales and Scotland. See data from www.parliament.uk/about/how/elections-and-voting/constituencies/.

24 In 2006 in the Netherlands, one candidate—supported by Turkish immigrants—moved up on the party list thanks to individual votes and won election to parliament.

25 In 2015 elections, four parties crossed the threshold, and the percentage of votes for other parties was under five percent. This older election is included here both for illustrative purposes and because it represents "the norm" prior to the 2015 elections.

26 Proportionality is also determined by the mathematical formula used to determine winners of seats (e.g., the d'Hondt method versus Sanite-Lague). These issues are rather technical. For more details on proportional representation systems, see David Farrell, *Electoral Systems: A Comparative Introduction* (New York: Palgrave, 2001), and Michael Gallagher and Paul Mitchell, eds. *The Politics of Electoral Systems* (Oxford: Oxford University Press, 2006).

27 Details as well as arguments for and against can be found in Gallagher and Mitchell, *The Politics of Electoral Systems*, Chapter 25.

28 This discussion borrows heavily from the contributions of Arend Lijphart—a well-known defender of proportional representation—as well as Guy Lardeyret and Quentin Quade in Larry Diamond and Marc Plattner, eds. *Electoral Systems and Democracy* (Baltimore: Johns Hopkins University Press, 2006).

29 Shocking as it might be to some, not *every* vote counts in a plurality system. Consider, for example, an election in which Candidate A, two hours before the polls close, has already won more than 50 percent of the votes from all eligible voters in a district. True, no one knows the results until the votes are tallied, but in this case the votes of all who vote in the last two hours of voting, after A has already "won," have no effect on the outcome. Put another way, why should a Labour voter turn out to vote in a "safe" Conservative district if she is certain the Conservative candidate will win? In contrast, under PR, hypothetically at least one extra vote could make a difference in terms of the proportional distribution of seats. There are fewer "wasted" votes.

30 Tiny parties, such as the British Monster Raving Loony Party, which, among other things, advocates a 99 pence coin to save on change, may appear on the ballot, but everyone knows they have no chance of winning. Candidates from this party—really—actually received 6,311 votes in the 2005 elections. In order to cast a vote that "matters," voters may be compelled to vote for a party that is not their first or second choice.

31 Lijphart, "Constitutional Choice for New Democracies," in Diamond and Plattner, *Electoral Systems.*

32 Ken Gladdish, "The Primacy of the Particular," in Diamond and Plattner, *Electoral Systems.*

33 Maurice Duverger, *Political Parties: Their Organization and Activity in the Modern State* (London: Methuen, 1954).

34 Stein Rokkan, *Citizens, Elections, Parties* (Oslo: Universitetsforlaget, 1970), p. 147–168, and Lijphart, *Democracies.*

35 Canada and India, which use SMDP, have more than two parties, but this is largely a consequence of religious, linguistic, and/or ethnic diversity. The US and Australia remain two-party systems, although they use different types of plurality systems.

36 Data from Inter-Parliamentary Union, available at www.ipu.org/wmn-e/classif.htm, accessed on September 22, 2009.

Turkish President Recep T. Erdoğan has forcefully argued for expanded executive power

Chapter 6

Executive authority in Europe

Recep Tayyip Erdoğan has dominated Turkish politics in the first two decades of the twenty-first century. He led the Justice and Development Party (JDP) to election victories in 2002, 2007, and 2011, and he served as prime minister from 2003 to 2014. He was forced to surrender this post not because of an electoral defeat, but because of internal JDP term limit rules. Rather than retire from politics, however, Erdoğan sought a nominal promotion, running for the Turkish presidency in 2014 in the first popular elections for this office. He duly won, becoming head of state. However, the powers of the Turkish president are relatively limited. Erdoğan therefore lobbied for constitutional changes to create a stronger presidency, one that, in his reckoning, would allow for more efficient exercise of power and confirm the *de facto* reality that even lacking formal power, he remained the country's true political executive. Critics charged that his plans for "*à la Turca* presidentialism" would erode checks and balances and weaken Turkish democracy.[1] While his party failed to gain enough seats in 2015 elections to change the constitution unilaterally, in January 2017 the JDP garnered the support of small nationalist party and pushed through changes creating a presidential system in Turkey. This change, however, will need to be approved in a referendum in April 2017.[2]

Debates over executive actions and power are not unique to Turkey. The three tenures of Italian Prime Minister Silvio Berlusconi (1994–1995, 2001–2006, and 2008–2011) were marked by multiple scandals and disputes among the prime minister, president, and the courts. Many saw Berlusconi's growing power and weak commitment to the rule of law as a major threat to Italian democracy. In Romania, President Traian Băsescu was twice impeached by parliament (in 2007 and in 2012), a manifestation of a long-running power struggle between him and the legislature. Băsescu called these efforts a "putsch" and both times was re-instated to the presidency after a popular referendum failed to garner enough votes to confirm his removal.[3] In 2009, Czech President Václav Klaus, who was named to his post by parliament, not Czech voters, created controversy by asserting his right to refuse to ratify the EU's Lisbon Treaty (he ultimately signed it after securing some opt-outs for Czechs).[4] In 2015, Portuguese President Anibal Cavaco Silva, who was formally empowered to grant elected representatives the opportunity to form a government, refused to offer a coalition of left-wing parties in a chance to form a new government, even though they won over 50 percent of the popular vote and possessed a majority in parliament. Critics accused him of abusing his powers and suggested that Portugal should make constitutional changes to its semi-presidential system, although in contrast to Erdoğan's aim in Turkey, the objective would be to weaken the power of the presidency.[5]

This chapter examines the role and power of the executive branch in governments throughout contemporary Europe. Because many countries have a parliamentary system of governance, in which parliamentary and executive authority are linked together, this chapter builds upon the previous one. However, one can, at least for analytical purposes, separate the parliament or the legislature from the executive branch of government, which can be defined as the one responsible for implementing or administering the law. Executive authorities in Europe, however, often do much more than that, and, as suggested in Chapter 5, some believe that in terms of actual exercise of political power, executives have eclipsed parliaments; in this respect developments in Turkey may reflect a broader pattern. In all cases, however, individual chief executives, acting as heads of state and/or heads of government, hold important powers. They are responsible for representing their country overseas, for crafting legislation and setting the legislative agenda, and for shepherding their proposals through parliaments. They oversee vast bureaucracies. Some can issue executive orders with the force of law. They represent their country at the EU level. Typically, they are leaders of a political party. Chief executives are also often better able than parliaments to rally public opinion one way or another, and in some states they can call referenda to have the public vote on a favored proposal.

Because European states are democratic, the top executive authority with real, effective political power—the president, prime minister, or chancellor—is elected (directly or indirectly) and is accountable to voters. As with parliaments, however, the nature of executive authority varies from country to country. This chapter highlights the main patterns of how executive authority is organized and how it functions in various settings in contemporary Europe.

Head of state vs. head of government

head of state
individual that is the chief public representative or symbol of the state; can be elected or unelected.

One distinction that can be made among executive authorities is the difference between the roles of head of state and head of government. **Head of state** refers to the individual who serves as the chief public representative of the state, including representing the state abroad. This role suggests that this individual comes to personify the state and assume the mantle of the state's legitimacy. Charles de Gaulle, former French president and architect of France's current constitutional order, stated that a head of state, as he envisaged it for France, would embody the spirit of the nation. The head of state can thus be understood as a living symbol, and in this role he or she is removed from and placed above day-to-day political squabbles. In sum, the office of head of state, although it may be granted various political duties, can be thought of mainly as a symbolic or affective power that is designed to unite all the people of the country.

The **head of government**, in contrast, is the individual who is responsible for running the machinery of government. He or she is empowered to direct the activities of the government (administering laws, proposing legislation, appointing officials) and typically oversees a **cabinet** composed of government ministers who in turn oversee various departments or ministries (e.g., foreign affairs, defense, transportation, the environment). The head of government does not, as a head of state would, represent the country primarily in a symbolic fashion. Rather, he or she exercises real political authority. However, the head of government is also an expressly *political* figure, and is often involved in partisan policy debates.

head of government
individual who holds executive authority in the government and is responsible for running the government; this post is elected in European states.

In some countries, particularly those with a presidential system of government, such as the United States, these two positions are embodied in a single person. However, because most European countries do not have a presidential system, these two offices, head of state and head of government, are often separated. In parliamentary systems—discussed more below—there is often a largely symbolic executive head of state. In eight European states[6]—Great Britain, the Netherlands, Sweden, Norway, Spain, Denmark, Luxembourg, and Belgium—this takes the form of a monarch (king or queen). These states are **constitutional monarchies,** meaning that the monarch, although often powerful in the past, is constrained by significant constitutional limits on his or her authority. These figures usually serve symbolic or ceremonial roles, at times with great fanfare (e.g., as with the royal family in Great Britain) but sometimes in a more low-key manner (e.g., as in the Netherlands, Sweden, and Norway). At times, monarchs exercise *de jure* political power—meaning that they are given formal, legal power to oversee the operation of government, approve laws, and appoint government officials—but *de facto*—in actuality—they are merely signing off on decisions taken by the elected officials who exercise real political power. For example, the Dutch monarch is formally responsible for naming the country's prime minister, but the king or queen of the Netherlands could not impose his or her own selection as prime minister on an unwilling parliament. Typically, any formal powers given to a monarch are delegated to an elected head of government. In contemporary Europe, any monarch who attempted to overrule or even influence democratic institutions in order to exercise real political authority would rapidly lose much of his or her public standing. A curious episode occurred in Belgium in 1990, when the king, a practicing Catholic, refused to sign a law that would permit abortion. In response, the parliament temporarily suspended the king, promulgated the law, then reinstated him.

cabinet
collection of ministers who oversee departments of the government.

constitutional monarchy
form of government in which a monarch serves as head of state but his or her power is severely limited, with real political authority vested in an elected head of government.

In several parliamentary republics (e.g., Germany, Italy, Austria, Hungary) where sovereignty is formally vested in the people as opposed to in a monarch, there is a largely symbolic president who serves a similar role as head of state. Whether elected directly by voters (as in Austria) or by some type of electoral college involving parliamentary and/or regional authorities (as in Germany, Hungary, and Italy), this individual largely fulfills ceremonial roles (e.g., recognizing and receiving ambassadors, formally opening parliament). Some of these figures possess, at least formally, wide powers. For example, the Austrian president is empowered to appoint cabinet ministers, judges, and military officers and can dismiss parliament. Like European monarchs, however, the Austrian president is constrained by traditions not to interfere in political decision-making. He or she in effect rubberstamps decisions made by the chancellor or parliament. Similarly, in Italy, the president has a variety of powers, including nominating judges to the Supreme Court, calling referenda, declaring a state of war, and issuing decrees with the force of law. Any act of the president, however, must be countersigned by a minister from the government, meaning that the Italian president's political autonomy is limited.

These symbolic presidents are thus largely figureheads, nothing like the American or Russian or (as we'll see below) the French president in terms of actual political power. They are supposed to represent national unity rather than a particular political party or ideology. At times, however, these leaders can play important mediating roles in the political life of their country. For example, the president of Italy was called upon in early 2007 to broker talks among factions within parliament to hobble together a continuation of its coalition government. For the most part, however, such symbolic figures are rarely politically relevant. Thus, when we discuss executive authority in states such as these, we are talking about politically empowered actors (heads of government), not the affective, symbolic ones (heads of state).

Several countries (France, Portugal, Finland, Romania, Turkey) have semi-presidential systems, which feature a popularly elected president who serves as head of state and shares executive authority with a prime minister, who serves as head of government. This "hybrid" type of system is more complex than a pure presidential or parliamentary system, and, as suggested at the outset, can lead to political struggles. The precise division of powers between the two offices vary from country to country, with the French president ranking as the most powerful. How this type of system functions is discussed later in this chapter.

Organization of executive authority

The exact form of executive authority will not be the same from country to country. Some items that vary include length of term of office for chief executives, how they are elected, their precise constitutional powers, and the size and effectiveness of the bureaucracy that administers the law. More relevant in terms of categorizing types of executive authority is how executive authority relates to parliamentary bodies. Thinking about pure, ideal types with respect to the last factor, one can envision a system in which executive and parliamentary power are linked or fused together, one in which they are separated, and one that combines these types, with one executive separate from parliament and one connected to it in some fashion. These are, respectively, a parliamentary system, a presidential system, and a semi-presidential system.

Parliamentary systems

parliamentary system
form of government in which the executive authority (the prime minister) is chosen by the parliament, not directly by voters.

As noted in the previous chapter, most European democracies have parliamentary forms of governance, with executive power vested in the prime minister (or chancellor in Germany and Austria) and his or her cabinet. The essence of the **parliamentary system** of government is that the prime minister is chosen by the parliament (not the voters), and he or she is, typically, a member of the legislative body.[7] The executive and the parliamentary bodies are thus said to be fused together. The prime minister typically nominates members of the cabinet and runs the government, but he or she remains directly accountable to the legislature, which not only voted him/her into office but retains the power to oust the prime minister

vote of no confidence
procedure by which a parliament can remove the executive authority from office.

at any time by a **vote of no confidence.** In this way, although there are clear lines of accountability, there is no separation of powers as understood in a presidential system (see below), and election cycles can also be less predictable than in a presidential system with a fixed term of office where it is impossible, save for impeachment, to remove the chief executive from office. Table 6.1 lists key differences between a parliamentary system and a presidential system, the later of which is found in the United States and in much of Latin America, but is, as we shall see, very rare in Europe.

In states with bicameral legislatures, the prime minister is selected by the "lower house"—for example, the House of Commons in Great Britain, the *Bundestag* in Germany, the *Seim* in Poland. If one party has a majority in the legislature, then the leader of that party is typically selected to be prime minister, and he or she then names cabinet ministers, who frequently are members of parliament from the same party of the prime minister. Such has been the norm in Great Britain, which, because of its plurality electoral system (see Chapter 5), typically gives one party a majority in parliament. Such was the case in the 2015 elections (see Table 6.2), which allowed David Cameron of the Conservative Party to be Prime Minister and appoint members of his party to the cabinet. Together, the prime minister and cabinet—in effect the executive branch but more commonly referred to in parliamentary system as simply "the government"—are then charged with presenting proposals to the parliament and ensuring that laws passed by the legislature are duly implemented. Single party governments, as of 2016, also prevailed in Poland (see Table 6.2), Turkey, and Hungary.

TABLE 6.1 Features of parliamentary and presidential systems

Features	*Parliamentary systems*	*Presidential systems*
Head of government	Prime minister, selected by legislature	President, elected by voters
Head of state	Separate individual; largely symbolic office	President; both roles are fused together
Head of gov't part of legislature?	Yes, in most cases	No
Can legislature remove head of gov't?	Yes	No (except for impeachment)
Can head of gov't dissolve the legislature?	Yes	No
Separation of powers?	No—"fused government"	Yes
Set term of office?	No	Yes
Divided go'vt possible?	No	Yes
Can executive be a coalition?	Yes—cabinet positions can be divided among parties	No—president is sole executive body
Examples	Great Britain, Italy, Germany, Netherlands, Sweden, Hungary, Estonia	Cyprus (pure presidential); France, Poland, Portugal, and Romania are semi-presidential

Because most European countries have multi-party (three or more significant parties) systems—in large part due to the proportional representation electoral system, discussed in the previous chapter—it is difficult for one party to win a majority in the parliament. Most European countries therefore are ruled by a coalition of parties, meaning that a group of two or more parties within the parliament form an alliance for the purpose of constituting a majority and selecting a prime minister and cabinet, whose members will come from the coalition partners. Typically, the formation of a coalition is subject to negotiation, both in terms of the individuals who will serve in the government positions and in terms of the policy priorities to be pursued by the government. Because the coalition should be based on some sort of common political ground, they are often based upon ideological affinity, meaning parties that share similar outlooks join together and elect the leader of one of the parties (typically the larger or largest party) as the prime minister. For example, as seen in Table 6.2, as of 2016 Finland and Germany had coalition governments: Finland's government is fundamentally right-wing in orientation, combining three parties that ideologically range from centrist to far-right. Parties on the left serve in the opposition. Usually coalitions contain only the necessary number of parties to obtain a majority; there is no need to add an "extra" party to the coalition, as this would only make governing more difficult. In the Finnish case, the Christian Democrats, a small party on the right, were thus excluded from the government, as its small number of parliamentary mandates made its inclusion unnecessary.

Note that it does not have to be the case that the largest party becomes the leading party in government. In 2015 parliamentary elections in Portugal, for example, the center-right Social Democratic Party (yes, the name is deceiving!) won the largest number of seats (eighty-nine), but, together with the other right-wing party, the People's Party, it lacked a parliamentary majority, claiming between the two of them only 107 of the 230 seats. Three left-wing parties, led by the Socialist Party (eighty-six seats) did possess a majority (122 of 230), and, after some controversy over whether they would be asked to form a government (noted above), these three parties formed a government, with Antonio Costa, leader of the Socialist Party, becoming prime minister.

At times, when other possibilities do not exist, one may see the formation of a "grand coalition," an alliance of the two largest parties, usually on opposite sides of the political spectrum, that will command the overwhelming majority of votes in parliament. In recent years, Germany has been the best example of this phenomenon. In 2005, because no one would form a coalition with the pariah Left (*Die Linke*) Party, and neither of the smaller parties on the left (Greens) or the center-right (Free Democrats) would join in a coalition with parties on the other side of the spectrum, there was no "natural" center-left or center-right majority. After protracted negotiations, the Christian Democrats and the Social Democrats agreed on a grand coalition. In 2009, after new elections, the Christian Democrats were able to form a government with the Free Democrats, their traditional partner, but, as seen in Table 6.2, this arrangement ended in 2013, when the Free Democrats failed to enter parliament. While the Christian Democrats came close to an outright majority of seats (311 of 631), they needed a coalition partner, and, unwilling to work with the Left Party or the Greens, they again formed a grand coalition with the Social Democrats, with Christian Democratic leader Angela Merkel remaining chancellor.

TABLE 6.2 Governing parties in various European countries

	Great Britain (2015)	*Poland (2015)*	*Finland (2015)*	*Germany (2013)*	*Sweden (2014)*
Party/Orientation/Seats*	**Conservatives (center-right) 331** Labour (center-left) 232 Scottish Nationalist (regional) 56 Liberal Democratic (liberal) 8 Other 23	**Law and Justice (right) 235** Civic Platform (liberal) 138 Kukiz '15 (far right) 42 Nowoczena (liberal) 28 Polish People's Party (agrarianism) 16	**Centre Party (center-liberal) 49** **Finns (far-right) 38** **National Coalition Party (center-right) 37** Social Democrats (center-left) 34 Greens (center-left) 15 Left Alliance (left) 12 Swedish People's Party (minority) 9 Christian Democrats (center-right) 5	**Christian Democrats (center-right) 311** **Social Democrats (center-left) 193** The Left Party (far-left) 64 Greens (left) 63	**Social Democrats (center-left) 113** Moderate Party (center-right) 84 Swedish Democrats (far-right) 49 **Greens (center-left) 25** Centre Party (liberal) 22 ^Left Party (Left) 21 ^Liberal People's Party (left) 19 Christian Democrats (center-right) 16
Total Seats	650	460	200	631	349
Prime Minister or Chancellor	David Cameron (Conservative)	Beata Szydlo (LJ) (Moderate)	Juha Sipila (Centre)	Angela Merkel (CD)	Stefan Lofven (SD)

*Seats are in the parliamentary body that chooses the prime minister. Governing parties are in bold. Smaller parties and independents are not listed. ^Party offers support to minority government.

Source: Parties and Elections in Europe (www.parties-and-elections.eu, accessed on February 20, 2016)

minority government
a government that relies upon the permanent support of only a minority of members of parliament but that can survive with case-by-case support from other parties.

It is possible that a **minority government**, one that does not possess a majority of votes in the legislature, can form if the majority in the legislature does not actively oppose it. For example, in post World War II Sweden and Denmark, most governments have been minority governments, with the Social Democratic Party in both states often able to pass measures thanks to *ad hoc* deals with centrists or far-left parties, with these parties preferring to eschew the formal creation of a coalition government. As seen in Table 6.2, this situation once again prevailed in Sweden after 2014 elections, as the Social Democrats formed a formal coalition with the Greens (both of which have positions in the cabinet) but rely on the support of other small, left-oriented parties to pass legislation. The situation in Denmark after 2015 elections is perhaps even more complicated. There, Denmark's Liberal Party (Venstre) is the sole governing party, even though it is the third largest in parliament and commands only thirty-seven of the 179 seats in the Danish Folketing. It governs, however, with the support of center-right and far-right parties, which together possess a majority but, for a number of reasons (including controversy that would ensue by inviting the far-right Danish People's Party formally into government), prefer to grant Venstre a monopoly of cabinet positions. In April 2016, Ireland also formed a minority government, after elections failed to produce a parliamentary majority, three attempts in the Dáil (parliament) to elect a taosieach (prime minister) failed, and there was too much enmity between the two leading parties for a grand coalition. Under the "political ceasefire," the center-left Fianna Fáil party allowed the center-right Fine Gael party to govern with the support of independent MPs while it formally remained in the opposition.[8] One can imagine that this is a delicate arrangement. For this reason, minority governments, because they are not based on a formal coalition, are often more unstable compared to those with clear majority support.

Note that prime ministers or chancellors do not "run" for office in the same way that the American, Russian, or French presidents do. They are not elected directly by the country's voters. Typically, they are the head of a party, elected to parliament either from a party-list or, as in the British case, from a particular district. Most European voters thus do not vote for their chief executive. They vote for his or her party or for another representative from that party. Ideally, however, voters know that their votes will contribute to the possibility of the leader of a party to become prime minister. The central point, though, is that voters, in parliamentary systems, do not directly elect the executive. If voters want to change the chief executive in a parliamentary system, they must do so by voting in legislative elections.

In between elections, however, the prime minister remains accountable to the legislature, and his/her position depends upon maintaining parliamentary support. Just as prime ministers are selected by the legislature (or, more accurately, typically by those parties within the legislature that command a majority of seats), they can also be removed by a vote of no confidence, meaning that a majority in the legislature votes, in essence, to "fire" the prime minister. This vote can either be an explicit one on the future tenure of the prime minister or on a matter of such importance that, should the prime minister lose, he or she would feel it impossible to continue serving and would thus resign. In practice, this means prime ministers, despite all of their authority, can be ousted from office if only a few members of parliament decide to vote against them. For example, looking at Table 6.2, one can see that if either the National Coalition Party or the Finns (formerly True Finns) Party were to withdraw its support from the government led by the Centre Party, the Finnish government would lose majority support. If this occurred, either a new coalition would have to form to assume governance (potentially a minority government) or there would be new elections to produce a new parliament. While Finnish political leaders may not wish to risk such an outcome, this can occur. For example, in 2010, in the midst of Ireland's economic crisis, the small Green Party defected from the ruling coalition, causing the government to fall and necessitating new elections. Similarly, in 2010 in Belgium and in 2011 in Slovenia, governments collapsed because coalition partners withdrew their support. After trying unsuccessfully to form a new coalition with different parties, the governments in all these countries called for new elections, hoping that a new parliament would produce a more workable government, although, as noted in the previous chapter, it took nearly a year for parties in Belgium to form a government after the elections. As seen in Figure 6.1, across the multi-party parliamentary systems in Europe, where coalition governments are frequently the

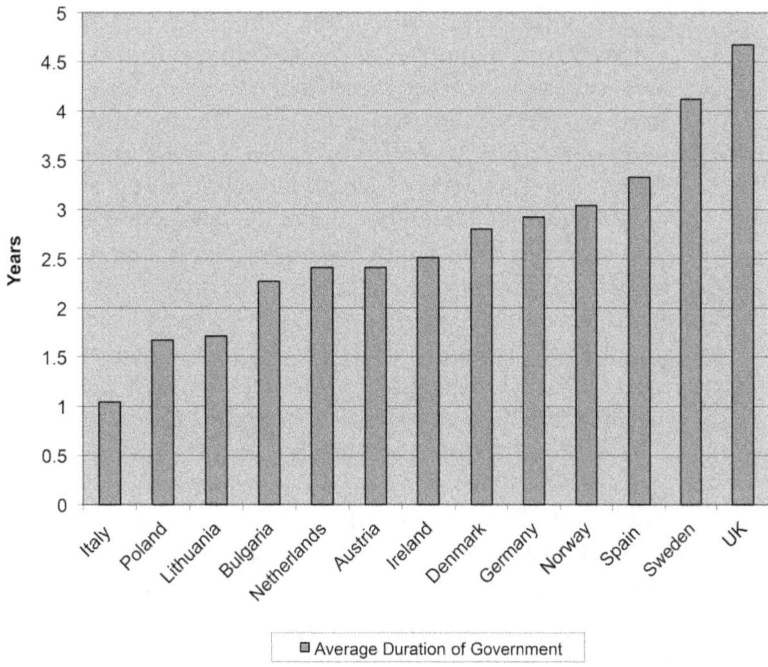

FIGURE 6.1 Average duration of parliamentary governments

Author's calculations. Years are 1945–2015, except for Ireland (1937–2015), Poland (1990–2015), Bulgaria (1990–2015), and Lithuania (1991–2015)

norm, the average duration of governments varies considerably, with some countries (e.g., Poland and Italy) prone to more fragile coalitions than those in Scandinavia, where governments frequently manage to serve their entire term of office. In Germany, government longevity is enhanced by a provision that requires the *Bundestag* to pass a constructive vote of no confidence, meaning that a majority must not only reject the chancellor but also vote in favor of an alternative candidate.

In Great Britain, single-party governments have been the norm, and, as seen in Figure 6.1, British governments tend to be among the most stable in Europe. However, governments can, potentially at any rate, fall in countries with parliamentary systems in which only one party serves in government. For example, in the 2000s, both Prime Ministers Tony Blair and Gordon Brown in Great Britain faced opposition on important questions (e.g., the Iraq War, education reform, economic policy) from members of their own Labour Party, who threatened at times to vote against the prime minister and potentially necessitate new elections. In 2016, Prime Minister David Cameron did resign, but this was the result not of a parliamentary vote of no confidence but of the rebuke handed to him by British voters, who opted for "Brexit." In 2011, the ongoing economic crisis in Greece put great pressure on the single-party government of the Pan-Hellenic Socialist Movement. Although it narrowly survived a vote of no confidence in November of that year, its leader agreed to resign to allow formation of a broader national unity government, akin to a grand coalition, which some hoped would be better able to weather the storm and enact EU-mandated reforms.

Typically, if a prime minister is removed by a vote of no confidence, the legislature either selects another individual—from the same party or from another party—

to serve as prime minister or the country holds new elections. If a prime minister resigns either voluntarily—as David Cameron did in Great Britain in 2016—or under pressure—as Sigmundur David Gunnlaugsson of Iceland did in the same year—new elections are not necessary; the parliament—in practice the majority party or coalition—has the prerogative to select a new person as prime minister to finish out the government's term of office. In addition, in a parliamentary system the prime minister can, at his or her discretion, dissolve the legislature and call for new elections. This is an important power, as the prime minister can time an election at the height of his or her popularity in order to gain a fresh term of office. Thus, election cycles are irregular, as new elections can be held at any time, although each state has a maximum term (typically four or five years) after which new elections must be held. Provided that the prime minister's party wins elections—"winning" meaning that the party gains a majority of seats or can organize a coalition to form a government—the prime minister can stay in office for multiple terms.

Because the chief executive is responsible to the legislature (not directly to voters) and is typically a member of the legislature, the executive and legislative branches are in effect fused together. The composition of the executive—either a single-party executive or a coalition—reflects the will of the majority in the legislature, making divided government, in which one party controls the executive and one the legislature, impossible. Thus, in parliamentary systems, it is usually easier for the government to pass its proposals through the legislature, although managing coalitions, minority governments, or bicameralism can at times be complicated because the prime minister will be less certain that he or she will command a majority of votes at all times. For example, many in the German government in 2010 wanted to make substantial reforms in health care, but this was problematic, given disputes among the coalition partners, interest associations, and the federal and regional governments.[9] In the 2010s, Greece has experienced instability with governments serving short terms of office because of the difficulty of accepting painful austerity measures.

In most parliamentary systems, the initiative to propose legislation is assumed by the government, with relevant cabinet ministers (and, at times, the prime minister) appearing before the legislature for question time, during which they can be grilled by members of the opposition. Although question time provides some form of accountability, it is often entertaining to watch (in the British case during heated sessions insults are hurled across the political aisle), and requires government ministers to be able to speak extemporaneously and defend their policies in a rough-and-tumble forum, the outcome of the final vote is usually known in advance.

Although parliamentary systems are structured similarly, the actual power wielded by prime ministers varies. The British prime minister, for example, tends to be very powerful. Because Great Britain has—more or less—a two-party system, the prime minister, in most cases (a coalition government between the Conservatives and Liberal Democrats from 2010–2015 being the most recent exception), can count on a majority in the House of Commons. Party discipline is also high, meaning that members of his or her party will usually cast their votes as they are instructed. The upper house of parliament, the House of Lords, if it wants to stop a measure proposed by the prime minister, can only delay adoption of legislation passed by the House of Commons. Lastly, there is no judicial review to overturn any act of parliament. Parliament can do, in a strictly legal sense, whatever it wants, which gives the party that controls the House of Commons virtually a political blank check.

For some, this may amount to little more than "elected dictatorship," but in practice the prime minister is constrained by what is politically acceptable to his own cabinet, the majority of his party, and, ultimately, the British public. For example, in the early 2000s Prime Minister Tony Blair on numerous occasions expressed some support for Britain joining the euro. However, powerful figures in his own cabinet opposed this. Blair thus did not push the issue, either in parliament or in a referendum among the larger public. In 2013, David Cameron, recognizing the divisiveness of Britain's EU membership within his own party, agreed to hold a referendum on Britain's continued EU membership. He calculated that this would give Britain some leverage to negotiate a better deal with the EU and that the proposal to leave the EU—"Brexit"—would be defeated, allowing him to silence the more Euroskeptic voices among the Conservatives. In the end, of course, Britons opted for Brexit, compelling Cameron to resign and creating great uncertainty both within Britain and the EU as a whole.

In contrast, the Italian prime minister has traditionally been far weaker. Italy has several parties represented in parliament, and the typical Italian prime minister has had to manage a coalition of several parties. Finding common ground to get agreement on many policies is difficult. If the prime minister cannot maintain the support of his or her coalition partners, he or she risks losing office. In addition, the Senate has co-equal legislative powers with the Chamber of Deputies, meaning that even if the prime minister and the government get a bill through the Chamber of Deputies, they may encounter opposition in the Senate. Lastly, there is a Constitutional Court, to which the opposition may appeal, claiming that proposals violate the constitution.

Thus, even though the two countries both have parliamentary systems, they function quite differently. The consequences are clear for all to see: Great Britain generally has had stable, powerful, durable governments, whereas governments in Italy have been politically weak and fragile. Italy went through fifty-six governments in fifty-six years between 1945 and 2001. Silvio Berlusconi, the richest man in Italy and the melodramatic, arguably megalomaniac leader of the *Forza Italia* (Go Italy) party, was the first Italian prime minister to serve a full term of office (2001–2006) in fifty years. Italy's problems are sometimes trotted out by those who would argue that parliamentary systems are too unstable. After all, they might say, the government in a parliamentary system can be voted out at any time, and this can be chaotic—look at Italy! However, Italian politics suffers from a number of problems: a high degree of political polarization, the fact that some parties (e.g., the traditionally large Communist Party) have been treated as pariahs by other parties (thereby constraining possibilities for coalition governments), and a proportional electoral system that encouraged the proliferation of small parties. Changes in the electoral law in 1993 to reduce the number of seats decided by proportional representation, however, did not appreciably reduce the number of parties, and Italian politics today remains far more unstable than, for example, British politics. For example, Tony Blair, after serving as prime minister for ten years, managed to hand power over to Gordon Brown in 2007 without much difficulty, and in 2010 the Conservative Party leader David Cameron led a coalition government with the Liberal Democrats that honored its pledge to serve a full five terms until the next election. After securing a majority in 2015 elections, Cameron did resign in 2016, but this was not because of jockeying among political parties in Parliament. Rather, the British vote for "Brexit" was a rebuke to his preference for Britain to remain in the EU; after the referendum, Cameron's position was untenable, and the Conservatives selected Theresa May, who had served as Home Secretary in Cameron's cabinet, as the new prime minister.

Consider the contrasts with Italy. In February 2007, Prime Minister Romano Prodi, leader of an unwieldy nine-party center-left coalition, tendered his resignation, less than a year after his razor-thin victory over the center-right government of Silvio Berlusconi, who had changed the electoral law again in a misplaced hope that such a change would contribute to his victory. Prodi was reinstated by parliament the following week (the various parties could not agree on a replacement), but a year later, in February 2008, after a small party in the Senate withdrew support from the coalition, Prodi narrowly lost a vote of confidence in the Senate and was forced to resign. Italy held new elections, and Berlusconi, whose popularity had increased since his 2006 defeat, became prime minister (for a third time) in another center-right coalition government. However, in November 2011 Berlusconi resigned after he lost his parliamentary majority due to various scandals as well as chronic economic difficulties. From 2011–2016, Italy has had three prime ministers, two of which headed "technocratic" governments charged with adopting difficult economic measures to pull Italy out of crisis.

In addition to managing the government, prime ministers or chancellors also have other duties. Although they are not nominally head of state, in practice they represent the country in international affairs and make important decisions with respect to foreign policy. The prime minister, in most cases, is also the head of a political party, giving him or her discretion in managing the affairs of that party, including how to assign members of his or her party to cabinet positions.

Varieties of presidentialism in Europe

Although most governments in Europe are parliamentary and thus headed by prime ministers or chancellors, many countries also have presidents, although many of these, as noted above, tend to have only symbolic powers. While they do serve as head of state, most European presidents (with a few exceptions) co-exist with more powerful prime ministers. In general terms, one can identify three different types of presidentialism in Europe, and some features of all European countries with presidents is presented in Table 6.3.

Pure presidentialism

presidential system form of government in which executive authority is vested in an individual who is typically elected by voters separately from the parliament.

When most people speak of a **presidential system**, they would be referring to a "pure" presidential system are like those found in the US and in much of Latin America, in which a directly elected president[10] is the undisputed head of the executive branch, not sharing power with a prime minister and serving as both head of state and head of government. Presidential power is entirely separated from the legislature, meaning that the two branches have distinct powers, are elected separately, and a person cannot simultaneously serve as president and in the legislature. Usually, there is a system of checks and balances (e.g., presidential veto, right of the legislature to approve presidential appointments) that, in theory at least,

TABLE 6.3 Forms of presidentialism in Europe

Country	*Who elects?*	*Substantial powers?*	*Prime minister?*	*Type of presidentialism*
Cyprus	Voters	Yes	No	Pure presidentialism
France	Voters	Yes	Yes	Semi-presidentialism
Finland	Voters	Some	Yes	Semi-presidentialism
Lithuania	Voters	Some	Yes	Semi-presidentialism
Poland	Voters	Some	Yes	Semi-presidentialism
Portugal	Voters	Some	Yes	Semi-presidentialism
Romania	Voters	Some	Yes	Semi-presidentialism
Turkey	Voters	Some	Yes	Semi-presidentialism
Czech Republic	Parliament	Some	Yes	Semi-presidentialism[c]
Austria	Voters	No	Yes	Symbolic
Bosnia and Herzegovina[a]	Voters	No	Yes	Symbolic
Bulgaria	Voters	No	Yes	Symbolic
Croatia	Voters	Some	Yes	Symbolic
Ireland	Voters	No	Yes	Symbolic
Macedonia	Voters	No	Yes	Symbolic
Montenegro	Voters	No	Yes	Symbolic
Serbia	Voters	No	Yes	Symbolic
Slovakia	Voters	No	Yes	Symbolic
Slovenia	Voters	No	Yes	Symbolic
Albania	Parliament	No	Yes	Symbolic
Estonia	Parliament	No	Yes	Symbolic
Germany	Parliament	No	Yes	Symbolic
Greece	Parliament	No	Yes	Symbolic
Hungary	Parliament	No	Yes	Symbolic
Italy	Parliament	No	Yes	Symbolic
Latvia	Parliament	No	Yes	Symbolic
Malta	Parliament	No	Yes	Symbolic
Switzerland	Parliament[b]	No	Yes	Symbolic

Source: Author's compilation, drawing from the state's constitution and political practice

[a]In Bosnia and Herzegovina, the presidency consists of a three-person council composed of one Serb, One Croat, and one Bosniak (Muslim). The chair of this body rotates every eight months.

[b]The Swiss president is a member of the seven-member Federation Council, which as a collective body functions as the head of state. The president rotates among the members of the Council on a yearly basis.

[c]Even though the Czech president is not elected by voters, he/she enjoys powers similar to other European presidents in semi-presidential systems.

are designed to foster limited government. Note as well that a presidential system can have a divided government, meaning that the executive branch and the legislative branch are controlled by two different parties (e.g., the situation in the US from 2010 to 2016 when the Democrats had the presidency but the Republicans controlled the House of Representatives). This would be impossible in a parliamentary system, in which the majority party or coalition of parties in the parliament chooses the political executive. Differences with the more common parliamentary system were presented earlier in Table 6.1, and an extended discussion about the relative merits of presidential and parliamentary systems can be found in the **In focus** feature.

In focus

The relative merits of presidential and parliamentary forms of government

Earlier in the chapter we discussed general differences between presidential and parliamentary forms of governance. As noted in Chapter 5, there is a longstanding focus in political science on the study of institutions. The goal typically is not just description or classification but to demonstrate how institutions matter. In other words, there are consequences to how institutions are set up, and implicitly there is often a normative element as well: Some designs are better than others. This is not just an exercise in abstract argument. In the 1980s and 1990s, when numerous states—including those in Eastern Europe—began to move toward democracy, a lively debate emerged about which institutions should be adopted. One of the core areas of argument revolved around the choice between parliamentarism and presidentialism.

Each has its defenders.[11] Those favoring presidential systems of governance would claim that it has several advantages[12]: first, because the term of office of a president is fixed. Whereas in a parliamentary system the prime minister can lose office at any time through a vote of no confidence, presidential systems are said to be more stable and facilitate predictable policy planning. Americans, for example, know literally centuries in advance when presidential elections will be held (on Tuesdays in early November every four years), whereas elections in European states with parliamentary systems could occur, literally, at any time. Second, a president (forgetting for a second about the vagaries of the Electoral College in the US) is directly elected, and thus can claim a mandate from the people, whereas a prime minister is elected by parliament and does not therefore stand before all of the country's voters. Third, presidential systems are said to have a more effective system of checks and balances, as the executive and legislative branches are independent of each other. Fourth, one could also argue—in somewhat of a contrast to the point just made—that presidential systems, because the executive branch is controlled by a single individual not beholden to maintaining parliamentary approval, will produce more decisive executive leadership than prime ministers whose hold on power depends upon their ability to manage complex coalitions.[13]

Those favoring a parliamentary system offer different arguments. First, they would maintain that presidential government, with all of its checks and balances, can lead to "gridlock" when the executive and legislative branches are controlled by different parties. This is not only inefficient, but also makes political accountability difficult, as each branch blames the other if they cannot agree on what policy to adopt. This has been an issue in France, which has seen "cohabitation" between its president and prime minister, and it can make governance more complicated. In contrast, parliamentary systems—particularly those in which a single party is able to form the government—can be very efficient and have clear lines of accountability for policy. Second, one could argue that presidential systems are too rigid. Presidents having a fixed term of office can turn into "lame ducks," whereas a parliamentary system can make more rapid adjustments to respond to changing circumstances or public opinion. True, in extreme cases—such as Italy with over sixty governments since World War II—this can lead to instability; in more moderate cases, one might deem such "flexibility" a positive feature. Third, presidential systems rest on a "winner-take-all" logic, meaning that only one individual can be president. Although one could argue that the president thus represents the entire nation, this may be problematic in ethnically divided societies, where the minority group would find it difficult to have one of its own elected president. A power-sharing arrangement that would allow for the possibility of executives made up of coalitions of parties might therefore be more inclusive. Fourth, there is a problem of representation. For example, in the first round of French presidential elections in 2002, when sixteen candidates ran for office, Jacques Chirac, the eventual winner, polled only 20 percent of the vote. True, he prevailed with 82 percent of the vote in the run-off against the extreme xenophobe Jean Marie Le Pen, but, given his low vote total in round one, can one really say that Chirac's election represents the will of the people of France? Lastly, one could argue that presidential elections are often akin to celebrity beauty contests and hinge too much on personalities and personal lives and not enough on the issues (e.g., this is a chronic complaint in every US election). Because voters in a parliamentary system are typically not voting for the prime minister directly, they may focus more on the party platforms than the personalities.

In a simple sense, then, there are trade-offs between the two systems. Moreover, one could argue that each system can work: parliamentarism has a successful track record in Great Britain, the Netherlands, Sweden, and many other countries; presidentialism works in the US, and few Americans would even dream of the idea of adopting a parliamentary form of government; and semipresidentialism, despite some of its complexities, has succeeded in France. Does this demonstrate that all systems are equal?

Not quite. In empirical work looking at the performance of "new democracies" since World War II, several analysts have noted that parliamentary systems perform better, as they have greater stability and are far more likely to become consolidated, successful democracies.[14] Why? Alfred Stepan and Cindy Skach suggest that a major problem is that the mutual independence of presidents and legislatures can produce political impasses for which there are no easy remedies. The consequences are military coups, suspension of the constitution, and instability—a dramatic example being the stand-off in 1993 in Russia between President Yeltsin and the Russian parliament, which was "resolved" only after Yeltsin ordered tanks to fire on the parliament building. In contrast, the mutual dependence between prime ministers and parliaments provides a means to break political impasses and ultimately contribute to the stability of the democratic system.[15]

What does one find in Europe? In a recent study of post-communist countries, Steven Fish examined how the powers of legislative branches—as opposed to presidents—affect democracy. He concludes that there is a relationship, with presidential or even semi-presidential systems, such as Belarus, Ukraine, and Russia—far less democratic in the 2000s than countries with parliamentary systems with stronger parliaments, such as Latvia, Slovenia, Hungary, and Slovakia.[16] Moreover, one can argue that the adoption of semi-presidentialism in countries like Poland and Romania complicated governance in both countries. For example, President Lech Walesa (1990–1995) in Poland tried to gain more powers by pushing a "Little Constitution" and undermining parliament by using his status as a heroic figure to appeal directly to public opinion.[17] In Romania, disputes between President Emil Constantinescu (1996–2000) and parliament led to the collapse of several cabinets and slowed the course of reform, and the country was once again severely handicapped in the late 2000s–early 2010s as parliament twice impeached the president.

Critical thinking questions

1. Can you make an argument that one type of system (presidential or parliamentary) is more "democratic" than the other?
2. Why might it be that parliamentary systems are more common than presidential ones in Europe?

The only example of "pure" presidentialism in Europe is in Cyprus, where the president is elected by voters for a five-year term, is both head of state and head of government, and has numerous political powers, including veto power over legislation. The fact that Cyprus—under British control from 1878 until gaining independence in 1960—adopted presidentialism may seem peculiar, but it developed as a means of power-sharing between the island's majority Greek population (which elects the president) and minority Turkish population (which is supposed to elect a vice president who wields some political power). After the Turkish invasion of Cyprus in 1974, the island has been politically divided, with the Turkish population having their own government (not internationally recognized) on the northern third of the island. Since this time, the office of the vice president has been unfilled.

Semi-presidentialism

semi-presidentialism form of government in which executive authority is shared between a president and prime minister; combines features of both the presidential and parliamentary systems.

More common in Europe is **semi-presidentialism,** sometimes called a "dual executive" system.[18] The classic definition of this arrangement, set forth by Maurice Duverger, has three elements: the president should be elected by direct popular vote; the president should possess considerable political power; and the president must co-exist with a prime minister and cabinet ministers who possess powers over the government and can stay in office only if the parliament does not show opposition to them.[19]

Among European governments, the best example of semi-presidentialism is found in France. This arrangement evolved as a compromise in 1958 between Charles de Gaulle and forces in the French legislature. After World War II, France adopted a parliamentary form of government, but it was weak and unstable. De Gaulle, hero of the French resistance to the Nazis, was called back to rescue the government from a grave crisis in the French colony of Algeria, but he agreed to serve only if France would adopt a new constitution with strong presidential powers—which, of course, he would be able to use. Forces within the French legislature agreed to accommodate this demand, but were unwilling to cede all power to the office of the presidency. Thus, the Fifth Republic in France—its current constitutional system—has both a president, popularly elected by the people and serving as head of state, and a prime minister, who is accountable to the French National Assembly (the lower house of parliament) and is considered the head of government.

The French president, however, is quite powerful, reflecting de Gaulle's belief that "parliaments should be seen, not heard." The French president, by the Constitution, directs the military and is responsible for foreign policy; he or she, unlike the US president, can dissolve the legislature;[20] he or she can also call referendums, declare a state of emergency, force the National Assembly to vote on proposed laws, and appoint numerous bureaucratic, judicial, and military officials. He or she is also charged with naming the prime minister, but, since the National Assembly can censure the prime minister and remove him or her from office, *de facto* the president must name someone acceptable to the majority of the representatives in the legislative branch. The prime minister in turn nominates the other cabinet ministers, who are also accountable to the National Assembly.

The precise division of power between the president and the prime minister is rather vague. Whereas the Constitution enumerates several specific presidential powers, the prime minister is given, in Article 21, more general directives such as directing the action of the government and being "responsible" for national defense. How this squares with the powers of the president—who, after all, directs the military!—is not explicitly stated. When de Gaulle was President (1958–1970), there was little question who was in charge: Prime ministers did the bidding of the president. Indeed, given the fact that the president can dismiss the National Assembly and the prime minister[21] and not vice versa, it is clear that there is a lopsided relationship, with the prime minister and government—in most periods of the Fifth Republic—expected to execute the president's political program and serve as a lightning rod to deflect public criticism away from the president. Indeed, if the president's party commands a majority in the National Assembly and thus can count on a reliable prime minister, the French president can in practice exercise more power than virtually any other democratically elected leader.

However, matters have not always been that simple. Naturally, the French prime minister does not want to be the president's lap dog. He or she has a personal interest in carving out an individual political identity, if for no other reason than to gain stature and, perhaps, as was the case for Georges Pompidou (1962–1968), Jacque Chirac (1974–1976 and 1986–1988), and Lionel Jospin (1997–2002), later running for president. However, France's semi-presidential form of government creates opportunities for tension and conflict that goes beyond personalities. It is possible that the president and prime minister could be political rivals from different parties, because the president must appoint a prime minister acceptable to the National Assembly.[22] If the Assembly is controlled by a different party than the one that occupies the presidency, the president is *de facto* compelled to appoint as prime minister someone outside his or her own party. This situation, known as **cohabitation**, has occurred three times: in the periods from 1986 to 1988, from 1993 to 1995, and 1997 to 2002. In these cases, there was rivalry between the two executives, and the president could not expect the prime minister and National Assembly to go along with his initiatives. During cohabitation, there are more "checks and balances" in place, and the prime minister gains power, although the precise arrangements depend as much upon personalities and willingness to compromise as upon the rather vague prescriptions in the French Constitution. In general, the pattern has been for the president concentrating on foreign policy and representing France in more symbolic ways as the head of state, but with the growing power of the European Union on French domestic issues, the line between foreign and domestic policy is increasingly blurry. In the 1997 to 2002 cohabitation period between President Jacques Chirac (from the political right) and Prime Minister Lionel Jospin (from the Socialist Party), France experienced a weak government that did not or could not take major initiatives. Chirac won 2002 presidential elections, and his party—named at the time the Movement for a Presidential Majority—reflected in its very name a desire to be rid of cohabitation, which may be less likely in the future because the Assembly and the President are now, thanks to a constitutional amendment, on the same five-year election cycle. For example, in 2007 French voters elected as president Nicholas Sarkozy and gave Sarkozy's party, the Union for a Popular Movement (UMP), a majority in the National Assembly, allowing Sarkozy to name François Fillon of the UMP as prime minister. In 2012, the Socialists returned to power, gaining both a parliamentary majority and the presidency. President François Hollande was thus able to name a fellow Socialist, Jean-Marc Ayrault, as prime minister.

cohabitation
arrangement in a semi-presidential system in which the president and prime minister come from different political parties.

As seen in Table 6.3, other countries in Europe also have semi-presidential systems, although in most cases their presidents are constitutionally weaker than the French President.[23] Examples include Finland, Poland, and Portugal. Notably, in these cases, the powers of the president have diminished in recent years. In Finland, the president is popularly elected and in the post–World War II era has often exercised control over foreign policy and enjoyed the power to dissolve parliament, but constitutional changes in 2000 stripped the president of many of his or her domestic political powers and diminished his or her role in foreign policy. In Poland, from 1992 to 1997 under the so-called "Little Constitution," the president enjoyed a range of powers ranging from a veto over legislation to a designated special role in defense and foreign affairs. The 1997 constitution took away many of the president's powers, although he or she can still refer bills to the Constitutional Tribunal, nominate state officials, and possesses a veto that requires a 60 percent (as opposed to two-third vote, as before) vote in the Polish lower house to override it. In Portugal, the president enjoys, on paper, a host of powers, although since the transition to democracy, the president has generally not exercised them, deferring instead to the prime minister. Exceptions, however, have occurred, often the result of political partisanship. For example, in 2004 President Jorge Sampaio of the Socialist Party dismissed the controversial government of Pedro Santana Lopes of the center-right Social Democratic Party, despite the fact that Lopes still enjoyed the support of the majority in parliament. As noted earlier, in 2015 center-right President Anibal Silva initially refused to give the left-wing parties in parliament a chance to form a government, even though they, not the center-right parties, possessed a majority of seats. In 2014, Turkey became formally semi-presidential when the president, for the first time, was popularly elected by voters. However,

David Cameron faces his critics during question time

as noted at the outset of the chapter, reforming the constitution to give more power to President Erdoğan, who now claims a mandate to govern, is a source of contention. The Czech Republic could also be called a semi-presidential system, even though it does not mean Duverger's definition because the president is not elected by voters. However, this post has not been purely ceremonial; in addition to approving treaties, the president can veto laws passed by parliament, although parliament may override the veto.[24]

Symbolic presidentialism

symbolic presidentialism form of government in which a president (elected or unelected) has weak powers and serves, like a constitutional monarch, as a largely symbolic head of state.

As noted earlier in this chapter, several European republics have a system of **symbolic presidentialism**, in which presidents are heads of state and perform functions similar to those of kings and queens in constitutional monarchies. While the president in such countries may enjoy a variety of enumerated powers (e.g., appointment of judges and other officials, commander-in-chief of the armed forces, signing laws), typically he or she defers to parliament in exercising power. Thus, these countries should be properly understood as parliamentary, with the president serving a more symbolic role and not typically interfering in issues of governance.[25]

It is worth noting that not all symbolic presidential systems are structured in the same way. In some cases (e.g., Ireland, Bulgaria, Austria), the president is popularly elected and thus can claim some democratic legitimacy to insert him- or herself into political debates. This was true, for example, in Ireland in 1994, when President Mary Robinson refused to grant the dissolution of parliament and call for new elections, although in the past the president had always granted such requests.

Other presidents are selected by the legislature, with the president often a well-respected, older, non-divisive figure. In such cases, the office of the presidency is seen as a political reward for a distinguished career of public service. Whereas one would expect presidents of this type to adhere more closely to the non-political role than those that are elected, such is not always the case. For example, in Italy in the 2000s, Italian presidents challenged Prime Minister Berlusconi, including rejecting some of the ministerial nominees and vetoing a measure in 2003 that critics claimed would have strengthened Berlusconi's already substantial control over Italian media. In 2016, German President Joachim Gauck inserted himself into rancorous debates over the refugee crisis in Europe, asserting that limitations or quotas on admission of refugees should be adopted.[26] Occasionally, such presidents can also become embroiled in political scandals. This occurred in Germany in 2012, when President Christian Wulff resigned amid reports of corruption when he served as leader of a regional-level government.

The cabinet

Whereas the prime minister or chancellor serves as the political chief executive in European parliamentary democracy, the political executive as a whole—often referred to simply as the government—is the cabinet, which functions like a board of directors. The cabinet—called the Council of Ministers in some countries such as Spain, Belgium, and Albania—comprises a set of ministers, each of whom is typically responsible for overseeing a government department.[27] The precise number of ministers will vary, depending upon the number of executive departments: As of 2016, Germany has sixteen members of the cabinet (including the chancellor); Greece has eighteen; Britain, twenty-two. In Switzerland, seven individuals comprise the Federal Council, which also serves as a collective head of state. Ministries can be created (or eliminated) from time to time. Whereas some ministries will be specific to a particular country (e.g., the British minister for Northern Ireland, the Danish minister for Nordic cooperation), many ministries are in common across countries. These include foreign affairs, finance, education, agriculture, culture, defense, health, science, justice, and environment.

The cabinet is appointed by the prime minister or chancellor, but, as noted above, he or she may not have complete discretion in choice. This is especially true in coalition governments, where the coalition partners will negotiate over what party and what individual will assume a cabinet post. Frequently, cabinet positions are political appointments, meaning they are given out to top party officials on the basis of seniority or patronage. In such cases, appointees are often members of parliament or officials from regional governments. However, for those ministries that are deemed less "political" (e.g., science, tourism, or health), appointments may be made from unelected civil service officials or academics who have expertise in the area.

Cabinet officials serve two major roles. First, they manage a particular department or ministry. This means they oversee personnel and the functioning of the department and during cabinet meetings advance agendas emanating from that department. If there is a problem in a department, responsibility rests with the cabinet minister, who may be, depending upon the severity of the problem, expected to resign from office. Secondly, however, the cabinet official is a member of the government, a collective entity. He or she participates in policy decisions, and, regardless of his or her particular position, each cabinet official is expected to take collective responsibility for decision-making. This means he or she is expected to defend the government's decision in public. If one cannot go along with the decision, one is expected to resign, as British Foreign Secretary Jack Straw did in 2003 over decisions relating to the war in Iraq. This role of collective responsibility distinguishes ministers in parliamentary democracies in Europe from those in presidential systems such as the United States, where the cabinet minister merely oversees a department and is not typically responsible for collective decision-making. Collective responsibility provides protection for individual ministers for unpopular decisions. All cabinet ministers are expected to sink or swim together.

This does not mean, however, that each cabinet minister actively participates in every decision made by the government. Given the thousands of decisions made by a government in the course of a year, proposals are typically developed within a particular department or ministry that has expertise in a given area. The minister in charge of that department will present the proposal at a cabinet meeting, and other ministers will typically defer to that member, who is more familiar with the proposal. This means that there is a division of labor within cabinets, and ministers typically abide by a policy of non-intervention in the affairs of other ministries. In some countries, ministries may include junior ministers or undersecretaries. In coalition governments, they often come from parties different from those of the minister. For example, the minister of education in Sweden may be from the Social Democratic Party, but a junior minister responsible for higher education may be from the Green Party. Although the junior minister may answer to the minister, the fact that he or she is from a different party may provide some sort of oversight on the working of the ministry.

presidentialization
term that refers to the growing power of prime ministers in parliamentary systems over both the cabinet and the parliament.

Within a cabinet, the prime minister is typically considered *primus inter pares*, first among equals. In point of fact, however, the prime minister—by virtue of his or her control of a political party, ability to dismiss ministers, access of information from all components of government, and political visibility—occupies the commanding position. In some countries—most notoriously Great Britain—the prime minister has become so powerful and dismissive of the cabinet for decision-making that some speak of "prime ministerial" government or the "**presidentialization**" of the system.[28] As noted above with the example of adopting the euro, however, this can be exaggerated, as prime ministers, even in the British system, do not always get their way. This topic of "presidentialization" and concentration of power is explored more fully in the **Is Europe one?** section.

The civil service

civil service
government bureaucracy that is considered part of the executive branch.

Most people who serve in the government or work for the state are not prime ministers, cabinet officials, members of parliament, or judges on a Constitutional Court. Moreover, on a day-to-day level, such high-level officials have little contact with the wider public. Most people encounter "government" on a personal level in the form of the building inspector, policeman, mail carrier, register of deeds, schoolteacher, or the like. Of course, thousands of "faceless bureaucrats"—those that process tax forms, ensure that pension checks are delivered on time, distribute government grant money, and perform countless other tasks—operate behind the scenes, albeit often in little cubicles that give them little contact with real live human beings. These government employees—often referred to as the **civil service** or the bureaucracy—are the human machinery of government, ensuring that government implements the laws and performs the services it is assigned to do. Because most members of the civil service ultimately answer to a government representative at the national or sub-national level and because their primary duty is to execute the laws, they are properly understood as part of the executive branch of government.

Government bureaucracies are often criticized. Indeed, the inventor of the very word bureaucracy, the Frenchman Vincent de Gournay, endowed it in 1765 with a negative connotation, opposing it to the alleged efficiencies of a *laissez-faire* or market-based system. One scholar argues the following:

> In study after study produced from the 1960s on, state bureaucracies have been presented as endlessly demanding, self-serving, prone to lie in order to cover the blunders that they commit, arbitrary, capricious, impersonal, petty, inefficient, resistant to change, and heartless.[29]

Perhaps many of you have your own horror story from an encounter with a government official. However, it is worth asking, what would one do in modern states without large government bureaucracies? Who would enforce the laws? Who would administer government programs? Whereas an anarchist or a libertarian would argue for no or very limited government, the fact is that today governments

Is Europe one?

Concentration of power and movement toward informal "presidentialism"

As noted earlier in this chapter, most European democracies have parliamentary forms of government. In this respect, there is a sort of uniformity across the continent. Parliamentarism also distinguishes "European style" democracy from the presidential system used in the United States. The irony, however, is that one can discern movement in numerous European states to something that looks increasingly like presidentialism.

This is not to say that the formal, legal institutional arrangements have changed. European voters, by and large, are not electing powerful presidents. Instead, presidentialization refers to a "process by which regimes are becoming more presidential in their actual practice without, in most cases, changing their formal structure."[30] "Presidential" in this case means that the core executive (prime minister or chancellor) acquires more power and autonomy vis-à-vis other political actors (cabinets, parties, and parliaments) and that politics as a whole becomes much more centralized and personalized, tied to a leader as opposed to collective entities or an ideology. A "presidential" type of executive would, for example, have more control over the agenda of government, appointments to the cabinet, decisions taken by his or her party, and play a central, very visible role in elections.

Several factors may drive this process. One is the internationalization of politics, meaning, particularly in Europe, that as more and more decisions are subject to inter-governmental negotiations, power is shifted to the head of government. Increasingly, parliaments are called on only to ratify decisions that have been taken elsewhere. Examples include EU treaties but also directives issued from the EU that require parliamentary action. Secondly, one can point to the increasing complexity of governments and bureaucracies that require more executive oversight and less parliamentary involvement. As the head of government, the prime minister is at the nexus of communication flows and is uniquely empowered to oversee the entire governmental operation. This gives the office of prime minister more power and resources and makes him or her more necessary to coordinate sectoral policy-making, in which the cabinet plays more the role of a rubberstamp than a locus of decision-making. Third, one can point to the erosion of ideology, traditional cleavages, and interest associations, which tends to make voters focus more on specific issues and leaders. Finally, the role of the media, especially television, is central, as prime ministers can gain easier access to the media, and parties feel the need to put forward charismatic, media-friendly leaders. According to one study, "presidentialism would appear to be a characteristic of modern parliamentary elections that is unlikely to go away, largely because political parties have become more dependent in their communications with voters on the essentially visual and personality-based medium of television."[31]

There are numerous examples of European prime ministers exhibiting both the style and substance of presidentialism. These include Margaret Thatcher (1979–1990) and Tony Blair (1997–2007) in Great Britain, Silvio Berlusconi (1994–1995, 2001–2006, and 2008–2011) in Italy, Václav Klaus (1992–1997) in the Czech Republic, and Recep T. Erdoğan (2003–2014) in Turkey. In all of these cases, the movement toward presidentialization was abetted by their outsize personalities, and, in Berlusconi's case, his ownership of a media empire. In the late 2000s, the British Conservative Party, out of office for over a decade, "remade" itself thanks to the selection of a more youthful, camera-friendly David Cameron as its leader, much as the Labour

Party did in the 1990s by choosing Blair as its leader. Some in Britain pointed to presidentialization (or, "Americanization") in the 2010 elections, when, for the first time ever, there were televised debates among the three major party leaders. In cases such as these, the focus is more and more on the individual, less and less on policy or ideology. Italy may have been the extreme case, where politics (and media) were so dominated by Berlusconi that the main cleavage in Italian politics boiled down to one's view of him. Studies have also presented evidence of presidentialization—in terms of the resources at the disposal of prime ministers and diminishing power of cabinets and parliaments—in Spain, Finland, Belgium, Denmark, and the Netherlands. The authors of the leading study on the subject conclude that "it is reasonable to talk of the 'presidentialization' of contemporary democracy."[32] A more recent example could be seen in 2015, amid the refugee crisis in Europe, in which case German Chancellor Angela Merkel's leadership, which often meant taking positions at odds with many in her party, did less to facilitate consensus than to cement her status as, to use a term from former US President George W. Bush, "the decider."

How much is one to make of this trend? While the specific traits of some leaders may facilitate presidentialization more in some countries than in others—and the more majoritarian British system might foster it even more—some of the factors that promote it, such as bureaucratic complexity, electronic media, and internationalization, will only continue to grow in prominence. Those who favor old-style politics driven by political machines and clear ideological lines and those who worry about centralization of power may decry signs of presidentialization, but such a development may be both functionally necessary for governance and create affective links between the political system and citizens.

Critical thinking questions

1. The notion that political executives—presidents and prime ministers—have gained at the expense of parliaments is not confined only to Europe. Why might this be the case?
2. What might be done to prevent concentration of executive power?

do a lot and require civil servants to administer their duties. Certainly, bureaucracies have problems—many can be inefficient, predatory, or even unnecessary—but given the size of modern states, public administration based upon a bureaucracy is necessary. Max Weber (1864–1920), for example, wrote about how bureaucracy is an inherent and productive component of modern life and how bureaucratic rule engenders its own sense of legitimacy, as it allows political life to move beyond personalized politics—where all depends upon the will of the leader—and instead be based on the rule of law. Perhaps donning some rose-colored glasses, he praised it as a mechanism that provides, among other things, "precision, speed, unambiguity, [and] knowledge."[33] Updating Weber's terms, bureaucracies produce **state capacity,** endowing them with the resources to perform their essential duties or maintaining law and order and implementing laws. In many parts of the world (e.g., sub-Saharan Africa, Pakistan, Iraq), the problem is *not* "big government" but low state capacity, as governments do not have the means to perform basic tasks, often because they lack well-trained personnel in government bureaucracies.

state capacity the ability of a state to perform its essential duties; depends heavily upon the quality and resources of the civil service.

In contrast, European states have large bureaucracies. From 1950 to 1980, for example, the number of civilian employees of the government grew in Western Europe from 11 percent to 23 percent of the workforce. Communist countries in Eastern Europe had even larger public sectors, as the state owned most of the property and administered a great number of economic and social programs. Despite the rhetoric of "new public management" and various efforts to slim down government—through, for example, privatization of state enterprises, contracting out services to private providers, or by employing technology such as the Internet to perform some basic services—today in Europe government, by far, is the largest employer, although there is a lot of variation.[34] For example, according to the Organization for Economic Cooperation and Development (OECD), in 1997 government employment constituted 25 percent of all employment in Finland, 23 percent in Hungary, 21 percent in France, 13 percent in both Great Britain and Germany, and (remarkably given the subsequent blowup over the Greek financial crisis in 2010) only 7 percent in Greece.[35] True, not all of these individuals are the "faceless bureaucrats" that are the usual target for derision. These figures include garbage collectors, teachers, mail carriers, and transportation workers, all of which, in most people's view, perform essential tasks. Still, there is little doubt that government is, so to speak, "big business."

Why are civil services so large? Much of the answer has to do with the tasks assumed by European states, particularly after World War II, when large social-welfare states became the norm and the state began to do more to regulate the economy. Despite, in many cases, cuts in regulations and state spending, European governments still administer a variety of economic and social programs, and the workers of a number of institutions—hospitals, public works, universities, state-owned firms—can be considered employees of the government. In a broader sense, one could argue that democracy itself is the cause of an expanded bureaucracy, insofar as democratic government produces demands for redistribution of income and social welfare programs.[36] Indeed, in many European states government spending accounts for over 40 percent of the gross domestic product (GDP)—the figure comes closer to 60 percent in Sweden, the Netherlands, and Denmark—and obviously part of that money is the salaries of civil service personnel.[37]

Of course, beyond size, not all European civil services are the same. Some speak of the differing political cultures within the civil service. One can compare, for example, the British tradition of pragmatism based upon a staff of "generalists," meaning that public administration relies upon civil servants that typically possess only general administrative and managerial skills, whereas most European states have a more technocratic civil service that relies upon specially trained, more "elite" bureaucrats. This is the case in France, where the administrative corps is recruited, trained, and socialized in a higher education system that lies outside of the regular university sector. The two main training grounds both for French bureaucrats and politicians are the École Polytechnique and the École Nationale d'Administration. Both are highly competitive, as the prospect of a well-paying job in the French civil service is an extremely attractive proposition to many young French men and (increasingly so) women. Whereas defenders of this system stress the skills of their graduates, others complain that the upper echelon of the French civil service is too elitist and is composed of "drones" that lack sufficient initiative and individualism.

politicization
term that refers to whether the government civil service is politically neutral or whether it reflects the partisan composition of the government.

nomenklatura
system of appointments in communist countries in which appointments were strictly controlled by the Communist Party.

In addition, there are differences in the degree of **politicization** of the bureaucracy. The question here is whether bureaucratic officials—and here we are discussing those serving in the top ranks of the bureaucracy—should be strictly professionals independent of any particular political party or whether they should reflect the partisan composition of the government. Those favoring professionalism—which is well reflected in practices in Great Britain and Sweden—would stress the need for continuity and expertise in the bureaucracy and that the bureaucracy should only faithfully administer the laws, not have a partisan position. In contrast, one could argue that the bureaucracy will work better with elected officials if those elected are allowed to put some of "their people" in top positions. France, Austria, and Belgium, among other countries, have a more politicized civil service with a higher turnover of top officials when governments change. Of course, political appointments can be abused, with plum government jobs going to partisan "hacks" who may have little knowledge about the tasks they are expected to fulfill. In communist Eastern Europe, the entire bureaucratic apparatus was politicized under the ***nomenklatura*** system, which meant that virtually all of the officials appointed to the civil services in these countries were vetted and approved by the Communist authorities, with loyalty to the Communist Party (if not actual membership in the Party) usually a necessary qualification. Depoliticizing the civil service in post-communist states in the 1990s was an important task of democratization, albeit one that rarely captured headlines.[38]

Finally, there are significant differences among civil services in terms of their performance. Consider, for instance, corruption—are civil servants fundamentally honest or not? While one could argue that bureaucracies are inherently corrupt, as they are interested in advancing their own political and budgetary agendas, caring little about the broader public interest,[39] there is nonetheless a vast divergence in Europe in terms of corruption. Data for several countries from Transparency International, a non-governmental organization that monitors corruption, are reported in Figure 6.2. Here one sees that countries in Northern Europe, which have both a high level of economic development and a long tradition of democracy, fare quite well, among the very best in the world. In contrast, one sees more corruption in the poorer countries of post-communist Europe such as Romania and Albania—but also low scores for Greece and Italy, which have long histories battling—often unsuccessfully— against corruption. If one considers additional data—for example that 28 percent of Bosnians, 22 percent of Greeks, 21 percent of Turks, and 19 percent of Latvians personally reported in 2013 of having to bribe a public official in the past year[40]—one can understand that creating an honest—let alone efficient—bureaucracy remains a serious problem in some countries in Europe. The leaks in the "Panama Papers" in 2016 revealed additional problems relating to the offshore deposits of sizeable funds and creation of shell companies to avoid taxes by prominent government and business officials throughout Europe. Several officials were forced to resign, including government ministers in Spain and Malta and, perhaps most surprisingly, the Prime Minister of Iceland.[41] While problems such as these *per se* do not make these countries undemocratic, it does raise questions about the quality of leadership and breaches of public trust.

Although executive authority in Europe is, formally at least, typically beholden to parliaments, there is little doubt that prime ministers, chancellors, and presidents command great authority. In short, leaders matter. More so than parliaments, they are the face of political authority to their own publics and to the outside world. This

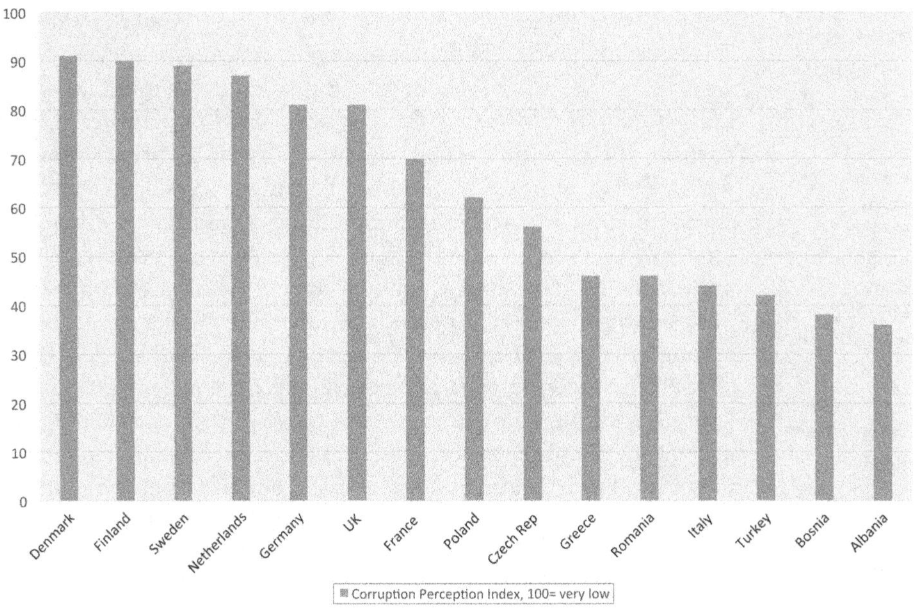

FIGURE 6.2 Corruption Perceptions Index, 2015

Transparency International (TI), at www.transparency.org/cpi2015. Data come from questionnaires completed by experts that interact with each country. Score is on a scale of 0 (highly corrupt) to 100 (very little corruption)

chapter has focused more on institutional arrangements across Europe, and less so on policy preferences and impacts. However, it is clear that leaders' actions shape the politics of their own countries and, at times, European politics as a whole. While some leaders are advocates of a stronger and more united Europe, others, such as Turkish President Erdoğan, mentioned at the beginning of this chapter, are more ambivalent, if not hostile, to deeper European integration. Fashioning a consensus among European leaders about how to tackle the multiple challenges facing the continent is obviously difficult. These issues will be taken up in later chapters in this volume.

Application questions

1. Why have several European states retained a constitutional monarchy? What purposes do monarchs serve? Why are they often popular with their subjects?
2. Coalitions can be hard to manage. What might be some advantages of a coalition government?
3. Some data seem to suggest that parliamentary systems perform better than presidential ones. From this record, would you suggest that a country with a presidential system or semi-presidential system (e.g., France, the US) adopt a parliamentary system? What problems might a parliamentary system create?
4. Why do you think some countries are more corrupt than others? What practical steps can be undertaken to combat corruption?

5. Is "presidentialization" a worrying trend? How might this affect the quality of democracy (e.g., accountability, efficiency) in Europe?

Key terms

Additional reading

Elgie. Robert, ed. 1999. *Semi-Presidentialism in Europe*. Oxford: Oxford University Press.
The seminal source on the phenomenon of semipresidentialism, this book examines both what it means in terms of institutional behavior and how it functions in a number of settings.

Lijphart, Arend, ed. 1992. *Presidential versus Parliamentary Government*. Oxford: Oxford University Press.
A collection of essays examining the pros and cons of each form of government, both in theoretical terms and in particular case studies.

Müller, Wolfgang, and Strøm, Kaare, eds. *Coalition Governments in Western Europe*. 2003. Oxford: Oxford University Press.
This book, which examines both theories of coalition formation and how governments have behaved in Western Europe, might be especially helpful for American students, who are less familiar with the premises and practices of coalition governments.

Poguntke, Thomas, and Webb, Paul, eds. 2005. *The Presidentialization of Politics: A Comparative Study of Modern Democracies*. Oxford: Oxford University Press.
An exploration of the development of presidential style and substance in European democracies, based upon examination of this trend in a number of countries, including Great Britain, Italy, Spain, Portugal, Sweden, and Finland.

Shugart, Matthew S., and Carey, John. 1992. *Presidents and Assemblies: Constitutional Design and Electoral Dynamics*. Cambridge: Cambridge University Press, 1992.
Written for a scholarly audience, this book examines the interplay between institutional design and voting, including voter turnout, coalitions, and development of political parties.

Notes

1 Ersin Kalaycioğlu, "The Challenge of à la Turca Presidentialism in Europe," Global Turkey in Europe (Instituto affari internazionali, Rome), November 2014, available at www.iai.it/en/pubblicazioni/challenge-la-turca-presidentialism-turkey.
2 In May 2016, Prime Minister Ahmet Davutoğlu announced his resignation, which was seen by many as a resolve of his disagreements with Erdoğan on several issues and that Erdoğan forced him from office, as Erdoğan had the support of most of the JDP members of parliament.
3 "Romania Votes on Whether to Remove Its President," *New York Times*, July 29, 2012.
4 Interview in *Lidove Noviny* (Prague), October 17, 2009.
5 Manuel Nunes Serrano, "Reengineering Democracy in Portugal," *Open Democracy*, January 22, 2016, available at www.opendemocracy.net/democraciaabierta/manuel-nunes-ramires-serrano/reengineering-democracy-in-portugal.
6 Small states such as Monaco, Andorra, Liechtenstein, and the Vatican are also properly considered monarchies, but we do not discuss them in the text.
7 In some cases, this does not hold. For example, in the Netherlands and Sweden, it is constitutionally prohibited for a person to be a member of the legislature and a member of the executive branch simultaneously. Any member of parliament named to a ministerial post, including the Prime Minister, must resign his/her seat in parliament.
8 "Ireland Set for Minority Government After Two Main Parties Reach Deal," *The Guardian*, April 29, 2016.
9 "Dr. Rosler's Difficult Prescription," *The Economist*, May 1, 2010.
10 The president of the US is actually indirectly elected through the Electoral College, a feature that is extremely difficult to explain to many Europeans.
11 A good review of arguments can be found in Arend Lijphart, "Introduction," in Lijphart, ed., *Parliamentary vs. Presidential Government* (Oxford: Oxford University Press, 1992).
12 These arguments apply best to a "pure presidential" system such as that in the US, but they can also apply to a semi-presidential system with a strong president, such as France.
13 This argument blends parliamentarism and multiparty systems together. The two do not have to go hand in hand (e.g., Great Britain has in essence a two-party system), but in Europe one frequently encounters multi-party parliamentary democracies.
14 See Alfred Stepan and Cindy Skach, "Constitutional Frameworks and Democratic Consolidation: Parliamentarism versus Presidentialism," *World Politics* 46:1, October 1993, 1–22, and Juan Linz and Arturo Valenzuela, eds. *The Failure of Presidential Democracy* (Baltimore: Johns Hopkins University Press, 1994).
15 Stepan and Skach, "Constitutional Frameworks."
16 M. Steven Fish, *Democracy Derailed in Russia* (Cambridge: Cambridge University Press, 2006), p. 194–209.
17 Alfred Stepan with Ezra Suleiman, "The French Fifth Republic: A Model for Import? Reflections on Poland and Brazil," in H.E. Chehabi and Alfred Stepan, eds. *Politics, Society, and Democracy* (Boulder: Westview Press, 1995).
18 Some offer different terms to describe the French system. Saalfield, for example, dubs it a "premier-presidential" system, as he emphasizes the fact that *de jure* the French President (unlike the Russian one) cannot fire the Prime Minister (called premier in French) and that governance on most issues—save foreign policy—looks like a parliamentary system. See Thomas Saalfield, "Government and Politics," in Richard Sakwa and Anne Stevens, eds. *Contemporary Europe*, 2nd edition (New York: Palgrave Macmillan, 2006), p. 90–91.
19 Maurice Duverger, "A New Political System Model: Semi-Presidential Government," *European Journal of Political Research* 8:1, June 1980, p. 165–187. Note that the definition does not say that the parliament names the prime minister, as *de jure* (and in some cases *de facto*) this is often done by the president.
20 Note that this does not reflect the standard view that presidential systems have a separation of powers between the executive and legislative branches of government.

This right applies to the National Assembly, not the Senate, which is a much weaker legislative body.

21 The Constitution does not explicitly give the president this power, but in 1962 de Gaulle asked his first prime minister, Michel Debré, to resign, and Debré did so. Whether a president under cohabitation could succeed in dismissing the prime minister has yet to be tested.

22 Technically the president could nominate anyone he or she wants, but if the assembly censures the selection, it would produce a political crisis, for which the president would likely be blamed. No French president has pressed his authority in such a fashion.

23 Elgie defines semi-presidentialism in such a way that any state with a popularly elected president (e.g., Austria, Ireland, Iceland) would qualify as semi-presidential, even if presidential powers are minimal. See Robert Elgie, ed. *Semi-Presidentialism in Europe* (Oxford: Oxford University Press, 1999). I tend to follow Duverger, with the exception of the Czech Republic and Turkey, and consider how presidents function in the political system.

24 For example, in 2006, Klaus vetoed a measure to legalize same-sex partnerships; the veto was, however, overridden by the Czech Parliament.

25 Some constitutions do give the president the power of commander-in-chief of the military and some authority in foreign affairs, but, in most cases, the norm has been for the president to allow the prime minister to exercise real authority, even in these fields.

26 "German President Backs Refugee Quotas as Austria Sets First Caps," *Financial Times*, January 20, 2016.

27 At times, some members of the cabinet may be a "minister without portfolio," meaning that he or she does not oversee a particular department. Deputy prime ministers with various duties may also be included in the cabinet.

28 Thomas Poguntke and Paul Webb, eds. *The Presidentialization of Politics: A Comparative Study of Modern Democracies* (Oxford: Oxford University Press, 2005).

29 Martin van Creveld, *The Rise and Decline of the State* (Cambridge: Cambridge University Press, 1999), p. 408.

30 Poguntke and Webb, *The Presidentialization of Politics*, p. 1. This section borrows heavily from this volume.

31 Anthony Mughan, *Media and the Presidentialization of Parliamentary Elections* (New York: Palgrave, 2000), p. 129.

32 Poguntke and Webb, *The Presidentialization of Politics*, p. 347.

33 Max Weber, from "Wirtschaft und Gesellschaft," reprinted in Richard Stillman, ed. *Public Administration: Concepts and Cases*, 8th edition (New York: Houghton Mifflin, 2006), p. 59.

34 Van Creveld, *The Rise and Decline of the State*, p. 361.

35 OECD, at www.oecd.org/dataoecd/37/43/1849079.xls, accessed March 5, 2006. Regular OECD *Labour Force Statistics* publications do not include such data.

36 Margit Tavits, "Size of Government in Majoritarian and Consensus Democracies," *Comparative Political Studies* 37:3, April 2004, p. 340–359.

37 Data on government spending as percentage of GNP can be found at www.oecd.org.

38 Jan-Hinrik Meyer-Sahling, "Civil Service Reform in Post-Communist Europe: The Bumpy Road to Depoliticisation," *West European Politics* 27:1, January 2004, p. 69–101.

39 A classic view on this question can be found in Aaron Wildavsky, *The Politics of the Budgetary Process* (Boston: Little Brown, 1964).

40 2013 Global Corruption Barometer from Transparency International, available at www.transparency.org/gcb2013/results. In contrast, only 1 percent of Finns reported paying a bribe.

41 See, for example, report "5 Ways the Panama Papers Swept Up EU Figures," *Politico*, April 4, 2016.

Members of parliament from the opposition party in Poland display copies of the constitution to protest government plans to place its supporters on the Constitutional Tribunal

© Czarek Sokolowski AP/PA Images

Chapter 7

Legal structures and judicial systems

In 2016, Poland found itself embroiled in a constitutional crisis. At stake was the composition and powers of the country's Constitutional Tribunal, its highest court. In October of the previous year, the conservative Law and Justice Party won a parliamentary majority. Anticipating that the court might rule against some of its policies, the government named five new justices to Constitutional Tribunal, disregarding the five justices appointed by the outgoing center-right government who had yet to be formally seated because Andrzej Duda, the President and former Law and Justice Party member, suggested they had been improperly appointed and refused to swear them in. Furthermore, the new government passed measures to restrict the Tribunal's power, including requiring that cases be decided by a two-thirds as opposed to a simple majority and that thirteen (as opposed to the previous nine) judges be required to hear each case. Given that it is composed of fifteen justices, the clear goal of these measures to pack the court was to neutralize it politically. Critics charged that it amounted to a coup and "Putinization" of Polish politics, a reference to anti-democratic actions by President Vladimir Putin in Russia.[1] The Tribunal itself ruled that most of these moves were unconstitutional. The government, however, rejected the court's ruling and refused to publish it (as required for it to take effect), creating a political impasse.

In addition to protests by Poles, these developments elicited reactions by the European Union and other bodies. The European Commission, the European Parliament, and the Council of Europe all passed measures condemning the actions of the government as an endangerment to democracy, human rights, and the rule of law. Donald Tusk, the President of the European Council and a former Polish prime minister, was also critical of the new government's actions, as were several past Polish presidents, who signed a public letter warning that they undermined the country's democratic record. Members of the Polish government and Law and Justice Party rejected such criticism as "absurd," coarse," and "vulgar," and condemned what they viewed as undue interference by the European Union. Prime Minister Beata Szydlo pointed to an East-West divide and suggested that haughty West European politicians feel superior to those from post-communist states and "like to instruct others."[2] Potentially, failure to resolve this issue could lead to sanctions by the EU, including loss of Poland's voting rights. This, however, is unlikely, as it would require unanimity, and the Hungarian government, which has also raised the ire of many in Europe for breaches of the rule of law and liberal democratic norms, has indicated it will support the Polish government.

The drama in Poland is exceptional, in part because courts, while at times rendering controversial decisions, rarely generate international headlines. They are also seen, typically, as the least "political" of all political institutions, although, as we'll see in this chapter, at times they do weigh in on significant political questions. More generally, courts, and the broader constitutional system they are empowered to uphold, can play important roles in structuring political institutions, defining what is and what is not legally permissible, and safeguarding the rule of law and democracy.

judiciary
institutions of government that are designed to apply and interpret the law and adjudicate legal disputes.

This chapter takes up the institutions of the **judiciary**, which are designed to apply and interpret the law and to adjudicate cases in which one party is alleged to have violated the law. Often, these lack an explicit political character, as they involve private parties in civil disputes or trials against those accused of criminal offenses. Judges in Europe—unlike in many areas of the US—are not elected to their posts. They are thus assumed to be impartial and immune from popular or political pressure. We know, of course, that courts can at times play a political role in numerous ways, such as by ruling on the constitutionality of certain questions, by adjudicating disputes in which the government is a party, or by expanding or constricting individual rights. In Europe, courts play an important role insofar as they are expected to uphold both national and EU-level laws and directives. Because of the growing importance of European-level law, an issue explored in the **Is Europe one?** section of this chapter, the judiciary is the political institution that arguably has witnessed the most Europeanization.

This chapter takes up judicial systems in Europe as well as broader issues relating to the legal structure of power, concerns that did not fit neatly into our previous discussions of parliaments and executives. These questions include the scope of individual rights and the division of powers among national, regional, and local governments.

Constitutions

constitution
set of rules for a particular country that define how political power is distributed, how political decisions are to be made, and the nature and extent of citizens' rights.

The good starting place to begin examining the overall legal structure of European polities is with their **constitutions**, meaning sets of rules that define how power is distributed among political bodies and actors; how political decisions are to be made, applied, and interpreted; and the nature and extent of citizens' rights. In short, constitutions define the rules of the political game. They are not the only source of law, but they serve as a foundation for all laws and rules of governance, an idea nicely captured by the Turkish term for constitution, *Anayasa*, meaning "mother law."

The adoption of a constitution is an exceptional event in a country. No countries in Europe can boast of a written constitution as old as the United States' Constitution (1787). The oldest European written constitution that is still functioning, that of the Netherlands, was adopted in 1815, and most states' current constitutions were adopted in the twentieth century. However, the old joke that one had to look for the French Constitution in the periodical section of the library is a bit of an exaggeration. Constitutions are designed to last, although from time to time a state may decide to adopt a new constitution. Typically, there are three main occasions that necessitate adoption of a constitution. First, as one would expect, when a country gains independence, it adopts its own constitution. Such was the case, for example, with Finland in 1919 and Ireland in 1922, and, most recently, in 2008 for Kosovo, Europe's newest country, albeit one not recognized by all states. Secondly, when there is a major change in political regime, either through revolution, defeat in war, or democratization, a new constitution is usually necessary to define the rules of the new system of government. Thus, Germany and Italy adopted constitutions after World War II, Spain did so in 1978 as it began a transition to democratic government, and most countries in Eastern Europe adopted new constitutions after the collapse of communism. Third, countries may adopt new constitutions as a solution to a political crisis or to facilitate major political adjustments. For example, France adopted a constitution in 1958 to resolve a crisis that put the country on the brink of civil war, and Denmark adopted a new constitution in 1973, the same year it joined the European Community. In some cases, constitutions are adopted by supermajority of votes (more than 50 percent) in the legislature or through some sort of constitutional convention, although in other cases (e.g., Switzerland in 1874, France in 1958, Spain in 1978, and Poland in 1997) constitutions are approved by popular **referendum,** meaning that the people vote directly on the constitution.

referendum procedure by which political questions are put directly to voters; an example of direct democracy.

Constitutions vary widely from country to country, and each state can claim a unique set of constitutional traditions. However, one can identify a number of common tasks served by virtually all constitutions. Typically, they set forth who is to carry out the major functions of politics; how power is divided among different branches of government; who controls the military; how citizenship is defined and acquired; how people occupying positions of authority are to be chosen; areas in which the state is given authority; what rights citizens retain; the role of religion; and how the constitution can be changed. Many constitutions also contain provisions on symbolic aspects of the state, such as the flag, the national anthem, and the national motto.

They can vary in some basic and obvious ways. One is length. Some constitutions are short, focusing only on basic principles of governance. The US Constitution is famously short, as constitutions go, at 4,620 words. In Europe, France's stands out as relatively short (7,686 words).[3] Others are much longer, detailing many specific tasks of government. As a general rule, the more recent constitutions tend to be longer, delving into policy areas that are largely ignored in older constitutions when the state's role in society was more limited. For example, both the Spanish Constitution (17,976 words) and the Polish Constitution (20,750 words) enumerate a number of socio-economic rights, including rights to education, health care, housing, social security, workplace safety, and paid vacations, that would not have been considered "rights" a century ago. In addition, both states commit themselves to protect the natural environment, to strive for full employment, and to foster a more equitable distribution of income. These documents, however, are shorter still than Germany's Basic Law (the *de facto* constitution), which was adopted by West Germany in 1949. It was envisioned as a temporary document (pending long-hoped-for reunification, which, although it occurred in 1990, did not produce a new constitution) and totals 21,941 words.

Which is better? While some might like a document that is more detailed and specific, it can be a problem if the government cannot fulfill all of its constitutional obligations. No constitution can foresee every political exigency, and shorter and vaguer constitutions have the advantage of flexibility, although their adaptability may depend upon the ability of courts to interpret centuries-old provisions for use in the contemporary world. Indeed, one could say that court decisions, legislation, and traditional understandings make up, albeit in a less formal manner, the constitution in many states. For example, the Spanish Constitution recognizes the right of autonomy of nationalities and regions within a common, unitary "fatherland." What this means in practice for the various regions of Spain (e.g., Catalonia, Valencia, Basque areas) has been the subject of negotiations with the central government and has evolved over time, making up, so to speak, an aspect of the Spanish constitution (little *c*).

Constitutions also vary in strength. One dimension of strength is whether a political institution—typically a court—can defend the constitution against the actions of another institution. This is captured in the idea of **judicial review,** the idea that courts can declare legislation or actions of the executive branch unconstitutional. This means that nothing can contravene the Constitution, at least as it is interpreted by the courts. As we shall see later in this chapter, several European states, among them France, Germany, Poland, and Italy, have judicial systems with elements of judicial review. However, in other cases, such as Sweden, the Netherlands, and Great Britain, judicial review is much weaker or non-existent, meaning that legislatures can pass measures without any explicit check on whether they pass constitutional muster.

judicial review mechanism through which courts can declare legislation or actions of other governmental actors as unconstitutional.

Another way of defining strength is how easy it is to change the constitution. Obviously, constitutions must be subject to change. If they were not, citizens would be stuck with the arrangements adopted by their forebears, a predicament hardly compatible with popular sovereignty and democratic governance. Constitutional provisions that can be easily changed or annulled, however, are not particularly powerful. In most states, supermajorities of the legislature and/or a popular vote are necessary to change the constitution. For example, the proposed constitutional changes in Turkey to create a stronger presidency, discussed in the previous chapter, require an affirmative vote of two-thirds of the National Assembly or a 60 percent vote by the legislature plus approval by voters in a national referendum. Provisions such as these make it relatively difficult to change the constitution. However, in some states, a simple majority vote in the legislature is sufficient to alter the constitution. Such is the case in Sweden, where the constitution can be amended by a majority vote in the Swedish parliament, although the parliament must vote twice: once before and once after a general election. Not coincidentally, the Swedish "constitution" is called "The Instrument of Government," a moniker that signifies a lesser status than that of a constitution.

A third way in which constitutions differ is how they are assembled. In most countries, the constitution, formally understood, is a single document. The exception is Great Britain, which is commonly described as having an "unwritten constitution." This is not really accurate, as the British Constitution is composed of numerous written documents, including such famous treaties as the Magna Carta of 1215 and landmark acts of Parliament such as the 1707 Act of Union, which brought Scotland into the United Kingdom, and the Reform Acts of 1832 and 1867, which expanded suffrage. Other elements of the British Constitution include treaties (e.g., EU treaties to which Britain has acceded), common law, tradition and convention, and "works of authority" developed by scholars of the constitution. There is no judicial review, in part a reflection that there is no single authoritative document on which a court could rely to make a constitutional judgment. In general, the principle of

TABLE 7.1 Constitutional features in selected European states

Country	*Const. monarchy/ Republic*	*Parliamentary/ Presidential*	*Unicameral/ Bicameral*	*Federal/ Unitary*	*Judicial Review?*
Germany	Republic	Parliamentary	Bicameral	Federal	Yes
France	Republic	Semi-presidential	Bicameral	Unitary	Yes
Great Britain	Const. monarchy	Parliamentary	Bicameral	Unitary*	No
Spain	Const. monarchy	Parliamentary	Bicameral	Unitary*	Yes
Austria	Republic	Parliamentary	Bicameral	Federal	Yes
Netherlands	Const. monarchy	Parliamentary	Bicameral	Unitary	No
Sweden	Const. monarchy	Parliamentary	Unicameral	Unitary	No
Poland	Republic	Semi-presidential	Bicameral	Unitary	Yes
Hungary	Republic	Parliamentary	Unicameral	Unitary	Yes
Serbia	Republic	Parliamentary	Unicameral	Unitary	Yes
Romania	Republic	Semi-presidential	Bicameral	Unitary	Yes
Turkey	Republic	Semi-presidential	Unicameral	Unitary	Yes

*Devolution of authority in Great Britain and Spain has been significant, but most observers would still classify them as unitary.

"parliamentary supremacy" reigns in Britain, meaning that anything passed by the British parliament carries constitutional weight. As a result, one could say that since the mid-1990s Britain has experienced a constitutional revolution, considering the major reforms such as devolution of greater political authority from the central government to the non-English regions of Scotland, Wales, and Northern Ireland, changes in the House of Lords, and adoption of the European Convention on Human Rights.[4] The overall result is that the constitutional order, so to speak, is more flexible in Great Britain; there is nothing formally standing in the way of even radical changes, including, as proposed in a 2014 referendum, the secession of Scotland, which failed to win majority support. Some, including those in Britain lobbying for a written constitution, worry that parliamentary supremacy could be dangerous, as there is nothing to prevent, for example, the parliament from ending democracy by cancelling future elections. In practice, however, elections are strong enough of a constitutional feature—one that exists through tradition—that no British Parliament could, in practice, actually do such a thing.[5]

Finally, constitutions differ in how they define the type of government in a given state. Again, within Europe we are always talking about democratic governments, but among democracies there are various subtypes. Table 7.1 highlights some features of the constitutional structures in several European states. Some of these aspects have been covered in earlier chapters, and some will be discussed more in depth below.

Sub-national governance

A basic question within any political system is what institution is empowered to act on certain issues. In most countries, different bodies have different political competencies; these can be divided among type of institution (e.g., parliaments versus executives) but also by the level of government. In the last two chapters, we have largely discussed political institutions at the national level, those that are located in the capital city and make decisions affecting the entire country. However, these are not the only governments in Europe. Voters also get to elect mayors and city councils, and in most countries there are regional or provincial level governments as well. These sub-national governments have a more restricted mandate, typically tending to such issues as road maintenance and transportation, education, sanitation, law and order, public recreation, and housing, and their reach is obviously more geographically constrained. This level of government is a layer in what was earlier labeled multi-level governance in Europe, and is often far more connected to the day-to-day concerns of citizens—and more trusted by them[6]—than those in the pan-European level or even the national level. Developments at this level rarely generate headlines—the election in 2016 of Sadiq Khan, a British-born Muslim of Pakistani heritage as mayor of London stands out as an exception—and the minutiae of the powers and performance of regional and local governments across Europe need not concern us here.[7] However, it is worth making distinctions based upon the degree upon which political power is centralized or decentralized within a given country.

federal states
countries in which political power is legally and formally divided between the national government and regional (sub-national) government.

Some countries in Europe are **federal states,** meaning that political powers are formally divided between the national government and regional (sub-national) governments. The precise division of powers is constitutionally defined and varies among federal states, but the key point is that "some matters are exclusively within the competence of certain local units and are constitutionally *beyond* the scope of the authority of the national government."[8] Of course, sub-national governments are not free to countermand any aspect of national law as they see fit, but federalism does mean that in areas under their purview (e.g., law enforcement, culture, education, housing), the national government is expected not to interfere, and sub-national governments have legal recourse to defend their "turf" against encroachments from the central government.

subsidiarity
principle that political decisions should be taken at the closest level possible to the individual citizen.

There are several rationales for federalism. One is to give ethnic or linguistic minorities, who are often concentrated in a particular region, group autonomy and powers of self-government on issues (e.g., education, culture) that are important to their identity.[9] Within Europe, this type of federalism is exemplified by Switzerland, a very decentralized state made up of German, French, and Italian speakers and twenty-six *cantons* (regions) with long traditions of autonomy, and Belgium, which has a complicated territorial/linguistic federalist system to ameliorate disputes between the Walloons (French speakers) and the Flemish (Dutch speakers). After horrific fighting in the early 1990s, Bosnia and Herzegovina also became a federal state, with power divided between the Republika Srbska (dominated by ethnic Serbs) and the Confederation of Croats and Bosniaks.

Federalism may also be defended as a means to check potential abuse of power by national governments and electoral majorities.[10] This, together with a nod to a history of local or regional self-rule, provided the rationale for the creation of a federal state in (West) Germany and Austria after World War II, as many believed that having a weaker national government would safeguard democracy and make it less likely for a figure like Hitler to emerge.

Third, one could make an argument for federalism by invoking the principle of **subsidiarity,** meaning that political decisions should be taken, for reasons both of democracy and of efficiency, at the closest possible level to the individual citizen. Some issues, such as defense, national tax rates, and management of the national currency, must be left to the central government. Uniformity across the nation, however, is not required in all policy areas. Some issues, such as education, might be better handled at the sub-national level, which can take into account the preferences of citizens in a particular region and provide more accountability. Local experimentation, it could also be argued, might serve as a laboratory to test out new ideas or policies that, if successful, could later be adopted across the entire country. Subsidiarity, one might recall from Chapter 4, has also been invoked in debates about the EU's powers, and as such it stands as a core concept to bolster democracy and accountability under conditions of "multi-level governance."

Federalism can co-exist with a number of different forms of government and electoral systems, but it typically requires two institutional arrangements. One, described in Chapter 5, is bicameralism, as the second chamber of the legislature provides a means for regional governments to be represented at the national level and thus gives, to some degree, regions a say over national policy.[11] Secondly, federal states should have some form of judicial review, discussed more in the next section of this chapter. This is necessary to prevent the national parliament or executive authorities from adopting any measure that they see fit. Without some sort of credible, constitutional guarantee that the national government could not simply abrogate federalist arrangements, it would be difficult to defend the rights of sub-national governments and make federalism work.[12] In these respects, the German federal system is fairly typical. Each of Germany's seventeen different regions (*Länder*) has responsibility in fields such as education and transportation and is also responsible for implementing much of the national legislation adopted by the federal government. *Länder* have a direct say in policy-making, as they are represented in the upper house of the German parliament (the *Bundesrat*), which must give its approval to all legislation affecting the *Länder*, which in effect means approximately two-thirds of all laws. Lastly, as discussed more below, Germany has a very powerful Constitutional Court, and the *Länder* can appeal to it to rule on the constitutionality of legislation if they believe the central government in Berlin has overstepped constitutional boundaries.

unitary states
countries in which the national government has exclusive political powers, although it may delegate some of its powers to regional or local governments.

Most states in Europe, however, are non-federal or **unitary states**, meaning that only the central government has exclusive political powers. In many cases, it delegates its authority to sub-national governments; there are, for example, regional administrative political units in France, Sweden, Poland, Hungary, and other countries. The key points, however, are that these administrative units enforce national law and do not make their own laws and that the central government is not *constitutionally* compelled to share any of its powers with other structures, which possess no autonomous powers on their own. Furthermore, the central government can take away its delegated powers at any time. Perhaps the fact that most European states are unitary can be explained by the fact most federal states in the world (e.g., the United States, Canada, Russia, Australia, India, Mexico, Brazil, Nigeria, Malaysia) tend to be very large and/or be ethnically diverse, whereas most European states are small and many are rather ethnically homogeneous. However, the lack of federalism in some states can also be attributed to political choices made by political elites. For example, after the collapse of communism in Eastern Europe, one might have thought, on democratic grounds, that federalism would be appealing, among other reasons, as means to bring government closer to the people and prevent the emergence of another centralized dictatorship. Moreover, as seen in Figure 7.1, many Eastern European states have sizeable ethnic minorities. Moreover, these minorities, unlike the immigrant minorities in West European countries such as France, Germany, and the Netherlands, are indigenous or have long resided in these countries in which they are citizens. They include ethnic Albanians in Macedonia, ethnic Hungarians in Slovakia and Romania, ethnic Turks in Bulgaria, and ethnic Russians in the Baltic states. The presence of such groups might have augured well for federalist arrangements. However, the example of Czechoslovakia and Yugoslavia—post-communist federal states that broke up, in part, due to ethnic-based separatism—as well as the desire to create a strong national government to serve the interests of the titular (dominant) nationality, made federalism less attractive to most states.

devolution process by which more authority is granted to regional or sub-national governments, although the powers of these governments are not constitutionally protected as they are in federal state.

However, in several non-federal states, things have been moving in a "federal direction," although as of yet they are not, by most accounts, truly federal. Most European countries guarantee language and cultural rights for their ethnic minorities, although, as in Slovakia and Macedonia, they may lack a territorially defined federal unit. Sometimes, as with the case of France's island of Corsica, Sicily and Sardinia in Italy, or the Åland islands of Finland (dominated by Swedish speakers), a territorial unit is granted a measure of autonomy or a special status. This is closer to federalism, but in France, Italy, and Finland, other regions do not enjoy autonomy, and political authority ultimately is in the hands of the national government. Matters have gone further in Great Britain, where since the 1990s the central government pursued a policy of **devolution,** granting more authority to regional governments in Scotland, Wales, and Northern Ireland.

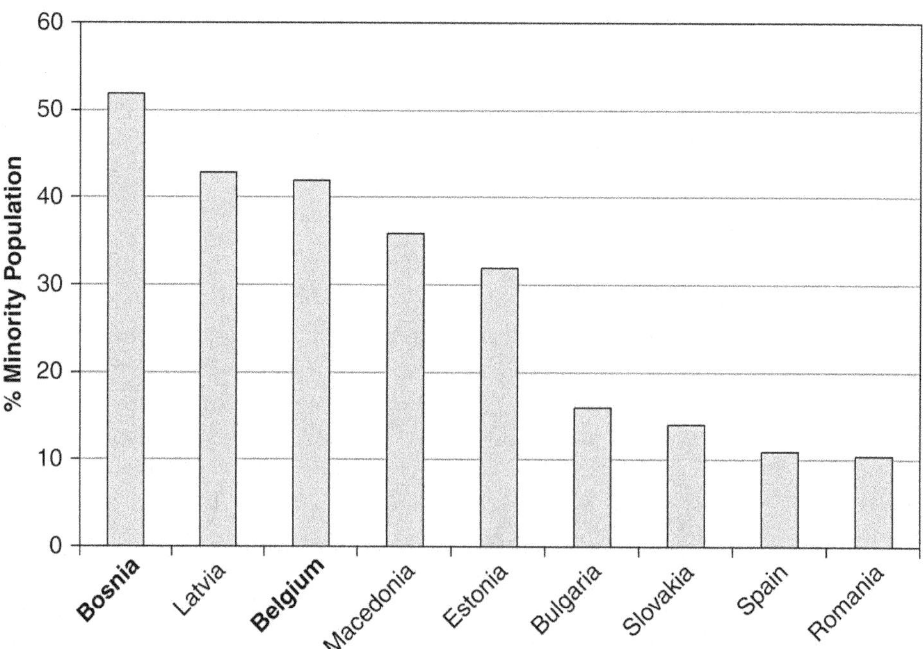

FIGURE 7.1 Indigenous minorities in select European countries (federal states are in bold)

Christoph Pan and Beate Sibylle Pfeil, *National Minorities in Europe* (West Lafayette IN: Purdue University). These figures do not include immigrants from outside of Europe

In some states, such as Spain, regions are pushing for even greater power, including independence from the central government. This raises a variety of political and constitutional questions. However, an irony of sorts is that as Europe is coming closer together through economic, political, and social integration, separatist impulses are present in many countries. This issue is taken up in the **In focus** section.

Legal traditions

Because laws vary widely from state to state—despite the growth of EU law—it is hard to make comprehensive comparisons about each state's legal system. True, as noted in the **Is Europe one?** section, there has been a certain amount of Europeanization of legal codes, as EU directives and regulations have been adopted in all member states. However, laws on a variety of topics such as freedom of expression, government surveillance, abortion, gay marriage, drug use (just to take a few controversial topics) vary across the continent, although there are some commonalities, including a ban on capital punishment. Rather than focus on individual issues, some of which are covered elsewhere in this book, we can speak more generally about the bases for the legal system as a whole.

common law
system of law developed in Great Britain in which judicial precedents obtain the status of law; judges have more power and discretion under this system.

code law
system of law in which laws are defined exclusively as statutes adopted by the government, and courts and judges merely apply the law.

There are two primary legal traditions in Europe.[13] In England, Wales, and Ireland (but, interestingly enough, not Scotland), Anglo-Saxon or "**common law**" legal traditions prevail. This system also exists in the US and Canada (with the exception of Quebec), as they were subject to English influence. Under this system, laws include statutory law as enacted by a legislature, regulatory law promulgated by executive branch agencies, and common law or "case law," which are decisions issued by courts or quasi-judicial tribunals within government agencies. Put another way, the law contains not only explicit provisions approved by elected officials but also is composed of judicial precedents that are binding on lower courts, other government agencies, and individual citizens. The reasoning for reliance on "common" or "case" law is that enacted statutes often give only terse statements of general principle, and for the fine boundaries and definitions necessary to apply the law, one must consult previous judicial decisions on the topic and reason from those by analogy. From time to time, precedents may be overturned, meaning that the law can evolve over time thanks to discretion and judgment offered by individual judges. Think of, for example, how the idea of "equality" has changed over the years to include women's rights and minority rights. However, in England, Wales, and Ireland today, common law traditions are weaker than they were in the past, thanks in large measure to the body of EU law—which must be applied by English, Welsh, and Irish judges—and their governments' accession to the European Convention of Human Rights.

Most European states—as well as Scotland—rely upon Roman or "**code" law**. This means that law is codified in detail by the government and then expected to be applied by qualified judges. The classical code law was adopted by Napoleon in France—the Napoleonic Code—and under French influence this system spread to many parts of Europe. In systems based on code law, judges do not enjoy much discretion. They are merely civil servants who determine the relevant facts to which codified laws are then applied. Judicial precedent plays much less of a role, as the

In focus

Devolution and separatist impulses in Europe

The idea of a single Europe may be equated with movement to a federal Europe that will bring European states closer together under a single political structure. However, federalism can evolve not only as a means to bind political units closer together. It also can emerge to devolve political authority to lower-level political structures (e.g., regions, provinces). Indeed, while Europe as a whole has been drawing closer together for several decades, devolution is occurring in a number of European states. Some formerly unitary states are looking more and more federal, stoking the fears (or hopes) that they may break apart into several states. In this respect, some national governments are being squeezed in both directions, with pressures to surrender sovereignty both to European institutions and to sub-national governments. These issues are particularly acute in Italy, Great Britain, Spain, and Belgium.

Italy was unified as a single state only in 1861, and vast economic and cultural differences remain between a more prosperous north and a poorer south.[14] The *Lega Nord* (Northern League), a right-wing political party, was founded in 1991 to champion the cause of *Padania*, part of northern Italy that claims to be a separate nation united by its own history and culture. Many would argue that *Padania* is pure invention, but there is no denying that since the 1990s the *Lega Nord* has been an important force in Italian politics, garnering over a sixth of the seats in both the Chamber of Deputies and Senate in 1994 and winning over 10 percent of the national vote in 1996 elections. It joined a coalition to install Silvio Berlusconi as Prime Minister in 1994 (withdrawing from it the following year, thus bringing down the government) and obtained cabinet positions in Berlusconi's government from 2008–2011. Thanks in large part to the influence of the *Lega Nord*, the Italian government has adopted reforms to devolve authority over health, education, and police to the regions, although some, including most leaders within the *Lega Nord* itself, want Italy to devolve further and become a federal state.

The government of Prime Minister Tony Blair (1997–2007) pursued devolution in Great Britain as part of an ambitious constitutional reform agenda.[15] Scotland now has its own parliament, enjoying control over police, culture, education, and housing, and it also has the right to levy its own taxes. Wales has an assembly, albeit one without the ability to tax. London and other localities now elect their own mayors. Northern Ireland, a land troubled since the 1970s by violence between its Catholic and Protestant communities, also has its own assembly, although power-sharing arrangements envisioned by the 1998 Good Friday Accord were implemented only in 2007. Some have even broached the idea of regional assemblies within England—where most of the population lives—but this was rejected by voters in 2004. The endpoint of devolution in Great Britain remains unclear, particularly with regard to Scotland. While a referendum on Scottish independence in 2014 failed to a gain majority support among Scotland's residents—they were the only ones allowed to vote—45 percent did vote in favor of secession. The Scottish National Party also became the dominant party in Scotland after 2015 national parliamentary elections, and it has pledged to keep the issue of separatism alive, as many Scots believe independent Scotland would be better off economically (thanks to revenue from oil in the North Sea) and could implement its own policies free from a Conservative-led government in London. After the British vote for "Brexit" in 2016—favored by the English and the Welsh, but not by Scots, who were over 60 percent in favor of remaining in the EU—the question of Scottish independence has been re-opened, with leading figures in the Scottish National Party advocating another referendum for secession.

All seventeen of Spain's regions are officially "autonomous communities," and devolution has given the regions broad powers over issues such as health and education. Sixty percent of public spending in Spain is now at the sub-national level.[16] Some already list Spain as a "semi-federal" state or one with "asymmetric federalism,"[17] although many in Spain would like to take matters further. One survey suggested eleven of the seventeen regions desire more autonomy.[18] The desire for outright independence from Madrid is strongest among the Basques, an ancient people who speak a language unrelated to Spanish, and Catalans, who have their own language (related to Spanish and French), culture, and cosmopolitan "capital," Barcelona.

Many Basques support separatism, and the Spanish government in Madrid has battled against the group ETA (Basque Homeland and Liberty), generally considered a terrorist organization, whose attacks since the 1960s have claimed more than 800 lives, including those of prominent Spanish politicians.[19] Basque political parties, while distancing themselves from violence, nonetheless seek as much power as they can obtain from Madrid. Since 2003, the regional Basque government has been led by the Basque Nationalist Party, which calls for the region to be a "freely associated state" with Spain and to have its own representation in the EU. The government has tried to reach accommodation with the Basques, including negotiating with ETA, which in 2011 announced an end to its armed activity. This does not mean, however, that the goal of separatism has been abandoned.

It is, however, in Catalonia, the most prosperous region in Spain, where Madrid faces its most serious separatist threat that has involved numerous legal battles. In 2006, the Catalonian parliament passed a declaration declaring Catalonia a "nation," a move the Spanish Constitutional Court declared had no legal value, as the Constitution recognizes the "unity of the Spanish nation." In 2009–2011, several Catalan municipalities held non-binding independence referendums—all of which were "won" by separatists—and in November 2014 the Catalan government organized a controversial non-binding vote in a "citizen participation process on the political future of Catalonia," which was conducted in defiance of the Spanish Constitutional Court's suspension of the vote. This was overwhelmingly "won" by those favoring separatism, although it remains unclear both whether the Catalan government will be able to find a legal or political means to advance its separatist cause, and how the Spanish state can maintain legitimacy among Catalans given the expressed desire for independence.

Belgium may rank as the most divided country in Europe. Nearly 60 percent of Belgian citizens are Flemish (Dutch-speakers), who reside mostly in the north of the country. The south is populated mostly by Walloons (French-speakers). Brussels, the capital, is the capital of Flanders but is predominantly French speaking. Belgian national identity has always been weak,[20] as people identify more with their language community, which includes linguistically segregated churches and political parties. Belgium is a federal state, and power is exceptionally de-centralized. In addition to the linguistic divide, there is also an ideological one: The Walloons tend to support leftist parties, the Flemish Christian-Democratic or Liberals, and both have their share of separatist nationalists. It took the divided political parties over a year and a half—a global record—to form a government after June 2010 elections. As one commentator noted, all Belgians have in common is a monarchy and a soccer team.[21] After terror attacks in 2016, another report suggested it was "the world's wealthiest failed state."[22]

Nonetheless, Belgium has managed to remain a single country. While some parties campaign for secession, the issue has yet to be put to a vote. After 2014 elections, it took Belgian parties only five months to form a government, which is led by a Walloon, even though the coalition is dominated by Flemish political parties. In part, Brussels itself may hold the country together. Despite being, in many ways, unloved ("Brussels" is used derisively in Belgium and beyond as shorthand for a bloated and overbearing EU), neither the Walloons nor the Flemish want to give it up.

Critical thinking questions

1. How should countries beset by regional or ethnic divisions try to preserve their unity? What are the advantages/disadvantages of policies such as federalism and devolution?
2. Some have suggested that the growth of the EU has encouraged regionalism within European countries (think of Scotland, Flanders, or Catalonia). Why might there be such a connection?

judiciary becomes "merely an administrative tool for the implementation of legislatively determined policies."[23] In addition, defendants typically do not enjoy the presumption of innocence—although France adopted such a provision in 1999—or protection against self-incrimination. In this tradition, the judge is also not a neutral arbiter; he or she is an agent of the state, frequently entering into arguments during trial. In contemporary practice, this means working to determine the pertinent facts, not siding with the state, although in Eastern Europe under communism, judges were clearly on the side of the authorities, rendering the judicial system fundamentally unfair. Even though judges are not supposed to be biased with respect to the outcome of cases, there can be real difficulties with this type of system when the state itself is the defendant (e.g., sued by a citizen for violating her rights). To handle questions like these, many states with code law systems have created a whole separate system of administrative courts, and these courts do make laws by precedent.

Court systems

Most European states have a hierarchical court system, in which the decisions of local or lower-level courts can be subject to appeal to higher courts, culminating in some sort of supreme court. Federal states have their own courts to administer laws passed at the sub-national level, and there are often courts for civil and criminal matters as well as separate juvenile and tax courts. In Turkey, military courts have played a role in prosecuting those deemed to be threatening to the state, although this feature of the Turkish state has been subjected to criticism by the EU, compelling the Turkish government to curtail their role.

Judges are expected to be well-trained professionals, and thus the naming of judges is typically not left to voters. In most states, the president and/or parliament appoints the judges, although rules are established that create a minimum level of qualification (e.g., law degree) for judges. In many states (e.g., Italy, Spain, Hungary), a non-political judicial committee made up of judges and/or lawyers screens and recommends potential judges to the authorities. Although judges are supposed to be above politics, a strict separation is often impossible to maintain, as political actors or bodies are prone to appoint judges that share their general orientation. The independence of the courts from interference by other branches and the expectation of political impartiality in judicial decisions are enshrined in many constitutions and are crucial to maintaining the integrity of the court system. If the courts seem packed with political cronies—a problem at times in states such as Spain and Italy, hence generating a system whereby appointments to courts are made by fellow judges—the credibility of the court system suffers. However, as seen in Figure 7.2, surveys from many countries reveal that the judiciary is typically far more trusted by citizens than more "politicized" institutions such as parliament or political parties.

constitutional courts
special courts whose primary purpose is to rule on the constitutionality of proposed or adopted legislation; they are the main agents who exercise judicial review.

The most explicit political role normally undertaken by courts is to exercise judicial review, meaning that the courts can nullify or declare invalid a law or regulation passed by parliament or an action taken by the executive branch. Although generally thought of as a US innovation and at odds with principles of code law that served to constrain judges, judicial review has spread throughout Europe. Reflecting in part the tradition of code law, constitutional questions are usually reserved for special **constitutional courts** or constitutional councils. Some courts, such as France's Constitutional Council and Romania's Constitutional

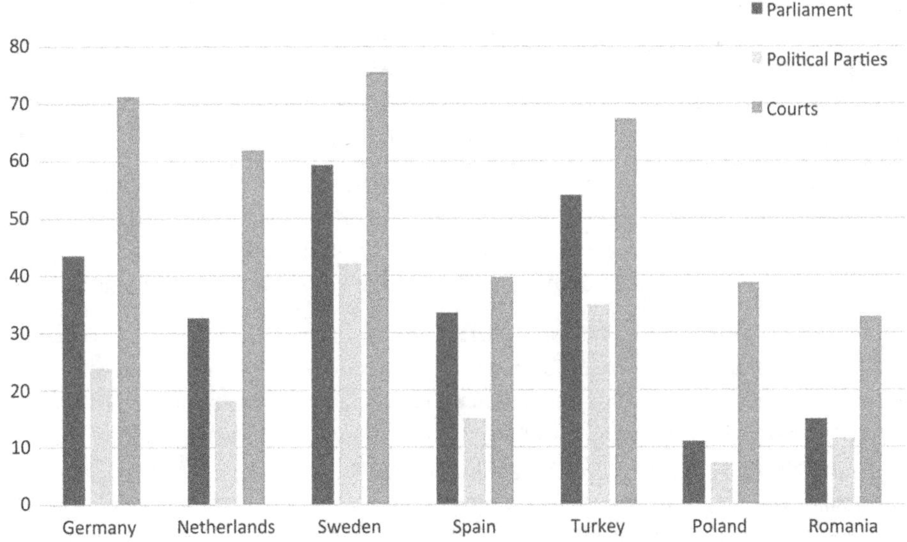

FIGURE 7.2 Confidence in courts and other political institutions

World Values Survey, Wave 6, at www.worldvaluessurvey.org. Data are from 2011 for Spain, Sweden, and Turkey; 2012 for Poland, Romania, and the Netherlands; and from 2013 for Germany. Responses are percentage of those indicating a great deal or quite a lot of confidence in a particular institution

Is Europe one?

Europeanization of judicial systems

Europeanization requires that national-level political institutions work with the EU and coordinate some of their activities. As we saw in Chapter 5, national parliaments are increasingly tied to the EU. Headv§s of government work through the European Council to set EU priorities. However, coordination between EU-level and national-level institutions may go furthest in the court system, reflecting the supranational reach of the EU into its members' legal systems.[24]

As we learned in Chapter 4, European-level law is extensively developed. Application of this law is often through national court systems. Europeanization of the legal system thus means that, when it considers a case, national-level judges must apply, if relevant, European-level law in domestic-level legal proceedings. In order to facilitate uniform application of the law, Article 177 of the 1957 Treaty of Rome provides the European Court of Justice (ECJ) with power to make preliminary rulings on questions raised by national courts concerning the interpretation of EU law. In other words, one responsibility of the ECJ is to make sure courts apply EU law similarly throughout the union. National level courts operate as *de facto* European courts when they interpret EU directives that have been transposed into national law and can, in principle, request legislatures to "re-do" legislation that does not meet EU requirements. In this way, via national courts, European-level rules can be introduced into domestic legal orders.

Additionally, the ECJ requires national courts to enforce European law. By the doctrine of direct effect of Article 189 of the Treaty of Rome, provisions of EU law confer rights and impose obligations on individuals and public authorities. National courts can apply these directly, without the need for national-level legislation. Litigants in court can appeal to these EU-level measures, which, due to the doctrine of supremacy that holds that EU law is supreme to national law, means that if EU law contradicts national-level law, EU law prevails. This later principle was established in the case of *Costa v. ENEL* in 1964, in which an Italian citizen invoked European law to sue his government when the Italian government nationalized ENEL, an energy company. Although the ECJ ruled against Mr. Costa, it noted that he did have a right to invoke EU law, and, if there were a conflict between European law and Italian law, the former would prevail. In the ECJ's words,

> [i]t follows from all these observations [in the case] that the law stemming from the treaty, an independent source of law, could not, because of its special and original nature, be overridden by domestic legal provisions, however framed, without being deprived of its character as community law and without the legal basis of the community itself being called into question.[25]

In practice, this means that there is judicial review at the EU level, which can be done both at the ECJ if a case comes before it but also at the national-level, as courts are expected to override domestic level law where it conflicts with EU law. National level courts can even order compensation in cases where individuals suffer losses from inadequate implementation of EU law.

In effect, what this means is a legal hierarchy has taken hold in Europe, with EU law at its pinnacle. The EU, however, does not have the resources to oversee an entire legal structure. Whereas the ECJ does adjudicate some disputes, it relies upon national-level courts to do much of its job. The courts thus partner up in a manner far more extensively than do executives or parliaments, and, because the doctrine of supremacy is well established, the turf battles and disputes over subsidiarity that might affect relations between national parliaments and the EU are relatively absent.

This does not necessarily mean, however, that all functions smoothly all the time. Examination of how national courts interact with the ECJ reveal that links between the ECJ and the French and British courts, are, in comparison with the Dutch, Italian, Belgian, and German courts, not very extensive. In the French case, the lack of *posterior* judicial review as well as concentration of power works against litigants trying to appeal to EU law. In the British case, judges may, as they can under common law, cite EU law as precedent, but many of the direct appeals to the ECJ for preliminary rulings concern social issues, an arena in which British law is relatively undeveloped and/or in conflict with prevailing EU law, and thus British litigants are more able to make appeals for the use of EU law. In contrast, German use of EU law is facilitated by its decentralized federal system and stronger judicial review, which provides more opportunity for litigation. In the words of one writer,

> German courts are the most active participants in the European judicial dialogue, and German political structure provides the best "institutional fit" with European political structure. The dispersion of power in both systems promotes the organization of societal interests into groups that can pursue legal action. German society has long been prepared to seize the opportunities of Europeanization through judicial forums.[26]

Critical thinking questions

1. Countries typically accept judgments against them at the European Court of Justice. Why would they do so instead of simply ignoring the ECJ?
2. "Europeanization" of judicial systems is fairly extensive, yet the ECJ is typically viewed more favorably and is less controversial than the European Commission or European Parliament. Why might this be?

Court, only have the power of *a priori* review, meaning they can consider the constitutionality of a measure only *before* it is adopted into law. Most constitutional courts have the power of *posterior* review, meaning they review the constitutionality of legislation after it becomes law. In these cases, for example, an individual may argue that a law violates his or her constitutional rights and take the matter to court or to an **ombudsman**, an office usually attached to parliament that is expressly designed to handle citizen complaints about government abuse of power. Cases may also be brought before a constitutional court if one believes a law contravenes an international treaty. These matters, if judged to have merit, can then be referred to a constitutional court for a definitive ruling. Germany, Italy, Poland, Spain, and the Czech Republic, among others, all have constitutional courts with these powers, and they have been politically important. For example, in the 1990s the Polish Constitutional Tribunal struck down some of the government's "shock therapy" economic reforms and intervened in political disputes by declaring efforts to President Lech Walesa to extend his powers as unconstitutional. To the extent that rulings such as these set precedents and give the courts power over the other branches of government, the use of judicial review in continental Europe is helping to erode some of the distinctions between common law and code law systems.

ombudsman
government official charged with handling citizen complaints about governmental abuse of power.

Not all states have formalized judicial review. For example, courts do not have such power in Great Britain, the Netherlands, Sweden, and Finland. This does not mean, however, that there is no review of legislative proposals. For example, in Sweden, a Legal Council of judges from the Supreme Court can be asked whether controversial measures are compatible with the constitution, and its judgment carries considerable weight. In Great Britain, the highest court for normal civil and criminal appeals is composed of Law Lords from the House of Lords. Judges ensure that political entities follow existing law, but they are not empowered to review the laws themselves and declare the acts of the House of Commons as unconstitutional. Similarly, in the Netherlands, Article 120 of the constitution expressly prohibits courts from considering the constitutionality of laws. However, because both Great Britain and the Netherlands have ratified treaties such as the European Convention of Human Rights, the courts can now ask that laws be considered in light of their respect for such treaties. This is not merely theoretical: Issues such as granting of political asylum, a controversial issue in the wake of terrorist attacks in London in 2005, have involved the British courts ruling that government proposals to restrict applications for asylum run afoul of the country's international commitments.

The Swiss case deserves special mention because constitutional questions are often decided not by courts but by voters themselves in a referendum. Referendums, an example of direct democracy, give people a direct say in the adoption of laws. In Switzerland, questions can be put to voters if 50,000 signatures are put on a petition. Any bill decided by parliament can be subject to referenda, and all constitutional amendments must be submitted to voters. A referendum passes if it is approved by the majority of voters and by voters in a majority of the twenty-six cantons. If voters wish to amend the constitution, neither parliament nor the courts can stand in their way.[27] Swiss voters have decided a number of important issues, including granting women the right to vote (1971), joining the UN (2002), and acceding to the Schengen Agreement (2005).

In order to gain more understanding of the importance of the judiciary and, in particular, judicial review, let us turn to a few examples in contemporary Europe.

Germany: The growing importance of the Constitutional Court

Germany has one of the strongest constitutional courts in Europe. It is separate from the regular system of civil, criminal, and administrative courts, ruling only on the constitutionality of legislation and international treaties. Cases can come before it by referral from members of the *Bundestag*, regional governments, ordinary courts, or individuals. Notably, there was no such court prior to World War II, which meant that no institution could overturn Hitler's laws and decrees. Much of the rationale for creating this court after the war therefore was a desire to avoid a repeat of this experience. Members of the court are nominated by political parties and appointed to a twelve-year term by a two-thirds vote in both houses of parliament. The court is comprised of two eight-member Senates, one of which is for issues arising out of ordinary litigation and one is for disputes between branches of government. The federal government, *Länder* governments, and a collection of one-third of *Bundestag* members can request an abstract review of any existing law,

The German Constitutional Court in session

and individual citizens can request a concrete review of suspect law if they believe they have been harmed by it. The constitutional court is based not in Berlin but in Karlsruhe, a medium-sized city in southwestern Germany.

This court has made many noteworthy rulings and exerts real influence both in Germany and within the EU as a whole.[28] In the first fifty years of its existence, it declared about 5 percent of the bills passed by the *Bundestag* to be unconstitutional.[29] Alone among German institutions, it can ban a political party, which it did in the 1950s in the case of neo-Nazi and communist parties. Since the 1990s, the German Constitutional Court has ruled on such diverse issues as public financing of political parties; the liberalization of abortion laws; religious symbols in the schools; allowing German military units to participate in international operations; approval of the euro; granting equal legal treatment to homosexual unions; and ruling on the constitutionality of the EU's Maastricht Treaty. In some cases, as with rulings on whether smoking can be allowed in bars or whether commuters can deduct transport costs from their taxes, the Court has waded into minutiae of public policy, leading some to call it the third chamber of the legislature. Nonetheless, there is no evidence that Germans are dissatisfied with such "judicial activism." The Constitutional Court is trusted by over 80 percent of Germans, double the number who trust the federal government and the *Bundestag*.

Germany's Constitution Court is also powerful beyond the country's borders, as it has ruled on the constitutionality of EU treaties, specifically whether those treaties violate German principles of federalism and individual rights of Germans. Since 1974, the German Constitutional Court has made the transfer of powers to the EU conditional on the protection of Germans' basic rights; if they are infringed, Germany could, therefore, reclaim them. Because it has asserted itself in this manner, the German Constitutional Court is often the last legal hurdle needing to be overcome when the EU adopts major reforms. This was the case with the Lisbon Treaty, which was held up by a court ruling in June 2009 that said that the EU was not democratic enough to support more integration. In this case, the Constitutional Court asked the German parliament to pass new laws to give itself more say over EU affairs so that Germany will retain power to shape "citizens' circumstances of life" in areas such as education, religion, and criminal law.[30] This ruling delayed final German ratification of the treaty, which finally occurred in September 2009. In 2012, the German Constitutional Court was asked to rule on the legality of the EU's "bailout" package for Greece under the European Stability Mechanism (ESM) (for more, see Chapter 10). It ultimately gave its approval, but only after placing a cap on Germany's contribution to the ESM and requiring the *Bundestag* to approve all future activations of the ESM. Reports noted that this ruling allowed "Project Europe" to move ahead.[31] This feature of the German judiciary is interesting, because Europeanization is often conceived as a one-way process, with power and influence flowing from the EU to member states; here is a case of a domestic political body ruling on the legitimacy of EU actions. In this way, the German Constitutional Court becomes an important arbiter of future EU integration.

France: Abstract, *a priori* review

Judicial review in France functions very differently than in Germany, or, for that matter, in the US. France's equivalent of a constitutional court is a Constitutional Council, created in the 1958 constitution of the Fifth Republic. The Council is composed of nine regular members,[32] who are appointed to a nine-year term. Three each are appointed by the president, the president of the National Assembly, and the president of the Senate.

France has abstract and *a priori* judicial review, a system that some would not consider to be a true system of judicial review.[33] This means that the Council reviews a law or executive order *before* it is enacted into law, not afterwards (as in the US) and that it reviews the law without having a specific complainant (again, as in the US). "Organic bills," those which fundamentally affect government and treaties, must be vetted by the Council. Other proposed measures may be brought before it, but, unlike in Germany or the US, only certain individuals can bring a case before it: the president, prime minister, president of the National Assembly, president of the Senate, or (since 1974) a group of sixty individuals from either legislative body.[34] Ordinary citizens who feel they might be harmed by the legislation, in other words, cannot take a case to the Constitutional Council. If the proposal does not meet with the Council's approval, it goes back to the legislature or president for revisions. Interestingly, in addition to the 1958 Constitution and international treaties (e.g., the European Convention on Human Rights), the Council has stated it may void measures that violate the 1789 Declaration of Rights of Man, which dates to the French Revolution. In this way, the Council can exercise real power, but, because only elected officials can make appeals to it, it reviews fewer cases than the German Constitutional Court and traditionally has been far less likely to issue rulings against the government's wishes. Since the 1980s, however, the Council has been both more active and been more politicized: Members of the opposition party in the National Assembly now regularly bring controversial bills before it, and, if the political makeup of the Council differs from that of the incumbent government, disputes are more likely.[35] Some of its more controversial decisions have touched on bills to limit immigration and government funding for church-run schools, and after terrorist attacks in Paris in 2015, it has been asked to rule on a host of emergency security measures, most of which it has approved.[36] The Constitutional Council also supervises and certifies elections and referenda.

Post-communist Europe: Ensuring an independent judiciary

Whereas several West European states adopted judicial review after World War II, in Eastern Europe the court system, like all political and social institutions, was subjugated to the Communist Party. Courts were not independent, and often they enforced measures (e.g., censorship, imprisonment for public dissent) that were not compatible with democratic governance. Judges were servants of the government, and rather than having independent powers, they were expected to fall into line with the demands of the communist authorities. In the words of one writer, communism "translated into corruption and 'telephone' justice," the latter phrase meaning decisions were made with the help of a phone call to a Party official.[37]

One of the priorities, therefore, in post-communist Europe has been the establishment of a well-functioning, independent judiciary that will uphold principles of democracy and the rule of law. Eastern European states, inspired in part by the French and German systems, also established constitutional courts with the power of judicial review. New measures—either in statutes or in new constitutions—were passed relatively quickly to create these courts and uphold the principles of separation of powers and judicial independence. Appointment of judges for the regular civil and criminal court system is either by the executive authority (as in the Czech Republic), an expert judicial committee (as in Bulgaria), or a combination of the two (as in Poland). Appointment procedures for constitutional courts are more similar, usually involving legislative and executive authority and putting judges on the court for a fixed term of seven to ten years.

Whereas putting changes on paper was relatively easy, creating well-functioning courts, in some cases, has been more problematic. Communist-era judges, for example, were frequently disqualified from continued service on the bench, and finding new, qualified individuals willing to work as a judge on a civil servant's salary has not always been easy. Although judges are supposed to be politically independent, the fact that they are, in many cases, appointed by presidents or parliaments has made some question their independence. In some cases, such as Bulgaria, the parliament has tried to interfere in the workings of courts. This interference took various forms: changing the qualification of judges in order to get rid of certain troublesome (from the perspective of the parliamentary majority) judges; cutting the budget of the courts; even trying to evict the Constitutional Court from its building![38] Throughout the region, connections between judges and political and/or business figures have led to accusations of corruption, and judicial reform and the elimination of corruption were major concerns of the European Union in the 2000s in accession talks with Romania, Bulgaria, and Croatia. Whereas in some countries, notably Hungary, Constitutional Courts have been very active in asserting their powers—one observer suggested that Hungarian Constitutional Court, which rules on approximately 1,000 motions a year, may be the "most powerful constitutional court in the world"[39]—in other cases the culture of judicial review has been harder to establish, as parliaments have tried to ignore or override the courts, as evidenced most recently by the attempt to weaken and pack the Constitutional Tribunal in Poland.

Spanish courts and universal jurisdiction

universal jurisdiction controversial idea established by Spanish courts that they have the ability to try human rights crimes regardless of where such crimes allegedly occurred.

The Spanish court system is structured and functions similarly to those elsewhere on the continent. However, it has one special feature: Its courts claim **universal jurisdiction** over human rights crimes. What this means is that one does not have to commit such a crime in Spain in order to be tried by Spanish courts. Spanish law allows Spanish courts to investigate and try these cases wherever they occur in the world.

Spaniards who defend this provision argue that it helps to ensure justice. If human rights crimes (e.g., genocide, mass murder) are "crimes against humanity," then there is no logical reason why those who commit such crimes must be tried only by one certain country. Moreover, in some cases—think of government officials in Sudan accused of genocide or Saddam Hussein when he ruled Iraq—it would be impossible to bring the accused to justice in their home countries. This does not mean that Spanish courts seek indictments against all alleged human rights abusers. However, they have sought such indictments in a couple of high-profile cases. One involved Augusto Pinochet, who ruled Chile from 1973 to 1990 and was accused of being complicit in the murder and torture of thousands of civilians, including Spanish citizens living in Chile. Spain's warrant against Pinochet led to his arrest in Great Britain in 1998, as the latter was obligated by European law to honor it. This was a watershed event in the history of international law, as no previous head of state had been arrested on the principle of universal jurisdiction.[40] Cases have also been opened against officials in Israel and China for human rights abuses in Gaza and Tibet, respectively. Perhaps even more controversially, in 2009, Baltasar Garzón, a Spanish judge, opened an investigation against six former officials in the Bush Administration for providing legal cover for torture allegedly committed at the prison in Guantanamo Bay, Cuba. Because of the fallout of this action, the Spanish parliament passed a measure to change the law that allows the courts to claim universal jurisdiction.[41] Henceforth, the accused will have to be arrested in Spain, a victim will have to be a Spaniard, or there will have to be some other clear connection to Spain before the court will be allowed to proceed. There will also have to be proof that no other national court system has taken up a given case. Interestingly as well, Garzón was indicted in 2010 for opening up examination of crimes committed under the dictatorship of Francisco Franco (1936 to 1975) in Spain that were, according to those who sought his indictment, covered by an amnesty law that forbids prosecution of anyone for these actions.[42]

Constitutional arrangements and court systems rarely capture political headlines, although there are some exceptions, including those in Poland noted at the outset of this chapter. Courts may also become important (and perhaps politicized) actors as a possible check on government power with respect to anti-terrorism measures, an issue explored in Chapter 12. In normal circumstances, however, constitutions and legal systems are generally accepted as givens, the neutral "rules of the game" for political actors as well as the citizenry as a whole. However, as we've seen in this and in other chapters, these rules have real consequences and help account for differences in institutions and policies across Europe. Moreover, as actors question the fairness or legitimacy of these rules, courts can take on real political importance and become a source of both controversy and change.

Application questions

1. Do you think a constitution should include socio-economic rights, such as right to education and right to health care?
2. Why do you think judicial review has become common in Europe? Why might some be against it?
3. What are the advantages and disadvantages of extensive use of referenda? Should some matters be reserved for decisions by referenda?
4. Should a constitution or courts be able to prevent something that a majority of people wants to see adopted as a law or policy?
5. How seriously, in your view, does the power of the ECJ erode the sovereignty of states and their voters?

Key terms

Additional reading

Bell, John. 2006. *Judiciaries within Europe: A Comparative Review*. Cambridge: Cambridge University Press.
This book presents an overview of the workings of court systems in France, Germany, Spain, Sweden, and Great Britain, with an effort to make comparisons across these cases.

International Constitutional Law website, sponsored by University of Bern, at www.servat. unibe. ch/law/icl/index.html.
This is a portal through which one can view constitutions (in English) of many countries in the world, as well as retrieve basic information about elections and party systems; an excellent resource.

Sweet, Alec Stone. 2000. *Governing with Judges: Constitutional Politics in Europe*. Oxford: Oxford University Press.
This work examines constitutional courts' function in a number of countries, as well as the workings of the ECJ.

Sweet, Alec Stone. 2004. *The Judicial Construction of Europe*. Oxford: Oxford University Press.
This work focuses on the legal development of the EU and how this has affected national-level legislation and judicial systems.

Swenden, Wilifried. 2005. *Federalism and Regionalism on Western Europe*. New York: Palgrave Macmillan.
This book, a thematic treatment of how sub-national governments work in European states such as Germany, Spain, and Austria, focuses on political decision-making and the allocation of resources among levels of government.

Notes

1 "Das ist gelenkte Demokraite nach Putins Art," *Frankfurter Allgemeine*, January 9, 2016. See also "A Challenge to Poland's Anti-Democratic Drift," *New York Times*, April 15, 2016.
2 "Polish Government Undermines Democracy, E.U. Says," *New York Times*, April 12, 2016, and "Ex-Presidents of Poland Issue a Rebuke to Government," *New York Times*, April 24, 2016.
3 Calculations come from English translations found through a website sponsored by the University of Bern (Switzerland) at www.oefre.unibe.ch/law/icl/index.html, accessed on April 5, 2010. This website is an excellent site to view and compare constitutions.
4 For more on the unique features of Great Britain, see Anthony King, *Does the United Kingdom Still Have a Constitution?* (London: Sweet and Maxwell, 2001).
5 Elections during World War II were postponed, but were held in July 1945. Ironically, the Conservatives, led by Winston Churchill, lost this election, despite Churchill's courageous leadership of Britain during the war.
6 Jennifer Fitzgerald and Jennifer Wolak, "The Roots of Trust in Local Government in Western Europe," *International Political Science Review* 37:1, 2016, p. 130–146.
7 Details of local government structures in many European states can be found in Peter John, *Local Governance in Western Europe* (London: Sage, 2001).
8 Robert Dahl, *Democracy, Identity, and Equality* (Oslo: Norwegian University Press, 1986), p. 114.
9 Federalism is thus part of a "consociational" system, long advocated by the political scientist Arend Lijphart, to make democratic governance easier in ethnically divided societies. See Arend Lijphart, *Democracy in Plural Societies* (New Haven: Yale University Press, 1997), and Andrew Reynolds, ed., *The Architecture of Democracy: Constitutional Design, Conflict Management, and Democracy* (Oxford: Oxford University Press, 2002).
10 For a classic treatment of federalism on this front, see William Riker, *Federalism: Origin, Operation, Significance* (Boston: Little Brown, 1964).
11 Exceptions are the tiny Federated States of Micronesia and Canada, which has an appointed Senate as its upper legislative chamber.
12 By this definition, non-democratic systems such as the Soviet Union and Yugoslavia, despite the façade of federalism, could be said not to have true federal governments, since, particularly in the Soviet case, sub-national governments did not have effective means to defend themselves against the political center.
13 Prior to the collapse of communism, one could speak of principles of "socialist law" that animated legal systems in Eastern Europe. These have largely been eradicated.
14 Robert Putnam with Robert Leonardi and Raffaella Nanetti, *Making Democracy Work: Civic Traditions in Modern Italy* (Princeton: Princeton University Press, 1993).
15 Colin Pilkington, *Devolution in Britain Today* (Manchester: Manchester University Press, 2003).
16 James Graff, "Regional Ruckus," *Time*, February 29, 2004, and "All Must Have Prizes," *The Economist*, August 1, 2009.

17 John Gibbons, "Spain: A Semi Federal State," in D. McIver, ed. *The Multinational State* (London: Macmillan, 1999), and Kenneth McRoberts, *Catalonia: Nation-Building Without a State* (Oxford: Oxford University Press, 2001).
18 "Homage to Barcelona," *The Economist*, June 18, 2005.
19 "Survey of Spain," *The Economist*, May 19, 2001.
20 A Walloon socialist was said to have told King Albert II in 1912, "Il n'y a pas des Belges" (There are no Belgians). See Jochen Bittner, "Europe, After Brussels," *New York Times*, March 24, 2016.
21 Ian Buruma, "In the Capital of Europe," *New York Review of Books* 53:6, April 7, 2016, p. 39.
22 "Brussels Attacks Underscore Vulnerability of an Open European Society," *New York Times*, March 22, 2016, at www.nytimes.com/2016/03/23/world/europe/belgium-security.html.
23 Robert Utter and David Lundesgaard, "Comparative Aspects of Judicial Review: Issues Facing the New European States," *Judicature* 77, 1994, p. 241.
24 This section relies heavily on Paul Mullen, "Legitimate Options: National Courts and the Power of the European Court of Justice," *European Community Studies Association Review* 11:1, Winter 1998, p. 2–7, and Lisa Conant, "Europeanization and the Courts: Variable Patterns of Adaptation among National Judiciaries," in Maria Green Cowles, et al., *Transforming Europe: Europeanization and Domestic Change* (Ithaca: Cornell University Press, 2001).
25 European Court of Justice, Case 6/64, *Falminio Costa v. ENEL* [1964] ECR 585, 593.
26 Conant, "Europeanization and the Courts," p. 113.
27 An exception occurs if a proposed measure violates international law. Such was the case in 1996 with an anti-asylum measure.
28 Much of this section comes from "Judgment Days," *The Economist*, March 28, 2009, p. 59–60.
29 Manfred Schmidt, *Political Institutions in the Federal Republic of Germany* (Oxford: Oxford University Press, 2003), p. 120.
30 "Constitutional Concerns," *The Economist*, July 25, 2009, p. 51.
31 Ian Traynor, "Project Europe Clears Legal Hurdle but Merkel Holds Key to Political Union," *The Guardian*, September 12, 2012.
32 Former French presidents are *de jure* members of this council, but they do not always participate in its proceedings.
33 Such is the presentation in Michael Gallagher, et al., *Representative Government in Modern Europe*, 4th ed. (New York: McGraw-Hill, 2006), p. 99.
34 Constitutional reforms in 2008 provide for appeals to the Council from lower courts, but statutory law to spell out how this would function have not been adopted as of 2010.
35 For more on developments in France, see Paul F. Mullen, "Legitimate Options."
36 See for example, "French Constitutional Court Approves New Powers for Intelligence Services," *Wall Street Journal*, July 24, 2015.
37 A.E. Dick Howard, "Judicial Independence in Post-Communist Central and Eastern Europe," in Peter Russell and David O'Brien, eds. *Judicial Independence in the Age of Democracy* (Charlottesville: University of Virginia Press, 2001), p. 91. Much of this section borrows from this chapter.
38 Albert Melone, "The Struggle for Judicial Independence and the Transition Toward Democracy in Bulgaria," *Communist and Post-Communist Studies* 29:2, June 1996, p. 231–243.
39 Jon Elster, "On Majoritarianism and Rights," *East European Constitutional Review* 1, 1992, p. 11.
40 Pinochet was eventually taken back to Chile to stand trial, where, up until his death in 2006, he was in and out of house arrest and fought prosecution by claiming legal immunity and health problems, including dementia.
41 "Push in Spain to Limit Reach of the Courts," *New York Times*, May 21, 2009.
42 "Spain Allows Case Against Noted Judge," *New York Times*, March 25, 2010, at www.nytimes.com/2010/03/26/world/europe/26spain.html.

The far-right Jobbik Party: What does it demonstrate about democracy in Hungary?

Chapter 8

Political parties and elections

A European political party that campaigns against Jewish control of the world's financial system and a party leader who instructs Jews to "go back to playing with their tiny circumcised tails." A party with a militia dressed in black that patrols Roma (Gypsy) ghettoes and threatens to deport or send the Roma to prison. A political campaign that features attacks on a rabbi's house and defacement of a Jewish memorial.[1] When the votes are counted, the party is claimed the big winner of the elections, threatening to upend the established political order. Could this be Germany in the 1930s, perhaps Italy in the 1920s? No, this is Hungary in 2010, where the Jobbik Party,[2] which warns voters against the rise of "Judapest," surprised observers by winning 16.7 percent of the vote in parliamentary elections and became the third-largest party in the Hungarian parliament. Afterwards, MPs from Jobbik caused numerous scandals, including protesting the holding of the World Jewish Congress in Budapest as a Jewish attempt to buy up Hungary, commemorating a nineteenth-century blood libel case against Jews, and suggesting that Hungarian Jews be placed on a national register because they pose a security risk to Hungary.[3] While these actions were all condemned both inside and outside Hungary, Jobbik did not suffer at the polls; indeed, it improved upon its 2010 performance, winning over 20 percent of the vote in 2014 elections. In 2015, amid the refugee crisis in Europe, Jobbik proposed changes in the Hungarian constitution that would both limit the ability of individuals to receive asylum and authorize declaration of a state of emergency, giving the military the right to shoot those attempting to cross the border.[4]

Is this a cause for alarm? Perhaps not. Jobbik itself claims that it is a principled and "radically patriotic" party committed to defending "Hungarian values." It is not a coalition partner in the Hungarian government, so its actual political influence is somewhat limited. Hungary's economy also suffered a severe blow during the global economic crisis in the late 2000s–early 2010s, and many may have voted for Jobbik, which campaigned extensively in areas with high unemployment, as a means to protest. However, nationalist, xenophobic, anti-immigrant parties such as Jobbik are not a purely Hungarian or Eastern European phenomenon, although Jobbik may qualify as the most explicitly racist among such parties. Many have done well in several Western European countries such as France, Switzerland, Austria, Sweden, and Denmark, and, given fears over refugees, migrants, and terrorism in Europe in the 2010s, they have promised to do even better in coming years. Moreover, radical or "anti-system" parties on the left have also done well in some European elections in recent years, including in Germany, Portugal, and Greece. At minimum, issues of whether these types of parties threaten democracy or liberal values aside, what these phenomena demonstrate is that the political spectrum in Europe, with parties representing highly controversial and combative views, is exceptionally diverse and dynamic.

This chapter takes up the topics of political parties and elections, subjects that have been mentioned at various points in the text but have yet to receive concerted, systemic treatment. These are, of course, core subjects both in European politics and in the study of democratic governments more generally. After all, the main attributes that distinguish democracies from other forms of government are political competition among various groups or parties, and that power is won through free and fair elections. All governments have some form of executive, legislative, and judicial power—even if in extreme cases powers are fused and all held by a single individual—but only in democracies do elections determine who holds power and only in democracies are people given a meaningful choice when they vote.[5] The choices that are presented to voters are usually determined by political parties, which are the primary organizations that nominate candidates for public office and contest elections. Political parties are thus a necessary component of modern democracies, and, insofar as parties structure political life and provide the key personnel for government, they are often considered a political institution.

Functions of political parties

The key actors in any democratic electoral system are political parties. Political parties serve several essential roles in modern democracies, making politics as we know it today "unthinkable" without them.[6] Indeed, political parties arose with the expansion of suffrage and introduction of democratic politics, first in the US in the early 1800s and later in Europe in the late 1800s through early 1900s.[7] Their primary function is to contest elections and nominate candidates for public office. This activity distinguishes political parties from other organizations such as interest groups, which are involved in political life but do not nominate candidates and seek formal governmental authority. Across Europe, party organizations have a great deal of control in recruiting and nominating candidates for office. Typically, they choose individuals that they believe will be loyal to the goals and top leadership of the party, thus helping to ensure, as we noted in Chapter 5, a high degree of party discipline among elected officials.[8] MPs are typically hesitant to vote against the stated party line, knowing that they risk losing their party's nomination in the next election cycle.

catch-all parties
parties whose platforms and programs try to appeal to the broadest range of voters.

single-issue parties
parties whose programs typically are restricted to a single or a very narrow set of issues.

In addition to nominating candidates to stand for office, parties also hope, obviously, to win elections. This implies several things. First, they need to motivate and mobilize voters to get them to the polls. Indeed, near election time, parties care about little else. Between elections, though, parties must also stake out positions to attract members and sympathizers. This means they must develop programs and try to voice and represent the interests of a wide number of individuals. Most parties therefore aim to be **catch-all parties** (e.g., the British Conservative Party or the German Social Democratic Party), meaning that they try to broaden their base as far as possible to attract the most supporters. Others, though, are **single-issue parties** (e.g., the Dutch Party for Animals or the now-defunct Polish Beer-Lovers Party), seeking to generate support by emphasizing an issue that they hope will be popular and/or drawing attention to an issue otherwise ignored by other parties. In some cases (e.g., the Greens) single-issue parties can broaden their base by moving beyond just a single issue and developing a wider political platform. In either case, parties help to organize the political life of a country, provide individuals with a sense of political identity, and make a potentially myriad of possible choices simpler and more intelligible to voters. Whether in or out of government, they also can provide input to policymakers and organize actions (e.g., protests, rallies, petition campaigns) to influence state leaders.

Parties are organizations, and as such have their own internal structures and rules. Most parties are hierarchical, having national, regional, and local branches. With a few relatively minor exceptions, European political parties embrace democracy,[9] and thus one would expect parties themselves to function democratically. Although most parties do give local bodies and the general membership some sort of say (e.g., through a national convention), ensuring intra-party democracy is a problem. Nearly a century ago, Robert Michels, in a study of the German Social Democratic Party, developed his **iron law of oligarchy**, noting the propensity of any organization, even those committed to democracy, to produce bureaucratic, elite leaders, who, by virtue of control over finances and information, tend to gain control of the organization and use it to promote their own interests.[10] Rather than serving as democratic vehicles, many parties become corrupt, or at least are perceived to be so, using their power to dispense patronage (e.g., jobs, government contracts, access to public housing) to their supporters. These phenomena are captured in the German term *Parteibuchwirtschaft* and the Italian term *Partitocrazia*. Although most political parties in Europe receive public (government) funding, many also rely upon private funding. The corrosive effect of money on politics is a concern in many European states, although the cost of campaigning in Europe has yet to reach the billions of dollars spent in each election cycle in the US.[11]

iron law of oligarchy

idea that all organizations will produce bureaucratic, elite leaders who tend to gain control of an organization and thereby limit internal democracy.

Perhaps for these reasons, as well as diminishing ideological polarization in many European states, party membership in most European states has declined. Accurate membership figures are hard to come by, as parties have an incentive to exaggerate their membership, but many surveys have confirmed that fewer and fewer Europeans belong to political parties. Party membership figures from several countries—as taken from the 2010 European Social Survey—are presented in Table 8.1. This table also shows the percentage of respondents who say they tend to trust political parties. Both figures must be troubling to party leaders. The drop in membership since peaks in the 1950s and 1960s ranges, depending upon the country, from 30 to 80 percent.[12] In post-communist Europe, the relative newness of the party system and "partyphobia"—a disgust with political parties thanks to the negative experience of living under single-party, communist rule—is invoked to explain the particularly low figures of party membership. In the British case, the decline has been so precipitous that by 2005 more Britons belonged to birdwatching clubs than all political parties combined![13] Party identification is also on the decline, making it less likely that parties can rely upon a base of loyalists. The term **dealignment** is used to refer both to the failure of individuals to attach themselves to a particular party and the general mistrust toward political parties. Indeed, given the rise of single-issue interest groups, social media, and new media such as blogs, not to

dealignment

declining attachment to and increasing distrust of established political parties.

TABLE 8.1 Membership and trust in political parties

Country	*% party members*	*% trust political parties**
Germany	3.2	6.6
France	2.4	4.4
Great Britain	2.2	9.5
Spain	2.0	4.4
Netherlands	5.5	23.6
Sweden	7.3	24.5
Denmark	6.5	**26.3**
Cyprus	**11.2**	10.3
Greece	4.1	**1.8**
Hungary	1.2	8.8
Czech Republic	3.2	6.4
Slovakia	2.3	4.7
Poland	**0.7**	3.4
Total (24 states)	4.2	9.1

Source: European Social Survey, 2010, online analysis available at http://nesstar.ess.nsd.uib.no/webview/

*Scores of 7–10 on 0–10 scale of trust, with 10 being complete trust. Results in bold are lows and highs for the entire survey.

mention a more general withdrawal from political life, one might wonder if the traditional idea of a mass-based party makes much sense today. Because of declining membership subscriptions, parties are relying more and more on public financing and/or large donations, and some worry about growing reliance in campaigns on professional consultants and the mass media instead of grassroots mobilization of the membership.

Party families in Europe

There are literally hundreds of political parties in Europe, and no two are exactly alike. Obviously, they differ in size, power, and particulars in their party platforms. In a broad comparative perspective, however, today most European political parties are similar insofar as they accept the basic tenets of individual rights and democratic government, although there are some, as discussed above, which espouse views that, at least according to their critics, would endanger democracy if they would come to power.

political cleavages
divisions within a society that acquire political importance and become political markers that divide supporters of one party from those of another.

How should one try to classify the myriad of parties in Europe? The simplest way is delineate party families, based upon a combination of shared origins and ideological or policy orientation. In the broadest terms, one can speak of parties of the Left and parties of the Right. The division between Left and Right dates to the French Revolution and refers to how members of the post-revolutionary French assembly seated themselves according to their ideological viewpoints.

Historically speaking, the Left and the Right have been defined on the basis of several social or political cleavages, divisions within a society that acquire political importance and become political markers that divide supporters of one party from

Left
political orientation that tends to appeal to those from lower classes and minorities and is more secular and cosmopolitan in outlook.

Right
political orientation that tends to appeal to upper classes, is often concerned with preserving traditions, and frequently puts priority on religion and/or nationalism.

cosmopolitanism
the degree to which a person is interested in the wider world and sees him- or herself as part of a wider community outside of his or her own country; usually associated with the political left.

nationalists
those who are suspicious of the outside world and tend to put priority on the interests of their particular country; usually associated with the political right.

those of another.[14] Historically, probably the most important political cleavage has been class, meaning a group defined by its social standing and relative economic and political power. The parties of the **Left** have traditionally catered to those in the lower and working class (manual or industrial laborers), arguing for (among other items) redistribution of wealth, more government intervention in the economy to create more economic equality, and a welfare state to provide basic needs (e.g., education, health care) to the population. The parties of the **Right** tend to appeal to the middle or upper classes, and favor, compared to the Left, less government involvement in the economy, emphasizing the responsibility of the individual to provide for his or her own needs and the greater efficiency achieved by free markets. Class voting—meaning that voters choose parties on the basis of their own class position—has traditionally been the primary prism to view electoral behavior and party systems in Europe, although since the 1990s many analysts have suggested that class voting is on the decline and that other cleavages matter more both in terms of defining parties and in terms of explaining voting behavior.[15]

Another cleavage that has been important historically is religion. The Left tends to be more secular, favoring less involvement of religious authorities in political and social questions. The Left also tends to be less "traditional," endorsing measures that make it easier to divorce, obtain an abortion, or (most recently) allow homosexuals to marry. Parties of the Right, in contrast, tend to espouse "traditional values" and often, as in the case of Christian Democratic parties, adopt an explicitly religious moniker. Even though most European states today are very secular, the individual voter's level of religiosity remains a potent predictor of her vote in many countries. For example, Russell Dalton, utilizing survey evidence from 1999 to 2002, finds that frequency of church attendance is a more powerful explanatory factor in voting than class in countries such as the Netherlands, Belgium, Finland, Denmark, Italy, and France.[16]

One can also identify a cleavage between those who are more cosmopolitan and those who are more nationalist in orientation. **Cosmopolitanism** refers to the degree to which a person is interested in the wider world and sees him- or herself as part of a wider community outside of his or her own country. Those who are more cosmopolitan would, for example, be more likely to embrace the EU, economic and cultural globalization, and the rights of immigrants and ethnic minorities. **Nationalists,** on the other hand, are more suspicious of the outside world, put priority on the interests of their particular country and/or national group, and worry that the EU, globalization, and immigrants are changing their country in negative ways. The emergence of this cleavage, a reflection of increased globalization, EU powers, and growing immigration, has fueled the rise of nationalist-oriented parties (discussed more below) that have challenged traditional parties on both the left and the right.

More recently, Ronald Inglehart and his collaborators have argued for the existence of a different sort of cleavage in Europe, between "post-materialists" and "materialists."[17] Post-materialists are most interested in quality of life issues, such as expansion of political and social freedoms and in protection of the environment, and tend to gravitate toward the political Left. The Greens, discussed below, are the archetype of a "post-materialist" party. Post-materialists tend to be younger, wealthier, and better educated. Materialists, in contrast, emphasize economic and physical security, putting emphasis on achieving the most basic needs. Greater discussion of manifestations of post-materialism within Europe can be found in the next chapter.

There are other cleavages in Europe, although some are less salient than before. The pioneering study on political cleavages by Seymour Lipset and Stein Rokkan, who based their work on how parties emerged in the 1920s, pointed to the existence of an urban-rural divide and a center-periphery one.[18] Urbanization in most European countries has made the traditional urban-rural cleavage less salient, although it may be manifested today as an element of the cosmopolitan-nationalist cleavage.[19] The center-periphery cleavage refers to battles over the consolidation of the nation and of state authority. In most states, as noted in Chapter 2, the center prevailed, imposing its rule over the disparate regions of the country, but the push for decentralization, federalism, and even separatism in some European states reveals that this cleavage has not wholly disappeared. However, it is hard to put this dimension on a traditional Left-Right spectrum. Scottish and Catalan separatists, for example, might be more leftist in their general orientation, but the *Lega Nord* in Italy would be better classified as on the political right.

Note that although some social cleavages may appear to be similar and thus reinforce each other (e.g., secularism may be correlated with post-materialism or cosmopolitanism), they can also "crosscut," meaning that they work in such a way that individuals do not fall on one side on all dimensions. Consider, for example, an unemployed worker in the French city of Marseilles. Is he, based upon social class, likely to vote for the Communist or Socialist Party (left-wing parties in France)? Or, because he may believe a North African immigrant has "stolen" his job and/or that France is becoming too "Americanized" due to globalization, will he vote for a more nationalist party such as the National Front? Or, consider a wealthy businesswoman in Vienna. By virtue of class, one might imagine she is on the political right, but she might also be supportive of environmental causes or embrace the multicultural nature of her city, positions that might incline her to vote for the Social Democratic or Green Parties on the left. Electoral politics often boils down to how parties pitch their programs and whether and how they can persuade voters that a particular cleavage matters more than others and thus earn their votes.

The saliency of a given cleavage can also change over time, producing shifts in voters' orientation. Some parties benefit from this and grow; others contract or disappear; and still others may be created to address a new issue or fill a gap on the political spectrum. These dynamic phenomena are captured by notion of party system volatility, which is taken up in the **In focus** section.

Let us now examine in brief the main party families in Europe, moving from left to right across the spectrum. Not all states have all types of parties. Party systems will vary in terms of the number of parties, their relative strength, and their volatility from election to election.

Communists
parties on the far left that try to appeal mostly to urban, blue-collar workers and emphasize government ownership of industry and generous social welfare policies.

Communist parties

Communist parties occupy the far left of the spectrum. They have been in sharp decline since the collapse of communism in Eastern Europe and the Soviet Union in 1989 through 1991, but they have been, historically, important forces in European politics. Obviously, they were the ruling parties in all of the communist countries in Eastern Europe,[20] although their "success" depended upon more on their ability to outlaw or suppress any form of political opposition than to attract voluntary support. In Western Europe, Communist parties emerged as the largest parties immediately after World War II in both France and Italy, although in both states they were unable to capture a majority of the votes and form the government. Nonetheless, they were the dominant party on the left in both states for several decades. In Greece, the Communist Party was also a sizeable force and fought a civil war after World War II against its centrist and right-wing opponents to win power. It lost the war and was banned until 1974. Communist parties have also had a sizeable presence in (Greek) Cyprus. In Sweden and Finland, communist parties regularly won parliamentary seats and at times offered their support to left-wing governments. Elsewhere, Communist parties did not fare so well, either because their ideas never caught on with voters (e.g., in Great Britain and West Germany) or because they were actively suppressed by virulently anti-communist governments (e.g., in Spain and Turkey).

All Communist parties claim fealty to the ideas of Karl Marx (1818 to 1883), who railed against the injustices of the capitalist system. The actual program of Communists, taken from Karl Marx, includes state ownership of the "means of production" (meaning factories and land), government planning of the economy, and generous provision of social welfare benefits. Over the years, communism acquired an unsavory reputation thanks to its association with the Soviet Union and Eastern Europe, where some of Marx's core ideas—state ownership and planning—were implemented but were accompanied by political repression and eventually economic stagnation. After 1989, most of the Communist parties in Eastern Europe changed their names, usually dropping any reference to communism in favor of a less-tainted socialist or social democratic label. This includes the Left Party (*Die Linke*) in Germany, which is the successor to the ruling party of East Germany, but it is still considered a pariah by many in Germany because of its links to the repressive communist regime. Some of these reformed communist parties returned to power (e.g., in Lithuania, Poland, Slovenia, Hungary, Romania), but they have abandoned the core communist program of government control over the economy, and they have agreed to play the game of democratic politics.

In Western Europe, the once-mighty Communist parties in France and Italy are no more. Although popular among urban workers and some intellectuals, they were always burdened with an association with the repressive Soviet state, even though from the 1950s onward they condemned numerous actions of the Soviet government and tried to fashion their own "Euro-communism." Whereas they were able to appeal to more than 20 percent of voters even through the 1980s, the collapse of communism in Eastern Europe left many wondering about the feasibility or attractiveness of communism. By the time of the 2012 French parliamentary elections, the Communists, as the leading member of the Left Front (*Front de Gauche*) won less than 7 percent of the vote—compared with 10 percent in 1997—and in 2013 elections the Communist Party in Italy polled only 2.2 percent of the vote. Elsewhere, the Communist parties of Finland and Sweden have renamed themselves (the Left Alliance and Left Party) and abandoned much of the hard-core communist program, joining the Nordic Green Left Alliance cross-national group as a reflection of their desire to maintain respectability. They still win enough of

In focus

The stability and volatility of party systems

How stable and dynamic are party systems in Europe? For much of this chapter, we have described the existing spectrum of parties in Europe, but have not explored in depth how they have evolved, how they might be changing, and whether some countries have a more volatile system than others.

In the initial post-World War II period, stability appeared to be the norm. Seymour Lipset and Stein Rokkan, who did much of the pioneering work on political cleavages, maintained that cleavages were frozen, producing stable political alignments and electoral results. One set of authors, writing at the end of the 1960s, maintained that rather than explaining change, the primary need was to explain the absence of change in democratic countries of Western Europe.[21]

It would be difficult to make such an argument today. Already by the 1970s scholars were noting the breakdown of traditional (e.g., class) voting patterns, the formation of new cleavages, and the creation of new political parties.[22] Politics became more volatile and in some cases unpredictable as social structure began to change (e.g., growth of the service sector at the expense of manufacturing and agriculture), and voters switched allegiances and in some cases their identities (e.g., declining prominence of religion). New issues (e.g., the environment, immigration) rose to prominence, and the realignment of the European party systems around new sets of cleavages (e.g., post-materialism) became a subject of concerted inquiry. Moving the discussion forward in time, in the twenty-first century, new technologies have also changed the ways people learn about and participate in politics.

That being said, how dynamic are party systems? The answer is that it depends—both on what one examines and which country is the subject of discussion. Consider, for example, established democracies such as Germany, the Netherlands, and Great Britain. In each, politics since World War II has been dominated by catch-all parties on the center-right (Christian Democrats in Germany, Christian Democrats and Liberals in the Netherlands, Conservatives in Britain) and on the center-left (Labour in the Netherlands and Britain, Social Democrats in Germany). Whereas each election has its ups and downs, the results of the major parties in these states have stayed rather similar over several decades. Moreover, continent-wide, if one looks at the overall vote of parties of the left and parties of the center and right over time, there is remarkable stability—parties of the right and center command approximately 55 percent of the vote, parties of the left about 40 percent of the vote.[23]

This statistic, however, may obscure more than it reveals. Within general left/right divides, there have been important changes. On the left, the Communists have declined in the past two decades, whereas the Greens have established themselves as important political players in several states. Xenophobic parties, which focus mostly on the issue of immigration and preservation of "traditional culture," are commonly placed on the political right and are now well entrenched in many states. These developments are driven not only by changing issues (demand) but also by the electoral system (supply), as the proportional representation system in most European countries facilitates the emergence of new, smaller parties. In the parlance of political science, their "entry cost" is relatively low. In other cases, such as Italy's Christian Democrats, volatility has meant their complete disappearance (destroyed by corruption scandals), although they have been replaced by other parties with a different focus or ideology on the right wide of the political spectrum.

Even in countries with plurality systems, however, there has been volatility and movement away from established parties. For example, in France, there has been an increase in votes for fringe or "anti-system" parties (e.g., the FN, various Trotskyite and other Marxist parties), so that by 2012 the leading center-left and center-right parties commanded only 64 percent of the vote, compared to 77 percent in 1981 and 73 percent in 1988. In Britain, despite the odds against them posited by Duverger's Law, the Liberal Democrats became a well-established third party, picking off votes from those disillusioned by the two main parties. In 2015, the relatively new United Kingdom Independence Party garnered the third-largest share of the vote (over 12 percent), and the Scottish National Party tripled its share of parliamentary seats, becoming the third largest party in the House of Commons.

However, it is in the eastern half of the continent that we see the most volatility, as parties disappear and are replaced by entirely new creations. This is hardly surprising, as most parties in post-communist Europe are of recent vintage, and thus few command party loyalty of the type that Labour in Britain or the Christian Democrats in Germany might enjoy. What is interesting, however, is how parties in the region have broken up and new parties (or offshoots) take their places and gain electoral traction, a reflection of the dissatisfaction many people feel with the existing political parties. Examples include Jobbik, noted at the outset of this chapter; *Smer* (Direction), which won 2006 elections in Slovakia and had broken from the Party of the Democratic Left in 1999; and New Era, which was founded on a platform to combat corruption in 2001 and in elections the following year became the largest party in the Latvian *Saeima* (parliament). Poland deserves special mention. Of the dozens of parties that arose since the end of communism, only one, the Polish Peoples' Party, lasted over twenty years. The Law and Justice Party won elections in 2005 after being created by the Kaczynski twins in 2001 as a replacement for the defunct Solidarity Electoral Action bloc. In 2015, three of the top five vote-getters did not exist in 2011, whereas two of the five parties from 2011 did not field candidates in 2015 (see Table 8.5 later in this chapter). Some of this is driven by personality. The quintessential new party-turned-governing-party centered on one central political figure was the National Movement for King Simeon II in Bulgaria, which won elections in 2001, the same year it was formed, but whose fortunes (along with the king's) quickly faded, so much so that by 2007 it changed its name to remove reference to its eponymous founder and by the 2010s garnered less than 1 percent of the vote. Elsewhere, as in Albania, the party system is, at best, poorly structured, evidenced by the fact that over sixty parties contested the 2013 parliamentary elections, although most were in one of two electoral blocs.

Critical thinking questions

1. Is the instability of party systems in post-communist Europe a sign that democracy is weak in that region, or merely evidence of transition or growing pains?
2. Some have suggested that recent global changes are more challenging for the left than the right. Would you agree? Which side has, in your estimation, changed more since the end of the Cold War?

the vote (7.1 percent in 2015 Finnish elections and 5.7 percent in 2014 Swedish elections) to make a difference, and both parties served in coalition governments in the 1990s and 2000s. In the 2010s, the most successful communist—or, perhaps more accurately—far-left party in Europe is Greece's Syriza, which won 2015 parliamentary elections campaigning against EU-imposed austerity. This party was founded in the early 2000s from among several small left-wing parties; the Greek Communist Party is a separate party and garnered over 5 percent of the vote in 2015 elections.

Green parties

Greens
parties on the left of the political spectrum that emphasize environmentalism as well as peaceful approaches to international relations and minority rights.

Green parties, so named for their focus on environmental protection, emerged in the 1970s and 1980s. Green parties typically grew out of Socialist, Communist, or other left-wing parties, but they are less concerned about social class issues and more about quality of life issues. As such, they are a prototypical post-materialist phenomenon. As one would expect, environmental concerns—nuclear power, alternative energy, water and air quality, species protection, recycling—figure prominently in their platforms. Many of them also have a pacifist streak, growing out of the nuclear disarmament movement. Green parties have thus been critical of the deployment of European troops overseas (e.g., Afghanistan, Iraq) and favor cuts in their own states' military budgets. As left-wing parties, they also tend to support government regulation over aspects of the economy, the welfare state, grassroots democracy, women and minority rights (including those for homosexuals), and, controversially in some cases, the legalization of marijuana. Some—such as those in Germany and the Netherlands—are decidedly pro-European integration, whereas others, such as those in Sweden and Great Britain, tend to be less keen on the idea.

Green parties have fared best in northern European countries such as Sweden, the Netherlands, Finland, Germany, and Belgium, all of which also have strong environmental movements and multi-party political systems. In these states, since the early 1980s Greens have averaged 7 to 8 percent of the vote, giving them, potentially at least, a great deal of power in the formation of government coalitions. In 1995, the Finnish Green Party became the first Green party to enter into government, and from 1998 through 2005 the German Green Party served as a coalition partner to the Social Democrats in a "Red-Green Coalition." Joshka Fischer, leader of the German Greens, became German foreign minister and Germany's most popular political figure, in part due to his arguments against the war in Iraq, which was widely unpopular in Germany. Greens have also served in governments in France, Sweden, Belgium, Italy, Ireland, and the Czech Republic. Whereas some in the 1980s might have thought of the Greens as a short-term, "protest" type of development, it is clear that they have become a fixture in European politics, and, thanks in part to their efforts in drawing attention to environmental concerns, European states have gone "green" in terms of their environmental laws and regulations.

Green parties elsewhere are small, either because the electoral system works against small, start-up parties (as in Britain) or because there is not such a strong environmental consciousness (arguably true in Greece, Spain, and much of post-communist Europe). Nonetheless, they do exist in virtually every country, winning a few seats in national elections or those for the European Parliament. In February 2004, Indulis Emsis of the Latvian Green Party became the first Prime Minister from any European Green Party, although he managed to hold his coalition government together for less than a year.

Social Democratic parties

The largest parties on the Left are Social Democratic parties. They are known by different names (Social Democratic, Socialist, the Labour Party in the British or Dutch cases) and some countries (e.g., Portugal) have more than one, but most trace their roots back to the mid-late 1800s and the emergence of a social-democratic movement in Europe. Although influenced by Marx, their primary intellectual forebears are so-called Marxist "revisionists" such as the Germans Karl Kautsky and Edward Bernstein. They endorsed a more moderate perspective than revolutionary communists, rejecting the need for a violent revolution or complete government control over the economy. Instead they believed that the lower and working class could take advantage of the democratic process to elect parties that would serve their interests and reform capitalism to create a more just economic and social system. Trade unions were historically a crucial ally of Social Democratic parties, supplying funds, reliable voters, and party officials, and solidifying the identity of **Social Democrats** as the party of the working class.

Social Democrats term used to refer to a variety of parties on the left that have traditionally embraced a strong role for government in the economy and generous welfare policies.

Although Social Democratic parties did come to power in some European states in the 1920s and 1930s, they really emerged as a powerful electoral force after World War II, best shown with the victory of the Labour Party over Winston Churchill's Conservatives in Great Britain in 1945, months after Churchill had played such a heroic role in the defeat of Hitler. In office, Social Democrats in many states established sizeable welfare states, expanded workers' rights, and set up corporatist systems of governance that gave unions a voice in setting economic policy. Although many Social Democratic parties were skeptical of European integration in the 1950s and 1960s, today most embrace the EU as a positive economic and political institution. In post-communist Europe, Social Democratic parties are frequently successors to the former Communist parties, moderating themselves and pledging to work for social and economic reforms within a democratic and capitalist framework. Today, parties from the Social Democratic "family" dominate the left side of the European political spectrum across Europe, and in the 2000s and 2010s they led governments in countries as diverse as Spain, France, Great Britain, Sweden, Germany, Poland, Romania, Italy, Greece, and Slovakia.

Although these parties have a tradition of representing the working class and advocating a larger role for the state in the economy, this has changed in recent years, particularly as the number of blue-collar manufacturing jobs has shrunk in favor of more white-collar jobs in the service sector, where employees are less likely to view themselves as members of the "working class."[24] As a consequence, Social Democratic parties have tried to broaden their base, appealing in particular to state employees, workers in the arts and in education, and students, and they are the overwhelming choice of voters in European urban centers such as London, Paris, Madrid, Vienna, Berlin, and Rome. One challenge for Social Democrats, as we shall examine in greater detail in Chapter 10, is that the welfare state is under assault across Europe due to demographic and global economic pressures, making it harder for parties on the left to advocate "tax and spend" policies as they did in the past. Thus, since the 1990s, many parties on the left have moved towards the political center in search of a so-called **Third Way** between capitalism and communism.

Third Way
term used to refer a middle ground between capitalism and communism and embraced by some on the political left who moved toward the political center in the 1990s.

This phenomenon can be seen in many countries, and, as noted in the **Is Europe one?** feature, has even taken on pan-European dimensions in an effort to force greater transnational links among like-minded parties. In Great Britain, Tony Blair, who became leader of the Labour Party in 1994, argued for a "New Labour," one that would move to the center to appeal to more middle-class British voters. Under Blair, the Labour Party renounced previous policies such as state ownership of economic enterprises and curtailed the powers of the trade unions. Blair became Prime Minister in 1997, and pushed through so many economic programs associated with the right (e.g., tax cuts, welfare reform) that critics accused him of being Margaret Thatcher in a suit. In Germany, Gerhard Schröder of the Social Democratic Party became Chancellor in 1998 and, like Blair, advocated a series of reforms such as tax cuts for businesses and less generous welfare policies. In France, which has a long tradition of state intervention in the economy, François Mitterand, elected in 1981 as the first Socialist President, turned away from a left-wing platform and oversaw numerous privatizations of state-owned firms.[25] His successor as head of the Socialist Party, Lionel Jospin, ran for president in 2002 claiming that, "My program is not socialist."[26] In the 1990s in Poland, Lithuania, and Hungary, left-wing Social Democratic parties, which were the reformed successor organizations of the old, discredited communist parties, continued the free-market economic reforms pursued by right-wing governments after the collapse of communism.

This is not to say that all Social Democratic parties have abandoned their beliefs. There are still real differences between the left and right on economic questions. However, in the ten years prior to 2016, which includes the most acute period of the global economic crisis, social-democratic parties (and all those on the left more generally) fared poorly in many European states, constituting the main governing party in the eight largest European countries for only twenty-nine out of a possible eighty years, including none in Germany, Poland, and the Netherlands.[27] Nonetheless, center-left parties can still garner support, especially as some voters want some protections from globalization and free market capitalism. Social-democratic parties were the leading vote-getters in the 2013 Italian election, narrowly defeating the center-right coalition led by scandal-plagued former prime minister Silvio Berlusconi and the anti-establishment, Euroskeptical Five Star Movement led by comedian Beppe Grillo, and in Portugal, where a coalition of center- and far-left parties won the majority in 2015 elections. Both of these countries had been hard-hit by the economic crisis. Arguably the center-left's most significant victory in the 2010s, however, occurred in France in 2012, when François Hollande of the Socialist Party, running on an unrepentant leftist platform of higher taxes on the wealthy and more state spending, won the presidency and his party and its allies gained a majority in the National Assembly. Hollande, however, has not governed as a hard leftist, and in 2016 he controversially used an executive order to implement changes in the labor law to erode some protections for workers, sparking protests from labor unions and splits within his party.[28]

Is Europe one?

The Europeanization of political parties

Political parties are quintessentially national organizations, succeeding or failing on the basis of their ability to appeal to national-level voters. Even within party families, one finds significant differences in both style and substance among different national parties. At the same time, however, as European countries face a host of common problems (e.g., immigration, pressures on the welfare state, globalization) and the power of the EU is growing, might one see greater convergence or coordination among political parties? In other words, are parties becoming "Europeanized," adapting to the demands, constraints, and opportunities of European integration?

Evidence is mixed, and in many ways one could say that parties—as opposed to courts, parliaments, and executives—are the least Europeanized of all political institutions in Europe. True, as explained in Chapter 4, similar political parties form groups within the European Parliament, where parties sit and caucus on a pan-European, not national, level. For example, most Christian Democratic parties belong to the European Peoples' Party, most Social Democrats belong to the Progressive Alliance of Socialists and Democrats, and Greens belong to the Greens-European Free Alliance group. These umbrella organizations provide a means for different national political parties to consult with each other and forge common positions on European issues. However, these groups do not always vote as a bloc, and MEPs (Members of the European Parliament) are far more accountable to their national parties than any pan-European organization. Moreover, because elections to the European Parliament are conducted on a national level with national parties, national-level issues (e.g., is the government popular? is unemployment falling?) often figure more than cross-national, European issues. Just as there is no "European" electorate, there are no "European"—as opposed to national—political parties.[29]

Additionally, there is little to suggest that European issues have significantly changed the organizational structure of most European political parties. Surveys among parties reveal that there has been little structural adaptation to pan-European or EU concerns. Moreover, MEPs are not usually particularly influential within their respective political parties, which serves to minimize any sort of socialization effect one might hope is provided by work in the European Parliament.[30]

This is not to suggest that party leaders are unaware of the need for more cooperation on the pan-European level. This is arguably gone furthest with the Greens and the center-left parties, which are among the keenest for European integration. For example, in the 1990s Tony Blair and Gerhard Schröder, then leaders of Great Britain and Germany, together with former US President Bill Clinton, sponsored a series of high-level meetings to discuss the previously mentioned "Third Way." They issued a well-publicized manifesto ("Europe: The Third Way/The New Middle") on this concept in 1999, and subsequent meetings involved leaders from the political left in Sweden, Italy, the Netherlands, as well as Latin American and African countries. The aim was to fashion a common response among left-wing parties to social and economic challenges of globalization and how best to reform welfare states. Blair even reached out to the Conservative leader of Spain, José María Anzar (1996–2004), for his input into how to transform European social democracies. Many, however, were skeptical that these efforts had any lasting impact, and some political parties (e.g., the French Socialist Party) clearly had little enthusiasm for the idea.[31]

Meanwhile, Angela Merkel, who has served as German Chancellor since 2005, has tried to forge a common approach among center-right parties. While she found some backing, particularly with respect to the European debt crisis, from leaders in Finland and the Netherlands, this effort has been hampered by the Euroskepticism pervasive in the British Conservative Party. In the 2010s, one has seen the rise of anti-EU, nationalist parties in many states. Interestingly, while one might think that they could easily forge a bloc in the EP, in fact they are divided (due to both personality disputes and different points of emphasis in their programs) into two: the more Euroskeptic Europe of Freedom and Direct Democracy and the more nationalist, anti-immigrant Europe of Nations and Freedom. In short, it seems that Europe remains a long way from forging cross-party links that would be congruent with the notion of a single European polity.

Critical thinking questions

1. Assuming one wanted greater "Europeanization" among political parties, how might one accomplish that goal?
2. Is the relative lack of "Europeanization" among political parties evidence that the powers of the EU are exaggerated? Or does it tend to reflect more on *how* the EU has acquired power?

The Liberals

Liberals
parties of the political center that combine a commitment to free markets with a belief for social tolerance and individual rights.

The political definition of "liberal" is an example of how the same English word can have different meanings on different sides of the Atlantic Ocean. In the United States and Canada, "liberal" is associated with the left. In Europe, however, **Liberals** occupy what could best be described as the political center. Their use of the term "liberal" refers back to the classic expositions of European liberalism by, among others, John Locke, Alexis de Tocqueville, Adam Smith, and John Stuart Mill. The common thread for European Liberals is a belief in limited government and individual freedom. The Liberals' primary political basis is businesspeople and urban professionals, although in Scandinavia, the Liberals (or Centrists, as they are frequently known) are successors to powerful Agrarian Parties and still try to appeal to rural voters. Most Liberal parties also tend to be pro-European integration.

Liberalism, however, contains two main components. One is free-market (or "conservative") liberalism, a belief that the state should minimize interference with the market. Liberal parties are often—but not always[32]—the loudest champions of free markets in Europe, although most European Liberals accept the need for some sort of limited welfare state as a social safety net. The other strand of liberalism is social-liberalism, a more post-materialist orientation that emphasizes the need for individual rights and more progressive state policies. These include civil rights, legalized abortion, more opportunities for political participation, LGBT rights, and, frequently, government spending in areas such as education to expand opportunities. Examples of Liberal parties that emphasize the first component are the Free Democratic Party in Germany, the Civic Platform in Poland, and the Estonian Reform Party. Examples of those more focused on social-liberalism include the Liberal Democratic Party in Great Britain and the Center Party in Finland. In some cases, such as the Netherlands, a country might have two different parties reflecting these different points of emphasis. In the Dutch case, the People's Party for Freedom and Democracy (whose leader, Mark Rutte, became Prime Minister in 2010) represents free-market liberalism, whereas Democrats 66 is more of a social-liberal party.

Liberals are rarely the dominant political party in any European country, but, because in many respects they occupy a middle ground between the left and right, they have been attractive coalition partners. For example, the German Free Democratic Party and the Dutch People's Party for Freedom and Justice have served in several post-World War II coalition governments, allying themselves at times with Social Democrats and at other times with Christian Democratic parties on the right. In the 2000s and 2010s, Liberal parties supplied the Prime Minister in Finland, Denmark, Estonia, Iceland, the Netherlands, and Romania, and served in coalition governments in Belgium, Germany, Great Britain, and Sweden.

The Christian Democrats

Christian Democrats parties on the center-right that tend to favor a mixed economy while making some appeals on the basis of traditional "value" issues.

The center-right portion of the political spectrum in Europe is represented by two groups of parties. One is the **Christian Democrats.** The Christian Democrats have been the dominant political party on the right in Germany, the Netherlands, Austria, Malta, Switzerland, and Belgium, and, until 1992, Italy.[33] Some—those in Austria, Italy, Belgium, and (formerly) Italy—are Roman Catholic in origin, whereas Scandinavian Christian Democratic Parties—the strongest one is in Norway—are Protestant in origin. In Germany, there are technically two Christian Democratic Parties (the Christian Democratic Union and Christian Social Union, the latter centered in the overwhelmingly Catholic region of Bavaria), and the Netherlands, with a history of separate parties based upon religion, has a tri-confessional party alliance, the Dutch Christian Democratic Appeal.

Obvious questions about these parties are, what do they mean by "Christian" and what place do they have in a secular Europe? These are not easy questions to answer. Many of them—particularly the Catholic ones—originally appeared as a response to secular, left-wing Social Democratic parties, and they stood for (among other things) defending the interests of the Church. Today, they are more secular in their orientation, although most still campaign for traditional values such as restrictions on abortion, opposition to gay marriage and euthanasia (the latter very sensitive in Germany due to Nazi policies), and have even engaged in quixotic campaigns to restrict alcohol and pornography in famously liberal, permissive countries such as Sweden. Some of their Christian inclinations, however, have also pushed them (compared to Conservative parties on the right) toward the left, as most Christian Democratic parties accept the need for consensual politics between different class interests as well as the idea that society has an obligation toward the poor and less advantaged. Consequently, they not only have supported many aspects of the welfare state but actually oversaw construction of strong welfare states and mixed forms of economic statism and capitalism (e.g., the "social market economy" in Germany, strong corporatist institutions in Austria that give a voice to trade unions and try to promote social consensus) when they were the dominant political parties in some countries in the 1950s and 1960s. Many social-welfare policies (e.g., maternity leaves, subsidized child care) are also supported by Christian Democrats as "pro-family." While it would be fair to say that Christian Democratic parties are more to the right (meaning more pro-market) than Social Democratic parties, the former have not rushed to embrace radical neo-liberalism that seeks to remove the state from the economy. Indeed, in one of her first initiatives after becoming German Chancellor in 2005, Angela Merkel of the Christian Democratic Union supported an increase in the value-added-tax in Germany, a move that a stalwart Conservative such as British Prime Minister Margaret Thatcher would have found anathema. Christian Democrats have also tended to be in favor of European integration.

Christian Democrats were strong—one might even say dominant—in many Western European countries in the years immediately following World War II. Since the 1980s, their share of vote has dropped in many countries, including former strongholds such as Germany, the Netherlands, and Belgium, reflecting in large part the rise of both Liberal and nationalist parties. In post-communist Europe, Christian Democratic parties—typically embracing a combination of nationalism, market economics, and at times economic populism—have done best in Slovakia, Hungary, and Poland, all countries with a Catholic tradition. Smaller Christian Democratic parties exist in the Czech Republic, Romania, and Slovenia.

Although it may seem peculiar, one could place Turkey's Justice and Development Party (JDP) in the Christian Democratic family. True, the JDP has Islamic roots, thereby obviously meaning it is not a *Christian* Democratic party. However, it won elections in the 2000s and 2010s emphasizing not only a more public role for religion in a state which since the 1920s has enforced secularism, but also a communitarianism rooted in social responsibility. To the extent that the JDP advocates "traditional values" and more open markets tempered with policies to help the disadvantaged, it is, ironically, closer to the Christian Democratic tradition than any other party in Turkey, and has aligned itself with the Christian Democratic-dominated European People's Party in pan-European party forums.

Conservatives parties on the center-right that tend to emphasize free markets, "law and order" issues, and upholding traditions; they are often opposed to greater European integration.

The Conservatives

The other center-right parties in Europe belong to a family that might best be described as **Conservatives**, although they go by various names.[34] Although they may make reference to defending "traditional values" and appeal to more religious voters, Conservative parties do not carry a religious label. Conservatives are generally associated with pro-business policies and traditionally received most of their support from the upper and middle classes, although, as class-based voting has dissipated throughout Europe, many Conservative parties try to appeal to lower-class voters by touting the ability of freer markets both to be more efficient than state intervention and to create economic opportunities for all members of society. Conservatives in general tend to be more skeptical of the EU than parties on the left, perhaps because they associate the EU with excessive regulation and assaults on the traditional prerogatives of the state. Many also emphasize the need for a strong national defense and "law and order" issues. As immigration and multi-culturalism have emerged as major issues—and fed the growth of nationalist, xenophobic parties—Conservatives have espoused programs to limit immigration and to defend cultural traditions and national patriotism.

Whereas all Conservative parties occupy the right side of the political spectrum, they do vary, especially in how far they embrace free market principles. The British Conservative Party, especially during the reign of Margaret Thatcher (1979–1990), has been most strongly associated with free-market policies, advocating privatization, tax cuts, cuts in government programs, and reforms in fields such as education to get more room for personal choice and non-state initiatives. Whereas the Conservatives succeeded under Thatcher and support for the free market became the new orthodoxy in Britain—breaking with more than three decades of political consensus on the necessity for a strong state role in the economy—by the end of the 1990s they were seen as out of new ideas and out of touch with British voters, and since lost three straight elections (1997, 2001, 2005) to the Labour Party. Elsewhere, the closest party to the British Conservatives is the Czech Civic Democratic Party, led in the 1990s by Václav Klaus, then the prime minister and an open admirer of Margaret Thatcher and other advocates of the free market such as Milton Friedman and Friedrich Hayek. Like Thatcher, Klaus was also critical of what he saw as socialist tendencies in the EU, suggesting at one point that he did not think the Czechs should "lower" themselves to enter the EU.

Elsewhere, Conservative parties have been more accommodating to statist economic policies. For example, in France, the political right is associated with the legacy of Charles de Gaulle who, among other things, advocated a strong state role in the economy (*dirigisme*) to advance the French nationalism and power. Although France has curtailed the state's role in the economy in the past two decades, there has been no Thatcherite revolution. Indeed, the "Right" in France, on questions of the state's role in the economy, has often been more to the "Left" than that of the Labour Party in Britain or the Democratic Party in the US. Indeed, the idea of adopting Anglo-American free-market principles is anathema to many in France. In the late 2000s and early 2010s the center-right government led by President Nicholas Sarkozy (2007–2012) backed away from significant free-market oriented reforms in labor policy amid widespread popular opposition. In Scandinavia, Conservative parties have traditionally played by the rules of consensus politics, often cooperating with the political left and accepting many aspects of the welfare state. However, as the idea of free-market economics has spread in popularity across the globe, they have become more aggressive in attacking some elements of statist policies (e.g., high marginal tax rates) that are not particularly popular with the public. This has proved a winning strategy, as Conservative parties joined coalition governments after elections in Denmark (2001, 2005), Norway (2001), and Sweden (2006, 2010). Conservative parties are also a major political force in Greece, Spain, Ireland, Poland, Croatia, and Hungary, and they do best where they do not have to compete on the right with Christian Democratic parties.

Xenophobic, nationalist parties

Xenophobic and nationalist parties, often described as "far-right" political parties, have emerged in numerous European states. While clearly they are on the nationalist side of the cosmopolitan-nationalist cleavage—they rail against immigrants as well as the EU and globalization more generally in what they portray as a platform to protect national sovereignty and traditional cultural practices—many endorse economic policies (e.g., restrictions on trade and multi-national businesses, favoritism for locally based companies, opposition to some privatization plans, maintenance of regulations and social welfare) that are at odds with free-market ideology typically espoused on the political right. For that reason, it may be more accurate to simply refer to them as xenophobic, nationalist parties—some also call them "populist," a label that highlights their anti-elite orientation—which emphasize rights for the titular nationality (e.g., France for the French!) and worry about the erosion of sovereignty, including, in particular in the 2010s, the loss of control over state borders in the EU.

They are, in some respects, protest parties, galvanized by economic and cultural changes that they feel are causing irreparable harm to the established order. While some of their complaints about immigrants are grounded in economic concern about job loss, some of these parties, such as Hungary's Jobbik mentioned at the outset of this chapter, have a racist edge, attacking the perceived dirtiness, dishonesty, sexual voraciousness, criminality, and inferiority of non-white or non-Christian peoples (e.g., Algerians and Jews in France, Moroccans in the Netherlands, Pakistanis and Africans in Great Britain, Turks and Bosnians in Austria, Jews and Roma in Eastern Europe). They represent, in many people's views, an ugly side of European politics, one that harkens back to fascist movements and earlier incarnations of anti-Semitism and racism.

A few quotes from some prominent leaders of the radical right will suffice. Jean Marie Le Pen, the long-time leader of the FN in France, remarked in 1987 that the gas chambers were a "mere detail" of World War II, complained that the French national soccer team (which won the 1998 World Cup) was made up of too many Arabs and blacks, and that the Islamic veil "protects us from ugly women."[35] He was convicted in 1987 for inciting racial hatred by casting doubt on Nazi persecution of the Jews and in 2000 was banned from political office for a year for assaulting a Socialist opponent. In Italy, Umberto Bossi, head of the *Lega Nord*, suggested that "immigration consists of Muslim invaders and common criminals from the Third World." In Austria, Jorg Haidar, former leader of the Freedom Party—which won more votes (27 percent) than any other party in 1999 elections and briefly served in the government—was quoted as saying, "There is something of a problem with the blacks . . . There is just not much of a brain about."[36]

If these parties polled only 1 or 2 percent of the national vote—as was long the case with the British National Party or the German National Democratic Party, both accused by critics of supporting fascism[37]—one might not have much cause for concern. However, xenophobic parties have done well across Europe, including in Denmark, Switzerland, the Netherlands, France, Sweden, Serbia, Romania, Hungary, and Great Britain, where the anti-immigrant UK Independence Party spearheaded the 2016 Brexit vote.

For example, in Denmark, the anti-immigrant Danish Peoples' Party won over 12 percent of the vote in three elections in the 2000s and garnered over 20 percent of the vote in 2015, becoming, in the process, a central party in Danish politics that has lent its support to minority liberal-conservative coalition governments. In 2007 parliamentary elections, the Swiss People's Party won the largest share of all parties (29 percent), running on a platform to expel immigrants and their family members if someone commits a crime. It retained its position as the leading party in parliament after the 2011 and 2015 elections. One of the more interesting anti-immigrant parties in Europe was the List Pim Fortuyn, founded in the Netherlands by Pim Forutyn, a gay university professor who objected to Muslim immigration on the grounds that Islam was incompatible with Dutch traditions of liberalism and tolerance. He was killed by an animal rights activist in 2002, and posthumously his party won 17 percent of the vote in 2002, becoming the second largest party in the Dutch parliament. Its anti-Islamic and anti-immigration platform has been picked up by the Dutch Freedom Party, which won 16 percent of the vote in 2010 elections and 10 percent in 2012. It is led by Geert Wilders, who has suggested, among other things, that the Koran, the Muslim holy book, be banned in the Netherlands. In France, Marine Le Pen, Jean-Marie's daughter, became leader of the FN in 2011. She has tried to re-craft the party in a somewhat more tolerant position, including speaking out against anti-Semitic actions committed by Muslims in France. She has expelled FN members linked to neo-Nazism and racism, including, most dramatically, her own father, the FN's founder. She won nearly 18 percent of the vote in 2012 presidential elections, and the FN was the leading vote-getter in France in the 2014 EP elections. She has railed against the Lisbon Treaty as the "gravedigger of the independence and identity of European nations," has advocated France leave the eurozone, and has pushed for closer ties with Russia while suggesting the US cannot be a global partner for France. Many believe (or fear) that she will at least make it to the run-off in 2017 presidential elections, if not prevail.[38]

In the past two decades, these parties have gained strength in many countries, and in 2016—thanks in no small part to Brexit and the surprise victory in United States presidential elections by Donald Trump, who championed Brexit and employed similar rhetoric to many European nationalists—the wind appeared to be at their backs, as polls showed them doing well across the continent. They have been able to expand their support by tapping into growing feelings of economic insecurity and being left behind in a more globalized world, one that is dominated by or serves the interests of cosmopolitan-oriented elites. In Europe (and the US), many of their voters come from rural areas, but they also do well in economically distressed areas that formerly depended on relatively high-paying manufacturing jobs.[39] The latter used to be a bastion of support for left-wing parties. Now, however, such jobs are scarce, and many backers of nationalist parties believe that the traditional elite and leaders of more mainstream parties—whether on the right or (especially) on the left—have neglected to defend their interests, as they are more beholden to global interests and supportive of the EU. Many Europeans are also quick to blame economic or social ills on immigrants, and thus the idea of curtailing immigration has become a political winner, even more so after various terrorist attacks in the 2000s and 2010s committed by radicalized Muslims as well as the massive inflow of refugees into Europe in 2015–2016, both of which are covered in later chapters.

As much as many Europeans express dismay at statements by some of the leaders of these parties, it is clear that they are not simply going to disappear. Indeed, as noted above, in many cases they appear to be increasing their support, and the success of Donald Trump in using an anti-immigration, anti-globalization platform to win the US presidency in 2016 may bolster them even further. However, even if these parties fall short of winning power outright, they have forced other parties, particularly on the right, to take up their issues, especially concerns about immigration, thus significantly changing both policy and overall political discourse.

Regional parties and parties of ethnic minorities

Outside of the classic left–right framework, one could also mention parties that try to appeal to voters in a particular region or those belonging to an ethnic minority. Examples include the Scottish National Party (SNP), the *Lega Nord* in Italy, Convergence and Union in Catalonia, the Democratic Union of Hungarians in Romania, the Swedish Peoples' Party in Finland, and the Movement for Rights and Freedoms that is allied with the Turkish minority in Bulgaria. Some (e.g., the SNP) are more closely tied to the left. Others (e.g., the *Lega Nord*) are aligned with the right. What they do have in common are arguments for decentralization of power, if not national independence. Most tend to be pro-EU, seeing the EU as a source of protection against, in their view, national governments that are concerned with augmenting their own power. These parties, almost by definition, cannot win national power. However, they have served in coalition governments in countries such as Italy, Slovakia, Bulgaria, Romania, Finland, and, as noted in the previous chapter, are forces behind separatism in several states.

Campaigns and voter turnout

Let us now turn to the feature which interests all political parties and is present in all electoral systems: elections themselves. Because they have parliamentary systems, most European countries do not have elections on a regular, predictable cycle as in the US or Mexico, because Prime Ministers may see an advantage in calling for early elections. Thus while there is no fixed four- or six-year term of office, they cannot serve indefinitely without having elections: The maximum time between elections in most European states is four years (as in Germany, Sweden, Spain, Romania, and Poland) or five years (as in France, Great Britain, and Italy).

In addition to selecting members of national, regional, and local governments, Europeans may also participate in referendums.[40] Referendums provide for "direct democracy," allowing citizens to vote directly on a policy question. As noted in the previous chapter, this practice is most common in Switzerland, where it has a history of more than one hundred years. Constitutional questions also require a referendum in Spain, Ireland, Denmark, and Estonia, and in many states governments have the option of putting a question before voters. Referendums have been important on numerous occasions and often receive more attention than normal governmental elections. Examples from recent European history include French voters' approval for a directly elected president (1962), a British referendum affirming its membership in the European Community (1975), rejections of membership in the European Community/European Union by Norway (1972, 1994), votes for independence from the Soviet Union in Lithuania, Estonia, and Latvia (1990–1991), Italy's change of electoral system (1991), narrow French approval of the Maastricht Treaty on EU (1992), liberalization of abortion (1992) and divorce (1995) in Catholic Ireland, referendums for devolution in Scotland and Wales (1997), accession to the EU and joining NATO in a number of former communist states in the 1990s and 2000s, Sweden's rejection of the euro (2003), French and Dutch rejection of the proposed EU Constitutional Treaty (2005), Montenegro's separation from Serbia (2006), Irish rejection (2008) and subsequent approval (2009) of the Lisbon Treaty, the failed vote on Scottish independence (2014), Irish approval of gay marriage (2015), and the vote in Britain for "Brexit" (2016). Advocates of direct democracy claim that it reflects the true meaning of democratic government—the people rules themselves and make their own laws—whereas critics claim that the process is unwieldy, favors more mobilized "special interests," can be a divisive way to resolve complex and controversial issues, and can be abused by national leaders to further their agenda. Hitler, for example, subjected some of his plans to referenda, which is one reason referendums are prohibited in Germany today.

Regardless of whether candidates, parties, or policy questions are on the ballot, there is certain to be a campaign to mobilize public opinion and ultimately get people to the polls. Campaigns, by their very nature, are idiosyncratic affairs, conditioned upon the nature of the candidates, parties, political culture, and electoral system. A couple of observations about European campaigns, however, generally hold. The first is that the "official" campaign season in most European states is relatively short. The precise dates of European elections, in most cases, are not known. Instead, with a few exceptions, the government announces them only a few weeks in advance. While this period is considered the actual campaign, in reality in Europe (as in most every democratic state) campaigning never really stops. In the parliamentary systems of Europe the opposition must be prepared for elections to be called at virtually any time. Rather than going through a long US-presidential primary cycle to choose a challenger, the opposition usually has its leader in place. In Great Britain there is even a shadow cabinet, an assembly of members of the opposition that signals to voters who will assume positions of leadership should the opposition come to power. The shadow cabinet also provides a means for the opposition to criticize the government, as, for example, the "shadow" finance minister is in charge of explaining why the government's economic plans are ill conceived or not as successful as their proponents claim.

Secondly, at least compared to the US, campaigns in Europe are far less expensive. Most countries prohibit widespread television or radio advertising, preferring instead to offer parties a quota of limited advertisements (e.g., in Great Britain parties get five 5-minute slots on national television, in Germany each party can produce one ninety-second ad that airs in proportion to its past electoral performance).[41] Nonetheless, during the time of a political campaign, parties find ways of getting their message across—rallies, social media, public forums, banners, leaflets, and (as I discovered in Austria in 2005) giveaways such as t-shirts, balloons, chocolates, and even free yogurt drinks emblazoned with a party's label. Several countries do offer parties state-financing, usually tied to their past electoral performance, which of course favors the more established parties. Most countries put caps on party or candidate spending and/or on the amount individuals can contribute to a campaign, although enforcement is frequently a problem, not only in newer democracies in post-communist Europe,[42] but also in Italy, France, Germany, and Great Britain, which were all afflicted by major campaign finance scandals in the 1990s and 2000s. The Electoral Integrity Project, a multinational academic effort to assess the quality of elections worldwide, ranked elections from 2012–2015 in 139 countries. Overall, European countries fared well; nine of the top ten countries were all in (northern) Europe. Post-communist European states, all newer to democracy, fared the worst in the region: Hungary ranked 68th; Albania, 75th; Romania, 93rd; and Macedonia, 99th. Turkey (101st) was the lowest of all countries included in this volume. In these cases, blatant disregard for campaign finance laws, as well as a tilted media playing field, was a prime reason for the low ranking. However, some West European states (Italy [33rd], Greece [36th], and Great Britain [39th]) failed to distinguish themselves.[43] While reliable data is often hard to come by, most would argue that spending for campaigns in Europe is overall much less than in the US. For example, one study concluded that in 2001 a grand total of $1.65 was spent per voter in British elections compared with $13.50 spent in 2000 in the US.[44] In 2013, the campaign costs for the Christian Democrats amounted to between €20 and €30 million, compared to a single US Senate seat costing over $10 million or Obama's 2012 re-election campaign that cost over $700 million, not including contributions from political action committees (which are illegal in Germany and most of Europe).[45]

Notions that one can distinguish between European and US political campaigns may be less true than they used to be. Modern campaign techniques—including polling, use of focus groups, and utilization of the Internet and social media—are now widespread, and even well-known US pollsters such as Stan Greenberg (a Democrat) and Frank Luntz (Republican) regularly work in Europe.[46] Ségolène Royal, the first female major party candidate for the French presidency, took a page out of Hillary Clinton's playbook with her campaign with a well-publicized "listening tour" that included more than 6,000 (many virtual) town meetings.[47] At times European political campaigns can also be dirty or nasty, as evidenced by incidents such as when John Prescott, a deputy prime minister from the British Labour Party, punched a citizen on the campaign trail in 2001 after the man allegedly threw a tomato at him, or when Prime Minister Silvio Berlusconi in Italy called supporters of his opponents "vampires" and "dickheads" during the 2006 campaign.[48] However, because most European democracies have vibrant multi-party systems, there is less incentive to engage in negative advertising. One reason is that one would not want to alienate a potential coalition partner. Moreover, it would be hard to target negative ads against several parties, and there also may be good reason to believe that a third party (neither the author nor target of negative ads) would stand to gain.

Irrespective of current restrictions on their campaigning, there is little doubt that most European parties outperform their US counterparts in the final result: getting voters to the polls. In general, turnout in European elections is high, particularly when compared with the US. Some states—Austria, Belgium, Cyprus, Italy, Luxembourg, and Turkey—have mandatory voting, although enforcement of this law varies (strongest in Cyprus and Belgium). Turnout tends to be better when voters think there is more at stake, which may explain (in part) why turnout is markedly lower for elections to the European Parliament (discussed in Chapter 4). Continent-wide, there is wide variation in turnout in national elections, as seen in Figures 8.1 and 8.2. The highest turnout in a country without a mandatory voting law is in Iceland, whereas the lowest turnouts in Western Europe are in Great Britain and, interestingly, Switzerland, which has a strong tradition of direct democracy. The figures give some evidence to support the argument that turnout has declined over time, perhaps reflecting a general disengagement with things political. This trend is most marked in post-communist states, as seen in Figure 8.2, where voting turnout has fallen precipitously since the first free, democratic elections in the early 1990s. By the 2010s, turnout in some countries such as Bulgaria, Poland, and Romania had fallen to about 50 percent. To combat this trend, in 2016 the Bulgarian parliament passed a measure to make voting compulsory; those not supporting any party would be able to select "not voting for anyone."[49] Whether this is the most effective solution or whether it can be enforced are good questions.

However, not all European states have seen a significant decline in voter turnout. As for the question of who votes, older and better-educated citizens tend to vote more in higher numbers. Gender gaps that appeared in the 1950s have now closed, with recent data showing no significant difference in turnout between men and women.[50]

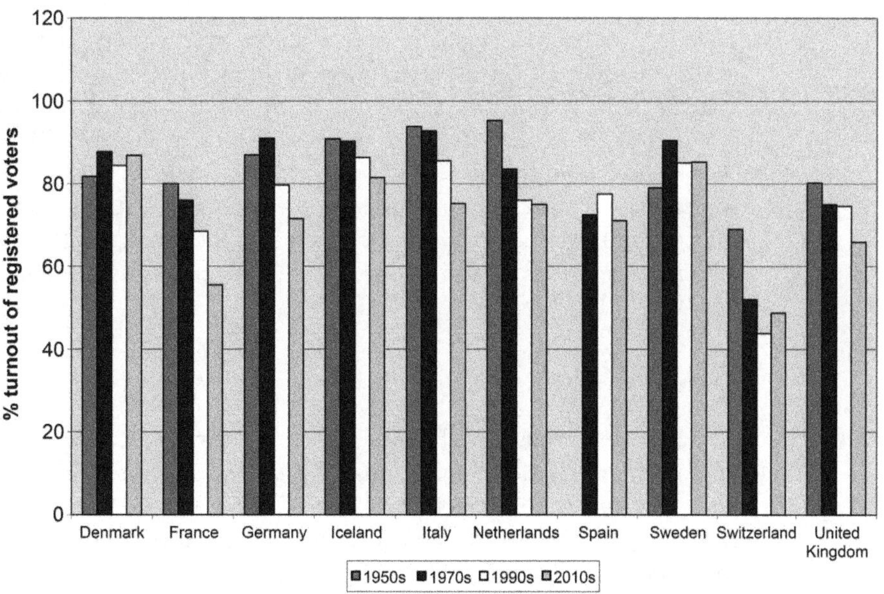

FIGURE 8.1 Trends in voter turnout in Western Europe

International Institute for Democracy and Electoral Assistance, www.idea.int/vt. Elections refer to national parliamentary elections

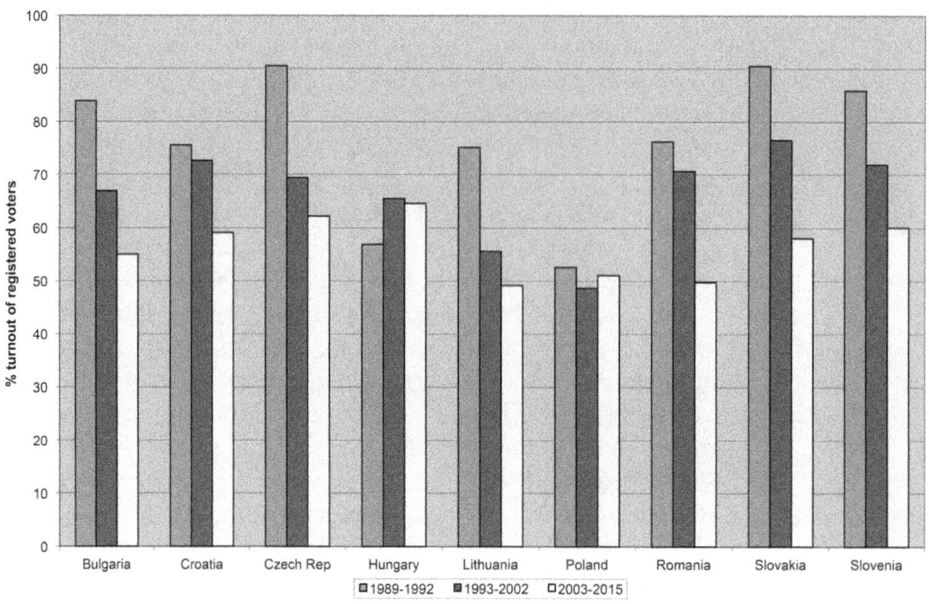

FIGURE 8.2 Trends in voter turnout in post-communist Europe

International Institute for Democracy and Electoral Assistance, www.idea.int/vt. Elections refer to national parliamentary elections

Recent European elections

Thus far, we have discussed parties, elections, and voting primarily in very general terms. In order to get a better grasp of both how political parties and electoral systems actually function as well as learn about some of the issues that concern electorates, let us look at some recent elections in Europe. Obviously, one could choose any number of cases, and arguably each country's elections generate something worthy of discussion. Here we examine elections from 2012 to 2015 in four of the larger countries in Europe, using these cases both to shed light on the individual countries as well as to illustrate some points made earlier in the chapter.[51]

The 2012 French elections

French voters went to the polls in the spring of 2012 for presidential and parliamentary elections amid a host of problems. Although France was not as hard-hit by the euro-zone economic crisis as Greece, Spain, or Italy, it was experiencing rising public debt, decreasing competitiveness, and over 10 percent unemployment. Many observers suggested it could no longer afford its generous welfare provisions and needed to make some "tough choices" to stimulate the economy.[52] Many in France were also fearful of rising immigration, and in March of 2012 a French Muslim of Algerian descent made three attacks in southern France on French soldiers and a Jewish school in southern France.

French Prime Minister Manuel Valls on the campaign trail

As noted in Chapter 6, in order to win the French presidency, a candidate must receive a majority of the votes. If no candidate receives a majority, the top two vote-getters advance to a run-off election. In 2012, ten candidates entered the race, but only three were given a serious chance of advancing to the second round. The incumbent was President Nicholas Sarkozy, leader of the center-right Union for a Popular Movement (UMP) and son of a Hungarian immigrant. Sarkozy won the election in 2007 promising a tougher line on immigration and to adopt free-market oriented reforms to create jobs and economic growth. In office, however, Sarkozy abandoned much of this latter agenda, pledging in 2008—in the early stages of the financial crisis—to create 100,000 state-subsidized jobs and create a strategic fund to protect French companies from foreign takeovers. He declared laissez-faire capitalism "dead" and rallied against the "dictatorship of the market."[53] He followed this up with austerity plans that featured more tax hikes than budget cuts, leading one observer to remark that "that's not the kind of welfare state dismantling many market liberals abroad might have banked on."[54]

Sarkozy's leading rival was François Hollande, the candidate of the Socialist Party. He backed a variety of measures to preserve and expand the welfare state, including rolling back the retirement are (changed under Sarkozy to 62) to 60, raising the minimum wage, creating more jobs for teachers and subsidized jobs for young people (over 20 percent of French youth were unemployed), re-negotiating EU rules on public debt, raising taxes on French companies, and, most controversially, raising the top rate of the income tax to 75 percent for those earning more than €1 million a year. Hollande explicitly appealed to anti-capitalist sentiments of the French, and proclaimed that "the soul of France is equality."[55] He did not, in contrast to Sarkozy, make immigration a major concern for his campaign, and he also endorsed same-sex marriage.

The third major candidate was Marine Le Pen, who had succeeded her father in 2011 as leader of the FN. She brought, in style if not substance, a softer image to the FN, and tried to broaden the party's appeal. Her core issues, however—anti-globalization, anti-immigration, concern about "Islamization" of France, and

TABLE 8.2 2012 elections in France

Presidential elections			*Parliamentary elections*				
Candidate	*% vote Round 1*	*% vote Round 2*	*Party*	*% vote in Round 1*	*% vote in Round 2*	*Total seats*	*% seats*
F. Hollande	28.6	51.6	Socialists	29.4	40.9	280	48.5
N. Sarkozy	27.2	48.4	UMP	24.7	38.0	194	33.6
M. Le Pen	17.9		FN	13.6	3.7	2	0.3
J.L. Mélenchon	11.1		Left Front	6.9	1.1	10	1.7
			Greens	5.5	3.6	17	2.9
			Others	19.6	12.7	74	12.8

Turnout: 80 percent in the presidential elections; 57 and 55 percent in parliamentary elections.

Source: www.electionresources.org/fr

withdrawing France from the euro zone—were familiar FN themes. Still, she hoped to do well, perhaps replicating her father's feat in 2002, when he placed second in the first round, thereby advancing to a run-off.

In the first round of voting in April, Hollande placed first (see Table 8.2). Sarkozy managed to stave off the challenge from Le Pen on his right flank, who performed substantially better than her father did in 2007 (10.4 percent of the vote). This set up a run-off with Hollande. Hollande seemed well-poised for victory, as he could easily blame Sarkozy for France's problems and position himself as the agent for change. He was also confident of capturing the support of those who voted for several leftist candidates, including Jean-Luc Mélenchon of the Communist Party who placed fourth and echoed Hollande's call for higher taxes and wages while also calling for civil insurrection. Sarkozy veered to the right, pledging to do more to restrict immigration, including potentially withdrawing France from the Schengen Agreement if other EU states could not control their borders. The goal was to win over FN voters, but this had limited success: Le Pen said she would turn in a blank ballot in the second round.[56] Ultimately, Hollande prevailed with a narrow majority.

Elections for the National Assembly followed in June, again in a two-stage process given France's two-ballot plurality system of voting (see Chapter 5). Over a dozen parties fielded over 6,600 candidates, meaning on average eleven candidates contested each constituency. Hollande, fresh from his victory, urged voters to give him a parliamentary majority so he could implement his reform agenda. The UMP ran largely on a platform to deny Hollande too much power, painting the Socialists as extremist. The FN was the largest "anti-system" party; nearly one-third of voters opted for radical parties on either the left or right, which shows that a large number of French people are not satisfied with more established, mainstream options when given a large array of options. As shown in Table 8.2, the Socialists garnered the most votes in the first round, and in the second round they were able to make alliances with leftist parties and woo enough voters to ultimately gain 280 seats, a near majority. The UMP became the largest opposition part. The FN, because it was largely unable to make alliances in the second round, gained only two seats; Marine Le Pen herself failed to win her district. The Socialists cobbled together a parliamentary majority with the support of the Greens and small leftist parties. This had the effect of enabling Jean-Marc Ayrault, a Socialist leader who had been appointed Prime Minister by Hollande immediately after the latter's election, to retain his post, as he enjoyed the support of the majority in the National Assembly.

The 2013 German elections

The four-year term of the German *Bundestag* ended in September 2013, necessitating new elections. In 2009, Angela Merkel's Christian Democrats won the highest number of votes, and they were able to form a center-right coalition with the liberal Free Democratic Party (FDP). Since that time, Merkel had clearly established herself as the *de facto* leader of Europe, playing a key role in developing mechanisms to bail out indebted nations such as Greece. This was not popular with some Germans, but many of her harshest critics came from her party. The parties on the left—the Social Democrats, the Greens, and the Left Party (*Die Linke*)—are all pro-EU, and, if anything, they advocated policies that would be more generous and less demanding of indebted EU members. Merkel was thus able to pursue a middle, pragmatic ground (e.g., favoring a bailout but with conditions), and she also was given credit for pragmatic, steady leadership in helping Germany weather the global economic crisis. By 2013, German unemployment was at a post-reunification low of 5 percent, German exports were up, and the government could even boast of a budget surplus.[57] All pre-election polls forecast a victory for the Christian Democrats. The only question was how large this would be.

The results of the 2013 elections can be seen in Table 8.4. Without question, Merkel and the Christian Democrats were the big winners. The Christian Democrats had their best performance since the immediate post-reunification 1990 elections. They came within five seats of obtaining an outright parliamentary majority. However, they did fall short, thus requiring a coalition partner to form a majority government. Their previous coalition partner, the FDP, failed to clear the 5 percent electoral threshold for the first time in their history. FDP officials acknowledged this was a "bitter defeat," created in part by disappointment after its failure to achieve tax reform while in the coalition with the Christian Democrats and also because some of its more Euroskeptic voters may have opted to back the newly

TABLE 8.3 2013 Bundestag elections in Germany

Party	*% vote*	*Total seats*	*% seats*	*+/- from 2009*
Christian Democrats*	41.5	311	49.3	+72
Social Democrats	25.8	193	30.6	+47
The Left (Die Linke)	8.6	64	10.1	–12
Greens	8.4	63	10.0	–5
Free Democrats	4.8	0†	0	–93
Alternative for Germany	4.7	0	0	0

Turnout: 71.5 percent *Includes both the Christian Democratic Union and the Christian-Social Union of Bavaria †Parties must receive 5 percent of the vote to receive any of the seats awarded on a proportional basis.

International Institute for Democracy and Electoral Assistance, www.idea.int/vt. Elections refer to national parliamentary elections

formed Alternative for Germany party, which advocated (among other things) German withdrawal from the Eurozone.[58] A paradoxical situation emerged. While the Christian Democrats were clearly victorious and Merkel easily was the most admired political figure in Germany—immediate post-election polls revealed that 80 percent of Germans approved of her leadership[59]—the three left-wing parties possessed a majority of the seats in the Bundestag. Technically, they could have formed a government. The twist, however, is that both the Social Democrats and the Greens refused to govern in a coalition with *Die Linke*, whose origins lay in the old communist party of East Germany and was still considered by many to be a pariah.

The options, therefore, were either a minority government—which was not preferred because it could be weak and unstable and undermine Germany's European leadership role—or a coalition between the Christian Democrats and either the Social Democrats or the Greens. More conservative Christian Democrats ruled out a coalition with the Greens, leaving the Social Democrats as the only viable partner. Many Social Democrats were leery of serving in a "grand coalition," as they had done so before (2005–2009) and felt their concerns had not been taken into account. The two parties required nearly two months to hammer out a deal, one in which the Christian Democrats compromised on issues such as creation of a minimum wage, lowering the retirement age, and establishing rent controls in some German cities.[60] Merkel remained chancellor, with Social Democratic chairman Sigmar Gabriel becoming vice-chancellor.

The elections thus re-confirmed Merkel's leadership, but they also pointed to a possible cloud on the horizon. The right-wing and Euroskeptic Alternative for Democracy party, which was formed only in April 2013, won nearly 5 percent of the vote. It played upon concerns that Germany was giving away too much to the EU. It has been compared to the anti-establishment "Tea Party" on the political right in the United States. Opposition to immigration and concerns over Islam in particular later became top issues for the party as well.[61] It gained over 7 percent of the vote in 2014 EP elections, and has won representation in several German regional parliaments as Merkel's popularity has declined, as many in Germany believe the country is taking in too many refugees, an issue we'll explore more in Chapter 11.

The 2015 British elections

In May 2015 British voters went to the polls to elect a new House of Commons. Five years earlier, no party had won a parliamentary majority, necessitating a coalition government, a relatively uncommon phenomenon in Great Britain. The coalition paired the Conservatives, who had received the largest share of the votes, and the Liberal Democrats, who had long sought the power and credibility of serving in government. The Conservative leader David Cameron served as Prime Minister. The election therefore was in part a referendum on this government, but it was also clouded by the rise of the anti-EU, anti-immigrant United Kingdom Independence Party (UKIP) and the surprising surge of the Scottish National Party (SNP) after the failure of a referendum in 2014 for Scottish independence.

The Conservatives had fared well in 2010 in part to the global economic crisis that hit Britain in the late 2000s, which included the collapse of several banks and housing prices and a spike in the state's budget deficit. Cameron also made a conscious effort to re-make the Conservatives, as he was young (43), telegenic, a good speaker and debater, and embraced new, more moderate issues (e.g., environmentalism) in an attempt to appeal to younger, centrist voters. He presented himself as a problem-solver, someone capable of leading Britain in the twenty-first century. In office, the Conservatives presided over an austerity program that included cuts in public services, in particular to education. This was unpopular in many quarters, but from 2010–2015 Britain had the fastest rate of growth of any major European economy, and at the time of elections the unemployment rate stood at 5.6 percent, far less than the 10 percent in France.[62] Just as importantly, the Conservatives pinned the economic problems of the 2000s and the subsequent need for austerity on the previous Labour government. Conservatives, in short, saw the economy as a winning issue.[63]

Their coalition partner, the Liberal Democrats, did not gain a similar edge. The Liberal Democrats were defeated in 2011 in a popular referendum to change Britain's voting system away from first-past-the-post. This was one of their key issues. While Cameron agreed to put this to a vote, he extracted from the Liberal Democrats their support for austerity measures, which were very unpopular with their core voters. Well before the election, opinion polls predicted they would suffer large losses, with the Liberal Democratic leader, Nick Clegg, held in low regard by the party's past voters.[64]

The main opposition party, Labour, elected a new leader, Ed Milliband, in the wake of its 2010 defeat. Milliband barely defeated his brother, David, for this post, and began pushing the party to the left. He relied heavily on the support of trade union leaders, and harshly criticized the government's austerity program. He touted Labour as the party that would defend the working and middle class by fighting against inequality and delivering "fairness." He also pledged to protect the beloved National Health Service and warned the Conservatives would significantly cut it. However, questions about whether he had the experience to lead the country, the divisiveness of his campaign rhetoric, and doubts about whether he and Labour as a whole had a credible economic program—as opposed to slogans and populist policies like capping prices on rail fares—dogged the party's campaign. Significantly, his standing among Labour's core supporters was much lower than Cameron's among Conservatives, creating concerns of an enthusiasm gap.[65] Furthermore, as it became clear that the SNP would gain seats (largely at Labour's expense) so that Labour could not win a majority on its own, Conservatives raised the specter of a Labour-SNP coalition that would preside over Scotland's exit from the United Kingdom.

The final results of the elections are shown in Table 8.4. The Conservatives claimed victory, gaining less than 1 percent more of the overall vote compared to 2010 but, significantly, winning more districts to garner a majority of the seats. Notably, many of the seats they picked up came from the Liberal Democrats, who were decimated. Labour slightly improved its vote share as well, but lost over two dozen seats, many of which were claimed by the SNP, which won half of the vote in Scotland and all but two of its districts, thus demonstrating that the dream of

TABLE 8.4 Results of 2010 and 2015 elections in Great Britain

	2010 elections			*2015 elections*		
Party	*% vote*	*Seats won*	*% seats*	*% vote*	*Seats won*	*% seats*
Conservative	36.1	307	47.1	36.9	331	39.8
Labour	29.0	258	39.8	30.4	232	47.1
Liberal-Democrats	23.0	57	8.8	7.9	8	1.2
UK Independence Party	3.1	0	0	12.6	1	0.2
Scottish National Party	1.7	6	9.2	4.7	56	8.6
Greens	0.9	1	0.2	3.8	1	0.2
Others	6.2	21	3.2	3.9	21	3.2
Turnout		65.1%			66.1%	

Scottish independence is still very much alive. The UKIP, which some had predicted would cut into the Conservatives' vote—Cameron may have helped forestall this by pledging to hold a referendum on Britain's EU membership—fared well in gaining an eighth of the overall vote, but it won a plurality in only one district. Both the UKIP and SNP are now powerful forces in British politics. Other parties—mainly regional parties in Northern Ireland—also picked up seats in the 2015 elections.

As one can see from the table (and appreciate from the discussion of plurality election systems in Chapter 5), the results are far from proportional, as the Conservatives won a parliamentary majority with just over a third of the vote. The UKIP's public support did not translate into seats, whereas the SNP, whose voters are more geographically concentrated, "over-performed" in relation to their overall national vote. Whether the Liberal-Democrats can rescue themselves from irrelevance and once again gain a sizeable presence in parliament is a genuine question. For its part, Labour was the other clear loser in these elections, particularly given that it was ahead of the Conservatives until about six months before the vote. Afterward, Milliband resigned as Labour Party leader; Jeremy Corbyn, a maverick far-left MP, assumed that post in September 2015. Whether he could gain support from moderate, centrist voters was an open question. In the wake of the election it looked as if Cameron and the Conservatives were in good stead, although as noted in Chapter 4, they suffered sharp internal divisions on the 2016 Brexit referendum, whose results compelled Cameron to resign. Theresa May, chosen by the Conservatives to serve as the new Prime Minister, inherits Cameron's small parliamentary majority, but given the splits within her own party (she herself campaigned tepidly for "Remain"), her ability to lead Britain in uncertain times will likely be sorely tested.

The 2015 Polish elections

In October 2015, Poles elected both a new *Sejm* (lower house of parliament) and Senate, the eighth parliamentary elections since the end of communist rule in 1989. Poland obviously does not have the venerable traditions of democracy as in Western

Europe, but it had been hailed as a post-communist success story. Notably, previous elections revealed both a great deal of electoral volatility, with power alternating between parties of the left and right, and volatility in the party system, as new parties formed and others folded. Only one Polish party survived intact from 1991 to 2009.

By 2015, the two leading parties in Poland both had their genesis in the anti-communist Solidarity movement and could be classified as on the right side of the political spectrum. The main governing party, which had prevailed in 2007 and 2011 elections, was Civic Platform (PO in Polish). It is more center-right or even liberal in its orientation. It tends to be pro-EU and pro-free market and appealed to those voters who felt that they were better off as a result of post-communist reforms, including the 2 million Poles working in Western Europe. Its main challenger was the Law and Justice Party (PiS in Polish), which was founded in 2001 by twin brothers, Lech and Jaroslaw Kaczynski. It is more of a classic conservative party, supportive of the Catholic Church and "traditional" values (e.g., anti-abortion, anti-homosexual), backed heavily by rural voters, and more nationalistic (particularly vis-à-vis Germany and Russia) and critical of the EU. PiS came to power in 2005, with Lech serving as President (from 2005 until his death in a plane crash in Russia in 2010) and Jaroslaw serving as Prime Minister (2006–2007) and remaining leader of the party. In May 2015, Andrzej Duda won election as Poland's president, a position with relatively limited powers.

Notably, Poland's once-prominent center-left party, the Alliance of the Democratic Left, which had ruled the country in the early 2000s, had collapsed as a major political force due to corruption scandals and joined forces with other small left-oriented parties for the 2015 elections. The other main parties, Kukiz 15 and Modern (*Nowoczesna*), were recent creations, the former an anti-establishment party founded by punk musician Pawel Kukiz, who burst on the political scene by winning over 20 percent of the vote in the 2015 presidential elections, and the latter a liberal party founded only five months before the elections by a former World Bank economist.

One might have expected the PO to be re-elected, as Poland was the only major European economy to avoid a recession during the global economic crisis and it possessed one of the EU's fastest growing economies. However, it looked increasingly stale after eight years in power and was implicated in "Waitergate" in 2014, which involved secret recordings of politicians eating in restaurants. In addition, Duda's victory in the presidential election signaled a shift to the right in the Polish electorate, as he campaigned as a champion of those who felt left behind by the surging economy and as a leader who would protect Poland's interests in an integrated Europe.[66] One of his proposals included taxes on foreign banks, a move that would violate EU policy. Significantly, by the fall of 2015 the refugee crisis in Europe raised great concern in Poland about a possible flood of people across Poland's borders and that the EU (read: Germany) would "order" Poland to take in more refugees. The PiS, which had long embraced nationalism, including past calls for a "pure" Poland (this in the country with the largest concentration camps in World War II) and that Poland be given more voting rights in the EU because it would have more people if not for Nazi Germany (a suggestion that did not sit well with Angela Merkel), both profited from and stoked these concerns, with

TABLE 8.5 Results of 2015 Polish parliamentary elections

Party	*% vote*	*% seats*	*Total seats*	*+/– from 2011*	*Seats in Senate*
Law and Justice	37.6	45.4	235	+78	61
Civic Platform	24.1	36.1	138	–69	34
Kukiz 15	8.8	11.5	42	+42	0
Modern (*Nowoczesna*)	7.6	16.7	28	+28	0
United Left	7.6	0	0*	–50	0
Polish Peoples' Party	5.1	0	16	–12	1
Others	9.2	.1	1	–17	4

Turnout: 50.9 percent *The threshold for single parties is 5 percent; it is 8 percent for electoral blocs with combined lists, hence the result for the United Left coalition.

Jaroslaw Kaczynski warning that migrants carry dangerous diseases. Others warned that Poland had become Germany's "lap dog" in the EU and that Polish workers were being exploited in Teutonic sweatshops offering "junk" contracts.[67]

PiS was the big winner in the election, as seen in Table 8.5. It became the first party in post-communist Poland to win an outright majority in the *Sejm*, and it also gained control of the Senate. Beata Szydlo, vice-chair of PiS, became Poland's third female prime minister. As noted in Chapter 7, however, the PiS's victory generated concerns in Poland, including the government's attempts to limit the power of the Constitutional Tribunal as well as rising anti-Semitism, the latter evidenced by the burning of an effigy of a Jewish figure holding an EU flag and a statement by the nominee to be defense minister that the anti-Semitic forgery *The Protocol of the Elders of Zion* may be legitimate.[68] Most significantly, this election could be a harbinger for how parties across Europe can use xenophobia and concerns about the refugee crisis to win office, a development that, if repeated enough, could have continent-wide implications.[69] Certainly, as suggested in this chapter (and developed more in Chapter 11), many European parties would be quite comfortable doing so.

Elections are among the most important, interesting, and, at times, unpredictable, political phenomena in Europe. What one sees across the continent is that political leaders are under pressure to respond to a variety of issues (e.g., economic worries, foreign policy challenges, immigration, the role of the EU), and that many voters are discontented both with individual politicians and with political institutions as a whole. In some cases, incumbents are re-elected, but one trend is that "change" —whether in substance, style, or purely as a rhetorical device—is often a powerful political mantra. In many respects, of course, this is perfectly understandable as voters look for something new and parties try to respond to voters' preferences. In many countries, this helps create a very dynamic political environment, particularly when more novel, "protest" parties, such as Jobbik, are on the ballot and capture the public's discontent with more established parties. One problem worth bearing in mind, however, is that "change" can be for the better or for the worse. In the case of Jobbik and other parties on the political fringes, one might worry that what they represent is less something new and more of a return to an uglier past.

Application questions

1. What are advantages/disadvantages to strong party discipline? Does party discipline undermine or support the basic notions of democracy and representative government?
2. Is there a big difference among political parties in terms of how they are organized and allow for internal democracy? How might parties or other organizations make reforms to prevent the "iron law of oligarchy" from taking hold?
3. What cleavage do you think is most pronounced in your country? Do more traditional lines of cleavage (e.g., class, religion) still matter? What might constitute new forms of political cleavage?
4. In the 2010s, parties on the right, including nationalist, xenophobic parties have tended to do better across Europe than parties on the left. Why might this be? Why haven't many parties on the left been able to respond successfully to economic anxiety felt across Europe?
5. How would you explain variance in voter turnout in Figures 8.1 and 8.2? Is it enough to say that voters in post-communist Europe are not "used" to democracy? Do you think compulsory voting is a good idea?

Key terms

catch-all parties	228
Christian Democrats	241
Communists	232
cosmopolitanism	231
Conservatives	242
dealignment	229
Greens	236
iron law of oligarchy	229
Left	231
Liberals	240
nationalists	231
political cleavages	230
Right	231
single-issue parties	228
Social Democrats	237
Third Way	238

Additional reading

Briter, Michael, and Deloye, Yves. 2007. *Encyclopedia of European Elections*. New York: Palgrave.

This useful resource reviews political issues and electoral outcomes throughout Europe.

International Institute for Democracy and Electoral Assistance (IDEA), at www.idea.int
An excellent database on electoral systems, voter turnout, and regulations on parties and campaign finance.

Luther, Kurt, and Muller-Rommel, Ferdinand, eds. 2003. *Political Parties in the New Europe: Political and Analytical Challenges*. Oxford: Oxford University Press.
This collection of essays by leading scholars who study political parties includes considerations of how parties are changing organizationally, how they are responding to a new ideological environment, how they maintain bases of support, and how "Europeanization" offers challenges and opportunities.

Mudde, Cas. 2007. *Populist Radical Right Parties in Europe*. Cambridge: Cambridge University Press.
This book examines the factors contributing to the emergence of a "radical right" and how such parties have performed in a number of countries.

Party Politics, journal published by Sage Publishing. Consult www.partypolitics.org.
This premier scholarly journal publishes research on the theory and practices of political parties, with frequent articles on European political parties.

Notes

1 See articles in *The Economist* on June 20, 2009 and April 10, 2010.
2 The full name of the party is Jobbik—The Movement for a Better Hungary (in Hungarian: *Jobbik Magyarországfért Mozgalom*).
3 "Hungarian MP Denounced for 'Jewish List' Call," *Al-Jazeera*, November 28, 2012, available at www.aljazeera.com/news/europe/2012/11/2012112722413396434.html.
4 "Jobbik on Refugees: Shoot First, Ask Questions Later," *Budapest Beacon*, August 28, 2015, available at http://budapestbeacon.com/public-policy/jobbik-on-refugees-shoot-first-and-ask-questions-later/26588.
5 Most countries in the world do have elections—including China, Iran, Cuba, and Iraq under Saddam Hussein. The key point is that these elections must be fair and there must be political competition. The above examples do not meet these criteria.
6 E.E. Schattschneider, *Party Government* (New York: Rinehart, 1942), p. 1.
7 The Whigs and Tories, factions in Britain that date to the eighteenth century, are best thought of as elite factions than as political parties, considering the fact that until 1867 less than 10 percent of Britons enjoyed the right to vote. Nonetheless, today many in the Conservative Party in Britain claim the "Tory" tradition.
8 Party discipline may also be high because of the nature of parliamentary government, as the members of the party must stick together in order to assure that "their" prime minister and cabinet remain in office.
9 Here I mean that they support the idea that those in power should be chosen by the people. Whether all parties support more liberal ideas such as expansive freedoms and rights for minorities is another matter.
10 Robert Michels, *Political Parties: A Sociological Study of the Oligarchical Tendencies of Modern Democracy* (New York: Hearst's International Library, 1915).
11 Information about campaign finance is often hard to find. One useful source is the Electoral Integrity Project (www.electroralintegrityproject.com), directed by Pippa Norris of Harvard University. This analyzes problems of flawed elections, including those of corruption or non-transparent campaign finance.
12 "Political Parties: Empty Vessels," *The Economist*, July 24, 1999.
13 "Party Time," *The Economist*, September 24, 2005.
14 The classic work on political cleavages is Seymour Lipset and Stein Rokkan, eds. *Party Systems and Voter Alignments* (New York: Free Press, 1967). For a more recent presentation of cleavages based upon economic and social changes in Europe, see Ronald

Inglehart, *Culture Shift in Advanced Industrial Society* (Princeton: Princeton University Press, 1990).

15 For an obituary on the idea of class voting, see Mark Franklin, et al., *Electoral Change: Responses to Evolving Social and Attitudinal Structures in Western Countries* (Cambridge: Cambridge University Press, 1992). For an alternative view, see Geoffrey Evans, *The End of Class Politics?: Class Voting in Comparative Context* (Oxford: Oxford University Press, 1999).

16 Russell Dalton, *Democratic Challenges, Democratic Choices: The Erosion in Political Support in Advanced Industrial Democracies* (Oxford: Oxford University Press, 2004).

17 Good coverage of this theme is in both Inglehart, *Culture Shift*, and in Dalton, *Democratic Challenges.*

18 Lipset and Rokkan, *Party Systems.*

19 "Like Trump, Europe's Populists Ride a Wave of Rural Discontent to Victory," *The New York Times*, December 7, 2016.

20 Some of these parties went by different names, e.g., the Polish United Workers' Party. Nonetheless, in terms of their orientation, they clearly were "Communist" parties.

21 Lipset and Rokkan, *Party Systems*, and Richard Rose and Derek Urwin, "Persistence and Change in Western Party Systems since 1945," *Political Studies* 18, 1970, p. 287–319. See also Stefano Bartolini and Peter Mair, *Identity, Competition, and Electoral Availability: The Stabilization of European Electorates, 1885–1985* (Cambridge: Cambridge University Press, 1990).

22 The classic source is Mogens Pedersen, "The Dynamics of European Party Systems: Changing Patterns of Electoral Volatility," *European Journal of Political Research* 7:1, 1979, p. 1–26.

23 Author's calculations using Parties and Elections in Europe database.

24 Herbert Kitschelt, *The Transformation of European Social Democracy* (Cambridge: Cambridge University Press, 1994).

25 Tony Judt, *Postwar: A History of Europe Since 1945* (New York: Penguin, 2005), p. 553–554.

26 "The Lady in Red," *The Economist*, February 17, 2007.

27 Author's calculations.

28 "France's Socialist Government Survives Vote, but Remains Fractured," *The New York Times*, May 13, 2016.

29 For a view that is more optimistic on the role of the European Parliament in "Europeanizing" political parties, see Amie Kreppel, *The European Parliament and the Supranational Party System* (Cambridge: Cambridge University Press, 2001).

30 Thomas Poguntke, et al., eds. *The Europeanization of National Political Parties: Power and Organizational Adaptation* (London: Routledge, 2007).

31 John Lloyd, "Prepare Ye the Way of the Blair," *The New Statesman*, May 10, 1999, and "Third Way Club Gathers Members," *The Guardian*, May 3, 1999. See also Richard Dunphy, *Contesting Capitalism? Left Parties and European Integration* (Manchester: Manchester University Press, 2004).

32 Compare, for example, the more interventionist policies favored by the British Liberal Democrats with the more free-market orientation of the Conservatives.

33 In 1992, the once-dominant Christian Democratic Party in Italy was torn apart by corruption scandals. The Right in Italy is now dominated by explicitly secular parties.

34 Examples include the Spanish People's Party, France's Republicans, Forza Italia in Italy, and FIDESZ and Hungary.

35 "The True Face of the National Front," *The Guardian*, April 25, 2002.

36 Both of these quotes are from John Lloyd, "Le Pen Is Mightier. . ." *New Statesman*, April 29, 2002.

37 Although neither have seats in the national legislature, the British National Party won seats in some local elections in 2006 and in the EP in 2009. It experienced a decline in votes in the 2010s and was briefly de-registered in 2016. The German National Democratic Party won seats in regional elections in the former East Germany 2006 and 2011.

38 For a good review of the FN under Marine Le Pen, see Robert Guttman, "France's Socialist Prime Minister Warns That Far-Right Leader Marine Le Pen Could Wind-Up

as President in 2017," *Transatlantic Magazine*, March 10, 2015, available at http://transatlantic-magazine.com/frances-socialist-prime-minister-warns-that-far-right-leader-marine-le-pen-could-wind-up-as-president-in-2017/.

39 "Like Trump, Europe's Populists Ride a Wave of Rural Discontent to Victory," *The New York Times*, December 7, 2016.

40 A good source on the topic is Mads Qvortrup, *A Comparative Study of Referendums: Government by the People* (Manchester: Manchester University Press, 2002).

41 An excellent source is Lynda Lee Kaid and Christina Holtz-Bacha, eds. *The Sage Handbook of Political Advertising* (Beverly Hills: Sage, 2006).

42 Janis Ikstens, et al., Campaign Finance in Central and Eastern Europe: Lessons Learned and Challenges Ahead (Washington DC: IFES, 2002).

43 Electoral Integrity Project, *The expert survey of Perceptions of Electoral Integrity*, Release 4 (PEI-4.0, 2016) www.electoralintegrityproject.com. The US ranked 47th (lower than Mongolia, Argentina, and Tunisia), mainly because of campaign finance concerns.

44 Patrick Basham, "Campaign Finance Fantasyland," Paper from the Cato Institute, June 9, 2001, at www.cato.org/dailys/06-09.01.html, accessed on March 31, 2007. British parties were capped at a measly $28 million for the campaign, the cost of an individual Senate campaign in a large US state.

45 See Olga Khazan, "Why Germany's Politics Are Much Saner, Cheaper, and Nicer Than Ours," *The Atlantic*, September 30, 2013.

46 Joe Klein, "The Party's Over," *The Guardian*, May 24, 2001.

47 "Lady in Red," *The Economist*, February 17, 2007.

48 Berlusconi reference is from "A Sad Italian Story," *The Economist*, April 8, 2006.

49 Reuters, "Bulgaria Approves Compulsory Voting to Boost Turnout," April 21, 2016.

50 The best central source on voter turnout can be found at the website of the International Institute for Democracy and Electoral Assistance, www.idea.int/vt, accessed on April 25, 2010.

51 All the results from these elections, unless otherwise noted, come from the Parties and Elections in Europe database, available at www.parties-and-elections.eu/.

52 See for example "An Inconvenient Truth," *The Economist*, March 31, 2012.

53 "Is Sarkozy a Closet Socialist?," *The Economist*, November 13, 2008.

54 Bruce Crumley, "More Taxes Please, We're French," *Time*, December 26, 2011.

55 "An Inconvenient Truth," *The Economist*, March 31, 2012.

56 BBC News, "France Election: Le Pen to Cast Bank Vote in Run-Off," May 1, 2012, available at www.bbc.com/news/world-europe-17906203.

57 Deutsche Welle, "Germany Achieves Budget Surplus as Recovery Continues," February 25, 2014, available at www.dw.com/en/germany-achieves-budget-surplus-as-recovery-continues/a-17454992.

58 Stefan Wagstyl, "German Election: FDP Faces Worst Result Since Second World War," *Financial Times*, September 22, 2013.

59 Olga Khazan, "Why Is Merkel Still So Popular?" *The Atlantic*, September 22, 2013.

60 Philip Oltermann, "Angela Merkel Agrees to Form German Coalition with Social Democrats," *The Guardian*, November 27, 2013.

61 Alexandra Sims, "Alternative for Germany: The Anti-Immigration Party Even Scarier than Donald Trump," *The Independent*, March 14, 2016.

62 Data from www.tradingeconomics.com

63 See Steven Swinford, "Election 2015: How David Cameron's Conservatives Won," *The Telegraph*, May 8, 2015.

64 "General Election 2015: Why Has Labour Lost Its Lead in the Polls?" *The Guardian*, October 6, 2014.

65 Ibid, as well as Peter Mandelson, "Why Labour Lost the Election," *The New York Times*, May 18, 2015.

66 "Andrzej Duda Victory in Polish Presidential Election Signals Shift to the Right," *The Guardian*, May 25, 2015.

67 "Fear and Xenophobia Poison Polish Polls," *The Guardian*, October 23, 2015.

68 Joshua Keating, "Anti-Refugee Polish Nationalists Didn't Get the Message That They're Not Supposed to Hate Jews Anymore," *Slate.com*, November 20, 2015.

69 The gains of the Danish Peoples' Party in June 2015 elections may have been the first clear sign of this phenomenon. After the Polish elections, one could also mention results from the first half of 2016, including the strong performance of the new, anti-immigrant Alternative for Germany party in regional elections and the victory of Nobert Hofer of Austria's Freedom Party in presidential elections.

Despite numerous scandals, Silvio Berlusconi dominated Italian political life for two decades

Chapter 9

Political culture and political behavior

How can one explain the phenomenon of Silvio Berlusconi? Italy's richest man, he made his fortune as head of a media empire and has served as prime minister three times (1994–1995, 2001–2006, 2008–2011). Long dogged by allegations of corruption, connections to organized crime, and concerns about his near-monopoly control over Italian television, he has been the consummate political survivor and is Italy's only post-war prime minister to serve a full five-year term of office. In office, he was also embroiled in a series of sex scandals, including allegations of an improper relationship with the 18-year-old daughter of a political ally and payments to prostitutes who worked parties at his presidential residence, as well as exhibiting what most outsiders would consider bizarre behavior (e.g., nominating showgirls to run from his party for the European Parliament). His wife filed for divorce, but Berlusconi claimed that he was the victim of a plot by the media and communist judges to remove him from office. Critics contended that he had turned Italian politics into a "Mexican soap opera" and a "whore-ocracy."[1]

Whereas shenanigans like Berlusconi's would end the career of most political leaders in Europe, his resignation in 2011 was a result primarily of severe economic problems and parliament's rejection of his proposed budget. In 2012, an Italian court sentenced him to four years in prison for tax evasion and banned him from holding political office.[2] Even so, he did not leave the political scene. He led the center-right People of Freedom coalition into 2013 elections, in which it was less than half a percent point of coming in first. Afterward, he revived his *Forza Italia* (Forward Italy) party, although prospects for his return as prime minister look rather remote.

How can one account for all of this? Perhaps, one could say, Berlusconi's mix of flamboyance and *machismo* is a reflection of Italian culture, some sort of "bizarre Italian anomaly in which sexist macho men and successful businessmen and swindlers are admired rather than villified?"[3] Many Italians, of course, would bristle at such an explanation; lechery, bombast, and corruption are hardly unique to Italians. However, this type of cultural explanation has a certain resonance. Governments in Europe are elected by voters; their leaders and their policies should therefore reflect aspects of the country's cultural milieu. Of course, cultural arguments can degenerate into lazy analytical shortcuts, and stereotypes (e.g., hardworking Germans are thrifty, slothful Greeks are profligate spenders, "backwards" Eastern Europeans vote for pugnacious nationalists) are often difficult to support with hard evidence, and are often poorly equipped to explain political change. Nonetheless, they are frequently invoked, and the study of political culture figures prominently in political science.

Political culture, and, by extension, various forms of political behavior that are a manifestation of cultural values, are therefore worthy topics of serious consideration. In the previous chapter we looked at political parties and voting patterns among European publics, but this only captures a small part of political behavior or what might also be called citizenship politics. We should also consider peoples' basic political values and orientations, as these core beliefs inform and color their political participation. We should also recognize that citizens engage in political activity in a myriad of ways, and that voting, although certainly the most obvious and perhaps most common form of political participation, is not always the most effective or even important form of political engagement. This chapter steps back from examination of institutions and macropolitics and focuses more at the individual, micro level. It seeks both to analyze fundamental attributes of political culture across a wide range of European countries and to examine individuals' political behavior through participation in interest organizations and social movements, which have at times played crucial roles in shaping political, economic, and social life in Europe.

Defining and refining political culture

political culture set of attitudes, beliefs, and sentiments that provide the basic assumptions and rules that govern political behavior.

One of the most venerable and popular topics of study in political science is **political culture**. One can define political culture as "the set of attitudes, beliefs and sentiments which give order and meaning to a political process and which provide the underlying assumptions and rules that govern behavior in a political system."[4] As employed by social scientists, it refers to enduring, fundamental sets of beliefs that can be studied across time and across countries. It is thus not the same thing as public opinion *per se*, which is often something more specific and time-bound. For example, asking a rather generic question about trust toward political parties or courts would be tapping into an aspect of political culture. A question more specific to a particular party (e.g., the German Christian Democratic Union) or its leader (Angela Merkel) would be better described as probing public opinion. Put differently, the study of political culture aspires to look at a broader, longer, and moving picture of citizens' values—with more of a psychological or even anthropological aspect—whereas public opinion is often more of a snapshot view, limited in scope and time.

Why study political culture? The basic reason should be obvious, especially when considering democratic political systems. If government is "of the people" and "by the people," the people matter, and their beliefs and values should be reflected in their government. Some invoke a "theory of congruence," meaning that the durability of a political system requires the congruence or resemblance between governmental authority and the values and other authority patterns found within a society.[5] Less prosaically, people get the government they deserve. Aristotle (384–322 BCE), often considered the first political scientist, recognized this, arguing that a successful democracy depended upon the virtue of its citizens.

It is worth mentioning, however, a couple of problems in the study of political culture. One is identifying what aspects of political culture matter most. For example, tolerance and a commitment to equality are usually argued to be an important feature of a democratic political culture. However, sexism, racism, and homophobia have been—and in some cases continue to be—prominent features in democratic polities. A second problem is whether one can isolate political culture as a *cause* of political phenomena. For all the popularity of cultural arguments, they are frequently hard to prove and often end up as tautologies (e.g., Great Britain is democratic because the British have a democratic orientation). There is clearly a chicken and egg type of problem here, and it can be hard to isolate culture as the sole or primary cause. Perhaps, culture should be treated as an effect, as other factors (e.g., economic development or government policies) help produce a given political culture. One could take a more agnostic view on causality, maintaining that various factors affect each other in a complex fashion, as pictured in Figure 9.1. Such a perspective would still treat political culture as an important, but not necessarily the only, factor in explaining political phenomena. It would also recognize that political culture can change through **political socialization**, the process through which an individual acquires information, attitudes, and orientations concerning

political socialization process through which an individual acquires information, attitudes, and orientations about political life.

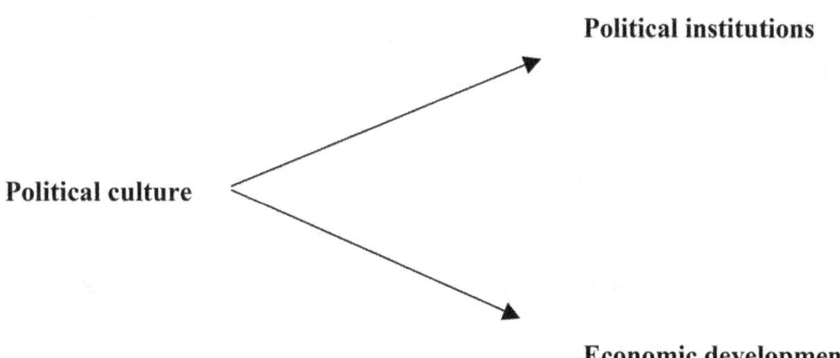

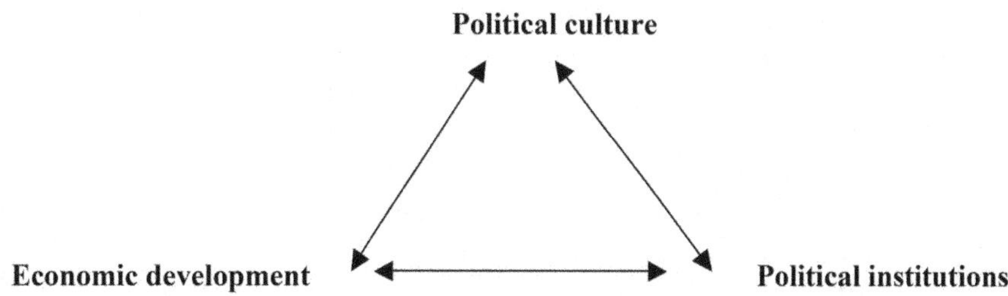

In the top diagram, political culture is the primary causal variable. In the bottom diagram, political culture is inter-related with other variables, acting both as a cause and as an effect.

FIGURE 9.1 How might political culture function?

Is Europe one?

How strong is the feeling of Europeanness?

European countries are drawing closer and closer together in terms of economic cooperation and political institutions. One of the goals of the EU, however, is social integration, including the development of a broader sense of European identity or European values among various national publics. In other words, on a cultural level, one would think of oneself less and less as German, Swedish, or Romanian and increasingly as simply "European," one who shares common values with citizens in other countries across the continent.

This idea of a European identity has been wrapped up in various projects to fashion a united Europe. True, a prominent theme in European history is the rise of nation-states, but many thinkers saw the nation-state as a stepping-stone to a larger Europe. Jean-Jacques Rousseau, in his *Considerations on the Government of Poland*, suggested—no doubt wishfully—that there "are no more French, German, Spanish, even Englishmen. Whatever one says, there are only Europeans. They all have the same tastes, the same passions, the same habits."[6] Of course, Rousseau's vision has not yet been realized. Identity is based upon symbols, myths of common origins, stirring narratives, and heroes, and, as debates in the late 1990s over whose face should appear on the euro revealed, these are in short supply on the pan-European level.[7] Yet, identities can be crafted or emerge out of political arrangements. Borrowing from Italian statesman Massimo D'Azeglio, who wrote, "We have made Italy, now we must make Italians," can we say that "Europeans" are being made today?

There are good reasons to be skeptical. Both the World Values Survey (WVS) and the Eurobarometers ask questions about citizenship and identity, about how "European" people feel as opposed to French, Italian, Swedish, and so on. Not surprisingly, the surveys reveal that people feel primarily local or national identities as opposed to a pan-European identity. For example, in the WVS of 2005–2007, on average only 16.7 percent of respondents in nine EU countries[8] "strongly agreed" that they saw themselves as part of the EU, which was lower than those who felt the same about their country (50.2 percent), locality (34.5 percent) or even as a citizen of the world (18.8 percent). Interestingly, the country in which people were most inclined to "strongly agree" that they see themselves as part of the EU was Norway (54.1 percent), which is *not* an EU member! Since 2010, Eurobarometers have regularly included a battery of questions on European citizenship. A 2015 survey found fairly strong (especially compared to the above-mentioned WVS results) support for a feeling of EU citizenship. Over half of respondents "definitely" (27 percent) or "to some extent" (40 percent) felt themselves to be an EU citizen. Younger respondents, those with more education and a better personal financial situation, and those in older member states were more likely to feel this way, and the total of those feeling themselves an EU citizen was higher than when the questions were first asked in 2010 (67 percent v. 62 percent). Figures were, perhaps not surprisingly, lower for newer member states as well for countries such as Greece, Italy, and Cyprus, which had recently experienced economic problems and procured, albeit with conditions, assistance from the EU. At the same time, only 10 percent of respondents felt that, in terms of their identity, they feel purely "European" (2 percent) or "European" and then their own nationality (8 percent). However, over half (52 percent) stated they do identify as "European" secondarily after their own national identity, which can be interpreted as a stronger feeling of Europeanness than in 2005, when only 17 percent said that they "often" thought of themselves as European in addition to identifying with their own particular nationality.[9]

Beyond affective feelings, is there evidence of behaviors that might give rise or support a common European identity? A Eurobarometer survey from 2013 found that only a minority of Europeans participate in cross-border "European" activities: 49 percent reported they had socialized with people from other EU countries, 39 percent reported they had visited another EU country, and only 25 percent claimed to have read a book or newspaper in a language other than their native tongue. On all measures, this is a slight increase from a previous 2006 special Eurobarometer. On all these questions, those in northern European countries (especially Luxembourg, Denmark, the Netherlands, and Sweden, where fluency in English is common) were more likely to report participation in such activities than those in Southern or Eastern Europe. Analysts for the Eurobarometer concluded from the 2013 survey that two-thirds of Europeans have "low openness" to other Europeans, with the figures highest for tiny Luxembourg (85 percent) but much lower in countries such as Bulgaria, Hungary, and Italy.[10] On all questions, younger respondents, those with more education, those in "white-collar" professions, and those who regularly use the Internet were more likely to be knowledgeable or participate in "European" activities. Knowledge about basic facts of the EU—including the number of countries in the EU, how the European Parliament is elected, and whether Switzerland is an EU member (it is not)—is also low. A 2014 Eurobarometer found that only 39 percent of respondents knew the answers to all three questions, with the most knowledgeable respondents in Slovenia (62 percent), Luxembourg (61 percent), and Croatia (60 percent and also the newest EU member). Respondents in Great Britain fared the worst, reflecting perhaps both disdain and disinterest in the EU.[11]

While these data may be disappointing for those hoping to forge a self-conscious citizen of Europe, there are some signs pointing toward the emergence of a growing feeling of "Europeanness." In a Eurobarometer survey in 2015, 51 percent of respondents felt that EU member-states were close in terms of values, an increase of 6 percent from 2006. Younger and better-educated respondents were more likely to claim there are "European values," and, in this case, the highest levels of support for this proposition came from newer members such as Slovakia (72 percent), the Czech Republic (68 percent), and Poland and Croatia (67 percent in each), with the least support in Latvia (30 percent), Cyprus (34 percent), and Spain (36 percent). When pressed about what the EU represents, peace, human rights, democracy, and individual freedom are the top responses, and respondents suggested that culture, economy, history, and values (as opposed to factors such as religion, languages, and scientific achievement) helped create a sense of community among EU citizens. As noted throughout this section, it is also young people who feel the most "European," and, in many cases, responses supportive of a shared European identity have grown over time. One set of analysts, looking at trend data, suggest that the feeling of "Europeanness" should continue to grow, thanks in part to generational effects and socio-economic factors (e.g., rising education) but also to socialization factors such as European media, tourism, and labor mobility.[12] True, the data do not suggest that national-level identity will melt away and be replaced exclusively by a European one; people still proudly identify with their own country. However, given the fact increasing numbers of people believe one identify as both a German, Italian, Dane, and so on, and as European, one can be somewhat sanguine about the prospects for a more united Europe.

Critical thinking questions

1. Does globalization and the spread of various technologies (e.g., Facebook) make the growth of a feeling of "Europeanness" almost inevitable? What might work against the growth of feeling of "Europeanness"?
2. Can you find evidence from contemporary events that there is a pronounced feeling of "Europeanness"? What might bring such feelings out?

political phenomena. Political socialization can include parental and peer influence, life experiences, education, and exposure to media. The key point from this perspective is that political culture is not an innate characteristic like hair or skin color. One is, in a real sense, not born French, Irish, or Hungarian. One *becomes* these only through political socialization. To the extent that there is a growing pan-European media as well as academic, business, and social networks, one can discuss the emergence of a broader *European* political culture and identity, a topic in this chapter's **Is Europe one?** feature.

Aspects of European political culture

Although political culture has a long tradition in political science, until recently it was hard to examine rigorously or systematically. Frequently, assessments of political culture were rooted in impressionistic evidence or travelogues. Hard data, unfortunately, was lacking, although scholars debated aspects of political cultures in historical cases (e.g., how might German political culture explain the rise of Hitler?).

In recent decades, the data problem has been solved thanks to systematic survey research that has been conducted across a number of countries. We can now rely upon broad cross-national research that has traced European values and attitudes for several decades. One source is the WVS, which has completed six iterations in Europe since the early 1980s and is now conducted globally by academic researchers in more than seventy countries. The European Values Survey (EVS), whose genesis was in the WVS but in recent iterations includes more countries and asks a different battery of questions, is also another useful source of data. Another is the European Social Survey (ESS), which is similar in many ways to the WVS and has been conducted every other year (with a varying mix of countries) since 2002. Finally, there is the Eurobarometer series, which is commissioned by the European Commission and has been conducted for more than thirty years.[13] All are publicly available online, and we shall draw upon them in the analysis below. Note that we cannot here present comprehensive data on all measures for all countries. The results are meant to be illustrative, and, if you want to know more about certain countries, you can look up results and/or, in many cases, conduct your own data analysis.

A democratic political culture?

One core question would be whether or not there is political culture that is supportive of democracy. To begin, one could define a democratic political culture as one that embraces values generally supportive of democracy, including belief in a democratic system of government, priority on individual rights and freedoms, and confidence in the ability of political competition to produce a well-functioning political system. It should also embrace **political tolerance** and respect for equality, not only in general terms of race and/or gender, but also tolerating the rights of your political opponents or disliked groups, which often can be more trying. In addition, many point to **interpersonal trust**—how much citizens trust each other in the most general terms—as important for democracy because it facilitates the growth of citizens' organizations and makes groups willing to bargain with and cede power to others. Trust is often assumed to be a central component for **social capital**, meaning the skills and attitudes necessary to promote active citizenship and social networks. Lastly, *per* Aristotle, one would expect democratic citizens, given the responsibilities they have within the political system, to take an interest in politics, which, hopefully, contributes to their general political competence as citizens.

political tolerance
belief that respects the views and rights of others, even those with whom you disagree or do not identify; considered important for democratic government.

interpersonal trust
the degree to which one trusts fellow citizens, often linked to development of associational life and democracy.

social capital
skills and attitudes necessary to promote active citizenship and social networks.

What do we find with regards to a democratic political culture? First, there is strong evidence for the idea that Europeans attach value to democracy. For example, in the 2012 iteration of the ESS, vast majorities across 26 countries expressed the view that it is "important to live in a democratically governed country."[14] The average was 78.5 percent, with over 90 percent in Cyprus, Denmark, Sweden, Norway, and Iceland. The lowest figures came from Portugal (66 percent) and several post-communist states, including Lithuania (55 percent), the Czech Republic (67 percent) and Slovakia (68 percent). Similarly, there is near universal acceptance of democracy as a very good or good system of government. For example, respondents in seventeen European countries surveyed in the WVS between 2005 and 2007 in the WVS[15] overwhelmingly (92.1 percent) agreed that having a democratic system is a good thing. The lowest figure was 80 percent in Serbia and the highest was 98 percent in Sweden. Lastly, in the most recent publicly available EVS (from 2008, covering twenty-eight countries), over 90 percent of respondents agreed with the aphorism—usually attributed to Winston Churchill—that democracy may have its problems but it is better than any other form of government.

These results might give one confidence that the vast majority of Europeans possess democratic values, but these questions are rather vague (e.g., what do people understand "democracy" to mean?) and tend to produce a positive response to democracy throughout the world, even in non-democratic countries. More telling are questions that ask respondents if a specific alternative might be preferable to democracy. Interestingly, as seen in Table 9.1, in the 2011–2013 iteration of the WVS many Europeans agreed that rule by experts or rule by a strong leader that would not have to bother with elections would be good. On these questions, one sees some differences between Western and Eastern Europe, a result also present in the EVS 2008 when majorities in all seventeen post-communist states[16] endorsed rule by experts and majorities in eight of these countries favored a strong leader (in no West European country did a majority express that view). Indeed, just looking at Table 9.1, it is hard to be sanguine about prospects for democracy in a country

political legitimacy
the voluntary acceptance of the validity of a country's political system by its citizens.

such as Romania. How to explain these results? One possible answer is that many Europeans—again, particularly in, but not only in, Eastern Europe—are not satisfied with the democracy that they have. Thus, while they may not (yet) have soured on democracy in principle, they are more ambivalent about democracy in practice, and perhaps in some states that have experienced instability, corruption, or economic crisis—again more common in Eastern Europe—the idea of a strong leader or dispassionate experts sounds good. These issues touch upon the broader question of **political legitimacy**, the voluntary acceptance of the validity of a country's political system by its citizens. If citizens feel their system of government is not performing well and another alternative would be preferable, they may seek systemic political change. Popular assessments of democratic performance and the broader question of whether there is a crisis of legitimacy for democracies in Europe is a topic taken up below in the **In focus** section.

Another component of a democratic political culture is valuing rights and freedoms. Surveys in Europe typically do not ask whether people think freedom of speech, religion, assembly, and so on, are important, primarily because not many would be opposed when questions are asked in such fashion. Some surveys, however, have probed respondents about how important freedoms are compared to other things. For example, the 2012 ESS asked respondents about personal freedoms, specifically whether they are a person who considers it important to make one's own decisions and be free or whether they are more inclined to do what one is told and follow the rules. The results revealed that many more Europeans (68 percent) described themselves as a person who believes it is important to make one's own decisions as opposed to one who does what one is told (40 percent). However, on these questions one sees substantial evidence of an East-West divide. Those from the ten post-communist European states in the survey were less likely (61.7 percent) to consider themselves as someone who places importance on individual decision-making and more likely (47.4 percent) to describe themselves as someone who tends

TABLE 9.1 Preferences for non-democratic alternatives

% saying "good" or "fairly good" to each statement

Statement	*Germany*	*Netherlands*	*Spain*	*Sweden*	*Poland*	*Slovenia*	*Romania*	*Turkey*
Having experts, not government, make decisions according to what they think is best for the country	56.7	49.8	43.6	36.9	74.6	74.6	79.6	49.8
Having a strong leader who does not have to bother with parliament and elections	20.7	26.9	39.5	26.3	20.0	23.6	69.7	49.8

Source: WVS, Wave 6, 2011–2013

to do what he/she is told, with majorities in five countries (Albania, Bulgaria, Poland, Slovakia, and Kosovo) expressing this latter perspective. In 2008, Eurobarometer surveys asked for respondents to prioritize national goals for the near future, choosing two among fighting rising prices, maintaining order, giving people more say over government decisions, and protecting freedom of speech, the latter of which would be considered post-materialist values (developed more later in the chapter). Overall, fighting rising prices (66 percent) and maintaining order (53 percent) were much more preferred than giving people more say (45 percent) or protecting freedom of speech (28 percent). Fighting rising prices was the top choice of respondents of twenty-three of the twenty-seven countries in the survey. Maintaining order was most preferred in Great Britain and in Sweden; freedom of speech the top priority only in Denmark and the Netherlands (both of which had recently experienced violence directed against those championing free expression).[17]

What of tolerance, particularly respect for equality and acceptance of differences? Social scientists try to get at this question in various ways. Sometimes they ask about opinions toward certain groups. On this score, one does find discriminatory views toward racial minorities, Jews, immigrants, Muslims, homosexuals, and Roma in many European countries, as seen in reports from the 2008 EVS and reported in Table 9.2. Intolerant, discriminatory views are particularly marked in post-communist Europe and in Turkey, although intolerance toward Roma, Muslims, and immigrants is significant in several West European states.

Another tactic to ascertain levels of tolerance is to ask more general questions about equal treatment of people and respect for differences in opinion. This touches upon tolerance for various forms of difference, including expressly political (as opposed to racial, ethnic, or religious) aspects. Some data from such questions from the 2012 ESS are presented in Table 9.3. They reveal that most Europeans would rank as tolerant—at least when they answer survey questions—but we also know that anti-immigrant and at times explicitly racist parties have attracted sizeable followings in some countries. Notably, fewer claim it is important to understand

TABLE 9.2 Social intolerance in Europe

% replying rhey would not like to have as neighbors

Country	*Jews*	*Muslims*	*Roma*	*People of different race*	*Homo-sexuals*	*Immigrants*
Germany	6.1	26.2	27.2	4.6	17.1	11.6
France	2.4	7.6	25.5	3.4	5.7	4.3
Great Britain	3.2	12.9	33.8	5.8	10.8	14.9
Italy	12.1	22.7	62.8	15.6	21.7	16.1
Netherlands	8.0	18.9	30.2	11.1	10.8	15.4
Poland	17.9	25.1	33.4	12.2	52.7	17.5
Hungary	6.4	11.0	38.7	9.0	29.5	15.2
Bulgaria	14.9	19.5	49.5	21.2	54.9	18.8
Albania	37.2	28.5	41.0	36.2	56.7	31.3
Turkey	68.9	6.0	67.4	42.7	90.5	48.7

Source: EVS 2008, online analysis at http://zacat.gesis.org

different people, although this need not imply that they would suggest banning some groups from exercising rights to express their viewpoints. As to whether or not individuals experience discrimination—for reasons such as gender, race, national origin, or religion—one sees that the figures in many countries are relatively low, although, interestingly, highest in established democracies such as France and Great Britain, where immigration and multi-culturalism, issued covered in more detail in Chapter 11, are hot political issues.

Interpersonal trust, as noted above, is also considered an important attribute in a democracy, providing a means for social networks and organizations to form and contribute to a culture of tolerance. Several surveys ask respondents if people can generally be trusted or if one cannot be too careful. Data from the 2014 ESS are presented in Table 9.4. Following the pattern already established, we see more trust in countries with longer practice of democracy, although overall levels of trust even in several established democracies (that, also, it is worth mentioning have low crime rates) is not overly high. Those who emphasize the importance of social capital would be disappointed with these data, although one could ask how relevant a question is of this sort since people usually associate, both socially and politically, not with complete strangers but with likeminded people in secure settings. Still, with sufficiently high levels of distrust, one might wonder about the ability of civil society to take root and how different groups will be able to work together for common national goals.

Lastly, how knowledgeable and empowered are citizens about politics? Data from the ESS in 2014,[18] displayed in Table 9.5, reveal sizeable differences in political interest, with majorities in many counties of Western Europe asserting they are "very" or "quite" interested in politics, although this is not universally the same, as majorities in France, Ireland, Belgium, and, perhaps most surprisingly, Norway,

TABLE 9.3 Levels of tolerance and discrimination among European publics

Figures are % agreeing

Country	*Treat people equally*	*Need to understand different people*	*I am a member of a group discriminated against*
Germany	80.1	76.4	4.5
France	77.7	61.8	10.5
Great Britain	78.9	69.9	11.9
Italy	81.0	77.3	5.6
Netherlands	62.8	74.5	7.4
Poland	84.7	68.9	5.0
Czech Republic	63.8	69.7	6.8
Bulgaria	57.1	41.3	9.9
Albania	86.3	74.5	5.5

Source: ESS, 2012. Questions ask whether the respondent identifies with a particular type of person, such as one who believes that everyone should be treated equally and have equal opportunities and one who believes that one should try to understand others, even if he or she disagrees with that person. Those who say that such a person is "very much like me" or "like me" are included in the table. The question on discrimination asks simply whether the respondent feels him- or herself to be a member of such a group

TABLE 9.4 Interpersonal trust in European countries

Country	*% saying people can be trusted*
Germany	29.8
France	21.6
Austria	28.9
Netherlands	51.7
Sweden	54.0
Denmark	59.5
Poland	16.4
Slovenia	16.9
Czech Republic	20.8

Source: ESS, 2014. Question: "Would you say that most people can be trusted, or that you can't be too careful in dealing with people?" Responses are 0 ("can't be too careful") to 10 ("most people can be trusted"), with responses of 7–10 included in the table

confess they are "hardly" or "not at all" interested in politics. Interest in politics also tends to be low (below 50 percent) in most of post-communist Europe. This latter finding does little to support claims of a "civic culture" of political engagement across Europe. Moreover, as seen in Table 9.5, most citizens—East and West—report that they do not believe that it is easy to participate in politics or that the political system allows people to have influence on politics. These questions get to their own knowledge and/or interest as well as how they believe political actors and institutional arrangements function in their country. They also get at the critical notion of **political efficacy**, the belief that one is capable of participating effectively in political life. If people find politics complicated or a fruitless area of activity, or, for whatever reason, are simply not interested, it is hard to imagine them being active, well-informed citizens. If too many citizens withdraw from political life, the crucial link between elected officials and citizens may be very weak, allowing those with greater resources or possessing narrow, particular interests to hold sway over the country.

political efficacy
the feeling that one is capable of participating effectively in political life.

TABLE 9.5 Political interest and efficacy

	Germany	*France*	*Netherlands*	*Sweden*	*Poland*	*Czech Republic*	*Slovenia*
How interested in politics ("Very" or "Quite")	66.8	49.3	63.8	67.5	36.6	17.7	44.4
It is easy to take part in politics	23.4	17.7	10.6	7.4	16.6	18.7	26.1
Political system allows people to have influence	30.5	7.0	8.4	11.9	5.4	7.8	3.5

Source: ESS 2014. The last two questions are on a 0–10 point scale. Reported responses are those expressing agreement, registered as a score of 7–10

In focus

Is there a crisis of democracy?

In addition to learning about European political culture in terms of what people consider should be the direction of political, economic, and social policy, we might also ask about how they assess the political systems under which they live. Given our interest in democracy, one might ask about the health of democratic institutions as registered by public attitudes towards their political systems. Charles Maier of Harvard University, in an influential article in 1994, argued that many of the well-established democracies in Europe (and, for that matter, in North America and Japan) were suffering from a "moral crisis," fuelled by resentment about corruption, social inequality, and a perceived abyss between publics and political leaders.[19] While he did not suggest that democratic governments would collapse, he did draw parallels between the 1990s and the 1920s and 1930s, when many European democratic governments failed. Many Europeans, he claimed, suffered from "weariness with politics" (*Politikverdrossenheit* in German) and were either withdrawing from political and social life or turning to more extremist movements, particularly on the xenophobic, nationalist right. Several years later, *The Economist*, drawing upon data from surveys in the late 1990s, suggested that there were genuine signs of worry, pointing to a long-term decline in trust in political leaders and in confidence in political institutions.[20] Ralf Dahrendorf, a prominent German social scientist, wrote in 2000 that "representative government is no longer as compelling a proposition as it once was."[21]

These issues get to the important question of political legitimacy. All political systems, but especially democracies, require political legitimacy.[22] Over the long term, a system that lacks legitimacy will either be removed by one more acceptable to the people or will have to resort to large levels of coercion in order to stay in power. One way of measuring political legitimacy is to ask general questions about the trust or confidence one has in various political and public institutions. Whereas a decline in confidence in generally stable European polities may not mean immediate revolution, it does point to a potential crisis of democracy and may signal that citizens will begin to look for new, possibly more extreme, political groups for remedies and redress of grievances.

Are these exaggerated statements and fears? Over two decades after Maier's article, do we see signs that this "crisis" is deepening, or, instead, are there more positive signs? One can point to some disturbing developments, some of which were mentioned in previous chapters: the growing emergence of intolerant, nationalist political parties that embrace xenophobic and racist views; lower voter turnout; fewer members in traditional political parties; and elections of populist leaders with dubious commitment to liberal democracy and rule of law. One might also mention corruption scandals in recent years, which have engulfed not only the new democracies in post-communist Europe (where corruption has been a prominent leitmotif since the fall of communism) but also states such as Great Britain (expense accounts for parliamentarians), Germany (fundraising impropriety with the Christian Democratic Union), and, most notoriously, Italy, where, among other problems, Prime Minister Silvio Berlusconi seemed to be under a constant cloud of some financial or sex scandal. The Irish political scientist Peter Mair points to the "hollowing out" of Western democracy—a phenomenon at work in the US as well—in which politicians are removed from average citizens, as they are more and more dependent upon donors or insider connections and are then "sold" to increasingly less engaged voters through the media.[23] And, lastly, the financial crisis of the late 2000s–early 2010s, which hit many countries in Europe quite hard and was often blamed on poor leadership, obviously would not be expected to bolster one's confidence in political authority or perhaps, even, democracy itself.

Survey evidence confirms a sense of alienation, distrust of political institutions, and widespread dissatisfaction with democratic performance across Europe. For example, in the 2014 ESS, majorities in most countries tended to favor the view that politicians do not care about what people think. Respondents were asked to answer on a 0–10 scale, with 0 indicating they believed politicians did "not at all" care. Majorities responded in the 0–3 range, exhibiting a fairly strong sense of disillusionment with politicians, in eight of the fifteen countries included in the survey, including 76 percent in Slovenia and Poland, both generally considered post-communist success stories, and 65 percent in France and 60 percent in Germany. Across the survey, only a minority (13 percent) responded in the 7–10 range (10 = politicians "completely" care), with the highest figures coming in Norway (30 percent) and Denmark (29 percent). This question connects with the aforementioned issue of political efficacy, insofar as people are not likely to feel empowered or that their voice matters if they believe that their elected representatives do not care about their views.

One can also ask more specific questions about confidence in institutions, including parties, parliaments, and the courts. The WVS wave from 2011–2013 asked respondents whether they tended to have confidence in certain institutions. Trust in political parties averaged 21 percent, ranging from 3 percent (!) in Slovenia to 42 percent in Sweden. Just over a third of respondents expressed trust in parliament or the government as a whole, with lower figures, under 20 percent, in Poland, Romania, and Slovenia. Trust in the courts (54 percent average) and police (64 percent) were higher. Time-series analysis, looking at several surveys that date back to the 1980s or early 1990s, reveal that trust in parliament dropped in most countries—East and West—whereas trust in the courts held fairly steady, with the exceptions of Romania and Slovenia, where it had declined by half since the collapse of communism.

The upshot is that many Europeans are not satisfied with their democratic governments. For example, Eurobarometer 81, conducted in June 2014, found only 50 percent of those surveyed in twenty-eight countries were satisfied with the way democracy works in their country. Forty-eight percent were dissatisfied. The lowest performers tended to be in Eastern Europe (only 20 percent satisfied in Croatia and Bulgaria, 22 percent in Slovenia, 23 percent in Romania) and in Greece (20 percent), a country still embroiled in economic crisis. As we've seen many times in this chapter, the Scandinavians fared better, with Danes (88 percent), Swedes (84 percent), and Finns (80 percent) reporting a much higher level of satisfaction.

Are these data capturing a snapshot, or is there a trend at work, one perhaps identified by Maier? Looking back over a decade at previous surveys, one does find—with some variation—a rather consistent low level of trust in many institutions, a sense of alienation, and at best a mixed assessment about democratic performance. The biggest declines have not been in Western Europe, which was Maier's focus, but in Eastern Europe, where many of the high hopes engendered by the collapse of communism have not, at least according to citizens there, been realized. With respect to the most general question from the Eurobarometer about satisfaction with democracy, one does see a decline, from 57 percent satisfaction in 2004—the year the EU expanded to eight post-communist states—to 50 percent by 2014. Again, the economic crisis no doubt plays a role, accounting for the low (30 percent or less) level of satisfaction not only in Greece but also Spain, Portugal, Italy, and Cyprus. If and when the effects of the economic crisis dissipate, one would expect satisfaction with democracy to go up. However, not only is this still an uncertain prospect in many states—the EU as a whole

returned to its overall 2008 level only in 2016—it is also clear that some problems are chronic and not simply the result of economic turbulence. Democracy, for all of its promises, has not, in many cases, led to overall satisfaction with government or, for that matter, generated a widespread sense of citizen empowerment.

Critical thinking questions

1. **What might contribute to lack of political efficacy among Europeans? Is this, in your view, a false or exaggerated perception or capturing the reality that citizens are increasingly disempowered?**
2. **"The problems of today's world are too complex for traditional institutions of democracy." Would you agree? In what way?**

What do these numerous data illustrate? Most clearly, one can still see a difference in political culture between Western Europe and Eastern Europe (including Turkey). Whether the years of democratic experience in Western Europe have created more democratic values or whether the values spawned the institutions—a sort of chicken-and-egg argument—cannot be resolved here. What is interesting, though, is that on many measures—social trust, interest in politics, tolerance, political efficacy, and support for democracy versus a strong leader—there is weak or uncertain evidence of a "democratic political culture" in several countries. Of course, democracy does not require that everyone be the ideal democratic citizen, but the data presented above—and analyzed in detail in other studies[24]—could make one worry about the future of democracy in Europe, a topic examined in more detail in the **In focus** section.

The role of the state in the economy

Another important set of issues is what expectations or preferences people have about the responsibilities of the state on socio-economic questions. This would include items such as whether the state should guarantee people employment, redistribute income, take a role in directing the country's economic life, and provide generous social welfare benefits. While these are not as explicitly political as what was discussed above, they address a fundamental aspect of political economy: How far should the state, as opposed to market forces, go in shaping the direction of the economy? Answers to these questions have been traditionally one of the main lines of cleavage between the left and right. Whereas the next chapter in this volume looks more closely at actual policies, here we can probe values and orientations on this topic.

At first glance, one can find substantial evidence that Europeans support a strong role for the state in the economy. For example, the ESS in 2008 asked whether Europeans agreed the government has a responsibility to provide a job for everyone and that the government should reduce income levels. Data are presented in Figure 9.2. One sees that there is strong support for government action to reduce inequality, although it is worth noting the question does not suggest precisely what should be done. This holds across both halves of the continent, although a bit less in Great Britain, Poland, and the Netherlands, where recent governments have been stauncher supporters of liberal, free-market policies. As for government responsibility to provide everyone with a job, one sees substantial support for this notion, with overwhelming majorities backing it in Spain and Hungary, both of which were hit hard by the global economic crisis at the time of the survey. Interestingly, however, when the survey asked more directly about higher taxes and state spending—the traditional hallmark of the left—there was decidedly less support, perhaps because few people relish the certainty of paying higher taxes without knowing what the precise personal benefit would be of more state spending.

Indeed, other evidence shows that Europeans are actually more ambivalent about the role of the state. For example, a Eurobarometer survey in 2012 asked people whether they believed that free competition is the best guarantee of economic prosperity and whether they thought that at present the state intervenes too much in their lives. Results for several countries are presented in Table 9.6. While majorities support free competition in every EU country, there is significant variance. Interestingly, respondents in nine of the ten post-communist countries (Hungary is the exception), support free competition more so than the overall EU average (65 percent). France, with a narrow majority endorsing competition, ranked lowest of all states, even lower than countries such as Spain, Greece (64 percent), and Portugal (69 percent), all of which had been hit hard (and, at the time of the survey, were still severely affected) by the global economic crisis. These data—along with

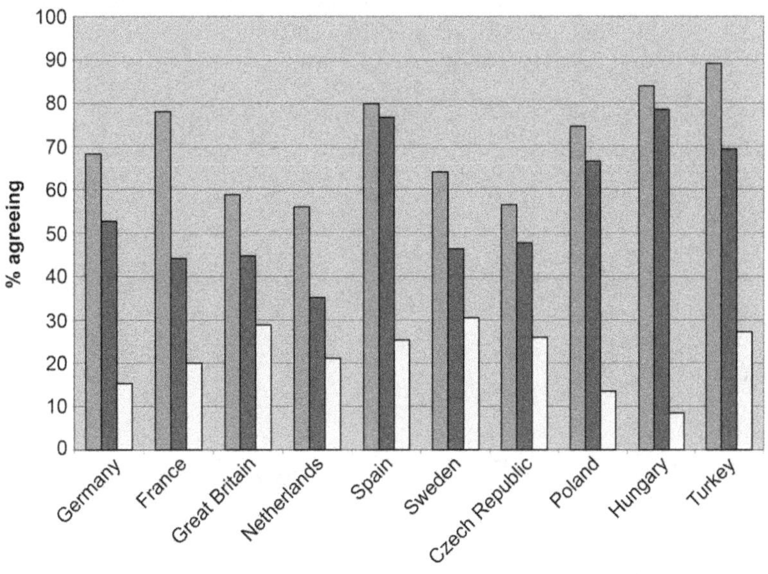

FIGURE 9.2 Views of the role of government in the economy

ESS, 2008. The table reports those agreeing with the proposition that the government should reduce income inequality and those answering 7–10 on a 0–10 scale on the last two questions, with 10 representing that it is "entirely the government's responsibility" and "much higher taxes and spending"

other reports that show the French skeptical of capitalism[25]—help explain why market-oriented efforts to reform the French economy in the 2000s and 2010s (e.g., by reducing protections for workers) repeatedly evoked protests. Interestingly, across the survey there was no discernible difference by age or education level, and even a majority (58 percent) of those who reported themselves to be under financial pressure supported free competition. Overall support for free competition was similar to that found in earlier Eurobarometers in 2006 (pre-crisis) and in 2009.[26]

As for the more general question about state intervention, again one finds that a majority agrees that the state does intervene too much. What the nature of this state intervention is was not specified, and the strongest majorities on this question were in Portugal (86 percent) and Greece (84 percent), where it was state-imposed austerity, not socialist-oriented policies, that likely rankled most respondents. At the same time, however, as seen in Table 9.6, the same 2012 Eurobarometer survey finds solid majorities across Europe agreeing to the proposition that more equality and justice is needed even if individual freedom is reduced. The Netherlands and Denmark, both of which have strong welfare states, were the only two countries in which a majority disagreed, and respondents in eight of the ten post-communist states were more in agreement than the survey average (66 percent). This is admittedly puzzling: One finds that Europeans simultaneously aver that free competition is best for the economy while at the same time agreeing that more justice and equality is needed at the expense of freedom. Perhaps individuals are reacting favorably, on the one hand, to the generic notion of competition, but, on the other hand, living in a society in which individuals already have much freedom, they embrace the lofty goals of equality and justice.

As one might suspect, these data can hide more than they reveal. Clearly there are both pro-market and pro-statist Europeans, just as there are those who are unequivocally democrats and those who are more ambivalent about democracy and

TABLE 9.6 Pro-market or pro-state?

% agreeing to each proposition

	Germany	*France*	*Great Britain*	*Spain*	*Sweden*	*Hungary*	*Poland*	*Romania*
Free competition best guarantee of economic prosperity	74	51	66	57	59	54	71	72
State intervenes too much in our lives	57	60	55	68	68	56	73	66
We need more equality and justice even if this means less freedom for the individual	48	58	79	73	59	70	59	79

Source: Eurobarometer 77, "The Values of Europeans," May 2012, available at http://ec.europa.eu/public_opinion/archives/eb/eb77/eb77_value_en.pdf

democratic values. The more interesting and complicated questions are those that try to assess what sorts of people harbor what attitudes and, implicitly, what variables or factors account for aspects of political culture. It is to these questions that we now turn.

Parsing the data

Thus far we have presented national-level data and made comparisons primarily across countries. However, just as we know that there are identifiable differences in political culture across Europe, there is also marked variation among groups of people within a given country. Just as some Germans are Christian Democrats and some are Social Democrats or Greens, one can also, using survey evidence, point to those that are more pro-market, more tolerant, more interested in politics, and so on, as well as to the factors that contribute to or at least help account for the strength or weakness of various dispositions.

Scholars of political culture would point to several prime candidates that lend themselves to cross-national analysis: education, income, age, religion, and gender.[27] Education is generally associated with pro-democratic attitudes and behaviors as well as a stronger belief in a less interventionist role for the state. Income functions similarly, although the precise effect of income versus education—seeing as how the better educated tend to be wealthier—are hard to disentangle. One would imagine that age could matter, although it would be hard to ascertain if it is a reflection of socio-economic status or a distinct generational effect that might divide older and younger citizens. Religion, traditionally at any rate, has been associated with a less democratic orientation and, to the extent that the religious tend to support the political right, arguably more free market. Gender has been found to be significant in some survey research, with males, perhaps because they are often in a stronger economic position, tending in particular to support free-market policies whereas women are stronger backers of the welfare state.

What do we find among the issues we have discussed? Tables 9.7 and 9.8 present a simple analysis, identifying how various sub-groups (e.g., the better educated, those older than 50) rank versus the average across all European countries in the survey on two selected questions: whether one endorses a strong leader that could dispense with parliament and elections (from the 2011–2013 WVS), and whether one believes one needs more equality and justice even if it means less freedom of the individual (from the 2012 Eurobarometer). We reported country-level findings on these questions in Table 9.1 and Table 9.6. Here we are looking at all European countries in the survey, and that each country could (and probably does) have its own particular pattern and its own, unique cleavage structures that do not lend themselves to cross-national comparison.

A few comments are in order about each figure. First, as seen in Table 9.7, those living in larger cities, with more education and higher incomes, are *less likely* to endorse the hypothetical non-democratic alternative, although, as one sees, just because one is in one or more of these categories is no guarantee that that person would reject the idea of a strong leader dispensing with democracy. These three variables are also found to be associated with "democratic attitudes" on a host of measures. Additionally, one sees a fairly modest gender difference on this question,

TABLE 9.7 Socio-demographic factors on democratic attitudes

Attribute	*% positively inclined to strong leader who does not need elections*
Women	32.8
Men	35.6
Higher education	24.5
Only primary education	38.9
High income	30.5
Low income	39.8
Over 50	33.1
Under 30	36.7
Very religious	42.9
Not religious	25.8
Believe country being run democratically	32.4
Does not believe country being run democratically	49.4
Urban (> 500,000)	24.1
Rural (< 10,000)	33.0
Survey mean	34.2

Source: WVS, 2011–2013, from ten European countries (Cyprus, Estonia, Germany, the Netherlands, Poland, Romania, Slovenia, Spain, Sweden, Turkey); online analysis

TABLE 9.8 Socio-demographic factors on equality vs. freedom

Attribute	*% agreeing need more equality and justice even if freedom declines*
Women	71.2
Men	64.1
20+ years of education	65.6
15 years or fewer of education	73.7
High level in society (self-placement)	64.1
Low level in society (self-placement)	70.7
Over 55	72.5
Under 25	63.3
Very good personal financial situation	51.4
Very bad personal financial situation	69.3
Survey mean	67.6

Source: Eurobarometer 77.2, from all EU-27 members; online analysis with weighted survey at http://zakat.gesis.org

although on some other measures that try to get at attributes of a "democratic political culture," there is such a gap (e.g., 55 percent of males compared with 41 percent of females in this survey assert they are interested in politics). Age also has modest effect—although it may be surprising to some that younger respondents are more likely to favor rule by a strong leader. Older people in the survey, however, are much more interested in politics (45 percent of those older than 50, compared with 38 percent of those younger than 30), reflecting the widespread observation that young people have other concerns besides politics. Table 9.7 does show a fairly strong effect of religion, with those claiming religion is very important to them—perhaps more "traditional" individuals—more likely to endorse the "law and order," strong leader option than those who say religion is not at all important. Not surprisingly, one also finds that general assessment-type variables also matter. For example, those who believe their country is not being governed democratically are more likely to favor a strong leader, perhaps because they do not see positive results from their current government.

Table 9.8 reveals a variety of factors that affect the propensity to value justice and equality over individual freedom. Age (younger respondents more likely to value freedom), gender (women more inclined to favor equality and justice), and income/education/placement in society (those with higher incomes and education or believing they are in the "upper level" of society less inclined to support equality and justice over freedom) all have a discernible effect.[28] Many of these results may not be especially surprising, as those in a better socio-economic situation—which also includes, on average, men—would have less demand for "justice" or "equality." The more surprising variable may be age, as older respondents, as one might think older respondents would be more financially secure than younger ones and therefore respond akin to those with higher incomes. However, in this survey, correlational analysis finds age negatively related both to positive assessment of one's own situation and with respect to expectations for the future, which might explain a positive relationship between youth and value of freedom over justice and equality.

This discussion is by no means meant to be definitive, and one could employ more advanced statistical techniques such as regression analysis to delve into the data ore deeply and isolate the effect of particular variables. The point, however, is to alert you to the fact that there are various cleavages within countries, making it difficult to generalize about "typical" French, Italian, Turkish, and other national attitudes. It also shows that one can demonstrate some effects of economic, social, and demographic factors on various attributes of political culture, allowing one to suggest what might explain differences across countries and changes over time.

Post-materialist values

As noted briefly in the previous chapter, scholars of European politics in recent decades have noted the emergence of orientations and political cleavages that transcend traditional concerns such as economic security. Characterized as **post-materialism**, these orientations focus more on quality of life (not simply economic growth), expansion of rights, and personal expression and empowerment. Scholars have associated the rise of post-materialist values with various campaigns and movements in Europe in the 1960s and 1970s, including feminism, the student movement, the "sexual revolution," nuclear disarmament, and environmentalism. What stood out, however, was that the main protagonists in many of these "movements" were relatively well-to-do, and their primary concerns were not material, economic gains. In the words of Ronald Inglehart, the scholar most associated with the study of post-materialism, "[a]fter a prolonged period of almost uninterrupted economic growth, the principal axis of political cleavage began to shift from economic issues to life-style issues, entailing a shift in the constituency most interested in obtaining change."[29] In short, what distinguishes a "post-materialist" from a "materialist" is that whereas the latter gives top priority to

post-materialism
orientations that focus more on quality of life issues, such as rights and political participation, than economic or security concerns.

physical sustenance and safety, the former places emphasis on belonging, self-expression, and quality of life.[30]

Inglehart suggested that the rise of post-materialism was caused by two factors. First, after World War II, Europeans enjoyed peace and prosperity. Having their most basic needs met, Europeans began to aspire to "higher order" needs such as expanding personal freedoms and maintaining a clean and healthy environment.[31] In addition, there was a **socialization effect**.[32] In other words, individuals acquire basic value orientations at a young age. Those that grew up with affluence—as did the initial post-war generation in Western Europe—were more likely to possess a post-materialist orientation than their parents or grandparents that had experienced the Great Depression and World War II. As time wore on, more and more individuals became part of the "post-materialist" generation. Writing in the 1980s, Inglehart maintained that post-materialism had "moved out of the student ghetto" and was being more commonplace among technocrats and the professional class in Western societies.[33]

socialization effect
notion that individuals acquire basic political values at a young age and that different environments can therefore produce lasting, generational differences.

Inglehart, who was one of the pioneers behind the WVS, identified and measured post-materialism through public opinion surveys. One common method was to ask respondents to choose, among several possible national priorities, which are most important to them. Precise measures have varied from survey to survey. For example, in the 2011–2013 wave of the WVS, respondents were asked:

> If you had to choose among the following things, which are the *two* that seem the most desirable to you?
>
> - A high level of economic growth
> - Strong defense
> - Giving people more say about how things are done
> - Try to make our cities and countryside more beautiful

Based on these responses, one can calculate a simple materialist/post-materialist index. Those that chose the first and second options would be deemed "materialists"; those choosing the third and fourth were "post-materialists"; those opting for one from each category were labeled "mixed."[34]

Consistent with his hypotheses, Inglehart and his collaborators have consistently found that post-materialist attitudes are most prevalent in wealthier societies and among the younger generation. They have also become more pronounced over time due to the generational and socialization effects. By the late 1980s, post-materialist orientations had grown throughout the continent, with the highest levels found in the Netherlands (25 percent), West Germany (24 percent), and Denmark (18 percent), whereas the lowest figures were in the relatively poorer countries of Spain (12 percent), Greece (8 percent), and Portugal (6 percent).[35] Surveys from Eastern Europe in the 1990s revealed, as one might have predicted based upon levels of economic development, fewer numbers of post-materialists. Data from the above-mentioned 2011–2013 WVS are reported in Table 9.9. As expected, post-materialism is more pronounced in wealthier countries with longer experience with democracy, although "pure" post-materialists remain a minority across all countries. There is also a modest age effect. Across all 10 European countries in the survey: Those under 30 are more likely to be post-materialists than those over 50 (13.3 percent to 12.3 percent) and less likely to be "pure" materialists (22.5 percent to

TABLE 9.9 Materialism/Post-materialism in contemporary Europe

Country	*% materialist*	*% mixed*	*% post-materialist*
Germany	19.6	55.8	22.4
Netherlands	22.4	60.8	12.8
Spain	32.6	55.1	9.3
Sweden	7.6	59.9	30.0
Poland	23.5	64.5	7.0
Romania	29.9	58.6	8.2
Serbia	39.0	34.0	3.2
Turkey	32.2	53.3	10.7

Source: WVS, 2011–2013

27.9 percent). As for the impact of this shift in values, Inglehart maintained that the emergence of post-materialism and its concomitant emphasis on individual liberty and expression has been contributed to democratization in Europe and beyond, as there is a strong link between percentage of post-materialists in a country and its level of democracy.[36]

As noted, the rise in post-materialist values is often invoked to explain the emergence of "new" political issues in the 1960s and 1970s. Some post-materialist concerns, such as feminism and environmentalism, have substantially altered the political landscape, especially in Western Europe. Feminism has experienced various waves, beginning with campaigns in the late nineteenth century to give women the vote and improve social welfare benefits for women and children.[37] In the 1960s and 1970s, "second-wave feminism" began mobilizing forces to press for broader cultural and social change. In the 1970s these movements were able to organize literally millions of women, particularly in the large cities, raised public consciousness, and eventually achieved victories on policies such as equal pay, equal rights, maternity leaves, divorce, and abortion. It is worth noting as well that many elements on the feminists' agenda have been enshrined in EU law and directives, including policies on maternal leave (fourteen weeks paid with full job protection), parental leave (three months unpaid with job protection), and recommendations on expanded access to childcare.[38] Today, by most standards, European states rank among the most progressive in the world in terms of protecting women's rights and creating more equality between the sexes.

Many of the basic notions underlying feminism are now enshrined in the political culture, but, arguably, there is still progress to be made. For example, in the 2011–2013 wave of the WVS, 21.9 percent of respondents (with 59.4 percent in Turkey and 39.8 percent in Romania) agreed that when jobs are scarce men have more right to a job than women. In response to another question, 30 percent (68 percent of Turks and 41.1 percent of Romanians) believe men make better political leaders than women. In line with what one would expect from the above discussion, post-materialists and those with more education were far less likely to express the sexist viewpoint. However, there was no discernible difference across age groups.

Environmentalism is manifest in many ways in contemporary Europe, including policies at all levels of government. Green parties have become important political players in several countries, and their very emergence in the 1980s can be taken as

Bicycles are a popular form of green transport in the Netherlands

© Janine Wiedel Photolibrary / Alamy

a sign of the rise of post-materialism. Survey research since the 1970s has noticed a growth in environmental consciousness, participation in environmental causes, and a willingness among large sections of the public to favor "green" policies even if they cost more. Data from a 2014 special Eurobarometer survey are reported in Table 9.10. Respondents were given several choices about how important they rated environmental protection. Not only is environment personally important to the

TABLE 9.10 Attitudes of Europeans toward the environment

Country	*Environmental protection very important to you personally*	*Protecting the environment can boost economic growth*	*Willing to buy environmentally friendly products even if cost is higher*	*Authorities should favor environmental considerations over cost considerations*
Germany	94	61	80	63
France	95	79	78	60
Great Britain	94	68	82	65
Italy	95	84	67	58
Denmark	96	70	87	58
Sweden	100	87	94	75
Poland	91	69	71	36
Czech Republic	93	72	71	70
Bulgaria	94	77	62	53
EU-28	95	74	75	59

Source: Special Eurobarometer 416, "Attitudes of European Citizens Towards the Environment," April–May 2014, available at http://ec.europa.eu/public_opinion/archives/ebs/ebs_416_en.pdf

overwhelming majority of Europeans, most—both in Western Europe and in Eastern Europe—would be willing to pay more for environmentally friendly products and believe that public authorities should pay more attention to environmental considerations than financial costs when developing and implementing policy. Most respondents also reported engaging in some sort of environmental activity (e.g., recycling, reducing water or energy use, using eco-friendly means of transport, etc.). Lastly, it is worth noting that protection of the environment is one area where there is strong support for EU-level policy (e.g., 60 percent in the survey believe environmental policy should be made jointly between national-level governments and the EU), although those in some more Euroskeptic countries such as Great Britain (45 percent) and the Czech Republic (42 percent) are less supportive of granting the EU a say over environmental policy.

The declining importance of religion

Another element of a cultural shift in Europe is the rise in most countries of a predominantly secular orientation and the corresponding decline of religiosity. Whereas in the past religion played a major role both in the lives of individuals and in politics, as well as in European culture more generally, this is no longer the case. This is reflected not only in declining church attendance but also in a shift in attitudes on a number of issues that challenge "traditional values" and tend to favor, similar to post-materialism, the rights of individuals over the preferred orientation of traditional religious authorities.

How religious are Europeans?

The decline of organized religion in Europe has been commented upon by many observers. Since World War II, religion's role in politics has declined, and European Christians, both Catholics and Protestants, have become less and less personally religious. Part of this is due to the rise of post-materialism and the willingness of many to question traditional authorities. This has also been accompanied by changes within religious establishments. For example, Tony Judt writes that the Vatican II Council, which began in 1962, was a crucial event, as the Catholic Church began to reconcile itself to liberal democracy, mixed economies, modern science, other religions (including Judaism), and secular politics. Vatican II accelerated movement toward what was already becoming a "post-religious" society, marking the "final divorce between politics and religion in continental Europe" and playing a critical role in "the making of 'the sixties.'"[39]

Available evidence suggests that lack of religious faith has grown over time, a reflection of what Matthew Arnold lamented as early as 1867 in "Dover Beach" as the "long withdrawing roar" of faith. For example, in subsequent waves of the WVS, respondents have reported less religious belief. The WVS wave of 1999–2001 found high numbers of self-professed atheists in many countries, including the Czech Republic (52 percent), Sweden (41 percent), the Netherlands (39 percent), Estonia (39 percent), and France (35 percent). Similarly, the numbers of those asserting that

God is important in their lives has also declined in most states, so that by the 1999–2001 survey wave, the average score on this question (on a ten-point scale) in the Czech Republic (3.63), Denmark (4.02), Sweden (4.10), and Estonia (4.23) was less than half the figure for the US (8.47), which stands out among Western countries for its religiosity. Pippa Norris and Ronald Inglehart also report a decline in both religious belief and participation in religious organizations in Western Europe from the 1970s to the 2000s, and find a strong correlation to individual religious belief to one's socio-economic status, seemingly confirming modernization theory's hypothesis that economic development leads to a decline in religious belief.[40] Longer-term data from surveys in Great Britain is even more striking: Whereas in 1957 71 percent of Britons declared that Jesus was the Son of God, only 38 percent claimed so in 2001, and in 2004 only 44 percent of British respondents admitted belief in God.[41]

Just how non-religious are Europeans today? The 2012 ESS asks several questions about religious belief in twenty-six European countries. Notably, most (62 percent) claimed to belong to a religious denomination, although this figure was markedly lower in several countries, including the Czech Republic (20 percent), Sweden (32.5 percent), and the Netherlands 37 percent). Claiming that one belongs to a particular faith tradition, however, need not suggest that one is actually religious. Figure 9.3, based on responses in the 2012 ESS, provides additional data about religious belief and practices. It reports responses to a question asking respondents, on a scale from zero to ten, with those ranking themselves zero to two coded as "not religious" and those ranking themselves eight to ten as "very religious." The data show wide variation, with the greatest levels of religiosity in predominantly Greek Orthodox Cyprus (Greece was not included in the survey) and in Catholic Poland, Slovakia, and Italy. Levels of religiosity are lower elsewhere, particularly in northern Europe,

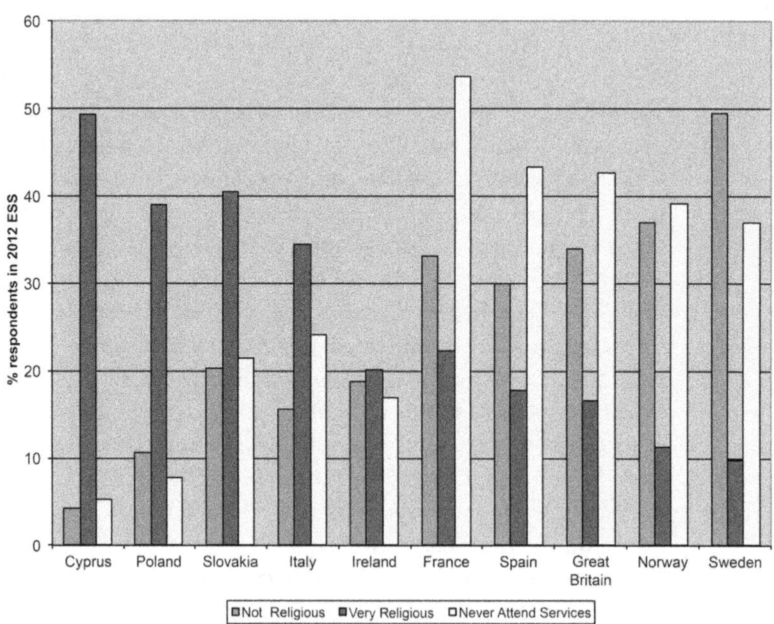

FIGURE 9.3 Levels of religiosity in Europe

ESS 2012

but also in some post-communist states such as Bulgaria (13.6 percent), Estonia (10.8 percent), and the Czech Republic (5.9 percent). Many Europeans also never formally attend religious services. Interestingly, although anecdotally some report that European churches are empty whereas mosques are full, two-thirds of Muslim respondents in the survey say they attend services "never," "less often," or "only on special holy days," figures higher than that of Catholics (52 percent) but lower than that of Protestants, three-quarters of whom report never or rarely attending services.

The relative decline of individuals' religious commitment is reflected as well in a widespread belief that religion should not play a political role. For example, in a 2007 survey conducted by the Pew Global Attitudes Project in nine European countries, there was consensus that religion should be a matter of personal faith and should be kept separate from government policy. Agreement with this statement ranged from a low of 84 percent in Sweden, to 94 percent in very Catholic Poland, with, it is worth adding, a clear majority of Muslim Turks (86 percent) also agreeing.[42] This sentiment was expressed by former British Prime Minister Tony Blair, who converted to Catholicism in 2007 after leaving office, who noted that while it is acceptable that religious belief shape one's policies, "it's probably best not to take it too far."[43] Religion was, notably, a subject of debate over the draft EU Constitutional Treaty in the 2000s, with the Poles in particular insisting that it contain some reference to God. In the end, the document referred to Europe's "cultural, religious, and humanist inheritance" but failed to include mention of either the Almighty or Christianity. Its primary author, former French President Valery Giscard d'Estaing, justified this decision, arguing, "Europeans live in a purely secular political system, where religion does not play an important role."[44] It is no wonder then that most European countries do not have the equivalent of groups such as the Moral Majority, Focus on the Family, or Christian Coalition that exist in the US and, despite the presence in several countries of Christian Democratic Parties, religious officials do not exercise significant political influence. Indeed, some would argue that secularism has become a cultural feature of contemporary Europe, one that distinguishes it from the United States.[45] On the other hand, others have bemoaned this development, arguing that as Europeans increasingly live "*etsi Deus non daretur* (as if God does not exist)" they are forfeiting part of their heritage, and that a civilization based purely on secular values "can only burn down to the last waxed threads of its wick."[46]

"Values" issues

The decline of religion and traditional values has manifested itself in shifts in public opinion and, often, state policy on a variety of "moral" or "values" issues. Here I am referring to practices that, until relatively recently, were considered sinful or immoral by both prevailing opinion and religious authorities and were often prohibited under the law. This shift also touches upon the notion of post-materialism as viewpoints and policies are increasingly reflecting preference or priority on choice and individual autonomy. Since the 1960s, thanks in part to the sexual revolution and its attendant social movements, Europeans tend to be liberal or permissive on previous taboo issues including abortion, divorce, pre-marital sex, and homosexuality.

Abortion

Beginning in the 1930s in Protestant countries (e.g., Iceland, Sweden), abortion was legalized. In the 1960s and 1970s, abortion was legalized in most of Western Europe, with Great Britain (1967) adopting one of the most liberal abortion laws. Catholic countries such as France (1975), Italy (1978), and Spain (1985) also legalized abortion. More recently, in 2002 and 2007 respectively, Switzerland and Portugal, each of which had some of Europe's more restrictive abortion policies, liberalized their laws after referendums indicated that abortion rights had the support of a majority of voters. In communist Eastern Europe, abortion was legal in all countries except Romania, and it was a popular form of birth control.

Abortion laws today vary from state to state.[47] In some countries, such as Germany, Austria, Hungary, and Switzerland, all women are required to undergo counseling before having an abortion. Abortions are paid for under many national health insurance programs. Among European countries, the most restrictive anti-abortion policies—abortion is legal in Ireland only to save the life of the mother and in Poland it is legal for that reason as well as in cases of rape and incest and if the fetus is seriously malformed—are in two countries where the Catholic Church has often played a major political and social role: Ireland and Poland. In both countries, pro-choice advocates have attempted to overturn restrictive abortion laws, and public opinion, especially in Ireland, has changed in a more pro-choice direction. In 2016, Ireland indicated some willingness to adopt a more liberal policy in line with recommendations made by a UN human rights report.[48] On the other side, anti-abortion forces tried to make a case to ban abortion before the ECHR, but, in *Vo v. France* in 2003, the court ruled that the European Convention on Human Rights does not give the fetus legal rights. The Catholic Church continues to lobby for restrictions on abortion in many European countries, but abortion rights have wide support throughout most of the continent,[49] and EU foreign aid even includes funding for abortions in developing countries.

The rate of abortions in Europe, as seen in Table 9.11, varies widely, with the highest rates of abortion in post-communist Europe, reflecting, perhaps, little use of birth control in these countries. Although the figures in the table may seem high,

TABLE 9.11 Abortion rates in Europe

Figures are number of abortions per 1,000 live births

Country	*1980*	*1990*	*2000*	*2010*
Great Britain	231	247	291	259
Germany	290	200	176	163
Italy	325	278	258	200
Denmark	407	325	234	258
Sweden	359	302	343	326
Czech Republic	448	852	381	205
Hungary	544	719	607	448
Romania	1,036	3,153	1,100	480
Bulgaria	1,217	1,375	1,318	418

Source: Database of the UN Economic Commission for Europe, http://w3.unece.org/PXWeb/en/, accessed on May 13, 2016

even alarming to some, it is worth noting that according to studies carried out by the World Health Organization (WHO), Europe, even with its liberal abortion laws, has a lower abortion rate than in Africa and Asia, where laws are more restrictive but where women turn to illegal and often dangerous abortions.[50] The table also shows that abortion rates have declined in most countries in recent decades. Nonetheless, there is no denying that the legalization of abortion—together with widespread availability of other forms of contraception—helps account for the fall in European birthrates, which became more marked in the 1960s.[51]

Drug policy

Ask many college students who have been to Amsterdam something about the city, and the answer, if it is honest, is not likely to be about Rembrandt, van Gogh, Dutch architecture, Anne Frank, or even Amsterdam's famous canals. No, instead you will likely hear something about "coffee shops," a code word of sorts for establishments that sell, in addition to coffee, marijuana (cannabis).

The Dutch amended their drug laws in 1976 to distinguish between "hard" (e.g., heroin, cocaine) and "soft" (e.g., marijuana) drugs. Although the sale of marijuana remains technically illegal in the Netherlands, more than 800 "coffee shops" are tolerated as points of sale, provided they meet certain conditions (e.g., no sales to those under 18, no advertising, no alcohol).[52] Several states (e.g., Austria, Belgium, Switzerland, Great Britain, the Czech Republic) have decriminalized possession of cannabis for personal use, and in 2010 Spain legalized members-only "cannabis clubs," which have become very popular and have earned Barcelona—where over 165,000 people are members of these clubs—the moniker "Amsterdam of the South."[53] Portugal has gone further than any other state by decriminalizing all drug use in 2001. Those caught with drugs—including heroin and cocaine—are sent to treatment and therapy instead of jail. Interestingly, according to studies conducted in the Netherlands, use of marijuana among the Dutch—not taking into account the tourists for whom "legal" marijuana is a novelty—is actually lower than in the US, and drug use in Portugal has also declined since the law was changed.[54]

Not all of Europe is so "soft" on drugs. In France, possession of marijuana can still land one a jail term. Scandinavian countries also have tough drug laws on their books, even if enforcement of the law against individual users is minimal. With the exception of the Czech Republic, post-communist countries also maintain stricter drug laws and punishments. European public opinion as a whole has moved somewhat toward a more "liberal" or "tolerant" attitude, but data from a special Flash Eurobarometer in 2014 conducted among young people aged 15 to 24 in the EU show not only that over 90 percent favor existing criminalization of heroin, cocaine, and ecstasy, but also that a majority (!) (53 percent) believe marijuana should be illegal. In only eight member states did respondents think marijuana should be legal, with the highest percentage in the Czech Republic (71 percent). Interestingly, and perhaps surprisingly, legal marijuana was supported by only 47 percent of young Dutch respondents.[55]

Prostitution

Prostitution is, as the cliché states, the "oldest profession," but, despite almost universal presence, it has usually been met with moral censure. However, it has persisted, if only as part of the "shadow" or "black market" economy. In the 1970s, in part because of the sexual revolution, in part because some women argued they had a right to engage in the trade of their choice, and in part because of worries of the consequences of pushing it underground, some began to argue that it should be legalized. The purported advantages of legalized prostitution were several: legal protections for sex industry workers; improved public health; and tax revenues for the state.

In the Netherlands, prostitution was *de facto* legalized in the 1970s, and in 1988 it was recognized as a legal profession. By the 1990s, Amsterdam, the Dutch capital, had become the "sex capital" of Europe. In 2002, Germany legalized prostitution, which was estimated to bring in €6 billion of revenue a year and "serve" up to a million customers a day.[56] Other states that have legalized prostitution include Greece, Austria, Switzerland, Great Britain, the Czech Republic, and, perhaps most interestingly, Turkey. In Norway, France, and Sweden, the selling of sex is legal but the purchasing is not, meaning that the "john" or buyer, not the prostitute, can be subject to criminal charges.[57]

The legalization of prostitution has not been without controversy. While traditional moral opprobrium has dissipated, there is great concern in Europe about the problem of human trafficking, especially among young women. Most of these women—there are estimated to be more than 500,000—come from Eastern Europe and the former Soviet Union, and are lured to Germany, the Netherlands, Greece, and elsewhere with promises of a "normal" job. Instead, they are essentially enslaved, subjected to violence, and forced to become prostitutes. For this reason, states such as Bulgaria—a source of many trafficked women—that had considered liberalizing their laws have had second thoughts. In addition, liberalization of prostitution laws in several European countries has been linked to a growth in the sex industry, and research has shown that a majority of the workers are not native to Western Europe. Many are also under the age of consent. This has led to fears that liberal prostitution laws are only abetting human trafficking in women and children.[58] Reflective of such concerns, Sweden recriminalized the purchasing of sex in 1999. As a consequence, today's Stockholm, although liberal on many issues, does not have the red-light districts of Amsterdam or Hamburg, although some complain that the sex trade has simply been pushed underground, to the detriment of many women.[59]

Homosexuality and gay marriage

Homosexuality, throughout most of European history, has been condemned by religious authorities and penalized by state law. Italy (1890) and Poland (1932), interestingly, were the first European countries to decriminalize homosexual behavior, but homosexuals were harshly punished in Mussolini's fascist Italy and in Franco's Spain and were sent to concentration camps in Hitler's Germany.

After World War II, there was more active campaigning to extend legal protections to homosexuals. Inspired in part by activism in the US in the 1960s and 1970s, a European gay rights movement emerged in several countries. Homosexuality was decriminalized throughout most of Europe in the 1960s and 1970s. In 1986, in *Norris v. Ireland*, the European Court of Human Rights (ECHR) ruled that the criminalization of homosexuality violated the European Convention on

Human Rights. In 1974, the Netherlands became the first country to allow openly gay people to serve in the military, and in 1999 the ECHR struck down a British law banning gays from military service.[60] Removal of anti-gay legislation has also become a requirement for EU membership, which became an issue when some post-communist states entered the accession process. In 1989, Denmark became the first state to create registered partnerships for homosexual couples, granting partners inheritance and property rights. In December 2000, the Netherlands, over the objections of the Catholic Church, became the first country to legalize gay marriage. As of 2017, same-sex marriage is also legal in Belgium, Spain, Norway, Sweden, Iceland, Portugal, Denmark, Luxembourg, France, Finland, most of Great Britain (northern Ireland is the largest exception), and, perhaps surprisingly, in Ireland, where voters in November 2015 became the first to legalize same-sex marriage via popular vote, in this case over the vociferous objectives of the Catholic Church. Many other states, including Greece, Germany, and, as of 2016, Italy (which overcame intense opposition by the Church), recognize same-sex civil unions, giving same-sex couples many legal rights.[61] In some countries, mostly in post-communist Europe (e.g. Bulgaria, Poland, Hungary, Latvia), only heterosexual marriage is constitutionally recognized; a bill to legalize same-sex marriage in Slovenia passed through parliament but was rejected by voters in a referendum in 2015.[62] Notably, in July 2015 the ECHR, in *Oliari and Others v. Italy*, found Italy's lack of recognition of same-sex couples (later recognized) in violation of the European Convention on Human Rights, which may put pressure on other states to change their laws as well.[63]

Changes in policy have been accompanied by a shift in the public mood with respect to homosexuality, as seen in Table 9.12. Whereas in the early 1980s homosexuality received wide condemnation, by the 2000s there was far greater acceptance, particularly in Western Europe. A special Eurobarometer survey in 2015 found a sizeable majority (71 percent) believed gay people should have the same rights as everyone else, and 61 percent favored same-sex marriage. Notably, majorities supported the latter in every EU-15 country (except Greece), whereas

TABLE 9.12 Changing attitudes toward homosexuality

Percentage of people who say they accept homosexuality		
Country	*1981–1982*	*2005–2007*
Germany[a]	21	60
Great Britain	20	49
France	17	60
Spain	14	63
Sweden	29	82
Poland	n/a	17
Bulgaria	n/a	30
Turkey	n/a	3
US	9	31

Source: Analysis from WVS. Figures are those reporting 6–10 on a ten-point scale asking whether they considered homosexuality justifiable, where 10 was always justifiable

[a] For West Germany only

majorities in every post-communist state except the Czech Republic and Slovenia were against same-sex marriage. Overall, support for same-sex marriage had grown from 2006, when it was backed by 44 percent of respondents in another Eurobarometer, and its strongest proponents were younger and better-educated respondents.[64] Gay individuals have won political office, serving as mayors of Berlin and Paris and the head of the German Free Democratic Party. In 2009, Johanna Sigurdardottir, a lesbian, became prime minister of Iceland and the first openly gay person to serve as leader of a country; in 2015, Xavier Bettel, Luxembourg's prime minister, became the first national leader to marry a same-sex partner.[65]

Interest organizations and social movements

Political culture—defined as attitudes and values—is only one part of what we might call citizen politics. Behavior and participation, or what one *does* based upon one's attitudes and values, is also an important topic to study. People can participate in politics in a number of ways. In the previous chapter we looked at membership in political parties and voting, the latter an important and most commonly studied form of political participation. Another type of political engagement is membership in **interest groups**, associations of individuals united around a common goal that organize and express needs or demands to decision-makers. Unlike political parties, they do not nominate candidates for office and typically they are concerned with a narrower set of issues. They seek to use their resources—financial, access to media, ability to mobilize their members and supporters—to lobby for their causes and influence policy.

interest groups associations of individuals, united around a common goal, that organize and express needs or demands to decision-makers.

There are different types of interest groups. Anomic interest groups are spontaneous associations that respond to a particular policy or event but do not possess much of an organizational structure (e.g., student protesters, impromptu demonstrators). Institutional groups have more of a structure but are part of organizations that have other functions besides political interest articulation. Examples would be business corporations, bureaucracies, local governments, or the military. Associational groups are organized to represent the interests of a particular collectivity. They have well-developed structures, formal membership, and usually employ professional staff. Associational groups are the ones that political scientists examine as interest groups. Of course, not all associational groups have a political orientation. For example, one could classify chess clubs, film societies, or fan clubs of a particular sports team as associational groups, but, except perhaps in exceptional moments, they would not capture the interest of political scientists. Instead, political scientists are more apt to focus on associational groups that frequently engage with political and economic institutions, such as trade unions, business chambers, professional organizations, and environmental groups. In the European context, it is worth noting as well that powerful interest groups seek to influence policy not only at national level but also at the EU level. Thus, for example, the National Federation of Trade Unions in Sweden has to mind not only what transpires in Stockholm but also seek influence in Brussels, insofar as what the EU decides on social policy or labor law can have a significant effect on their Swedish members.

There is a debate in democratic theory about the contribution and functions of interest groups. Traditionally—in writings such as the *Federalist Papers* or Alexis de Tocqueville's *Democracy in America*—interest organizations have been defended as important mechanisms to express and defend the interests of citizens, provide a means of political participation in between elections, educate the population, and check excessive governmental power. Organized groups of citizens that are independent of the government—in other words, civil society—have been lauded as an essential component of democracy, constituting the means through which people acquire democratic norms and can exercise active citizenship.[66]

Some, however, would complain about the activities of such groups, often deriding them as "special interests." In this view, interest organizations, which have a particular agenda to benefit their members, do not represent the common good of the citizenry. Moreover, not all groups are equal, and their political activities may lack transparency. "Special interests" can therefore hijack the political system, using their funds and lobbying ability to craft policy to suit their own interests, weakening both representative democracy and economic performance. For example, the aforementioned National Federation of Trade Unions in Sweden could seek higher wages for their members, making it both more costly for employers to retain and hire workers and pushing up costs of Swedish-made products for Swedish and European consumers. The same could be said for business, agricultural, or other associations that seek policies than would benefit their membership exclusively. To the extent that people believe their political system has been commandeered and compromised by these groups and that their individual votes no longer matter, this feeds public disillusionment with their political system.

How extensive is participation in various organizations among Europeans? A 2013 Eurobarometer survey asked about participation in a number of organizations. Data from the survey are presented below in Table 9.13. A few items stand out. First, participation is significantly higher in Western Europe, which has a longer tradition of independent associational life, than in Eastern Europe, where, until 1989, virtually every interest association was controlled by the Communist Party and many of the older, communist-dominated groups collapsed after communist power fell. Second, even within Western Europe there is marked variance, with the Finns, Dutch, and the Swedes standing out as far more involved in associational life than, say, the Spanish, French, and Italians. Third, more in-depth analysis of the data reveal that income and education—factors identified above as strongly linked to more "democratic" values—are positively related to associational membership, meaning that those with higher incomes and more education are more likely to join associations. Finally, it is worth noting that most, East and West, believe these organizations can be effective in influencing political decision-making, with members of these organizations more likely (61 percent to 49 percent) to express this view.

Let us look in more detail at some of the largest and politically most important interest organizations in Europe.

Trade unions

Trade unions grew in strength throughout much of the twentieth century as Europe became more and more industrialized and more and more individuals left the farms

TABLE 9.13 Participation in various social/interest organizations

Percentage of respondents claiming they were a member				
Country	*Trade union*	*Professional association*	*Economic, social, environmental, cultural or sporting interest*	*Believe these organizations can be effective in influencing decision-making*
Great Britain	19	19	19	52
France	12	8	17	63
Germany	15	13	19	52
Netherlands	24	15	26	56
Italy	15	6	7	54
Spain	15	11	22	49
Sweden	54	17	35	55
Finland	37	23	37	51
Poland	8	7	11	53
Romania	3	4	3	65
Bulgaria	9	8	7	47
Hungary	6	16	4	11
EU-27	6	20	50	54

Source: Flash Eurobarometer 373, "Europeans Engagement in Participatory Democracy," 2013, available at http://ec.europa.eu/public_opinion/flash/fl_373_en.pdf

and joined the industrial "working class." Postwar reconstruction bolstered the positions of trade unions in many states, and unions dwarfed all other interest groups, at least in terms of membership. Union membership grew throughout the first three decades after World War II, so that, for example, in 1980 union density (the percentage of workers belonging to unions) was 34.8 percent in the Netherlands, 34.9 percent in Germany, 49.6 percent in Italy, 50.7 percent in Great Britain, 54.1 percent in Belgium, and a staggering 78 percent in Sweden.[67] Moreover, union density was near 100 percent in communist Eastern Europe, although unions in these countries were not independent from the authoritarian Party-state and did not truly represent the interests of workers. While some might view unions as primarily economic organizations—concerned first and foremost with wages and working conditions—they were and are often explicitly political. In many European countries, trade unions enjoy close ties with social democratic or left-leaning political parties, influencing party platforms, helping with campaigns, and placing leaders in the party hierarchy. Like all interest organizations, they also lobby the government for policies that would benefit their members, and, with considerable assets and power over the economy, they have often been successful in procuring pro-worker policies.

pluralism
system of interest mediation in which a number of different interest groups compete for power and influence.

The way that trade unions interact with political authorities varies from state to state. In some countries, interest mediation is based on **pluralism**, meaning a number of different unions and other interest groups jockey for power and influence over policy-making. The presence of multiple unions may be due to how unions are organized by occupation, with, for example, separate unions for those in blue-collar and white-collar professions or divisions among unions between workers in more competitive export-oriented sectors and domestically protected ones. Such is the case in Hungary, with seven national-level union confederations, and in Great Britain, which, even though it has an umbrella Trade Unions Congress confederation, is usually categorized as a pluralist system due to the divisions among many unions. More typically, however, unions are divided along ideological or party lines. For example, in France and Italy there are union confederations with a communist orientation, more moderate socialist ones, and still others that identify with Catholic social thought. Turkish unions are similarly divided along ideological and religious lines, with different organizations appealing to secular and more Islamic workers. In Poland, the two main union groups are Solidarity, which emerged in 1980 to challenge communist rule, and the OPZZ, the formerly "official" unions linked to the communist authorities.

corporatism
system of interest mediation in which centralized, singular interest groups, such as a single trade union federation, work closely with the government to coordinate economic policy.

social partnership
a feature of a corporatist system, these are bargains among unions, employers, and government designed to foster growth, employment, and peaceful labor relations.

In other European countries, one finds corporatist systems of interest representation. Under **corporatism**, unions enjoy a formal, institutionalized seat at the policymaking table. Rather than just lobbying or competing for influence as in pluralist systems, corporatist systems unions, together with business organizations and government officials, have a prescribed political role and help set national economic policy. For example, wages are set at a nation-wide or industry-wide level by a bargaining process involving not just unions and employers but the government. In corporatist systems, there is typically one primary or peak interest organization that is centrally organized. This makes negotiations easier, and arguably such an organization, representing a wide swath of workers or employers, is better able to look to common good and oversee enforcement of agreements. Many in the 1970s and 1980s praised the corporatist systems and the resulting "**social partnership**" in such countries as Austria, Sweden, the Netherlands, and Germany as producing economic growth, greater equality, generous welfare states, and being less disruptive and chaotic than the more pluralist systems of Great Britain, Italy, and France, in which multiple competing trade unions did not have guaranteed access to policymaking and often engaged in protests against government policy.[68]

Corporatism's heyday, both in real life and as a subject for study, is long over. Unions, once powerful political forces across much of Europe, have suffered a precipitous decline in membership and in influence in the past three decades, as seen in Table 9.14. One could point to several factors that have negatively affected trade unions: anti-union governments (most notoriously Margaret Thatcher's in Great Britain [1979–1990]), privatization of state-owned industries, the decline of blue-collar manufacturing enterprises, shifts in the nature of work to provision of services and more part-time work, and global pressures on European businesses to cut costs. In most European countries, the public sector (e.g., educational and health care establishments, government bureaucracies, state-owned firms) is the strongest redoubt of trade unions. A few states, such as Sweden and Finland, still have sizeable labor organizations, but these are the exception. Across Eastern Europe, for example, the dream of trade union leaders to replicate the "Swedish model" and create powerful corporatist institutions was not realized.[69] As for unions' political influence, many of the unions' chief political allies on the left end of the political spectrum (e.g., the French and Italian Communist and Socialist Parties, the British Labour Party, the German Social Democratic Party, Social Democratic parties throughout post-communist Europe) have either lost much of their former appeal or they have gravitated to the center in the hope of winning more middle-class voters. In 2016, for example, unions opposed the actions of the Socialist government

TABLE 9.14 Unions' decline in European countries

Union density in select years and countries					
Country	*1970*	*1980*	*1990*	*2000*	*2012*
Great Britain	44.8	51.7	39.3	30.2	26.0
France	21.7	18.3	9.8	8.0	7.7
Germany	32	34.9	31.2	24.6	18.3
Italy	37	49.6	38.8	34.8	36.9
Spain	n/a	13.5	13.5	16.6	17.1
Netherlands	36.5	34.8	24.6	22.9	17.9
Sweden	67.7	78.0	80.0	79.1	67.5
Finland	51.3	69.4	72.5	75.0	69.8
Poland	n/a	n/a	36.7	17.5	12.7
Hungary	n/a	n/a	58.9 [a]	22.0	10.7

Source: Online data from Organization for Economic Cooperation and Devlopment (OECD), available at https://stats.oecd.org/Index.aspx?DataSetCode=UN_DEN#

[a] Data from 1994, earliest available year

in France to reform labor laws to make it easier to dismiss workers.[70] Notably, a Eurobarometer survey from 2010 found that only 38 percent of European citizens trusted trade unions, which placed them lower on the trust scale than the police, army, religious institutions, and the EU itself; one should note, trust in unions was higher than in big companies, national parliaments, and political parties.[71]

This is not to say that unions are now irrelevant. Strikes, particularly among transportation workers, remain virtually yearly rituals in countries such as France and Italy. Protests by unions in Germany have weakened or stopped labor-market reforms that would have made it easier to fire workers. In Poland, vestiges of the Solidarity labor movement were a major force in Polish politics for over a decade after communism's fall. In the wake of the global economic crisis in the 2000s, unions took the lead in protesting austerity measures in several European states. However, it would be safe to say that the general trend in Europe—and globally, for that matter—has worked against unions, as elements of the welfare state, one of the trade union movement's primary accomplishments, have come under assault, and workers, facing both competition from less expensive overseas labor and, in many cases, double-digit unemployment rates, are in a poor position vis-à-vis their employers. These issues are taken up in greater detail in the next chapter.

Business organizations

Trade unions' main rivals—or, in corporatist systems perhaps, partners—are business organizations. Since they represent corporations, they are not mass membership organizations like trade unions, but, nonetheless, thanks to their resources and organizational capacity, they yield considerable influence in many European states. Typically, business associations press for benefits such as lower corporate taxes, fewer protections for workers, start-up monies for investment, and subsidies for business. In some cases, relations between business groups and workers can be very adversarial, and both groups lobby the government for their own cause. In states with corporatist systems, social partnership is the ideal, and business-labor relations, in general, are less conflictual. Even though many business organizations bring together thousands of different enterprises, their corporate-based membership is dwarfed by mass membership organizations such as trade unions.

Like workers, however, not all employers are the same, and thus often—especially in non-corporatist systems—one finds several business associations within a given state. For example, one (e.g., the League of German Industry or the Movement of French Enterprises) might represent large companies, while another (e.g., the National Association of German Employers or the French General Federation of Small and Medium Enterprises) primarily represents small or medium-size enterprises. Whereas most business associations are associated with Conservative (in Great Britain), Christian Democratic (in Germany), or Liberal (in the European sense) parties (as in the Netherlands), they may be divided on other grounds. For example, some business associations may represent older industries and lobby from protection from cheaper foreign imports (e.g., steel producers); others in more competitive industries may favor free trade (e.g., automakers who don't want to pay more for steel). Some businesses are owned in whole or in part by the state (e.g., the giant multinational Airbus) and rely upon state support for their survival, and they may have different agendas from businesses or business associations of privately owned companies that by and large favor more *laissez-faire* policies. In most countries, there are separate business associations on the regional level (e.g., Catalan business groups in Spain, Bavarian ones in Germany, those concentrated around Milan and other industrial centers in northern Italy) that implicitly compete with business associations representing firms in other parts of the country. In Turkey, one finds two main business groups: the Turkish Businessmen and Industrialists' Union that is grounded in the secular establishment and another, the Independent Businessmen and Industrialists' Union that caters to businesses with a more Islamic orientation. Finally, unlike the individual worker, individual large companies (e.g., Shell, Renault, Siemens) can be effective political actors in their own right, either through support of candidates or through lobbying efforts. In post-communist Europe, with its nascent capitalist systems, business organizations are not as well organized, and lobbying of individual firms is more commonplace, although in many countries the close connections between business and politics has fueled political corruption.

Agricultural associations

Several countries also have sizeable agricultural organizations. The largest ones are the National Federation of Agricultural Enterprises in France and the Italian General Confederation of Agriculture, each of which claims to represent hundreds of thousands of agricultural producers and enterprises. Although the largest number of farmers in Europe today is in post-communist countries such as Poland and Romania, farm associations are weaker there, in part a vestige of the communist experience. As with business groups, there are scores of sector-specific agricultural associations, ranging from those that represent French wine makers to those of Greek olive producers to British beekeepers. Agricultural associations have had a great deal of success in the past in lobbying for financial support from the state. In France, because rural political districts are over-represented, farmers have traditionally been an important lobby, generally connected to parties on the right and, at times, mobilizing to protest government policies. In Italy, the General Confederation of Agriculture, tied to the Christian Democratic Party, enjoyed for years a corporatist type of relationship with the state, becoming almost a quasi-state agency as it administered credits, subsidies, and other services to farmers. Generally speaking, however, as fewer and fewer Europeans are employed in agriculture, agricultural organizations have lost much of their political importance, and, since agricultural policy is now by and large established at the EU level with the Common Agricultural Policy (CAP), more and more of their lobbying efforts concentrate on activities in Brussels.

Other interest organizations

Traditionally, most discussions of interest organizations among political scientists center on economic organizations, those representing workers, employers, and farmers. There are, of course, many other interest organizations that are not strictly economic in orientation. Examples would include professional organizations (e.g., medical societies, academic societies), human rights and humanitarian organizations (e.g., Amnesty International and *Médecins sans frontières*, religious organizations, environmental groups, and ethnic organizations). Although some of these organizations are not expressly political, concentrating on items such as maintenance of professional standards, education, and social networking, they can be "political" by lobbying for particular government policies (including, in some cases, higher wages for their members), special "rights," or access to public monies. At times, they can be controversial. For example, ethnic-minority groups such as Basques and Catalans in Spain, Turks in Germany, and ethnic Serbs in Kosovo have their own organizations to advance their particular set of demands, at times creating conflict with the ethnic majority. Some ethnically defined groups go even further, advocating separatism, and a few (e.g., ETA for the Basques in Spain, the PKK for the Kurds in Turkey) have engaged in terrorist activities.

Social movements

social movement conscious, collective, organized attempt to bring about or resist large-scale change in the social order by non-institutionalized means.

Citizens can participate in politics in means beyond voting and formal membership or support to an organized interest group. One could assess their level of civic engagement by considering, for example, whether they attempt to have their voice heard by contacting their representatives, signing a petition, or engaging in protests or demonstrations. Such activities might be part of grassroots politics, a more informal, neighborhood or community-based effort to produce some sort of political change. Some grassroots campaigns remain entirely local. Examples might be an effort to secure better funding for the municipality's library or dedicate a monument to some local notable. Others, however, can be transformed into a broader-based **social movement**, meaning "a conscious, collective, organized attempt to bring about or resist large-scale change in the social order by non-institutionalized means."[72]

Social movements can be distinguished from interest groups in various ways. For one, they usually aim for something big; they are less interested in day-to-day, piecemeal change as a permanent, bureaucratic organization might be. Instead, they strive to produce fundamental political change (e.g., think of suffrage, civil rights, or environmental movements). They also tend to be more ephemeral than interest organizations; they either run out of energy or achieve their goal, obviating the need for a movement. Moreover, social movements usually are based upon and require active participation (e.g., marches, protests, sit-ins, etc.)—what one scholar identifies as "politically confrontational and socially disruptive tactics"[73]—as opposed to interest organizations that often rely upon people to pay dues in order to hire a professional staff to do the work of the group. Social movements thus seek to gain influence primarily through the power of social mobilization—bringing people out for the cause—as opposed to relying more on behind-the-scenes lobbying or campaign donations. True, some social movements can spawn organizations (e.g., the labor movement of the late nineteenth and early twentieth century leading to trade unions), but it is the masses of people in the streets or otherwise gaining exposure in the media that comprise the labor *movement*, peace *movement*, the anti-nuclear *movement*, the women's *movement*, and so on.

In recent European history, one can point to a few prominent social movements. Several (e.g., environmentalism, feminism), as noted previously, were linked to the rise of post-materialist values. A more contemporary example might be the movement against the war in Iraq in the 2000s in several European countries, which was able to draw millions of people into the streets to protest the deployment of troops to Iraq by the US and several European governments. While it is harder at present to identify pan-European social movements, there have been widespread protests in a number of countries focusing on rather specific concerns. Examples include German students protesting higher fees for university attendance, French farmers and workers protesting globalization, Polish workers protesting pro-market policies of their government, and Turkish organizations mobilizing for human rights. In the wake of the economic crisis in the late 2000s, protests became commonplace in countries such as Greece and Spain. Whereas social movements are often associated with the political left, they can also represent the political right. One example would be Pegida (Patriotic Europeans Against the Islamization of the West), which has organized mass protests in Germany and has branches in other countries. One could argue that social movements, or, at least, the politics of protest, are becoming more and more commonplace, a feature seen, in some form or another, in most European states and around the world.[74]

While protests can often generate headlines, one still might ask how much Europeans participate in social movements or other forms of active citizenship. A precise answer is hard to come by, in large part because people may have different conceptions of what constitute a social movement and surveys typically do not employ the term. However, surveys do regularly ask about different modes of political participation as well as the degree of participation in organizations, including whether one has performed volunteer work. This line of inquiry gets at the idea of active participation, something more than vicarious membership in an association.

Data from the 2012 ESS reveal sizeable variance in these forms of political participation.[75] Across the 26 countries surveyed, the most popular form of activity was signing a petition (19.1 percent) and contacting a politician or an elected official (12.3 percent). Only 6.8 percent stated they had taken part in a lawful demonstration in the past year—what might be considered a hallmark of a social movement—and fewer still (3.7 percent) reported they had worked in a political party of action group. As one might expect, there is wide variance. For example, over a third of Swiss, Germans, and Swedes reported they had signed a petition, compared to fewer than 10 percent of Hungarians, Bulgarians, and Slovenians, a result largely in line with findings of more interest in politics and higher levels of political efficacy in wealthier countries with longstanding democratic traditions. However, residents of Spain (25.9 percent), Iceland (17.8 percent), and Italy (17.3 percent), countries all hard-hit by the economic crisis, were far more likely to engage in protests than people in Denmark, Finland, and the Netherlands (all of which were under 5 percent), perhaps because the latter believed they had less to protest. As for a more general question about social or civic engagement—how involved are you in work with voluntary or charitable groups—a majority in the survey (64 percent) reported "never," a figure that reached over 75 percent in several post-communist states, including Bulgaria, the Czech Republic, Hungary, and Poland. If one's "ideal citizen" is one that is *actively* involved in associational life—in other words, a participant in civil society—one finds many countries fall short, especially in post-communist Europe. Again, the usual variables—the younger city dwellers who are better off and better educated—are associated with non-voting political activity of all types.

What do these data mean? Are too few people engaged in political life? Is democracy the province of the elite, with most people watching passively from the sidelines? Does democracy really require active citizenship? Would politics function better if everyone was constantly protesting, advancing a grassroots initiative, or contacting officials? Can there be "too much" civil society? Many would argue, of course, that Swedish or Dutch democracy functions better than Bulgarian or Romanian democracy, but does that mean that the Swedes or Dutch are better citizens? Are the shortcomings of democratic government in parts of Europe the fault of citizens of those states?

These questions return us to those posed at the beginning of this chapter: How much does political culture matter? Can it be employed to explain specific political outcomes or a particular national style of politics? How can one conclusively isolate political culture from other possible explanatory variables? These are difficult questions, and while it might be easy to make links based on anecdotes or casual observations, such positions are often hard to prove with solid evidence and analytical rigor. Learned political scientists frequently debate the overall importance of political culture. As you familiarize yourself with the development and functioning of European governments, you can offer your own hypotheses and assessments.

Application questions

1. Make a simple argument that political culture causes a particular outcome. How can one prove it to be true?

2. At the same time post-materialism, which in many respects is about greater freedom, was appearing in Europe, the welfare state, which created a more pronounced role for the state in many spheres of life, was also expanding. What, if anything, is the relationship between the two phenomena?
3. Based upon your responses to the question (on p. 252) that tries to gauge post-materialism, what are you? Does the causal type of explanation offered by Inglehart seem compelling in your case? In other words, what factors (e.g., family economic status, future expectations, world events) helped produce your values?
4. Some suggest that the decline of religiosity in Europe is a cause for concern and that Europe will lose part of its heritage and perhaps its moral compass. Would you agree? Does secularization come at a price?
5. Have unions outlived their usefulness in modern, developed democracies? What explains the varying rates of unionization in European countries?

Key terms

Additional reading

Dalton, Russell. 2004. *Democratic Challenges, Democratic Choices: The Erosion of Political Support in Advanced Industrial Democracies*. Oxford: Oxford University Press.
Based on examination of survey research, this work looks at various challenges to contemporary democracies, in particular the lack of trust in political institutions.

Inglehart, Ronald, and Welzel, Christian. 2005. *Modernization, Cultural Change, and Democracy*. Cambridge: Cambridge University Press.
This book, building upon previous works by Inglehart, is global in scope and more explicit in linking the emergence of post-materialism and economic growth with democratic development.

Jenkins, Philip. 2007. *God's Continent: Christianity, Islam, and Europe's Religious Crisis*. Oxford: Oxford University Press.

A well-written and comprehensive account of the decline of Christianity in Europe and how this, together with immigration, is transforming Europe.

Montero, José, and Torcal, Mariano, eds. 2006. *Political Disaffection in Contemporary Democracies: Social Capital, Institutions and Politics*. London: Routledge.
Looking in particular at public attitudes and low levels of civic engagement, this collection of essays takes up the question of whether modern democracies are experiencing some sort of crisis.

Rose, Richard. 2009. *Understanding Post-Communist Transformation: A Bottom Up Approach*. New York: Routledge.
Based upon almost two decades of survey work in post-communist Europe, this book analyzes the role of public opinion and civil society in the transformation to democracy and capitalism.

Notes

1 Alexander Stille, "The Corrupt Reign of Emperor Silvio," *New York Review of Books*, April 8, 2010, p. 18–22. See also the film, *Videocracy*, directed by Erik Gandini, which appeared in 2009.
2 The actual time served is one year, and can be done either through house arrest or a community service program. He did not go to a regular jail.
3 Stille, "The Corrupt Reign," p. 18.
4 Lucian Pye, "Political Culture," in *International Encyclopedia of the Social Sciences* (New York: Macmillan, 1968), p. 218.
5 Harry Eckstein, *Regarding Politics* (Berkeley: University of California Press, 1992).
6 Quoted in Ariane Chebel d'Appollonia, "European Nationalism and European Union," in Anthony Pagden, *The Idea of Europe: From Antiquity to the European Union* (Cambridge: Cambridge University Press, 2002), p. 174.
7 Unlike most currencies, the euro notes do not feature a human face. Instead, representative, somewhat banal examples of European architecture appear on the bills, although each country was free to put its own design(s) on euro coins.
8 These were Cyprus, Germany, Poland, Spain, Finland, Sweden, Slovenia, Hungary, and Italy.
9 Eurobarometer 83, May–June 2015, and Eurobarometer 64.2, conducted in October–November 2005.
10 Eurobarometer 79, conducted in May 2013, and Special Eurobarometer, "The Future of Europe," published in May 2006.
11 Eurobarometer 81, Spring 2014.
12 Wolfgang Lutz, Sylvia Kritzinger, and Vegard Skirbekk, "The Demography of Growing European Identity," *Science* 314:425, October 20, 2006, p. 425–426.
13 All of these surveys are conducted according to rigorous social science standards, including selection of a random sample of respondents, face-to-face interviews with trained surveyors, and questions that lend themselves to cross-national and longitudinal (across-time) analysis. The results from all are available online. Data from the World Values Survey can be found at www.worldvaluessurvey.org. Data from the EVS can be accessed through the GESIS system of Leibniz Institute for the Social Sciences at http://zacat.gesis.org. Data from the ESS are available at http://ess.nsd.uib.no. Eurobarometers are archived at http://ec.europa.eu/public_opinion/standard_en.htm, and on-line analysis can be performed through the GESIS system.
14 This question was asked on a 0–10 scale, with 10 being "extremely important." I am interpreting those rating 8–10 as reflecting the view that it is "important" to live in a democracy.
15 These are France, Germany, Italy, Spain, the Netherlands, Great Britain, Cyprus, Turkey, Finland, Norway, Sweden, Serbia, Slovenia, Romania, Bulgaria, Andorra, and

Switzerland. Other rounds of the WVS surveyed other countries. Online data for the most recent round (2011–2013, round 6) includes only ten European countries (as defined in this text), hence reporting of the older data. All results reported in this chapter come from these sources.

16 Defined here as current EU members plus states in the western Balkans. It excludes post-Soviet states such as Georgia, Armenia, and Ukraine, which were also surveyed.

17 Eurobarometer 69, "Values of Europeans," March–May 2008, published in November 2008.

18 Only fifteen countries were surveyed in this round, a much smaller number (twenty-six, not counting Israel, Russia, and Ukraine) than in the 2012 survey. However, the mix of questions for political efficacy was more limited in 2012.

19 Charles Maier, "Democracy and Its Discontents," *Foreign Affairs* 73:4, July–August 1994: p. 48–64.

20 *The Economist*, "Public Opinion: Is There a Crisis?" July 17, 1999, p. 49–50.

21 Ralf Dahrendorf, "Afterword," in Susan Pharr and Robert Putnam, eds. *Disaffected Democracies: What's Troubling the Trilateral Countries?* (Princeton: Princeton University Press, 2000), p. 311. See also Russell Dalton, *Democratic Challenges*.

22 The classic treatment of legitimacy is Max Weber, *Economy and Society* (1925). Weber makes a distinction between *Herrschaft* (Rule) and *Macht* (Power or Force), maintaining that a state cannot survive solely on force.

23 Peter Mair, Ruling the Void: The Hollowing of Western Democracy (London: Verso, 2013).

24 Russell Dalton, Democratic Challenges, Democratic Choices: The Erosion of Political Support in Advanced Industrial Democracies (Oxford: Oxford University Press, 2004).

25 For example, a 2010 survey reported in *The Economist* found a third of French respondents strongly or somewhat agreed with the statement that the free market is best, down from 42 percent in 2002. See *The Economist*, "Market Troubles," April 6, 2011.

26 Eurobarometers 66 and 71.

27 This list is by no means exhaustive. Again, the goal is to illustrate some basic patterns, not answer complex issues within political science.

28 The GESIS online platform allows for tests of statistical significance as well. In bi-variate correlations with the query on equality/freedom, all of these variables were statistically significant at the .01 level.

29 Ronald Inglehart, *The Silent Revolution: Changing Values and Political Styles Among Western Publics* (Princeton: Princeton University Press, 1977), p. 285.

30 Ronald Inglehart, *Culture Shift in Advanced Industrial Society* (Princeton: Princeton University Press, 1990), p. 66.

31 Central sources for Inglehart are Abraham Maslow, *Motivation and Personality* (New York: Harper, 1954), and Karl Deutsch, *The Nerves of Government* (New York: Free Press, 1963).

32 Inglehart, *Culture Shift*, p. 68.

33 Inglehart, *Culture Shift*, p. 331.

34 The survey also includes a twelve-item materialist/post-materialist index, based on two additional questions that offer other choices, including (for post-materialism) progress toward a society in which ideas count for more than money and protecting freedom of speech.

35 Inglehart, *Culture Shift*, p. 93, and Inglehart, *Modernization and Postmodernization: Cultural, Economic and Political Change in 43 Societies* (Princeton: Princeton University Press, 1997), p. 38.

36 Ronald Inglehart and Christian Welzel, *Modernization, Cultural Change, and Democracy*. (Cambridge: Cambridge University Press, 2005), p. 154–155.

37 For an excellent web resource on European feminism, see "Feminism in Europe" at www.cddc.vt.edu/feminism/eur.html, accessed October 8, 2009.

38 Catherine Hoskyns, *Integrating Gender: Women, Law, and Politics in the European Union* (London: Verso, 1996).

39 Tony Judt, *Postwar: A History of Europe Since 1945* (New York: Penguin, 2005), p. 375.

40 Pippa Norris and Ronald Inglehart, *Sacred and Secular: Religion and Politics Worldwide* (Cambridge: Cambridge University Press, 2004).
41 Data reported in Philip Jenkins, *God's Continent: Christianity, Islam, and Europe's Religious Crisis* (Oxford: Oxford University Press, 2007), p. 27.
42 Pew Global Attitudes Project, "World Publics."
43 Philip Jenkins, *God's Continent*, p. 41.
44 Quoted in Jenkins, *God's Continent*, p. 39.
45 Charlemagne, "A European Values Debate," *The Economist*, December 9, 2006.
46 Michael Novak, quoted in Jenkins, *God's Continent*, p. 9.
47 See BBC News, "Europe's Abortion Rules," February 12, 2007, at http://news.bbc.co.uk/2/hi/europe/6235557.stm, accessed on March 30, 2010.
48 See "Middle Ireland Has Spoken: Now the Government Should Act on Abortion," *Sunday Independent*, September 21, 2014, and "Government to Consider UN Abortion Law Recommendations," *Irish Times*, May 13, 2016.
49 Analysis from data from the 1999–2001 WVS show that in Europe the percentage of people saying abortions are never justified is largest in Ireland (49.7 percent), Croatia (42.8 percent), Poland (41.7 percent), all of which are overwhelmingly Catholic, and in Turkey (63.9 percent).
50 "Safe, Legal, and Falling," *The Economist*, October 20, 2007.
51 Tony Judt, *Postwar* p. 490.
52 The best source by far on drug policies in Europe is the European Legal Database on Drugs, available at http://eldd.emcdda.europa.eu, accessed on March 30, 2010. In particular, see its 2005 report, "Illicit Drug Use in the EU's Legislative Approaches."
53 "Barcelona's Booming Cannabis Clubs Turn Spain into the 'Holland of the South,'" *The Guardian*, August 4, 2014.
54 *International Herald Tribune,* November 7, 2007. The Netherlands has not actually legalized cannabis, a move that would cause trouble within the EU and arguably be against existing UN agreements on combating controlled substances. On Portugal, see "Drugs in Portugal: Did Decriminalization Work?" *Time,* April 26, 2009.
55 Flash Eurobarometer 401, "Young People and Drugs," 2014, available at http://ec.europa.eu/public_opinion/flash/fl_401_en.pdf, accessed May 13, 2016.
56 "Rethinking a Legal Sex Trade," *Christian Science Monitor,* May 11, 2005.
57 Information on laws regulating prostitution available at http://prostitution.procon.org/view.resource.php?resourceID=000772.
58 See *International Herald Tribune,* October 5, 2007, and Richard Poulin, "The Legalization of Prostitution and Its Impact on Trafficking in Women and Children," February 6, 2005, at http://sisyphe.org/spip.php?article1596, accessed March 30, 2010.
59 "Britain Eyes Swedish Law on Sex Workers," *Christian Science Monitor,* January 10, 2008.
60 By 2005, the British government was actively working to recruit more gays into the service. See *International Herald Tribune,* February 23, 2005.
61 "A History of Same-Sex Unions in Europe," *The Guardian*, January 24, 2016.
62 "Slovenians Vote Against Same-Sex Marriage in Referendum," *The Guardian*, December 20, 2015.
63 Edward Delman, "An Ambiguous Victory for Gay Rights in Europe," *The Atlantic*, July 24, 2015.
64 Special Eurobarometer 437, "Discrimination in the EU in 2015," May–June 2015, available at www.equineteurope.org/IMG/pdf/ebs_437_en.pdf.
65 "Luxembourg Premier Is First E.U. Leader to Marry Same-Sex Partner," *The New York Times*, May 15, 2015.
66 Jean Cohen and Andrew Arato, *Civil Society and Political Theory* (Cambridge: MIT Press, 1992), and Robert Putnam, *Making Democracy Work: Civic Traditions in Modern Italy* (Princeton: Princeton University Press, 1993)
67 Data from Jelle Visser, "Union Membership Statistics in 24 Countries," *Monthly Labor Review*, January 2006, p. 45.
68 Miriam Golden. "The Dynamics of Trade Unionism and National Economic Performance, *American Political Science Review* 87:2, June 1993: p. 439–454.

69 Paul Kubicek, *Organized Labor in Postcommunist States: From Solidarity to Infirmity* (Pittsburgh: University of Pittsburgh Press, 2004). The one exception may be Slovenia, which inherited a different type of communism that gave greater authority to workers.
70 "France's Socialist Government Survives Vote, but Remains Fractured," *The New York Times*, May 13, 2016.
71 Eurobarometer 74 conducted in November 2010, available at http://ec.europa.eu/public_opinion/archives/eb/eb74/eb74_publ_en.pdf. Notably, the lowest levels of trust were in Eastern Europe (Bulgaria, 21 percent, Romania, 21 percent, and Hungary, 31 percent) and in Greece (29 percent), whereas the highest were in the more "corporatist" countries: Denmark (66 percent), Finland (67 percent), and the Netherlands (59 percent).
72 John Wilson, *Introduction to Social Movements* (New York: Basic Books, 1973) p. 8.
73 Cyrus Zirakzadeh, *Social Movements in Politics: A Comparative Study* (London: Longman, 1997), p. 5.
74 Sidney Tarrow, *Power in Movement: Social Movements and Contentious Politics*, 2nd ed. (New York: Cambridge University Press, 1998). This was epitomized in 2011, when in the wake of Arab Spring, *Time* magazine declared 2011 the year of the protester.
75 Flash Eurobarometer 373, "Europeans' Engagement in Participatory Democracy," February 2013, available at http://ec.europa.eu/public_opinion/flash/fl_373_en.pdf.

Tens of thousands of Greeks have protested austerity measures

© NurPhoto/NurPhoto via Getty Images

Chapter 10

Economic issues in Europe

The global financial crisis, which began in 2007 with banking and housing market crises in the United States, hit many countries in Europe hard. Economies contracted, stock markets experienced sharp downturns, many financial institutions teetered on the brink of collapse, and many governments were compelled to devise rescue plans to bail out their financial systems. Greece faced the most dire situation, as the country was unable to pay its immense sovereign debt, calculated at €262 billion in 2009, over 50 percent higher than in 2004 and over 125 percent of GDP.[1] As a member of the eurozone, Greece had long been able to borrow funds at low interest rates, despite longstanding concerns about corruption, waste, and poor economic management. As growth slowed, Greece's budget deficit ballooned and it found itself unable to pay its massive debt. It required €53 billion just to cover its debt obligations in 2010.[2] The problem, however, was that lenders had little confidence in Greece. They now demanded high interest rates, which Greece could not afford. Greece was therefore forced to turn to the EU and international financial institutions for assistance. Many, particularly the Germans, were reluctant to help and insisted that Greece had to take measures, such as raising taxes and cutting spending on everything from pensions, civil servant salaries, education, and infrastructure, to get its economic house in order. Many Greeks mobilized against the prospect of economic austerity. Voices in and outside of Greece suggested Greece might be forced to leave the eurozone. Some even lobbied for "Grexit" from the EU.[3] As the debt crisis spread to other countries, including Ireland, Portugal, and Spain, it assumed more dimension, becoming not just a financial market crisis or a sovereign debt crisis but an institutional crisis for the EU itself.[4] Euro-pessimism reached new lows, with scholars of EU integration asking whether the EU was now "doomed."[5]

The EU, led by Germany's Angela Merkel, eventually pushed through bailout provisions to give Greece, and other highly indebted states, access to funds. Those states were expected to maintain fiscal discipline in addition to making structural reforms (e.g., raising the retirement age, ending certain protections for workers). The last part of this chapter details these arrangements and the political battles over their development and implementation. The primary point, however, is that generating growth and employment under such conditions has been a serious problem in many states. It was only in the first quarter of 2016 that overall gross domestic product (GDP) in the eurozone eclipsed its previous high set in early 2008.[6] Unemployment has gone up in numerous states, reaching over 20 percent in both Greece and Spain, generating widespread protests and the emergence of new parties and political actors that railed against EU-imposed reforms. In January 2015, Greeks elected Alexis Tsipras, a former Communist Party youth member, as Prime Minister. He hailed from the Syriza Party, whose full name is translated as Coalition of the Radical Left. Tsipras promised to re-negotiate a better deal for Greeks, but later, even after Greeks voted in a referendum against the conditions tied to an EU bailout proposal, he was forced to agree to another round of austerity measures in return for EU funds. Economic recovery, at least for Greece—whose economy has shrunk by 25 percent from 2010 to 2016 and whose debt by 2015 had grown to 175 percent of the country's GDP—remains at best a long-term prospect, as many (both in and outside of Greece) question the economic and political viability of continued austerity.

The Greek case, as well as that of other states hit hard by the crisis, dramatically and vividly demonstrates the importance of economic issues, both to individual countries and to Europe as a whole. It also shows how the economic connections that have developed since World War II—most clearly seen with the euro—can also have negative repercussions. Europe is more tightly connected than ever before, but the flip side of the benefits of greater trade and investment is that each country becomes more vulnerable to events and forces beyond its borders. In this sense, the Greek crisis is a statement not only about Europeanization but also about the more general phenomenon of globalization.

This chapter takes up a variety of economic issues in contemporary Europe, looking both at longer-term trends that present challenges to the European social-welfare state as well as the domestic and international aspects of the economic crisis that by 2016 has yet to fully pass. Although Greece has perhaps garnered most of the headlines related to the economic crisis, economic issues *writ large* typically rank as a top concern for citizens and are a major subject of public policy. As noted in Chapter 1, some would contend that the European socio-economic model, which includes a much more developed welfare state than in the US, is one of the cornerstones of European identity. This model took root after World War II and helped ensure economic growth, a high standard of living, and economic security for millions of Europeans.[7] Although Europe, compared to other regions of the world, remains rich, many Europeans became increasingly concerned about their economic situation even before Greece's collapse threatened to spread to other corners of the continent. For years, many countries were plagued by chronically high (10 percent or more) unemployment, weak economic growth compared to the US and high-flying emerging economies, and high labor costs and regulations that were, arguably, leading to the loss of jobs to other countries such as China and India. The European social-welfare model—which, as we'll see, varies across the continent—was challenged on both pragmatic (e.g., can European governments afford it?) and on ideological grounds (e.g., does the high-tax, high-government spending model really outperform alternatives?). The global economic crisis, although generated by developments in the US, laid bare some of the weaknesses in European economies, and even produced dire economic conditions in previously heralded "success stories" such as Iceland, Ireland, Latvia, and Hungary.

The introduction of the euro, discussed in Chapter 3, was, according to its proponents, supposed to contribute to overall economic growth as well as the economic unity of the continent. Nearly two decades after its formal creation, it seems clear that it has not delivered on these promises.[8] Indeed, as evidenced by the debt crisis in Greece (and elsewhere), the euro can easily be blamed for many of the continent's problems; at minimum, it made what could have been simply a Greek, Spanish, or Portuguese problem a European problem. While the worst of the crisis may have passed, much still remains to be done in many states to reduce debt and stimulate growth and employment.

This chapter thus takes up the challenges facing the European economies and the welfare state, noting debates over and challenges to the post-war economic model, highlighting different economic strategies in various countries, and, finally, discussing the causes, impact, and solutions to the debt crisis that had ripple effects across Europe in the 2010s.

Challenges to the welfare state

We'll begin our discussion by backing up a bit and continuing the chronological narrative of Chapter 2. One might recall that we ended the discussion of the European welfare state in the 1970s, when several states began to experience lower growth and higher inflation and unemployment. This was especially acute in Great Britain, where there was a series of political crises in Britain (e.g., nationwide strikes) and many began to rethink previous assumptions about the "collectivist consensus" that endorsed a strong role for the state in the economy. In the British case, Prime Minister Margaret Thatcher (1979–1990) identified the "nanny state" as the source of Britain's troubles. Her reforms changed not only Great Britain but inspired a global re-orientation away from state control and toward more market-oriented policies. However, Thatcher left a mixed legacy, and some resisted implementing Thatcher-style reforms. By the turn of the century, however, chronic problems in many states propelled discussions about the need to dismantle elements of the welfare-state model.

Thatcher's reforms

As noted in Chapter 2, Great Britain was, compared with other European states such as West Germany, a relative poor economic performer in the post-war period. One could list numerous reasons for this development—ill-conceived state planning, an aging industrial base, lack of investment in new technologies—but Thatcher and like-minded conservatives saw Britain's economic stagflation in the 1970s—rising unemployment, accelerating inflation (24 percent in 1975), and low growth—as an indication that the post-war big government model needed to be replaced. Her answer was relatively simple: The state needed to get out of the way to let free markets function more efficiently.

Margaret Thatcher had bold and, at the time, controversial ideas. She was ardently committed to principles of smaller government, leading the Conservative Party by proclaiming that it was time to end the quest for political consensus. In the early 1970s, she served as education minister. In order to meet budget targets, she abolished free milk in Britain's schools, earning her the sobriquet "Maggie Thatcher Milk Snatcher."[9] Although many found her style abrasive, enough Britons believed that she was right, or, at least, offered a more convincing program than the hapless Labour Party.

Thatcher came into office in 1979 with a clear, ideological mission. She did not merely want to reform the welfare state. She intended to scrap many elements of it and remake British culture. Taxes were cut to help stimulate investment and spending. The government also pursued **privatization**, meaning that state-owned assets such as oil companies, mines, public housing, and marquee firms such as British Airways, British Telecom, and Rolls Royce were sold to private investors. Government regulations, which she viewed as hampering business growth, were scaled back. She sought to cut government spending, particularly on social welfare programs. She attacked the trade unions, ending corporatist tripartite arrangements that gave unions access to policy-making, passing legislation that made it more difficult for workers to strike, and effectively destroying (with great relish) the once-powerful miners' union. She was pro-American and highly skeptical of European integration, claiming that all problems came from across the English Channel and all solutions from across the Atlantic. No child of the 1960s, she fought to reestablish traditional values, and, even though she was Britain's first female prime minister, she did not consider herself a feminist.

privatization the selling of state-owned enterprises to private owners, pursued in numerous states to promote efficiency and raise revenue.

The overall theme of her program was stress on the individual, freeing the individual from a predatory and paternalistic state and demanding that individuals be responsible for their own fate. In a 1987 interview, she said,

> I think we've been through a period where too many people have been given to understand that if they have a problem, it's the government's job to cope with it. "I have a problem, I'll get a grant." "I'm homeless, the government must house me." They're casting their problem on society. And, you know, there is no such thing as society. There are individual men and women, and there are families. And no government can do anything except through people, and people must look to themselves first.[10]

Thatcher's rule—in substance and style—was controversial.[11] Former Conservative Prime Minister Harold MacMillan, critical of privatization, accused her of selling "the family silver" and others condemned what they saw as her promotion of greed and "the unacceptable face of capitalism."[12] Her combative style was off-putting to many, and many thought she had no compassion for the less fortunate. There were, however, some positive effects: In the early 1980s, the economy began to rebound, thanks in part to the collapse of inefficient firms, increased competition, and foreign investment. Millions of British citizens became shareholders in privatized firms. Inflation was tamed to single digits, productivity rose, and profits soared. Growth rates in the late 1980s were over 4 percent, although inequality increased, with the wealthiest 10 percent of Britons seeing a 65 percent increase in after-tax income in the 1980s, compared to a 14 percent decline for the bottom 10 percent.[13] Public services, in particular housing and transport, were squeezed of funds. Private affluence, in the words of one critic, was accompanied by "public squalor."[14] Nonetheless, Thatcher's Conservatives trounced Labour in 1983 and 1987 elections.

It is worth mentioning, however, what Thatcher did not do. While spending was cut for public housing and transport, she did not seek to dismantle the National Health Service, a state-body that dispensed "socialized medicine." British universities remained tuition-free. Total government spending, as percentage of the economy, still remained over 40 percent of GDP, roughly the same as it was in the late 1970s, in part because unemployment rose—by 1985 twice as many Britons were unemployed as ten years before—and the government was obligated to pay unemployment benefits. Thatcher, then, did not wholly destroy the welfare state, although her policies did refashion both the economy and state-society relations and, perhaps most importantly, changed the political discourse by suggesting that markets, not states, were the best organizers of economic life.

Thatcher's international impact

Despite mixed effects of her policies and her polarizing personality, the latter of which helped cost her leadership of the Conservative Party in 1990, Thatcher's political legacy is substantial. Together with the "Reagan Revolution" in the United States that saw markets as the solution and government as a problem—President Ronald Reagan liked to say that the scariest words in the English language are "I'm from the government. I'm here to help."—and the collapse of communism in the late 1980s, old statist approaches were widely discredited. **Neoliberalism** became a powerful ideology, as economists, international financial institutions such as the World Bank and International Monetary Fund, and political leaders in several states (particularly those on the political right) embraced the power of markets and scaled back the powers of the state. True, few embraced the market and denigrated the state with Thatcher's relish, but there was no doubt that defenders of the old order were on the defensive.

neoliberalism an economic perspective that gained prominence in the 1980s and 1990s; advocated a smaller role for government and market-based approaches such as low taxes, privatization, deregulation, and trade liberalization in order to produce economic growth.

Her ideas carried on both beyond Britain and beyond her time in office. Reagan was clearly influenced by her, and by the end of the 1980s a neoliberal approach became the orthodoxy of the so-called "Washington Consensus" of international development agencies. In Europe, Francois Mitterrand, the first Socialist president of France (1981–1995), abandoned ideas of state ownership and instead embarked upon his own privatization program. Privatization also featured prominently in government programs in Italy, Spain, and Austria. Criticism of the previously sacrosanct welfare state was heard in Scandinavia. In the 1990s, free market reformers such as Václav Klaus in the Czech Republic and Leszek Balcerowicz in Poland were open admirers of Thatcher. They advocated rapid reforms to dismantle communism and helped make their states more business friendly than most countries in Western Europe. In the 1990s, under the leadership of Tony Blair, the opposition Labour Party in Great Britain also moved toward the political center, and once Blair became prime minister in 1997, he built on some of Thatcher's successes while trying to be softer around the edges, a development we'll discuss later in the chapter.

The case for reforming the welfare state

Thatcher's "revolution" in Britain demonstrated both that there was an alternative to the post-war European political-economic model and that such an alternative could be, arguably, more productive and dynamic. By the 1980s, average growth rates in several countries, including West Germany, France, Italy, Sweden, and the Netherlands were under or just above 2 percent a year, hardly an impressive accomplishment and far less than these countries had experienced in previous decades. In the early 1990s, much of Europe, including Britain, fell into economic crisis because the reunification of West and East Germany dragged down the German economy, whose problems spilled over to other countries. Recovery in some countries was quite modest. Average growth from 1993–2000 in Germany was 1.9 percent; in Italy, 1.6 percent; in France, 2.3 percent. In contrast, states that had adopted a more free-market approach had higher growth. Great Britain averaged 3.1 percent growth, and Ireland, a country with relatively low taxes and policies to encourage foreign investment (discussed more in the **In focus** section), enjoyed average growth of over 10 percent a year.[15]

One might note as well that as much of Europe had modest or low growth in the 1990s, the economy of the United States, which has lower taxes and less state spending than most countries in Europe, performed quite well, with average growth of 3.5 percent. More impressive, perhaps, was the relative performance on unemployment. Whereas unemployment in the US averaged 5 percent from 1993–2000 (declining to 4 percent in 2000), comparable figures in most of Europe were much higher: 8.4 percent in Germany, 10.9 percent in Italy, 11.1 percent in France, and 7.6 percent in Great Britain. Even after the worldwide economic downturn after 9/11 and the world economic crisis at the end of the 2000s, the US recovered faster than most states in Europe. Comparative data on growth and unemployment immediately before the global financial crisis and afterward are presented in Figures 10.1 and 10.2, which show that since 2012 the US has both higher growth than the larger economies in Europe and markedly lower unemployment than the EU average.

The last part of this chapter features an extended discussion of the global economic crisis and its aftermath. As for the more chronic problem of low to modest growth and high unemployment in much of Europe, numerous factors could be invoked as causes. Possible culprits include globalization, higher energy prices, aging

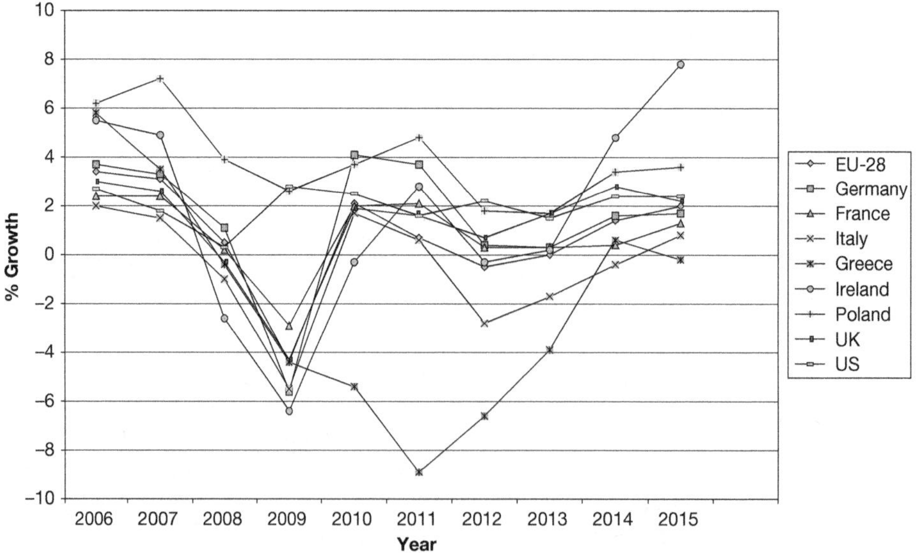

FIGURE 10.1 Real GDP growth 2006–2015

Eurostat, available at ec.europa.eu/Eurostat, and (for US) Statista

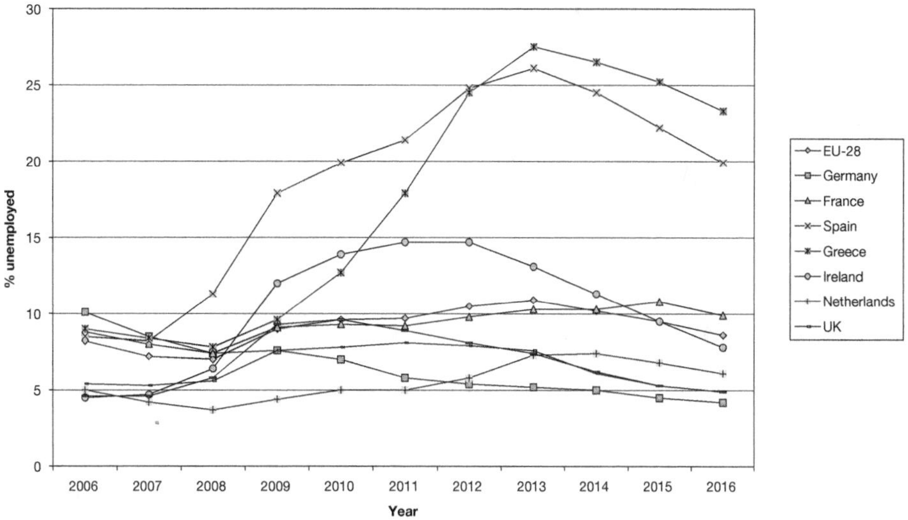

FIGURE 10.2 Unemployment rates 2006–2016

Eurostat, available at ec.europa.eu/eurostat. Figures for 2016 are through June

infrastructure, and a growing number of retired workers. However, the contrast in performance, particularly prior to the economic crisis of the late 2000s, between Britain and the US, on the one hand, and France, Italy, and Germany (among others) suggests another, more politically driven answer: Those states with more free-market oriented economies and pro-business policies have tended to perform better in terms of growth and job creation. In contrast, continental Europe's more generous social welfare provisions and less flexible labor markets (e.g., it is very difficult to fire workers in Italy and France) are held up as problems, arguably creating less incentive for people to look for jobs and for businesses to hire new workers.[16]

In short, "big government" is upheld as one of the main problems. This raises the following question: How big is "big government" in Europe? Table 10.1 compares the size of government—looking at taxes and government spending—across several West European states as well as the US. The results indicate that the overall tax burden, which includes income taxes, value-added and sales taxes, and corporate taxes, is lower in the US than in any country in Western Europe (Switzerland, at 26.6 percent, is closest to the US).[17] On the other hand, government spending in Europe, and, in particular, state social spending (e.g., health, education, pensions, welfare provisions) is significantly more pronounced. Table 10.2 presents an "Economic Freedom Score" from the Fraser Institute for several countries. This takes into account taxes and spending but also the extent of government regulation, protection of property rights, monetary policy, and trade barriers. As one can see, there is wide variance across Europe. Some countries, again Ireland and Great Britain, but also several post-communist states (discussed in a separate section in this chapter), as well as the US, rank among the most "economically free" in the world. Several other West European states, including Germany, Finland, Denmark, and the Netherlands, also rank as relatively economic free, a reflection that even though they may have (compared to the US) high taxes and government spending, they also have embraced policies, especially in terms of ease of establishing businesses and labor market regulation, that are more market-oriented. They were also the least hard-hit in Europe during the economic crisis, functioning as the creditors in pledging bailout funds for countries such as Greece and Portugal, which rank much lower in terms of economic freedom. They also have much lower unemployment. For example, as of mid-2016, Germany had 4.2 percent unemployment and

TABLE 10.1 Tax burden and state spending in Europe and the US

Country	*Total Tax Revenue as % of GDP, 2014*	*Gov't Spending as % of GDP, 2013*	*Public Social Spending as % of GDP, 2014*
Great Britain	32.6	44.9	21.7
Germany	36.1	60.8	25.8
France	45.2	57.1	31.9
Italy	43.6	51.1	28.6
Spain	33.2	45.1	26.8
Netherlands	36.7[a]	46.4	24.7
Sweden	42.7	52.4	28.1
Finland	43.9	57.5	31
Ireland	29.9	39.7	21
US	26.0	38.8	19.2

Source: Organization for Economic Cooperation and Development (OECD), available at www.oecd.org

[a] Data from 2013. Spending data includes national and sub-national government spending.

TABLE 10.2 Economic Freedom Scores

Country	*Fraser Freedom Score (1–10)*	*Rank among 157 countries*
Switzerland	8.16	4
Ireland	7.90	8
Great Britain	7.87	10
US	7.73	16
Romania	7.69	17
Finland	7.61	19
Lithuania	7.61	19
Denmark	7.58	22
Germany	7.50	29
Netherlands	7.42	30
Czech Republic	7.33	42
Sweden	7.33	42
Poland	7.29	47
Italy	7.13	68
France	7.12	70
Greece	6.87	85
Slovenia	6.44	111

Source: James Gwartney, Robert Lawson, and Joshua Hall, Economic Freedom of the World 2015 Annual Report (Vancouver: Fraser Institute, 2015). Scores are based upon data from 2013

Denmark and the Netherlands had 6 percent. In contrast, France had 9.9 percent unemployment, Italy 11.6 percent, and Greece a whopping 23.3 percent.[18]

Those who argue against "big government" contend that that high taxes, extensive regulations, and state spending policies are harmful to growth and job creation and/or are simply unsustainable, particularly in light of a long-term decline in European birthrates. Advocates of these positions—which can be found in virtually every article on European economic issues in *The Economist*, a conservative (in American parlance) British publication—would advise that European governments seriously rethink the large role of the state in the economy, something many Europeans have taken for granted since World War II. However, as we'll examine in discussion of a few case studies, it has been politically difficult to implement many market-oriented reforms and curtail spending.[19] The economic crisis at the end of the 2000s, which resulted in exploding budget deficits in a number of countries (see Table 10.6 later in the chapter), was thought by some to be the final blow for the welfare state, as many governments were hypothesized to have little choice but to cut back on spending. However, according to the Organization for Economic Cooperation and Development (OECD), state social spending as a percentage of GDP since 2000 has increased in many states, including France, Italy, Spain, and Great Britain, a reflection in part of the aging workforce but also, in several states, due to sustained unemployment and underemployment and demands on the system.[20]

The case for a "European social model"

The "European social model," which varies from state to state but rests, in most cases, on relatively high levels of state spending and high taxes, has proven to be fairly resilient, as seen in Table 10.1. True, marginal income tax rates have significantly declined in recent decades, dropping from over 80 percent in some countries to 45 percent or less in countries such as France, Germany, Italy, and Sweden. EU policies, particularly with respect to management of the euro, have also put pressure on fiscal policies, as states face (to date more in theory than in practice) punishment for running large budget deficits. Most governments work to attract, not discourage, foreign investment. Competition among economic actors is widely assumed to produce positive results (e.g., lower prices, better service), and few today would argue for state ownership of large economic enterprises. However, despite economic problems in many European countries, many would continue to defend the "European" model, in which the state plays a larger role in the economy, as opposed to the "American" or "Anglo-American" variant.[21] As noted above, the global economic crisis of the late 2000s originated with the sub-prime mortgage crisis in the United States, a development that some blame on lax oversight of the financial sector, not overly intrusive statist policies.[22]

In the wake of the crisis, some European countries have recovered and fared relatively well, as seen in Figures 10.1 and 10.2. Moreover—and surprisingly, perhaps, especially for Americans—some European countries (e.g., Norway, the Netherlands, Ireland, Belgium, Germany, France) have comparable or even greater productivity per worker than the US, although US workers are still more productive than EU workers on average.[23] More than anything else, perhaps, these data suggest that it is difficult to speak about a common European economic experience in the

In focus

The lessons of Ireland and Finland

Although many European economies have not been strong performers over the past two decades, some have done quite well. Several Eastern European states, as noted later in this chapter, saw solid and steady growth in the 2000s and 2010s. Norway has taken advantage of oil wealth to become one of the richest countries in the world. Switzerland and Luxembourg, which rely heavily on banking, are both wealthier, *per capita*, than the US. Two of the more impressive European "success stories" have been Ireland and Finland.

Ireland, of course, has a history of underdevelopment and poverty. Millions of Irish people left Ireland to find a better life elsewhere. Ireland joined the European Community (EC) in 1973, but, by Western European terms, it was relatively poor, making it a recipient of European regional development funds. Its standard of living lagged well behind that of Great Britain, the country's former colonial master.

Starting in the 1990s, however, Ireland became the "Celtic Tiger," a country that experienced high and sustained economic growth like the so-called "Asian Tigers" of Singapore, Taiwan, and Hong Kong. From 1993 to 2007 economic growth averaged nearly 8 percent a year. Unemployment dropped from 16 percent in 1993 to 4.3 percent by 2007. By 1997, Ireland had caught up to Great Britain in terms of GDP *per capita*, and by 2006 its average GDP *per capita* was 33 percent higher than that of Great Britain and 44 percent higher than the EU average. It was running budget surpluses, not deficits. Among EU states, Ireland ($52,000) in 2007 was the second-wealthiest country in *per capita* income (Luxembourg [$89,700] was first), markedly higher than even the US ($44,000).[24] The Irish diaspora reversed a long historical trend by coming back to Ireland, and thousands of other workers from around the world followed suit.

What accounted for Ireland's success?[25] Some of the answers would warm the heart of Margaret Thatcher: tax reduction, cuts in spending, and opening up of markets, particularly for foreign investment. At 12.5 percent, Ireland has, by far, the lowest corporate tax rate in Western Europe, and the government spending also accounts for a lower percentage of GDP than in most European countries. Low taxes, relatively (compared to Britain, say) lower labor costs, and, no less crucially, a well-educated labor force whose native language was English encouraged various companies, particularly in the high tech sector, to set up both production and service sectors in Ireland and use Ireland as a base to enter European markets. Foreign investment flooded into Ireland. In 2003, for example, $25 billion in foreign investment came to Ireland, more than to Great Britain or Germany. Fewer regulations also allowed new, Irish firms to develop. Some flourished, most famously Ryanair, which has become a leading low-cost airline in Europe and provides a great boost to the tourism industry.

These policies were adopted in the 1990s with a large degree of political consensus. Unions signed on to tax cuts and cuts in state spending in return for modest wage increases. The depth of Ireland's crisis in the 1980s—rising debt, slowing growth, high unemployment—made it clear to all parties that reforms were needed. The government worked with interest groups in the National Economic and Social Council on its market-oriented Program for Economic Recovery. Pragmatism and creativity, not ideology, have been the guiding features of Irish political life.

An additional explanation for Irish growth is that Ireland has benefited immensely from EC (later EU) membership. Regional funds in the 1970s and 1980s were devoted to infrastructure development and education. Membership in the EC also meant, however, that Ireland was subjected to competitive pressures from Europe—meaning it could no longer protect failing domestic industries—but also gained access to wider markets. Lacking well-established industrial sectors, it could direct, through the government's Industrial Development Authority, investment and tax incentives into new industries, establishing a niche as a pharmaceutical and high-tech research and development site for Europe. By virtue of being in the EC, production in and export from Ireland made sense for multi-nationals seeking access to the European market.

Finally, one should mention human capital and demographics. Ireland produces more engineers *per capita* than the US or any West European EU state and was well positioned to capitalize on the growth of high-tech sectors. In addition, years of out-migration meant that were plenty of well-trained Irish workers and managers in multi-national corporations. By European standards, Ireland also had a lot of young workers, with almost half of the population under 25 years of age. Growth in the labor force helped drive overall economic growth.

This is not to say that Ireland was free of problems. As the economy grew, prices (particularly for housing) increased dramatically, and inequality rose. Ireland, particularly its banking and housing sector, was also hit very hard by the global financial crisis, with the economy contracting by nearly 10 percent in 2009, twice the average in the eurozone. The popping of the housing bubble and drying up of foreign investment put severe pressure on Irish banks, which were bailed out by the government. This in turn put pressure on state finances, putting Ireland in the mix with countries such as Greece and Portugal that faced heavy burdens to pay off their debt. Ireland appealed to the EU for help, and in December 2010 the EU approved a €85 billion bailout for Ireland, with Ireland in turn slashing public spending and adopting tax increases. Unemployment soared to nearly 15 percent. However, as seen in Figures 10.1 and 10.2, by 2014 Ireland was on the rebound, a reflection (in contrast to Greece) of the country's solid economic fundamentals and institutions. Although the crisis did take some shine off the "Irish model," there is little doubt that reformers across the continent will still draw some positive lessons from the Irish experience.

Finland's economic accomplishments are also extremely impressive. In the early 1990s, thanks in large measure to a dramatic drop in trade with Russia, Finland slid into a recession. Unemployment soared to 18 percent in 1993. Since the late 1990s, however, Finnish economic growth has been higher than the European average. Even after the global financial crisis, GDP *per capita* in Finland is higher than in France and Germany.[26] The World Economic Forum ranked Finland as the most competitive economy in Europe in its *Europe 2020 Competitiveness Report,* and it placed eighth among all countries in the world in its 2015 *Global Competitiveness Report*.[27]

What accounts for Finland's success? As one can see from Table 10.1, Finland did not dismantle its welfare state. Its tax rate remains high, as does government spending. Rather, Finnish growth has been predicated on development of a homegrown technology sector, best exemplified by Nokia (which accounted for over half the value of the Finnish stock market in the early 2000s), but also by literally thousands of smaller companies. In 2005, for example, Finland was the world's *per capita* leader in patent applications.[28]

How did this occur, or, to put it more dramatically, how did the leading industry in Finland change from paper production to high tech? One answer is government policy.[29] Research and development has become an increasingly important part of the state's budget, tripling as a percentage of GDP from the 1980s to the 2000s. Since 2000, Finland has been one of two European countries (Sweden is the other) to consistently spend over 3 percent of its GDP on research and development.[30] Technological development has been furthered by government-business cooperation, exemplified by the government's National Technology Agency, which dispenses funds to universities and businesses and helps identify markets and products for companies to develop and manufacture. Finnish firms began reorienting their outputs, and money was provided for spin-offs and start-ups. Market liberalization, particularly in terms of financial sector development and development of flexible labor contracts, has also helped. As seen in Table 10.2, Finland ranks among the top countries in Europe in terms of the "economic freedom index." However, there was no Thatcher-like attack on unions or push to eliminate all government regulation. Instead, government, employers, and trade unions have cooperated in focusing on growth in new sectors that provide Finland with high-paying jobs and the funds necessary to maintain a generous social welfare state.

Part of the answer, however, also has to do with Finland's education system, which is ranked among the best in the world.[31] Finnish students consistently score at the top among students globally in math, science, and reading. What is the secret to Finland's educational system, which, in the 1960s and 1970s, was nothing exceptional? Many conventional answers from American debates on education policy do not seem to apply. Finns start school at age 7 (although most youngsters attend government-subsidized preschools and daycare) and go to school on average only five hours a day through elementary school. Per-pupil spending ($5,000) is half of that in many US localities, and Finns place little emphasis on national-level student examinations. Instead, answers appear to lie in teaching training (all teachers have masters' degrees), limits on the number of teacher-training programs so that the supply of teachers is low but the quality of teachers is high, and flexibility within the curriculum to encourage innovation.

Does Finland offer a model for other countries? Certainly, Finland is unique: It is ethnically homogeneous, not hobbled by government or private sector corruption, enjoys a high degree of consensus in political life, and, perhaps more so than France or Italy, is willing to embrace change. It is also relatively small (5 million people), meaning modest investments by French or German standards can go a long way. Yet, one could argue that aspects of its educational system and research and development policy could easily be adopted elsewhere. Moreover, the Finnish experience illustrates that one does not have to embrace the Anglo-American-Irish reform model in order to succeed.

Critical thinking questions

1. Both Ireland and Finland are small, relatively homogeneous countries. How successfully can they serve as a "model" for others?
2. Of the two, which country's policies do you think are more likely to be successful over time? Have recent developments made either or both less worthy of being called a "success story"?

past decade. Moreover, on some economic comparisons, Europe (or, at least, many countries in Europe) fares better than the US. The US has the world's largest trade deficit ($500 billion in 2015), is the world's largest debtor nation, and, like Europe, has lost hundreds of thousands of jobs as companies have outsourced production in lower-wage countries. Finally, and perhaps most significantly, even if Europeans might concede that the US has been more dynamic and efficient, at least measured by average incomes or total growth over the medium and long term, many would still maintain that the European "model" remains more "humane" in various ways and therefore superior to the US system.

Indeed, it is on this point that Europeans and various "Europhiles" defend the European system against the US model.[32] For example, while the richest Americans have fared very well since the 1980s, average wages have been flat. The average European worker, in relative terms to the economic elite in her country, has fared better. Consider the following. In 1980, the average American CEO earned forty times the wage of the average workers in manufacturing. In 2000, the ratio was 475:1, compared to 24:1 in Britain, 15:1 in France, and 13:1 in Sweden.[33]At the low end, poverty rates—levels are defined differently by country—are under 10 percent in many European countries, including France, Austria, Poland, the Netherlands, Switzerland, and Ireland, compared to 15 percent in the US.[34] In the UN's **Human Development Index (HDI)**, which rates countries in terms of income, education, and health, most European countries score quite high, as seen in Table 10.3. Twenty-one of the top ranked thirty countries in the world are European, including some post-communist states. Several also rank higher than the US. Furthermore, as seen in the same table, inequality on the factors assessed by the HDI is much higher in the US than in most of Europe. This is largely because European governments more actively pursue **economic redistribution** to provide basic goods and services to large swathes of the population. Some amenities, such as housing subsidies, cash transfers, and unemployment benefits, are directed to the poor or those in economic distress. Others, however, are provided more broadly. They include free daycare, state-provided health care or guaranteed low cost health insurance, free higher education, job training, family allowances, and guaranteed pensions. The result is a stronger safety net, resulting, in many states, lower poverty levels and more equality. Some deride this as overly costly. However, the World Health Organization found that the US—not France, Sweden, or Germany—by far spends more on health care *per capita* than any other country. Much of the spending in the US is by private individuals, not the government (thus it is not reflected in Table 10.1)—yet ranks lower than many European states in terms of outcomes such as infant mortality and life expectancy, well-established indicators of public health.

Human Development Index (HDI)
index developed by the United Nations that takes into account income, health, and education. Its proponents maintain that it presents a more complete assessment of a country's living standard.

economic redistribution
policies, usually based on taxation and government spending, that redistribute money from the wealthy to poorer segments of the population; often a key component of the welfare state.

Americans are, by most standard measures, wealthier. GDP *per capita* is higher in the US than in most of Europe. Americans tend to own bigger houses, cars, and refrigerators and have more "stuff." Yet, they work far more hours than the typical European—who enjoys four to six weeks of vacation—and, as many Europeans would be sure to note, such conspicuous US-style consumption is not environmentally friendly or sustainable.[35] Moreover, GDP figures measure items such as military spending, "wasteful" health care spending, and prisons (far more populated in America than in Europe), factors that do not necessarily reflect a higher quality of life. Interestingly, as seen in Table 10.3, in many European states, people are more satisfied with their standard of living than in the United States.

TABLE 10.3 Data from the 2015 UN Human Development Report

Country	*Rank on HDI*	*Coefficient of inequality**	*% state spending on education*	*% satisfied with standard of living*
Norway	1	5.3	6.6	95
Australia	2	7.9	5.1	83
Switzerland	3	7.3	5.3	94
Denmark	4	7.1	8.7	91
Netherlands	5	6.5	5.9	85
Germany	6	6.7	5.0	90
Ireland	7	8.5	6.2	77
US	8	15.7	5.2	74
Canada	9	8.6	5.3	79
Sweden	14	6.5	6.8	89
Great Britain	15	8.4	6.0	79
Belgium	21	7.9	6.5	81
France	22	8.6	5.7	74
Finland	24	5.5	6.8	76
Slovenia	25	5.8	5.7	61
Spain	26	11.0	5.0	68
Italy	27	11.3	4.3	64
Czech Rep	28	5.3	4.5	68

Source: UN Human Development Report 2015: Work for Human Development

*Combined inequality in income, life expectancy, and education. Higher value indicates greater inequality.

The politics of economic reform in Western Europe

To be sure, the European welfare state has staunch defenders, particularly when the government tries to reduce or take away benefits (such as free higher education) enjoyed by large numbers of people. At the same time, however, many have argued that for the sake of greater growth or due to economic realities—whether it be that international markets require a more business-friendly environment or that a rapidly aging Europe cannot afford many social welfare programs—economic reforms are now required. Various political parties have put forward plans to foster economic growth and job creation. Some, mostly those on the left, seek to preserve key elements of the welfare state and make public investments in fields such as education and infrastructure. Others, mostly on the right, seek lower taxes, less regulation, and/or reduced government spending, leaving it more to the private sector to provide essential services. Some reformers can claim success; in other cases, reforms have been resisted both by political actors and by society at large. The global economic crisis in the late 2000s made these issues particularly acute in heavily indebted countries such as Greece, which in effect ceded its economic sovereignty to the EU.

To understand how debates over economic reform have played out, let us turn to specific cases in Western Europe.

New Labour and beyond in Great Britain

One of the most interesting developments occurred in Great Britain, where, after nearly two decades (1979–1997) of rule by the Conservatives, the left-wing Labour Party won elections after moving to the political center. Tony Blair, who championed the slogan "New Labour," spearheaded this transformation. Blair pushed through changes in the party's platform, including the abandonment of the goal of state ownership, control over taxes and expenditure, welfare reform, and decreasing the power of trade unions over the party. Blair's moves were both pragmatic and political, bowing to the reality that "Old Labour" was being trounced in elections. Some accused Blair of selling out, that the party had "abandoned virtually all that it had once stood for" and that Blair helped cement the reforms of the 1980s under Thatcher, so that "the economic principles of Thatcherism had become the conventional wisdom."[36]

Blair's defenders did not see things quite this way. As noted in Chapter 8, Blair and New Labour touted the idea of a "Third Way," meaning that they hoped to offer an alternative between the excesses of state-led socialism and complete reliance on free markets.[37] Under the "Third Way," the government would not work against markets or globalizing economic forces. Rather, the government would help create conditions for economic growth while expanding opportunity for individuals to participate in economic life by supporting education, job retraining, and entrepreneurship. The Third Way thus envisioned a "social investment state," one that focused on human capital, not excessive regulation to constrain markets.

Blair's reforms proved to be economically and politically successful. As seen from the figures above, economic growth in Britain in the 2000s was higher than in many European states and unemployment was lower. The stock market soared, and, even though Britain remained outside of the euro zone, London became the unquestioned financial capital of Europe. Taxes, by European standards, remained low, and Blair held the line on public spending, pushing through welfare reform that sought to get people back into the workforce, and, controversially, raising fees at British universities. Not all was well with Britain—many complained of a deterioration in health care, public transport, and school performance, and Blair lost much of his popularity thanks to his support for the invasion of Iraq[38]—but Labour retained its parliamentary majority in 2001 and 2005 elections, reflecting the fact that many middle-class Britons—Thatcher's core constituency—believed that "New Labour" was competent on economic matters. By the end of the 2000s, however, Britain's economy, particularly its banking sector, was jolted by the global financial crisis. Blair's successor, Gordon Brown, pushed through ambitious bailout plans, which initially won him praise.[39] However, as seen in Figure 10.1, the British economy, like most of Europe, experienced a severe economic contraction in 2009. Brown and the Labour Party began to suffer politically.

In 2010, the Conservatives, led by David Cameron, returned to power as the leading party in a coalition government. Interestingly, Cameron had tried to re-make the Conservatives in Blair's image, emphasizing the notion of competent government, not simply, as under Thatcher, less government. Cameron, however, faced some difficult choices given Britain's economic problems, particularly growing budget deficits, which had soared to 11 percent of GDP. Rather than opting for government spending to potentially stimulate growth, the government decided that debt had to be top priority. It thus pushed through programs to raise some taxes and slash state spending by $130 billion over five years, including in areas such as education, child support, transportation, and public sector employment.[40] As seen in the figures in this chapter, the economy did rebound, although by 2015 the budget deficit remained over 5 percent of GDP and there were intense debates as to whether it was because of or in spite of the government's policies.[41] Whereas Cameron's critics, mainly on the left, pushed for a return to state spending, Cameron led the Conservatives to victory in 2015 elections.

However, lingering long-term problems in Britain, including decline in Britain's industrial north (blamed in no small measure on globalization) and insecurity among working class voters, produced a startling development in 2016: British voters' decision to leave the EU. While "Brexit" can be seen in part as a protest against the establishment—and in this respect there was common ground on the nationalist right and many on the left—it is also a reflection that the Remain's primary argument—that Brexit risked the country's economic prosperity—fell on deaf ears as many felt they had no prosperity to risk.[42] As a result of this vote, Cameron resigned his post and Britain was compelled to re-negotiate its relationship with the EU.

Reviving Germany to become Europe's engine of growth

Germany suffered from high unemployment and sagging growth in the 1990s. This stood in contrast with the German "economic miracle" of the 1950s and 1960s. This was built around political consensus, participation of business and labor in important economic decisions, and a "conservative welfare state," which was managed by semi-public agencies (social security and health funds), was based in part upon worker payments so that those who paid in more received more, and was designed in many respects to support traditional family values (e.g., tax breaks for married couples, family allowances, provisions that discouraged mothers from working). Many pinpointed Germany's problems to borrowing for reunification as well as high **payroll taxes** and social insurance premiums, both of which substantially raised labor costs.[43]

payroll taxes taxes on employers that are used to pay for health insurance, unemployment benefits, and pensions; these can substantially add to the cost of employing workers.

In 1998, thanks in large part to concerns over the economy, Gerhard Schröder returned the Social Democrats to power in coalition with the Greens. Schröder had been influenced by Blair's ideas of a Third Way and pulled the Social Democratic Party to the center. In 2000, he pushed through major cuts in both income and corporate taxes. The government also pushed measures to give tax breaks to investors and stabilize public spending. The economy, however, did not markedly improve: It experienced no growth from 2002 to 2003, debt soared, Germany became less competitive internationally, and unemployment increased.

In 2003, recognizing that the situation was increasingly dire, Schröder unveiled a more ambitious reform plan, labeled Agenda 2010. Sounding like Margaret Thatcher, he declared that social welfare programs would be cut and that individuals would have be more responsible and assume more financing of programs such as health insurance and university education. Some benefits, especially unemployment benefits, were to be put on the chopping block. The government also changed the labor laws, making it easier for employers to fire workers. Individuals were encouraged to set up private retirement accounts to make up for cuts in pensions.

Agenda 2010 was highly controversial. Unions organized mass protests in opposition, and many within the Social Democratic Party accused Schröder of betraying long-standing principles. With the help of the opposition Christian Democrats, Schröder got Agenda 2010 through parliament, but he failed to win re-election in 2005, when Angela Merkel of the Christian Democratic Union became Chancellor as part of the "Grand Coalition" with the Social Democrats.

Although she is the leader of a party on the political right, Merkel has proven to be a centrist, adopting the slogan *Die Mitte* ("the middle").[44] She helped push through new laws to create more labor-market flexibility by allowing companies to make local or plant-level agreements with workers and continued some cuts in social programs. She also raised the retirement age to 67 to save on pensions. However, over the objections of some on the right, she was forced to increase both sales taxes and income taxes on high earners to ensure that the state's budget deficit remained within the EU's allowable limits. She also pushed through ambitious plans to invest in renewable energy, and in 2014 the government adopted Germany's first ever-minimum wage, €8.50 an hour. Under her leadership, the German economy weathered the global economic crisis, outperforming all other major European economies. She resisted calls on the left for a massive stimulus package, but did bail out German banks and large companies such as Opel, angering some on the right who chaffed at such government intervention. Nonetheless, the government's budget remained in surplus, not deficit. Unemployment, nearly 11 percent in 2005, declined in Germany in the late 2000s–early 2010s (even as it rose elsewhere), falling to just over 4 percent by 2016 (see Figure 10.2). Growth has been above the EU average, although after 2012 it slowed to under 2 percent a year, leading some to suggest that Germany might take advantage of low interest rates to be less fiscally austere, including taking steps to invest in infrastructure and encourage consumer spending. Adoption of such a course could also boost growth throughout Europe.[45]

For some, Germany is a model country. It adopted structural reforms and has been fiscally prudent. In less than twenty years, it has gone from being the "sick man of Europe" to the economic leader. "What we have done, everyone else can do," Merkel has declared.[46] Matters may not be that simple, as some countries lack Germany's advantages (e.g., a competitive export sector) and political difficulties in making economic reforms.

Resistance to reform in France

Such has been the case in France. Despite some reforms to cut back the size of the state under President Francois Mitterrand (1981–1995), French economic performance was not particularly impressive. Unemployment remained in the double digits throughout the 1990s, and the French became increasingly uneasy with the economic costs of globalization. Some began to call for more reform, with *The Economist*, in a magazine cover, suggesting that France needed its own Margaret Thatcher.[47]

Certainly, there was much about France in the 1990s and the 2000s that a person with Thatcher's ideological leanings would not like. The bureaucracy remained large and in many cases stifling. One out of four workers was in the public sector. Taxes and state spending were high, even by European standards; government regulations numerous; pensions and other welfare provisions generous; and the state continued to own or subsidize major industrial enterprises (e.g., Airbus). Whereas in the late 1970s income *per capita* was roughly 25 percent higher in France than in Great Britain, by 2005 the British had overtaken the French.[48]

In the late 1990s and 2000s French leaders began proposing various reforms. One idea, put into effect with much fanfare in 2000, was to mandate a thirty-five-hour work week, under the assumption that firms would hire extra workers to make up the difference. Various programs—including job training and tax breaks for businesses—were also put into place to help young people find jobs, as a quarter of those younger than 25 years old were unemployed. The government also tried to get its fiscal house in order, in part to meet the criteria to join the eurozone. The government embarked on privatizations (raising €30 billion from 1997 to 2002), cut income taxes, and trimmed pensions, while investments were made in energy and new technologies (e.g., nuclear power plants, grid computing, high-speed trains).

Nonetheless, the reforms were rather limited and not overly effective. Unemployment, while down from the double-digit highs of the late 1990s, was still above the European average for most of the 2000s. Rather than hire more workers because of the thirty-five hour work week, many firms made do with what they had. Per worker productivity did go up, but many people remained unemployed or could find only part-time employment. Part of the problem was with the French labor market, which imposes high payroll taxes on employers for social security. For example, in 2007, over 40 percent of all tax revenue in France went to payroll taxes and social security contributions, the highest rate in Western Europe.[49] The norm in France was also for workers to be on long-term contracts, making it difficult to fire them, which also has the effect of making employers hesitant about hiring new workers. Meanwhile, France's government debt (75 percent of GDP in 2007) was also high, a reflection that state spending (52 percent of GDP in 2007) remained high, even by European standards.[50]

Despite the case for market-oriented reforms to reduce spending, taxes, debt, and regulations, they have been difficult to adopt. Lionel Jospin, France's Socialist prime minister (1997–2002) spoke for many French when he rejected notions of a "Third Way" and vigorously defended socal democracy as an "inspiration" and declared that "we reject the market society."[51] Even though Jacques Chirac, the 1995 candidate from the center-right, campaigned for lower taxes and reforms, he was no Margaret Thatcher. His proposals to cut welfare payments, raise the retirement age, and increase health-care premiums were abandoned in the wake of nation-wide strikes. Under Chirac, the state bureaucracy and public debt grew, and growth remained under 2 percent a year. When he tried to make changes in the labor market to make it easier to fire (and thus, presumably hire) younger workers, French students and unions launched large-scale protests, compelling Chirac to withdraw the law.[52]

In 2007, Nicholas Sarkozy, who served as interior minister under Chirac, sensed that France was ready for change, adopting "La Rupture" as a campaign slogan.[53] Unabashedly pro-US, he campaigned on a platform of reform, urging the French to swallow some bitter pills in order to get the economy moving. His opponent, Socialist Ségolène Royal, promised more state protection and higher wages. Sarkozy prevailed, creating possibilities for economic reform. While no one doubted Sarkozy's energy—he maintained a daily jogging regimen and, after a divorce, globe-hopped with his new, ex-supermodel wife—his reform plans, not surprisingly, encountered opposition. When he proposed cuts in pensions for public sector workers and liberalizing the labor law in 2007, there was another round of strikes, shutting down the country's transportation network. Sarkozy pledged that he would push forward, including plans to reform the thirty-five-hour workweek law.[54] Progress, however, was modest at best, and by 2009, as the global economic crisis hit France, Sarkozy changed focus, advocating more spending to prop up employment, as unemployment crept back up to nearly 10 percent. Overall, however, by the time Sarkozy left office, French debt (100 percent of GDP) was much higher than what it had been when he assumed office. Taxes for social security and government spending were also higher.[55] The French labor code remained longer than the Bible.[56]

As noted in Chapter 8, Françoise Hollande, a Socialist, defeated Sarkozy in the 2012 presidential elections. Hollande rode a wave of popular dissatisfaction, and he tapped into anger on the left by promising, among other items, a 75 percent income tax on millionaires. This was highly controversial—some high-profile wealthy French, including actor Gérard Depardieu, moved and renounced French citizenship (he took a Russian passport), the Constitutional Council ruled against it, and even the Economic Minister confessed it made France "Cuba without the sun."[57] The tax was formally abandoned at the end of 2014. In 2016, Hollande sparked nationwide protests by using an executive order to push through labor market reforms, in particular making arrangements between employers and workers more flexible and making it easier for employers to dismiss workers. While these policies have long been advocated by French businesses and even by centrists within the Socialist Party, many on the left accused Hollande of betraying sacrosanct principles.[58] Hollande seems unlikely to win re-election in 2017, and whether these reforms will actually be implemented or what difference they make remains to be seen.

France's predicament points to the difficulty of reforming an entrenched system by imposing costs on those vested in the system. It was one thing, as under Thatcher, to privatize housing (thereby creating home owners) or large companies (thereby creating shareholders). It is far more difficult to take away people's benefits. Many French are used to job security; they do not want to give it up so somebody else can get a job. They also want to be able to retire—as railway and public transit workers, National Opera employees, and Bank of France officials can—with full pensions as early as the age of 50. They like their state-run health system, which is ranked among the best in the world, and, compared to others in Europe, are skeptical of both capitalism and globalization. Arguments about economic efficiency or competitiveness have yet to win them over.

Swedish model
term used to describe the high-tax, extensive welfare state in Sweden, which centered on economic redistribution in an effort to maintain greater economic equality.

Challenges to the Swedish Model

As noted in Chapter 2, Sweden, as well as other Scandinavian states, developed a very extensive welfare state. The "**Swedish model**," however, was not predicated on state ownership or government planning. Rather, it was based upon redistribution of resources with the goal of promoting full employment, social security, and greater economic equality. Corporations and individuals paid high taxes, and in return the government devoted resources to health, education, infrastructure, housing, and family allowances. The Social Democrats dominated Swedish politics, and corporatist institutions ensured cooperation among the government, business, and unions. Businesses remained privately owned, but employees were granted extensive job security protection, and wages were decided through national-level collective bargaining. Swedish politics and society rested upon this consensual model.

Cracks began to appear as early as 1976, when the Social Democrats lost power for the first time since 1932. Part of the reason for their defeat was Sweden's deteriorating economic performance: Growth slowed, unemployment rose, inflation crept up to nearly 10 percent. The center-right government tried to stimulate growth by cutting taxes, creating investment incentives, (ironically) socializing the ailing shipbuilding industry, and international borrowing. There was, however, no dramatic improvement in the economy.

The Social Democrats returned to power in 1982, but they began to pursue a more moderate course. Bowing both to domestic and international economic realities, the government announced that while it would seek to maintain the welfare state, it would not add new programs. Taxes would be cut to be more in line with other European states. The government, risking the wrath of the unions, also put a cap on wage increases to limit inflation.

In 1991, amid another economic downturn, another center-right coalition assumed power. It announced its intention to end the "age of collectivism" in Sweden. Its plans included tax and spending cuts, economic deregulation, and partial privatization of education and social services. However, the government failed to pass many of its proposals, and it was voted out in 1994. Sweden joined the EU in 1995, necessitating some deregulation in favor of market principles. In the latter half of the 1990s, the Social Democrats, again in power, put priority on deficit reduction and price stability, both of which were pursued with an eye to meet the criteria for the euro, which Sweden did not, as it turned out, adopt. The Social Democrats (barely) survived elections in 1998 and 2002, finally succumbing to a center-right coalition in 2006, which focused its efforts on stimulating job growth by cutting payroll taxes and trimming unemployment benefits, not radically overhauling the system. It won re-election in 2010, but in 2014 the Social Democrats won the most votes and were able to form a minority government with the help of the Greens.

Despite some retrenchment over the years, the "Swedish model" is not dead. As seen in Table 10.1, Sweden continues to have high tax rates and greater than average government spending and redistributive policies. Swedish trade unions also remain strong. Yet, Sweden has one of the most competitive economies in the world, boasting world-class companies such as Ericsson, Volvo, and Telia. In the World Economic Forum's 2015 Global Competitiveness Index, Sweden ranked ninth, just after Finland and before Great Britain. Sweden received strong marks for innovation, technological readiness, and business sophistication.[59] Immigration—over 10 percent of the population was born outside of Sweden, and Sweden was one of the more welcoming countries in the 2015–2016 refugee crisis—has put some strains on the system. Whereas in 2015 the overall unemployment rate (7.4 percent) was below the EU average, youth unemployment was over 20 percent.[60] Successive Swedish governments have moved to trim the welfare state due to chronic fiscal concerns, but it would be an exaggeration to suggest that there is a broad ideological push to dismantle the "Swedish model." Consensus, which admittedly is less solid than a few decades ago, rests on the idea that much of it should be preserved.

For a non-Swede who might balk at some aspects of this system—particularly the high taxes—one pertinent question might be, what explains the resiliency of the Swedish model? There are several possible answers to this query.[61] One is that Swedish society rests on notions of solidarity, meaning reciprocal responsibility or mutual obligation. In other words, the "Swedish model" is grounded in a social commitment. Second, welfare provisions in Sweden are universal in scope, not restricted just to the poor. Students, the elderly, parents, children, and workers—all can take advantage of particular features of state largesse, although, because many universal benefits are taxable, the wealthier in effect receive less than those with low incomes. Thus, while there is without question economic redistribution, most get something. According to one saying, "the richest 90 percent help support the poorest 90 percent." Lastly, considering that Sweden, by virtually any measure, has been politically and economically successful, there is no widespread call to abandon the current system. This is not to say that Sweden is paradise or that there are not potential threats to the current system (e.g., a rise in immigration, an aging population), but, overall, Sweden's continued success shows that the European welfare state is not (yet, anyway) passé or good as dead.

The impact of globalization

Europe 2020
adopted in 2010, this is a plan of the EU to bolster economic innovation and competitiveness across Europe.

Pressures to reform European economies, however, have not come only from within Europe. The argument that the high-tax and high-spending model is untenable comes less from the fact that voters have grown tired of it than from the fact that they may no longer ensure that Europe can grow and prosper in a global economy. Indeed, it is Europe's need to compete with other countries and regions that is putting pressure on European countries to become more market and business-friendly.[62] Strategies to bolster European competitiveness have been debated at both the national level and in the EU as a whole, which in 2000 unveiled its Lisbon Strategy to make the European economy more dynamic and innovative. This is followed by the **Europe 2020** plan, which had similar goals. Whether or not these strategies have borne fruit is discussed more in the **Is Europe one?** feature.

globalization
multifaceted process of growing political, economic, and social connections among countries and individuals; it is putting pressure on Europe to become more economically competitive.

Economic challenges of globalization

Western European countries, starting in the 1950s, took the lead in eliminating barriers to cross-border economic activity. The EU, in many ways, is a leading institution that promotes **globalization**, a multi-faceted process that promotes the flow of goods, information, ideas, and cultures across borders. Today the entire world is becoming globalized, whether measured by growth in trade, foreign investment, immigration, and labor flows. Individual European countries and the EU as a whole are major actors in the area of international economics. Globalization, however, has many consequences on domestic European economies and societies.

Globalization, without question, poses a challenge to the advanced industrialized states of Western Europe. Their labor costs—both in terms of wages and payroll taxes—are high. Government regulations (e.g., on the environment, safety standards, worker protections) are numerous. Other countries or regions may be more business-friendly in terms of lower taxes, fewer regulations, and labor costs that are only a fraction of those in Europe. True, German or Swedish workers may be more productive than their Chinese or Indian counterparts, but, with the difference in labor costs between Western Europe and developing countries up to fifty-fold, one might ask whether European workers are fifty times more productive. If not, there can be a real temptation to outsource jobs to lower-cost locales. Consider, for example, the highly successful Danish toymaker LEGO. LEGO maintained design and production plants in Denmark, Switzerland, and the United States. In 2006, in a cost-cutting move, LEGO agreed to outsource its production to Flextronics, a Singapore-based firm that has plants in Mexico and the Czech Republic, where wages are much lower than in Denmark or the United States. Nine hundred employees in Denmark lost their jobs as a result.[63] This story is not unique. High-end design jobs—for electronics, clothing, furniture, or any number of products—may remain in Europe, but it often makes more economic sense to move production and assembly, which requires less-skilled workers, to other places. As another example, the iconic Swedish furniture firm, IKEA, has most of its production facilities in Asia and Latin America.

In addition to worries about outsourcing, Europeans worry about how they can compete in global markets against low-cost producers. China, in particular, has been a giant exporter, producing a vast variety of goods at low cost. In 2014, the EU as a whole ran a €140 billion trade deficit with China.[64] European firms that produce similar products to those made overseas will likely, because of labor costs, find their products uncompetitive. They will be unable to sell their products, at home or for export, and thus be put out of business. One answer, of course, is to close Europe off to world markets. As tempting as this may be for some, it would be costly and is not very realistic. Another possibility is to trim labor costs and various regulations, but many fear that this will result in a "race to the bottom," with the lowest wages and standards prevailing. It is preferable, from the European standpoint, to keep a high-wage, high-productivity economy, but as China and others "catch up," many Europeans feel threatened, particularly as automation drives many productivity gains, meaning that there is strong pressure on firms to cut labor costs.

While globalization will, without question, generate "losers" who go out of business or are forced to take salary and benefit cuts, one should be careful not to exaggerate the threat. The challenge is to adjust to a globalized world and find comparative advantages so that one can compete successfully. Germany is the second-largest trading nation in the world (eclipsed by China in 2009), and numerous countries, including Sweden, the Netherlands, Ireland, and Finland, have embraced globalization and developed high-tech sectors and export-oriented firms. Tourism, which is booming globally, is boosting many European economies, particularly those in Italy, Spain, and France. As noted in Chapter 1, many European firms are global leaders in a variety of sectors ranging from aerospace to publishing to food processing. Expanding global trade can also create jobs. For example, while Chinese imports into the EU have more than doubled from 2004 to 2014, exports to China grew over three-fold,[65] meaning that some European firms are selling more to China, which is presumably creating jobs within Europe.

Is Europe one?

Can the EU help turn European economies around?

Until this point, we have primarily discussed individual European economies. While each country has its own unique features, one can nonetheless point to similarities across many European cases, particularly in Western Europe. Whereas one could argue that individual European governments can or should make many reforms to stimulate economic growth, one might also ask what can be done on the European level to strengthen economic performance.

Not surprisingly, the EU has considered this question. Many of the issues discussed in this chapter on a country-by-country basis were included in the EU's Lisbon Strategy (2000–2010) and its successor, Europe 2020 (2010–2020).[66] The Lisbon Strategy recognized that unemployment and declining international competitiveness plagued many European states. It declared that by 2010 the EU should become "the most dynamic and competitive knowledge-based economy in the world capable of sustainable economic growth with more and better jobs and greater social cohesion and respect for the environment."[67] The Lisbon Strategy placed priority on creating a healthy climate for business, modernizing education, scientific research and development, completion of the internal common market, environmental protection, and combating social exclusion by investing in human capital and putting more Europeans to work. Targets were set for growth, research investments, and employment. The EU defended the need for a broad strategy, noting that

> [o]ur economies are interdependent. Prosperity in one Member State creates prosperity in others. Sluggishness in one Member State holds others back. So Europeans need to work together to achieve economic reform, sharing policies that work. In addition, national policies alone are not enough to allow the Lisbon Growth and Jobs Strategy to succeed. European Union policies are also central to the Strategy. For example, an efficient internal market, the right policies on external trade, the updating and enforcement of EU competition law, well-targeted European research programmes, the effective use of EU Structural and Cohesion funding and the application of EU environmental policies are all crucial to delivering the prosperous and modern society which is the ultimate aim of the Lisbon Strategy.[68]

Europe 2020, devised in 2010 as Europe grappled with the global financial crisis, recognizes some new difficulties, but is not substantially different. It focuses on employment, spending in research and development, climate/energy, education, and social inclusion. Progress is monitored via the "European Semester," a yearly cycle of economic and budgetary coordination. In 2015, the Council of the European Union adopted new guidelines for Europe 2020. Among other provisions, they stipulate that:

> Moving the Union to a state of smart, sustainable and inclusive growth and job creation is the key challenge faced today. This requires coordinated and ambitious policy action at both Union and national levels, in line with the Treaty and Union economic governance. Combining supply and demand side measures, that policy action should encompass a boost to investment, a renewed commitment to structural reforms and exercising fiscal responsibility.[69]

The goals of both the Lisbon Strategy and Europe 2020 are rather unobjectionable. Europe needs more growth and employment. The more difficult question is how the EU and member countries intend to realize these objectives. As plans that reflected consensus within the EU, both the Lisbon Strategy and Europe 2020 understandably eschewed radical reforms that would be impossible to adopt and implement. Instead, the main idea was that through coordination and strategic investments, Europeans could reinvigorate their economies.

The Lisbon Strategy was, overall, a disappointment. A 2004 mid-term report, authored by a panel of experts led by former Dutch Prime Minister Wim Kok, was bluntly critical.[70] It noted that the Lisbon Strategy had an "overloaded agenda," "poor coordination," "conflicting priorities," and, most crucially, a "lack of determined political action." Heeding many aspects of the Kok Report, the EU relaunched the Lisbon Strategy in 2005. Highest priority was put on government funding for research and development (the target was 3 percent of GDP) and raising employment to 70 percent of the working age population. The opening paragraph of the relevant EU document presented an almost utopian vision:

> Just think what Europe could be. Think of the innate strengths of our enlarged Union. Think of its untapped potential to create prosperity and offer opportunity and justice for all of its citizens. Europe can be a beacon of economic, social, and environmental progress for the rest of the world.[71]

This lofty goal was far from realized. Most of the self-imposed targets of the revamped Lisbon Strategy were not met. In 2009, Swedish Prime Minister Fredrik Reinfeldt bluntly declared it a "failure." While some pointed to the voluntary nature of the Lisbon Strategy—there was nothing to compel a state to undertake reforms—others questioned the will of voters (and governments) to sacrifice security for economic dynamism.[72] By 2010, when the Lisbon Strategy officially ended, Europe found itself in the midst of economic crisis. Plans for growth and reform were largely shelved as focus turned to management of debt.

Europe 2020 recycled many aspects of the Lisbon Strategy, including setting benchmark targets for improvement. Extra emphasis is placed "smart growth" and sustainability. The EU offers recommendations to member states based upon their annual reports, but, as with the Lisbon Strategy, there are no binding commitments or punishments for states that fail to meet targets. A 2014 mid-term report noted progress in some areas, such as reducing greenhouse gas emissions and development of renewable energy, but there was limited progress in increased workforce participation, spending on research, and reducing the numbers those living at or near poverty levels. The EU noted pronounced regional divides, with more indebted states in the south and less economically developed states in the east making less progress. While the lingering effects of the global crisis was cited as one factor that limited progress, the EU often noted that "ambition" also varied, indicating that many countries were less than fully committed to the goals of Europe 2020 or, perhaps, had other priorities.[73]

Expecting much from plans such as these may be unrealistic. The EU can encourage and coordinate all it wants, but its resources are limited as the budget is under great strain. Its ability to require states to undertake difficult reforms is limited. European labor markets will always be "stickier" than trade or capital movements, for the simple reason that people may be reluctant to leave their home country for the sake of employment. The EU has no jurisdiction over issues such as payroll taxes to stimulate employment, and room to maneuver on fiscal policy is limited, as states must be worried about debt and the European Central Bank's top priority, by statute, is maintaining low inflation, not loosening the purse strings to bolster economic growth. Finally, most of the gains of integration—elimination of trade and investment barriers—have already been made. In other words, the EU has been effective in *removing* obstacles to economic growth. Arguably, it is not so well positioned with respect to *creating* structures that actively promote economic vitality.

Discussion of various targets and coordination in Europe 2020 aside, it is clear in the 2010s that Europe is increasingly divided, both in terms of economic circumstances and preferred policy response. Whereas richer states in the north such as Sweden, Germany, and the Netherlands can pursue increased competitiveness with investments in training and technology, the remedy for states in the south such as Greece and Italy may be to let wages fall so that their workers can become competitive. Chronic trade deficits in the south, combined with trade surpluses in the north, may necessitate a long-term need for intra-EU transfers of funds. Neither of these paths will be politically popular, and the viability of the eurozone can easily be questioned, particularly given divisions between those, like Germany, which favors more restrictive monetary and fiscal policy, and France and Italy, which would like to see some rules governing the euro loosened.[74] As we'll note later in the chapter, the EU did manage, with great difficulty, to put together bailout packages for Greece and other heavily indebted countries. While this may have prevented disaster, battles over how to respond to difficult economic conditions in much of the EU in the 2010s have done little to advance the cause of European unity.

Critical thinking questions

1. What additional steps can the EU take to foster economic growth and employment in Europe? Would these require strengthening the powers of the EU?
2. Does it make sense for the EU to make ambitious, multi-year growth strategies? Why can't these issues be handled at the state level?

The political problem posed by globalization

Globalization, however, is more than simply an economic phenomenon or problem. One element of globalization is immigration, an issue discussed in the next chapter and deemed threatening by many in Europe for a host of reasons. Globalization, arguably, also erodes the sovereignty of states. States are compelled to react and adapt to market forces, many of which derive beyond their own national borders. States no longer control their economic borders like they once did, as goods and services flow from country to country with fewer hindrances. Various international bodies, including the EU and the World Trade Organization (WTO), make rules that states are required to obey.

This has several repercussions. First, to the extent that states are no longer truly sovereign, it means that voters have been stripped of power as well, compromising democracy. In other words, if political actors in Paris, Athens, or Rome no longer have the power to make decisions to affect the country's economic life, then the votes of French, Greek, and Italian citizens become less relevant. Simply put, it matters less who voters elect because elected officials are at times more answerable to or influenced by other actors (e.g., the EU, international markets) than their own citizens. An example might be the euro, which was unpopular in several states. No one directly voted *for* the euro (Swedes, when given a choice in 2003, voted against), and the criteria to join the euro were devised by EU officials. These types of decisions, some argue, compromise democracy. The "democratic deficit" of the EU, discussed more in Chapter 4, is one of the reasons it is unpopular in many quarters. Indeed, the Brexit vote in 2016 was driven by many Britons desire to "take back" their country from the powers of the EU.

One could retort, however, that claims of diminished sovereignty are overblown. States have held out against some elements of integration and globalization (e.g., Sweden, Denmark, and Britain did not adopt the euro). Political leaders can resist international market pressures. In other words, leaders do not have to fall lockstep in line with market dictates. They can still do what they (or voters) want. While in principle this is true, the key point is that the consequences can be more severe today than in an era with less globalization. Global markets can harshly punish states (e.g., by withdrawing investments) if they do not abide by or adopt policies deemed to be most market-friendly. Global capital is extremely mobile. States risk angering markets at their own peril. Thus, what one has seen in a variety of countries is politicians campaigning on left-wing or populist policies (e.g., maintain or expand the welfare state, workers rights, etc.), but, once in office, they change course and begin to fall into line with expectations from the marketplace. Such was the case with Mitterrand in France in the 1980s, and in Poland, Hungary, and Sweden in the 1990s. As noted in the outset of this chapter, the left-wing Syriza party won elections in Greece in January 2015 vowing to defy the EU and resist imposition of more **austerity measures**. However, *even after* the Greek public re-affirmed his anti-austerity position in a referendum, Prime Minister Alexis Tsipras was forced to capitulate, agreeing to bailout terms including required cuts in public spending, increased taxes, pension reforms, and privatization of state assets. While hardly popular—Tsipras resigned in August as thousands of Greeks protested this change of course—the government really had little choice, as leaving the Eurozone would entail high costs and a default on its debt would have worsened the situation.

austerity measures
politically difficult measures, such as tax increases and sharp cuts in public spending, necessary to solve debt crises.

This issue, which extends to many countries in Europe, creates problems of public trust and confidence in political leadership. Politicians always campaign on the notion that they can devise policies to improve living standards, create jobs, and so on. Perhaps some can; good policies, as noted in the **In focus** section, can make a difference. However, national leaders cannot simply roll back globalization. They cannot easily bring back the jobs lost to outsourcing. Thanks to EU and global trade rules, they have lost some of their freedom to maneuver. Finally, it is hard to hold domestic political leaders accountable if the nation's economy suffers because of global economic problems (e.g., a recession in the US, an increase in energy prices, etc.). Globalization suggests the idea that large, structural economic forces, often those beyond the borders of one's own country, have more and more importance in each individual's daily life. Political leaders, arguably, are less and less relevant, less able to make a real difference. While this point remains somewhat speculative, one could, in this way, tie globalization to the loss of confidence in political institutions mentioned in Chapter 9.

Public attitudes

Public opinion surveys capture European anxiety about globalization. When asked in 2014 about whether they had positive or negative feelings about globalization, a plurality (43 percent) of respondents in the EU-28 said they viewed it positively, with 42 percent saying they viewed it negatively. Responses varied considerably across countries, with Danes (75 percent), Swedes (70 percent), and Finns (62 percent) (all of which have relatively robust, competitive economies) all more supportive of globalization, whereas the Greeks (28 percent), Cypriots (32 percent), and French (32 percent) were less likely to view globalization positively.[75] Across Europe, younger and better-educated respondents—often those more capable of adapting and functioning in a more globalized world—tend to view globalization more positively, whereas those in the working class or lower middle class do not.

When asked about how globalization affected different domains, answers are rather mixed. Table 10.4 reports results from a 2010 Eurobarometer survey. On the one hand, when asked if globalization was an opportunity for economic growth, most respondents, with the exception of the Greeks, were inclined to agree. One sees, however, significant differences between countries, with respondents in Denmark and the Netherlands, which are relatively strong economic performers, more pro-globalization than those in Italy or France, whose economic performance has not been as strong. However, when asked about different effects of globalization, one sees more skepticism. Most respondents, even in countries where people overwhelmingly saw globalization as an opportunity for growth, thought globalization increased social inequality and most also thought globalization tended to favor large companies, not individual citizens. On the latter question there is again some variance, with the Greeks and French on one extreme and the Dutch and Danes at

TABLE 10.4 Public opinion on globalization

	Globalization is opportunity for economic growth		*Globalization increases social inequalities*		*Globalization profits large companies, not citizens*		*Globalization makes global rules necessary*	
Country	*Agree*	*Disagree*	*Agree*	*Disagree*	*Agree*	*Disagree*	*Agree*	*Disagree*
Germany	63	27	69	22	64	30	81	13
France	44	41	76	14	77	14	68	17
Great Britain	62	17	49	25	60	21	58	19
Italy	49	30	54	28	55	25	67	15
Netherlands	76	15	45	41	45	43	62	28
Denmark	87	8	52	39	46	47	72	21
Greece	42	55	81	16	81	17	62	30
Finland	71	20	62	30	56	36	73	18
Ireland	60	20	56	22	60	19	62	14
Poland	53	24	54	21	61	19	65	13
Hungary	70	21	71	18	68	24	68	21
EU-27	56	27	60	23	62	23	68	16

Source: Eurobarometer 73, May 2010, available at http://ec.europa.eu/public_opinion/archives/eb/eb73/eb73_anx_full.pdf

the other. There is more consensus, however, on the idea that globalization requires more global rules, a notion that is regionally applied within the EU itself. A 2014 Eurobarometer found that only a minority (22 percent) of respondents believed that their country could cope with negative effects of globalization by itself, and a plurality (48 percent) believed that the EU enables Europeans to better benefit from the positive effects of globalization.[76] On the latter question, Greeks, Italians, and Belgians tended to disagree, whereas there was movement in favor of the EU in countries such as Portugal and Cyprus, which by 2014 had overcome the worst of the economic crisis.

Interestingly, according to data from a 2014 global survey carried out by the Pew Global Attitudes Project, Europeans tend to be less supportive of trade and foreign investment than publics in developing states such as China, Vietnam, Brazil, Indonesia, and Nigeria. For example, 28 percent of Germans, 39 percent of Greeks, 49 percent of the French, and 59 percent of Italians think that trade results more in job losses than in job creation. That view is shared by only 13 percent of Nigerians, 11 percent of Chinese, and 5 percent of Vietnamese. Americans also rank among the least enthusiastic about globalization. Overall, perhaps contrary to some expectations, there is a negative relationship between wealth and support for globalization, with poorer countries more likely to support free trade and activities of foreign companies in their country.[77]

Environmentalism

An increasingly important part of what could be dubbed the European socio-economic model is a focus on the environment and sustainable growth. Chapter 9 included some discussion on the growth of environmentalism, which manifests itself in the programs of political parties across the political spectrum. For example, when Tony Blair's Labour Party came to power in Great Britain in 1997, its election manifesto acknowledged that environmental protection is "not an add-on extra, but informs the whole of government, from housing and energy policy through to global warming and international agreements."[78] Angela Merkel of the center-right Christian Democrats in Germany—whose leader in the 1980s dismissed the Green Party as "the Trojan horse of the Soviet cavalry"[79]—has established herself as a global leader on environmental issues. As noted in the previous chapter, surveys reveal widespread support for green causes, even if they would cause economic growth to slow. Concepts such as "**sustainable development**" are now part of the political mainstream across Europe, as well as a condition for the provision of EU regional funds and development assistance to countries outside of Europe.

sustainable development
idea that economic growth must take into account its environmental impact and its consumption of natural resources so that it can be sustained over time.

The impact of environmentalism in Europe can, literally, be seen. Air quality in most European cities has improved in recent decades and is much better than that of most American cities, let alone the rapidly growing cities in Asia and Latin America. Gasoline is expensive due to high taxes, but this encourages purchase of small, fuel-efficient cars and use of bicycles and public transport. Urban planning also stresses the need for more "livable" cities, with a compact core and many pedestrian zones. Behind the scenes, environmental regulations (e.g., on water use, on energy development) are also often quite restrictive, more restrictive than those in the US. Many Europeans criticize Americans' high energy use (e.g., Americans make up 5 percent of the world's population and consume 25 percent of the world's oil) and uphold their concern for the environment as proof of the superiority of the European "model."

One should note that environmental policies have been enacted on many different levels. At the European level, as noted in Chapter 4, the EU, since the 1980s, has had an environmental policy. Over the years, the EU has set standards on items ranging from air and water quality to better farming practices and food safety to reduction of noise pollution. EU funds have been used to enhance transportation networks, in particular development of freight and passenger rail. As noted in this chapter's **Is Europe one?** feature, the EU's Europe 2020 strategy cites the need for sustainable growth. Its environmental targets—reducing greenhouse gas emissions, developing renewable sources of energy, and improving energy efficiency—are, according to a mid-term report on Europe 2020, the ones that the EU is most likely to hit.[80] Globally, as will be developed in Chapter 12, the EU aspires to environmental leadership, particularly on enacting binding cuts in carbon missions to combat global warming. Because EU environmental policy has been driven by the more environmentally conscious countries (e.g., Denmark, the Netherlands, Germany), EU mandates on the environment have progressively become "greener," compelling national governments to adopt EU standards as their own.

This is not to say that national governments have been forced to adopt "green" policies. On the contrary, many European governments have become "greener" without prodding from Brussels. Much of this stems from the environmental movement itself. For example, Great Britain adopted some laws (e.g., the Protection of Birds Act, the Litter Act) in the 1950s, but in the 1970s and 1980s legislative activity on environmental issues expanded (creation of a Department of the Environment [1970], Deposit of Poisonous Wastes Act [1972], Water Act [1973], Endangered Species Act [1976], Agriculture Act [1985], and Environmental Protection Act [1990]).[81]

Much of the push toward environmentalism, however, occurs and is supported at the local level. Recycling—everything from glass, paper, and plastics, to organic and yard waste (for composting)—is *de rigueur* in Europe, even in smaller towns. Many larger European cities, such as Paris, Vienna, Brussels, and Copenhagen, have public bicycle stations, allowing people to rent bicycles at various places around the city at low or no cost. Numerous cities have set their own targets for carbon emission cuts. London, most famously, imposed in 2003 a hefty (£8) surcharge on cars and trucks entering the city, and, in 2008, a variable fee of up to £25 was introduced for SUVs and trucks. Stockholm has followed suit. Munich has launched a major campaign to re-insulate older buildings and hopes to reduce its carbon emissions by 50 percent by 2030. Barcelona has required new buildings to install solar panels to supply at least 60 percent of the energy for hot water, a measure that Swedes, Finns, and Danes could probably not adopt. Nonetheless, perhaps the most environmentally ambitious projects are on the Danish island of Samsø, which is run almost entirely by wind energy, and in Växjö, Sweden, which pledged in 1996 to eventually stop using fossil fuels and within ten years had already cut its emissions by 30 percent by using low-emitting, leftover wood chips for heating.[82]

Lessons from Eastern Europe

To this point, this chapter has largely focused attention on the advanced industrialized states of Western Europe. However, post-communist Eastern Europe faces some different circumstances. As noted in Chapter 2, in the 1990s these states, with varying enthusiasm and degrees of success, implemented market-oriented reforms to move away from the communist economic system. These reforms included privatization, opening to international trade and finance, freeing of prices, elimination of many state subsidies, and cuts in the social safety net. These reforms were painful, producing inflation, unemployment, and decreasing living standards for many. By the end of the 1990s, however, most countries were experiencing an economic upturn. The purpose here is not to revisit that experience but to make some contemporary comparisons with Western Europe in light of what has been discussed throughout this chapter.

How are post-communist states faring?

Looking at post-communist Europe today one could argue that many of these states, economically speaking, are on the right track. True, they remain poorer than most Western European countries. For example, in 2015, Slovenia, Estonia, and the Czech Republic—three of the wealthiest post-communist countries—each had average GDP *per capita* which was about half that of wealthier West European countries such as Germany, the Netherlands, France, and Great Britain. Even taking into account purchasing-power parity, all post-communist states rate below the EU-28 average. The Czech Republic came closest (85 percent of the average), but others were much lower, such as Hungary (68 percent), Romania (57 percent), and Montenegro (41 percent). Nonetheless, for many countries the trend line is up, with growth rates for most post-communist states in the 2010s much higher than the

TABLE 10.5 Economic indicators in several post-communist states

Country	*UN HDI rank*	*Unemployment (2015)*	*Labor productivity, 2015 (100 = EU average)*	*% at risk of poverty or social exclusion,* 2014*	*UN HDI coefficient of inequality*
Slovenia	25	9.0	81.3	14.5	5.8
Czech Republic	28	5.1	79.7	9.7	5.3
Estonia	30	6.2	70.7	21.8	8.9
Slovakia	35	11.5	82.5	12.6	6.2
Poland	36	7.5	73.4	17.0	9.6
Hungary	44	6.8	69.1	15.0	7.1
Romania	52	6.8	59.2	25.4	10.2
Bulgaria	59	9.2	43.6	21.8	10.4

Source: UN Human Development Report 2015 and Eurostat

*defined by Eurostat as those with 60 percent or less of median equivalized income after social transfers

EU average. For example, in 2014 and 2015 the Czech Republic, Poland, Romania, Slovakia, and Macedonia all had economic growth at twice the average level compared to the (mostly West European) countries in the eurozone.[83]

Economic growth may not be everything, of course. Table 10.5 provides additional economic indicators for several post-communist states. As might be expected—due primarily to lower incomes—most post-communist countries rate lower on the UN HDI, although some now do crack the top thirty and rank roughly the same as countries such as Spain (26) and Italy (27). For much of the 2000s, unemployment was above 10 percent in many of these countries. Over time, however, unemployment has declined, even, in some cases, during the global financial crisis. In Table 10.5, one sees that unemployment in many countries is below the 2015 EU average of 9.4 percent. On the other hand, labor productivity lags behind the EU average in all post-communist states, a reflection, in part, of lower levels of technology in many economic sectors. In terms of poverty and inequality, one sees significant variance. Some, such as the Czech Republic and Slovakia, are well below the average "poverty" figure (17.2 percent) reported by Eurostat. Bulgaria and Romania, both significantly poorer on average, also have higher poverty rates. In terms of inequality, the higher-ranked countries on the HDI perform well compared to many states in Western Europe (see Table 10.1 for comparison), whereas, again, Romania and Bulgaria fall short, with higher levels of inequality in income, education, and health, as captured by the HDI. However, the trend on many indicators—including income, productivity, employment growth, investment, and foreign trade—is up, reflecting that several Eastern European states in the 2000s and 2010s showed more signs of economic vitality than some larger West European economies such as France and Italy.

Are they doing anything differently?

If we accept the notion that post-communist states—or, at least, some of them—have weathered the worst of the reform period in the 1990s and are on a fairly solid economic trajectory, then one logical next question is what accounts for this success? There are several possible answers. One is simply that they started at a relatively low level. After experiencing decades of problems under communism and then declines in growth in the early 1990s, post-communist states were able to reconfigure their economies, get rid of non-productive enterprises, and employ new technologies to experience high levels of growth, following up on what China, India, and other fast-growing economies have done. Most of the growth in Eastern Europe has been with new, "greenfield" investments, not in turning around moribund communist-era enterprises. In other words, many East European states began to realize their "untapped potential," something West European states cannot currently do. Secondly, one could argue that they benefitted from EU largesse in the 1990s, access to European markets, and the enlargement process itself. EU monies helped rebuild infrastructure and offset some costs of reforms; EU markets provided a convenient market for export; and enlargement helped ensure that post-communist states would implement sound economic policies and practice good governance. Eastern European states, despite years of communist mismanagement of the economy, also had a relatively highly skilled workforce. Given that labor costs in

Since the fall of communism, many companies have built factories in Eastern Europe, such as this factory in Slovakia

© AP Photo

Eastern Europe are a fraction of those in Western Europe, some, as noted in the LEGO example earlier in this chapter, were able to take advantage of economic globalization to gain foreign investment. Finally, many East European countries (like Ireland and Finland, discussed earlier) are rather small, meaning that the presence of one or two large investments or companies can make a considerable difference in total economic output; the same cannot be said for larger economies in Western Europe.

However, one could also make a strong case that many Eastern European countries benefitted themselves by adopting sound policies. In the 1990s, they implemented various reforms to encourage efficient, competitive private enterprise and move out of non-productive sectors. This was economically painful (e.g., thousands of industrial workers lost their jobs), but by the 2000s new jobs were being created in new sectors. Post-communist states were pro-active in courting foreign investors, offering relatively easy access to resources and lower corporate tax rates. For example, corporate taxes in Hungary (16 percent), Poland (19 percent), and Slovakia (19 percent) were well below the EU's average rate (31.1 percent).[84] Foreign investment in most of Eastern Europe—in sectors ranging from automobile production to software engineering to food processing to steel—grew dramatically in the 2000s. Eurostat reports that in 2011, for example, the value added by foreign owned firms totaled over a third of all the added economic value in countries such as Slovakia, Poland, Hungary, Estonia, and the Czech Republic.[85] Personal income taxes are also lower in post-communist Europe, and many states have adopted a simple flat tax system that some celebrate as much more efficient and growth-friendly.[86] Several post-communist states, including Estonia, Latvia, Lithuania, and Romania, now rank in the top forty of the Fraser Institute's Economic Freedom Index (see Table 10.2).

All of this is not to say that these states have adopted the American or Thatcherite model. Many welfare benefits have been trimmed, but overall government spending accounts for over 40 percent of GDP in several states, including Poland, the Czech Republic, Hungary, Slovakia, and Slovenia. Tax revenue totals 30 percent of GDP. In this respect, they are well within West European norms (see Table 10.1).[87] Politicians in countries such as Poland, Hungary, Slovakia, and Romania have won office on appeals to increase state spending on popular programs such as pensions. The state still provides free or low-cost health care and higher education, although private providers of both exist in many states. By joining the EU, these states have also agreed to a host of regulations over economic activity.

In terms of structural conditions, they also share some similarities with Western Europe, in particular an aging population and declining birth rates. As we'll investigate more in the next chapter, one solution would be immigration, but this has been very highly contested, to say the least, in many post-communist countries, where anti-immigrant sentiment has grown even in the absence of large-scale immigration. Arguably, one structural advantage that they do retain is that most—as of 2016, Slovenia, Estonia, Slovakia, Lithuania, and Latvia are the exceptions—are not part of the eurozone, meaning they retain control over their own currency. This means they are not subject to rules such as the Stability and Growth Pact, which (in theory at least) limits the size of a state's budget deficit. They thus have more flexibility over both fiscal and monetary policy. However, when they joined the EU, all post-communist countries pledged to eventually adopt the euro, and maintaining fiscal stability and sound monetary policy, whether using the euro or Polish zlotys or Hungarian forint, is still seen as a secret to economic success. When Hungary experienced a debt crisis in 2008, the fact that it was not in the eurozone meant that it was able (unlike Greece) to escape EU-mandated austerity, but it also meant that EU members did not feel an urgency or obligation to come to the rescue. In the end, Hungary was forced to allow the forint to fall in value against other currencies and appealed to the International Monetary Fund (IMF) for funding, but it also was able to pass legislation to allow debtors to make discounted payments on their foreign currency loans. However, when Hungary experienced another crisis in 2012, the EU did step in, temporarily suspending €495 million in cohesion funds because of the country's insufficient attention to its budget difficulties.[88]

The challenge of the global financial crisis

The difficulties of Hungary, however, were rather insignificant, at least in terms of their impact on the EU and, for that matter, the world economy, compared to the debt crisis within the eurozone itself. This was, to put it mildly, not supposed to happen, as the EU had agreed on rules to limit government debt. While some pushed the envelope in terms of the allowable three percent budget deficit, overall debt, including debt obligations of banks and individuals, rose as borrowing increased, particularly in countries with "hot" real estate markets such as Great Britain,

Ireland, and Spain. This was, perhaps, sustainable as long as depositors put money in banks and economic conditions were stable and solid enough that people were able to pay their mortgages and states could fund their debt obligations.

In retrospect, however, there were signs of trouble, even before the meltdown of fall 2008, when the collapse of the New York-based investment bank Lehman Brothers led to widespread panic, prompting many global stock indices to lose over 30 percent of their value. Growth was already slowing. Higher energy and commodity prices were stoking inflation and lowering domestic demand for many products. A sluggish US economy made it harder to export products across the Atlantic. In Eastern Europe, worries about budget deficits, growing wage costs and labor shortages, and diminishing international competitiveness meant that several states that had in the recent past seen double-digit economic growth (e.g., Estonia, Latvia, Slovakia) were dramatically lowering growth forecasts.[89]

When the global credit crunch did occur, some Europeans initially reacted with a bit of *Schadenfreude*, as they felt that America had brought this upon itself due to its financial recklessness. One Dutch newspaper crowed, "European capitalism is better suited to meet the challenge of the current financial crisis," and French President Sarkozy and then-British Prime Minister Gordon Brown suggested that there should be a fundamental re-ordering of the global financial system.[90] However, Europe was soon engulfed in the crisis, as many European banks were also heavily indebted and held mortgage assets, which, as housing prices dropped and homeowners defaulted on their loans, had less and less value. Many banks became insolvent, requiring bailouts. Credit cried up. Companies slashed their labor forces. Some heavily indebted governments found it impossible to make payments on their debt. The result was a severe economic turndown. The eurozone had a 4 percent economic decline in 2009, and unemployment began to rise, climbing to over 10 percent for the EU as a whole by 2012 and topping over 20 percent in Greece and Spain. Individual countries as well as the EU faced tough choices, as the crisis threatened to suck in more countries and perhaps lead to the collapse of the eurozone.

sovereign debt
debt assumed by country, often accrued by running chronic budget deficits and financing them by issuing bonds to domestic or foreign investors. As debt mounts, countries often have to offer higher interest rates to attract bond buyers. Also referred to as "public debt" or "national debt."

As seen in Figure 10.1, the crisis lingered for several years. After a modest recovery in 2010, growth throughout the EU was under 1 percent in 2011 and actually fell by half a percent in 2012. While by the mid-2010s the worst of the crisis seems to have passed, Europeans are still grappling with what lessons can be learned from this experience and what changes can be made to prevent a similar crisis from developing.

This final section reviews the economic crisis, focusing mostly on those states that experienced the worst problems, but also highlighting the EU's role, including the schisms that were exposed within the EU as the crisis unfolded.

The collapse of Greece

As noted in the beginning of this chapter, Greece was most seriously affected by the global financial crisis. The Greek crisis was a classic **sovereign debt** crisis, as the government accumulated far more debt than it was able to sustain. This was supposed to have been prevented, or at least made less likely, when Greece joined the eurozone in 2001. Even at that time, however, observers warned that Greece

TABLE 10.6 General government surplus/deficit as percentage of GDP

Country	*2006*	*2009*	*2012*	*2015*
EU-28	–1.6	–6.7	–4.3	-2.4
Germany	–1.7	–3.2	–.1	.7
France	–2.3	–7.2	–4.8	-3.5
Italy	–3.6	–5.3	–2.9	-2.6
Spain	2.2	–11.0	–10.4	-5.1
Ireland	2.8	–13.8	–8.0	-2.3
Greece	–5.9	–15.2	–8.8	-7.2
Sweden	2.2	–.7	–.9	0
Finland	3.9	–2.5	–2.2	-2.7

Source: Eurostat. Positive figures indicate a surplus, negative ones a deficit

had not done enough to get its economic house in order, as both its inflation and overall debt levels remained above the stated EU criteria.[91] In retrospect, reports came to light that Greek leaders had fudged the numbers to get Greece in, while at the same time EU officials did little to dig into the numbers or strongly enforce spending rules.[92] Be that as it may, once in the eurozone, Greece was able to issue bonds denominated in euros and borrow at roughly the same interest rates as countries such as Germany and the Netherlands. The Greek economy did grow in the early 2000s, but borrowing was also high. As seen in Table 10.6, even before the crisis hit, Greece's budget deficit was over 3 percent of GDP (the threshold in the EU's Growth and Pact for EU members).

All of this, perhaps, was sustainable as long as the Greek economy was growing and creditors were willing to lend at low interest rates. However, in 2008, as the global financial crisis began to gain momentum, the Greek economy began to contract. Tax revenues declined, pushing the budget deficit and overall debt up. By the fall of 2009, Greek leaders acknowledged the economy was in "intensive care," and "black holes" in government accounts meant that the budget deficit would double to 12 percent of GDP.[93] Credit rating agencies downgraded Greece's credit rating to "junk" status, meaning it would have to borrow money at higher interest rates to finance its debt. The government announced tax hikes and massive budget cuts, leading to strikes and political crisis. By early 2010, it became clear that Greece would be unable to solve this problem on its own, and it requested a bailout from the EU and the IMF.

To be sure, such a scenario was not envisioned by the architects of the euro, although in retrospect one might have been able to predict it, given Greece's overall economic record. There were, however, sharp differences in the EU about how to respond to this crisis. France, which had long championed changes in rules governing the euro to allow states to run higher deficits, took the lead in arguing in favor of a bailout. The Germans, who pushed for tighter rules on debt and saw themselves as paragons of macroeconomic management, were far more reticent to loan money to the Greeks, who, many in Germany would note, on average worked less and retired earlier than Germans and had repeatedly turned a blind eye to corruption, tax evasion, and the doctoring of economic statistics. The Germans, however, could not be entirely let off the hook, as German banks, among others, had loaned money to Greece, and other reports surfaced showing that the global investment bank Goldman Sachs had helped Greece conceal the true extent of its debt problems.[94] In short, there was enough blame to go around. Furthermore, it became clear that the consequences of not assisting Greece would be devastating: collapse of banks across Europe, more countries going under, possibly the end of the euro and the unraveling of much European economic integration.[95]

In March 2010, as it became clear that the debt crisis was spreading to other countries (discussed in the next section), Angela Merkel agreed, under pressure, to a "last resort" €40 billion bailout, but this proved insufficient to reassure markets or meet Greek needs. The EU (together with the IMF) eventually pledged €110 billion to Greece in this first bailout. It is worth noting that Slovakia, a relatively new EU member that had received EU aid to help develop its economy, refused to participate in this plan, indicating that the schisms in the EU on this issue were more than those of the rich opposed to the relatively poor. Greece was required to make numerous reforms to help balance its books, including cuts in wages of public-sector employees, tax hikes, and an increase in the retirement age. These reforms were unpopular and led to large protests, but Greece's finance minister indicated that the government had little choice, as the option was "'destruction' or saving the country."[96]

This was but the first of many EU commitments to rescue indebted countries. Also in May 2010, the EU created the European Financial Stability Facility (EFSF), which was authorized to borrow up to €440 billion to assist eurozone states in economic difficulty. EFSF funds were to be supplemented with those from the IMF and the European Financial Mechanism (EFSM), which raised funds from financial markets that would be guaranteed by the European Commission. All three were later utilized by Ireland and Portugal (see below).

In 2011, as the Greek budget deficit again topped 10 percent of GDP and the country was on the brink of another crisis, its government declared it could not meet its debt obligations and appealed for more loans. The EFSF enlarged its capital guarantee to €780 billion. In October 2011, the EU offered Greece €130 billion in EFSF funds, and put together a bailout package that included a "haircut" for lenders, as banks accepted a 50 percent write-off of some of the Greek debt. However, Greek leaders were upset with the package's austerity demands, and, as the crisis festered, they tried to bargain for a better deal with the EU. Eventually, in February 2012, the two sides reached a deal, with Greece pledging cuts in public-sector employment, wages, and pensions, and the EU offering lower interest rates and longer-term maturities for loans. The goal was to make Greece's debt sustainable and reduce it to 120 percent of GDP by 2020.

European Stability Mechanism (ESM)
established in 2012 as a crisis resolution mechanism for countries in the eurozone. It is authorized to lend up to €500 billion in conjunction with economic adjustment programs.

In October 2012, the EFSF and EFSM were replaced by the **European Stability Mechanism (ESM)**, which was established by an EU treaty and is authorized to lend up to €500 billion.[97] It, unlike the EFSF, is a permanent agency, headquartered in Luxembourg. Its financial foundation is capital provided by EU governments, which can be used to buy bonds in capital markets or provide direct financial assistance. Its shareholders are all nineteen members of the eurozone. Germany (27 percent) is the largest source of capital, followed by France (20 percent) and Italy (18 percent). One of the ESM's primary functions is to offer reassurance to investors, as it—not the indebted, borrowing state—is on the hook for loans, essentially mutualizing debt. It can therefore obtain funds at lower interest rates than what a high-risk borrower (e.g., Greece) could. States, however, have to apply for funding, which is envisioned to be conditional under adoption of reforms and budget cuts in borrowing countries. Creation of the ESM is a significant development, as it institutionalizes rescue mechanisms and provides a firewall for the euro.

The fundamental problem, however, is that while the bailouts may have stopped Greece from going off a financial cliff, it is still in dire economic trouble. Part of the problem, many believe, is the economic "medicine" prescribed by Greece's creditors, austerity, is counter-productive, as it hampers growth. Tens of thousands of Greeks have been forced off the government payroll; many more have seen wage cuts. Taxes are higher (which presumably reduces consumption and adds to the financial burden on households) and more effort has been devoted to tax collection. However, the economy has shrunk (by 25 percent from 2010–2015), meaning that, measured both in absolute terms and as a percentage of GDP, Greek debt has actually gone up even as the EU has provided emergency funding and "haircuts" and debt swaps have written off part of the debt. By early 2015, Greek debt was over €320 billion, €40 billion more than in 2012.[98] Furthermore, as younger Greeks who have economic prospects have left the country—youth unemployment in Greece is nearly 60 percent—older citizens make up more and more of the population. According to one report from 2014, nearly half (48.6 percent) of Greek families rely on pensions as their main source of income and 3.5 million employed people are supporting 4.7 million unemployed or economically inactive citizens. Such a situation, the author of the report concluded, is not a recession but the utter collapse of the Greek economy.[99]

This is the context for the emergence of Syriza and Greek voters' rejection in 2015 of EU austerity measures, mentioned at the outset of the chapter. Greeks have grown increasingly hopeless and frustrated with the EU, as well as their own political leaders. The problem, however, is that their "democratic" preference—the end of austerity, debt forgiveness, ideally more state spending to help relieve the pain of the crisis—is both subject to veto by outside forces (in particular, the Germans) and not economically feasible given Greece's financial state. Even though Syriza won elections and Greeks rejected the EU's conditions on further loans, neither, by itself, was a solution to Greece's insolvency, which generated a new crisis in June 2015 when it defaulted on a €1.6 billion payment due to the IMF. This put in jeopardy access to funds the country needed to pay wages, pensions, and other core budgetary needs, and the EU pushed its demands for more austerity and reforms in order for Greece to have access to more funds through the ESM. The government, in a surprise move, called for a referendum on conditions attached to a new bailout plan. While Greek voters decisively rejected the terms of the bailout (61 percent voted to reject the EU's proposal), this did not strengthen Greece's negotiating position, whose threatening play was massive default and withdrawal from the eurozone. It is worth noting that some economists have advocated this step, noting that continued austerity and trying to pay off debt for decades is a dead-end.[100] However, there is no doubt that it would be, at least in the short term, also highly costly for Greece. As the EU stood its ground, the Greek government closed banks and adopted capital controls to prevent complete collapse of the country's finances. Eventually, in August, Greece agreed to an €86 billion bailout plan to recapitalize Greek banks, albeit one that had harsher conditions in terms of tax increases, spending cuts, and EU oversight than the one rejected by Greek voters. Many

Greeks labeled this a "coup," and Prime Minister Tsipras resigned, although he was re-elected a month later.

In the end, while European leaders praised the deal for staving off the worst and keeping Greece in the eurozone, the Greek crisis promises to drag on. Previous austerity measures did not generate growth, and one could rightly ask why it would be different this time. Even the IMF—which did not contribute to the 2015 bailout—admits that its debt burden is unsustainable and that it will need more debt relief.[101] Politically, mending fences between Brussels and Athens will also be difficult, as will devising new rules on the euro to prevent such crises in the future.

Crisis in other EU states

Although Greece, among all European countries, has experienced the most serious and persistent economic problems in the wake of the global financial crisis, it was far from alone. In several countries, problems in banking and financial sectors led to debt, bankruptcies, rising joblessness, and economic contraction.

Iceland was among the first victims of the crisis.[102] Iceland is not in the EU or a member of the eurozone, but it is heavily integrated into the larger European economy. This was especially true for its banking sector, which expanded after deregulation in the early 2000s and accumulated significant debt obligations, particularly in real estate in Great Britain. Tiny Iceland became an important global financial player. By 2008, Iceland's three largest banks held €50 billion in debt, about €160,000 per resident and eight times the country's GDP. To offset this debt, the banks attracted overseas depositors, thanks to the country's relatively high interest rates, which led to sharp appreciation in the Icelandic króna. When American and British banks and investment houses began to experience a crisis in 2007, foreign depositors began withdrawing their money from Icelandic banks, making it impossible for them to make their debt payments. In essence, the speculative bubble popped. Because the debt was so large relative to the size of the economy, the government could not bail them out, and an EU bailout was not an option. The banks therefore went bankrupt. Afterwards, many other Icelandic companies also collapsed, the stock market lost 95 percent of its value, unemployment quadrupled to 8 percent, and the government devalued the króna by 60 percent, dramatically raising the prices of imported goods. The political fallout included the collapse of the government in January 2009 and subsequent dismissal of the Central Bank governors.

Ireland also experienced a banking crisis. Its primary cause was massive lending by Irish banks to home buyers and construction firms in the red-hot Irish real estate market in the 2000s, which grew to over 20 percent of the country's GDP. By 2008, loans to households and non-financial institutions accounted for 200 percent of GDP.[103] Most of this lending was supported with bonds issued by Irish banks, which were purchased by German, British, French, and other European investors. As with Iceland, when foreign creditors withdrew their funds and quit supplying liquidity, the banks faced bankruptcy. Unlike in Iceland, the government stepped in to guarantee the bank loans, passing emergency legislation in September 2008 to provide up to €440 billion to Irish banks, effectively putting Irish taxpayers on the hook for the debts of the privately owned banks.[104] It also appealed to the EU and

IMF for emergency loans to limit the economic damage. Still, Ireland fell into a deep economic crisis; the stock market lost 80 percent from its 2007 high, unemployment rose to over 14 percent, and thousands of foreign workers who had flocked to Ireland during its boom years left.

Although crises in both Iceland and Ireland were like Greece's debt crises they were not, as in Greece, sovereign debt crises caused by state borrowing. They were centered on private banks, which engaged in speculative loans, made possible by foreign deposits and investments. In hindsight, many also pointed to the lack of regulation in both countries. What is most striking, however, is the different responses in the two countries. In Iceland, the government let the banks go bankrupt. They did not rescue depositors or creditors. On the contrary, the Icelandic government passed an emergency law that temporarily prevented depositors from withdrawing their funds and later refused to put more money into its guarantee fund to refund bank depositors their money. This caused a political crisis with Great Britain, as many British citizens had money in Icelandic banks thanks to an "Icesave" program that had been heavily promoted.[105] Iceland was also (unlike Ireland) able to devalue its currency, which allowed it to restore its international competitiveness. In contrast, Ireland nationalized the problems of the banks, making private debts public ones. Some cheered Iceland's response, as it was evidence of a small country standing up to international pressure and defending its citizens from mistakes made by its bankers.[106] Iceland also experienced a fairly rapid post-crisis recovery, although, as seen in Figures 10.1 and 10.2, by the mid-2010s the Irish economy has also turned around.

In 2010, the European debt crisis began to spread. One victim was Portugal, which had experienced solid growth in previous years but had also been borrowing heavily. By 2009, its budget deficit approached 10 percent of GDP. Its credit rating was lowered, meaning it would now pay higher interest rates to borrow money. Initially, the government tried to solve the problem itself, through austerity measures of tax hikes and spending cuts. These proved to be insufficient. Unemployment surged above 10 percent, and in 2011 the government lost a vote of no confidence over its economic proposals. Afterward, Portugal became the third eurozone country to turn to the IMF and EU for a bailout.[107]

Greece, Iceland, Ireland, and Portugal are all relatively small economies, but even bailing them out put a clear strain on their own and European resources. When Spain and Italy—both of which had high levels of private debt and long-term problems of economic competitiveness—began showing signs that they too might require a bailout (thus leading to the rise of the acronym PIIGS [Portugal-Ireland-Italy-Greece-Spain]), there was a real fear that the EU might simply be overwhelmed, as it lacked the means to support these larger states. Like Ireland, Spain's economy rapidly grew in the early 2000s; indeed, as late as 2007 it had a budget surplus thanks to surging wages and tax revenues. However, it also, like Ireland, had a housing bubble, along with lax oversight of the banking sector. When the real estate market crashed, there was a predictable banking crisis. The economy contracted, unemployment surged, and the government adopted several unpopular reforms, including raising the retirement age, welfare cuts, and eliminating some protections for workers, leading to massive protests by the *Indignado* ("The Indignant" or "The Outraged") movement. The government also debated leaving the eurozone and then devaluing its currency to restore competitiveness.[108] In 2012, unable to solve the banking crisis with its own resources, the Spanish government applied to the EU for €100 billion to bail out and restructure its banks.[109] It became the first country to receive funds from the newly created ESM.

As for Italy, it had long been plagued by corruption, instability, and declining international competitiveness. For years its debt levels had been high compared to the rest of the other eurozone members, and as it fell into recession as a result of the global financial crisis, its debt problems mounted. By 2011, it had become the third most-indebted country in the world, topping over $1 trillion, far more than the EU could help re-finance.[110] The government struggled to come up with a response, leading to the resignation of Prime Minister Silvio Berlusconi in November 2011. His government was replaced with a technocratic government led by Mario Monti, which passed a series of austerity measures that allowed Italy to avoid asking for a bailout. Even so, Italy has struggled economically—see its low growth into the 2010s on Figure 10.1—and remains hobbled by many problems, including weakness in its heavily indebted banking sector.[111]

As a "domino effect" began to take hold, there were mounting fears that the euro could collapse.[112] Pressure was brought to bear on national and EU leaders to restore economic stability. However, as suggested with respect to the crisis in Greece, not everyone agreed on what needed to be done. Several countries, including Denmark and Germany, acted unilaterally to guarantee deposits in their own banks, but pledging funds to prop up foreign banks was a tougher sell."[113] Similarly, countries such as the Netherlands and Germany resisted adopting a stimulus program—as was done (on a rather limited scale) in the US under President Obama and in Great Britain under the Labour government that was voted out in 2010—to spur growth in Europe, in part because they already had larger social safety nets, but also for fears of exploding budget deficits as well as concern that the benefits of any national-level stimulus programs would accrue to other states as well.[114] Others, such as the French, suggested that protectionist measures might be necessary. The French government, for example, extended bailouts to French auto manufacturers, but wanted to require these companies to save jobs in France, not in factories in Slovakia or Slovenia. Other common European policies—including its competition policies, and the commitment to reduce greenhouse gases—also came under assault. Italy's Foreign Minister disparaged market-oriented economists, grouping them together with "bad teachers, exorcists, faith healers, shamans, and witch doctors."[115] The requirements of the Growth and Stability Pact, which required states to keep budget deficits under 3 percent, were also hotly debated. As seen in Table 10.6, several countries (not just the PIIGS) violated it, and many began questioning the wisdom and viability of a policy that envisioned fines as punishment for countries with high budget deficits.[116] At present, much of the debate in Europe is over the relative priority of adhering to the 3 percent threshold and reducing debt—still high in many states—or generating growth, which arguably would be facilitated by government spending and higher deficits.

Ultimately, as noted in the discussion on the Greek crisis, the EU developed a variety of mechanisms—the EFSF, the EFSM, and, finally, the ESM—to provide funds for indebted countries. These were the result of a realization that the crisis in Greece, Ireland, Portugal, etc. did not just affect those countries. Their problems had the potential to bring down others, due to, among other reasons, the fact that much Greek and Irish debt was held by German, Dutch, and French banks.

Convincing leaders of creditor countries to extend billions of euros to countries that, particularly in the cases of Greece and Spain, had mismanaged their economies, was not easy. They demanded tough conditions on borrowers, including politically unpopular austerity measures. However, increasingly there was a recognition that the costs of doing nothing or adopting piecemeal half-measures was not enough. As Mario Draghi, President of the European Central Bank (ECB), noted in 2012 in the immediate aftermath of the Spanish bailout, the ECB would do "whatever it takes" to save the euro.[117] While this did not end the crisis, together with the creation of the ESM, it did signal to markets that European leaders were more unified in facing the crisis. By 2017, even as Greece remains dependent on EU largesse and could, perhaps, still leave the eurozone, the EU appears, at high economic and political cost to be sure, to have weathered the worst of this storm.

The post-crisis agenda

The global economic crisis deeply affected many countries as well as European unity. By the mid-2010s, most states were beginning to experience economic recovery. The worst may have passed. Figure 10.1 shows that growth is up in most states, and one sees in Table 10.6 that budget deficits are down, although still rather high in Spain and Greece. Worries remain, however, that recovery is fragile and that banks in some countries still have too many bad loans on their books.[118] Without question, generating robust growth over time and ameliorating chronic problems of unemployment remain challenges in several countries. In some cases, as noted in this chapter, they pre-date the crisis. One might ask, however, whether recent developments have changed the terms of debate over economic policy, both in terms of what individual states can do as well as what the EU can do both to ensure that there is no similar crisis in the future as well as to preserve, if not strengthen, European integration.

In terms of the first issue—what political and economic actors can or should do within individual countries—there is, as one might expect, a wide diversity of views. This is reflected, in part, in traditional left/right divides, with the former advocating a greater state role in the economy and the latter generally in favor of lower taxes and pro-business policies. While many still advocate for smaller government, lower wages in countries such as Greece and Italy to restore competitiveness, and market-oriented reforms—read virtually any article in *The Economist* to find this view—what is striking is that the neoliberal agenda of Thatcher and her acolytes has lost a great deal of support. Merkel, Europe's leading figure on the center-right, is no Thatcher. While she has advocated tough reforms for indebted countries such as Greece, she has made deals at home to put off labor market reforms, establish a minimum wage, and expand family benefits.[119] This is perhaps not that surprising, as austerity or wage cuts are rarely vote winners. To the extent there is momentum in several states on the political right, it is more with anti-immigrant, nationalist parties, whose economic agenda often includes a strong state to protect (native-born) workers and restrictions on free movement of people and capital.

What is striking is that there does seem to be momentum on the political left. This is particularly true in states hardest hit by the economic crisis. Left-wing governments have won post-crisis elections in Greece, Portugal, and Italy, where austerity measures have been politically unpopular. Socialists prevailed in France in 2012, featuring a promise to raise taxes on millionaires. In Spanish elections in both 2015 and 2016, the left-wing party *Podemos*, which emerged out of the *Indignado* protest movement (which in turn was an echo of Occupy Wall Street in the US), won over 20 percent of the vote, effectively ending Spain's two-party system and complicating the formation of a new government.[120] Many economists have panned the austerity policies imposed by the EU and IMF as failures, as they did not produce growth and only imposed pain on countries already in crisis. In their analysis, the solution is more investment—not cuts—and a loosening of fiscal policy, meaning more state spending in countries such as Great Britain, Germany, and the Netherlands.[121] The economic agenda of many on the left has been influenced by the surprise best-seller *Capital in the Twenty-First Century* (2013), written by the French economist Thomas Piketty, which points to problems of economic inequality and recommends a global tax on wealth to facilitate economic redistribution.[122] Others have embraced the idea of a basic income, meaning that everyone would receive a guaranteed payment regardless of employment status, as a solution to inequality.[123]

Concerns over inequality are reflected in public opinion. A Eurobarometer survey from 2010—in the middle of the crisis—found that 88 percent of respondents across the EU believed that differences in income were too high. Eighty-five percent agreed that the government should ensure that wealth is redistributed in a fair way to all citizens, and 79 percent favored higher taxes on the wealthy to help reduce poverty.[124] Similarly, the European Social Survey (ESS) in 2014 found that over 70 percent of respondents across 20 European countries agreed that the government should do more to reduce income levels, with over 80 percent in favor in Spain, Hungary, and Portugal.[125] In terms of specific policy preferences, many Europeans believed that the financial sector should be subject to more oversight and taxes. For example, a 2013 Eurobarometer found that 81 percent of respondents favored a special tax on bank profits, 80 percent backed regulations on wages in the financial sector, 78 percent supported tighter rules for credit rating agencies, and 62 percent backed a tax on financial services.[126]

At the same time, however, European publics embrace a certain degree of economic "realism," knowing that debt is a real problem that cannot be wished away. For example, in the same 2013 Eurobarometer, most respondents (77 percent) agreed that measures to reduce debt cannot be delayed. Greeks (59 percent) were least keen on this proposition, but it found strong support (80 percent or more) among the Irish, Italians, Portuguese, as well as (more predictably) Finns, Germans, and Swedes. In June 2016, Swiss voters were given a chance to approve a basic income measure that would guarantee each adult 2,500 Swiss francs ($2,555) a month, a figure that reflects Switzerland's high cost of living but that undoubtedly would entail high costs to taxpayers. This was overwhelmingly (77 percent against) rejected. [127] Furthermore, as noted earlier in the discussion on France, even if parties on the left are elected, they may abandon some of their policies and even press ahead with reforms championed on the right that give more power to employers while stripping away some protections for workers (e.g., 2016 changes in French labor law). In other words, there is no certainty that a vote for parties that reject austerity or endorse state spending or social welfare protections will lead to a policy shift in that direction.

In light of the crisis, there have also been intense debates about what (if anything) the EU can do.[128] Obviously, there are some, such as those championing Brexit, who have given up on the EU. They would like to see their countries leave it or, if this proves impossible, undo certain aspects of integration (e.g., open borders) and/or take away many of the EU's powers, returning them to national governments. Particular attention has been devoted to the euro, which, one might note, was never popular in some quarters of Europe, especially Germany, where the anti-euro Alternative for Germany party has emerged in the 2010s as a potent political force. Those arguing for the end of the euro do so both in terms of national sovereignty and economic rationality, noting that the ability to devalue one's currency unilaterally (as Iceland was able to do) can be an effective means to restore competitiveness. While such a position may attract adherents on the fringes of the nationalist right and the far-left, this position has yet to be embraced by more mainstream parties or leaders.

There are, however, others who believe that the proper response to the crisis is not to slow down or retreat from integration but to push forward with new reforms to strengthen the EU, both to ensure economic stability but also improve governance by eliminating the EU's "democratic deficit" and connecting better with citizens. Piketty, for example, advocates mutualization of debt, creation of a separate eurozone parliament to promote greater fiscal integration and development of a common social safety net, the loosening of strict fiscal criteria in the governance of the euro (e.g., increasing the threshold on allowable budget deficits), and a common corporate tax.[129] The German sociologist Claus Offe, also on the political left, also supports more integration, including tax harmonization, development of EU-wide unemployment insurance and poverty relief, a commitment to combat inequality, a write-off of some sovereign debt, EU-wide guarantees for youth employment, and more redistribution from richer states to poorer ones. He also believes the EU must empower and develop elected bodies, which would have more control over the European Central Bank and the European Commission. He believes the EU must become a "supranational democracy."[130] One idea that has been floated by the European Commission is issuing of **Eurobonds**, debt investments which would be issued and guaranteed jointly by all nations in the eurozone. These would allow indebted countries—which by themselves would have higher interest rates on bonds because of the perceived high-risk in loaning them money—to borrow at lower interest rates, as they would be able to take advantage of being part of a group that is presumably less of a credit risk.[131] If enacted, these reforms would create a much stronger EU, one with powers akin to a national government and one, arguably, more capable of ensuring the continent's economic success.

Eurobonds
jointly issued bonds that would allow the higher-risk, more indebted euro members to borrow at lower interest rates. Proposed by the European Commission in 2011, they were rejected by creditor states such as Germany.

Leaving aside the question of their desirability, one might also ask how politically realistic these proposals are. Certainly, European publics have not given up on the EU, and there is ample evidence to suggest citizens would support some expansion of EU powers. For example, the aforementioned 2013 Eurobarometer found that respondents were equally split on whether the EU or national governments would be the most effective agent to help resolve the economic crisis, and over 90 percent favored greater cooperation among EU members. In terms of policy recommendations, there was broad support for more EU regulation of financial services and more accountable governance of the euro (75 percent for each), a Banking Union (70 percent), and imposition of fines for countries that borrow too much (63 percent).

Majorities also favored what might be viewed as more "radical" moves against national sovereignty, including EU approval of state's budgets (58 percent) and creation of an EU finance minister (52 percent).[132] Most of these proposals, one might note, are directed at the more indebted states. When asked about Eurobonds—which could impose costs on creditor states, as they would be on the hook if another euro member threatened to default on them[133]—respondents were less enthusiastic, with only 44 percent in favor. Not surprisingly, one found a large difference between Greeks (58 percent in favor) and Germans (25 percent in favor).

This divide points to a larger political problem, one that both Piketty and Offe acknowledge, which is that most of these suggested measures to strengthen or reform the EU are not likely to be politically palatable. Germans, for example, are not going to favor transferring management of the euro to elected bodies or a eurozone parliament or introduction of Eurobonds, the latter of which was rejected by Merkel in 2012. While in the short term Greeks may have little choice but to submit to EU-imposed measures, in effect handing over their economic sovereignty to Brussels (and Berlin), how long this can be sustained is a good question. Offe makes the key point that the problem is that European leaders must respond to the given preferences of their national voters. They gain little—in fact, they could lose a lot—by appealing to a pan-European constituency. He thus notes that the necessary reforms, to which everyone can agree "in principle," are "virtually impossible" to carry out, as they cannot be "sold" to the voting publics of both the "core" and "periphery." The solution, he suggests, is that political leaders must have the courage to re-shape existing preferences to overcome "widespread fears, sentiments of distrust, suspicion, a propensity to victim-blaming, and the prevalence of national frames."[134]

This assessment was given in early 2015, before the political drama that surrounded the 2015 bailout package for Greece, a development that clearly runs counter to ideals envisioned by Offe and others who hope for a more unified and democratic Europe. It is fair to say that the EU still has work to do, politically as well as economically, to deal with the fallout of the global financial crisis. By the end of 2015, however, European unity was perhaps even more seriously tested by a new crisis, an influx of refugees and migrants from the Middle East and North Africa. This is taken up in the next chapter.

Application questions

1. Few people relish paying taxes, yet tax rates in much of Europe are, by world standards, quite high. Why do you think Europeans have been willing to pay higher taxes?
2. The European social welfare state is derided by critics—both in Europe and (in particular) in the United States—as outmoded, too costly, inefficient, and inimical to growth. Do you think this is a fair assessment, or would you defend elements of the welfare state?
3. Do all people benefit equally from globalization? Who "wins"? Who "loses"? Can governments and the EU take action to lessen the negative effects of globalization?

4. How did the Greek economic crisis become a large-scale political and economic crisis for Europe as a whole? What does this crisis say about European political unity and about the future of the euro?
5. What are the differing priorities and values of the political right and left in terms of economic policy? Do you believe the arguments of the political right or left are currently more ascendant in terms of debates over the economy and steps needed to generate growth? Which do you find more compelling?

Key terms

Additional reading

Alesina, Alberto, and Giavazzi, Francesco. 2008. *The Future of Europe: Reform or Decline?*. Cambridge MA: MIT Press.
An accessible analysis of many economic problems facing Europe today. In particular, the authors point to problems of overregulation in fields ranging from business development to education. They also offer a variety of solutions which they believe will enhance competitiveness and growth, most of which are more market-oriented.

Eurostat (Statistical service of the European Union), available at http://ec.europa.eu/eurostat.
A wealth of data on economic and other topics. User-friendly, includes links to publications that provide more analysis on topical issues.

Laqueur, Walter. 2007. *The Last Days of Europe: Epitaph for an Old Continent*. New York: St. Martin's.
Laqueur presents a useful contrast to more positive accounts of contemporary Europe, arguing that Europe faces the prospect of an immense long-term economic crisis because it has declining birth rates and can no longer pay for its welfare system.

Offe, Claus. 2015. *Europe Entrapped*. Cambridge: Polity.
A short but incisive analysis of the financial crisis in Europe. The author points to numerous problems, including poor management of the euro. He argues that solutions that would strengthen Europe and prevent such crises are available, but they require political leaders to take bold, perhaps unpopular actions.

Reid, T.R. 2004. *The United States of Europe: The New Superpower and the End of American Supremacy*. New York: Penguin.
Within a larger argument explaining the emergence of Europe as a "superpower," Reid makes a favorable evaluation of European economies in terms of provision of social welfare, technological innovations, and maintenance of equality.

Russell, James. 2014. *Double Standard: Social Policy in Europe and the US*, 3rd edition. Latham MD: Rowman and Littlefield.
This book traces the development of the welfare states on both sides of the Atlantic, analyzing why they evolved so differently. It compares policies on issues such as education, health care, and family support, and, although not as one-sided as some treatments, it makes a fairly strong case for the superiority of the European model.

Wallace, Paul. 2015. *The Euro Experiment*. Cambridge: Cambridge University Press.
A clear, analytical guide to the origins of the euro crisis. It focuses on issues of sovereign debt, banking, private debt, macroeconomic imbalances, defective economic governance, and the interplay of national and European politics. While not overly Euroskeptic, the account is a sober assessment of problems plaguing both European economies and the EU.

Notes

1 For background on the crisis, see "Greece Debt Crisis: Timeline," *The Guardian*, May 5, 2010 and May 9, 2012, at www.theguardian.com/business/2010/may/05/greece-debt-crisis-timeline and www.theguardian.com/business/2012/mar/09/greek-debt-crisis-timeline.
2 Greece's budget deficit as percentage of gross domestic product (GDP) soared to 13 percent in 2010, and the ratio of its public debt to GDP swelled to 130 percent, both far above EU guidelines for the eurozone. Articles from *The Economist*, March 6, 2010 and March 27, 2010.
3 For a good review of the origins and dynamics of the Greek crisis, see Nicos Christodoulakis, *Greek Endgame: From Austerity to Growth or Grexit* (Lanham MD: Rowman and Littlefield, 2016).
4 For more detailed analysis, see Damian Chalmers, Markus Jachtenfuche, and Christian Joerges, eds. *The End of the Eurocrats Dream: Adjusting to European Diversity* (Cambridge: Cambridge University Press, 2016), and Claus Offe, *Europe Entrapped* (Cambridge: Polity, 2015).
5 Jan Zielonka, *Is the EU Doomed?* (Cambridge: Polity, 2014).
6 "Eurozone GDP Returns to Pre-Crisis Levels," *Financial Times*, April 29, 2016.
7 For more on the development of social and welfare policy in Europe, see James Russell, *Double Standard: Social Policy in Europe and the United States*, 3rd edition (Lanham MD: Rowman and Littlefield, 2014).
8 For more, see Paul Wallace, *The Euro Experiment* (Cambridge: Cambridge University Press, 2015).
9 Tony Judt, *Postwar: A History of Europe Since 1945* (New York: Penguin, 2005), p. 540.
10 Interview in *Woman's Own*, September 23, 1987.
11 For extended discussions, see Earl Reitan, *The Thatcher Revolution* (Lanham MD: Rowman and Littlefield, 2003), and Anthony Seldon and Daniel Collings, *Britain Under Thatcher* (New York: Longman, 1999).
12 Judt, *Postwar*, p. 541–542.
13 Reitan, *The Thatcher Revolution*, p. 77–78.
14 Judt, *Postwar*, p. 544.
15 All data compiled from OECD (Organization for Economic Cooperation and Development), *Main Economic Indicators* (various issues).

16 For extended discussion of Europe's economic problems prior to the global economic crisis, see Alberto Alesina and Francesco Giavazzi, *The Future of Europe* (Cambridge MA: MIT Press, 2008).
17 This indicator is far better than comparing, for example, marginal tax rates, because it takes into account deductions and rebates that create lower actual tax payments, and it also takes into account the higher value-added taxes that account for much of the difference between the US and Europe.
18 Data from Eurostat, at ec.europa.eu/Eurostat.
19 For more details on this, see Alesina and Giavazzi, *The Future of Europe*, 2008.
20 Data from OECD, same as in Table 10.1.
21 For example, a 2014 Eurobarometer survey found that 69 percent of respondents had a positive view on both competitiveness and competition, but 63 percent also had a positive view of the welfare state. See Eurobarometer 82, Autumn 2014, at http://ec.europa.eu/public_opinion/archives/eb/eb82/eb82_anx_en.pdf, accessed August 18, 2016.
22 For example, see Joseph Stiglitz, *Freefall: America, Free Markets, and the Sinking of the World Economy* (New York: Norton, 2010).
23 Data are from the OECD, GDP per hour worked. Belgium, the Netherlands, and Norway had higher figures than the US for 2007–2008, but by 2014 only Norway was higher than the US.
24 Data from *OECD in Figures, 2007* (Paris).
25 Good reviews of the turnaround in Ireland can be found in Joseph Harris, "Ireland Unleashed," *Smithsonian*, March 2005, and Sean Dorgan, "How Ireland Became the Celtic Tiger," The Heritage Foundation, June 23, 2006, at www.heritage.org/Research/WorldwideFreedom/bg1945.cfm.
26 Data from Eurostat. Finnish GDP was $38,200 in 2015.
27 Reports from World Economic Forum available at www3.weforum.org/docs/WEF_Europe2020_CompetitivenessReport_2014.pdf and http://reports.weforum.org/global-competitiveness-report-2015-2016/economies/#economy=FIN, accessed August 18, 2016.
28 Robert Kaiser, "Innovation Gives Finland a Firm Grasp on Its Future," *Washington Post*, July 14, 2005.
29 Darius Ornston, "Reorganising Adjustment: Finland's Emergence as a High Technology Leader," *West European Politics* 29:4, September 2006, p. 784–801.
30 Data from Eurostat at http://ec.europa.eu/eurostat/tgm/table.do?tab=table&init=1&plugin=1&pcode=tsc00001&language=en, accessed August 18, 2016.
31 See "Suutarila Journal: Educators Flocking to Finland, Land of Literate Children," *The New York Times*, April 9, 2004, and "Back to School," *The Economist*, March 23, 2006, and "How to Be Top," *The Economist*, October 18, 2007.
32 Useful (if dated) sources are Jeremy Rifkin, *The European Dream* (New York: Penguin, 2004), T.R. Reid, *The United States of Europe* (New York: Penguin, 2004), and Tony Judy, *Ill Fares the Land* (New York: Penguin, 2010). More sophisticated treatment is available in Jonas Pontusson, *Inequality and Prosperity: Social Europe vs. Liberal America* (Ithaca: Cornell University Press, 2005).
33 Tony Judt, "Europe vs. America," *New York Review of Books*, February 10, 2005.
34 Poverty data are very difficult to compare cross-nationally. The EU reports figures on those at risk of poverty or social exclusion; the US measures poverty based on income levels. These figures, from the 2010s, come from Index Mundi, www.indexmundi.com/map/?v=69.
35 The UN Human Development Report 2007/2008 notes that *per capita* electricity consumption in the US is double the rate in France, Germany, Italy, and Great Britain. Scandinavians, with their long and cold winters, use roughly the same as Americans.
36 Reitan, *The Thatcher Revolution*, p. 159, 167.
37 Anthony Giddens, The Third Way: The Renewal of Social Democracy (London: Polity, 1998). See also James Cronin, New Labour's Pasts: The Labour Party and Its Discontents (New York: Pearson, 2004).
38 For a critique of Blair, see Geoffrey Wheatcroft, "The Tragedy of Tony Blair," *The Atlantic Monthly*, June 2004.
39 Paul Krugman, "Gordon Does Good," *The New York Times*, October 12, 2008.

40 The National Health Service and international aid were the two areas free of cuts. See "Britain Announces Sweeping Austerity Measures," Radio Free Europe/Radio Liberty, October 20, 2010, at www.rferl.org/content/Britain_Announces_Sweeping_Austerity_Measures/2196108.html, accessed August 21, 2016.
41 "Cameron Promises Another Dose of Austerity as British Elections Near," *The New York Times*, March 16, 2015.
42 Jonathan Freedland, "A Howl of Rage," *The New York Review of Books*, 43:13, August 18, 2016, p. 4–8.
43 Total tax and nonwage costs of employment (e.g., health and unemployment insurance, sick pay, vacations, pensions) are estimated to add 40 percent to the basic wage earned by a worker.
44 "Merkel Is the Message," *The Economist*, June 27, 2009.
45 "Germany's Economic Policy Is Hurting Europe, the World, and Itself," *The Economist*, February 15, 2015.
46 "Going Backwards," *The Economist*, April 26, 2014.
47 *The Economist* (European edition), October 28, 2006.
48 "Survey of France," *The Economist*, October 28, 2006.
49 Data from OECD, at https://data.oecd.org/tax/social-security-contributions.htm#indicator-chart, accessed August 22, 2016.
50 Data from OECD, at https://data.oecd.org/gga/general-government-spending.htm#indicator-chart and https://data.oecd.org/gga/general-government-debt.htm#indicator-chart, accessed August 22, 2016. Comparable government debt figures were 64 percent of GDP for Germany, 53 percent for Britain, and 52 percent for Sweden. State spending in both Germany and Britain, meanwhile, was under 43 percent of GDP
51 Lionel Jospin, *Modern Socialism* (London: Fabian Society, 1999), p. 1.
52 William Pfaff, "France: The Children's Hour," *New York Review of Books*, May 11, 2006, p. 40–43.
53 Charles Grant, "Sarkozy—The New Napoleon," *The Guardian*, April 23, 2007.
54 "Attali the Hun," *The Economist*, January 26, 2008.
55 See notes 47 and 48.
56 "Working Nine to Four," *The Economist*, March 5, 2016.
57 "France Forced to Drop 75% Supertax After Meagre Returns," *The Guardian*, December 31, 2014.
58 "French President Bypasses Lower House on Labor Law Changes," *The New York Times*, May 10, 2016.
59 A fuller report on Sweden from the World Economic Forum can be found at http://reports.weforum.org/global-competitiveness-report-2015-2016/economies/#economy=SWE, accessed August 19, 2016.
60 Data from Eurostat.
61 Eric Einhorn and John Logue, Modern Welfare States: Scandinavian Politics and Policy in the Global Age (Westport CT: Praeger, 2003).
62 See Steven Weber, *Globalization and the European Political Economy* (New York: Columbia University Press, 2001).
63 "Outsourcing Move by Lego," *The New York Times*, June 21, 2006.
64 Data from European Commission, at http://ec.europa.eu/trade/policy/countries-and-regions/countries/china/, accessed May 2, 2016.
65 EU trade data, at http://ec.europa.eu/trade/statistics, accessed March 30, 2016.
66 More on Europe 2020 can be found at http://ec.europa.eu/europe2020/index_en.htm, accessed August 19, 2016.
67 "Facing the Challenge: The Lisbon strategy for growth and development," report from high level group chaired by Wim Kok, November 2004, at http://ec.europa.eu/growthandjobs/pdf/kok-reportem.pdf, accessed on February 4, 2008.
68 Taken from EU "Jobs and Growth" website, at http://ec.europa.eu/growthandjobs/faqs/background/index_en.htm, accessed February 4, 2008.
69 Taken from Council of the European Recommendation of July 14, 2015, at http://ec.europa.eu/europe2020/pdf/eu2020_20151407_economic_policies.pdf, accessed August 19, 2016.

70 "Facing the Challenge," 2004.
71 Commission of the European Union, "Working Together for Growth and Jobs: A New Start for the Lisbon Strategy," COM(2005) 24 final, February 2, 2005.
72 "Sweden Admits Lisbon Strategy Failure," *Euractiv.com*, June 3, 2009, and Charlemagne, "Do Europeans Want a Dynamic Economy?," *The Economist*, January 8, 2010. For more comprehensive treatment, see Laurent Cohen-Tanugi, *Beyond Lisbon: A European Strategy for Globalisation* (New York: Peter Lang, 2008).
73 Communication of the European Commission, "Taking Stock of the Europe 2020 Strategy," March 19, 2014, at http://ec.europa.eu/europe2020/pdf/europe2020stocktaking_annex_en.pdf, accessed August 19, 2016.
74 Meryn King, The End of Alchemy: Money, Banking, and the Future of the Global Economy (New York: Norton, 2016).
75 Eurobarometer 82, Autumn 2014, at http://ec.europa.eu/public_opinion/archives/eb/eb82/eb82_anx_en.pdf, accessed August 14, 2016.
76 Eurobarometer 82, Autumn 2014, at http://ec.europa.eu/public_opinion/archives/eb/eb82/eb82_anx_en.pdf, accessed August 14, 2016.
77 Pew Global Attitudes Project, "Faith and Skepticism about Trade, Foreign Investment," September 2014, at www.pewglobal.org/2014/09/16/faith-and-skepticism-about-trade-foreign-investment/, accessed August 17, 2016.
78 Cited in John Callaghan, "Environmental Politics, the New Left and the New Social Democracy," *The Political Quarterly* 71:3, 2000, p. 301.
79 Franz-Josef Strauss, quoted in Ramachandra Guha, *Environmentalism: A Global History* (New York: Longman, 2000), p. 97.
80 Communication of the European Commission, "Taking Stock of the Europe 2020 Strategy," March 19, 2014, at http://ec.europa.eu/europe2020/pdf/europe2020stocktaking_annex_en.pdf, accessed August 19, 2016.
81 Robert Garner, *Environmental Politics: Britain, Europe, and the Global Environment* (New York: St. Martin's Press, 2000), p. 153.
82 "Europe's Cities Take the Lead in Cutting Emissions," *Christian Science Monitor*, December 12, 2007.
83 Data culled from Eurostat tables, at http://ec.europa.eu/eurostat/web/national-accounts/data/main-tables, accessed August 18, 2016.
84 *OECD in Figures*, 2007.
85 Eurostat data, at http://ec.europa.eu/eurostat/tgm/table.do?tab=table&init=1&language=en&pcode=tec00024&plugin=1, accessed August 18, 2016.
86 See debate over this issue in "Flat Taxes," *The Economist Intelligence Unit*, January 18, 2007.
87 2014 data from OECD, at www.oecd.org, accessed August 19, 2016.
88 Akoa Valentinyi, "The Hungarian Crisis," Centre for Economic Policy Research, March 19, 2012, at http://voxeu.org/article/hungarian-crisis, accessed August 1, 2016.
89 "Dangers Ahead," *The Economist*, February 16, 2008, and "The Party Is Nearly Over," *The Economist*, August 16, 2008.
90 "Suddenly Europe Looks Pretty Smart," *New York Times*, October 19, 2008.
91 "Greek Joins Eurozone," BBC News, January 1, 2001, at http://news.bbc.co.uk/2/hi/business/1095783.stm.
92 "Greece Admits Fudging Euro Entry," BBC News, November 15, 2004, at http://news.bbc.co.uk/2/hi/business/4012869.stm, and "How 'Magic' Made Greek Debt Disappear Before It Joined the Euro," *BBC News*, February 3, 2012, at www.bbc.com/news/world-europe-16834815.
93 For more, see sources in note 1.
94 "How Goldman Sachs Helped Greece Mask Its True Debt," Spiegel On-Line, February 8, 2010, at www.spiegel.de/international/europe/greek-debt-crisis-how-goldman-sachs-helped-greece-to-mask-its-true-debt-a-676634.html.
95 One is reminded of a statement of the famous economist John Maynard Keynes, "If you owe a bank a hundred pounds, you have a problem. If you owe it a million, it has a problem." Multiply the latter by 250,000, and you can understand the dilemma posed by the Greek debt crisis.

96 See report from CNN, May 2, 2010, at http://money.cnn.com/2010/05/02/news/international/greece_bailout/.
97 Its website is www.esm.europa.eu.
98 See data from www.tradingeconomics.com/greece/government-debt-to-gdp and www.tradingeconomics.com/greece/government-debt.
99 "This Could Be the Moment for Greece to Default," *Financial Times*, April 13, 2014.
100 For example, see Paul Krugman, "Grexit and the Morning After," *The New York Times*, May 25, 2015.
101 "Will Greek Debt Deal Really Change Anything?," BBC News, May 25, 2016, at www.bbc.com/news/business-36376836.
102 This section draws from Rok Spruk, "Iceland's Financial and Economic Crisis: Causes, Consequences, and Implications," European Enterprise Institute Policy Papers, 2010, at http://papers.ssrn.com/sol3/papers.cfm?abstract_id=1574296, and Elizabeth Matsangon, "Failing Banks, Winning Economy: The Truth About Iceland's Economy," *World Finance*, September 15, 2015, at www.worldfinance.com/infrastructure-investment/government-policy/failing-banks-winning-economy-the-truth-about-icelands-recovery, both accessed September 5, 2016.
103 This section borrows significantly from Morgan Kelly, "The Irish Credit Bubble," University College Dublin Centre for Economic Research Working Paper, 2010, at www.ucd.ie/t4cms/wp09.32.pdf.
104 For a humorous take on this crisis that features cartoon robots while noting the dismay and anger of many in Ireland, see www.youtube.com/watch?v=vLniOkpl1QY.
105 The dispute dragged on for several years, but British depositors received only 2 percent of their claims on Icelandic banks, with the remainder being paid by British government guarantee funds. See "Icesave: Icelandic Government Winds Compensation Ruling," BBC News, January 28, 2013, at www.bbc.com/news/business-21231535.
106 See in particular Matsangon, 2015.
107 For a timeline of developments in Portugal, see reports from *The Wall Street Journal*, at www.wsj.com/articles/SB10001424052748704904604576335101867151090.
108 Indeed, the Spanish peseta was informally introduced in parts of Spain. See "The Spanish town That's Bringing Back the Peseta," *The Guardian*, February 14, 2012.
109 "Spanish Banks to Get up to 100bn in Rescue Loans," BBC News, June 9, 2012, at www.bbc.com/news/business-18382659.
110 "Debt Crisis Threatens Italy, One of Eurozone's Biggest Economies," *The Washington Post*, July 12, 2011.
111 "Italy Economy: IMF Says Country Has Two Lost Decades of Growth," *BBC News*, July 12, 2016, at www.bbc.com/news/business-36770311.
112 "In and Out of Each Other's European Wallets," *New York Times*, May 2, 2010, and "Acropolis Now," *The Economist*, May 1, 2010.
113 "The European Union's Week from Hell," *The Economist*, October 11, 2008.
114 Charlemagne, "Fingers in the Dyke," *The Economist*, March 21, 2009.
115 "Creeping Along," *The Economist*, September 27, 2008.
116 Charlemagne, "Rules of the Brussels Club," *The Economist*, September 11, 2010.
117 Draghi's July 26, 2012 speech, at www.ecb.europa.eu/press/key/date/2012/html/sp120726.en.html.
118 In 2016, the main worry is banks in Italy, which have some €360 billion in non-performing loans on their books. See report at www.cnbc.com/2016/07/26/italy-this-summers-euro-zone-crisis.html.
119 "Germany's Merkel Avoids Painful Economic Reforms," *Bloomberg News*, July 18, 2014, at www.bloomberg.com/news/articles/2014-07-17/germanys-merkel-avoids-painful-economic-reforms.
120 For more on *Podemos*, see a series of articles in *The Guardian*, at www.theguardian.com/world/podemos, accessed September 5, 2016.
121 For a critique of austerity focusing in particular on the British case, see Paul Krugman, "The Austerity Delusion," *The Guardian*, April 29, 2015.

122 An edition in English was published by Harvard University's Belknap Press in 2014. A shorter exposé of Piketty's core ideas can be found in Piketty, *The Economics of Inequality* (Cambridge: Belknap Press, 2015).
123 Tony Atkinson, *Inequality: What Can Be Done?* (Cambridge: Harvard University Press, 2015).
124 "Poverty and Social Exclusion," Special, Eurobarometer 355, 2010, at http://ec.europa.eu/public_opinion/archives/ebs/ebs_355_en.pdf.
125 Online analysis of the ES at http://nesstar.ess.nsd.uib.no/webview/.
126 "Europeans, the European Union, and the Crisis," Standard Eurobarometer 80, Autumn 2013, at http://ec.europa.eu/public_opinion/archives/eb/eb80/eb80_cri_en.pdf.
127 "Guaranteed Income for All? Switzerland's Voters Say No Thanks," *The New York Times*, June 5, 2016.
128 For example, see various contributions in Nikolaos Papakostas and Nikos Pasamitros, eds. *EU: Beyond the Crisis: A Debate on Sustainable Integrationism* (New York: Columbia University Press, 2016), and Hans-Wolfgang Platzer, "Rolling Back or Expanding European Integration," Freidrich Ebert Stiftung Policy Paper, 2014, available at http://library.fes.de/pdf-files/id/ipa/10527.pdf.
129 Thomas Piketty, "A New Deal for Europe," *The New York Review of Books*, February 25, 2016.
130 Offe, 2015, p. 119.
131 See proposal by the European Commission from November 2011 at http://europa.eu/rapid/press-release_MEMO-11-820_en.htm, accessed September 9, 2016.
132 "Europeans, the European Union, and the Crisis," Standard Eurobarometer 80, Autumn 2013, at http://ec.europa.eu/public_opinion/archives/eb/eb80/eb80_cri_en.pdf.
133 Perhaps the simplest way to understand this is that it is like parents co-signing a loan for their children. The children have little or no credit history. Banks would either not lend to them or charge them a much higher interest rate. By co-signing, the parents help the child obtain a lower interest rate, but should the child be unable to repay the loan, the parents are obligated to do so.
134 Offe, 2015, p. 4.

A German woman hands out chocolate bars to migrants from Syria, 2015

Chapter 11

Immigration and multi-culturalism in contemporary Europe

In September 2015, an important faultline running through contemporary Europe was exposed by scenes at two train stations located about 700 kilometers from each other.[1] At issue was how to respond to the refugee crisis, as tens of thousands of refugees,[2] mostly from Syria, were making their way through Turkey, Greece, and the Balkans into Central Europe, hoping to find refuge and asylum. Antonio Guterres, the UN High Commissioner for Refugees, declared it a "defining moment for the EU." In Budapest's Keleti station, thousands of desperate refugees were prohibited from boarding westward-bound buses or trains, creating a squalid refugee camp in the heart of the Hungarian capital. This was but one example of the general hostility displayed by the Hungarian government toward the refugees, as Hungarian officials blamed the crisis on the EU and Germany and Prime Minister Viktor Orbán claimed to be defending Europe against a Muslim invasion. Amid mounting international pressure, the Hungarian government eventually agreed to let the refugees leave for Austria and Germany. Upon arrival in Munich's *Hauptbahnhof*, thousands of refugees were welcomed by Germans with donations of food, blankets, medicine, and toys. Community centers across Germany provided shelter for refugees. This was hailed by many as an example of *Willkommenskultur* ("welcome culture"). Chancellor Angela Merkel was lauded by many for taking leadership on this issue, framing it as an expression of "European values" to help those in desperate need and stating that Germany would be willing to take in up to 800,000 refugees.

This was, by no means, the end of the crisis. Merkel's plan to assign each EU member a quota of refugees generated fierce opposition in several countries. The right of free movement of people within the EU was called into question by many. Some countries, including Slovenia and Denmark, closed borders and/or re-established border controls. Hungary built a three-meter high fence topped with razor wire across its entire border with Serbia. In October 2016, Hungarians voted overwhelmingly (98 percent) against the EU's quota-based re-settlement scheme, although the results were not valid because only a minority of voters (41 percent) bothered to vote.[3]

While Hungary may have adopted the most hostile position in Europe toward refugees, anti-immigration parties gained traction in several countries as the crisis deepened. Most notably, Merkel's own position was challenged both within her Christian Democratic party and by the nationalist Alternative for Germany party, which fared well in 2016 German regional elections. *Willkommenskultur* has given way to a plan to pay Turkey to keep and take back refugees, and in October 2016 the EU announced a plan to send tens of thousands of Afghan refugees/migrants back to Afghanistan.[4] The dramatic events surrounding the 2015–2016 refugee crisis are discussed more in the latter part of this chapter.

While the refugee crisis in Europe generated headlines and controversy, it is a more recent manifestation of a longstanding issue, as Europeans have been grappling with demographic changes and transformation of their countries into multi-cultural societies. On the one hand, the influx of refugees could be considered an affirmation of the accomplishments and ideals of "Europe" itself, as large numbers of people seek security, opportunity, and freedom that they cannot enjoy in their homeland. On the other hand, new arrivals may not share the traditional values and beliefs of native Europeans, and their presence can create economic, social, and political challenges. Debates over issues of immigration and multiculturalism rank among the most interesting and contested in Europe. Tony Judt, an esteemed historian of modern Europe, argued over a decade ago that issues of immigration and integrating existing minorities, particularly Muslims, constitute Europe's "true dilemmas."[5] By the 2010s, the problems had become arguably more acute. Thomas Friedman, a prominent cheerleader for globalization, conceded in 2016 that "the physical reality of immigration, particularly in Europe, has run ahead of not only host countries' ability to integrate people but also of the immigrants' ability to integrate themselves—and both are necessary for social stability."[6] How to respond to immigration constitutes a major political cleavage in many countries, propelling, as noted in Chapter 8, "far-right," nationalist parties, and featuring as a top concern among those voting for "Brexit" in 2016. Some of the fear is driven by special concerns about Muslims in Europe and terrorist attacks that have been committed by European Muslims. Some alarmist voices, pointing to high birthrates among Europe's Muslims, fear creation of "Eurabia," an Islamic takeover of Europe.[7] Terrorism is explored more in the next chapter as a security issue, but in many accounts it overlaps with the broader questions of immigration and devising effective policies to reflect and manage Europe's increasing ethnic and religious diversity.

These are great challenges, and go to the heart of many debates about what "Europe" is or should be. As noted in Chapter 1, some define Europe in cultural terms, which could include race, ethnicity, and religion. However, traditional notions of "Europe" and Europeans—the monochromatic vision of Europe's population found in dated films—increasingly bear little resemblance to Europe today. Walk down a street in Paris, Vienna, Florence, Zurich, Hamburg, London, Stockholm, Prague, or Copenhagen, and you will hear a host of non-European languages and see a variety of people who, based upon dress or skin color, would not traditionally be considered "European." Some may be tourists or business travelers, but many are refugees, permanent residents, or even citizens, the last in particular staking a claim that, however they look or pray, they too are Europeans. Thinking about Europe as a whole, it is easy, as the EU has done, to adopt "Unity in Diversity" as a motto. It is far harder, however, to manage diversity in ways that satisfy different groups that have diametrically opposed visions of what constitutes "Europe."

Immigrants in Europe

Historical patterns of immigration

Although the United States, Canada, and Australia claim some distinctiveness for being immigrant societies, Europe has its own long history of immigration. Germans made up a large percentage of people on historically "Czech" or "Polish" lands; many Italians, Portuguese, and Spaniards immigrated to France; and a Jewish diaspora lived throughout the continent. Even after the emergence of nationalism in the nineteenth century, migrants continued to settle in new countries. France, for example, became a melting pot for various peoples. By 1881, at roughly the same time that France gave the United States the Statue of Liberty to welcome the poor "huddled masses" to America, France had 1 million immigrants of its own.[8]

Until the latter half of the twentieth century, however, most of the immigration in Europe was intra-European immigration. This meant that people from poorer parts of Europe (e.g., Poland, Ireland, Portugal) moved to wealthier countries such as France, the Netherlands, and Great Britain. These immigrants, like the locals, were largely white and Christian. After learning the local language, they could be relatively easily integrated into their new home. Jews would be, of course, somewhat distinctive, and anti-Semitism could be found in all parts of Europe well before Hitler came to power.

Immigration patterns changed significantly after World War II. Many European states, experiencing a labor shortage, began to look for new sources of workers. Thus, in the 1950s and 1960s, millions of people, mostly young, single males, arrived in Europe as "guest workers" (*Gastarbeiter* in German). Many came from former European colonies, and frequently laws were very liberal in terms of allowing residents of the colonies to emigrate to the "mother country." Thus, hundreds of thousands of South Asians (e.g., Indians, Pakistanis, Bangladeshis) and Africans, as well as people from various islands in the Caribbean, moved to Britain; Moroccans, Tunisians, and Algerians came to France; Surinamese and Indonesians arrived in the Netherlands, which also invited large numbers of Turks and Moroccans as guest workers. Germany, which did not have overseas colonies, welcomed hundreds of thousands of Turks and Yugoslavs as *Gastarbeiter*. Suddenly, European countries had millions of new residents, many of whom were not, in traditional terms at any rate, "European." Many were also Muslims.

Gastarbeiter from German, it literally means "guest worker" and refers to workers, from countries such as Turkey, Algeria, and Morocco, that were allowed to work temporarily in Western Europe after World War II. Many, however, chose not to go back home.

Initially, this was not viewed as a large problem because these migrants were viewed as temporary guest workers. The plan was that they would eventually move back to their homeland. The problem, however, was that many chose not to move back: They could earn more, for example, in France or Germany, and they did not want to move back to poorer, often unstable or politically repressive states. Some European states began imposing immigration quotas, but, due to policies that allowed family reunification, natural reproduction, and liberal asylum policies, the number of immigrants and those with immigrant background grew. By the 1960s, non-European immigrants had assumed a larger and more open presence in European countries (e.g., more veiled women, new mosques) and an economic downturn led to competition for jobs. Consequently, immigration became a political issue, evidenced most dramatically in 1968, when Enoch Powell, a leading figure in the Conservative Party, gave his infamous "rivers of blood" speech, in which he fumed that "we must be mad, literally mad, as a nation to be permitting the annual inflow of some 50,000 dependents." This speech was widely condemned; the *Times of London* called it "an evil speech," and it effectively ended his political career.[9] However, one could invoke Powell as a precursor to the rise of nationalist, anti-immigrant political parties and figures, who have campaigned for more restrictive immigration policies or even expelling non-native peoples, arguing that these newcomers "stole" jobs and threatened "European" culture. By the 1960s and 1970s, however, many of the "guest workers" had been living in Europe for twenty or more years. In some states, such as France and the Netherlands, many were able to become citizens, and many had children born in Europe. Kicking them out was not (and is not) a realistic option. The challenge then became how to integrate immigrants and their descendants into European societies.

Immigrants in Europe today

Today Europe is home to millions of immigrants. Overall, approximately 9 percent of residents of the EU are foreign-born, with the figures much higher in countries such as Germany, Austria, and Luxembourg. Figure 11.1 highlights the percentage of foreign-born residents in each country, including a breakdown of where these residents come from for several states. A few caveats are in order. First, some of these foreign-born residents are Europeans, many of whom no doubt enjoy the EU-created freedom to live, work, and study wherever they wish in Europe. Indeed, among the 54 million EU residents born outside their current country of residence, over a third (36.6 percent) were born in another EU country. Still, that means roughly 34 million people living in the EU (6.7 percent of the population) were born in a non-EU country, with Morocco, Turkey, Russia, and Algeria ranking highest among places of birth. Second, some ex-patriate residents in Europe are not true "immigrants" in the sense that they have been temporarily re-located to Europe and their permanent home is elsewhere. This is the case in particular for Luxembourg and Switzerland, each of which have a very high number (44.2 percent and 27.4 percent, respectively) of foreign-born residents. Third, in the Baltic states, the foreign-born population is mainly ethnic Russians who moved to the region when it was part of the Soviet Union. They do not meet the typical profile of an immigrant. Fourth, the data do not take into account millions of illegal immigrants, who have been flocking to Europe—even prior to 2015—either through dangerous crossings of the Mediterranean or via overland routes from Turkey, the Middle East, and the former Soviet Union. Finally, while the data do take into account foreign-born individuals who have acquired citizenship in their new country of residence, they do not count the children or grandchildren of immigrants who were born in Europe. If one takes these generations into account, more than 20 percent of the population in many European countries has an immigrant background. In some cities, such as Amsterdam, Paris, and London, the number of such "foreigners" is similar to the number of "native" Dutch, French, or English citizens.

Immigration to Europe is higher compared to past decades, but it is subject to short-term fluctuations. For example, according to the World Bank, net migration

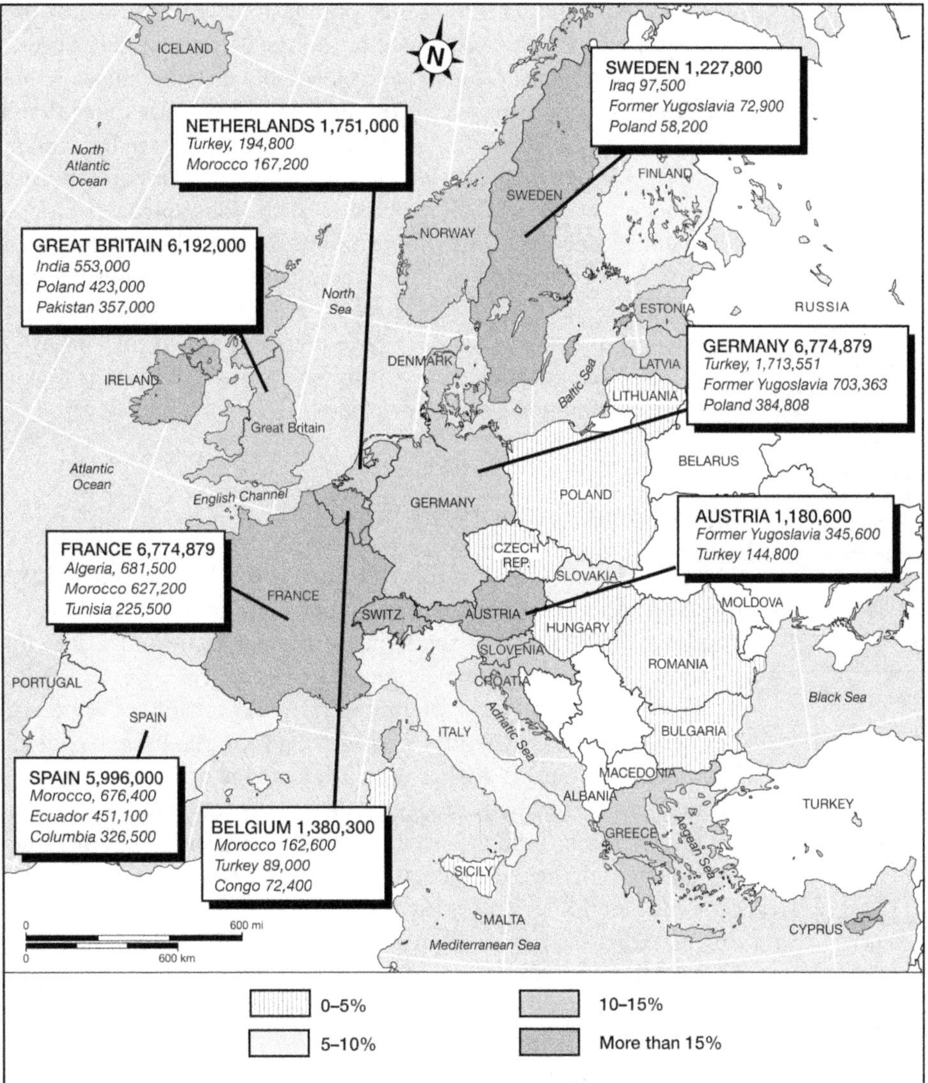

FIGURE 11.1 Foreign-born populations in Europe

Eurostat, data are as of 2015. County-of-origin data for France are from 2012 from the French National Institute for Demographic Studies (www.ined.fr) and for Germany from the Migration Policy Institute (www.migrationpolicy.org/programs/migration-data-hub)

to the EU was 5.9 million people in 2007, but only 2.3 million in 2012, reflecting, perhaps, fewer economic opportunities in the wake of the European economic crisis. Indeed, even in 2014 economically hard-hit countries such as Greece, Spain, Ireland, Cyprus, and Portugal were still experiencing net emigration as opposed to immigration.[10] The natural population growth rate for Europe in the 2010s—reflecting the difference of births and deaths and not counting immigration—is under half of 1 percent (it was actually –0.1 percent in 2012[11]), meaning to the extent Europe is gaining population, it is primarily due to immigration from outside the continent. As discussed later in this chapter, European countries will need more workers to support an aging population, and immigration is the obvious demographic (if more complicated political) answer. However, as is clear from Figure 11.1, immigrants are far from equally distributed across the continent. They tend to move to places with economic opportunity or those that adopt immigrant-friendly policies. After 2004, for example, Ireland, Sweden, and Great Britain were the only EU states to allow residents of new post-communist member-states to immediately work in their countries. As a consequence, large numbers of Poles, Latvians, Lithuanians, and others moved; by the 2010s, however, many moved back as economic conditions in their home countries improved. Immigration is also a function of geography—Italy, Greece, and Spain are often the first port of entry for migrants coming from across the Mediterranean or from Turkey—although, as seen in 2015, desperate migrants are willing to walk thousands of kilometers to find a more welcoming environment.

assimilation
a process through which immigrants are expected to adopt the practices, customs, and language of their host country.

How have immigrants fared?

Most immigrants come to Europe hoping for a better life. They want to live in a safe and secure environment, enjoy personal and civic freedoms, and find suitable employment. Relative to their status in their homelands, one can argue that most have fared better in their new places of residence.

integration
a two-way process through which immigrants make adaptations to life in their new country and in which governments help accommodate the needs of immigrants.

Nonetheless, the lives of immigrants in Europe are not without difficulties. Leaving one's native country and moving to a place where one does not know the language or culture is always difficult. If one is of a different religion or skin color, meaning one is clearly recognizable as an "outsider," there may be additional problems. Many immigrants, for a host of reasons, feel that they are unwelcome or can live only on the margins of European society. True, many countries provide economic assistance and cultural support (e.g., free language classes) to immigrants. Furthermore, insofar as all members of the EU are democracies, they are expected to prohibit discrimination and promote tolerance—although it is clear that discrimination still exists and many do not embrace a *Willkommenskultur*.

At the same time, many immigrants have found it difficult to assimilate or integrate into their new places of residence. **Assimilation**, usually endorsed by those who are skeptical of, if not opposed to, immigration, refers to a process whereby immigrants are expected to adopt the practices, manners, customs, and language of the host country. In so doing, they are expected to lose many of their own cultural characteristics, which is why most immigrants reject policies of assimilation. **Integration** suggests less of a wholesale transformation and is more a two-way process, in which immigrants make adaptations and governments adopt policies so that newcomers can live easily and productively in their new country. Integration nonetheless suggests, at minimum, that immigrants learn the host country's language and learn to respect the dominant culture.

multi-culturalism
the acceptance or promotion of multiple identities and cultures in a particular environment, often for practical reasons or for the sake of promoting diversity.

Some have advocated alternative approaches that endorse **multi-culturalism** as the preferred outcome, meaning there is less emphasis on fashioning a common culture and integrating newcomers into a common whole and more room for groups to retain their distinct cultures. While on some level this last approach may appear to be the least demanding of immigrants and the most tolerant, it has, as detailed later in this chapter, not always succeeded. Some argue it has isolated immigrants within their own communities and prevents them from participating fully in their country's economic, social, and political life.

Immigrants point to a number of problems, including scapegoating, discrimination and prejudice. Numerous political parties across Europe have campaigned successfully on anti-immigrant platforms, as immigrants are blamed for a number of social and economic problems. Expressions of their culture (e.g., female students wearing the *hijab* or *niqab*, two forms of Islamic head coverings) are viewed by many in Europe as threatening, or, at minimum, inconsistent with traditional expectations of public secularism. Extremist "skinhead" groups have also attacked immigrants and ethnic minorities. The European Social Survey (ESS) from 2014, conducted in twenty countries, found that those who are foreign-born are far more likely (19.4 percent) to report that they have been subjected to discrimination than the native-born (7.4 percent).[12] France (27.1 percent), the Netherlands (25 percent), Great Britain (23.1 percent), and Belgium (22.9 percent) rank among the countries where immigrants are more likely to claim they are a member of a group that is discriminated against. Figures are lower for Poland (6.2 percent) and Slovenia (3.1 percent), which have few immigrants, as well as for Germany (12.1 percent). Among religious minority groups, many Muslims (23.1 percent) and Jews (33 percent) reported discrimination based on religion.

What percentage of Europeans are in fact prejudiced against people of different races, faiths, or ethnic origins? Surveys on these questions may underestimate racism or prejudice because individuals may be reluctant to admit to holding such attitudes. Still, the 2013 British Social Attitudes Survey found that 29 percent of respondents admit to being "very" or "a little" prejudiced against people of other races, a drop from 1987 (38 percent) but an increase from 25 percent in 2001.[13] The 2014 ESS asked individuals if they believed some races or ethnic groups were born less intelligent or born harder working. Results are presented in Table 11.1. As one can see, many expressed agreement with both, with majorities in several countries expressing agreement with the more "positive" statement that praised some races or ethnic groups as "born" harder working. Racism appears to be less pronounced in Scandinavia and in the Netherlands; it is more apparent in central and southern Europe. A more detailed examination of the data from all twenty countries in the survey revealed, perhaps not surprisingly, that younger and better educated respondents, as well as women, were less likely to espouse racist sentiments. How racial prejudice may affect attitudes toward accepting more immigrants is explored more below.

Many immigrants, despite living better than they would in their native lands, fare worse economically than the native population. This is, perhaps, not entirely surprising, given the fact that many immigrants arrive with few resources and are relatively low skilled. Data, presented in Table 11.2, show that throughout most of Europe, foreign-born populations (which, again, includes other Europeans) tend to have higher unemployment rates than the native-born, and these figures probably understate the real issue—unemployment among people with non-European ancestry, which reaches over 20 percent in countries such as France and Germany. Part of the problem is discrimination. Indeed, studies in France—where unemployment among Muslim youth is twice as high as unemployment among non-Muslim immigrants with the same educational qualifications—reveal that, given identical resumes, a man with the name of "Ahmed" is far less likely to get a job interview

TABLE 11.1 Racist sentiments in Europe

Country	*Are some races or ethnic groups born less intelligent? (% agreeing)*	*Are some races and ethnic groups born harder working? (% agreeing)*
Austria	12.5	41.6
Belgium	17.0	40.8
France	10.8	50.7
Germany	9.1	38.3
Great Britain	18.8	46.5
Sweden	2.3	15.3
Norway	3.0	21.2
Netherlands	6.7	13.6
Switzerland	14.6	53.7
Portugal	39.5	68.1
Czech Republic	41.2	45.7
Hungary	34.5	35.7

Source: ESS, Round 7, 2014, online analysis at http://nesstar.ess.nsd.uib.no/webview/

than one named "Francois."[14] Data on wages are generally harder to come by, although there is little question that since immigrants are over-represented in the least remunerative jobs (e.g., agriculture, hotel and restaurant service, janitors) they earn less than the native-born. Many live in ethnic minority ghettos that have relatively poor housing, social services, and employment opportunities.

Another important issue for immigrants and their descendants is whether they can obtain citizenship in their new countries of residence. Citizenship, of course, confers important political rights (e.g., the right to vote) as well as putting immigrants on equal standing with native citizens for access to welfare provisions. Some countries, such as Sweden, the Netherlands, France and Great Britain, make fairly generous provisions for naturalization, meaning that those who lack a criminal record and maintained a period of legal residency (typically five years) can apply to become a citizen. In most cases, one must also demonstrate competence in the local language; in some, applicants must also prove they have been able to financially support themselves. Most European countries do not confer birthright citizenship upon children born in the country, a practice known as *jus soli* (right of the soil), one that holds in the United States.[15] Specifics, however, vary. In Great Britain, a child born to a legal non-citizen immigrant can obtain birthright citizenship, and in France if a child born in France has one parent who was also born in France, that child is entitled to French citizenship. In most other countries, the practice of *jus sanguinis* (right of the blood) is the norm, meaning that there is no birthright citizenship. One is "born" a citizen only if one has a parent who is also a citizen. In some countries, *jus sanguinis* was coupled with policies that made it very difficult to become a naturalized citizen. This was the case in Germany, meaning that a daughter of a Turkish immigrant in Germany, even if she was born in Germany, attended German schools, and spoke better German than Turkish, was not only not a German citizen by birth; she had no right to claim or apply for German citizenship. This has changed in recent years, as a new law on citizenship came into force in 2000 that is much closer to *jus soli*. It specifies that the children

TABLE 11.2 Unemployment rates among native- and foreign-born populations

Country	*% unemployed, native-born*	*% unemployed, foreign-born*
Austria	4.7	10.1
Belgium	6.9	17.6
Czech Rep	6.2	7.0
Denmark	6.0	12.3
France	9.1	16.0
Germany	4.5	7.9
Great Britain	6.1	7.1
Hungary	7.8	12.8
Italy	6.0	16.4
Netherlands	6.1	12.0
Spain	22.8	6.2
Sweden	33.3	16.4
Switzerland	3.3	7.7

Source: From OECD (Organization for Economic Cooperation and Development), 2014. Data available at https://data.oecd.org/

of foreigners born in Germany automatically obtain German citizenship if one of the parents has resided in Germany for at least eight years. Similarly, immigrants who have lived in Germany for at least eight years may now apply for German citizenship.

naturalization process by which immigrants become citizens of their adopted country; rules governing naturalization vary substantially among European countries.

Data reveal that rates of **naturalization** for foreign-born populations—meaning those who acquire citizenship in their new countries—vary throughout Europe. In 2014 Eurostat reported that on average 2.5 percent of non-citizen residents were naturalized in that single year, with over 6 percent in Sweden and (low immigrant) Hungary. Far lower figures (under 1 percent) were reported in Latvia, Estonia, and Lithuania, three countries in which knowledge of the language—all of which are unrelated to most major European languages and thus difficult to learn—is required to become a citizen. Given widespread concerns over immigration, some countries have changed naturalization procedures to make it more difficult to become a citizen. For example, Denmark has adopted a new citizenship test, which asks applicants numerous obscure questions (e.g., which Danish restaurant won a third Michelin star in 2016, the constellation in which a sixteenth century Danish astronomer discovered a new star) that many native Danes could not pass. Over two-thirds of those who took the new test failed it, but the Minister of Immigration and Integration was unapologetic, claiming applicants needed to study harder.[16]

Responding to a more diverse population

Many European states are now multi-cultural, possessing significant populations of non-European immigrants and their descendants. Their culture—in terms of dress, religion, food, values—may differ from that of native Europeans. While many celebrate Europe's greater diversity, this has also presented several challenges to European societies.

Conflicts between newcomers and natives

Some of these challenges rest with the immigrants, who may resist attempts at assimilation or integration. While this may partially be the result of conscious choice on the part of immigrants, it is often the product of housing policy, as many immigrants live (often placed there through a government agency or *de facto* confined there because of cost considerations) in ethnic ghettoes and are therefore unable to integrate into the broader community. Furthermore, identity is often a vexed question for the children of immigrants: Are they, for example, Dutch or Moroccan, Turkish or German? Some attempt to carve out a "third path," building their identities out of elements of both societies, and defend multi-culturalism as a human right.[17] **Hyphenated identity** (e.g., Dutch-Moroccan, Turkish-German), while familiar to American ears, is something new in Europe and challenges many pre-existing formulas. Some may also have a more ambivalent attitude about integrating in the host society, a reflection of what one writer calls "ambi-Europeanism"—respect for Western economic prosperity and power coupled with disgust over the allegedly spiritual emptiness of the West and how it uses its power.[18] For others, such as the European-born terrorists of immigrant heritage discussed in the next chapter that have attacked their fellow citizens in Spain, Great Britain, France, and Belgium, the answer is *jihad*, a war to "defend" the true faith against Western culture.

hyphenated identity
idea that a person can have multiple identities from two cultures or countries, e.g., Turkish-German or Asian-American.

In addition to terrorism, there can also be a broader clash over competing values and seemingly irreconcilable demands for tolerance and understanding. Some would demand that immigrants fully embrace all the norms and values of one's new country. Others might counter that one should be tolerant and respectful of the different values of immigrants. Achieving a balance, however, can be difficult. An example of this was the 2006 controversy over anti-Islamic cartoons published in a Danish newspaper, an event that had repercussions in Europe and globally and has been echoed in ongoing disputes between those fearful or prejudiced against Muslims and European Muslims that seek respect for their religious beliefs and values. This is discussed further in the **In focus** section of this chapter.

xenophobia
fear of foreigners.

Another concern is that many "native" Europeans oppose immigration and increased diversity as a threat. **Xenophobia**—fear or contempt of foreigners—is apparent in a number of ways. Immigrants are blamed for crime; accused of being lazy and living off welfare; or are charged with "stealing" jobs. Some accuse them of being insufficiently committed to integrating into their new place of residence and believe that they will never become "true" Frenchmen, Germans, Italians, and so on. This type of sentiment ranges from the more frivolous (do British-Indians root for the Indian or English international cricket team?) to the deadly serious (do they owe their fealty to a European state or to *fatwas* issued by the Islamic State?). Nationalist, anti-immigrant political parties across the continent have called for more restrictive immigration policies as well as measures to compel immigrants and their families to adapt to the dominant culture. These parties have performed well in a wide range of countries, including Denmark, France, Austria, Italy, the Netherlands, and Hungary. While some deny or try to conceal outright racism, others are less subtle. For example, in 2007, the Swiss People's Party, which railed against immigrants, won Swiss national elections with 29 percent of the vote. One of its campaign posters and mailings, which depicted white sheep kicking out a black one

Poster from the Swiss People's Party urging the country to "finally create security" by supporting an initiative to deport foreigners convicted of crimes

© Walter Bieri AP/PA Images

In focus

Responses to the Danish cartoon controversy

The presence of ethnic and religious minorities obviously complicates discussions of a united Europe, as Europe today is arguably more heterogeneous than at any time in its history. The issue, however, goes beyond racial or religious diversity. In some cases, conflicts over the presence of these groups touch upon deeper, philosophical questions and reveal that real tensions exist among the values or priorities that most Europeans hold dear. One concern that has come up repeatedly in Europe is how to balance the rights of free speech against the need and/or expectation for tolerance and respect for diversity.

This was manifested most clearly in the controversy and violence that erupted after the publication on September 30, 2005 of anti-Islamic cartoons in *Jyllands-Posten*, a Danish newspaper. The cartoons made connections between Islam and terrorism, with one depicting Muhammed, the revered prophet of Islam who by Muslim tradition is not to be drawn in any way, with a bomb as his turban. Once these cartoons had been discovered by a wider audience, which occurred months after their original publication when they were republished in newspapers across Europe,[19] there were violent protests against Danish, European, and US facilities in numerous Muslim countries that claimed dozens of lives—leading some to retort that such a backlash affirmed the accuracy of the depictions in the cartoons. In Europe, tens of thousands of Muslims protested in the streets. Many called for the newspaper to be shut down. Some threatened lawsuits. Many Muslim countries boycotted Danish products. Some Muslims, mainly outside of Europe, called for the death of the cartoonists and publishers. However, marchers in London who belonged to the extremist al Ghuraba group carried placards that read, "Butcher those who mock Islam" and "Europe, you'll pay, Bin Laden is on his way."[20]

The Danish cartoon controversy had antecedents in Europe. The most famous one involved Salman Rushdie, the Indian-born British author of *The Satanic Verses*. In 1989, Iran's leader, Ayatollah Khomeini, declared the book, which is mainly about Muslim immigrants in Europe but, like the Danish cartoons, includes an irreverent depiction of Muhammed, an insult to Muslims and issued a *fatwa* (religious order) enjoining Muslims to kill Rushdie and his publishers. Rushdie went into hiding. In several European states, Muslims burned copies of *The Satanic Verses*, and a terrorist killed himself in London in August 1989 in a failed attempt to assassinate Rushdie.

Then, as with the Danish cartoon controversy, the issue boils down to limits, if any, on free speech. Is this right absolute, or does the need not to offend (or, in some cases, spark violence) trump speech? If limits are placed on speech, are you not caving into those threatening violence, thereby letting those who want to repress freedoms prevail? Put differently, can one argue that freedom also carries responsibility? If so, who enforces this responsibility?

As Europeans grappled with these questions in light of the cartoons controversy, their responses varied.[21] Some fanned the flames. For example, an Italian minister was blamed for sparking riots in Libya, in which eleven people died, for wearing a T-shirt emblazoned with the most controversial cartoon. Others tried to contain the fallout by cracking down on anti-Muslim groups. Sweden's foreign minister, for example, tried to shut down a website that was going to publish more provocative cartoons about Mohammed. Both of these ministers, albeit for different reasons, were forced to resign. The original cartoonist, Kurt Westergaard, who was forced into hiding but avoided any legal prosecution, defended the decision to publish the cartoons, maintaining that Islam provided "spiritual ammunition for terrorism" and that Muslims could not simultaneously demand toleration for their own practices and then be intolerant of actions that offended them.[22] The editor of *Die Welt*, a German newspaper that published the cartoons, noted that, "It is the core of our culture that the most sacred things can be subjected to criticism, laughter, and satire. If we stop using our right to freedom of expression within our legal boundaries then we start to develop an appeasement mentality."[23] An American writer who lived in Oslo argued that Europe had reached a "Weimar moment" in which it had to stand up to Islamic radicals or watch their societies commit cultural suicide.[24] Others took a more measured view. *The Economist*, Britain's foremost newsweekly, rigorously defended the right of free speech, yet, recognizing the responsibility of publishers (or, less generously, fearing a backlash), opted not to publish the images. Some criticized this, arguing that *The Economist* had been cowed by fears of provoking Islamic extremists. Danish Prime Minister Anders Fogh Rasmussen, while regretting the violence and the offense caused to many Muslims and calling for tolerance, noted that he could not and would not tell newspapers what to print.

The controversy carried over for several years. In 2008, Danish police placed Westergaard under heightened security after they uncovered a plot to kill him. In January 2010, despite these precautions, he was attacked in his home by a Somali allegedly trained by al Qaeda. Later in 2010, al Qaeda published a "hit list" of prominent writers and public intellectuals, including both Rushdie and Westergaard. Interestingly, in 2013 a Lebanese-born Danish imam, who had spearheaded the protests in the Muslim world against the cartoons, changed his tune, claiming that he now believes the newspaper had a right to print them.[25] Both Rushdie and Westergaard, as of 2016, are still alive, although they continue to take security precautions. The same cannot be said of Stéphane Charbonnier, a French satirist who was killed in the January 2015 attack in Paris on the office of the magazine *Charlie Hebdo*. This event, which has clear echoes of the Danish cartoons, is discussed more in the subsequent chapter.

The questions that arise from these events pose a direct challenge to European values, or at least, to the idea that Europe represents a set of consistent, mutually supporting values. On the one hand, many claim Europe is a land of freedom, and rights of self-expression and dissent are upheld as fundamental. On the other hand, others claim Europe is a land of tolerance, a place upholding "Unity in Diversity." The two values can conflict, and several questions arise: Do expressions that are critical or hateful of others' culture or religion have a place in Europe? What is the line between criticism and hate? Can the tension between the values of freedom and tolerance be reconciled? More specifically, one could simply ask whether the cartoons should have been published, or whether analogous, controversial exercises of free speech, such as performance in 2006 in Berlin of Mozart's opera *Idomeneo* that featured a scene with the severed heads of Jesus, Muhammed, Buddha, and Poseidon, should have been cancelled? It ultimately was, to the disappointment of many. Questions such as these go beyond anti-Muslim cartoons, statements, or provocative performances. Similar issues arise with respect to Holocaust denial, a punishable offense in many European countries, openly racist statements, and condemnations of Western culture made by Muslims living in Europe.

The discourse is often shrill, and the choices appear to be stark. Tariq Ramadan, a Swiss Muslim academic (who was denied entry to the United States in 2004 to teach at the University of Notre Dame), argues, however, that this is not a clash of civilizations, a choice between inalienable freedom of speech and an inviolable sacred sphere. Rather, the lesson he learns from these controversies is that the various sides must have a reasonable and peaceful

dialogue, and that extremists on both sides must demonstrate respect for the other and build bridges based upon common values. He writes:

> **Disasters threaten that extremists on both sides would not fail to use for their own agendas. If people who cherish freedom, who know the importance of mutual respect and are aware of the imperative necessity to establish a constructive and critical debate, if these people are not ready to speak out, to be more committed and visible, then we can expect sad, painful, tomorrows. The choice is ours.[26]**

Critical thinking questions

1. **Should the publication of material that is intended to offend or provoke be protected? If one can anticipate that publication of such material will lead to negative outcomes such as violence, should the government prevent its publication?**
2. **After some discussion, the author and editor for this book decided not to reprint any of the anti-Muslim cartoons. Was this the proper decision? Is there anything wrong or anything to be gained by publishing them?**

with the tagline "For More Security," was decried by some as "dangerous" and "disgusting," a sign of blatant racism.[27] In 2009, its leaders successfully—and controversially—pushed for a change in Swiss law to ban the construction of minarets.

Much of the criticism is targeted at Islam as a cultural threat.[28] Noting that mosques are better attended than churches in many parts of Europe, some fear being inundated with Muslims, of Europe turning into "Eurabia." This sentiment is not confined to the most extreme nationalist political parties. Consider the statement in 2000 of Cardinal Giacomo Biffi of Italy:

> In the vast majority of cases, and with only a few exceptions, Muslims come here with the resolve to remain strangers to our brand of individual or social "humanity" in everything that is most essential, most precious: strangers to what it is most impossible for us to give up as "secularists." More or less openly, they come here with their minds made up to remain fundamentally "different," waiting to make us all become fundamentally like them . . . I believe that Europe must either become Christian again, or else it will become Muslim.[29]

More prosaically, the late Italian journalist and anti-Islamic crusader Oriana Fallaci worried that Muslim men would defecate in the Sistine Chapel.[30]

Public opinion

Public opinion on the issue of immigration is a bit more nuanced than might be inferred from the above quotations. Data on some attitudes toward immigration are presented in Tables 11.3 and 11.4. These data, from the 2014 ESS—notably *before* the 2015 refugee crisis—reveal that many Europeans believe that immigration has negative effects, such as more crime or job loss. Interestingly, with the exception of respondents in Poland and Hungary, people are more likely to be concerned about the effect of immigration on crime than on job loss. Looking at responses in the ESS over time, one sees that anti-immigrant sentiment, on some measures, as declined over time. For example, comparing the 2002 ESS with its 2014 iteration, one sees that the belief that immigrants make crime worse has declined in Germany (63 percent to 39.9 percent), France (48.5 percent to 34.7 percent), the Netherlands (64.9 percent to 51.7), Poland (53.1 percent to 23 percent), and even in Hungary (67.4 percent to 52 percent). Data on the question of job loss are more mixed, and may hinge on the country's economic performance, as one sees anti-immigrant sentiment drop precipitously in Germany (from 34.2 percent to 14.4 percent believing immigrants take away jobs) but rise modestly in Spain and France, where the economy was not as robust in the 2010s. Overall however, the data from 2014 do not suggest that the majority of Europeans harbor anti-immigrant sentiments.

A different question is what kind of immigrants people prefer. The 2014 ESS asked questions asking for support for immigration by both "professionals" and "unskilled" laborers. The former have been assiduously courted by the EU, which has developed a "**blue card**" procedure to allow more skilled immigrants from outside Europe to work in the EU.[31] In the 2014 ESS, strong majorities in virtually every country supported allowing "many" or "some" professionals from a poor European country to live and work in their country. Support reached over 80 percent in Sweden, Switzerland, and Germany; the only two countries among the twenty in the survey where there was not majority support for this view was Hungary and the Czech Republic, both countries with relatively few immigrants. When asked about professionals from a non-European country, overall support declined only modestly, as over 70 percent still supported admitting "many" or "some" in Germany, Switzerland, Denmark, France, Great Britain, Sweden, Norway, and Portugal. However, as seen in Table 11.3, Europeans are far less keen on unskilled immigrants. While one might expect that there would be a pronounced difference in regard to the hypothetical immigrant's country of origin, this is not always the case. Indeed, in a few countries, including Spain and Sweden, the data suggest people are more supportive of taking in immigrants from outside of Europe. With respect to religious minorities, few (except in Hungary) say their country should take in no Jewish immigrants—there is, one might note, no immediate prospect of large-scale Jewish immigration to any European country—but more Europeans support a ban on Muslim immigrants, including large numbers in post-communist Europe where there are, at present, very few Muslims. Many would see this as evidence of racism or Islamophobia, although, one might add, in most countries in the ESS survey a majority favors taking in "some" or "a few" Muslims.

blue card

a work-visa program that the EU hopes will attract high-skilled immigrants, who are viewed as less burdensome and threatening than lower-skilled immigrants.

However, it may not be racism *per se*, at least judging from this survey, that is the key problem. Rather, as seen in Table 11.4, Europeans are more supportive of immigrants if they are seen as likely to integrate and have skills to contribute to society. Of course, it is usually those coming from poorer countries outside of Europe that do not possess the marketable skills or language ability and will inevitably have more trouble fitting in. Being "white" or Christian, at least in this survey, is less of a concern, although in several post-communist states, including Poland, the Czech

Republic, Hungary, and Lithuania, 40 percent or more of respondents indicated that having a Christian background was an important qualification for an immigrant. This finding, a reflection perhaps of the lack of experience in these states both with immigrants generally and, more specifically, with Muslims (they have had significant Jewish populations, who have often been subject to discrimination) may help explain the divergent reactions to the 2015 refugee crisis, a topic we return to at the end of this chapter.

While anti-immigrant sentiment may not be "politically correct," is it nonetheless justified by experience? On the issue of crime, there is evidence that immigrants or those with foreign backgrounds do represent a disproportionate share of those in jails in Europe.[32] The same, of course, could be said for African Americans in the United States. By themselves, these data factors such as poor education, high unemployment, and policing and sentencing practices may be overly or disproportionately applied against immigrants and those with foreign backgrounds. As

TABLE 11.3 Attitudes toward immigration in Europe (percent agreeing with each statement)

Country	*Immigrants take jobs away*	*Immigrants make crime worse*	*Allow many or some unskilled laborers from Europe/outside Europe*	*Allow no Jews/Muslims*
Belgium	32.6	54.4	42.3/41.8	12.5/20.9
France	26.8	34.7	58.9/45.6	9/16
Germany	14.4	39.9	59.8/43.9	3.2/8.2
Great Britain	28.0	38.8	37.4/30.2	6.7/16.3
Netherlands	22.2	51.7	30.7/27.8	4.5/13.4
Sweden	7.8	43.4	65/68.2	1.2/4.2
Spain	33.8	50.9	25/28.3	12.7/22.3
Switzerland	17.1	47.9	59.8/38.7	5.4/12
Poland	33.6	23.0	50.4/37.4	12.7/32.2
Hungary	54.9	52.0	8/9.3	36.9/57.1

Source: ESS, Round 7, 2014, online analysis at http://nesstar.ess.nsd.uib.no/webview/. Responses for immigrants taking away jobs or creating crime are on a scale of 0–10, with 0 representing the most anti-immigrant sentiment. Responses from 0–3 on this scale are reported on the table

TABLE 11.4 Desired qualities in immigrants

Characteristic	*% saying it is important*
Committed to way of life in host country	78.3
Know local language	73.7
Has needed work skills	68.4
Educational qualifications	66.6
Christian	20.2
White	10.8

Source: ESS, Round 7, 2014, online analysis at http://nesstar.ess.nsd.uib.no/webview/. Percent saying important is taken from scale from 0–10, with responses 6–10 included here as agreeing it is important. Data are from a weighted sample from twenty countries

for the economic effects of immigration, numerous studies have been conducted on this matter. The consensus appears to be that immigration has a negligible effect on native unemployment and on wages, although there is some evidence to support the claim that low-wage or low-skilled native workers are harmed by immigration even as total income for the country increases with immigration.[33] Put differently, the benefits of immigration vary. Better-off Europeans can benefit by more maids and restaurants (where many immigrants work), but the low skilled can find themselves competing on the labor market with those willing to work for less. Even in these cases, however, much depends upon factors such as minimum wage laws, enforcement against illegal immigration, and the power of trade unions. Interestingly, Great Britain, which had seen more migration since 2004 than any other EU state—thanks mainly to policies that allow Poles and other East Europeans to come and work—had, prior to the banking and real estate crises of 2008 to 2009, one of the healthiest economies in Europe. Many Britons even expressed concern that as Poland grew wealthier the Poles would move back, creating a labor shortage in many sectors of the economy.[34] On the question of public finances, on average immigrants pay more into the system than they take out through social services. Estimates are that the "typical" migrant makes a net contribution of some €50,000 to public finances over her lifetime.[35] Whereas many in Germany and elsewhere in Europe worried about the economic cost of taking in so many refugees during the 2015 crisis, some reports suggested that the negative economic effects, for example, on depressing wages or requiring public expenditure (e.g., for housing, training, etc.) would be modest or primarily a short-term cost, with a strong likelihood that over time the new arrivals would boost output and become contributors to public finances.[36] One detailed study found that—contrary to what is typically heard from anti-immigrant voices—immigration on balance has a small but discernible positive economic effect with minimal impact on public welfare provisions.[37]

Lastly, the anti-immigrant argument overlooks one essential fact: Europe needs immigrants. Fertility rates are low in many European countries, with an average in Europe of about 1.4 births per woman. Some countries such as Italy, Germany, Hungary, and Slovenia are already having negative population growth. Immigration and children born to immigrants or those with foreign backgrounds are the main source of population growth in Europe. This is important, because whereas Europeans are having fewer children, they are living longer. There is a documented "graying" of Europe and, as noted in Chapter 10, this is putting pressure on European social-welfare systems. Put simply, Europe needs more workers to pay the taxes that fund pensions, health care, education, etc. Many European countries face prospective labor shortages, as fewer people will be entering the work force. They are going to have to either slash provisions of public services—not particularly politically popular—or attract more workers. Assuming natural population growth does not change, studies indicate that EU member states need more than 2 million net immigrants a year (roughly six times the pre-2015 figure) from 2000 to 2050 to maintain the same level of working-age population as in 1995 and even more to maintain the population ratio between older and younger workers.[38] From this perspective, the relevant policy prescription is not to close borders but to keep them relatively open—controls for legitimate security concerns certainly could be necessary—and allow immigrants to work as soon as possible, which would allow them both to contribute to the public coffers and foster more integration.[39]

Case studies

Policies toward immigrants and individuals' experiences vary widely from country to country. To understand better some of the dilemmas, let us examine in a little more detail the experience of two countries that have taken very different approaches on the question of immigration and multi-culturalism: France and the Netherlands.

France

More so than most European countries, France has a tradition of immigration. French policy, however, has always emphasized assimilation. This meant that one could become French if one learned the language and accepted the idea of a society composed of legally equal citizens. This did not, however, leave room for group rights or pronounced cultural difference; one was expected to conform to prevailing norms and practices. Hyphenated notions of citizenship (e.g., African-French) were explicitly rejected. The French do not even keep census data on race or religion, and "diversity," until recently, was not part of French political lexicon. Instead, membership in the political community is centered on the individual and predicated upon accepting French values. Since the early twentieth century, this has included *laïcité*, secular policies that preclude any role for religion in the public sphere. Even rather innocuous displays of religiosity (e.g., "In God We Trust" on coins, public officials swearing on the Bible) do not occur in France.

laïcité policy dating from the early twentieth century that religion should be excluded from the public sphere.

For most of French history, this policy worked. Spaniards, Portuguese, Italians, Russians, and Poles were able to become "French." After World War II, however, France became a destination for immigrants from the "Third World," particularly from former French colonies in Africa. Taking advantage of a liberal immigration policy, many Algerians, Tunisians, Senegalese, and Moroccans, many of whom did know French, moved to France. These immigrants did not "fit" the profile of past immigrants, particularly in terms of religion, as most of them were Muslim. By the 2010s it was estimated—there is no official data—that 5 to 6 million Muslims, mostly of North African and sub-Saharan (black) African heritage, lived in France. Over half are French citizens.

Although far-right political parties in France long complained of the economic effects of immigration, the cultural battle between Islam and traditional French values broke out in earnest in 1989. The issue was whether Muslim schoolgirls could wear the *hijab* to school. Muslims claimed they had a freedom to their religion and that head covering was mandated by their faith. The French pointed to the policy of *laïcité* that prohibited religious symbols in public schools. This issue was dragged through the French courts for over a decade. Finally, in 2004, the French government passed a law banning all conspicuous displays of religious affiliation from the public schools. Although the law could apply to Jewish yarmulkes, Sikh turbans, and even large Christian crosses, few doubted that the target was Muslims.

The ban on the *hijab* generated much controversy both inside and outside of France. The ban was, notably, popular among those both on the political right and the left, and research revealed that even a sizeable population of French Muslims—particularly women—were in favor of the ban.[40] Some Muslim girls, however, shaved their heads in protest. Some parents flatly refused to send their girls to school if they could not wear a *hijab*. Some threatened to sue in the European Court of

Human Rights, which in 2005 upheld a similar ban in Turkey. To those who embrace individual freedom, the French law seemed harsh, a violation of rights. The French government, however, upheld *laïcité* as a fundamental value and argued that wearing the *hijab* worked against the overarching goal of assimilation. Interestingly, the French found a backer of their policy in British Prime Minister Tony Blair, who defended a British school for firing a teacher who wore the *hijab*, noting it was a mark of separation.

The controversy over the *hijab* launched a broader discussion of the plight of France's Muslims and minorities. Although France celebrated its 1998 World Cup-winning soccer team that featured many Arabs and blacks, the upper echelons of French society remained white. No black or Arab, until 2007, represented mainland France in the National Assembly. The business elite, as well as the students at elite French universities, were, with few exceptions, white. There was not even a black or Arab newscaster until 2006. Many of France's minorities were consigned to live in ghettoes on the edges of large cities such as Paris and Marseilles, belying rhetoric of equality and assimilation. These areas featured sub-standard schools and few job opportunities, not to mention the numerous satellite dishes so residents could watch Algerian or Moroccan television. Some politicians began to talk about "**positive discrimination**" (in American parlance, affirmative action) to give minorities greater educational and employment opportunities. Others, noting that French law does not recognize any ethnic or group rights and that all citizens must be treated as equally legal, rejected such ideas as unacceptable.

positive discrimination
term from France that is akin to affirmative action in the US, whereby preferences for jobs and university placements would be given to minorities; as in the US, it is highly controversial.

Riots in the fall of 2005 across France, carried out largely by black and Arab youths in reaction to two young men dying while attempting to flee police, shocked France and Europe. Cars were burned; stores ransacked; even mosques were targets for vandalism. Remarkably, perhaps, some in France began to look at the US as a positive example about how one could integrate racial or religious minorities. Many, however, preferred to view the riots as more of a socio-economic problem than a cultural one. While conceding that much more would have to be done to ensure better, more integrated housing, education, and employment, the French model itself, defenders say, is not broken.[41] Immigrants know or learn French. Data from the 2000s revealed a relatively high rate of inter-marriage between Muslim men and French women (although not the other way around) and in a 2006 survey French Muslims were far less likely than their British counterparts (46 to 81 percent) to say they were Muslim first and French (or British) second.[42]

Still, all is not well in France. In 2006, some French cities saw a spontaneous movement to serve pork soup to the poor, thereby excluding Muslims. There were more violent outbursts directed against French police in some immigrant neighborhoods. Nicolas Sarkozy, the son of a Hungarian immigrant, appropriated part of the far-right National Front's platform in railing against immigration in the 2007 presidential elections. He won, but he conceded that some sort of "positive discrimination" might be necessary. His government created a Ministry for Immigration, Integration, and National Identity, and his cabinet included the daughter of North African immigrants.[43] Companies have been encouraged to set up "diversity charters" and elite French schools to establish special admissions tracks for students from disadvantaged areas.

Sarkozy's commitment to multi-culturalism, however, was limited, as he spoke out against the *burqa* (a full-length covering of women) as a prison that deprives women of identity. In 2010, the government's commission examining the question of the *burqa* recommended that it be banned in public institutions such as schools, hospitals, public transport, and government offices and that anyone wearing the *burqa* would be ineligible for public services. Amid some controversy, the French National Assembly adopted these recommendations in July 2010. While such a move was popular among many in France and was even supported by some French imams, it did little to get to socio-economic aspects of the issue. For example, unemployment in parts of Clichy-sous-Bois, where the 2005 riots started, reached 50 percent, there was still no government-run job center, and residents rarely went to central Paris, nine miles (but 1.5 hours by public transport) away. One French author acknowledged that "under the cover of an abstract concept of equality," French society still "practices a pitiless form of apartheid."[44]

Throughout the 2000s, France could, however, take solace in the fact that, unlike Spain or Great Britain, it did not experience a large-scale terror attack by radical Muslims. That ended in 2015, when in January the offices of the satirical magazine *Charlie Hebdo* were attacked and in November when over one hundred people were killed in Paris in a coordinated assault on a theater, stadium, and several cafes. The latter was the deadliest attack in France since World War II. In both cases, the attackers—European Muslim citizens—professed loyalty to ISIS and were responding to perceived insults against Islam and/or French policy in the Middle East. As a result of these attacks, France has implemented greater security measures, but it has also strengthened the political position of the nationalist National Front, which is well-known for its hostility to immigration and, in particular, Muslims. These attacks and how to prevent future tragedies will be top issues in the 2017 French elections.

Anti-Semitism has also been a significant problem in France, manifested both on the political left (which tends to oppose many policies of Israel and champion the Palestinian cause) and on the nationalist, xenophobic right, as well as by some French Muslims. Hundreds of anti-Semitic events, including attacks on synagogues and protesters' chants to "Gas the Jews," occurred yearly in the 2000s. Some were especially violent, including deaths during an attack on a Jewish school in Toulouse in March 2012 and during a hostage stand-off in a kosher supermarket in the immediate aftermath of the January 2015 *Charlie Hebdo* attack. In both of these cases, the attacker was a French Muslim. As a result of events like these, many Jews are leaving or considering leaving France.[45]

The Netherlands

Unlike the French, the Dutch developed a rather *laissez-faire* policy towards their immigrants, which include sizeable numbers of Moroccans and Turks as well as peoples from former Dutch colonies such as Indonesia and Suriname. While immigrants could become citizens and were assured of their rights to political inclusion and cultural and religious expression, there was scant effort to make them, beyond acquisition of the language, "Dutch." While they could partake of social welfare benefits, including free language instruction, little was done to integrate them into the broader society. They were generally expected to remain in their own communities, a reflection of the previous Dutch "pillar" system, under which there were separate institutions (e.g., schools, neighborhoods, newspapers, unions, hospitals) for Catholics, Protestants, and the nonreligious. Such a scheme did not envision much interaction among the groups, only a minimum of tolerance so that each group was able to do largely what it wanted to do. While such a policy was upheld by its defenders as one respectful of multiculturalism—after all, the Dutch were not forcing them to assimilate or even integrate into Dutch culture—critics charged that the Netherlands "let its immigrants rot in their own privacy."[46] Like immigrants in France, many were marginalized in ghettoes. Few were able to climb the socioeconomic ladder to achieve economic equality with the native population.

The Dutch model of tolerance was severely tested in the 2000s. First, Pim Fortuyn, a gay sociology professor who claimed that he understood Moroccans because he had had sex with many Moroccan boys, became, for a time, the most popular political figure in the country by campaigning against what he believed was Islam's intolerance. Praising Dutch tolerance (e.g., of soft drugs, homosexuality, women's rights), he suggested that Muslim immigrants, because of their culture, were a threat to Dutch values. He was assassinated in 2002 by an animal rights activist, but after his death his party, the Pim Fortuyn List, came in second with 17 percent of the vote and compelled the government to adopt more restrictive policies toward immigrants and asylum seekers.

Secondly, Theo van Gogh, a Dutch filmmaker and great-great-grandnephew of Vincent van Gogh, was murdered in November 2004 in broad daylight in Amsterdam by a Dutch-born Moroccan who shot and stabbed him multiple times. Van Gogh was a controversial figure: He had insulted Muslims in very crude terms and produced a film, *Submission*, which featured a young Muslim woman who claimed she had been raped by relatives and had words from the Koran (Muslim holy book) superimposed on her beaten and transparently veiled body. His assailant, Mohammed Bouyeri, who had grown up in the Netherlands, was a dual Dutch-Moroccan citizen and had been radicalized after 9/11. He proclaimed that Islamic law had compelled him to chop off the head of anyone who insults Islam. In the aftermath of van Gogh's murder, there were clashes between the native Dutch and Islamic communities, including attacks on mosques and churches, and death threats were directed at Ayaan Hirsi Ali, a Muslim Somali refugee who had co-written *Submission*, repudiated Islam as a violent and repressive religion, and been elected to the Dutch parliament.[47] Geert Wilders, another member of parliament, suggested that all Muslim schools be closed and that "The Netherlands has been too tolerant to intolerant people for too long. We should not import a retarded political Islamic society into our country."[48] He became leader of the Freedom Party. Among other things, he has called the Koran a fascist book and proposed it be banned in the Netherlands, referred to Muhammad as the devil, and in 2008 produced *Fitna*, a short anti-Islamic film.[49]

Since 2004, the Dutch government has adopted a tougher line toward immigration. Prospective immigrants from Muslim countries[50] are now required to pass a test on Dutch language and culture, which costs €350 and includes watching a film on the Netherlands which extols its tolerance for gays (one version features men kissing) and female emancipation (scenes include topless sunbathers) while noting that practices such as honor killings are not acceptable. While the film is no doubt patronizing and perhaps deliberately offensive, its backers would argue that immigrants need to be informed about Dutch society before they arrive and that the Dutch have every right to defend their cultural and legal traditions. One critic, however, alleged—probably correctly—that the testing program is much more about controlling immigration than promoting integration.[51] Ironically, Ayaan Ali herself got caught up in the anti-immigrant moment, as it was discovered she had lied on her application for political asylum and an unsuccessful attempt was made to strip her of Dutch citizenship. Some political figures have proposed banning the wearing of the *hijab* and the *burqa* on security grounds, and backed a national code of conduct that would require Dutch to be spoken on the streets. Immigration has played heavily in recent Dutch elections. Wilders' Freedom Party came in third place in both 2010 (15.5 percent) and 2012 (10.1 percent). For its part, the Dutch government proposed strengthening blasphemy laws so that inflammatory language could be more easily prosecuted. Thus, one could not, as Ayaan Ali did, call Mohammed a pedophile or suggest Islam is a "nihilistic cult of death." However, as with the Danish cartoon controversy discussed earlier, one might suggest that such restrictions on speech run counter to democratic freedoms.

The larger issue, however, is less about admitting (or not) more immigrants and more about what can be done to integrate the immigrants and those with immigrant backgrounds already in the Netherlands. The Dutch are seriously re-evaluating past policies upholding multi-culturalism. Neighborhoods with shrouded women, state-funded Islamic schools, and secretive mosques are no longer upheld as success stories of Dutch tolerance. There is pressure from nationalist forces to adopt policies to promote assimilation. A proposal to have current residents, not just prospective immigrants, take a Dutch language and culture test is dubious on legal grounds and does not directly address socio-economic issues or segregated neighborhoods. Many immigrants, on the other hand, have issued calls for civility from all actors and for more dialogue. The problem, however, is that it is hard to reach any consensus on what to do amid the shrill discourse on each side.

The European-level response to immigrants and refugees

Issues of immigration and cultural change rank among the most important issues discussed at the EU level. In 2015, amidst a wave of refugees coming from Syria and other lands of conflict, schisms on these issues were laid bare, galvanizing public opinion and provoking arguably Europe's greatest political crisis since World War II. Whether EU members can find common ground and reach a compromise remains very much to be seen.

The development of EU policy

Immigration was not originally within the scope of European institutions. However, in the 1980s, as Europe moved toward establishing a common market and more countries signed onto the 1985 Schengen Agreement creating a free travel area, the need to control and regulate the movement of migrants and third country nationals (e.g., Turkish, Algerian, or Pakistani citizens) became apparent. The Single European Act of 1986 included provisions that cited the need for a common immigration policy, and the Maastricht Treaty foresaw development of a common visa regime and policy toward third country nationals residing in European states under a Justice and Home Affairs pillar.

However, states have been reluctant to cede powers to the EU, preferring that action be taken through inter-governmental means. Border control, citizenship policy, and efforts to promote national integration are, arguably, core policies of a nation-state. Because of the peculiarities of local labor market conditions, cultural concerns about immigration, and historical patterns of immigration, many argued that would be inappropriate to adopt a common EU immigration policy. However, this argument is less persuasive than it might have been in the past. For example, because of the Schengen Agreement, the *de facto* external border for Denmark or Sweden is no longer in the Baltic Sea but is now the Mediterranean or the Polish-Ukrainian border, because once people are inside the Schengen zone—which by 2016 covered twenty-eight countries both inside and outside the EU—they can move about with relative ease. A common policy to regulate immigration might therefore make sense, although, as we'll soon see below, some are calling for individual states to take more control, meaning that Schengen could be re-visited or even scrapped.

One problem, however, has been that while many member states have become, in part due to domestic political pressures, more interested in restricting immigration, EU institutions, particularly the technocratic European Commission, tend to look favorably on data that suggest that Europe needs more immigrants. Thus, there has been a battle of sorts between the EU and member states over immigration policy, with directives of the EU falling far short of a comprehensive EU immigration policy.[52] Denmark, Great Britain, and Ireland have also opted out of common EU immigration policies, but in some ways this is more an expression of nationalism than a reflection of anti-immigrant sentiment.[53]

This is not to suggest that the EU has been completely inactive on the immigration front. The Amsterdam Treaty of 1997 incorporated the Schengen Agreement into the EU and put priority on the attainment of a European space of freedom, justice, and security. The European Commission has been charged with developing a common system for asylum and immigration. While the EU still lacks a comprehensive policy—the key issue of quantitative levels of immigration is still beyond EU control—the EU has adopted a number of directives and laws on immigration, most of which utilize the EU as a means to coordinate exclusion or prohibitions against immigration: a common standard on political asylum to prevent "asylum shopping" whereby asylum seekers would seek asylum in the state with the most liberal asylum laws; requirements in the Dublin Convention that asylum applications be processed in the first EU country a refugee enters; bolstering of EU external borders to prevent illegal immigration and cooperation for return of illegal migrants; agreements to combat human trafficking, whereby migrants, mostly females, are virtually enslaved in sweatshops or in brothels[54]; a visa information system; rules on family unification; a law on the status of long-term residents; police cooperation; joint initiatives with countries of origin; and monitoring of the status of non-EU citizens within the EU. The EU has also advanced a number of goals with respect to immigrants, including access to employment and education, fostering of entrepreneurship, fighting against discrimination, promotion of social inclusion, and protection. The EU has also set up a European Fund for the Integration of Third-Country Nationals and sponsors a Center on Racism and Xenophobia.[55]

In 2009, the EU, noting that it was far less successful than the US, Canada, or Australia in attracting skilled immigrants, adopted a "blue card" policy that aimed to bring 20 million skilled workers to Europe over a period of twenty years. This initiative is reflective of policies in many European countries, which try to differentiate between "bad" immigration (illegal or unskilled migrants) and "good" immigration that will contribute to growth and competitiveness. The rationale for the "blue card" (modelled after the United States "green card" that allows foreigners to work in the US) was in part to streamline conflicting admission procedures. The initial blue card would be good for three years, but it could be renewed and would allow its holder to change jobs and move within the EU. However, applicants had to be highly qualified (university degree or several years work experience), have a work contract with an EU employer, and demonstrate they have their own health coverage. Critics charged that such a policy would contribute to a "brain drain" in poorer countries, as highly skilled people, desperately needed in developing states, would move for more lucrative opportunities in Europe.

The blue card directive, however, has not had a major impact, and it is doubtful it will come anywhere close to its goal of bringing millions of people to Europe. Its supranational component was watered down, as member states were given the right to set quotas for blue cards or to decline to take in any workers. Several states also delayed transposing the blue card directive into their national legislation. In 2013, only 15,261 blue cards were issued; 14,197 of those were in Germany.[56] Whether or not the EU can in fact attract millions of highly skilled immigrants remains to be seen, and, more recently, political dynamics in many states have changed to make even these more "attractive" immigrants less welcome.

At the same time, however, the EU is aware that immigration is much more than an economic issue, declaring 2008 the European Year for Intercultural Dialogue. By 2015, one could argue that as immigration—a "least likely case" for EU supranational policy given traditional concerns over state sovereignty and its political salience—had become increasingly subject to EU-level discussions, if not yet comprehensive policy, one could be sanguine about a more united Europe, one that would make a "radical break with traditional notions of statehood and territorial control."[57]

The 2015 refugee crisis and beyond

Any such optimism, however, was sorely tested in 2015, when over 1 million refugees and migrants, mostly from Syria, but also from Iraq, Afghanistan, Eritrea, Somalia, and several states in North Africa, flooded into the EU.[58] Many had been living in Turkey, which had taken in over 2 million Syrian refugees since the outbreak of civil war in Syria in 2012. However, believing that they would fare better in the EU, many crossed the Aegean Sea, often at great cost and risk. Others braved the Mediterranean, fleeing conflicts and poverty in North Africa. Many did not make it. The International Organization for Migration reported over 3,770 fatalities in 2015 among those trying to cross these bodies of water.[59] Reaching Greece or Italy was often, however, the first step in their journey. Indeed, many did not—despite EU rules requiring them to do so—apply for asylum when they first entered the EU (Greece in particular also lacked the resources to process that many asylum applications). A widespread belief that Sweden and Germany would offer more generous asylum provisions lured many northward, again at great cost and risk, as evidenced by the seventy-one people who suffocated in the back of a truck in Austria in August 2015.

While the war in Syria had been, for several years, a humanitarian disaster, that conflict was suddenly brought into the heart of Europe. Pictures of dead refugees—one of a 3-year-old Syrian boy washed ashore on a Turkish beach went viral on the Internet in early September 2015—moved many in Europe to demand that their countries do something. As noted at the beginning of this chapter, Germany's Angela Merkel became the leading advocate of *Willkommenskultur*, condemning protests and violence against refugees and suggesting that Germany had both a moral and legal responsibility to help people in need. She indicated that the refugees would be welcome in Germany, which constitutionally guarantees the right of asylum. She also played to history and German pride, noting that "the world sees Germany as a country of hope and opportunity, [which] was not always the case." At the same time, she invoked the broader notion of European values and solidarity, arguing that, "if Europe fails on the question of refugees, if this close link with universal civil rights is broken, then it won't be the Europe we wished for."[60] While she pledged Germany would do more than its part—"*Wir schaffen das*" (We can do this) became a common mantra—she called on other countries to accept refugees. A majority of Germans rallied to her, and, for a time, her position won her accolades inside and outside of Europe, prompting *The Economist* to label her "the indispensible European" and *Time* magazine to name her "Person of the Year" for 2015 and "Chancellor of the Free World."[61] As explored in the **Is Europe one?** feature, her initial response to the refugee crisis bolstered her position as the leader of Europe.

Throughout the fall of 2015, the refugee crisis grew more acute. From January to October 2015, an estimated 1.2 million migrants/refugees had "illegally" entered the EU, a four-fold increase from 2014.[62] The voluntary agreement among EU members in early 2015 to take in just over 30,000 asylum seekers over two years was clearly insufficient.[63] Merkel pushed for a mandatory EU quota system similar to a decades-long system in Germany used to distribute refugees across the country. By year's end, Germany had taken in 1 million people, and tens of thousands were settled in Austria, Sweden, the Netherlands, Italy, and elsewhere.

However, *Willkommenskultur* was far from universal. As noted in the **Is Europe one?** section, some began to blame Merkel's open door policy—she declared that anyone from Syria would receive refugee status in Germany—for encouraging people to migrate. Many countries, citing security concerns and/or economic costs, put up fences and tightened security to keep them out, as seen in Figure 11.2. Hungary, due to geography and as well as its self-confessed "illiberal" prime minister, Viktor Orbán, took the lead in opposing the refugee wave and closed its border with Serbia and Romania to stop refugees from entering Hungary. There was some violence as police fired tear gas at refugees gathered outside border fences and refugees charged entry points. Images of hostility toward the refugees—including a dramatic case of a Hungarian journalist purposefully tripping a young refugee girl[64]—seemed out of place in a Europe that allegedly stood for open borders, freedom, rights, and dignity. A mayor of a small town in Hungary became a hero to nationalist parties across Europe for posting a video on YouTube, featuring intimidating security

Is Europe one?

Angela Merkel—Europe's chancellor?

To the extent Europe has been drawing closer and closer together as a political community, can one identify a single leader that can represent and lead this united Europe? With all due respect to both Jean-Claude Juncker, the former prime minister of Luxembourg and current President of the European Commission, and Donald Tusk, the former Polish Prime Minister and current President of the European Council, only one person in the 2010s can legitimately claim the title as the leader of Europe: German Chancellor Angela Merkel.

Merkel, even her ardent supporters would concede, does not claim leadership based upon her own personal charisma. Some find her dull and unimaginative, one who, in the words of former Chancellor Willy Brandt, practices "*Die Politik der kleinin Schritte*" (politics of baby steps). However, as discussed in Chapter 8, she has prevailed in German elections for her reassuring steady hand and pragmatism. As the EU's largest country, one would of course expect Germany's leader to have an important role to play in European politics. In a sense, then, one could say that European leadership has been more thrust upon Merkel than something she has ardently sought. Nonetheless, it would be fair to argue that during Europe's greatest crises in the twenty-first century, Merkel has stepped forward.

This was, as noted in the previous chapter, clearly evident in the European debt crisis in the late 2000s. Merkel's response to the crisis was not always popular, as she was the one holding the purse strings and was reluctant to give heavily indebted countries such as Greece a blank check. However, she proved willing to compromise, forcing debt holders to take a "hair cut" on Greek debt, and putting together the European Stability Mechanism to secure funds to help bail out indebted states.

It was in 2015, however, that Merkel's leadership most clearly stood out as the EU faced multiple crises. Among European leaders, she, the daughter of a pastor who grew up in communist East Germany, was the one who most forcefully stood up to Russian aggression against Ukraine and pushed for continuation of an EU sanction regime against Moscow. By summer, Greece again appeared on the verge of bankruptcy and possible expulsion from the eurozone. Merkel again intervened, forcing the hand of the Greek government, which reluctantly agreed to austerity measures in return for financial support. Immediately on the heels of this crisis, she took the lead on the refugee question. *Time* magazine waxed elegiac on her accomplishments and vision:

> Germany has spent the past 70 years testing antidotes to its toxically nationalist, militarist, genocidal past. Merkel brandished a different set of values—humanity, generosity, tolerance—to demonstrate how Germany's great strength could be used to save, rather than destroy. It is rare to see a leader in the process of shedding an old and haunting national identity. "If we now have to start apologizing for showing a friendly face in response to emergency situations," she said, "then that's not my country."[65]

Even George Soros, the Hungarian-American financier who had been a staunch critic of Merkel's approach to the economic crisis, praised her leadership over Russia/Ukraine and the refugees, conceding that she was far-sighted in realizing the refugee crisis had the potential to destroy the EU and that, contrary to being a cautious figure, she took "bold initiative" to change public opinion.[66]

A successful leader, however, not only needs to win followers; she must keep them. Initially, Merkel did win support among many Germans. The *Willkommenskultur* which she promoted was, at least in the short-term, a feel-good story, and it allowed the Germans to portray themselves as generous, as opposed to being (as Greeks and others had accused them with respect to the economic crisis) stingy and cold-hearted. However, as refugees continued to stream into Germany, she faced sharp criticism, particularly within her own Christian Democratic bloc. Finance Minister Wolfgang Schäuble, seen by some as an intraparty rival, accused her of acting like a "careless skier" and causing an avalanche by encouraging migrants to pour into Europe.[67] Her "Person of the Year" award, revealed in December, was derided by her critics.[68] As noted in the text, she had to backpedal on her enthusiasm for accepting refugees, conceding that Germany could not do it alone and placing some controls on the borders to control the flow and weed out economic migrants from those fleeing war and persecution. By February 2016, her approval rating within Germany (46 percent) was the lowest it had been in five years. Over 80 percent of Germans thought the government had mishandled the crisis; 40 percent of respondents wanted her to resign.[69] Even former chancellor Helmut Kohl, her mentor, spoke out against mass immigration, saying that Europe cannot become a home for people with fundamentally different values (read: Muslims).[70] While the EU's deal with Turkey—which featured a very awkward meeting between Merkel and Turkish President Erdoğan—may have won her a bit of a reprieve from those that believe the flow of refugees will be dramatically reduced, critics on her left expressed concerns about Turkey's reliability as a partner. Cem Özdemir, a German of Turkish descent who is co-leader of the German Green Party, rhetorically asked, "Does anybody seriously think that a country [Turkey] which hunts down and mistreats its own citizens can offer security to people in flight?"[71]

Outside of Germany, her standing in many places was even lower. Merkel had long been seen by many in Greece and others in Southern Europe as a bully, far more concerned with German voters (and taxpayers) than the plight of those suffering from the debt crisis. During the refugee crisis, as noted in the text, leaders in several EU countries openly derided her policies and refused to go along with EU-mandated quotas to redistribute refugees. One of her primary allies, Chancellor Werner Faymann of Austria, made a *volte-face* and closed Austria's borders. Even this, however, was not enough to save him politically. If the refugee crisis could have been viewed at first (perhaps naively) as a chance for Europeans to unite around a humanitarian disaster (and perhaps make some amends for its inaction to stop the conflict in Syria), it clearly fell short. Rather than keeping doors open for refugees, many leaders closed them. Overall, Europe looks far more divided in 2016—West versus East, North versus South, cosmopolitan European federalists versus nationalists—than it has at any time in the twenty-first century. If the refugee crisis was a test for Merkel and Europe, both, arguably, failed.

The political future of Merkel, who was first elected Chancellor in 2005, is uncertain. The German economy is performing well, and the main opposition parties do not have a compelling candidate to challenge her. Nonetheless, the Christian Democrats suffered defeats in regional elections in March 2016, both to the Social Democrats and Greens on the left and to the new (formed in 2013) Alternative for Germany party, which campaigned against the EU and a liberal immigration policy. Its strong showing in the east German state of Saxony-Anhalt (winning almost a quarter of the vote) generated headlines and concerns that the anti-EU forces prevalent in many other countries could gain real traction in Germany.[72] The German weekly *Der Spiegel* called the results a "black Sunday" for Merkel and her party.[73] Across Europe,

moreover, in 2016–2017 political momentum is now far greater among the Euroskeptics than with those that Merkel might believe to be her natural allies.

This book will go to press in early 2017. By the end of that year, one in which there will be national elections in both Germany and France, might Merkel be defeated and anti-EU, nationalist crusader Marine Le Pen of the French National Front win election and become "Person of the Year"? The very fact that such an outcome is even conceivable clearly shows how quickly things can change. Even though Le Pen clearly has no ambitions to lead a united Europe, the elevation of her (or someone like her) to prominent leadership would say much about prospects for a united Europe.

guards, in which he encourages refugees to stay out of both Hungary and his town. Helpfully, however, the video featured a map of alternative routes through Slovenia and Croatia.[74] Many, including anti-EU figures in Western Europe, suggested that the reanimation of border controls meant the death of the Schengen Agreement, which had eliminated border checks and allowed free travel within the EU, if not a broader unraveling of the EU.[75]

As refugees were turned away from Hungary, many did search for alternative routes west and north, leading, as seen in Figure 11.2, to more fences and more hostility and countries claimed they were unable to deal with the crisis. In September 2015, Merkel, recognizing that the situation was deteriorating, imposed checks along the Austrian border (she claimed it was both legal and temporary and was focused on ensuring that only those with valid claims of asylum were admitted as opposed to economic migrants), but also managed to secure agreement within the EU for her quota plan, although it only covered 120,000 refugees.[76] Nonetheless, it was staunchly opposed by several post-communist leaders, even though post-communist countries were required to accept essentially a token amount of refugees and, according to one report, were the European states most in "need" of immigrants, given both job vacancies and projected demographic decline in coming years.[77] Orbán openly balked at Merkel's refugee quota plan, calling it an example of "moral imperialism" and portraying himself as the protector of Europe. In December 2015, Slovakia, which was required to take in up to 802 refugees, went even further, filing a lawsuit against the plan in the European Court of Justice. Slovak Prime Minister Roberto Fico called the quota plan "nonsensical" and a "fiasco."[78]

It was not, however, only post-communist states that tried to close their borders to refugees. Denmark, wedged between asylum-friendly Germany and Sweden and upheld by some as a model of liberal, social democracy, shut down some of its borders, cut back on social benefits to refugees and passed a measure to confiscate any valuables they possessed to help pay for their care, took out ads in Middle Eastern newspapers warning would-be refugees not to come to Denmark, and ultimately said it could not accept the modest share of 1,000 refugees assigned to it in the EU's redistribution agreement. The Danish press and several politicians, echoing Orbán, spoke of a "Muslim invasion."[79] In January 2016, even Sweden, perhaps Europe's most friendly country to asylum seekers, imposed border controls, barring entry to those without proper documents.[80]

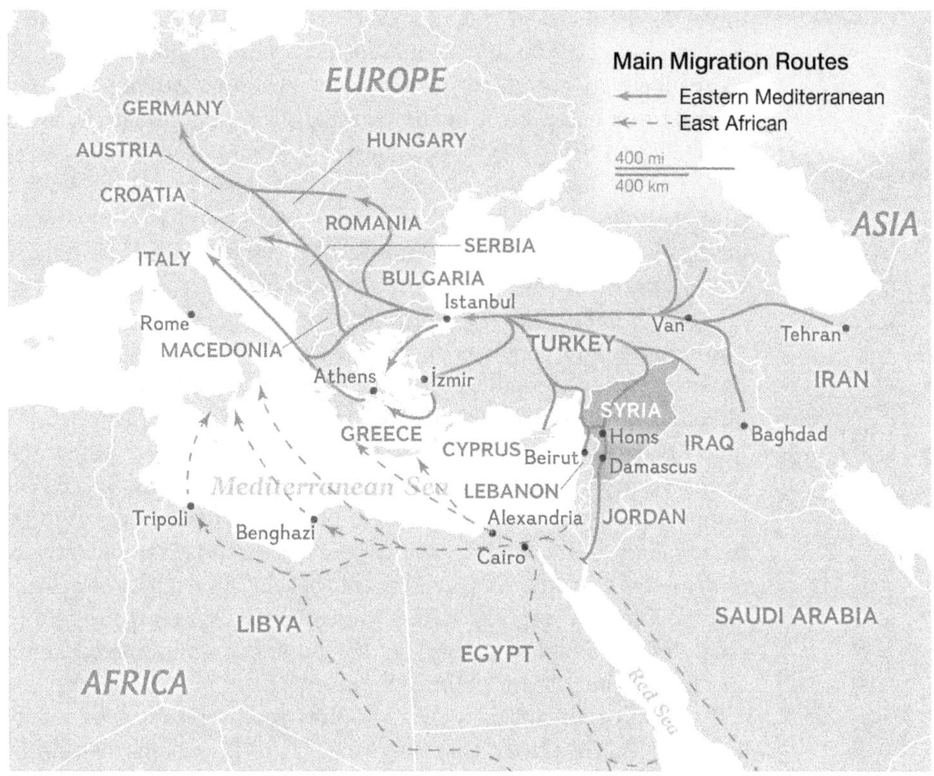

FIGURE 11.2 Refugee routes into Europe

Used with the permission of National Geographic

Policies such as these were also a reflection of deepening public concern across Europe about accepting more refugees. Partially, the issue was one of cost and the sheer ability of societies to absorb so many newcomers so quickly. There were also concerns about a possible crime wave or general poor behavior by refugees, including reports of sexual assaults by gangs of non-German men during New Year's celebrations in Cologne.[81] Most seriously, after the attacks in Paris in November 2015, investigations revealed that at least one of the terrorists had been in Syria fighting with ISIS. A passport of a Syrian refugee was also found at the scene of the attack. Although it was later demonstrated that all of the attackers were EU citizens, not Syrians, there was great fear that terrorists were embedded among the refugees.[82] Afterward, Poland announced that for security reasons it would not take in its mandated quota of refugees. As seen in Table 11.5, a pan-European survey conducted in the spring of 2016 found that Europeans, in general, are most worried about the link between refugees and terrorism, not fears of crime in general or economic costs. Interestingly, the fears (as well as general dislike of Muslims) are most pronounced in post-communist states such as Poland and Hungary, which have *not* been the destination of choice for most refugees. However, as seen from the table, Poles and Hungarians are far from alone in expressing concern about the refugees. French public opinion, interestingly, shows more concerns about the economic costs than terrorism. Older respondents, those with less education, and those on the political right also tend to be more fearful. The survey also revealed that in terms of defining national identity, Hungarians, Poles, and Greeks are much more likely to adopt an exclusionary position, valuing factors such as being a Christian or being born in the country than respondents in Sweden or Germany, who have on balance a more inclusive view of national identity.[83] Arguably, this is the case because these countries have less history dealing with immigrants, thus people are fearful of the new and unknown. Less charitably, one could suggest that publics in post-communist countries are rejecting ideas of diversity and tolerance which are ostensibly markers of cosmopolitan European identity.

By 2016, the *Willkommenskultur* was largely a memory. Anti-immigrant and anti-refugee sentiment was on the rise across Europe. Border controls in the Western Balkans effectively shut down the route many refugees had used to move from Greece to Central Europe, leaving thousands essentially trapped in Greece. Merkel's quota plan was in tatters, with only 3,000 refugees distributed to other countries.[84] In May, Austrian Chancellor Werner Faymann, who had backed Merkel's approach, resigned as his popularity plummeted. Concerns over immigration figured prominently in the June 2016 "Brexit" vote. Most significantly, as explored more in the **Is Europe one?** feature, Angela Merkel came under increasing pressure within Germany for her response to the refugee crisis. One report suggested that the refugee crisis could be her "undoing" as her popularity plummeted and anti-EU forces in Germany gained more political support.[85]

In March 2016, an unlikely "solution" to the crisis was found: The EU negotiated a deal with Greece and Turkey. Under its provisions, would-be asylum-seekers arriving in Greece must apply for asylum in Greece. The EU would provide financial assistance to facilitate processing. Those who failed to meet criteria as a legitimate refugee, including those coming from countries such as Afghanistan or Pakistan who were classified as economic migrants, would be sent back to Turkey. Those trying to enter Greece illegally would also be sent back. So that Turkey is not overwhelmed with people expelled from Europe, the EU agreed to re-settle one Syrian refugee from camps in Turkey for each person sent back. Turkey will be

TABLE 11.5 Widespread concerns over refugees

Table reports percent expressing agreement

Country	*Refugees increase likelihood of terrorism*	*Refugees are economic and social burden*	*Refugees bring more crime*	*Unfavorable view of Muslims*
Germany	61	31	35	29
France	46	53	24	29
Great Britain	52	46	28	28
Sweden	57	32	46	35
Italy	60	65	47	69
Greece	55	72	30	65
Hungary	76	82	43	72
Poland	71	75	26	66

Source: April–May 2016 survey by the Pew Research Center, reported at www.pewglobal.org/2016/07/11/europeans-fear-wave-of-refugees-will-mean-more-terrorism-fewer-jobs/ (accessed July 12, 2016)

paid €6 billion to accept them and maintain those already in Turkey, ostensibly helping to ensure that more people would choose to remain in Turkey.[86] In July 2016, the EU adopted new provisions, including giving states more latitude in accepting or rejecting refugee resettlement and offering €10,000 for each refugee they take in from Turkey or another non-EU country.[87]

The deal with Turkey was criticized for several reasons. Human rights organizations and the United Nations both claimed it violated international law on the treatment of refugees. Others saw it as a rebuke of the much-ballyhooed "European values," as Europe was now turning its back on desperate people who had suffered, both in their home countries and in their escapes, innumerable hardships.[88] The arrangement with Turkey, which also included provisions to approve visa-free travel for Turks into Europe, was also seen as a "deal with the devil," as Turkish President Recep Tayyip Erdoğan had, according to many in Europe, moved Turkey in an autocratic, non-democratic direction (this is discussed more in the following chapter). Refugees detained in camps in Greece protested being sent back to Turkey, claiming that Turkey was unsafe for them, as Turkey was not affording them full rights under international law and was rounding up would-be asylum-seekers and expelling them back to Syria.[89] In May 2016, a Greek judge sided with an asylum-seeker on this issue, preventing his expulsion from Greece to Turkey.[90] Refugees who have successfully won asylum in Germany and elsewhere also would not be sent back. While the deal has not stopped all illegal entries into Greece—Greece lacks the ability to completely secure its borders and will no doubt require substantial assistance in order to vet those who do arrive and apply for asylum—it has reduced the overall flow. The International Organization for Migration (IOM) reported that in the first two months of 2016, prior to the deal taking effect, over 2,000 people per day were entering Greece. By June 2016, the figure was only sixty-four people per day.[91] Figures compared to 2015 are also markedly lower.[92] While the deal has thus significantly reduced the overall flow of refugees and migrants into Europe, this deal does not cover crossings from North Africa across the Mediterranean, which increased after it became more difficult to enter Greece[93] and is arguably the more dangerous route, evidenced by the 400 migrants who died in April 2016 while trying to cross on overcrowded boats from Egypt to Italy.

Whether Europe can integrate the refugees remaining within EU borders—the prospect of them voluntarily returning to war-town Syria is, medium-term, exceptionally low—and weather the broader political fallout as anti-immigrant forces across the continent gain strength—the 2016 Brexit vote being the most significant but hardly only example—is an open question, one that is likely to be enduring as immigration is not an issue that is likely to simply go away. Both "push" factors (war, repression, lack of economic opportunity in home countries) and "pull" factors (relative stability, wealth, and freedom in Europe) will attract many to Europe even as, ironically, Europeans themselves have become more pessimistic about their own futures. Europe's response to this issue touches upon fundamental questions raised in this volume. Whether Europe presents as a hostile face (as displayed in Budapest's Keleti station), the *Willkommenskultur* witnessed in Germany and elsewhere, or something in-between that varies from country to country will go a long way in defining what Europe is and which direction it is heading.

Application questions

1. Can one apply lessons from the American "melting pot" and its experience with immigrants to Europe? Why or why not?
2. Sometimes there is a tension between free speech and other rights. When, if ever, might it be permissible to restrict speech for the sake of order or political harmony?
3. What are the costs and benefits of immigration? Should the religion or economic status of an immigrant matter when considering immigrant quotas or eligibility?
4. What policies would distinguish assimilation from integration? What mix of policies do you think would best serve your country with its immigrant population?
5. Some believe that if one leaves one's home country and takes up residence in another—either as an immigrant or refugee—one should fully embrace the norms and values of the country. If one cannot or will not do so, one should return to one's place of birth. Do you agree? What values and norms might be more essential? Which ones are more negotiable?
6. Conduct some research on responses to immigration in several European countries. Which one, in your view, has handled the situation best? What has it done differently from other countries?

Key terms

Additional reading

Buruma, Ian. 2005. *Murder in Amsterdam: Liberal Europe, Islam, and the Limits of Tolerance*. New York: Penguin.
Buruma investigates the context surrounding the murder of Theo van Gogh in Amsterdam. This book does an excellent job in raising questions about how liberal, democratic Europe can respond to the challenges of new immigrants.

Jenkins, Philip. 2007. *God's Continent: Christianity, Islam, and Europe's Religious Crisis*. Oxford: Oxford University Press.

Jenkins presents a well-written and comprehensive account of the decline of Christianity in Europe and how this, together with immigration, is transforming Europe.

Laqueur, Walter. 2007. *The Last Days of Europe: Epitaph for an Old Continent*. New York: St. Martin's.
This book presents an alarmist view of Europe focusing on how low birthrates and high immigration rates create social and economic challenges for European states.

Parson, Craig, and Smeeding, Timothy, eds. 2006. *Immigration and the Transformation of Europe*. Cambridge: Cambridge University Press.
This collection by a variety of writers assesses how immigration is changing Europe economically, socially, and politically.

Ramadan, Tariq. 2004. *Western Muslims and the Future of Islam*. Oxford: Oxford University Press.
A proponent of Euro-Islam who urges tolerance and mutual understanding, Ramadan argues that European Muslims can take the lead in fostering modernization and change throughout the Muslim world.

Notes

1 See "At Keleti Station in Budapest, the Refugees Could Wait No Longer," and "Cheering German Crowds Greet Refugees After Long Trek from Budapest to Munich," both appearing in *The Guardian*, September 5, 2015. *The Guardian* compiled a series of reports, including maps, on this crisis, at www.theguardian.com/world/ng-interactive/2015/sep/18/latest-developments-in-europes-refugee-crisis-a-visual-guide (accessed June 13, 2016).
2 "Refugee" denotes a particular legal status, as it confers protection, under international treaties, to those fleeing war or a well-founded fear of persecution. Refugees can be distinguished from "migrants," a term that notes only that an individual has left one country for another without noting his/her rationale or intention or conferring any legal protected status. I will typically use the term "refugee" when discussing the wave of new arrivals in 2015, as this was commonly referred to as a "refugee" crisis, and, in my view, those fleeing violence in countries such as Syria, Iraq, Libya, and Afghanistan all have solid grounds for claiming refugee status.
3 Malise Ruthven and Nick Thorpe, "On Today's Refugee Road," *New York Review of Books*, November 24, 2016, p. 27–30.
4 "Europe Makes Deal to Send Afghans Home, Where War Awaits Them," *The New York Times*, October 5, 2016.
5 Tony Judt, "Europe vs. America," *New York Review of Books*, February 10, 2005.
6 Thomas Friedman, "You Break It, You Own It," *The New York Times*, June 29, 2016.
7 Eurabia itself is a bit of a misnomer, as many of the Muslims in Europe are not Arabs. They are of Turkish, South Asian, or sub-Saharan African origin. For alarmist views of Islam in Europe, see Bat Ye'or, *Eurabia: The Euro-Arab Axis* (Madison NJ: Fairleigh Dickinson University Press, 2005); Oriana Fallaci, *The Rage and the Pride* (New York: Rizzoli International, 2002); and Bruce Bawer, *While Europe Slept: How Radical Islam Is Destroying the West from Within* (New York: Doubleday, 2006).
8 Gerard Noiriel, *The French Melting Pot: Immigration, Citizenship, and National Identity* (Minneapolis: University of Minnesota Press, 1996).
9 Others, however, found his points resonant; a poll conducted one week later found 74 percent of Britons agreed with it. See Sarfraz Manzoor, "Donald Trump and the 'Rivers of Blood,'" *The New York Times*, January 24, 2016.
10 Data from www.worldbank.org and Eurostat at http://ec.europa.eu/eurostat.
11 Data from www.worldbank.org.

12 European Social Survey, Round 7, 2014. Data are from the entire survey (minus Israel) using design and sample weights. Data available to registered users at http://nesstar.ess.nsd.uib.no/webview/.
13 "Racism on the Rise in Britain," *The Guardian*, May 27, 2014.
14 Jocelyne Cesari, *When Islam and Democracy Meet: Muslims in Europe and in the United States* (New York: Palgrave, 2004), p. 22, and Stephanie Giry, "France and Its Muslims," *Foreign Affairs* 85:5, September/October 2006, p. 93.
15 If a tourist or short-term visitor to these countries gives birth to a child, the child does not gain citizenship, and in France the child must have one parent who was born in France and must wait until the age of legal majority to formally obtain French citizenship.
16 "Tougher Test on Citizenship Stumps Even Native Danes," *The New York Times*, July 8, 2016.
17 Yasemin Nuhoğlu Soysal, *Limits of Citizenship: Migrants and Postnational Membership in Europe* (Chicago: University of Chicago Press, 1994).
18 Zachary Shore, *America, Islam, and the Future of Europe* (Baltimore: Johns Hopkins University Press, 2006), p. 7–8.
19 When the cartoons were originally published, the controversy was localized to Denmark. It was only later, after some Danish Muslims went to the Middle East and informed others of the event, that the issue acquired global significance. The cartoons can be found at www.brusselsjournal.com/node/698 (accessed on March 25, 2010).
20 "Arrest Extremist Marchers, Police Told," *The Guardian,* February 6, 2006.
21 A good archive of material, which includes various perspectives and is periodically updated, can be found through the website of *The Guardian*, at www.theguardian.com/world/muhammad-cartoons, accessed June 11, 2016.
22 *Glasgow Herald,* February 18, 2006.
23 "Q & A: The Cartoons Row," *The Guardian*, February 7, 2006.
24 Bawer, *While Europe Slept.*
25 Ahmad Akkari, "Danish Muslim: I Was Wrong to Damn Muhammad Cartoons," *The Guardian*, August 9, 2013.
26 Tariq Ramadan, "Cartoon Conflicts," *The Guardian*, February 6, 2006.
27 "Immigration, Black Sheep, and Swiss Rage," *New York Times,* October 8, 2007. A copy of the campaign poster was re-printed in the Daily Mail (London) and can be found at www.dailymail.co.uk/news/article-480493/Proposed-Swiss-immigration-laws-rise-new-racism-xenophobia.html. They also produced a campaign video, "Heaven or Hell," which contrasts the lives of immigrants with those of "real" Swiss. Unfortunately, I believe this has been taken down from online video sites.
28 For an overview of the many issues involving Muslims in Europe, see Kai Hafez, *Islam in 'Liberal' Europe: Freedom, Equality, and Intolerance* (Lanham MD: Rowman and Littlefield, 2014).
29 Quoted in Cesari, *When Islam and Democracy Meet*, p. 33.
30 See obituary for Fallaci in *The Economist,* September 21, 2006.
31 "Europe Tries to Attract Migrants It Prefers," *New York Times,* October 24, 2007.
32 For example, in Switzerland 70 percent of those in prison are non-Swiss. See "Immigration, Black Sheep, and Swiss Rage," *New York Times,* October 8, 2007.
33 For more discussion on these themes, see Herbert Brücker, Joachim Frick, and Gert Wagner, "Economic Consequences of Immigration in Europe," in Craig Parsons and Timothy Smeeding, *Immigration and the Transformation of Europe.* (Cambridge: Cambridge University Press, 2006).
34 "As the Poles Get Richer, Fewer Seek British Jobs," *New York Times*, October 19, 2007.
35 Brücker et al., "Economic Consequences of Immigration," p. 137.
36 See, for example, a December 2015 briefing from the European Parliament, "Economic Challenges and Prospects of the Refugee Influx," at www.europarl.europa.eu/RegData/etudes/BRIE/2015/572809/EPRS_BRI%282015%29572809_EN.pdf, accessed June 13, 2016, and *The Economist*, "For Good or Ill?," January 23, 2016.
37 Randall Hansen, "Making Immigration Work: How Britain and Europe Can Cope with Their Immigration Crises," *Government and Opposition* 51:2, 2016, p. 183–208.

38 Craig Parsons and Timothy Smeeding, "What's Unique about Immigration in Europe?" and Paul Demeny, "Europe's Immigration Challenge in Demographic Perspective," both in Parsons and Smeeding, *Immigration and the Transformation of Europe.*
39 Hansen, 2016.
40 "The War of the Headscarves," *The Economist,* February 7, 2004, p. 25.
41 Giry, "France and Its Muslims."
42 Pew Research poll cited in Jonathan Paris, "Europe and Its Muslims," *Foreign Affairs* 86:1, January/February 2007, p. 182.
43 Rachida Dati served as Minister of Justice from 2008 to 2009. She resigned in 2009 to take up a seat in the European Parliament.
44 "Survey: France 'Minority Report,'" *The Economist,* October 26, 2006.
45 Jeffrey Goldberg, "Is It Time for the Jews to Leave Europe?" *The Atlantic Monthly,* April 2015.
46 Jane Kramer, "The Dutch Model," *The New Yorker,* April 3, 2006, p. 63.
47 The premier source on the murder and its aftermath is Ian Buruma, *Murder in Amsterdam: Liberal Europe, Islam, and the Limits of Tolerance* (New York: Penguin, 2006).
48 Associated Press, November 19, 2004.
49 Over fears of possible violence, Wilders was denied entry into Great Britain in 2008.
50 Those wishing to immigrate to the Netherlands from Western states, including Canada, the US, Australia, and Japan, are exempt. One can find a version of the film at www.spike.com/video/to-netherlands/2710876, accessed on April 1, 2010.
51 Kees Groenendijk, head of Center for Migration Law at University of Nijmegen, in *RFE/RL Newsline,* April 5, 2006.
52 Adam Luedtke, "The European Union Dimension: Supranational Integration, Free Movement of Persons, and Immigration Politics," in Parsons and Smeeding, *Immigration and the Transformation of Europe,* p. 419–441.
53 Ireland and Great Britain, for example, have allowed workers from new members states in Eastern Europe to come and work, and Denmark allows members of a refugee's family up to the age of 24 to relocate to Denmark, whereas the EU norm in 21.
54 This is a major problem in both Western and Eastern Europe. See Caroline Moorehead, "Women and Children for Sale," *New York Review of Books,* October 11, 2007, p. 15–18.
55 European Commission. "Third Annual Report on Migration and Integration," COM 2007:512, September 11, 2007.
56 "Frequently Asked Questions: The EU Blue Card Directive," May 22, 2014, at http://ec.europa.eu/dgs/home-affairs/what-is-new/news/news/docs/20140522_faq_blue_card_report_june_2014_final_en.pdf. See also the immigration portal for the EU at http://ec.europa.eu/immigration.
57 Luedtke, "The European Union Dimension," p. 438.
58 As noted (note 2 above), refugee is a term denoting that the individual is fleeing violence or fear of persecution. Under international law, would-be refugees can apply for political asylum in another country. Eurostat reports that in 2015 there were 1.3 million applications for asylum in the EU. This was a marked increase from 2014 (627,000 applications) and 2013 (431,000 applications). The largest number of applicants were Syrians (29 percent), followed by Afghans (14 percent), Iraqis (10 percent), and Kosovars/Albanians (5 percent), the last of whom were viewed primarily as economic migrants. Data available at http://ec.europa.eu/eurostat/statistics-explained/index.php/Asylum_statistics (accessed July 13, 2016). Under the EU's Dublin Convention, refugees are required to apply for asylum in the first EU country they enter. However, many did not do so upon arriving in Greece. Consequently, some referred to the refugees as "illegal migrants" because they crossed borders without fulfilling their obligations.
59 International Organization for Migration, *Fatal Journeys: Volume 2*, 2016, available at https://publications.iom.int/books/fatal-journeys-volume-2-identification-and-tracing-dead-and-missing-migrants.
60 "Angela Merkel Calls for European Unity to Address Migrant Influx," *The New York Times*, August 31, 2015.

61 *The Economist*, November 7, 2015, and *Time*, December 9, 2015, online feature on Merkel available at http://time.com/time-person-of-the-year-2015-angela-merkel-choice/ (accessed July 13, 2016).
62 Jim Yardley, "The Breaking Point," *The New York Times Magazine*, December 20, 2015, p. 42.
63 "Looking for a Home," *The Economist*, August 29, 2015.
64 This can be seen at www.theguardian.com/world/video/2015/sep/08/journalist-appears-to-kick-and-trip-fleeing-refugees-video. The journalist was fired from her job but later said she would sue the refugee "as a matter of honor." See report from Canadian Broadcasting, at www.cbc.ca/news/trending/camerawoman-fired-for-tripping-refugees-plans-to-sue-facebook-and-a-refugee-1.3284591.
65 *Time*, December 9, 2015, online at http://time.com/time-person-of-the-year-2015-angela-merkel-choice/.
66 Interview with George Soros, "'The EU Is on the Verge of Collapse'—An Interview," *The New York Review of Books*, January 11, 2016, p. 35.
67 "Angela Merkel's Future Under Scrutiny for the First Time as German Asylum Process Criticized," *The Telegraph*, November 13, 2015.
68 For example, see "Angela Merkel, Person of the Year? Eine Katastrophe, More Like," *The Telegraph*, December 9, 2015.
69 "Could Europe's Refugee Crisis Be the Undoing of Merkel?," *The Washington Post*, February 4, 2016.
70 "Angela Merkel Is Warned by Her 'Mentor' Helmut Kohl that Europe Cannot Become Home for Millions of Migrants Whose Beliefs Are Different to 'the Foundations of Our Values,'" *Daily Mail*, April 18, 2016.
71 Quoted in "Merkel's Trust in Turkey and Greece to Stem Migrants Comes with Risks," *The New York Times*, March 21, 2016.
72 "German Elections: Setbacks for Merkel's CDU as Anti-Refugee AfD Makes Big Gains," *The Guardian*, March 14, 2016, and "Fury and the AfD: Inside the Revolt Against Angela Merkel," *Spiegel International Online*, March 21, 2016, at www.spiegel.de/international/germany/success-of-afd-populists-akin-to-revolt-against-merkel-a-1083147.html.
73 "*Blitzanalyse zu den Landtagswahlen: AfD triumphiert, schwarzer Sonntag für die CDU,*" Spiegel Politik Online, March 13, 2016.
74 Yardley, 2015, p. 40.
75 "Europe Starts Putting Up Walls," *The Economist*, September 19, 2015.
76 "Europe Starts Putting Up Walls," *The Economist*, September 19, 2015.
77 "More Vacancies Than Visitors," *The Economist*, September 18, 2015.
78 Reuters, "Slovakia Files Lawsuit Against EU Quotas to Redistribute Migrants," December 2, 2015, at www.reuters.com/article/us-europe-migrants-slovakia-idUSKBN0TL11K20151202.
79 Hugh Eakin, "Liberal, Harsh Denmark," *The New York Review of Books*, March 10, 2016.
80 "More European Nations Are Barring Their Doors to Migrants," *The Washington Post*, January 22, 2016.
81 BBC News, "Germany Shocked by Cologne New Year Assaults on Women," January 5, 2016, available at www.bbc.com/news/world-europe-35231046. A later report indicated that the majority of the fifty-eight men arrested were immigrants, mostly from North Africa, but only three were recent arrivals. See report in *The Independent*, February 14, 2016, at www.independent.co.uk/news/world/europe/cologne-only-three-out-of-58-men-arrested-in-connection-with-mass-sex-attack-on-new-years-eve-are-a6874201.html.
82 See "Paris Attacks: Eight Terrorist Suspects Named So Far Are Not Refugees and Have EU Passports," *The Independent*, November 18, 2015.
83 Report on the survey from the Pew Research Center is available at www.pewglobal.org/2016/07/11/europeans-fear-wave-of-refugees-will-mean-more-terrorism-fewer-jobs/ (accessed July 12, 2016).
84 "E.U. Offers a New Plan on Immigration," *The New York Times*, July 14, 2016.

85 "Could Europe's Refugee Crisis Be the Undoing of Merkel?" *The Washington Post*, February 4, 2016.
86 "E.U. Pact to Send New Migrants Back to Turkey," *The New York Times*, March 19, 2016.
87 "E.U. Offers a New Plan on Immigration," *The New York Times*, July 14, 2016.
88 "Migrants Lament Deal as a Betrayal by Europe," *The New York Times*, March 20, 2016.
89 "Clashes Erupt in Greek Refugee Camps as Deportation Threat Looms," *The New York Times*, April 1, 2016.
90 BBC News, "Migrant Crisis: Greek Judges Tell Syrian Refugee Turkey Is Unsafe," May 21, 2016, at www.bbc.com/news/world-europe-36345990.
91 International Organization for Migration (IOM) newsbrief, available at http://dtmodk.iom.int/docs/WEEKLY%20Flows%20Compilation%20No19%2030%20June%202016.pdf.
92 The United Nations reported 1,721 and 1,488 migrants arriving by sea to Greece in May and June 2016. Comparable figures for 2015 were 17,889 and 31,318. See "Migration to Greece From Turkey By Sea Has Plummeted, U.N. Says," *The New York Times*, July 9, 2016.
93 The IOM (note above) reported average daily entries into Italy in January–February 2016 of 150 people; by June, it was over 600 people per day.

Protesters in Ukraine in 2013 proudly display the EU flag as an emblem of their aspirations

Chapter 12

European security and foreign policy

In November 2013, tens of thousands of protesters converged on Kyiv's *Maidan Nezalezhnosti* (Independence Square), decrying the Ukrainian government's decision to reject an Association Agreement with the EU. Waving both Ukrainian and EU flags, the demonstrators chanted "Ukraine is Europe." The government responded with violence, but the protests only grew, recalling the 2004–2005 Orange Revolution that ushered in a new government that, briefly, buoyed hopes for the country's democratization and Europeanization. The protests climaxed in February 2014, after repeated attacks by security forces left over one hundred people dead. Protesters demanded an end to corruption and the resignation of the president, Viktor Yanukovych, who was accused of massive corruption, human rights violations, and trampling on democratic freedoms. Yanukovych, aware he had lost his grip on power, fled to Russia, and both the protesters and their supporters in Europe claimed victory. Independence Square gained a new moniker: Euromaidan.[1]

These events in Ukraine, at least initially, buoyed the EU. In contrast to the numerous harsh critiques directed against the EU in the 2010s in the wake of the global economic crisis and growing Euroskepticism in many member states—developments documented throughout this volume—in this case one witnessed a large-scale movement whose adherents sought to join Europe as well as an affirmation of the EU's soft power based on its commitment to peace, human rights, and democracy. However, the crisis in Ukraine did not end with Yanukovych's downfall. Amid the general breakdown in authority in Ukraine, Crimea, a Ukrainian region with an ethnic Russian majority, was annexed by Russia in March, and separatists, aided by Russia, shelled and occupied several cities in eastern Ukraine. The EU imposed sanctions on Russia, and Russia responded with sanctions of its own, including a ban on food imports from the EU.

The sanctions have proven to be a severe test for the EU. Leaders in several EU countries, including Hungary, Greece, and Czech Republic, claimed their countries were adversely affected and appealed for the sanctions against Russia to be lifted. Because they have been selective in scope and have failed to change Russian behavior—as of 2016 separatists still control significant territory in eastern Ukraine—the sanctions also highlight the EU's weakness in terms of hard power that it can deploy against an adversary that has demonstrated it is not willing to play by the EU's norms. More broadly, one could argue that the crisis over Ukraine has shattered the post-Cold War order within Europe, requiring actors within the EU and NATO to re-think some of their more sanguine assumptions about a relatively benign security environment.[2] The idea that the EU, by virtue of the now-signed Association Agreement—although final ratification of the Agreement has been complicated by a non-binding Dutch referendum that overwhelmingly rejected it in April 2016—as well as commitment of several billion euros in aid, could help turn around Ukraine itself has also been called into question amid persistent allegations of corruption in the new Ukrainian leadership, leading to the resignation of numerous officials, including the prime minister.[3] In short, the Ukrainian crisis has re-animated doubts about both European unity in foreign policy and the EU's ability to respond to security challenges, as well as raising the specter of a new Cold War with Russia.

This chapter takes up a wide range of security and foreign policy issues. Some foreign policy challenges are not exclusively "foreign," and have crossed into the EU itself, most literally in the case of refugee flows spurred primarily by conflicts in the Middle East, which was discussed in the previous chapter. Here the focus is more on the actions (or, in some cases, inaction) by the EU and EU members beyond the EU's borders. The Maastricht Treaty introduced a **Common Foreign and Security Policy (CFSP)**, whose goal is the coordination of states' foreign policies and development of a range of policy instruments to enhance international cooperation and security. While it is true that the CFSP, perhaps more than any other issue area, remains a work in progress, its very development is an indication that there was a global dimension to the goal of a more united Europe by creating a means to give European states a stronger presence on the world stage. Individual European states, of course, continue to have their own foreign policies and some, particularly larger and more powerful ones such as Great Britain, France, and Germany, are important international actors in their own right. This chapter, however, is less concerned about individual state's policies or comparative foreign policy and more focused on broad trends in a pan-European approach to security issues and international affairs. Foreign policy is a crucial case in the examination of the idea of a united Europe. The rationale is straightforward. For a number of reasons (historical experiences, power imbalances, divergent interests, desires to maintain state sovereignty), foreign policy is the area that arguably should see the *least* amount of integration. To the extent that one can remain optimistic about the development of a potent and coherent European foreign policy, one would likely think that movement toward "One Europe" could go quite far.

Common Foreign and Security Policy (CFSP)
created by the Maastricht Treaty, its goal is to develop a stronger, united approach on foreign policy and security issues by EU member-states.

Institutional bases for a "European" foreign policy

Origins

The origins of today's CFSP date to the earliest days of European integration, when proponents of a more politically unified Europe tried to create a European Political Community and a European Defence Community. Both of these plans were very ambitious, as they attempted to create supranational political and military organizations. The Treaty on the European Political Community was signed in 1952, but it was rejected by the French parliament, an action that also doomed the European Defence Community. Grandiose plans for European integration thereafter gave way to the more gradualist, functional approach epitomized by the Treaty of Rome and is described in Chapter 3.

The founding treaties of the then-European Community (EC) did not delegate to the common European institutions any of the powers of foreign policy-making traditionally exercised by the nation-state. The EC did, however, establish trade agreements with the outside world and offered association agreements to neighboring states such as Turkey and Greece that opened up the possibility of future membership to them. The EC also became an observer in many international organizations and established formal diplomatic relations with many countries throughout the world. Nonetheless, it was clear that the EC was *not* a state, and to the extent that there was an EC "foreign policy," it was the result of unanimous agreement among the member states. In 1970, the then six members of EC formed the European Political Cooperation (EPC), an informal consultation process on foreign policy matters with the aim of forming common policies. The establishment of the European Council in 1974 contributed to better coordination of EPC because of the role it gave to the heads of state or government in defining the general orientation of Community policy. Early successes for the EPC included the various Lomé Conventions, dating from 1975, which were trade and aid agreements between the EC and former colonies in the developing world, initiation of the Conference on Security and Cooperation in Europe (CSCE), and sanctions against states such as military-ruled Argentina and apartheid South Africa.

Incorporation in the Maastricht Treaty

By the early 1990s, however, there was a sense that the EC could and should do more. Purely inter-governmental consultations were unwieldy. European states had to play second fiddle to the US in the 1991 war against the Iraqi takeover of Kuwait, and European countries were unprepared to deal with crises closer to home, such as the breakup of Yugoslavia (analyzed in Chapter 2). It is in this context that adding a CFSP was viewed as a logical and necessary extension of the European project.

The Maastricht Treaty established the CFSP. By terms of the Treaty, the CFSP is supposed to safeguard the values and strengthen the security of the EU, preserve international peace in accord with the principles of the UN Charter, promote international cooperation, and develop democracy, rule of law, and respect for human rights. In addition, the Maastricht Treaty envisioned the "progressive framing of a common defence policy, which might in time lead to a common defence." To this end, it brought the **West European Union (WEU)**, which was formed in 1954 but remained largely dormant, into the EU. The WEU was later charged in the 1997 Amsterdam Treaty with humanitarian and rescue missions, peacekeeping, and crisis management. In contrast to NATO, the WEU is purely European and it includes (either as members, associates, or observers) all EU states, including formally "neutral" countries such as Ireland, Austria, and Sweden. As part of the WEU, France, Germany, Belgium, Spain, and Luxembourg have committed 60,000 troops as a Eurocorps, available for humanitarian and peacekeeping missions as well as combat. Eurocorps troops have been deployed to Bosnia, Kosovo, Afghanistan, and Mali.[4]

West European Union (WEU) defense organization within the EU, which is envisioned to play an important role in peacekeeping and humanitarian missions.

The EU was directed to pursue its CFSP by means of systematic cooperation between member states and the implementation of joint actions in areas where the member states have important interests in common. The individual states, however, retain sovereignty in the conduct of their respective foreign and security policy. In other words, cooperation is inter-governmental, with each state having a final say in policy. Particularly with respect to use of military force (e.g., Iraq in 2003, Libya in 2011, Syria throughout the 2010s), there have been divisions among European states, with some willing to deploy forces and others not. Nonetheless, the EU is supposed to ensure that countries refrain from any action that is contrary to the interests of the EU or likely to impair its effectiveness as a cohesive force in international relations. How successful the CFSP has been in producing a unified "European" foreign policy is taken up in the **Is Europe one?** section.

Procedures

How does European foreign policy work? This area has evolved rapidly since the 1990s, and the 2009 Lisbon Treaty transformed it even more. Under Lisbon, economic aspects of foreign policy (e.g., trade, development assistance) remain under "Community" decision-making principles, meaning that that policy is initiated by the European Commission, debated and voted on (usually by qualified majority voting) in the Council of the EU, and is subject to approval by the European Parliament (EP). CFSP decisions (e.g., use of force, adoption of sanctions) are made in a more inter-governmental fashion, with the European Council, the collection of heads of government, defining the strategic interests and objectives of the EU on the basis of unanimity, which also holds in the Council of the EU, which formally approves EU actions. The requirements of unanimity reflect the fact that foreign policy is an area where concerns about national sovereignty are important. The European Parliament may debate a given issue and may be consulted, but final approval of any CFSP rests with the Council of the EU.

There is, as one might expect, an elaborate bureaucratic structure for overseeing EU foreign policy and representing Europe to the world. The Amsterdam Treaty of 1997 created the office of the **High Representative** for the CFSP to coordinate the EU's foreign policy. Until the adoption of the Lisbon Treaty, however, the High Representative had to share responsibility for foreign policy with the EU Commissioner for External Affairs. The Lisbon Treaty altered this structure and created a single High Representative of the EU for Foreign Affairs and Security Policy. Catherine Ashton of Great Britain, who had served as EU Trade Commissioner but otherwise had little foreign policy experience, was the first person appointed to this post; she was replaced in 2014 by Federica Mogherini of Italy. The High Representative, not the European Commission, has the primary responsibility of making foreign policy proposals to the Council of the EU. As noted in Chapter 4, the Lisbon Treaty also created an individual president of the EU (as of 2014, Donald Tusk of Poland), who is also empowered to represent Europe globally. The Lisbon Treaty also created an EU External Action Force, which functions as an EU diplomatic corps.

High Representative the chief diplomat of the EU, who is given an enhanced role under the Lisbon Treaty and empowered to make foreign policy proposals to the EU Council of Ministers.

Is Europe one?

Is there a "European" foreign policy?

The CFSP is an important part of the EU, and over the past two decades European governments have taken a number of steps to give it more substance and teeth. However, one might fairly ask: Can one really speak of a *common* European foreign policy? Does it really make sense to speak of "One Europe" in terms of foreign and defense policies?

The CFSP has a clear rationale. Individually, most European states are too small to have much clout on the world stage. Collectively they can have more of a global role and exercise more influence. In theory, other states would have to deal with a strong and empowered "Europe," not Romania, Denmark, Finland, or Estonia. Some, particularly in light of the 2003 Iraq war, suggest that Europe needs to band together to balance the hegemonic power of the US.[5] Interestingly, survey data (as seen in Figure 12.1) reveals that majorities across Europe, even in some more Euroskeptical states, endorse multi-level governance in this field, believing that foreign policy decisions should be made not solely by national governments but jointly within the EU.[6]

Has CFSP been effective? In some respects, the answer is clearly yes. Again, Europe has more clout when it works collectively. Sanctions on human rights offenders, for example, are far more likely to be effective if adopted by numerous states than by only a few. The EU has adopted common positions on a number of questions—including sanctions against countries such as Zimbabwe, Myanmar, Sudan, and Iran, efforts to fight terrorism, nuclear safety, and cybersecurity—and functions as a collective whole on many issues. As will be highlighted more extensively in this chapter, it has been a leading actor on questions such as human rights, economic development, peacekeeping, removal of land mines and demobilization of combatants, election support, and climate change.[7]

Nonetheless, on many significant questions of international affairs, particularly those involving or requiring hard power, Europe has been less capable of acting with a single voice and/or less than effective in its chosen policy. A prime example was the former Yugoslavia in the early 1990s, where the "hour of Europe," in the words of Luxembourg's foreign minister, turned into four years of bloody fighting and ended only thanks to US intervention. Part of the problem in the Yugoslav case was lack of capability, but also lack of will and unity, as European leaders could not agree on a forceful common strategy. In the case of Kosovo in 1999, Greece, a NATO member, lobbied against bombing of Serbia, whereas some European leaders, notably Great Britain's Tony Blair, argued for a more forceful policy including use of NATO ground troops. After Kosovo declared independence in 2008, all EU members agreed to send an EU mission to develop its security and justice sector, but several states, including Spain, Romania, and Greece, all refused to recognize Kosovo as a sovereign state.

The decision to go to war against Iraq in 2003, however, posed perhaps the greatest challenge to the idea of a common European foreign policy. One writer suggested that Iraq "epitomizes everything that is wrong with the practice and even the concept of the CFSP."[8] The debate over what to do in Iraq, of course, took place in the UN, not within the confines of CSFP, but even there Great Britain was on one side and France and Germany on the other.

Whereas the election of Barack Obama as US President and the subsequent withdrawal of allied troops from Iraq may have healed some of the wounds created by the decision to invade Iraq, one still sees pronounced divisions within Europe on major foreign policy questions.

Yes, Europe can agree on relatively "safe" issues (e.g., sanctions on Myanmar, common measures against international terrorism), but it lacks a grand strategic vision (particularly with respect to its relationship with the US or Russia), and individual states still have their own interests that they feel obligated to pursue. CFSP remains essentially inter-governmental, revealing the limits of EU integration. In some cases that can be cited as an example of concerted European action, such as the 2011 military intervention in Libya which was designed to support UN resolutions and prevent large-scale atrocities against civilians, it was NATO, not the EU, that took the lead, and even then some states (e.g., Italy, Great Britain, France) participated and some (e.g., Germany, Poland) did not. Europe has struggled—to put it mildly—to deal with the Syrian refugee crisis as well as the war in Syria itself, which we'll examine later in this chapter. As noted above, there are even divisions about how to deal with Russian intervention in Ukraine, a state that clearly wishes to join the EU. In 2016, Viktor Orban, Prime Minister of Hungary, declared that Russia is a "partner" of Hungary and claimed that more and more EU countries wish to dispense with sanctions and normalize relations with Moscow.[9] Even at the UN, France and Great Britain retain their individual vetoes on the Security Council and have resisted calls for a common EU seat.

Whereas the motives behind the CFSP and Europe's desire to spread its values may be laudable, the effectiveness of the CFSP, as a grand strategy, is another matter. As one French writer dismissingly observes, "If Europe does not speak with a single voice, it is first and foremost because it lacks any strategic concept other than the wish to be friend to all, and notably the protector of widows and orphans."[10]

Critical thinking questions

1. Despite European concerns over human rights and genocide in areas such as Bosnia, Rwanda, Darfur, Congo, and Syria, European action in these areas has often been minimal or come far too late. Why has Europe been so hamstrung in responding to issues such as these?

2. Does the idea of a Common Foreign Policy for Europe seem attainable or unrealistic to you? Assuming such a policy was a goal, what could be done to realize it?

Instruments of policy

What can the EU do? The EU has four instruments for its CFSP: Common Positions, Joint Actions, Common Strategies, and Declarations. A Common Position means that EU members are obliged to comply with the EU position with regard to their own foreign policies. Examples include maintenance of economic or political sanctions. A Joint Action is designed to put into operation or support a Common Position. Examples include overseas deployment of police or human rights monitoring forces to support EU policy. A Common Strategy sets out broad policy guidelines with respect to a country or region. For example, the EU has a Common Strategy with both Russia and Ukraine and its European Neighborhood Policy (ENP) with countries to its south and east also fits into this rubric. A Declaration is simply a statement expressing the EU's position (e.g., condemnation of Russian action in Ukraine in 2014).

While the EU does have economic and diplomatic muscle to carry out foreign policy, it is relatively lacking when it comes to military capabilities. Individual states and/or NATO were counted on to provide security, and in several instances (e.g., the Italians in Albania in 1997, the British in Sierra Leone in 2000, the French in Ivory Coast in 2002 and in Central African Republic in 2013), separate countries have provided the military means to act while the EU has offered only diplomatic or political support. After the Kosovo crisis in 1999, the EU agreed that it must have "the capacity for autonomous action, backed by credible military forces, the means to decide to use them, and the readiness to do so, in order to respond to international crises without prejudice to actions by NATO."[11] To that end, the EU created a **Common Security and Defence Policy (CSDP)** (initially known as the European Strategic Defense Policy), which included efforts to bolster the EU's military capability. EU members agreed on a "Headline Goal" process that outlined the needs of the EU for its projected peacekeeping and military operations. Some, however, feared that the development of separate EU forces would undermine NATO. In 2002, NATO and EU agreed to cooperate in military affairs, and the EU is allowed to use NATO structures and assets if NATO declines to act in a particular situation. The first EU troops were sent on a peacekeeping mission to Macedonia in 2003, and, as noted below, the EU has participated in several peacekeeping or emergency operations. By 2008, the EU met its 2003 Headline Goal of 60,000 troops that can be deployed for up to a year and also has fifteen multi-national battle groups of 1,500 troops each at its disposal on a rotating basis as part of the ESDP.

Common Security and Defence Policy (CSDP)
EU program designed to increase its military capability; has already performed several peacekeeping and humanitarian operations.

The EU has deployed over thirty military and civilian missions from 2003 to 2015 in order to promote peace and security.[12] The EU's first mission outside of Europe occurred in 2003, when as part of Operation Artemis it sent 1,800 personnel, mostly French, to the Democratic Republic of Congo for two months to prevent the outbreak of wider violence. It also sent a force of more than 4,000 troops to Chad and the Central African Republic to assist in peacekeeping and support of refugees fleeing the Sudanese region of Darfur. EU police and monitoring groups have also been deployed in Georgia, Indonesia, Palestine, Moldova, Ukraine, and Sudan to assist in human rights and peacekeeping operations. While the EU touts such efforts as proof of the organization's positive record in promoting global security, critics would argue that the EU could and should do more (e.g., to stop atrocities in Darfur or Central African Republic, not simply protecting refugees that have already fled the area) and not confine itself to relatively low-risk peacekeeping or support operations.

Public support

Foreign policy and defense, perhaps more so than any other policy area, infringe upon traditional powers of state sovereignty. The right to defend territory and the ability to raise and deploy military forces are fundamental attributes of a state. Over its history, Europe has seen a variety of competing powers and military conflicts. The notion that European governments and publics would be willing to pool their sovereignty for the sake of common foreign policy or defense policies, particularly

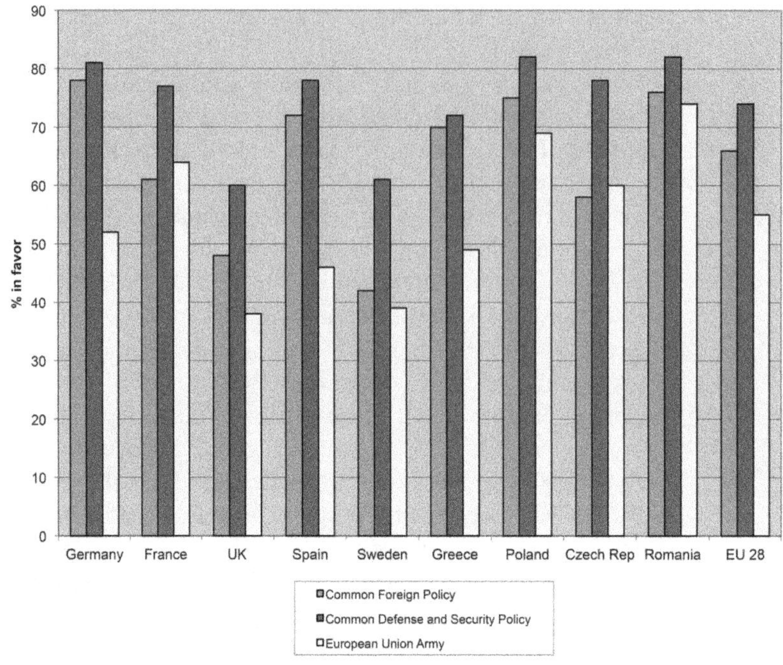

FIGURE 12.1 Support for Common Foreign and Security Policies, 2015

Eurobarometer 83, 2015, available at http://ec.europa.eu/public_opinion/archives/eb/eb83/eb83_anx_en.pdf

given the well-known shortcomings of the CFSP and divisions in Europe over core policies (e.g., how to respond to a resurgent Russia) might lead one to be skeptical about popular support for this project.

Figure 12.1 presents results of several questions for a 2015 Eurobarometer survey on foreign policy and defense-related questions. The results might be surprising, particularly given the levels of opposition to the EU and Euroskepticism we have encountered in previous chapters. Here one sees broad support for a common foreign and defense policy as well as majority support for creation of an EU army. True, support is lower in some countries, including (not surprisingly) Great Britain and historically neutral Sweden. However, even in France, which long had aspirations/pretensions as a great power, there is widespread support for a common European approach to foreign and security policy. Interestingly, support for these policies is higher than it is for both the euro (57 percent in the EU twenty-eight) and further expansion (39 percent), considered by many to be top achievements of the EU.

Other European security organizations

The fact that the CFSP is of relatively recent origin can be explained, partially, by the fact that other organizations in Europe focused on security issues. Two of these, NATO and the OSCE, continue to have relevance in the post-Cold War world.

The North Atlantic Treaty Organization (NATO)

NATO (North Atlantic Treaty Organization) military and political alliance of twenty-eight countries in Europe and North America; played key role during Cold War, and has since expanded to new countries and new missions.

The **North Atlantic Treaty Organization (NATO)** arguably remains the most important security institution in Europe. It is headquartered, like the EU, in Brussels, and its top official, the secretary-general, is a European.[13] NATO, however, is not, a wholly European organization. Because it includes Canada and the US—indeed, because of US military power, the US is the pre-eminent force in NATO—it is often described as a "trans-Atlantic" institution, one that creates a bond between the US and Europe.

NATO was the key player during the Cold War, serving to deter a possible Soviet attack on Western Europe. Fundamentally, NATO is a military alliance based on a system of collective security, whereby its member states agree to come to a member's defense if another actor attacks it. With its initial foe—the Soviet Union—no more, NATO has been compelled to look for a new role in the post-Cold War world.

One recent emphasis of NATO has been the addition of new members. In the 1990s many former communist countries sought NATO membership, less out of explicit security concerns (the possibility of a Soviet attack on Poland or Hungary seemed, at least then, quite remote) than as recognition that these states were part of the successful West. For their part, existing NATO states argued that NATO expansion (similar to EU expansion) would help consolidate democracy and prevent the emergence of a "security vacuum" in Eastern Europe. Despite objections by Russia, NATO added Poland, the Czech Republic, and Hungary in 1999; Bulgaria, Estonia, Latvia, Lithuania, Romania, Slovakia, and Slovenia in 2004; and Albania and Croatia in 2009. As of 2016, NATO's membership stands at twenty-eight countries, but it may expand further, in part as a response to a more belligerent Russia. Indeed, both Georgia (attacked by Russia in 2008) and Ukraine (subjected to Russian military intervention in 2014) ardently seek NATO membership. Whether this will occur is an open question, in part because of concerns about Russia's response to such a move and in part because it would be exceptionally risky to take on a member that has a border/security dispute with Russia.

NATO has also undertaken military missions outside of its primary responsibility to defend the territory of member states from outside attack. These cases included Bosnia (1994–1995) and Kosovo (1999), where NATO both bombed Serbian positions and took the lead in sending in peacekeepers once the fighting stopped. The intervention in Kosovo was particularly controversial because the UN did not authorize it and NATO's own treaty says members must "refrain from the use of force in any manner inconsistent with the purposes of the United Nations" (Article 1) and that the UN Security Council has "primary responsibility" for the maintenance of international peace and security (Article 7). Nonetheless, most NATO members felt compelled to act, given the juxtaposition of the possibility of another round of mass killing in the Balkans with NATO's fiftieth anniversary celebrations. Indeed, during the fighting NATO approved a new strategic concept that broadened its mission to "stand firm against those who violate human rights, wage war, and conquer territory" and stated that NATO would seek to "contribute to building a stronger and broader Euro-Atlantic community of democracy."[14]

The expansion of the activities and geographical reach of NATO grew even further after the September 11, 2001 attacks on the US. On September 12, 2001,

NATO, for the first time ever, invoked Article 5, its collective security provision, which declares that any attack on a member state will be considered an attack against the entire group. The US formally asked for and received NATO support for its military operations in Afghanistan against al Qaeda and the Taliban-led Afghan government. In April 2003, NATO agreed to take command of the International Security Assistance Force (ISAF) in Afghanistan, marking the first time NATO took charge of a mission outside of Europe. At its peak in 2010, ISAF operated out of 400 military bases and had 90,000 troops at its disposal, over half of which were American. In 2014, ISAF was formally disbanded as NATO's combat mission in Afghanistan ended.

The most contemporary military challenge for NATO may be the conflict in Syria, which is adjacent to NATO member Turkey. Turkey has supported the anti-government rebels in Syria, and artillery shells from Syria have landed in Turkey, killing some Turkish citizens. At Turkey's request, NATO deployed missile defense systems along Turkey's border with Syria. More seriously, in November 2015, a Russian military plane was shot down by Turkish planes along the border. The Turks claimed it had violated Turkish airspace, but there are fears that an escalating conflict in Syria could draw in more external forces, including, perhaps, NATO in support of Turkey.

The Organization for Security and Cooperation and Europe (OSCE)

OSCE (Organization for Security and Cooperation in Europe) pan-European security organization, includes former Soviet states, which has taken a lead in issues such as human rights, democratization, and arms control.

The largest security organization in Europe in terms of member states is the **Organization for Security and Cooperation in Europe (OSCE)**. It has fifty-seven members, including the US, Canada, all members of the EU, and all the former Soviet states. As the OSCE itself notes, it covers an area from Vancouver to Vladivostok (a Russian city on the Pacific Ocean), making it more than a European organization in the strictest sense of the term and the largest regional security organization in the world.[15]

The OSCE harkens back to the Cold War in the early 1970s, when the pan-European CSCE was created to serve as a multi-lateral forum for dialogue and negotiation between East and West. Meeting over two years in Helsinki and Geneva, the CSCE reached agreement on the Helsinki Final Act, which was signed on August 1, 1975. This document contained a number of key commitments on political, military, economic, environmental, and human rights issues that became central to the so-called "Helsinki process." This was important in many ways, not the least of which was putting human rights on the agenda in Eastern Europe, and many "Helsinki" organizations developed in communist countries to push for political reforms and respect for human rights.

Until 1990, the CSCE functioned mainly as a series of meetings and conferences that built on and extended existing commitments. However, with the end of the Cold War, the members of the CSCE sought to give the organization a stronger institutional basis. Thus, in 1994, it became the OSCE and has permanent headquarters in Vienna, Austria. OSCE decisions have to be taken by consensus. This means that there is no formal voting. If one or more delegations oppose an action, the issue goes back into negotiation. If all delegates agree, the decision becomes politically binding for all member states. Unlike the EU, it is therefore an entirely inter-governmental organization.

It has no military of its own, relying upon contributions from member states. The OSCE takes a comprehensive approach to security, however, emphasizing elements such as conflict prevention, early warning, and arms control. In addition, it includes dimensions that include economic development, respect for the environment, human rights, human trafficking, and development of democracy. As such, it works closely with EU efforts in these fields and contributes to the spread of European "soft power" in the global arena, which is discussed later in the chapter. As of 2016, the OSCE has permanent missions or field offices in fifteen different countries, most of which are in the Balkans and former Soviet states. These missions implement programs to support law enforcement, minority rights, legislative reform, the rule of law, and media freedom. Some of the OSCE's most visible work is in election monitoring; as of 2015, it had monitored 300 elections in fifty-seven different countries.[16] In some cases (e.g., Serbia in 2000, Georgia in 2003, Ukraine in 2004), OSCE observers reported irregularities that helped spur local citizens to the streets to demand another round of elections or drive the authorities from office. These efforts, however, are often controversial, particularly when the OSCE refuses to certify an election as free and fair. Since 2004, Russia has claimed the OSCE had a political agenda and has independently sent its own observers and certified as free and fair elections in countries with dubious democratic records such as Belarus and Azerbaijan. In 2014 and 2015, the OSCE (together with France and Germany) oversaw talks in Minsk, Belarus that led to a ceasefire among forces fighting in eastern Ukraine as well as plans for OSCE election observation in contested areas of Ukraine. However, these elections have been repeatedly postponed, and in February 2016 the German Foreign Minister lamented the failure of the ceasefire to hold amid renewed fighting and conceded that a lasting political solution to the war in Ukraine was still far away, meaning in effect that it may join the ranks of other ethnic/separatist "frozen conflicts" (e.g., in Moldova, Georgia, Azerbaijan) in the post-Soviet space.[17]

Security issues in Europe

Post-World War II Europe has often been called a "zone of peace." Indeed, a major, continent-wide war like the two witnessed in the first half of the twentieth century seems inconceivable today. This is not to say, however, that there has been no violence in Europe since 1945. In the 1970s, terrorism plagued a number of West European states (e.g., bombings by the IRA over Northern Ireland and by the Basque ETA group in Spain, radical leftist groups in Italy and Germany such as the Red Brigades and the Baader-Meinhof Gang). Military forces were also used to crush challenges to Soviet rule in Eastern Europe, including in Hungary in 1956 and in Czechoslovakia in 1968. The end of the Cold War eliminated the threat from the Soviet Union, but it opened up new possibilities for violent conflict, including in the former Yugoslavia in the 1990s.

Today Europe faces a series of security challenges, including some, such as human trafficking and the refugee crisis, that go beyond a purely military-centric view of security. In this section, we shall focus on three main concerns: establishing peace and security in non-EU states in the Balkans, a resurgent and aggressive Russia, and terrorism, particularly Islamic-inspired terrorism that has affected a number of countries across Europe after the September 11, 2001 attack on the United States.

Putting the Balkans back together

The collapse of Yugoslavia in the 1990s was briefly covered in Chapter 2. To review, the end of the Cold War created pressures to reform and democratize Yugoslavia. Nationalist politicians gained support in various regions of Yugoslavia. Fighting broke out in several regions, but it was fiercest in Bosnia, which experienced a three-sided conflict among ethnic Serbs, Croats, and Muslims (Bosniaks). After the failure of European diplomacy and UN peacekeepers to stop atrocities, NATO, led by the US, intervened, and the warring parties signed the Dayton Accord in 1995 to stop the fighting and establish a de-centralized federal state in Bosnia. When in 1999 there was a risk of more atrocities in the Serb-controlled region of Kosovo, where the ethnic Albanian majority was being attacked by Serbs, NATO again intervened, bombing Serb targets, including the capital, Belgrade. Tens of thousands of peacekeepers were sent into both Bosnia and Kosovo, and European monitors were also placed in Macedonia to prevent a major conflict from erupting there. All told, the fighting in the region claimed 200,000 dead and 2 million refugees, as well as, on a continent where most thought such things could never happen again, accusations of genocide.[18]

Large-scale fighting ended in 1999, and since then the EU and other international actors have taken significant steps to rebuild and reintegrate formerly war-torn states. The EU established a variety of programs to build state capacity in countries such as Bosnia and Kosovo, with a particular focus on establishing effective police forces and judicial systems. Money devoted to reconstruction has poured into the region from a host of international institutions and agencies. The OSCE has played an important role in overseeing elections. All the region's governments, including Serbia's, have been required by the EU to assist in the hunt for war criminals; one breakthrough development was the arrest in 2011 in Serbia of Ratko Mladic, who was indicted for his role as commander of Serb forces at Srebrenica in 1995.[19]

Progress in the two most war-torn countries, Bosnia and Kosovo, has been limited. One EU official in the former Yugoslavia told me in 2007 that Bosnia was basically an "American fiction." Most people continue to live in ethnically segregated communities. Its weak central government is plagued by corruption and exercises little control over regional and local authorities, who are dominated by nationalist politicians. Like the old Yugoslavia, it has a rotating presidency that is shared by representatives of the three main ethnic groups. This has not worked out very well as nationalist-oriented figures who are not prone to compromise have occupied this office. US Vice President Joe Biden traveled to Bosnia in 2009 and exclaimed in a speech before the Bosnian parliament that inflammatory nationalist rhetoric "must stop."[20] In 2015, ethnic Croatian leaders called for constitutional reforms to create a separate Croat entity within Bosnia, and ethnic Serbs have called for a referendum on judicial reform to weaken the country's national courts, which they believe are biased against Serbs in war-crime cases.[21] A long-delayed Stabilization and Association Agreement (SAA) with the EU finally went into effect in 2015, but the EU's own Progress Report in that year noted many problems, including corruption, poverty, high unemployment (60 percent among youth), poor maintenance of rule of law, and the fact that 1 million people (a quarter of the population) have been unable to return to their homes since 1995. It notes that "meaningful progress" in implementing a reform agenda to put Bosnia on a solid path to EU membership has yet to be demonstrated.[22] Overall, while the EU can take some credit in preventing the re-emergence of an overt military conflict among the formerly warring factions, it has found that the demands of state-building to provide stability and a solid security environment much more difficult.

A similar situation prevails in Kosovo. Efforts to reconcile Serbs and Albanians in the aftermath of the 1999 war failed, as Kosovo's Albanian majority voted for independence from Serbia in 2008. This event provoked outrage among Serbs, and there was violence in regions of northern Kosovo populated by Serbs and mob attacks on the US embassy in Belgrade. As noted above, not all EU members recognize Kosovo's independence. Even so, the EU has been heavily involved in security, rule of law, and state-building projects through its EULEX program, which maintains a staff of 1,500 people in Kosovo.[23] In October 2015 the EU concluded a SAA with Kosovo. Nonetheless, the EU recognizes a number of serious problems in the country, including rampant corruption and organized crime, political violence between Kosovo's government and its opponents, weak political institutions, unemployment, and problems of media freedom and women's rights.[24] A bright spot is that NATO and EU peacekeepers have been withdrawn from Kosovo and it is trying to normalize its relationship with Serbia—thus reducing the risk of cross-border conflict—but it is clear Kosovo has a long ways to go to meet the minimum political and economic criteria for EU membership.

As of 2016, the EU has close relations with all the countries in the western Balkans, and Macedonia, Albania (a NATO member), Montenegro, and Serbia are all formal candidates for membership. The region, broadly speaking, is stable in the sense that risk of conventional military conflict is low. The EU's influence in the region is strong, and it can claim some successes (e.g., mediating an agreement in Macedonia in 2015 that led to the holding of new elections and an accord between Kosovo and Serbia that gave Serb-dominated municipalities in northern Kosovo more rights).[25] However, all suffer from problems of corruption and weak judicial systems, relatively poor (by European standards) economic development, and insufficient protection of minority rights. While the EU hopes that it can produce progress on these fronts through the incentive of EU membership, accession to the union for most of these states—Macedonia may be the exception, although its dispute with Greece over its name has made its NATO and EU membership bid difficult[26]—is not likely in the nearest term. The refugee crisis in 2015–2016—a manifestation of geography as hundreds of thousands of refugees and migrants traversed Macedonia, Serbia, and Bosnia on their way from Greece to Central Europe—has also complicated both their domestic political situation and their relationship with EU members.

Russia's resurgence

If one can say that the situation in the Balkans in the 2010s—despite numerous, well-documented problems—is nonetheless better than in was in the 1990s, the same cannot be said with respect to dynamics created by a resurgent, nationalistic, and militarily assertive Russia. Indeed, in terms of conventional security challenges, Russia represents the greatest threat to Europe, as it tries to (re)establish a zone of influence in the former Soviet space, stands opposed to many EU norms, and has the ability to employ economic and political leverage against European states.

This is a relatively recent development. When the Soviet Union collapsed in 1991, Russia, the largest post-Soviet state, began to implement political and economic reforms and moved closer to the West. The EU and its member states provided sizeable economic assistance to Russia—both aid (€2.6 billion from 1991–2006) and investment—to assist in its transition from communism to capitalism. In 1994, the EU and Russia concluded a Partnership and Cooperation Agreement (PCA), which entered into force in 1997. The PCA envisioned a host of mechanisms to promote Russian-European cooperation on economic, security, political, cultural, energy, and environmental questions. The EU worked to get Russia accepted into international economic organizations such as the World Trade Organization (WTO). The EU and Russia set up dialogues and joint programs to work together on issues such as regional security, energy supplies, the environment, and human trafficking. Russia provided some assistance to NATO forces in Afghanistan in the early 2000s. By 2008, Russia had become the third-largest trade partner with EU countries, due mainly to its supply of energy, including 40 percent of the EU's natural gas imports and 30 percent of its crude oil imports. Reflecting the importance of the EU to Russia, Russia's embassy to the EU in Brussels is the largest Russian embassy in the world. In 2006 Russian president Vladimir Putin declared that while Russia did not necessarily wish to join the EU, it was nonetheless a "natural member of the European family."[27]

However, European-Russian ties (and Russia's relationship with the West more generally) are increasingly strained. Some of the problems are longstanding—for example, Russian objections in the 1990s and 2000s to the expansion of NATO, failures to solve ethnic conflicts in former Soviet countries such as Moldova and Azerbaijan, Russians' blaming the West for many of its economic problems[28]—but many are linked to the increasingly authoritarian and nationalistic approach taken by Putin in the 2000s. Many European governments and other international observers (e.g., Freedom House, Reporters without Borders) became increasingly critical of what they viewed as the erosion of democracy (e.g., rigging elections and limiting access on the ballot to the opposition, banning demonstrations, corruption, government control over the media, violence against government opponents) in Russia.[29] On top of this, Russia and the West in general have a series of policy disagreements, including Kosovo (Russia was and remains steadfastly against Kosovo's independence), Iran, which is an important trading partner for Russia, and, since 2012, Syria, where Russia maintains a military base and has openly backed the government of Bashir al-Assad in his battle against rebels supported by the US, Turkey, and many Arab states.

Russian interference in the domestic politics of some its neighbors and its military support for separatists have created fears of a new Cold War. An initial sign of this development was evident during the "Orange Revolution" in Ukraine in 2004–2005, when Russia backed Viktor Yanukovych, who was then accused of stealing the presidential election, while most European countries and the US backed the millions of anti-Yanukovych protesters and his opponent Viktor Yushchenko. Putin labeled the Orange Revolution a "coup" designed by Western powers, and afterwards was more assertive at home in attacking his opponents and the media lest a similar development occur in Russia. Russian forces openly intervened in a separatist conflict in Georgia in August 2008, crossing the border and threatening the Georgian capital. This further complicated Russia's relations with Europe, as Georgia had experienced its own "colored revolution" in 2003 and embarked upon a pro-Western course, including a desire to join NATO. Tellingly, however, European states were somewhat divided on how to respond to Russia, as former communist states such as Poland and Lithuania, together with Great Britain, took the lead in criticizing Russia, while others, such as Germany and France, were more restrained and sought to mediate between Washington and Moscow, and Italy even seemed to endorse Moscow's position.[30]

Russian troops eventually pulled out of Georgia proper (but remained in the breakaway regions of South Ossetia and Abkhazia, which have been formally recognized by Russia as independent countries), but this was arguably a prelude to the more consequential intervention in 2014 of both regular and irregular Russian forces into Ukraine, which, as noted in the outset of this chapter, wrested the region of Crimea away from Ukraine and has led to the creation of self-proclaimed, pro-Russia "republics" in parts of eastern Ukraine. By early 2016, this conflict had produced nearly 10,000 casualties, including 2,500 confirmed civilian deaths (as well as 298 killed in the downing of a civilian airliner [by most accounts by pro-Russian forces]), and thousands of cases of serious human rights violations, including kidnapping and torture.[31] As a result, EU countries imposed sanctions on Russia, which have had a deleterious effect on the Russian economy, but Russian counter-sanctions have also been costly for Europe, leading, as noted, for some to call for their end and for a normalization of relations with Russia. At the same time, several European post-communist countries, particularly the Baltic states of Lithuania, Latvia, and Estonia, feel threatened by possible Russian military action against them. Scenarios include overt or covert Russian intervention to "protect" Russian-speaking minorities in the Baltic states. In response to the perceived Russian threat, NATO has announced an increase in its military presence in Eastern Europe, including stationing of additional troops and conduct of military exercises.[32] While this might be reassuring to existing NATO members, including all the Baltic countries, it will do little to push pro-Russian forces out of eastern Ukraine.

The big question, of course, is what Europe (or the United States, for that matter) can really do about Russian actions in the post-Soviet space. Western countries are not going to go to war with Russia over Ukraine. While some military supplies have been shipped to Ukraine, it is doubtful if they would be used to dislodge the separatist forces, given fears in Europe (and in Kyiv for that matter) about escalating the conflict. Despite the sanctions and resulting economic pain, Putin seems secure in his position, and has railed against Western subversion against Russia.[33] Meanwhile, Russia retains great leverage over Europe due to the latter's dependence on Russian gas and oil; plans to develop alternatives (e.g., renewable energy, new supply routes) do not provide an immediate solution, thus handicapping Europe's ability to "get tough" with Russia. Most disturbingly, perhaps, authoritarian Russia has found supporters in the EU, including the self-proclaimed "illiberal" Prime Minister Orban in Hungary and Nigel Farage, leader of the United Kingdom Independence Party. Russia has given financial assistance to anti-EU, populist, nationalist parties such as France's National Front, Hungary's Jobbik, and Bulgaria's Ataka, invited a motley collection of European neo-Nazi, nationalist, and far-left political figures to oversee its "referendum" in Crimea, and proposed economic assistance to troubled Greece and Cyprus.[34] Russia has been accused of promoting "fake news" stories to discredit some Western institutions and politicians—Angela Merkel has been said to be a primary target[35]—and, perhaps, most disturbingly, is alleged to be behind hacks of Hillary Clinton's 2016 presidential campaign in an attempt to bolster the fortunes of Donald Trump, who has spoken approvingly of Putin and envisions the US and Russia working together on various issues (e.g., Syria).

Whether these actions will divide Europe (or divide Europe from the US) or create a change in the overall Western approach to Russia remains to be seen. Without a doubt, however, there is great concern in Europe (and beyond) about developments in Russia and their implications for regional and global security.

Terrorism in Europe after September 11, 2001

Developments in the Balkans or the post-Soviet space, as important as they may be, do not directly affect the security of most Europeans. The top security issue in Europe in the 2010s—one that has both domestic and international import—is terrorism, more specifically attacks by adherents of radicalized Islam. Several high-profile, high-casualty attacks by European citizens or immigrants who have professed allegiance to al Qaeda, the Islamic State (ISIS), or other Islamic groups have created fears across Europe about the loyalty of Muslim citizens and the wisdom of admitting more immigrants. Some of these issues were covered in the previous chapter. In addition, these attacks have generated a host of questions about how governments and societies can best prevent additional attacks in the future.

The first serious indication of this new threat came on September 11, 2001 (9/11). Although the terrorist attack on that day occurred in the US, 9/11 was a global event. The perpetrators were from Arab states. Many of them devised their heinous plot while living in Europe. The victims of 9/11 included peoples from dozens of countries. Europeans rushed to condemn the actions and express sympathy. *Le Monde*, a left-wing French newspaper typically critical of the US, ran a headline, "Nous sommes tous Américains [We are all Americans]" the day after 9/11.[36] Many European states joined the US in its fight in Afghanistan against al Qaeda and the Taliban, although all did not agree with all aspects of the American-led "war on terror" (e.g., the prison in Guantanamo Bay, the war in Iraq). As noted in the **In focus** section, some contended in the 2000s that the US and its European allies diverged in their worldviews in the wake of 9/11, although by the 2010s, given the rise of ISIS and several heinous terrorist attacks in Europe, this contention can be debated.

Since 9/11, the vast majority of radical Islamic terrorism in Western countries—as well as the vast majority of casualties—has occurred in Europe, not the US.

This is, perhaps, partially a reflection of geography, as the Middle East is adjacent to Europe and Middle Eastern and Muslim immigrants in Europe have been more likely than their American counterparts to engage in violence at home and travel to the Middle East to carry out *jihad* for groups such as ISIS.[37]

This is just a partial list of some of the most dramatic terrorist attacks in Europe since 9/11.

- In November 2003, two synagogues, the British Consulate, and a bank headquarters were bombed in Istanbul, Turkey. Fifty-seven people died. A local Turkish group with connections to al Qaeda claimed responsibility for these attacks.
- On March 11, 2004 (3/11), bombs exploded on four commuter trains in and around Madrid, Spain. One hundred and ninety-one people were killed, and more than 2,000 were wounded. The bombing took place three days before general elections in Spain. The government was accused of withholding or distorting information about the attacks, and, in the ensuing elections, the opposition Socialist Party prevailed. Notably, the Socialists had campaigned on a platform that included removing Spanish troops from Iraq, prompting some to declare that the timing of the attack indicated that the terrorists had achieved their objective of cowing Spanish voters and bringing down a government that had been a staunch ally in the US-led war in Iraq. In subsequent investigations, Spanish police arrested numerous suspects, most of whom are of Moroccan descent.[38]
- On July 7, 2005 (7/7), suicide bombers attacked three subway cars and one bus in London. Fifty-two people died and more than 700 were wounded. A group called "al Qaeda in Europe" claimed responsibility for the attacks. Investigators ascertained that the bombers were all British citizens, three of which were of Pakistani descent. Two weeks later, a similar plot to attack public transport in London was not successful, and police arrested the perpetrators, who included Muslim asylum seekers who had lived in Britain for several years. Seeking to deflect criticism from his own country, the Pakistani president suggested that Britain was now the primary breeding ground for the next generation of Osama Bin Ladens.[39]
- In June 2007, London police discovered two car bombs that, fortunately, did not go off. The next day, two men drove an explosive-laden vehicle into the front entrance of the Glasgow airport in Scotland. Their bombs also did not go off. British police arrested eight individuals, mostly doctors born in the Middle East or India, for these planned attacks.
- In May 2014, a gunman opened fire at the Jewish Museum in Brussels, killing four people. The suspect was a French citizen of Algerian descent who had spent a year in Syria fighting with Islamist rebels.
- In January 2015, gunmen attacked the office of the French satirical paper *Charlie Hebdo*, which had published a variety of materials that mocked Islam (among other religions). Twelve people died in that attack, which was followed by shooting of French police and a hostage crisis at a kosher supermarket which left four civilians dead. The main plotters, two French-born brothers who pledged fealty to al Qaeda in Yemen, claimed to be defending Islam. They and an accomplice were killed by French police.[40]

In focus

European and American Responses to the post-9/11 world

Anti-Americanism in Europe and anti-European feeling in the US both have long histories. Long before some Americans in the early 2000s took to calling French fries "freedom fries," Mark Twain declared, "There is nothing lower than the human race except the French," and the French diplomat Tallyrand (1754–1838) opined that the US is a "land of thirty-two religions and only one dish . . . and even that is inedible." Lest one think this is confined to the French, none other than Sigmund Freud (1856–1939), the famed Austrian psychologist, declared, "America is a mistake, a gigantic mistake."

Humor at the expense of each other and the occasional mean-spirited comments aside, Americans and Europeans also have a history of putting their differences aside during major crises. World War II and the Cold War come to mind, during which both sides affirmed the importance of human liberty. Victory over communism and the emergence of a more united Europe based upon democracy and capitalism seemed to bode well for US-European relations.

In the post-9/11 world, however, European-American relations have frequently been quite complicated and tense. Very quickly in the early 2000s, the goodwill and sympathy for the US created by 9/11 dissipated, with Europeans increasingly critical of the "cowboy"-like unilateralism of US President George W. Bush and many Americans upset at what they viewed as a wimpy and effete Europe. These sentiments were most strongly expressed by the neo-conservative writer Robert Kagan, whose essay "Power and Weakness" was widely read on both sides of the Atlantic. The opening lines of his polemic deserve to be quoted at length:

> It is time to stop pretending that Europeans and Americans share a common view of the world, or even that they occupy the same world. On the all-important question of power—the efficacy of power, the morality of power, the desirability of power—American and European perspectives are diverging. Europe is turning away from power, or, to put it a little differently, it is moving beyond power into a self-contained world of laws and rules and transnational negotiation and cooperation. It is entering a post-historical paradise of peace and relative prosperity, the realization of Immanuel Kant's "perpetual peace." Meanwhile, the United States remains mired in history, exercising power in an anarchic Hobbesian world where international laws and rules are unreliable, and where true security and the defense and promotion of a liberal order still depend on the possession and use of military might. That is why on major strategic and international questions today, Americans are from Mars and Europeans from Venus.[41]

If one is unsure whose side Kagan is on, one only need recall the title of a 1992 book on relationships, *Men Are from Mars, Women Are from Venus*.[42]

While one could argue that several long-term developments are behind the alleged differences in American and European views of the world, the shadow of 9/11 obviously looms large. Although many embraced the notion that the West—Europe *and* America—was embroiled in a "clash of civilizations" against radicalized Islam or "Islamofascism," some, like Kagan, were skeptical that Europe and America would come together against this common enemy.[43] Is it true, with respect to the multi-faceted battle against terrorism, that the US and Europe are living on different planets?

Certainly, there is some evidence to support Kagan's thesis. Differences over the war in Iraq are the most obvious example. The US government, with widespread popular support, attacked Iraq, believing such action was necessary to rid Iraq of weapons of mass destruction. European governments were far more divided on the wisdom of this course. France and Germany opposed the US within the UN Security Council. Hence "freedom fries" and *The New York Post* labeling France and Germany as part of the "axis of weasels."[44] Several European states—including Great Britain, Italy, Spain, Denmark, Poland, Romania, and the Czech Republic—sent military forces to Iraq, demonstrating that the division was not, contrary to an assertion made by US Secretary of Defense Donald Rumsfeld, strictly between "old" and "new" Europe. However, it is worth noting that European publics were overwhelmingly against military involvement in Iraq. As the conflict continued, several governments (e.g., Spain, Italy, Poland) lost elections and their successors pulled their troops out of Iraq. With the election of Barack Obama and the eventual withdrawal of US combat forces from Iraq by the end of 2011 (all European forces, including the British, had already left), a major irritant in US-European relations was removed.

There were also, however, sharp differences of opinion in the 2000s on other issues related to the struggle against terrorism. In Afghanistan, several of America's NATO allies initially contributed to efforts to fight the Taliban and al Qaeda, but as the war dragged on and casualties mounted, several countries had lost enthusiasm for this conflict by the end of the 2000s. Some questioned whether NATO (read: the Europeans) had the will to see the war in Afghanistan through.[45] Europeans have also voiced objections about other anti-terrorist policies adopted by the US. The US detention facility at Guantanamo Bay in Cuba has been roundly condemned by many in Europe both for alleged human rights violations. CIA secret prisons in Poland and Romania, whose existence was confirmed in 2005, were also roundly condemned, and the Council of Europe issued a report that noted that they had been sites of torture.[46] Some European citizens were even picked up by mistake in American anti-terror operations and have alleged that they subjected to torture.[47]

On other issues where Europeans and the US profess a common interest, strategies have differed. For example, both sides professed concern about Iran obtaining a nuclear weapon. Europeans, in line with Kagan's hypothesis, have emphasized negotiations and offering Iran a "carrot" (e.g., aid or trade benefits) to allow international inspectors of its nuclear program. Several US officials, on the other hand, were far more vocal about possibly using force against the Iranians. The two sides worked together to impose UN sanctions on Iran, and eventually in 2015 an agreement was reached with Iran over its nuclear weapons program, one that was (predictably perhaps) widely supported in Europe but condemned by many in the US as not strong enough to guarantee that Iran would not acquire a nuclear weapon.

As for the issue of homegrown terrorism, some were alarmed in the early 2000s at what they see as Europe's excessive tolerance and weak response to would-be terrorists within its own borders.[48] However, in the 2010s, particularly after the attacks in France in 2015, there has been a growing recognition within Europe, not just among the xenophobic, anti-immigrant parties, that European states must be more vigilant in stopping terror attacks.[49] Proposed measures include more monitoring of mosques and Internet sites, a more visible security presence at likely targets, greater powers to search and detain suspects, and more restrictions on immigration. There have been moves in a similar direction within the US, although no European leader has gone as far as US presidential candidate Donald Trump, who in 2016 called for a temporary ban on all Muslims (not just refugees or would-be immigrants) from entering the US.

Most significantly, perhaps, the 2015 attacks in Paris (and later attacks in 2016 in Brussels) elicited more than just shock and fear among Americans. There was an outpouring of sympathy, a recognition that Europe and America need to stand united in the face of this common threat. This was not only stressed by political leaders, who agreed that the West was under attack, but expressed in broader circles. "Je suis Charlie," a slogan of support in the wake of the attacks on the French satirical magazine *Charlie Hebdo*, can thus be seen as an echo of the post-9/11 "Nous sommes tous Américains." US and European intelligence services are working together with renewed purpose to eliminate the terrorist threat. France has conducted its own airstrikes against ISIS in Syria. There is no more talk of "freedom fries."

This does not mean, of course, that moving forward will be easy. Combating terrorists, both in and outside of Europe, as well as managing fear and avoiding overreaction, remain challenges. Anti-Americanism can still be harnessed as a political force. Isolationist impulses are strong in both the US and Europe, which may limit prospects for international engagement. Furthermore, there will be inevitable points of disagreement on various issues or strategies (as there were between Winston Churchill and Franklin Roosevelt in World War II). However, claims that Europeans and Americans are so far apart that it is as if we are living on different planets are less persuasive today.

Critical thinking questions

1. What might account for why Americans and Europeans often approach security challenges in different ways?
2. Did the presidency of Barack Obama fundamentally change US-European relations? If so, how? What did not change?

- In October 2015, over one hundred people were killed by two suicide bombers at a rally in Ankara, Turkey. The rally was designed as a pro-peace demonstration, attended by many supporters and leaders of opposition parties. The government blamed ISIS for the attack, claiming they were in retaliation for Turkish military attacks against ISIS in Syria.
- In November 2015, suicide bombers and shooters attacked several targets in Paris, including a soccer stadium, cafes, and a theater, killing 130 people and wounding nearly 400. ISIS claimed responsibility for the attack as retaliation for French attacks on ISIS-held territory in Iraq and Syria. All of the known terrorists were EU citizens who had plotted together in Belgium. Evidence suggested that some had travelled to Syria and possibly returned to Europe with the wave of Syrian refugees in the fall of 2015.[50] Afterwards, President François Hollande declared that France was "at war" and asked for extraordinary emergency powers to combat terrorism.
- In March 2016, days after a raid in Brussels arrested the last remaining suspect in the aforementioned Paris attack, three bombs exploded in Brussels, two at the airport and one at a subway station adjacent to the city's European Quarter. Over thirty people were killed. Two of the bombers were linked to the Paris attacks, and ISIS claimed responsibility, declaring it would continue to take

"Je suis Charlie" France, Paris, January 11, 2015 March for Charlie Hebdo

action against the "crusader states" fighting against it. This incident occurred despite intense anti-terror investigations in Belgium in the wake of the Paris attacks, leading many to question whether European states could develop an effective strategy to combat terrorism.[51]

- In June 2016, three ISIS suicide bombers attack Istanbul's largest airport, killing over forty people. The alleged mastermind of the attacked was a Russian citizen and an ethnic Chechen. As with the October 2015 attack in Ankara, many believe Turkey was the target because of its support for anti-ISIS forces in Syria.
- On July 14, 2016, Bastille Day, a Tunisian resident of France drove a truck into a crowd of celebrating people in Nice, killing eighty-four people before being shot by police. ISIS claimed the driver as one of its "soldiers." Afterward, French officials extended the country's state of emergency.

This list does not include smaller-scale incidents and the numerous plots that have been uncovered by police forces and intelligence services across the continent. These include plans to bring down trans-Atlantic airliners and attack targets such as police stations, museums, schools, soccer stadiums, and government buildings. One should, however, acknowledge that not every terrorist attack in Europe since 9/11 has been carried out by radicalized Muslims. One horrific incident occurred in Norway in July 2011, when bombings and shootings by a native, non-Muslim Norwegian left seventy-seven dead, most of whom were attending a youth camp of the left-wing opposition party, which the killer believed was too tolerant toward Muslims and other immigrants. Furthermore, after many attacks there have been reprisals against mosques and innocent, individual Muslims. However, it is true that most of the major terrorist attacks have been conducted by radicalized Muslims. Furthermore, most of the attackers were either EU citizens or had resided in Europe for many years. The suggestion that some European Muslims might be part of an al Qaeda or ISIS "fifth column" or that a "sympathetic milieu" exists for terrorist cells—the last apprehended attacker in the 2015 Paris bombings was able to hide out in a Brussels suburb for over three months—is deeply troubling and exacerbates concerns over multi-culturalism and immigration, issues discussed in the previous chapter.

European publics and governments, of course, have felt compelled to respond to this threat, which in 2015–2016 grew discernibly more acute. There have been marches and public campaigns against terror—the largest ones occurring in Paris in January 2015 when thousands, including many French Muslims, condemned the violence and declared "*Je suis Charlie.*" Government officials across the continent, particularly after the bombings in 2015 and 2016, announced that the continent was effectively "at war," echoing what US President George W. Bush declared immediately after 9/11.

However, as the US has discovered, it is difficult to conduct a "war on terror." In Europe, matters are even more complex than in the US, as terrorism in Europe can be seen as more of a "home-grown" problem, driven by alienation and radicalization and a rejection of many European norms and principles. One French intelligence official, in the wake of the 2016 Brussels bombings, called it a "favorable ecosystem," one in which would-be or actual terrorists can find support.[52] Surveys have revealed that substantial numbers of European Muslims favor introduction of Islamic law or express sympathy with those committing terrorist attacks.[53] To understand their predicament in combating radical Islam, some Europeans are prone to ask Americans to imagine what the US could or should do if Mexicans had been the perpetrators of 9/11.

Various approaches have been adopted to deal with this security threat. Even prior to the 2015 refugee crisis, immigration had been restricted, with some countries such as France even adopting DNA tests for immigrants that want their family members to join them. Great Britain and the Netherlands, which previously had liberal asylum laws, deported many people who claimed the right to asylum. In Belgium, where Dutch and French speakers agree on very little, there was a consensus, again, even before the 2016 attacks, that immigration and asylum should be made more difficult. However, after the Nice attack, Mariusz Blaszczak, Poland's Interior Minister, blamed "decades of multi-culti policy" for the attacks and said that many leaders have failed to learn anything from previous attacks, when they "just burst into tears." Geert Wilders, leader of the nationalist Dutch Freedom Party, suggested "[terror attacks] will not stop until we close our borders for Islam and de-Islamize our societies. No more terror. No more Islam."[54] Critics charge that such pronouncements amount to Islamophobia and only fuel more division and resentment. However, there is little doubt that the terror attacks have bolstered the political prospects of xenophobic, nationalist parties and put those defending multi-culturalism on the defensive.

In addition to military attacks against ISIS in Syria and Iraq (discussed more below), security measures have also been beefed up in Europe, reflecting recognition that terrorism in Europe is a criminal and law enforcement matter. For example, in Great Britain, the government has passed measures that include enhanced powers for the police, more surveillance, and indefinite detention of those suspected of or associated with terrorist activity. British intelligence issued a warning in 2007 that stated that 2,000 people in Britain "posed a direct threat to national security" and that terrorists were even recruiting youth as young as 15 to join their cause.[55] In France, even prior to the 2015 Paris attacks, many Muslim clerics (most of whom are not French citizens) were put under surveillance, and several dozen who were accused of inflammatory speech were deported. German authorities proposed a host of measures, including putting spy software on suspects' computers. Spain arrested hundreds of accused terrorists since the 2004 Madrid bombings, including one effort that broke up an Internet-based recruiting and propaganda network. Some intelligence also suggests that terrorist cells existed in Poland, the Czech Republic, and Bulgaria.[56] Religious education, in many cases sponsored by the government but taught by foreign imams, is also being assessed as a potential source of Islam-inspired violence. Known centers of Islamic political activism, including London's Finsbury Park mosque, Milan's Islamic Cultural Center, and the al-Quds mosque in Hamburg, have been placed under government surveillance.

However, especially with the rise of ISIS and attacks in 2015 and 2016 that have been blamed, at least in part, on European citizens who returned from fighting with ISIS in Syria, there are bigger, continent-wide issues at stake. This is most clear with respect to the open borders that were in the past celebrated as a sign of progress and European unity. These are now seen as security risks, and border security—if not a complete rejection of the Schengen Agreement—is a new priority. Monitoring of mosques and immigrant neighborhoods is being stepped up. After the Paris attacks, the French government claimed emergency powers, including powers for the police to act without judicial oversight and place people under house arrest and to shut down websites deemed a threat to public order. The government also proposed to strip dual citizens of French citizenship if they were convicted of terrorism-related charges. In May 2016, the parliament approved new laws to enhance police surveillance and give more leeway for use of deadly force, but the citizenship proposal, which had generated some controversy, was ultimately dropped.[57] Enhanced security at likely targets—train stations, stadiums, malls—is likely to become the norm, and all agree that more coordination among various European intelligence agencies would be useful.

However, no plans will be foolproof. In the wake of the 2016 Brussels bombing, for example, Turkey reported that it had detained one of the bombers on its border with Syria and had handed him over to the Netherlands, but he was freed because investigators could not definitively link him with a terrorist network.[58] The materials used in many of the bombings in Europe are relatively easy to obtain; purchases of such materials would not arouse unusual suspicion.[59] There is insufficient people power to secure all possible targets. The Istanbul airport, attacked in June 2016, had heavy security, including checkpoints as one entered both the parking area and the terminal itself. The "new normal" in Europe, at least as long as ISIS and its ilk remain a powerful force, is likely to include terror attacks. At the same time, there are also concerns about how to balance security versus freedom, and whether sweeps of mosques or immigrant neighborhoods might both violate constitutional principles and do more harm than good, as they will likely alienate an already marginalized population even further and fan Islamophobia and anti-immigrant sentiment, concerns that, as of the mid-2010s, are pushing xenophobic political parties to the forefront in many countries.

With respect to this last concern, there have been some efforts to try to engage the Muslim community and foster more integration. That is, beyond apprehending the existing "bad guys," governments and societies as a whole are trying to do more to prevent individuals from becoming "bad guys" in the first place. Blatant expressions of racism—such as unprovoked physical attacks on Arabs and Muslims, hostile letters sent to mosques, and rants posted to various websites—are routinely condemned by European leaders. Most European governments have attempted to foster a dialogue with their own Muslim organizations, such as the French National Federation of Muslims and the Muslim Association of Britain.[60] Education and jobs are also seen as ways to improve the lives of many of the poorer immigrants, but, as discussed in previous chapters, how they will be provided is unclear.

Europe as a global economic actor

Whereas the development of a common European security policy is relatively recent, the initial mission of the European project was economic integration. On this front Europe has had its greatest success, both within Europe and beyond. The members of the EU have created a common economic space, the world's largest single market and trading bloc. All members of the EU—even the relatively poorer ones that joined in 2004 and 2007—are wealthy compared to most of the world, and EU countries have great economic resources at its disposal. EU rules define global product safety standards, and its competition rules have affected mighty American companies such as General Electric and Microsoft. To the extent that it can act with a single voice in global trade talks or in the WTO, the EU rivals the US in power. Indeed, as noted in Chapter 1, for all the discussion of China and India as rising powers, the size of the Chinese and Indian economies are still dwarfed by the EU. In international economics, Europe is a central actor.

The European Union's global trade policies

The EU has been important in breaking down barriers to international economic activity. Moreover, by many measures, trade liberalization, both within Europe and in the wider world, has been a boon to Europe. However, as noted in Chapter 10, many Europeans are ambivalent or even hostile toward globalization, blaming it for their current economic problems and are unsure if Europe can successfully compete with rising global economic powers such as China. In contrast to free trade, those with these views would prefer to create "Fortress Europe," a walling off of Europe from the rest of world through various protectionist measures. Europe's trade policies reflect this ambivalence. In short, despite the idea that more open markets and freer trade and investment are supposed to spur growth—and indeed, most Europeans have embraced such principles with respect to the development of a common *European* market—Europe's record in promoting global free market is not entirely consistent.

True, Europeans regard themselves as champions for global trade liberalization. After World War II, European countries, together with other advanced industrialized states, embraced the idea of free trade as a measure to prevent economic nationalism and promote economic growth. Individual countries and later the then-EC were major players in various global trade talks that brought down tariffs on manufactured goods from more than 50 percent prior to World War II to less than 4 percent on most products by the 1980s. This spurred growth in world trade in the second half of the twentieth century, which grew on average 8 percent a year from 1945 to 1970. To the extent that the growth in trade eclipsed global economic growth (roughly 5 percent a year from 1945 to 1970), many have argued that freer trade has been a boon to growth across the world.[61]

The EU has concluded various bilateral and multi-lateral trade agreements (e.g., such as those made by the WTO), and, like all WTO members, EU trade agreements are made on the principles of **most-favored nation,** meaning that the EU cannot, with some exceptions, discriminate in favor or against a particular trading partner. Since the 1980s, the EU has worked to facilitate trade by reducing non-tariff barriers (e.g., quotas, regulations), applying WTO principles to trade in services, and securing protection of intellectual property rights. The EU also emphasizes trade as a means to promote sustainable development and regional integration. The EU's leadership on trade issues is underscored by the fact that by the 2000s the EU, as a collective entity, was the world's largest trader, accounting for roughly 20 percent of global imports and exports.

most-favored nation
principle in international trade whereby countries are granted the same level of trade liberalization as the "most-favored" nation; helps to ensure equal treatment of countries and is central idea to lowering barriers to trade.

That said, it is worth noting what Europeans have not liberalized. Tariffs on exports of manufactured goods fell, but Europeans continued to protect their textile and agricultural sectors, areas in which Europe did not have a comparative advantage in relation to the developing world. Thus, while touting free trade, "Fortress Europe" blocked—through tariffs, quotas, subsidies—importation of products produced by some of the poorest people on the planet. Noting EU policies on textiles and agriculture, the British charity Oxfam ranked the EU first—ahead of the US, Canada, and Japan—in its "Double Standards League" of free-trade rhetoric and protectionist practice.[62] In 1995, WTO members agreed to reduce quotas on textiles over a ten-year period, but, even so, European tariffs on textiles remain higher than those on other manufactured goods. Trade talks in the 2000s overseen by the WTO had agriculture high on the agenda, but there was no final agreement as many states, not just European ones, were reluctant to open up their markets to cheaper food from overseas, despite the fact that well over half the population in the poorest countries in the world work in agriculture and would greatly benefit from trade liberalization.

Cotonou Agreement
EU agreement, signed with less-developed states in 2000, that provides funds for development and promises to promote trade cooperation.

To be fair, Europeans recognize that not all states are equally ready to embrace or profit from globalization. For several decades the EU managed special trading arrangements with former European colonies, mostly in Africa, the Pacific, and the Caribbean (APC). In 2000, the EU concluded the more ambitious **Cotonou Agreement** (signed in Cotonou, Benin) with seventy-eight APC countries. In addition to providing funds and programs for development and means for a stronger political foundation for APC-EU relations (both discussed more below), the Cotonou Agreement is designed to promote trade cooperation by giving APC special access to the EU market. The EU also grants special trade privileges to those states that meet environmental or social (e.g., labor practice) standards. The Cotonou Agreement will be in effect until 2020, and on balance, as seen in Figure 12.2, the EU imports slightly more than it exports to APC countries. However, as seen in the

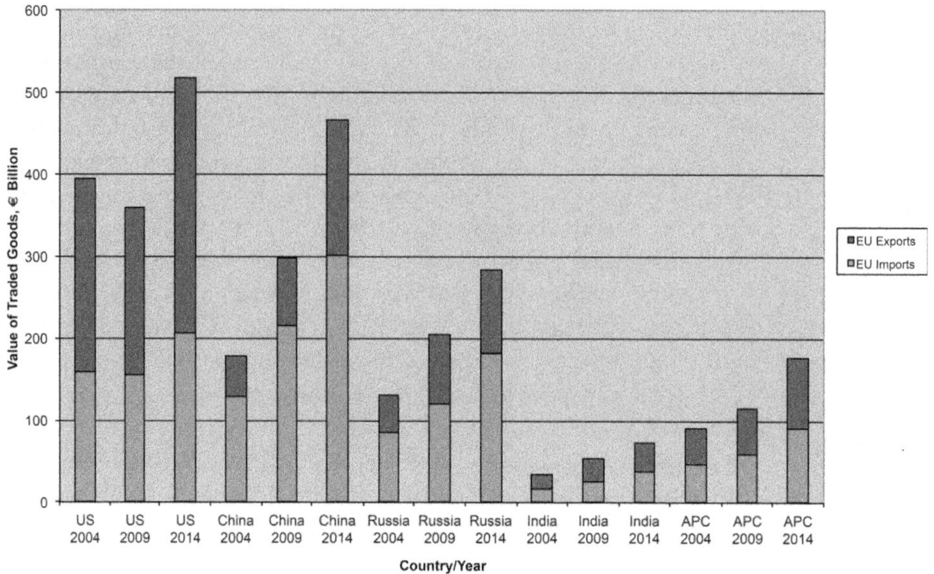

FIGURE 12.2 EU trade with selected countries, 2004–2014

EU trade data from http://ec.europa.eu/trade/statistics, accessed March 30, 2016

same figure, while trade between the EU and APC countries has grown from 2004 to 2014, on a percentage basis it has grown less than trade with China, Russia, and India.

Under Cotonou, trade relationships are expected to be reciprocal, meaning that the EU provides access to its market to the extent that individual APC countries open up their markets to European goods. However, there are still outcomes that are clearly unfair. For example, the cost of sugar from the developing world is half of that of European produced sugar, which is subsidized through the Common Agricultural Policy (CAP). The EU, until banned from such practices by the WTO, "dumped" its subsidized sugar in markets such as Brazil (!) where it was cheaper than locally produced sugar.[63] Thus, whereas Europeans in trade agreements may gain access to export machinery and other finished or higher-cost goods to developing states, those states do not have unfettered access to export agricultural products—their primary products—to Europe. With agriculture squarely on the global trade agenda, Europeans have found that their policies are targeted as being part of the problem in the global trading regime.[64]

Economic relations with the United States

Europe's economic relationships with the US is worthy of special consideration. The EU and US are the world's two largest markets, and one could argue that "much of what we associate with globalization is very largely the result of expanding economic exchange between Europe and America over the past twenty-five years."[65]

The European Commission itself notes that "no other commercial artery in the world is as integrated or fused together" as the transatlantic one.[66]

Statistics bear out these assertions. In 2014, total trade in goods and services between the US and the EU was over €500 billion (see Figure 12.2). The EU and the US are each other's largest trading partners. Reflecting the levels of integration between the US and EU, up to a third of EU-US trade is trade within firms that have operations on both sides of the Atlantic (e.g., Dell shipping components from its facilities in Ireland to the US or General Motors transferring equipment from the US to Germany). Significantly, the US runs a trade deficit with the EU, which ran to over $140 billion in 2014. The largest deficits in 2014 were with Germany ($74 billion), Italy ($25 billion), and France ($15 billion), but substantially less than the US trade deficit with China ($343 billion) in the same year.[67]

Foreign direct investment (FDI) is another important feature of the economic relationship. By 2012, the stocks of FDI held by Europeans in the US and Americans in Europe totaled $3.8 trillion.[68] Europeans account for approximately three-quarters of total foreign investment in the United States, with Great Britain, Germany, and the Netherlands constituting the largest European sources of investment. Even though foreign-owned firms are at times subjected to political backlash (e.g., consumers are told "Buy American"), foreign firms in the US tend to pay higher wages and are more productive than their US-owned counterparts.[69] Within the EU, the US is by far the largest source of foreign (non-EU) investment, accounting for 40 percent of overall stocks of FDI in 2012.[70] The EU estimates that the jobs of between 12 and 14 million people (roughly half in the US, half in the EU) are tied to transatlantic economic ties.[71] Looked at from this perspective, US-European economic ties are complementary, a win-win relationship.

This is not to say, however, that all is harmonious between the US and Europe. Protectionist tendencies are present on both sides, particularly in the agricultural sector. American development of genetically modified crops also worries some in Europe, creating a regulatory barrier against US imports. Some trade disputes between the EU and US have been taken to the World Trade Organization (WTO). These include complaints by both the EU and US about subsidies and support offered to Airbus and Boeing, EU action against the US for tariffs on steel, and the so-called "Banana War" in 2004 in which US companies complained of EU policies that favored banana producers in countries that were formerly colonies of EU member states. Given the importance of transatlantic trade and investment, American firms must also be aware of EU policies, and European actions that accused US companies such as Microsoft, Google, and Apple of unfair competition policies have been unpopular in the US.

Transatlantic Trade and Investment Partnership (TTIP)

Proposed agreement between the EU and US that would lower barriers to trade and facilitate greater international investment; critics suggest it will undermine various regulations and protections, including those for labor, the environment, and public services.

In the 2010s, negotiations were launched for a **Transatlantic Trade and Investment Partnership (TTIP)**, which aims to stimulate investment and reduce both tariffs and non-tariff barriers to trade, including numerous regulatory provisions. Backers of the TTIP suggested it could add over €200 billion yearly to the EU and American economies, which also means millions of new jobs.[72] European critics of the deal fear erosion of various standards (e.g., food safety, environmental protection), drops in wages and job protections, assaults on provision of public services, and the closed-door nature of the negotiations.[73] The EU has tried to remedy the latter by providing information on the status and content of the talks.[74] A Eurobarometer survey found a majority of respondents (56 percent) favored a free trade and investment agreement with the US.[75] The fate of the TTIP, however, is likely to hinge more on the American side, where anti-trade and anti-globalization sentiment took center stage in the 2016 election cycle.

Europe's growing economic relationship with China

After the US, the most important trade partner for the EU is China. This is a reflection both of China's sheer size and rapid economic growth since the late 1970s. Trade between Europe and China has increased sixty-fold since 1978, and by 2014 total two-way trade in goods and services was €467 billion, up from €177 billion from ten years before (see Figure 12.2). China is Europe's second largest trading partner, and EU countries collectively are China's largest trading partner. European investment in China has also been substantial, surging to over €140 billion by 2014.[76] European governments and companies have been eager to sell their goods to China, and European leaders regularly travel to China to conclude trade and purchasing agreements. Negotiations on a Partnership and Cooperation Agreement (PCA) with China began in 2007, with the EU declaring China to be a "strategic partner."[77] In 2013, the two sides published an EU-China 2020 Strategic Agenda.[78] Additional agreements with China are envisioned. For example, in 2016, EU and Chinese officials expressed hopes that the new sides could conclude a broad-based investment agreement in the near future.[79]

Nonetheless, there are some tensions in European-Chinese relations. Like the US, EU countries run a significant trade deficit (€140 billion in 2014) with China. While part of this reflects China's comparative advantage in labor costs, European governments and the EU also complain about market access obstacles as well as problems such as lack of protection for intellectual property rights. Many in Europe are also skeptical about the benefits of engagement with China, fearing that European investment in China and the flood of Chinese imports—which increased nearly six-fold from 1999 to 2014—mean European jobs are being lost to low-cost Chinese workers. A public opinion survey from 2013 found that 46 percent of Europeans (as opposed to 62 percent of Americans) see China's growing economy as a threat (41 percent described it as an opportunity), with fears most pronounced in France, Portugal, and Spain.[80]

Other problems also color EU-Chinese relations, including longstanding concerns about rule of law, human rights, environmental problems, and security concerns in East Asia.[81] China is not a democracy; efforts to link economic ties to political reforms in China have led to a deadlock in talks on the proposed PCA. China is also, in some respects, a rival for resources to Europe and the US in Africa, Asia, and the Middle East, and it has backed "rogue states" such as Sudan and Myanmar that have been subject to EU sanctions. In 1989, in response to the violent crackdown on pro-democracy demonstrators in China, the EU imposed an arms embargo on China, hoping that this would demonstrate EU concern about human rights and provide some incentive for China to make political reforms. Since then, progress, as the EU itself acknowledges, has been limited, as the Chinese government continues to repress religious, labor, and human rights organizations. The EU notes that it needs a more "focused and result-oriented" strategy, even though its expectations are "increasingly not being met."[82] The question, as with other cases, is what leverage the Europeans have. More comprehensive sanctions on China are not feasible given existing ties and China's size. Despite calls for some sort of protest during the 2008 Beijing Olympics, no country boycotted the games, although some leaders, including Angela Merkel, Britain's Gordon Brown, and Poland's Donald Tusk, boycotted the opening ceremonies.[83] Thus, rather than attempt to punish or coerce China, the EU has preferred to engage in a series of human rights "dialogues" with China, where it is able to express concerns about particular issues and obtain (on occasion) concessions, such as individual prisoner releases and Chinese agreement to sign international conventions on human rights.[84]

European use of "soft power"

European governments and the EU are major players on a number of important global issues. However, as should be clear from the above discussion, their international position is not based primarily on military power. Instead, Europeans have attempted to leverage what some have called their "**soft power**"—meaning the ability to get what you want through persuasion and attraction rather than coercion. Instruments of soft power include diplomacy, trade and investment, economic assistance, and the spread of one's values and culture. Soft power is contrasted with "**hard power**," meaning the use of the military and forceful measures such as economic sanctions to compel others to fall into line. Many actors, of course, engage in both, but in most formulations European countries are held to rely more on soft power, whereas the US, by virtue of its powerful military, is the exemplar of hard power.[85] Noting how European embrace of soft power makes sense given European capabilities and recent experiences of cooperation and integration, a French writer argues that:

soft power
use of non-coercive and non-military instruments of power, such as diplomacy, economic assistance, and power of example, to exert influence in world affairs.

hard power
use of the military and other coercive measures such as economic sanctions to exert influence in world affairs.

> [i]n contrast to the "imperialism" attributed to American power, the international ambition of Europe is supposed to consist merely in "humanizing globalization," organizing the "governance" of the planet, helping to resolve crises on the EU's periphery, ensuring the preservation of peace, and attempting to export around the world its model of cooperation and legal and diplomatic resolution of disputes.[86]

Application of soft power can be seen in a number of areas, including international aid, programs to bolster democracy and human rights, intensive efforts to protect the global environment, and promotion of the EU as a model for regional integration elsewhere.

Development assistance

One area of global economic policy that Europeans take great pride in is their relatively generous policy with respect to development assistance to poorer countries. European countries provide over half of the world's development assistance, and, as seen in Table 12.1, many spend much more on a *per capita* basis on development assistance than the US. On average, EU member states spend almost $150 a year

TABLE 12.1 Spending on Official Development Assistance (ODA)

Country	*Total ODA, (public and private funds) in $ Billion, 2014*	*ODA as % of national income, 2014*	*Top ODA recipients, 2014*
US	33.1	0.19	Afghanistan, Jordan, Kenya,
Japan	9.3	0.19	Vietnam, India, Indonesia
Canada	4.2	0.24	Ukraine, Ethiopia, Mali
Great Britain	19.3	0.70	Ethiopia, India, Pakistan
France	10.6	0.37	Morocco, Columbia, Ivory Coast
Germany	16.6	0.42	Myanmar, India, China
Sweden	6.2	1.09	Afghanistan, Mozambique, Somalia
Norway	5.1	1.00	Brazil, Afghanistan, Palestine
Denmark	3.0	.45	Tanzania, Mozambique, Ghana
Poland	0.86	.09	Ethiopia, Ukraine, Belarus
EU institutions	16.4	n/a	Turkey, Morocco, Tunisia

Source: OECD Development Statistics, available through https://data.oecd.org/oda/net-oda.htm and EU Development Atlas, https://euaidexplorer.ec.europa.eu/DevelopmentAtlas.do, accessed March 18, 2016

per citizen on official development assistance (ODA). Much of this ODA is provided bilaterally, from individual donor European states to individual recipient states. Some, notably the Scandinavians, are more generous than others, and they are among the few developed states that meet the pledge in the UN Millennium Development Goals to provide 0.7 percent of their national income in development assistance.[87]

In addition to bilateral (country-to-country) assistance, the EU runs its own development programs, dispensing funds to many regions throughout the world. ODA from various EU institutions and programs totaled over $16 billion in 2014. Most of the EU's aid programs are guided by the UN's Millennium Development Goals, which are directed at poverty reduction, education, gender equality, health (including AIDS and maternal health), environmental sustainability, and a global partnership for development. Much assistance is also tied to achievement of "good governance" and respect for human rights. Those states that systematically fall short in these fields (e.g., Zimbabwe, Sudan, Myanmar) have been subject to aid cut-offs and further sanctions. The top recipients of EU ODA in 2014 were all, however, in the EU's immediate neighborhood and/or in the queue for possible accession: Turkey, Morocco, Tunisia, Ukraine, Palestine, Serbia, and Bosnia, whereas the top recipients of bilateral ODA from EU member states were India, Myanmar, Afghanistan, Morocco, and China.[88]

A more focused comparison between US and European aid programs also reveal differences in areas of emphasis. The countries that received the most foreign aid (including military assistance) from the United States, since 2001, are Israel, Egypt, Columbia, Afghanistan, Iraq, and Pakistan, all of which are considered strategically valuable by the US and all of which have a substantial military/security component to their overall aid package. In contrast, European aid programs historically have been more directed to poorer African and Asian countries, with several countries emphasizing aid programs to their former colonies (e.g., Belgium to Congo, France to Senegal and Cameroon, Britain to Bangladesh and India, Portugal to Angola). Moreover, as noted above, the EU, through the Cotonou Agreement, grants privileged access to EU markets to the forty-nine least developed countries (mostly in sub-Saharan Africa), thus, in principle at least, supplementing aid with trade incentives to stimulate production and industries in poorer countries.

Although relatively generous foreign aid programs may make Europeans feel good about themselves and are an important element of soft power, it is debatable how effective these aid programs are. Critics of foreign aid note that countries can become dependent on aid, stifling their own development and incentive to adopt better economic policies.[89] Some also allege that European aid is too spread out and is poorly coordinated, and therefore would be better used in countries that either desperately need help or have the political institutions in place to use aid more effectively. As mentioned above, critics of EU would argue that it could do far more to eradicate poverty in the developing world by simply opening up its markets to agricultural imports. The EU does routinely assess the effectiveness of its aid programs, and has created EuropeAid, another EU bureaucratic organ that is charged with coordinating aid efforts. The Cotonou Agreement also stresses the need to build "performance-based partnerships" by channeling aid to those states that on political and economic grounds can be classified as "good performers." This sounds reasonable, but are Europeans therefore to abandon the poorest of the poor? Humanitarians would, of course, say no, but the fact that sub-Saharan Africa, traditionally the largest source of EU aid, has since the 1960s grown on average far less than other regions of the developing world and has done little to diversify exports beyond natural resources may give one pause about the efficacy of EU policies in this area.

Promotion of human rights and democratic values

Another example of Europe's use of soft power is in its various efforts to spread its core political values, including respect for human rights and democratic institutions. Of course, other countries, including the US, also have a longstanding interest in promoting democracy, but often Europeans are more prone to try to influence by example and by persuasion whereas the US is apt to try more direct political pressure and, in extreme cases such as Iraq in 2003, military invasion.[90] Several European and transatlantic institutions are interested in democratization, including the EU, OSCE, and the Council of Europe,[91] the last of which drafted the European Convention for the Protection of Human Rights, which is overseen by the **European Court of Human Rights (ECHR)**. The ECHR, which has jurisdiction across Europe, is an important institution through which individuals can take their own governments to court to redress human rights violations (e.g., unlawful imprisonments, discrimination).

European Court of Human Rights (ECHR) body of the Council of Europe, through which individuals can seek redress for alleged human rights violations; the ECHR can issue judgments against states and has been important in upholding human rights.

For the EU, a key element of a democratization strategy is construction of responsive and open political institutions. To this end, the EU gives over €100 million a year through its European Initiative for Democracy and Human Rights program as well as trade and other financial incentives to help build democratic institutions and encourage governments to be more respectful of human rights. Part of this push, however, is explicitly values-based, meaning that Europeans hope that various programs (e.g., training of civil servants, monitoring of media) will help spread democratic values to other parts of the world.[92]

How well has this worked out? Without question, the EU's greatest success has been in East-Central Europe. Given the prospect of joining the EU, states adopted the necessary reforms largely in line with EU expectations, although in some states (e.g., Romania) implementation has been a problem and some might question how "deep" or "values-based" these reforms are.[93]

Elsewhere, however, the EU has had, at best, modest success. European encouragement of good governance, respect for human rights, and democracy has found less fertile soil in the Middle East, sub-Saharan Africa, Russia, and China. True, there are some success stories (e.g., South Africa, Mozambique, Namibia), but it is very difficult to draw a line and say that EU policy was the "cause," for example, of the end of apartheid in South Africa. Often, when the EU has tried to implement sanctions, such as against Zimbabwe, offending governments can often find other supporters, particularly China, which is becoming more assertive in Africa and the Middle East and is far less particular about dealing with despots. Moreover, frequently Europe's commercial interests (e.g., need for energy, the desire to sell products) conflict with the human rights agenda, as noted above with respect to China.[94] In short, it is not clear that soft power gives Europe the means to deal with the more recalcitrant authoritarian leaders who possess their own resources (e.g., President Putin in Russia) or don't need Europe and thus have little interest or reason to make political reforms (e.g., arguably the case in places such as North Korea, Uzbekistan, and Sudan).

Efforts to protect the global environment

As has been noted in several places in this text, Europeans tend to care very deeply about the environment. Support for environmental initiatives comes from across the political spectrum. Europeans, however, have also attempted to take their environmentalism to the global level, trying to lead by example and through persuasion to get other states to make and abide by international environmental agreements. Arguably it is in this sphere that Europe is most clearly *the* global leader and even where Europe, as an idea or concept, may seek to carve out part of its identity.

Environmental concerns figure prominently in many European international programs, ranging from bilateral development assistance to help with water quality or deforestation or OSCE programs to foster good stewardship of the environment. However, it is in the most global of all environmental questions—climate change—that Europe hopes to make its mark. *The Economist* writes, "To Europeans, climate change embodies all the trends that will make the European Union exemplary in the next fifty years. The future, they think, will be about solving global problems by pooling sovereignty and setting up a framework of mutually accepted rules. This will be true for trade and conflict resolution as it is for environmental policy." In other words, some in Europe look to set up an international environmental regime modeled, in part, upon the experience of the EU. *The Economist*, with only the slightest sarcasm, concludes, "Europe will rescue the environment from destruction; the environment will rescue Europe from irrelevance."[95]

Kyoto Protocol global agreement signed in 1997 to limit carbon emissions, enthusiastically embraced by many European countries as a first step toward solving the problem of climate change.

Europe has tried to position itself as the "greenest" region in the world. In 1991, the EC issued its first Strategy to limit carbon dioxide emissions. In 2000, it created the European Climate Change Program, which was designed to identify and develop elements of an EU strategy to meet the goals of the 1997 UN's **Kyoto Protocol** on combating climate change. The EU and its member states officially ratified the Kyoto Protocol on global climate change in 2002. Under the terms of Kyoto, the then EU-15 pledged to reduce emissions of greenhouse gases by 2012 by an average of 8 percent from the level of 1990.[96] EU ratification helped the Kyoto Protocol enter into force as an international treaty, but not all countries, such as the US and China, ratified it. Europeans, however, generally embraced Kyoto with enthusiasm. Tony Blair, at that time the British prime minister, claimed that climate change is "probably the greatest long-term challenge facing the human race" and pledged that Britain would cut emissions by 20 percent by 2010, above its commitment through Kyoto.[97] Since 2002, EU members have also developed an emission-trading scheme, under which companies get a fixed number of permits to pollute. As they grow, companies must either reduce emissions or buy spare permits from others that have reduced their emissions. Such "cap-and-trade" schemes are upheld by many as a market-based model that could help reduce emissions globally.

Building upon its previous commitments, EU members are attempting to go further. Recognizing that the Kyoto Protocol would expire in 2012, EU members pledged at a 2007 EU summit to cut their emissions by at least 20 percent from 1990 levels by 2020 (and by 30 percent if other rich countries joined in) and to invest in solar, wind, and biofuels so that 20 percent of Europe's energy needs would come from renewable sources. Jacques Chirac, then president of France, hailed this so-called 20/20/20 plan as "a great moment in European history."[98] Much of the impetus for these pledges came from Angela Merkel, who also hosted the 2007 G-8 summit of leading industrialized states to highlight the EU's commitment on climate change. Merkel has made global warming a focal point for German foreign policy. Germany has adopted the world's most comprehensive climate-protection package, which includes measures to boost energy efficiency (including taxing or encouraging trade-ins of gas-guzzling cars) and promote renewable sources of energy. The aim is to reduce greenhouse gases by 36 percent from 1990 levels by 2020. These measures have a clear international orientation. Merkel noted, "We hope that the example set by our decisions will be followed and that we come together internationally to implement ambitious climate goals."[99]

The problem, however, is that Europeans' rhetoric on climate change and various investments (particularly with respect to wind energy) have not (yet) led to major accomplishments. Most of the energy used in Europe still comes from fossil fuels. Even as governments talk about renewable sources of energy, coal-fired power plants are under construction. In 2006, the British government admitted it would not meet its self-declared Kyoto target, and in 2007 it became apparent that most EU countries would not be able to uphold their own Kyoto commitments, in part because governments gave away too many pollution permits for free. Targets for production of biofuels also fell short, and investment in nuclear power, which is carbon-friendly but anathema for many in Europe, is not widely popular. The fears were that the EU, in failing to meet its own targets, would have to purchase excess carbon quotas from poorer countries, in effect telling poorer countries that they should not pollute so richer Europe can.

Furthermore, in the wake of the 2008 global financial meltdown, some Europeans began to revisit the commitments to reduce emissions that they made only a year earlier. A coalition of Eastern European countries, with support from Italy, argued that because they rely heavily on coal-fired power plants, they would have to assume far more costs to meet the 2020 targets than, say, the more wealthy Danes who already get much of their energy from renewable sources such as wind. Italy's Silvio Berlusconi suggested that it was not "the moment to push forward on our own like Don Quixote" and Donald Tusk, the Polish Prime Minister, insisted that states should have the right to veto EU environmental agreements.[100] In 2009, world leaders gathered in Copenhagen to discuss drafting a post-Kyoto agreement. Despite agreement that climate change was a problem, however, no binding agreement was reached, leading many to be disappointed with this outcome and the inability of Europe to forge a global consensus on the issue.[101]

Paris Agreement
2015 global agreement to limit carbon emissions, which places binding commitments on states; hailed by backers as a major step to addressing global climate change.

Those backing global efforts to combat climate change could celebrate good news in December 2015, when 195 countries (including, notably, China and the US) agreed to the first-ever binding climate deal, the **Paris Agreement**. This is planned to enter into force in 2020 and is designed to keep global temperatures from rising 2° Celsius from pre-industrial levels. Under this agreement, states pledge to reduce carbon emissions, regularly report progress, and aid developing states who may lack the funds or technology to adopt greener economic practices. EU countries invested significant efforts in producing this agreement, and the EU was the first major economy to announce its own emission-reduction plan prior to the Paris conference, pledging to reduce emissions by 40 percent by 2030.[102] However, real reductions (as opposed to limiting growth) of emissions is delayed for many countries, and it is very unclear what enforcement mechanisms will be employed, what (if any) penalties will be assessed for those who fail to meet their pledge, and if major polluters (especially the US) will adhere to the agreement under different political leadership.

multi-lateralism
strategy that relies upon the coordinated efforts of various countries and international institutions to produce a desired outcome; this is a cornerstone of EU policy.

unilateralism
strategy in which states pursue their foreign policy aims without cooperation of other states or international institutions.

Promotion of international cooperation and regional integration

As a final example of use of soft power, one could mention that emphasis European states place on **multi-lateralism,** meaning cooperative efforts by many states to resolve a particular international problem. As opposed to go-it-alone **unilateralism,** for which many have criticized the US, especially during the administration of George W. Bush (2001–2009), Europeans often prefer to take issues to international forums for discussion and development of consensus so that as many actors as possible are committed to a course of action. Examples are numerous: the effort to work out the Iraq crisis through the UN Security Council; international discussions and treaties on climate change and other environmental problems; support for international labor standards to prevent abuse of workers; utilizing the UN to dissuade Iran from building a nuclear weapon. Indeed, one item that is striking is how the UN is viewed quite favorably in Europe whereas the UN is the favorite punching bag for many US politicians.[103] Whereas some Europeans might attempt to explain their inclination for multi-lateralism as proof that they are inherently more "civilized" or disposed toward diplomacy, one can easily explain it by noting that European states, individually, are relatively small and it is only through multi-lateral forums that European countries can hope to exercise global leadership. With few exceptions, Europeans cannot go it alone.

At times, European efforts to create new international institutions have run up against American resistance. A primary example of this is the dispute over the International Criminal Court (ICC). The ICC, which is an outgrowth of *ad hoc* international tribunal for war crimes in the former Yugoslavia and Rwanda, was established in 2002 and is headquartered in The Hague in the Netherlands. As of 2016, 124 nations have ratified the treaty to form the ICC, including all EU states. The ICC is empowered to try individuals for genocide, war crimes, and crimes against humanity, and it has issued warrants of arrest with respect to several conflicts in Africa. Under 2005 revisions of the Cotonou Agreement, ratification of the ICC statutes was added as an obligation the EU expects APC states to fulfill. In contrast, the US nullified its signature of ICC treaties in 2002, expressing concerns over violation of national sovereignty and potential for politically motivated prosecutions (e.g., of US soldiers in Iraq). Whereas the EU has pressed other states to cooperate with the ICC, the US has linked military assistance to a number of countries to the latter's agreement that US personnel will be exempt from the jurisdiction of the ICC.

Another means by which Europe attempts to foster international cooperation is by promoting regional integration outside of Europe.[104] Such efforts are an explicit effort to put the "European model" into practice elsewhere. The EU has concluded cooperation agreements with a number of regional organizations, including the Association of Southeast Asian Nations (ASEAN), Mercosur in South America, and the African Union (AU). Promoting regional integration elsewhere coincides with Europe's attempt to define its place in the world. According to Romano Prodi, former head of the European Commission,

> [o]ur European model of integration is the most developed in the world. Imperfect though it is, it nevertheless works on a continental scale . . . I believe we can make a convincing case that it would also work globally.[105]

The influence of the EU is perhaps strongest in Africa, where the EU has tried to foster regional integration through the Cotonou Agreement, reciprocal trade agreements with different regional groupings of African states, and by supporting the AU, which was formally launched in 2002 and includes EU-like institutions such as Commission, Parliament, and Court of Justice. Several West African states have also discussed monetary union, and draft proposals of such a union follow closely the EU practice. Whether or not the AU can realize its stated goals of political integration remains to be seen, and Europe's relations with many African states are frosty given European concern over human rights violations.[106] Nonetheless, one could argue that the primary successes of the EU—in encouraging economic cooperation and lessening the risk of militarized conflict—give it the potential to be a model for other regions of the world.

Policies in Europe's neighborhood

The EU and various European governments trade, maintain diplomatic missions, provide humanitarian support, and work to improve global and regional security with countries across the globe. Some countries and regions, by virtue of geography, history, substantial economic ties, and worries over security, might be deemed "high priority" or "high involvement" regions. Leaving aside the US, Russia, and China (discussed above), one could easily rank Turkey, the post-Soviet space, and Middle East, all "neighbors" of the EU, as high priority concerns for European and EU engagement.

Possible EU expansion to Turkey

The EU has expanded several ties in its history, and it is likely that it will do so again. Indeed, several states, including Macedonia, Serbia, and Montenegro, are in the membership queue. However, the most problematic would-be member is Turkey, which is a large country (over 70 million people), overwhelmingly Muslim, and one in which there have been longstanding concerns about democracy and respect for human rights. Turkey concluded its Association Agreement with the then-EEC in 1963, and its geographic eligibility for membership has been continually affirmed since then. Since its foundation in the 1920s after the collapse of the Ottoman Empire, Turkish leaders have put the country on a Westernizing course (e.g., adoption of the Latin alphabet, secularism), and it joined NATO in 1952. As suggested in Chapter 1, however, there are ongoing debates on what "Europe" is or should be, and some believe that Turkey is not "European" enough. The EU's relationship with Turkey, and in particular whether it grants Turkey membership, is thus an important question, one that touches on the very definition of "Europe."

Turkey has long sought EU membership. However, the proclivity of the Turkish military to intervene against democratically elected governments (in 1960, 1971, 1980, and, albeit more subtly, in 1997), its spotty record in defending civil and human rights, and its economic underdevelopment prompted Brussels to reject its formal bids for membership in 1989 and in 1997. However, in 1999, after the EU agreed to take in several post-communist states as new members, it also declared Turkey a candidate member, offering the Turks the possibility of membership if Ankara could make the necessary political, economic, and legal reforms to meet the Copenhagen Criteria.

This decision produced a tidal wave of reform in Turkey. The EU put forward several short-term and medium-term goals for Turkey to meet in order for its application to proceed. These demands included greater freedoms for minorities, particularly the Kurds, who constitute perhaps 20 percent of the population, a ban on capital punishment, lifting restrictions on speech and assembly, a reduced role for the military in politics, and progress on resolution of the Cyprus problem (since 1974 Turkey has occupied the northern third of Cyprus and supports a self-declared Turkish Cypriot state). In response, the Turkish government pushed forward a series of reforms including thirty-four constitutional amendments in 2001 and 2002 that were in line with EU recommendations. By 2004, nine reform packages were passed that substantially liberalized the Turkish state and altered a third of its existing constitution.[107] Most of these measures were passed by a government led by the Justice and Development Party (JDP), which has Islamist roots but embraced a decidedly pro-EU agenda. The JDP ended the state of emergency in all provinces of the (largely Kurdish) southeast, established an EU Harmonization Commission, and adopted the UN Covenants on Civil and Political Rights and on Economic, Social, and Cultural Rights. It also pushed through controversial social reforms including a ban on discrimination against homosexuals, legalization of Kurdish-language media, and harsh punishments for "honor killings."

The EU deserves credit for much of this process. As one Turkish observer noted, Turkey has seen a "period of profound and momentous change in Turkish history . . . [A] change of this magnitude would have been impossible in the absence of a powerful and highly institutionalized EU anchor in the direction of full membership."[108] In 2005, the EU, impressed by the scope of reforms, agreed to open accession talks with Turkey.

Since then, however, progress has been limited. There are numerous problems: Little movement on the Cyprus question led to the suspension of talks on several chapters of the accession talks; outspoken objections by several EU political leaders, including Angela Merkel, of Turkish EU membership; and anti-immigrant and anti-Muslim feeling has sparked fears among some that Turkish membership would exacerbate some existing problems. Eurobarometer surveys have revealed sizeable doubts about Turkish membership. Over time, these have tended to grow: Whereas 55 percent were against Turkish membership in 2005, 59 percent expressed this view in 2010. Support for Turkish membership was lower than that of Croatia, Serbia, Ukraine, and Albania. One survey in 2006 found that 61 percent of respondents thought that cultural differences between Turkey and the EU are too significant to allow it to join the EU, with the highest support for this view coming from Austria (84 percent), Greece (79 percent), and Germany (74 percent).[109]

Turks tend to view the situation differently, as many believe European resistance to Turkey is rooted in Islamophobia and a desire to keep Europe a "Christian club." Turkish President Recep T. Erdoğan has argued that "the idea of 'Christian Europe' belongs to the Middle Ages. It should be left there. . . . There should be no doubt that Turkey's full membership will re-enforce the desire and will for co-habitation between Christians and Muslims."[110] Such arguments have been supported by some in the EU, particularly former British political leaders such as Tony Blair and Gordon Brown, who see Turkish accession to the EU as, if nothing else, symbolically important in the post-9/11 world. Turks also note how post-communist states—first Central Europeans, then Romania and Bulgaria (both poorer than Turkey), and now several former Yugoslav states—"cut" into the membership queue. They complain that additional criteria such as demands for official recognition of genocide against Armenians in 1915 and vague pronouncements about the "absorptive capacity of the Union" are placed on Turkey. Support for EU membership within Turkey has fallen. Whereas in the mid-2000s over 70 percent of Turks backed the country's EU bid, by 2015, only a third of Turks believed membership would be "good thing" for Turkey.[111] In the 2010s, Turkish foreign policy became less focused on the EU and looked to develop a stronger presence in the Middle East.

The most serious problem, however, is the weakness of democracy and rule of law in Turkey itself. Many have noted, particularly after 2011, rising authoritarianism within Turkey, characterized by arrests of journalists and political activists, use of force against protesters, utilization of anti-terror laws and closure of Internet sites to silence dissent, and large-scale corruption allegations. Some have linked this to an alleged Islamist agenda of the JDP, which by the 2010s controlled all the levers of power in Turkey.[112] The crackdown against the Gezi Park protests in Istanbul in 2013, which were broadcast globally and included denunciations by Erdoğan and his allies of Western plots to bring down his government, did much to undermine Turkey's EU bid. In 2016, Erdoğan complained to the German ambassador about the airing of a satirical anti-Erdoğan video on German TV, drawing more attention to his efforts to repress dissent, which have included hundreds of arrests in Turkey for insulting him.[113] In July 2016, the Turkish government survived an attempted military coup, but in its aftermath arrested thousands of people, including judges, prosecutors, and academics, leading some to fear that Turkish democracy will be compromised as Erdoğan centralizes power in his hands and effectively eliminates political opposition.[114]

However, as noted in the previous chapter, the EU needs Turkey to help solve the refugee crisis. It has offered Turkey over €6 billion in assistance to keep Syrian refugees in Turkey (and to take back Syrians who have fled to the EU).[115] It has opened up some of the closed accession chapters, and in 2016 approved measures for visa-free travel by Turks to the EU. Critiques of creeping authoritarianism and of renewed attacks by the government against Kurds, at least among many top European leaders, has been muted, particularly as terrorist attacks in Turkey in 2015–2016 and a coup attempt made many prioritize stability over civil liberties. This is not to say that the EU will be soon offering membership to Turkey. However, the backtracking away from democracy in Turkey points to limitations in the EU's democratization agenda, and the recent engagement with Turkey indicates, at least to some, the EU's priority on its self-interest (in this case, resolving the refugee crisis) and willingness to sacrifice principles such as support for democracy and human rights.[116] Furthermore, how the EU's relationship with Turkey evolves, particularly as Turkey is (re)evaluated as "European" or not, will inform us not only about Turkey but how Europeans define themselves.

European Neighborhood Policy (ENP)
EU policy initiated in 2004 to foster stronger ties with neighboring countries in post-Soviet Europe the Middle East and North Africa; it offered more aid and enhanced cooperation, but not the immediate prospect of EU membership.

Eastern Partnership (EaP)
EU policy, promoted by Poland and Sweden and launched in 2009, to develop closer ties with post-Soviet states; final objective of this policy is unclear.

The Post-Soviet space

The EU has made engagement with its eastern post-Soviet neighbors a foreign policy priority, concluding in the 1990s several Partnership and Cooperation Agreements (PCAs). While three—Estonia, Lithuania, and Latvia—gained EU membership in 2004, six other European post-Soviet states—Ukraine, Moldova, Georgia, Belarus, Azerbaijan, and Armenia—were included in the EU's 2004 **European Neighbourhood Policy (ENP)**,[117] which in 2009 was supplemented by the **Eastern Partnership (EaP)**,[118] a more focused initiative toward these states to promote economic ties and political development.[119] Both offered states financial and technical support and envisioned cooperation in a number of fields, including energy, the environment, security, and education. While some EU states, especially Poland, have lobbied for EU expansion to the east, neither of these programs promised or envisioned EU membership. Rather, the expectation was that each state would work with the EU to develop an "Action Plan" and that the EU would reward those that made more progress toward Europeanization. In the language of the ENP, the "pace of development of the European Union's engagement [with targeted countries] will depend upon commitment to common values," including, *inter alia*, democracy, human rights, and the rule of law. This was echoed in the EaP, which stated that "how far we [the EU] go in relations with each country will continue to depend on the progress made by the partners in their reform and modernization efforts."[120] The final goal of these initiatives is not explicitly stated; some envision a free-trade zone, with expansion perhaps a long-term goal. Some critics have criticized these initiatives for giving lip service to democratization while engaging with corrupt, authoritarian states, and Russia views them as a geo-political gambit by the EU to expand its sphere of influence.[121]

The rationale for this focus, however, is clear. Many post-Soviet states border the EU and/or are geopolitically important. They offer both opportunities (for trade, investment, energy) and risk (for instability and conflict). Russia, as already noted in this chapter, casts a long shadow over the region, and many states, such as Ukraine, Moldova, and Georgia, look to the EU (as well as NATO and the US) to help guard against Russian influence and threats. Developing relations with these countries, however, has proven to be a challenge, and not only because of Russian actions.

Among the non-Russian republics, Ukraine, the second-largest post-Soviet state, has been the largest target of EU assistance and engagement. The EU and Ukraine signed a PCA in 1994 and concluded a Common Strategy in 1999. Despite over €1 billion in EU assistance in the 1990s, relations with Ukraine were undercut by increasingly corrupt and undemocratic Ukrainian authorities, who also wanted to preserve good ties with Russia. In 2004, however, during Ukraine's "Orange Revolution," the EU took a leading role in mediating between rival parties and helping to ensure a third and fair round of voting that brought pro-Western Viktor Yushchenko into the Ukrainian Presidency.[122] Yushchenko claimed that one of his top aims was for Ukraine to join the EU, but progress toward this goal stalled. Viktor Yanukovych, far more pro-Russia in his orientation, assumed the presidency in 2010, and adopted a variety of illiberal policies that repressed his opponents and Ukrainian civil society. Despite this, the EU continued to be engaged with Ukraine, but, as noted at the beginning of this chapter, he ultimately walked away from signing an Association Agreement (AA) with the EU.[123]

The victory of the protesters on "Euromaidan" in Kyiv and installation of a pro-EU government buoyed hopes among many Ukrainians that they could join the Ukrainian family and also lessen Russian influence over their country, Alas, with the Russian seizure of Crimea and support for separatists in eastern Ukraine, together with continued problems of corruption at the highest levels of political authority (highlighted in the Panama Paper leaks in 2016), the moment of optimism from 2014 has seemed to have passed. Ukraine's economy is not growing; it is requesting billions more to turn around its economy. While the AA that establishes free trade went into effect in January 2016 and EU-Ukrainian trade has increased, investors remain leery of putting their money into much of the country, and, significantly, the EU has (despite the existence of a "free trade agreement") put in place limits on agricultural imports from Ukraine.[124] Whether the EU is willing to invest more in Ukraine—given the fact that its prior engagement paid few dividends—and whether and how the current "frozen conflict" in eastern Ukraine is resolved remains to be seen.

Elsewhere, the EU has attempted to facilitate conflict resolution in breakaway regions such as Abkhazia in Georgia, Nagorno-Karabakh in Azerbaijan, and Transdnistria in Moldova. EU efforts have been arguably undermined by Russian support for separatist parties, most clearly expressed when Russia invaded Georgian territory in 2008. In 2014, EU concluded an AA with Moldova, and Moldovans can travel without a visa to the EU. However, Moldova is the poorest country in Europe and is politically polarized between pro-Russia and pro-EU parties. Whether it could gain entry into the EU in the medium term is doubtful. Belarus also borders the EU, but its engagement with the EU has been limited, due in large part to the explicitly authoritarian and pro-Russian orientation of its government.[125] Further afield, the EU is very keen on bringing oil and gas from former Soviet states such as Azerbaijan, Kazakhstan, and Turkmenistan to Europe. European companies have invested heavily in energy fields and in new pipelines, including the Baku-Ceyhan pipeline, which ships oil from the Caspian Sea across Georgia and to a port on Turkey's Mediterranean coast. Other schemes involve pipelines that would circumvent Russia and ship oil and/or gas directly into Central Europe and Italy or from the Black Sea coast of Ukraine to the Baltic coast of Poland. While ambitious, these are best thought of as long-range plans that will require much political and economic investment and overcoming Russian objections, which at present controls many energy projects and export routes from the region.

The Middle East

Europeans have a long history of involvement in North Africa and the Middle East, including conflicts such as the Crusades and battles with the Ottomans, colonization, and significant trade and cultural ties. North Africans make up a substantial percentage of the immigrant population in Europe, and security concerns since 9/11 have focused global attention on the troubles of the region. Europe, far more than the US, depends upon the Middle East for energy resources. The Middle East, however, is also Europe's backyard, meaning that Europe has been compelled to engage with it to solve common problems and concerns. Many European efforts employ "soft power" and emphasize economic growth, integration, sustainable development, and good governance as factors that can contribute to regional stability.

Although the EU has had disparate elements of a "Mediterranean Strategy" since the 1960s, under the Maastricht Treaty it has attempted to create a more coherent, better-funded instrument to engage the region. This took shape in 1995 with the promulgation of the Euro-Mediterranean Strategy, also known as the Barcelona Process as it developed out of EU meetings in Barcelona, Spain. The Barcelona Process pledged a sizeable increase in EU assistance to the region—totaling €8.8 billion from the EU from 1995 to 2006 coupled with over €10 billion from the European Development Bank over the same period—in addition to more trade cooperation and regional integration. The EU signed Association Agreements with participating states, which, in addition to receiving privileged access to European markets, pledged to move to free-trade among themselves. The Barcelona Process also created a political dialogue designed to foster institutional reform and promotion of human rights.

In contrast to East-Central Europe, where in the 1990s the EU was also deeply committed, the Barcelona Process has been judged a relative failure. Aid and trade are unlikely to be enough to tackle the dire and deeply rooted poverty in the region

(North Africa on a *per capita* basis has income levels of approximately 10 percent of the EU average), and the Europe's agricultural markets, as noted above, were not open to free trade. Corruption also undercut much of the aid effort. In addition, the region's burgeoning population eclipses the economic growth that is occurring, meaning that Europe can do little, at least immediately, to improve markedly the region's economies and thereby dampen the allure of immigration. As for political reforms, with EU enlargement to North African and Middle Eastern countries not a possibility, there has arguably been less incentive to engage in political liberalization. With the exception of Israel and Turkey (which *is* a candidate to join the EU and thus treated differently), there was no well-functioning democratic state in the region, and most had serious human rights problems.

In 2004, the EU attempted to upgrade its relations with the Middle East through adoption of the aforementioned ENP, which includes North African/Middle Eastern states such as Morocco, Lebanon, Egypt, Israel, and Palestine. It was designed to provide a mechanism for enhanced cooperation. Like the Barcelona Process, it has an economic component of trade, investment, and sizeable aid (€12 billion for all sixteen ENP countries from 2007 to 2013) but has a significant security dimension as well, no doubt an outgrowth of both 9/11 and EU expansion in 2004 and 2007. The ENP is also designed to "build on commitments to common values, including democracy, the rule of law, good governance, and respect for human rights, and to the principles of market economy, free trade and sustainable development as well as poverty reduction."[126] Membership in the EU, of course, remains off the table, as Middle Eastern states (unlike, for example, Ukraine) can make no claim to qualify for EU membership. Instead, the EU holds out the prospect of deeper cooperation through individual tailored Action Plans with ENP countries.

By the 2010s, the EU found itself confronted with new crises in the region. The "Arab Spring" of 2010–2011 led to the overthrow of several authoritarian governments, including in Libya, where several European states intervened militarily to aid anti-government rebels. This was initially hailed as a success, and the Arab Spring in general generated some optimism that democracy and good governance would arrive in much of the Middle East. However, with the exception of Tunisia—which is receiving substantial aid from the EU—it has not resulted in greater democracy or stability. Egypt's new elected government, led by the Muslim Brotherhood, was ousted in a military coup in 2013. Libya has descended into chaos, with rival factions competing for power. Syria has been torn apart by a civil war, producing over half a million casualties and millions of internally displaced people and refugees.

The democracy and development agenda of the ENP, based on the EU's soft power, has largely been cast aside, as European leaders have focused on security questions and massive refugee and migrant flows from the region. While Europeans were reluctant to intervene in the Syrian conflict—the US also showed no appetite for another war in the Middle East—concerns over the growth of ISIS both within the Middle East and its broader terror network prompted some to call for a more pro-active policy. In the wake of the November 2015 attacks in Paris, France began striking ISIS targets in Syria. Britain has also been involved in the anti-ISIS campaign in Iraq. Turkey, which shares a border with both Iraq and Syria, has been backing forces opposed to the Syrian government and has also joined the anti-ISIS coalition. However, European military involvement in the Middle East has been rather limited, a reflection in part of Europe's own limited capabilities and fears of getting sucked into a conflict that has no easy solution and potential high costs. Suffice to say that stabilizing the region and eliminating terror networks will remain a difficult challenge, one that will no doubt require a long-term commitment and substantial international cooperation.

A common foreign and security policy for Europe remains, at best, a work in progress. Compared to the 1990s or 2000s, Europe in the 2010s faces a variety of difficult questions, including how to deal with a resurgent Russia, violence in the Middle East, and increasingly active home-grown terrorist networks. In many cases, Europeans are divided about how best to respond, and, as seen in the case of both the refugee crisis and ISIS-inspired attacks in Europe, it is clear that developments outside of Europe can have a significant impact on European societies. Without question, these challenges raise complex issues, ones that affect both individual countries as well as prospects for European unity.

Application questions

1. Does the EU have sufficient power and tools to be a powerful international actor? What factors might work against the emergence of the EU as a "superpower"?
2. Compare and contrast US and European policies toward a particular region or country. Do the policies complement or work against each other? Which one, in your view, is likely to be more successful?
3. How can one measure and assess the costs and benefits of globalization? What can European countries do to maximize benefits and minimize costs?
4. Can you make the case that "soft power" is more effective than "hard power"? Are there limits to the utility of "hard power"?
5. Can the EU model of integration be exported elsewhere? Did Europe have advantages on this front compared to Africa or Asia?
6. Should the EU expand to more states, such as Turkey or Ukraine? What would be the costs and benefits of such a decision?

Key terms

Additional reading

Ash, Timothy Garton. 2004. *Free World: America, Europe, and the Surprising Future of the West.* London: Penguin.
Written by a prominent British historian, this book counters European anti-Americanism and calls for renewed transatlantic unity. It offers an optimistic account on how Europe and the US can work together on issues such as global security and democratization.

Bretherton, Charlotte, and Volger, John. 2006. *The European Union as a Global Actor.* London: Routledge.
This book examines the emergence, role, and future of the EU as an actor in world politics. It looks at several areas of European foreign policy, including economy, trade, the environment, development, security, and identity. These are analyzed both theoretically and empirically and draw upon theory both from the development of the EU and from international relations more generally.

Holland, Martin, ed. 2004. *Common Foreign and Security Policy: The First Ten Years*, 2nd edition. London: Continuum.
This book provides a useful review of both the institutional development of the CFSP and case studies of how it has operated in specific circumstances, including Iraq, the developing world, and defense policy.

Kagan. Robert. 2004. *Paradise and Power: America and Europe in the New World Order.* New York: Atlantic Books.
This is a short, oft-cited, and polemical work by a noted conservative American commentator. Kagan's core thesis is that the US and Europe are fundamentally different in their international relations, with former relying on "hard power" and the latter establishing an international role based upon "soft power."

Leonard, Mark. 2005. *Why Europe Will Run the Twenty-first Century.* London: Fourth Estate.
A short and provocative book that argues that Europe has a broader and deeper influence on world affairs than the US, and that European power is likely to grow as more and more countries are brought into the "orbit" of Europe. Leonard argues that Europe constitutes a model for the future of international relations, as the growing power of Europe will transform world politics.

Notes

1 For a review of these events, see Nadia Diuk, "Euromaidan: Ukraine's Self-Organizing Revolution," *World Affairs*, March/April 2014, at www.worldaffairsjournal.org/article/euromaidan-ukraine%E2%80%99s-self-organizing-revolution, and Andrew Wilson,

Ukraine Crisis: What It Means for the West (New Haven: Yale University Press, 2014). See also the documentary from Netflix, *Winter on Fire: Ukraine's Fight for Freedom* (2015).

2 Richard Sakwa, "The Death of Europe: Continental Fates after Ukraine," *International Affairs* 91:3, 2015, p. 553–579.
3 Simon Saradzhyan, "Ukraine's Lost Cause," *Foreign Affairs* 24, February 2016, at www.foreignaffairs.com/articles/ukraine/2016-02-24/ukraines-lost-cause.
4 The Eurocorps dates back to Franco-German military cooperation and was formalized in 1993. See www.eurocorps.org.
5 For a very passionate argument along these lines, see Juergen Habermas and Jacques Derrida, "February 15th or What Binds Europeans Together," *Constellations* 10:3, September 2003, p. 291–297.
6 Eurobarometer 60, 2003, at http://ec.europa.eu/public_opinion/archives/eb/eb60/eb60_en.htm, accessed April 25, 2010.
7 For a review of the EU's accomplishments, see its website dedicated to the CFSP at http://eeas.europa.eu/cfsp/index_en.htm.
8 Brian Crowe, "A Common European Foreign Policy After Iraq?" *International Affairs* 79:3, May 2003, p. 534.
9 "Hungary: EU Sanctions on Russia Unlikely to be Renewed," *Euobserver*, February 17, 2016, at https://euobserver.com/foreign/132318.
10 Laurent Cohen-Tanugi, *Alliance at Risk: The United States and Europe Since September 11* (Baltimore: Johns Hopkins University Press, 2003), p. 71.
11 Declaration of the European Council on strengthening the Common European Policy on Security and Defence, June 3, 1999.
12 For more, see the website of the CSDP at www.eeas.europa.eu/csdp/.
13 In 2009, former Danish Prime Minister Anders Fogh Rasmussen was elected to this post by NATO members.
14 Quoted in Jeffrey Simon and Sean Kay, "NATO: European Security and Beyond?" in Ronald Tiersky, ed. *Europe Today: National Politics, European Integration, and European Security*, 2nd ed. (Lanham MD: Rowman and Littlefield, 2004), p. 104.
15 The OSCE maintains an excellent website at www.osce.org.
16 For more, see the election monitoring website at www.osce.org/odihr/elections/193741.
17 See report on Frank-Walter Steinmeier's remarks to *Deutsche Welle* at http://www.dw.com/en/german-foreign-minister-voices-deep-concern-over-ukraine-ceasefire-violations/a-19083641. See also Steven Pifer, "Letting Go," *Brookings Institution Policy Brief*, February 2016, available at www.brookings.edu/research/articles/2016/02/eu-us-minsk-ii-provisions-pifer.
18 Some disputed whether the atrocities in the region, especially in Bosnia, amounted to genocide. A premier source on this issue is Samantha Power, *A Problem from Hell: America and the Age of Genocide* (New York: Basic Books, 2002), Chapters 9 and 11. In 2006, the International Criminal Tribunal for the former Yugoslavia concluded that genocide did occur in Bosnia, at least during the 2005 Srebrenica massacre, but in 2007 the International Court of Justice ruled that the state of Serbia and Montenegro, while failing to prevent genocide, could not held accountable for it.
19 Charlemagne, "Arrest and Revival," *The Economist*, June 4, 2011, p. 64.
20 "Giving a Shunt Towards Europe," *The Economist*, May 23, 2009, p. 51–52.
21 "Bosnia and Herzegovina: A Hostage to Dayton?," *Al-Jazeera America*, December 14, 2015.
22 European Commission, "Bosnia and Herzegovina 2015 Report," November 10, 2015, at http://ec.europa.eu/enlargement/pdf/key_documents/2015/20151110_report_bosnia_and_herzegovina.pdf.
23 For more on EULEX, see www.eulex-kosovo.eu/?page=2,11,393.
24 European Commission, "Kosovo 2015 Report," November 10, 2015, at http://ec.europa.eu/enlargement/pdf/key_documents/2015/20151110_report_kosovo.pdf.
25 "Knocking on Heaven's Door," *The Economist*, August 29, 2015, p. 44.

26 Greece claims Macedonia is a region in Greece and that use of the name Macedonia suggests that the country claims dominion over part of Greece. Greece would prefer the name "Former Yugoslav Republic of Macedonia."
27 "The Bear Necessities of Life," *The Economist*, November 25, 2006.
28 See Michael Emerson, ed. *The Elephant and the Bear Try Again* (Brussels: Centre for European Policy Studies, 2006).
29 Coverage of these issues can be found in Karen Dawisha, *Putin's Kleptocracy: Who Owns Russia?* (New York: Simon and Schuster, 2014), and Steven Lee Myers, *The New Tsar: The Rise and Reign of Vladimir Putin* (New York: Knopf, 2015). Freedom House reports on Russia can be found at https://freedomhouse.org/country/russia.
30 "Differences Emerge in Europe of a Response to Georgia Conflict," *The New York Times*, August 12, 2008.
31 UN High Commissioner for Human Rights, "Report on the Human Rights Situation in Ukraine 16 November 2015 to 15 February 2016," at www.ohchr.org/Documents/Countries/UA/Ukraine_13th_HRMMU_Report_3March2016.pdf.
32 "NATO Will Expand Its Military Presence in Europe," *New York Times*, February 11, 2016.
33 "Vladimir Putin: West Has Tried to Contain Russia for Decades," *The Guardian*, December 4, 2014.
34 Luke Harding, "We Should Beware Russia's Links with Europe's Right," *The Guardian*, December 8, 2014.
35 "'Fake News' Threatens Germany's Election Too, Says Merkel," *The Washington Post*, November 23, 2016, at www.washingtonpost.com/news/worldviews/wp/2016/11/23/fake-news-threatens-germanys-election-too-says-merkel/?utm_term=.6644a696b68a.
36 Jean Marie Colombani, "Nous sommes tous Américains," *Le Monde*, September 12, 2001.
37 There is a vast and expanding literature on this topic. Useful sources include Zachary Shore, *Breeding Bin Ladens* (Baltimore: Johns Hopkins University Press, 2009); Robert Leiken, *Europe's Angry Muslims* (Oxford: Oxford University Press, 2011); and Angel Rabasa and Cheryl Benard, *Eurojihad* (Cambridge: Cambridge University Press, 2014).
38 In October 2007, twenty-one of the twenty-eight tried for the attacks were convicted on various charges. Some of the alleged ringleaders, however, were acquitted because of lack of evidence.
39 From Peter Neumann, "Europe's Jihadist Dilemma," *Survival* 48:2, Summer 2006, p. 71.
40 For details on these events, see BBC news archive at www.bbc.com/news/world-europe-30708237.
41 Robert Kagan, "Power and Weakness," *Policy Review*, June/July 2002.
42 John Gray, *Men Are from Mars, Women Are from Venus* (New York: HarperCollins, 1992).
43 See both Robert Kagan, *Of Paradise and Power*, (New York: Vintage, 2004), and Laurent Cohen-Tanugi, *Alliance at Risk*.
44 "Axis of Weasel—Germany and France Wimp Out on Iraq," *New York Post*, January 24, 2003.
45 "Shadows over NATO," *The Economist*, October 20, 2007.
46 "Secret CIA Prisons Confirmed by Polish and Romanian Officials," *The Guardian*, June 7, 2007.
47 "America Kidnapped Me," *Los Angeles Times*, December 19, 2005.
48 Bruce Bawer, While Europe Slept: How Radical Islam Is Destroying the West from Within (New York: Doubleday, 2006).
49 Mark Lilla, "How the French Face Terror," *New York Review of Books*, March 24, 2016, p. 37–39.
50 For profiles of the suspected terrorists, see BBC news archive at www.bbc.com/news/world-europe-34832512.

51 See series of stories under headline "Brussels Attacks Shake European Security," *New York Times*, March 23, 2016.
52 *New York Times*, March 23, 2016.
53 Walter Laqueur, *The Last Days of Europe: Epitaph for an Old Continent* (New York: Thomas Dunne Books, 2007), p. 72. For example, surveys in Britain in 2006 revealed that 40 percent of Muslims favored introducing Muslim law in parts of Britain and that 13 percent justified al Qaeda style terrorist attacks.
54 "Attack Builds Political Power of Anti-Immigrant Movements in Europe," *The New York Times*, July 17, 2016.
55 "British Intelligence Chief Sharpens Terrorism Warning," *New York Times*, November 6, 2007.
56 Neumann, "Europe's Jihadist Dilemma."
57 "France Broadens Authorities' Power to Fight Terror," *The New York Times*, May 26, 2016.
58 "Turkey Says It Deported One of the Brussels Suicide Bombers in Summer," *The Wall Street Journal*, March 23, 2016.
59 "Brussels Terrorists Probably Used Explosive Nicknamed 'the Mother of Satan,'" *Washington Post*, March 23, 2016.
60 These efforts have had mixed success in Britain. See "How the Government Lost the Plot," *The Economist*, February 28, 2009, p. 59–60.
61 Homages to the benefits of free trade can be found at the website of the WTO, www.wto.org, as well as that of the International Monetary Fund (IMF), www.imf.org.
62 Kevin Watkins and Penny Fowler, Rigged Rules and Double Standards: Trade, Globalisation, and the Fight Against Poverty (Oxford: Oxfam Publishing, 2004).
63 See Oxfam Briefing, "The End to EU Sugar Dumping," August 2004, at www.oxfam.org/sites/www.oxfam.org/files/dumping_0.pdf, accessed March 29, 2010.
64 For an economic analysis of EU trade policies on the developing world, see Simon Everett, *Do EU Trade Policies Impoverish Developing Countries?* (Washington, DC: Brookings Institution Press, 2006).
65 John Peterson and Alasdair Young, "Trade and Transatlantic Relations: Old Dogs and New Tricks," in Sophie Meunier and Kathleeen McNamara, *Making History: European Integration and Institutional Change at Fifty*, *The State of the European Union*, vol. 8 (Oxford: Oxford University Press, 2007), p. 283.
66 European Commission, Review of the Framework for Relations Between the European Union and the United States: An Independent Study, 2005, p. 13.
67 US Census Data, available at www.census.gov/foreign-trade/balance/index.html.
68 Data from https://ustr.gov/countries-regions/europe-middle-east/europe/european-union.
69 James Jackson, "Foreign Direct Investment in the United States: An Economic Analysis," Congressional Research Service, 2005, at http://fas.org/sgp/crs/misc/RS21857.pdf.
70 Data from http://ec.europa.eu/eurostat/statistics-explained/index.php/Foreign_direct_investment_statistics#The_United_States_was_the_main_holder_of_inward_FDI_stocks_in_the_EU-27.
71 European Commission, Bilateral Trade Ties with the United States, at http://ec.europa.eu/trade/issues/bilateral/countries/usa/index_en.htm.
72 Report of Centre for Economic Policy Research (2013), published on EU Commission's Website, http://europa.eu/rapid/press-release_MEMO-13-211_en.htm.
73 See for example, Stuart Jeffries, "What Is the TTIP About and Why Should We Be Angry About It," *The Guardian*, August 3, 2015.
74 http://ec.europa.eu/trade/policy/in-focus/ttip/.
75 Eurobarometer 83, Spring 2015, at http://ec.europa.eu/public_opinion/archives/eb/eb83/eb83_publ_en.pdf.
76 Data from European Commission, available at ec.europa.eu/trade/policy/countries-and-regions/countries/china/, accessed May 2, 2016.
77 Council of the European Union, "Joint statement of 9th EU-China Summit," 12642/06 (Press 249), Brussels, September 11, 2006.

78 Available at http://eeas.europa.eu/china/docs/20131123_agenda_2020__en.pdf.
79 http://trade.ec.europa.eu/doclib/press/index.cfm?id=1435.
80 2013 Transatlantic Trends Survey of the German Marshall Fund, available at http://trends.gmfus.org/files/2013/09/TT-Key-Findings-Report.pdf, accessed May 3, 2016.
81 An example would be European Commission, "EU-China: Closer Partners, Growing Responsibilities," COM(2006) 631 final, 2006.
82 "EU-China: Closer Partners," 2006.
83 Sarkozy, who earlier said he would boycott the ceremonies, did attend. Italy's Berlusconi was not in Beijing, but cited the hot weather as the reason.
84 For more, see http://eeas.europa.eu/delegations/china/eu_china/political_relations/humain_rights_dialogue/index_en.htm.
85 The term "soft power" is most associated with Joseph Nye, a political scientist at Harvard University. See his *Soft Power: The Means to Success in World Politics* (New York: Public Affairs, 2004).
86 Cohen-Tanugi, *An Alliance at Risk*, p. 75.
87 The Center for Global Development publishes an annual Commitment to Development Index, which utilizes several indicators in addition to aid. In 2015, the top-ranking countries in the entire world were, in order, Denmark, Sweden, Norway, Finland, the Netherlands, France, Great Britain, and Portugal. The US, in contrast, ranked twenty-first, behind Hungary and the Czech Republic. Taken from www.cgdev.org/cdi-2015, accessed March 30, 2016.
88 EU Development Atlas, at https://euaidexplorer.ec.europa.eu/DevelopmentAtlas.do.
89 See Paul Collier, The Bottom Billion: Why the Poorest Countries Are Failing and What Can Be Done About It (Oxford: Oxford University Press, 2007).
90 Whether or not the US has been effective or wholly consistent in use of such policies shall not detain us here. For a work analyzing differing US and European approaches, see Jeffrey Kopstein, "The Transatlantic Divide over Democracy Promotion," *The Washington Quarterly* 29:2, Spring 2006, p. 85–98.
91 Membership in the Council of Europe is open to any European state that agrees to adhere to democratic principles.
92 Sonia Lucarelii and Ian Manners, eds. *Values and Principles in European Union Foreign Policy* (London: Routledge, 2006).
93 A good selection of studies on these issues can be found in Paul Kubicek, ed. *The European Union and Democratization* (London: Routledge, 2003).
94 "Europe's Despot Dilemma," *The Economist*, October 13, 2007.
95 Charlemagne, "Climate Control," *The Economist*, March 17, 2007.
96 Precise targets varied from country to country. Germany, for example, pledged to cut gas emissions by 21 percent, France promised they would be at 1990 levels, and some countries such as Greece, Portugal, and Spain were allowed to have higher greenhouse gas emissions than in 1990.
97 "Hot Under the Collar," *The Economist*, April 1, 2006.
98 "European Nations Seek to Revise Agreement on Emissions Cuts," *The New York Times*, October 17, 2008.
99 "Germany Takes Dramatic Step on Climate," *Christian Science Monitor*, December 5, 2007, p. 10.
100 "European Nations Seek to Revise Agreement on Emissions Cuts," *The New York Times*, October 17, 2008.
101 "The Copenhagen Climate Conference," *The Economist*, December 18, 2009.
102 For a report on the EU's role in the Paris Agreement, see http://ec.europa.eu/clima/policies/international/negotiations/paris/index_en.htm.
103 According to a 2007 global survey, only 48 percent of Americans have favorable views of the UN, compared to 79 percent of Swedes, 68 percent of Poles, 67 percent of Italians, 66 percent of French, 64 percent of Germans, and 58 percent of Britons. Data from Pew Global Attitudes Project, available at http://pewglobal.org/reports/pdf/256.pdf, on November 14, 2009.

104 Mary Farrell, "From EU Model to External Policy? Promoting Regional Integration in the Rest of the World," in Meunier and McNamara, 2007.
105 Prodi, 2000, quoted in Farrell, "From EU Model," p. 299.
106 For example, a planned Europe-Africa Summit was delayed for seven years (until 2007), in large measure because of European opposition to the government of Robert Mugabe in Zimbabwe.
107 Ergun Özbudun, "Democratization Reforms in Turkey, 1993–2004," *Turkish Studies* 8:2, June 2007, p. 195.
108 Ziya Önis, "Domestic Politics, International Norms and Challenges to the State: Turkey-EU Relations in the post-Helsinki Era," in Ali Qarkoglu and Barry Rubin, eds. *Turkey and the European Union* (London: Frank Cass, 2003), p. 13.
109 See Dimitrios Dagdeverenis, "EU Public Opinion and Turkey's EU Membership," Bridging Europe, EU-Turkey Dialogue Initiative Working Paper, 2014, at www.bridgingeurope.net/uploads/8/1/7/1/8171506/working_paper_on_eu_public_opinion_on_turkey_dagdeverenis_august.pdf. For the 2006 survey, see Standard Eurobarometer 66, reported in http://ec.europa.eu/public_opinion/archives/eb/eb66/eb66_en.pdf. Both surveys accessed on April 1, 2010.
110 R.T. Erdoğan, "Why the EU Needs Turkey," Speech at Oxford University, May 28, 2004, at www.sant.ox.ac.uk/esc/docs/Erdogan1.pdf, accessed on March 30, 2010.
111 "Turkish People Indecisive Over EU Membership, Survey Reveals," *Daily Sabah*, August 3, 2015.
112 Useful sources include Cengiz Erisen and Paul Kubicek, eds. *Democratic Consolidation in Turkey: Micro and Macro Challenges* (London: Routledge, 2016), Berk Esen and Sebnem Gumuscu, "Rising Competitive Authoritarianism in Turkey," *Third World Quarterly*, 2016 (published online), and Cihan Tugal, "In Turkey, the Regime Slides from Soft to Hard Authoritarianism," *OpenDemocracy.net*, February 17, 2016.
113 "Erdogan's Attempt to Suppress German Satire Has the Opposite Effect," *New York Times*, March 30, 2016. The video is available at www.youtube.com/watch?v=R2e2yHjc_mc, accessed May 9, 2016.
114 "Failed Turkish Coup Accelerated Purge That Was Years in the Making," *The New York Times*, July 23, 2016.
115 "E.U. Pact to Send New Migrant Back to Turkey," *New York Times*, March 19, 2016.
116 "Merkel's Trust in Turkey and Greece to Stem Migrants Comes with Risks," *New York Times*, March 21, 2016.
117 The ENP grew out of the "Wider Europe—Neighbourhood" Communication of 2003. By 2004, this was transformed into the ENP, which included Middle Eastern and North African states as well. For more on the ENP, see its website at http://eeas.europa.eu/enp/index_en.htm, accessed May 2, 2016.
118 The EU's website for this initiative is www.eeas.europa.eu/eastern/index_en.htm.
119 EU-Russia relations have a different status outside the frameworks of the ENP and EaP.
120 Commission of the European Communities, 2004, European Neighbourhood Policy Strategy Paper COM(2004), 373 final, available at http://eur-lex.europa.eu/legal-content/EN/TXT/?uri=CELEX:52004DC0373, and Commission of the European Communities. 2009. "Eastern Partnership," press release, MEMO/09/217, 5 May, available at http://europa.eu/rapid/press-release_MEMO-09-217_en.htm?locale=en.
121 Gwendolyn Sasse, "The European Neighbourhood Policy: Conditionality Revisited for the EU's Eastern Neighbors," *Europe-Asia Studies* 60:2, 2008, p. 295–316.
122 Paul Kubicek, "The European Union and Democratization in Ukraine," *Communist and Post-Communist Studies* 38:3, June 2005, p. 269-292.
123 For more on relations between the EU and Ukraine under Yanukovych see Paul Kubicek, "Dancing with the Devil: Explaining the European Union's Engagement with Ukraine under Viktor Yanukovych," *Journal of Contemporary European Studies*, 2016.
124 Andrew Kramer, "Iffy Progress for Ukraine in Its Turn to Europe," *The New York Times*, May 10, 2016.

125 Giselle Bosse, "A Partnership with Dictatorship: Explaining the Paradigm Shift in European Union Policy Towards Belarus," *Journal of Common Market Studies* 50:3, 2012, p. 367–384.
126 GAER Councils of the ENP, June 14, 2004.

Final questions and possible trajectories

This book has offered a broad introduction to European politics, covering history, domestic political institutions, social actors, public policies, the EU, and Europe's place in the world. It has tried to relate where Europe and Europeans have been, what their concerns are at present, and the possible directions for future development. In order to make the last set of issues more explicit and in lieu of a final chapter, we conclude with a list of questions, suitable for reflection upon finishing this text, class discussion, a final exam or term paper, and/or further research.

1. Has Europe really overcome its history? Which historical attributes—for better or for worse—continue to color European politics?
2. How important do you think the old division between West and East is in Europe today? Is a North/South division now more salient?
3. What is the biggest threat to democracy in Europe today? How healthy do you think the state of democracy in Europe is?
4. The European project has made much progress in integrating states. Can it do the same in terms of integrating peoples? Can it do so without a strong notion of European "peoplehood" or citizenship?
5. The mission of the 1957 Treaty of Rome is largely complete with economic integration of the continent. After more recent setbacks, including the rejection of the Constitutional Treaty and intense disagreements on management of the euro and the refugee crisis, do you think Europe can regain its collective purpose? What will be the next big "narrative" for European integration?
6. Will Europe be able to compete with rising powers such as China and India? What must Europe do in order to be better served by globalization?
7. What is the future of US-European relations? Will the two sides continue to drift apart, or can rifts in the relationship be easily healed?
8. Can European states and societies adjust to their increasing multi-culturalism? Is immigration best understood as a threat or an opportunity? How is immigration changing the idea of what "Europe" is?
9. Are the European welfare states and the much-vaunted European social model dead? If so, what, perhaps, might be retained or salvaged?
10. What lessons can be learned in the wake of the global economic and European debt crisis? What reforms are necessary, both within states and in the EU, to prevent such crises from occurring in the future?

11. What lessons can be learned in the wake of the 2015–2016 refugee crisis in Europe? Is this a tipping point with respect to reversing elements of European integration?
12. What are the limits of European integration? Can the European Union really live up to its motto, "Unity in Diversity"?

Index

CPSIA information can be obtained
at www.ICGtesting.com
Printed in the USA
LVHW101627160120
643872LV00009B/439